GW01336943

THE BLOOMSBURY
POCKET
ENCYCLOPEDIA
OF THE WORLD

THE BLOOMSBURY POCKET ENCYCLOPEDIA OF THE WORLD

Bloomsbury
Books

Maps, text and index prepared and printed by Kartografie,
Prague, Czechoslovakia

Cartographic Editor:
RNDr. Jiří Novotný
Technical Editor:
Marie Pánková

© KARTOGRAFIE, PRAGUE, 1981, 1987, 1991

This edition published in 1991 by Godfrey Cave Associates Ltd,
42 Bloomsbury Street, London WC1B 3QJ, by arrangement with
Macdonald Illustrated, a division of Macdonald & Co (Publishers) Ltd
London & Sydney

All rights reserved
No part of this publication may be
reproduced, stored in a retrieval system,
or transmitted, in any form or by any
means, without the prior permission in
writing of the publisher, nor be
otherwise circulated in any form of
binding or cover other than that in
which it is published and without a
similar condition including this
condition being imposed on the subsequent
purchaser.

ISBN 1-870630-00-9

CONTENTS

	Text Page	Maps No	Maps Page
Afghanistan	91	22	100
Africa – *Physical Map*	115, 118	26	116, 117
Africa – *Political Map*	119, 122	27	120, 121
Alaska *(United States)*	–	33	144
Albania	50	13	65
Algeria	122	28	124
American Samoa	179	41c	177
Andorra	50	11	57
Angola	122	30	132
Anguilla	add 158	36b	157
Antarctica	182	42	181
Antigua and Barbuda	add 158	36b	157
Arctica	182	42	180
Argentina	163	39	168
Asia – *Physical Map*	86, 87	19	88, 89
Asia – *Political Map*	90	20	92, 93
Australia	175, 178	40	172, 173
Australia – *Physical Map*	171, 174	40	172, 173
Australia and Oceania – *Political Map*	175	41	176, 177
Austria	50	12	60, 61
Azores	71	11a	56, 57
Bahamas	151	35, 36	153, 157
Bahrain	91	21	37
Bangladesh	91	22, 22a	101
Barbados	154	36b	157
Baykal, Lake	–	16b	77
Belgium	51	11	57
Belize	154	36	157
Benin	122	29	129
Bermuda	add 158	32	141
Bhutan	91	22a	101
Bolivia	163	38	164
Botswana	122	30	132

page 3

	Text Page	Maps No	Maps Page
Brazil	163, 166	38, 39	164–169
British Antarctic Territory	add 182	42	181
The British Isles – *Physical Map*	38	7	40, 41
Brunei	91	23	104
Bulgaria	51	14	68
Burkina Faso	135	29	129
Burma/Myanma	91, 94	22	101
Burundi	122	30	133
Cameroon	123	29	129
Canada	142–146	33	144, 145
Canary Islands	–	26b	117
Cape Verde	123	28a	125
Caucasus and Transcaucasia	–	18a	84
Cayman Islands	add 158	36	157
Central African Republic	123	28	125
Chad	123	28	125
Channel Islands	50	6a	37
Chile	166	39	168
China	94	24	108, 109
Christmas Island	178	23	104
Cities of the World	add 30	–	–
Cocos Islands	178	4	29
Colombia	166, 167	38	164
Comoros	123	30	133
Congo	123	30	132
Cook Islands	add 178	41	177
Costa Rica	154	36	157
Countries of the World – *according to area*	26	–	–
– *according to population*	26	–	–
Crimea	–	16a	76, 77
Cuba	154	36a	157
Cyprus	95	19c	89
Czechoslovakia	54	12	60, 61
Denmark	54, 55	12	60
Dimensions of the Earth	23	–	–
Djibouti	123	28	125
Dominica	154	36b	157
Dominican Republic	154, 155	36	157

page 4

	Text Page	Maps No	Maps Page
Ecuador	167	38	164
Egypt	123, 126	28	125
El Salvador	155	36	156, 157
England	46	9	48, 49
Equatorial Guinea	126	27, 29	120, 129
Ethiopia	126	28	125
Europe – *Physical Map*	31, 34	5	32, 33
Europe – *Political Map*	35	6	36, 37
Explanations of Symbols	–	–	12, 13
Færoe Islands	55	6	36
Falkland Islands	171	39	168
Federated States of Micronesia	179	41	176, 177
Fiji	178	41b	177
Finland	55	15	72, 73
France	55, 58	11	57
French Guiana	171	38	165
French Polynesia	179	41	177
Gabon	126	30	132
Gambia	126	29	128
German Democratic Republic }	58	12	60
Germany, Federal Republic of }	add 58	12	60
Ghana	126	29	129
Gibraltar	59	5a	33
Greece	59, 62	14	69
Greenland	add 158	33, 42	145, 180
Grenada	155	36b	157
Guadeloupe	add 158	36b	157
Guam	179	41	176
Guatemala	155	36	156
Guinea	add 126	29	128
Guinea-Bissau	add 126	29	128
Guyana	167	38	164
Haiti	155	36	157
Hawaiian Islands	178	35a	153
Honduras	155	36	157
Hong Kong	114	19a	89
Hungary	62	14	68
Iceland	62	15a	72

	Text Page	Maps No	Maps Page
India	95	22	100, 101
Indonesia	98	23	104, 105
International Organizations	27, 30	–	–
Iran	98	21	97
Iraq	98, 99	21	96
Ireland	63	10	53
Islands of the World	add 26	–	–
Isle of Man	47	9	48
Israel	99	20b	93
Italy	63, 66	13	64, 65
Ivory Coast/Côte d'Ivoire	add 126	29	128, 129
Jamaica	158	36	157
Japan	99, 102	25	113
Java	–	23a	104
Jordan	102	20b	93
Kampuchea	102	22	101
Kenya	add 126	28, 30	125, 133
Kiribati	178	41	177
Korea, Democratic People's Republic of	102	25	112
Korea, Republic of	102, 103	25	112
Kuwait	103	21	97
Lakes of the World	add 26	–	–
Land Surface	26	–	–
Laos	103	22	101
Lebanon	103	20b	93
Lesotho	127	30	132
Lesser Antilles	–	36b	157
Levantine Countries	–	20b	93
Liberia	127	29	128
Libya	127	28	125
Liechtenstein	66	12	60
London *(Plan of the Town)*	–	7a	42
Luxembourg	66	11	57
Macau	114	19a	89
Madagascar	127	30	133
Madeira	–	28	124
Malawi	127	30	133
Malay Peninsula	–	19b	89

	Text *Page*	Maps	
		No	*Page*
Malaysia	103, 106	23	104
Maldives	106	22	100
Mali	127, 130	29	128, 129
Malta	66	13	64
Marshall Islands	179	41	177
Martinique	add 158	36b	157
Mauritania	130	28	124
Mauritius	130	30a	133
Mexico	158	36	156
Midway Islands	179	4	29
Military Pacts	add 30	–	–
Monaco	66	11	57
Mongolia	106	24	108, 109
Montserrat	add 158	36b	157
The Moon	19, 21	2	21
Morocco	130	28	124
Moscow *(Plan of the Town)*	–	17b	82
Mozambique	130	30	133
Namibia	add 130	30	132
Nauru	178	41	177
Nepal	106	22	100, 101
Netherlands	67	12	60
Netherlands Antilles, Aruba	167	36	157
New Caledonia	179	41a	177
New York *(Plan of the Town)*	–	32a	140
New Zealand	178	40a	173
Nicaragua	158	36	157
Niger	add 130	29	129
Nigeria	add 130	29	129
Nile Delta – Suez Canal	126	26a	116
Niue Island	add 178	41	177
Norfolk Island	178	41	177
North and Central America – *Physical Map*	138, 139	31	136, 137
North and Central America – *Political Map*	142	32	140, 141
Northern Ireland	47	10	53
Northern Mariana Islands	179	41	176

page 7

	Text Page	Maps No	Maps Page
The Northern Sky	15	1	16
Norway	67, 70	15	72, 73
Oceans and Seas	23	–	–
Oman	106	21	97
Pakistan	106, 107	22	100
Palau	179	41	176
Panama	add 158	36	157
Panama Canal Zone	add 158	34a	149
Papua New Guinea	add 178	41	176
Paraguay	167	39	168
Peru	170	38	164
Philippines	107	23, 23b	105
Pitcairn Island	179	41	177
Plain of Bengal	–	22a	101
Plain of Po	–	13a	65
Planetary Satellites	18	–	–
Planets	22	2b	22
Poland	70	12	61
Portugal	70, 71	11	56
Puerto Rico	151	36b	157
Qatar	107	21	97
Register	183	–	–
Réunion	135	30a	133
River Plate Countries, Southern Brazil	–	39a	169
Rivers of the World	add 26	–	–
Romania	71	14	68
The Ruhr Basin	–	12a	61
Rwanda	add 130	30	133
Saint Christopher and Nevis	add 158	36b	157
Saint Helena	135	4, 27	29, 120
Saint Lawrence Great Lakes Waterway	–	33b	add 146
Saint Lucia	add 158	36b	157
Saint Pierre et Miquelon	add 158	33	145
Saint Vincent	add 158	36b	157
Samoa	add 178	41c	177
San Marino	71	13	64
São Tomé and Principe	add 130	27	120
Saudi Arabia	107	20, 28	92, 125

	Text	Maps	
	Page	No	Page
Scotland	46, 47	10	52
The Seas on the Moon	20	2a	20
Senegal	131	29	128
Seychelles	131	27	121
Shetland Islands	–	10a	52
Sierra Leone	131	29	128
Singapore	110	19b	89
The Solar system	22	2b	22
Solomon Islands	179	41	176
Somalia	131	28	125
South Africa	131	30	132, 133
South America – *Physical Map*	159, 162	37	160
South America – *Political Map*	159, 162	37	161
The Southern Sky	15	1	17
Spain	74	11	56, 57
Sri Lanka	110	20a	93
Sudan	134	28	125
Suez Canal see Nile Delta	–	–	–
Surinam	170	38	165
Svalbard	74	16	76
Swaziland	134	30	133
Sweden	75	15	72, 73
Switzerland	75, 78	11	57
Syria	110	20b	93
Tahiti	179	41d	177
Taiwan	94, 95	25a	113
Tanzania	134	30	133
Thailand	110, 111	22	101
Time Zones of the World	14	–	14
Togo	134	29	129
Tokelau Islands	add 178	41	177
Tonga	179	41	177
Trinidad and Tobago	170	38	164
Tunisia	134	27a, 28	121, 125
Turkey	111	21a	96, 97
Turks and Caicos Islands	add 158	32	141
Tuvalu	179	41	177
Uganda	134	28, 30	125, 133

page 9

	Text Page	Maps No	Maps Page
Union Soviet Socialist Republics *(U.S.S.R.)*	79–83	16–18	76–85
United Arab Emirates	111	21	97
United Kingdom – *Political Map*	38–50	8	44, 45
The United Nations	27	–	
United States *(U.S.A.)*	146–151	34, 35	148–153
United States – Pacific Coast	–	31a	136
Upper Volta see Burkina Faso	–	–	–
Ural Region	–	17a	80
Uruguay	170	39a	169
Vancouver Area	–	33a	144
Vanuatu	179	41	177
Vatican City, State of	78	13	64
Venezuela	171	38	164
Vietnam	111, 114	22	101
Virgin Islands *(U.K.)*	add 158	36b	157
Virgin Islands *(U.S.A.)*	add 158	36b	157
Wake Island	179	41	177
Wales	46	9	49
Wallis and Futuna Islands	179	41	177
Waterfalls of the World	add 26	–	–
West Berlin (part of FRG)	78	12	60
Western Sahara	135	28	124
The World – *Physical Maps of the Hemispheres*	–	3	24, 25
The World – *Political Map*	–	4	28, 29
Tokelau	add 178	41	177
Tuvalu	179	41	177
Yemen,	114	28	125
Yugoslavia	78	13	64, 65
Zaire	135	28, 30	125, 132
Zambia	135	30	132, 133
Zimbabwe	135	30	132, 133

Index *of all geographical names* . . . . . 183 etc.

METRIC CONVERSION TABLE

The metric system is used throughout this encyclopedia. The following guide provides approximate Imperial equivalents for all quantities.

Altitude and *depth* are measured in metres. (m). To convert to feet, multiply by 3.28:
$$1 \text{ m} = 3.28 \text{ feet}$$
Mt. Kilimanjaro is 5,895m, or about 19,336 feet, high.

Distance is generally measured in kilometres (km), or thousands of metres. To convert to miles, multiply by 0.621:
$$1 \text{ km} = 1,000 \text{ m} = 0.621 \text{ mile.}$$
In 1982 Peru had 2,740km, or 1,702 miles, of railways.
Note: Most maps contain a scale with kilometres and miles.

Rainfall is measured in millimetres (mm), or thousandths of a metre. To convert to inches, multiply by 0.04:
$$1 \text{ mm} = 0.001 \text{ m} = 0.0394 \text{ inch}$$
The annual rainfall in Chicago is 843mm, or 33.21 inches.

Area is generally measured in square kilometres (sq.km). To convert to square miles, multiply by 0.386:
$$1 \text{ sq.km} = 0.386 \text{ square mile}$$
Cuba occupies 114,524 sq.km, or about 44,206 square miles.
Area is measured in square metres (sq.m) and hectares (ha):
$$1 \text{ sq.m} = 10.76 \text{ square feet}$$
$$1 \text{ ha} = 10,000 \text{ sq.m} = 2.47 \text{ acres}$$

Weight is measured in kilogrammes (kg) and tonnes (= 1,000 kg):
$$1 \text{ kg} = 2.205 \text{ pounds}$$
$$1 \text{ tonne} = 0.984 \text{ long ton, or} = 1.102 \text{ short tons}$$

Volume is measured in cubic metres; 1 cub.m = 35.32 cubic feet

Capacity is measured in litres (l) and hectolitres (hl):
$$1 \text{ l} = 61.02 \text{ cubic inches} = 1.76 \text{ pints}$$
$$1 \text{ hl} = 3.53 \text{ cubic feet} = 22.0 \text{ gallons}$$

Temperature is measured in degrees centigrade (°C). To convert to Fahrenheit, multiply by 1.8 and add 32:
$$(1.8)°C + 32 = °F$$
The mean July temperature in Manila is 26.9°C, or 80.42°F.

Natural gas is measured in joule (J), $TJ = 10^{12} J$ and $PJ = 10^{15} J$. A terajoule is a measure of energy equivalent to 23.46 tonnes of oil or 34.13 tonnes of coal.

EXPLANATIO

CITIES AND TOWNS

British Isles

⊖	**LONDON**	over 1,000,000 inhabitants
⦿	**GLASGOW**	500,000-1,000,000 inhabitants
⊙	Belfast	100,000-500,000 inhabitants
⊙	Bath	50,000-100,000 inhabitants
○	Perth	20,000-50,000 inhabitants
○	Douglas	less than 20,000 inhabitants

Other Maps

⊖	**NEW YORK**	over 1,000,000 inhabitants
⦿	**CALGARY**	500,000-1,000,000 inhabitants
⊙	Utrecht	100,000-500,000 inhabitants
⊙	Calais	50,000-100,000 inhabitants
○	Gibraltar	less than 50,000 inhabitants

Physical and World Maps

○ Ottawa

<u>Canberra</u>   National Capitals

CANADA

Victoria

St. Helena
(U.K.)

F SYMBOLS

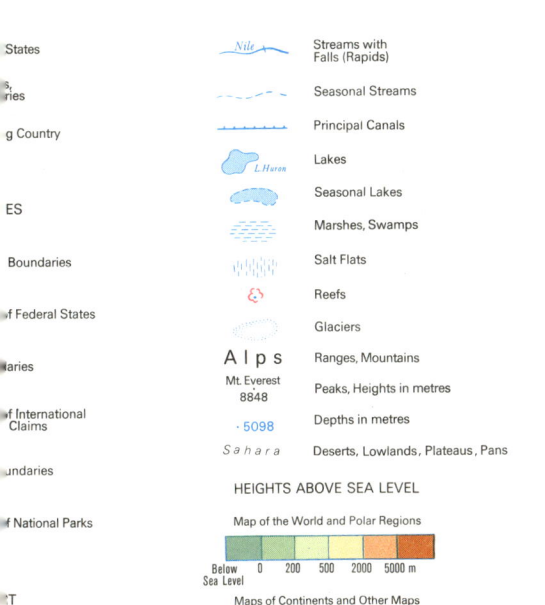

States

s,
ries

g Country

ES

Boundaries

f Federal States

aries

f International
Claims

undaries

f National Parks

T

er Construction

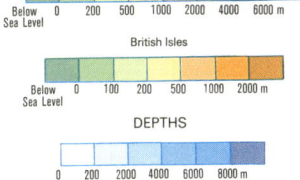

Nile	Streams with Falls (Rapids)
	Seasonal Streams
	Principal Canals
L. Huron	Lakes
	Seasonal Lakes
	Marshes, Swamps
	Salt Flats
	Reefs
	Glaciers
Alps	Ranges, Mountains
Mt. Everest 8848	Peaks, Heights in metres
· 5098	Depths in metres
Sahara	Deserts, Lowlands, Plateaus, Pans

HEIGHTS ABOVE SEA LEVEL

Map of the World and Polar Regions

Below Sea Level 0 200 500 2000 5000 m

Maps of Continents and Other Maps

Below Sea Level 0 200 500 1000 2000 4000 6000 m

British Isles

Below Sea Level 0 100 200 500 1000 2000 m

DEPTHS

0 200 2000 4000 6000 8000 m

TIME ZONES OF THE WORLD

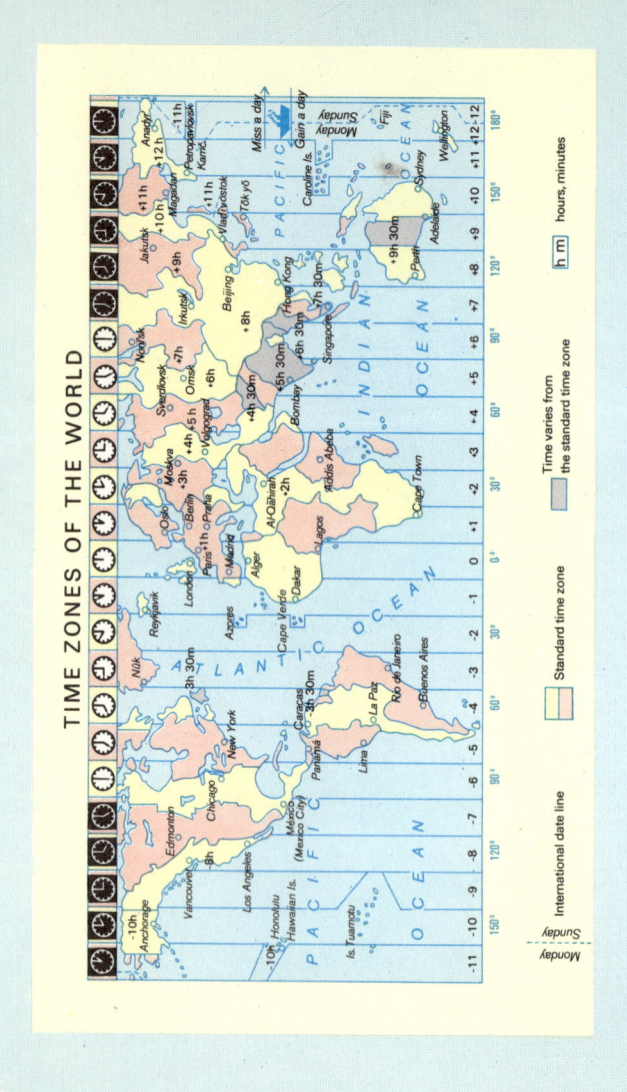

The Orbit of the Earth around the Sun

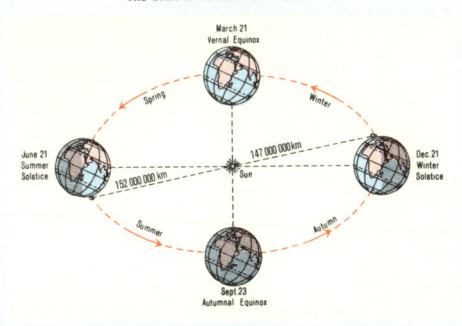

The position of stars on the celestial sphere and the position of places on Earth

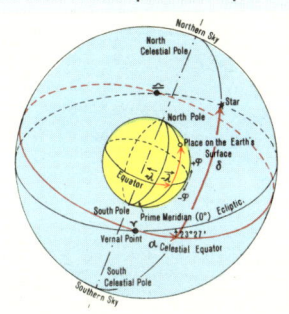

The coordinates of stars and the geographical coordinates. The position of places on the Earth is given by **the geographical coordinates** (λ, φ). **The geographical longitude** λ (lambda) is measured from the zero (Greenwich) meridian to the meridian of given point, to the West positively and to the East negatively, always from 0° to 180°. **The geographical latitude** φ (phi) is measured from the equator to the North positively and to the South negatively, always from 0° to 90°.
The position of stars is generally determined by using the equatorial coordinates (α, δ). They are analogous with the geographical ones. On the celestial sphere above the Earth's equator is the celestial equator. The position of Greenwich as a beginning point takes on the sphere **the first point of Aries** (vernal point) – the intersection of the celestial equator and the ecliptic in the place where Sun is going through the vernal equinox (its opposite is the autumnal point). Analogous with the geographical meridians are so-called declination circles; such circles go through both celestial poles and are perpendicular to the celestial equator. The equatorial coordinates are illustrated on the picture above.

The right ascension α (alpha) is an angle on the celestial equator measured from the vernal point to the declination circle of a given point. The right ascension is measured to the East from 0 to 24 hours (or from 0° to 360°).
The declination δ (delta) is an angle measured from the celestial equator to a given star, from 0° to 90° to the North positively and to the South negatively.

THE NORTHERN SKY

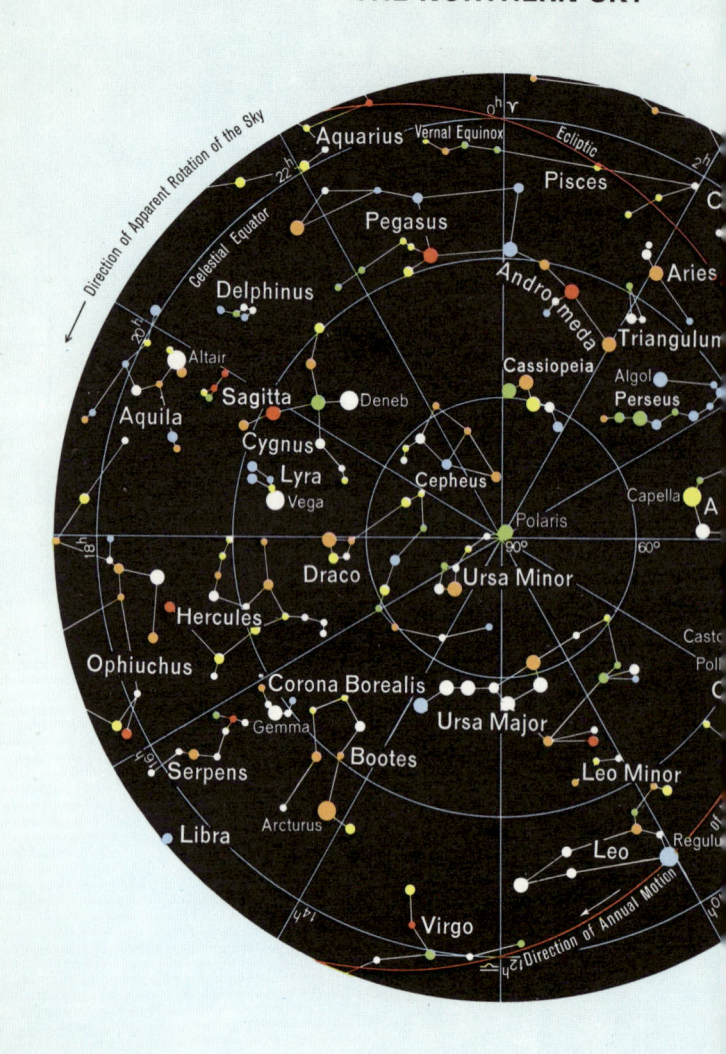

ctral Class
M K G

3,500° C 5,000° C 6,000° C

to to t

(surface ten

Hyades
Aldebaran
rus Rigel
Orion
Gemini
Monoceros
inor
Procyon

Stellar

1

PLANETARY SATELLITES

Planet	Satellite	Diameter (km)
Earth	Moon	3476
Mars	Phobos	27×19
	Deimos	15×11
Jupiter	Metis	40
	Adrastea	30
	Amalthea	270×150
	Thebe	70
	Io	3632
	Europa	3126
	Ganymede	5276
	Callisto	4820
	Leda	10
	Himalia	170
	Lysithea	20
	Elara	80
	Ananke	20
	Carne	20
	Pasiphae	30
	Sinope	20
Saturn	Atlas	40×20
	Prometheus	140×80
	Pandora	110×70
	Epimetheus	140×100
	Janus	220×160
	Mimas	390
	Enceladus	510
	Tethys	1050
	Calypso	34×22
	Telesto	34×28
	Dione	1120
	Helene	36×30
	Rhea	1530
	Titan	5150
	Hyperion	410×220
	Iapetus	1460
	Phoebe	200
Uranus	Cordelia	50
	Ophelia	50
	Bianca	50
	Cressida	60
	Desdemona	60
	Juliet	80
	Portia	80
	Rosalind	60
	Belinda	60
	Puck	170
	Miranda	485
	Ariel	1160
	Umbriel	1190
	Titania	1600
	Oberon	1550
Neptune	1989 N6	54
	1989 N5	80
	1989 N3	180
	1989 N4	150
	1989 N2	190
	1989 N1	400
	Triton	2705
	Nereid	340
Pluto	Charon	1192

THE MOON

Distance from the Earth: perigee 364 000 km
mean 384 400 km
apogee 406 700 km
Orbital velocity 3 680 km/h (1.02 km/s)
Diameter 3 476 km (0.27 Earth's diameter)
Mass 0.0123 Earth's mass
Mean density 3 340 kg/m^3 (0.60 mean Earth's density)
Surface temperature: daytime +130°C
nightime −150°C
Surface gravity 1.62 m/s^2 (0.165 Earth's gravity)
circular velocity (at the surface) 1.7 km/s
parabolic velocity (at the surface) 2.4 km/s
Sidereal month 27.321 661 days
Synodic month 29.530 588 days
Extreme libration: in latitude 6°50′, in longitude 7°54′

Almost 59 % of the Moon's surface can be observed from the Earth; 18 % is visible only at certain times and 41 % can never be seen from the Earth. Nevertheless, the whole of the Moon has been mapped (except for 1% of its surface) by means of space probes

THE MOON'S PHASES

The Moon does not shine by its own light; one of its hemispheres is illuminated by the Sun / a day / , the opposite is in a shadow / a night / . We can see only the part of the illuminated hemisphere which belongs to the Near Side. All Moon's phases change through 1 synodic month.

THE ROTATION OF THE MOON

The Moon's period of rotation on its axis is equal to its period of revolution around the Earth. Therefore the Moon always presents the same face to an observer on the Earth.

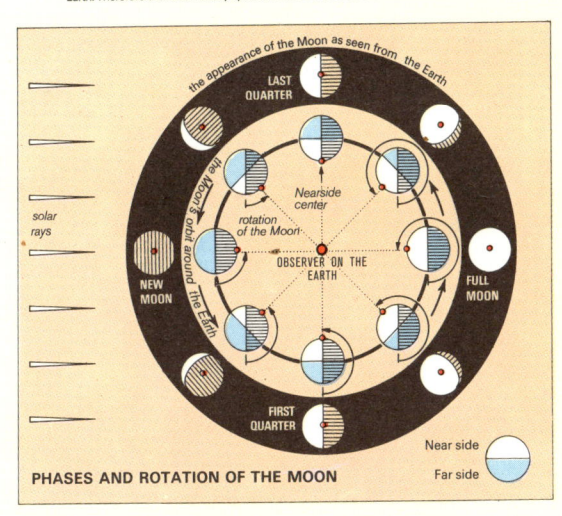

PHASES AND ROTATION OF THE MOON

THE SEAS OF THE MOON

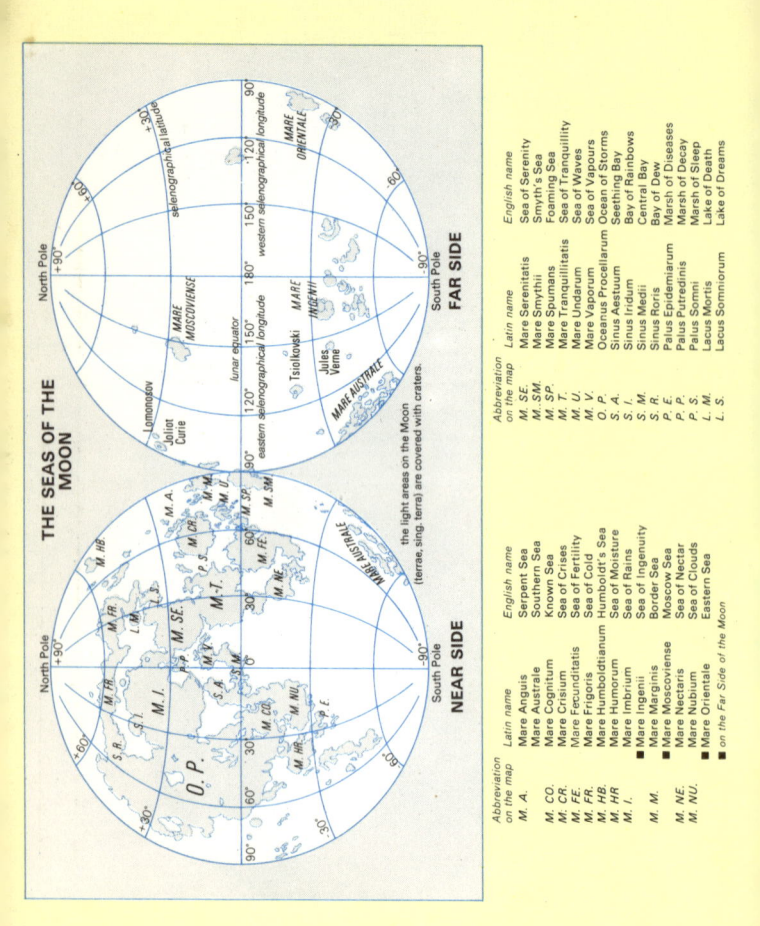

NEAR SIDE / **FAR SIDE**

the light areas on the Moon (terrae, sing. terra) are covered with craters.

Abbreviation on the map	Latin name	English name
M. A.	Mare Anguis	Serpent Sea
	Mare Australe	Southern Sea
M. CO.	Mare Cognitum	Known Sea
M. CR.	Mare Crisium	Sea of Crises
M. FE.	Mare Fecunditatis	Sea of Fertility
M. FR.	Mare Frigoris	Sea of Cold
M. HB.	Mare Humboldtianum	Humboldt's Sea
M. HR.	Mare Humorum	Sea of Moisture
M. I.	Mare Imbrium	Sea of Rains
■	Mare Ingenii	Sea of Ingenuity
M. M.	Mare Marginis	Border Sea
■	Mare Moscoviense	Moscow Sea
M. NE.	Mare Nectaris	Sea of Nectar
M. NU.	Mare Nubium	Sea of Clouds
	Mare Orientale	Eastern Sea

■ on the Far Side of the Moon

Abbreviation on the map	Latin name	English name
M. SE.	Mare Serenitatis	Sea of Serenity
M.SM.	Mare Smythii	Smyth's Sea
M.SP.	Mare Spumans	Foaming Sea
M. T.	Mare Tranquillitatis	Sea of Tranquility
M. U.	Mare Undarum	Sea of Waves
M. V.	Mare Vaporum	Sea of Vapours
O.P.	Oceanus Procellarum	Ocean of Storms
S. A.	Sinus Aestuum	Seething Bay
S. I.	Sinus Iridum	Bay of Rainbows
S. M.	Sinus Medii	Central Bay
S. R.	Sinus Roris	Bay of Dew
P. E.	Palus Epidemiarum	Marsh of Diseases
P. P.	Palus Putredinis	Marsh of Decay
P. S.	Palus Somni	Marsh of Sleep
L. M.	Lacus Mortis	Lake of Death
L. S.	Lacus Somniorum	Lake of Dreams

map 2b

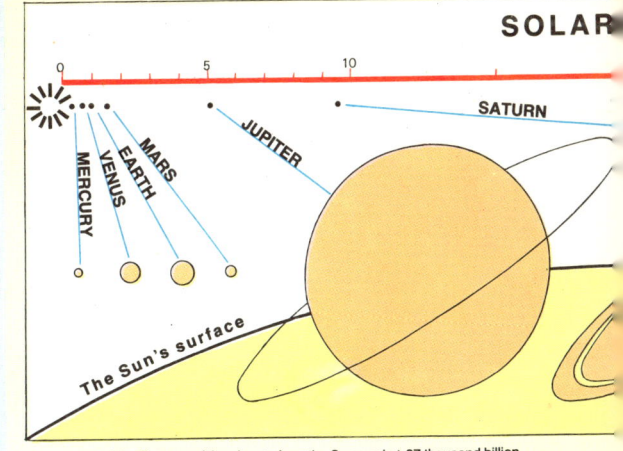

SOLAR

top: scheme of the distance of the planets from the Sun; scale 1:37 thousand billion
bottom: relative size of the planets and the Sun; scale 1:4.2 billion

PLA

Planet	Mean distance from the Sun in million km	Mean distance from the Sun in astronomical units	Sidereal period (years)
Mercury	57.9	0.387	0.24
Venus	108.2	0.723	0.62
Earth	149.6	1.000	1.00
Mars	227.9	1.524	1.88
Jupiter	778.3	5.205	11.86
Saturn	1432	9.576	29.46
Uranus	2884	19.281	84.01
Neptune	4509	30.142	164.79
Pluto	5966	39.880	247.7

△ Day side　　▲ Night side

SYSTEM

20   30   astronomical units   40

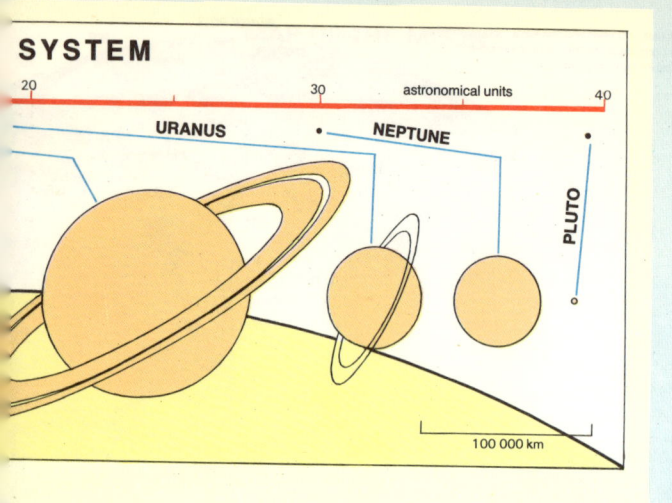

URANUS   NEPTUNE   PLUTO

100 000 km

NETS

Equatorial diameter in km	Mean density (in g/cm³)	Sidereal rotation period	Surface temperature in °C
4,878	5.4	58.6 days	+430 △ / −170 ▲
12,102	5.3	243 days	+480
12,756	5.5	23hrs 56mins.	+ 15 ●
6,794	3.9	24hrs 37mins.	− 50 ●
142,800	1.3	9hrs 50mins.	−130 ■
120,000	0.7	10hrs 14mins.	−185 ■
51,200	1.2	17hrs 18mins.	−220 ■
49,500	1.7	16hrs 07 mins.	−215 ■
2,280	2.1	6.4 days	−230

● Mean temperature   ■ Cloud's top

DIMENSIONS OF THE EARTH

	According to F. N. Krasovskij's ellipsoid	International Ellipsoid (year 1967)
Radius of the Equator (a)	6,378,245 m	6,378,160 m
Radius of the axis (b)	6,356,863 m	6,356,755 m
Flattening of the Earth $\left(\frac{a-b}{b}\right)$	$\frac{1}{298.3}$	$\frac{1}{298.25}$
Circumference of the Equator	40,075,704 m	40,076,600 m
Circumference of one of the meridians	40,008,548 m	40,009,150 m
Total surface area of the Earth	510,083,000 sq.km	510,100,933.5 sq.km
Area of dry land (29.2%)	148,628,000 sq.km	149,408,563 sq.km
Area of sea (70.8%)	361,455,000 sq.km	360,692,370 sq.km
Volume of Earth	1,083,319,780,000 cub.km	1,083,319,780,000 cub.km
Weight of Earth	5.978×10^{24} kg	5.970×10^{24} kg
Area of tropical zone (39.7%)	202,505,000 sq.km	
Area of temperate zones (52%)	265,418,000 sq.km	
Area of polar zones (8.3%)	42,160,000 sq.km	

Chemical composition of the Earth's surface: oxygen 49.13%, silicon 26%, aluminium 7.45%, iron 4.2%, calcium 3.25%, sodium 2.4%, potassium 2.35%, hydrogen 1%, titanium 0.61%, carbon 0.35%, chlorine 0.20%, phosphorus 0.12%, manganese 0.10%, sulphur 0.10%, fluorine 0.08%, barium 0.05%, nitrogen 0.04%, etc.

WATER

Chemical composition of sea water: oxygen 85.82%, hydrogen 10.72%, chlorine 1.89%, sodium 1.056%, magnesium 0.14%, sulphur 0.088%, calcium 0.041%, potassium 0.038%, bromine 0.0065%, carbon 0.002% etc.

Oceans and Seas

Name	Area in 1,000 sq.km	Volume in 1,000 cub.km	Greatest depth in m	Average depth in m
PACIFIC OCEAN	179,680	723,699	10,924	3,780
Philippine Sea	5,726	23,522	10,830	4,188
Coral Sea	4,791	11,470	9,174	2,243
South China Sea	3,537	3,622	5,559	1,024
Tasman Sea	3,336	10,960	5,944	3,285
Bering Sea	2,270	3,796	4,298	1,640
Sea of Okhotsk	1,580	1,316	3,916	821
Sea of Japan	1,062	1,630	3,699	1,535
ATLANTIC OCEAN	91,655	329,700	8,648	3,597
Weddell Sea	2,910	8,375	6,820	2,878
Caribbean Sea	2,776	6,745	7,535	2,429
Mediterranean Sea	2,556	3,603	5,121	1,438
Gulf of Mexico	1,554	2,366	4,376	1,522
Labrador Sea	840	1,596	4,316	1,898
North Sea	565	49	725	87
Baltic Sea	422	215	470	51
Black Sea	413	555	2,245	1,315
INDIAN OCEAN	76,170	282,600	7,725	3,710
Arabian Sea	4,592	14,514	5,803	3,160
Bay of Bengal	2,191	5,664	3,835	2,585
Arafura Sea	1,037	157	3,680	154
Andaman Sea	605	586	4,507	969
Red Sea	460	182	3,039	396
ARCTIC OCEAN	13,950	18,100	5,527	1,328
Barents Sea	1,424	316	610	222
Norwegian Sea	1,383	2,408	3,970	1,735
Greenland Sea	1,205	1,740	5,527	1,641
East Siberian Sea (Vostočno-Sibirskoje More)	913	49	915	54
Hudson Bay	848	92	258	128
Baffin Sea	780	593	2,414	861

Greatest ocean depth: in the Pacific Ocean – Mariana Trench 10,924 m (11°21′ N.Lat., 142°12′ E.Long.); in the Atlantic Ocean – Puerto Rico Trench 8,648 m (19°35′ N.Lat., 68°17′ W.Long.); in the Indian Ocean – Java Trench 7,725 m (10°15′ S.Lat., 109° E.Long. - approx.); in the Arctic Ocean – Eurasia Basin 5,527 m (82°23′ N.Lat., 19°31′ E. Long.).

1 : 150 000 000

0 1000 2000 3000 4000 Km

0 500 1 000 1 500 2 000 2 500 Mi

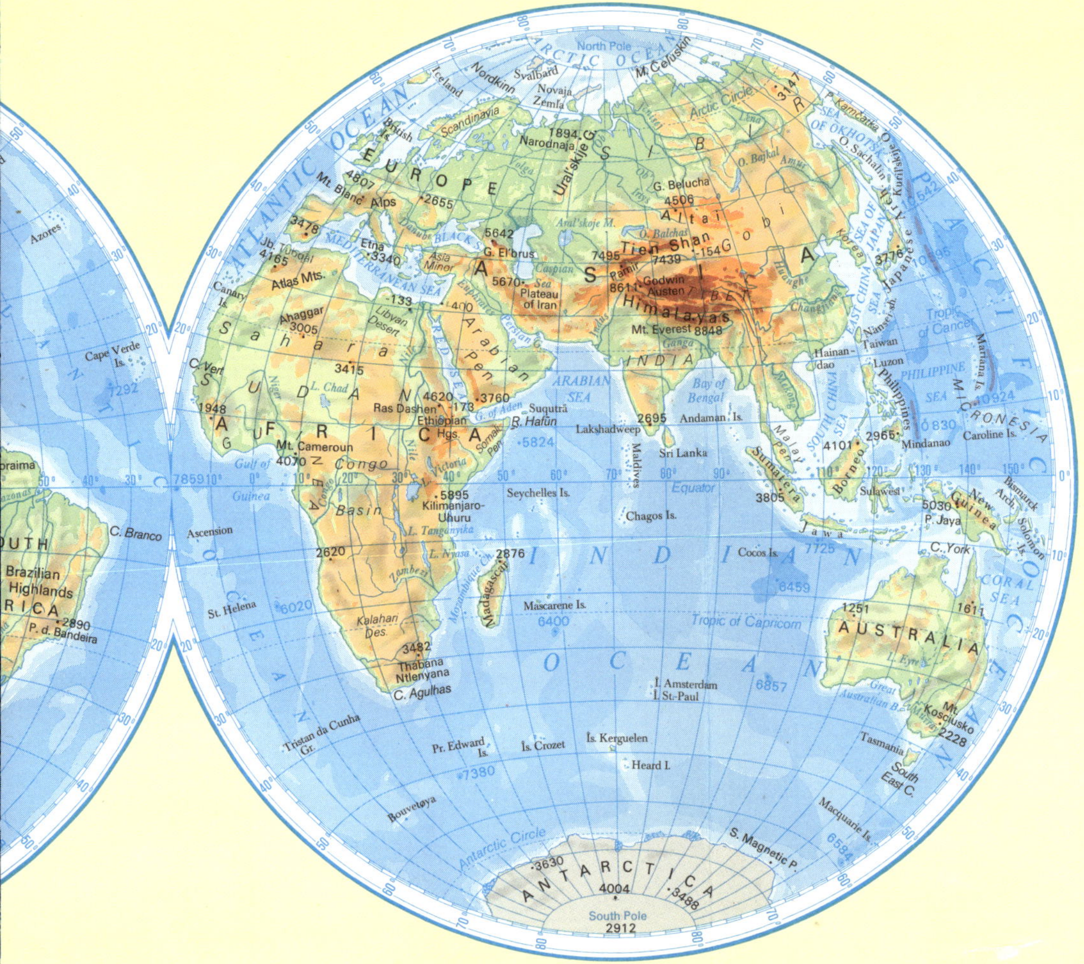

North Pole
ARCTIC OCEAN
ATLANTIC OCEAN
INDIAN OCEAN
PACIFIC OCEAN
EUROPE
ASIA
AFRICA
AUSTRALIA
ANTARCTICA
SIBIR
SOUTH AMERICA
Brazilian Highlands
P. d. Bandeira
2890
C. Branco
Azores
Cape Verde Is.
7292
Ascension
St. Helena
6020
Tristan da Cunha Gr.
Bouvetøya
Iceland
Nordkinn
Svalbard
Novaja Zemla
M. Čeluskin
British Is.
Scandinavia
Mt. Blanc
4807
Alps
2655
3478
Jb. Toubkal
4165
Etna
3340
Atlas Mts.
Canary Is.
MEDITERRANEAN SEA
BLACK SEA
Asia Minor
G. El'brus
5642
Caspian Sea
5670
Plateau of Iran
Narodnaja
1894
Ural'skije G.
Aral'skoje M.
O. Balchaš
G. Belucha
4506
Altai
Gobi
Tien Shan
7495
7439
Pamir
-154
Godwin Austen
8611
TIBET
Himalayas
Mt. Everest
8848
Ganga
Indus
INDIA
Arctic Circle
3147
P. Kamčatka
SEA OF OKHOTSK
O. Sachalin
Kuril'skije O.
O. Bajkal
Amur
Lena
Ob
Irtyš
Volga
Danube
Korea
SEA OF JAPAN
Japanese Arch.
3776
10542
10595
Huanghe
Changjiang
EAST CHINA SEA
Nansei-sh.
Taiwan
Tropic of Cancer
Mariana Is.
Hainan-dao
Luzon
Philippines
PHILIPPINE SEA
10924
MICRONESIA
Mekong
SOUTH CHINA SEA
Malay Pen.
Sumatera
3805
Borneo
4101
2965
Mindanao
10830
Caroline Is.
Sulawesi
Bismarck Arch.
New Guinea
5030
P. Jaya
Solomon Is.
Jawa
7725
C. York
CORAL SEA
1611
1251
L. Eyre
Great Australian Bight
Mt. Kosciusko
2228
Tasmania
South East C.
Macquarie Is.
6584
S. Magnetic P.
Sahara
Ahaggar
3005
Libyan Desert
-133
-400
Arabian Pen.
RED SEA
Persian G.
Euphrates
Nile
C. Vert
SUDAN
Niger
L. Chad
3415
1948
GUINEA
Mt. Cameroun
4070
Gulf of Guinea
Congo
Congo Basin
Ras Dashen
4620
-173
3760
G. of Aden
Ethiopian Hgs.
Somali Pen.
R. Hafun
Suqutrā
ARABIAN SEA
Bay of Bengal
Lakshadweep
2695
Andaman Is.
Sri Lanka
Maldives
5824
L. Victoria
Kilimanjaro-Uhuru
5895
L. Tanganyika
L. Nyasa
2620
Zambezi
2876
Mozambique Ch.
Madagascar
Kalahari Des.
3482
Thabana Ntlenyana
C. Agulhas
Seychelles Is.
Chagos Is.
Equator
Cocos Is.
6459
Mascarene Is.
6400
Tropic of Capricorn
I. Amsterdam
I. St-Paul
6857
Pr. Edward Is.
Is. Crozet
Is. Kerguelen
Heard I.
7380
Antarctic Circle
3630
4004
3488
South Pole
2912
7859

Longest Rivers of the World

Name	Length in km	River basin in sq.km
1. Amazonas (-Ucayali, -Apurímac)	7,025	7,050,000
2. Nile-Kagera	6,671	2,881,000
3. Mississippi-Missouri	6,212	3,250,000
4. Changjiang/Yangtze	5,520	1,942,000
5. Ob (-Irtys)	5,410	2,975,000
6. Huanghe/Yellow	4,845	772,000
7. Congo/Zaïre/Lualaba	4,835	3,822,000
8. Mekong/Lancangjiang	4,500	810,000
9. Amur (/Silka, -Onon)	4,416	1,855,000
10. Lena	4,400	2,490,000

Largest Islands of the World

Name (Continent)	Area in sq.km
1. Greenland (N.America)	2,175,600
2. New Guinea (Oceania)	785,000
3. Borneo/Kalimantan (Asia)	746,546
4. Madagascar (Africa)	587,040
5. Baffin I. (N.America)	507,414
6. Sumatera (Asia)	433,800
7. Honshū (Asia)	227,414
8. Victoria I. (N.America)	217,274
9. Great Britain (Europe)	216,325
10. Ellesmere I. (N.America)	196,221

Largest Lakes of the World

Name (Continent)	Area in sq.km	Greatest depth in m
1. Caspian Sea (Asia)	371,000	1,025
2. L. Superior (N.America)	82,414	393
3. L. Victoria (Africa)	68,800	125
4. Aralskoje More (Asia)	64,115	67
5. L. Huron (N.America)	59,596	226
6. L. Michigan (N. America)	58,016	281
7. L. Tanganyika (Africa)	32,880	1,470
8. O. Bajkal (Asia)	31,500	1,620
9. Great Bear Lake (N.America)	31,328	137
10. Great Slave Lake (N.America)	28,570	140

Highest Waterfalls of the World

Name (Country)	Height in m
1. Salto Angel (Venezuela)	979
2. Tugela (Natal, South Africa)	948
3. Yosemite (Cal., U.S.A.)	739
4. Cuquenán (Venezuela)	610
5. Sutherland (New Zealand)	579
6. Takakkaw (B.C., Canada)	503
7. Glétroz (Switzerland)	498
8. Ribbon (Cal., U.S.A.)	491
9. King George VI (Guyana)	488
10. Della (B.C., Canada)	440

LAND SURFACE

Continent	Area in 1,000 sq.km	% of Land surface	Altitude in meters highest	Altitude in meters average	Altitude in meters lowest	Population in millions (1988)	% of World Popul.
Europe	10,382	7.0	4,807	340	−28	498.008	13.7
Asia	44,410	29.7	8,848	960	−400	3,077.773	60.2
Africa	30,329	20.3	5,895	750	−155	609.8	11.9
North America	24,360	16.3	6,194	720	−86	416.3	8.1
South America	17,843	11.9	6,959	580	−40	285.2	5.6
Australia and Oceania	8,910	6.0	5,030	350	−16	26.2	0.5
Antarctica	13,175	8.8	4,897	2,020	(−2,538)		
WORLD	149,409	100.0	8,848	840	−400	5,116.0	100.0

Highest point on the Earth surface: Mount Everest 8,848 m.
Lowest point on the Earth surface: The Dead Sea −400 m below sea-level.
Highest active volcano: Volcan Guallatiri (in Chile) 6,060 m (eruption in 1960).
Largest island: Greenland 2,175,600 sq.km.
Largest peninsula: Arabian Peninsula 2,780,000 sq.km.
Longest mountain chain: Rocky Mountains Range – Andes (Cordilleras), length 15,000 km.
Largest lowlands: Amazonian Lowlands (S.America) approx. 5,000,000 sq.km.
Largest desert: Sahara (Africa) 7,820,000 sq.km.
Largest glacier (excl. Antarctica): Greenland, area 1,830,000 sq.km, volume 2,700,000 cub.km.
Largest lake: Caspian Sea 371,000 sq.km.
Deepest lake: O. Bajkal 1,620 m.
Longest river: Amazonas (-Ucayali, -Apurímac) 7,025 km.
Largest river basin: Amazonas (Amazon) 7,050,000 sq.km.
Highest average flow: Amazonas 120,000 cub.m per sec.
Highest waterfalls: Salto Angel (in Venezuela) 979 m.
Deepest cave system: Réseau de la Pierre-Saint-Martin (in French Pyrenees) depth 1,332 m.
Longest cave system: Flint Ridge-Mammoth Cave (Kentucky, U.S.A.) 297,080 m.
Highest absolute temperature: Al-Aziziyah (in Libya) +58°C.
Highest average annual temperature: Dalol (in Ethiopia) +34.4°C.
Lowest absolute temperature: Vostok (3,488 m high, Soviet base in Antarctica) −89.2°C (1983).
Lowest average annual temperature: Pole of Cold (in Antarctica) −57.8°C.
Highest average annual precipitation: Waialeale (Kauai – Hawaii, U.S.A.) 11,684 mm.
Lowest average annual precipitation: Arica (in Chile) 0.8 mm.
Largest national park: Wood Buffalo National Park, area 44,807 sq.km.

Countries of the World according to area

Country	Area in sq.km
1. U.S.S.R.	22,274,900
2. Canada	9,976,139
3. China	9,596,961
4. U.S.A.	9,372,614(*)
5. Brazil	8,511,965
6. Australia	7,686,848
7. India	3,287,590
8. Argentina	2,505,813
9. Sudan	2,381,741
10. Algeria	2,345,409
11. Zaïre	2,175,600
12. Greenland (Den.)	2,153,168
13. Saudi Arabia	2,027,087
14. Indonesia	1,972,546
15. Mexico	1,759,540
16. Libya	1,648,100
17. Iran	1,566,500
18. Mongolia	1,285,216
19. Peru	1,284,000
20. Chad	1,266,995
21. Niger	1,246,700
22. Angola	1,240,192
23. Mali	1,221,900
24. Ethiopia	1,221,037
25. South Africa	

(*) including Great Lakes 9,519,617

Countries of the World according to population (Mid-year estimates 1988)

Country	Population
1. China	1,103,983,000
2. India	796,596,000
3. U.S.S.R.	285,940,000
4. U.S.A.	247,083,000
5. Indonesia	174,951,000
6. Brazil	144,428,000
7. Japan	122,613,000
8. Pakistan	105,409,000
9. Nigeria	104,957,000
10. Bangladesh	104,532,000
11. Mexico	82,734,454
12. Vietnam	64,227,000
13. Federal Rep. of Germany	59,303,900(*)
14. Philippines	58,721,307
15. Italy	57,476,000
16. United Kingdom	57,077,000
17. France	55,874,000
18. Thailand	54,536,000
19. Iran	52,522,000
20. Turkey	52,422,000
21. Egypt	51,897,000
22. Ethiopia	47,882,000
23. Republic of Korea	41,975,000
24. Burma / Myanmar	39,966,000
25. Spain	39,085,000

(*) excluding West Berlin

map 4

THE UNITED NATIONS (UN)

The most important international organization in the world. The Charter of the United Nations was signed by 50 states at the San Francisco Conference held from 25 April to 26 June 1945, and it came into force on 24 October 1945 (United Nations Day). The Preamble to the Charter lays down the purposes and principles of the UN: to maintain international peace and security; to develop friendly relations among nations; to cooperate internationally in solving international economic, social, cultural and humanitarian problems and in promoting respect for human rights and fundamental freedoms; to support social progress and improve standards of living and to coordinate the fundamental principles of the member nations so as to attain these common ends.

Members of the UN are the sovereign states that established the organization and those admitted by the General Assembly upon recommendation of the Security Council. The UN had 159 members on 22 May 1990. Original member states (since 1945): Argentina, Australia, Belgium, Bolivia, Brazil, Byelorussian S.S.R., Canada, Chile, China, Colombia, Costa Rica, Cuba, Czechoslovakia, Denmark, Dominican Republic, Ecuador, Egypt, El Salvador, Ethiopia, France, Greece, Guatemala, Haiti, Honduras, India, Iran, Iraq, Lebanon, Liberia, Luxembourg, Mexico, the Netherlands, New Zealand, Nicaragua, Norway, Panama, Paraguay, Peru, Philippines, Poland, Saudi Arabia, South Africa, Syria, Turkey, Ukrainian S.S.R., United Kingdom, Uruguay, Union of Soviet Socialist Republics, United States of America, Venezuela and Yugoslavia. Other states admitted as members: in 1946 – Afghanistan, Iceland, Sweden, Thailand; 1947 – Pakistan, Yemen; 1948 – Burma; 1949 – Israel; 1950 – Indonesia; 1955 – Albania, Austria, Bulgaria, Finland, Hungary, Ireland, Italy, Jordan, Kampuchea, Laos, Libya, Nepal, Portugal, Romania, Spain, Sri Lanka; 1956 – Japan, Morocco, Sudan, Tunisia; 1957 – Ghana, Malaysia; 1958 – Guinea; 1960 – Benin, Burkina Faso (formerly Upper Volta), Cameroon, Central African Republic, Chad, Congo, Cyprus, Gabon, Ivory Coast, Madagascar, Mali, Niger, Nigeria, Senegal, Somalia, Togo, Zaïre; 1961 – Mauritania, Mongolia, Sierra Leone, Tanzania; 1962 – Algeria, Burundi, Jamaica, Rwanda, Trinidad and Tobago, Uganda; 1963 – Kenya, Kuwait; 1964 – Malawi, Malta, Zambia; 1965 – Gambia, Maldives, Singapore; 1966 – Barbados, Botswana, Guyana, Lesotho; (1967 – Democratic Yemen) 1968 – Equatorial Guinea, Mauritius, Swaziland; 1970 – Fiji; 1971 – Bahrain, Bhutan, Oman, Qatar, United Arab Emirates; 1973 – Bahamas, German Democratic Republic, Federal Republic of Germany, 1974 – Bangladesh, Grenada, Guinea-Bissau; 1975 – Cape Verde, Comoros, Mozambique, Papua New Guinea, Surinam, São Tomé and Principe; 1976 – Angola, Samoa, Seychelles; 1977 – Djibouti, Vietnam; 1978 – Dominica, Solomon Islands; 1979 – Saint Lucia; 1980 – Zimbabwe, Saint Vincent and the Grenadines; 1981 – Antigua, Belize, Vanuatu; 1983 – Saint Kitts and Nevis; 1984 – Brunei; 1990 – Namibia.

The principal organs of the UN: 1. The General Assembly – consists of all member states; each of them has juridically an equal position irrespective of size, power or importance; 2. The Security Council – bears the primary responsibility for the maintenance of peace and security (it has 5 permanent and 10 elected members); 3. The Economic and Social Council (54 elected members); 4. The Trusteeship Council (5 members); 5. The International Court of Justice (with its seat at 's-Gravenhage); 6. The Secretariat – carries out all administrative functions in the UN. It is headed by the Secretary-General, who is appointed by the General Assembly on the recommendation of the Security Council. **Secretary-General:** Javier Pérez de Cuéllar (since 1 Jan. 1982). **Headquarters of the UN:** New York. **Official languages:** Arabic, Chinese, English, French, Spanish and Russian.

The Economic and Social Council has **5 regional economic commissions**: the Economic Commission for Europe (ECE; H.Q.: Genève), the Economic Commission for Asia and the Pacific (ECAP; H.Q.: Krung Thep), the Economic Commission for Latin America (ECLA; H.Q.: Santiago), the Economic Commission for Africa (ECA; H.Q.: Addis Abeba), and the Economic Commission for Western Asia (ECWA; H.Q.: Bayrūt); functional commissions (Statistical Commission, Population Commission, Social Development Commission, Commission on Human Rights, Commission on the Status of Women, Commission on Narcotic Drugs, Commission on International Raw Materials Trade). **Special related agencies:** United Nations Children's Fund (UNICEF), Office of the United Nations High Commissioner for Refugees (UNHCR; H.Q.: Genève), United Nations Conference on Trade and Development (UNCTAD; H.Q.: Genève), United Nations Development Programme (UNDP), United Nations Industrial Development Organization (UNIDO; H.Q.: Wien), United Nations Institute for Training and Research (UNITAR), World Food Council (WFC; H.Q.: Rome), United Nations University (UNU, H.Q.: Tōkyō), as well as other commissions and agencies.

International specialized organizations in relationship with the UN (14): International Atomic Energy Agency (IAEA; H.Q.: Wien), International Labour Organization (ILO; H.Q.: Genève), Food and Agriculture Organization (FAO; H.Q.: Rome), United Nations Educational, Scientific and Cultural Organization (UNESCO; H.Q.: Paris), World Health Organization (WHO; H.Q.: Genève), International Bank for Reconstruction and Development (IBRD – World Bank; H.Q.: Washington), International Development Association (IDA; H.Q.: Washington), International Finance Corporation (IFC; H.Q.: Washington), International Monetary Fund (IMF; H.Q.: Washington), International Civil Aviation Organization (ICAO; H.Q.: Québec), Universal Postal Union (UPU; H.Q.: Bern), International Telecommunication Union (ITU; H.Q.: Genève), World Meteorological Organization (WMO; H.Q.: Genève), Inter-Governmental Maritime Consultative Organization (IMCO; H.Q.: London), General Agreement on Tariffs and Trade (GATT; H.Q.: Genève).

INTERNATIONAL ORGANIZATIONS

The Council of Europe – established on 5 May 1949 in London (H.Q.: Strasbourg). Membership: 21 European countries; founder members: United Kingdom, France, Italy, Belgium, the Netherlands, Luxembourg, Ireland, Denmark, Norway, Sweden, Turkey and Greece joined in 1949, Iceland in 1950, Fed. Rep. of Germany in 1951, Austria in 1956, Cyprus in 1961, Switzerland, Liechtenstein in 1963, Malta in 1965, Portugal in 1976, Spain in 1977. Finland and the Vatican City participate in the work of certain bodies. Control organs: the Committee of Ministers (usually 21 Ministers of Foreign Affairs), the Joint Committee (21 members), the Consultative Assembly (consists of 170 parliamentary representatives from 21 member countries) and the Secretariat. The Council's aim is to achieve a greater unity between its members and to co-ordinate policies on economic, social, cultural, legal, scientific and administrative matters. **European Communities** – short name for 3 communities established by 6 countries of Western Europe to integrate economic policies and move towards political unity. The original members are France, Italy, the Fed. Rep. of Germany, Belgium, the Netherlands and Luxembourg. Other members since 1973 are the United

A R
Barrow
Alaska
Fairbanks
U.S.A.
Anchorage
Victoria I.
Aleutian Is. (U.S.A.)
Gulf of Alaska
C A N A D A
Pine Point
Churchill
Hudson Bay
Prince Rupert
Edmonton
Vancouver
Winnipeg
Seattle
UNITED STATES
Montreal
Ottawa
San Francisco
Denver
Chicago
Los Angeles
St. Louis
New York
Philadelphia
Washington
Halif
El Paso
Houston
P A C I F I C O C E A N
Hawaii-U.S.A.
Tropic of Cancer
MEXICO
Monterrey
New Orleans
Miami
Bermuda (U.K.)
Gulf of Mexico
BAHAMAS
Guadalajara
La Habana
CUBA
Mérida
México
HAITI
DOMINICAN REP.
JAMAICA
Puerto Rico (U.S.A.)
Belmopan
Guatemala
CARIBBEAN SEA
Tegucigalpa
S. Salvador
NICARAGUA
Managua
Clipperton (Fr.)
San José
Panamá
Caracas
PANAMA
VENEZUELA
GUYANA
SURINAM
Fr. Guiana
KIRIBATI
Kiritimati
Bogotá
COLOMBIA
Equator
Quito
Arch. de Colón (Galapagos Is.Ec.)
ECUADOR
Amazonas
Manaus
Belém
B R A Z I
PERU
Îs. Marquises (Fr.)
BOLIVIA
Brasília
Lima
La Paz
Cook Is. (N.Z.)
French Polynesia
Iquique
Sucre
PARAGUAY
Paraná
Tahiti
Asunción
Sã
Pôr
I. de Pascua (Easter I.,Chil.)
URUGUAY
Pitcairn I. (U.K.)
Tropic of Capricorn
Santiago
Buenos Aires
Montev
Bahía Bl
CHILE
ARGENTINA
Pto. Montt
Pta. Arenas
Antarctic Circle
A
60°
40°
20°
0°
20°
40°
60°
160°
140°
1 : 150 000 000
0 1000 2000 3000 4000 Km
0 500 1 000 1 500 2 000 2 500 Mi

map 4

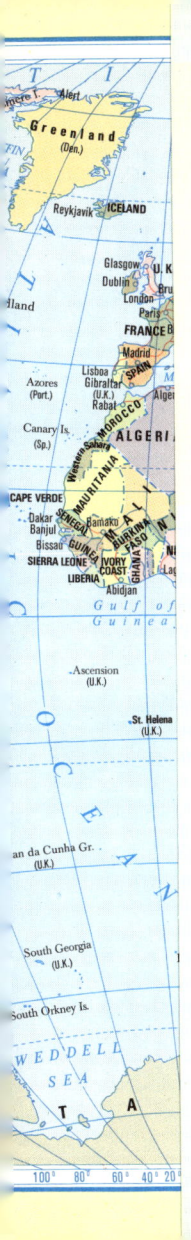

The General Agreement on Tariffs and Trade (GATT; H.Q. Genève) came into force in 1948. It deals with problems of international trade and lays down a code of conduct in international relations. 124 countries were associated in this organization at the beginning of 1986.
The World Council of Churches (office: Genève) was formally constituted in Amsterdam on 23 August 1948. In 1984, the Council had 301 members from more than 100 countries and territories.
The International Olympic Committee (H.Q.: Lausanne), founded in 1894, unites 159 National Olympic Committees.

MILITARY PACTS

NATO – the North Atlantic Treaty Organization (H.Q.: Bruxelles). The treaty was signed in Washington on 4 April 1949. A military and political grouping of western countries: Belgium, Canada, Denmark, France, Iceland, Italy, Luxembourg, the Netherlands, Norway, Portugal, the United Kingdom and the United States of America; Greece and Turkey since 1952, the Federal Republic of Germany since 1955, Spain since 1982. France withdrew from NATO in 1966.
The Warsaw Pact (H.Q.: Moskva), a military and political union of the European socialist countries for defensive purposes, signed in Warszawa on 14 May 1955. Members: Bulgaria, Czechoslovakia, the German Democratic Republic, Hungary, Poland, Romania and U.S.S.R.; Albania withdrew in 1962.
ANZUS – The Pacific Security Treaty, a military pact signed at San Francisco on 1 Sept. 1951 between Australia, New Zealand and the U.S.A.
SEATO – the South East Asia Treaty Organization (H.Q.: Krung Thep) – a military and political treaty signed in 1954. Members: Australia, France, New Zealand, the Philippines, Thailand, the United Kingdom of Great Britain and Northern Ireland and the United States of America.

Largest Cities of the World
(Population of the city proper)

Name (Country)	Population	(Year)
1. México (Mexico)	10,360,000	(1989)
2. Sŏul (Rep. of Korea)	10,280,000	(1988)
3. São Paulo (Brazil)	10,099,086	(1985)
4. Moskva (U.S.S.R.)	8,967,000	(1989)
5. New York (U.S.A.)	8,473,000	(1986)
6. Tōkyō (Japan)	8,379,385	(1986)
7. Bombay (India)	8,243,405	(1981)
8. Jakarta (Indonesia)	7,885,519	(1986)
9. Karāchi (Pakistan)	7,254,000	(1987)
10. Shanghai (China)	7,102,000	(1986)
11. London (U.K.)	6,775,200	(1986)
12. Al-Qāhirah (Egypt)	6,052,836	(1986)
13. Tehrān (Iran)	6,042,584	(1986)
14. Beijing (China)	5,968,000	(1986)
15. Rio de Janeiro (Brazil)	5,615,149	(1985)

Largest Cities of the World
(Population of the urban agglomeration)

Name (Country)	Population	(Year)
1. México (Mexico)	18,784,000	(1987)
2. New York (U.S.A.)	18,054,000	(1987)
3. São Paulo (Brazil)	15,880,000	(1985)
4. Los Angeles (U.S.A.)	13,471,000	(1987)
5. Al-Qāhirah (Egypt)	13,300,000	(1987)
6. Shanghai (China)	12,320,000	(1987)
7. Tōkyō (Japan)	11,906,331	(1986)
8. Moskva (U.S.S.R.)	11,850,000	(1988)
9. Sŏul (Rep. of Korea)	11,460,000	(1983)
10. Calcutta (India)	10,850,000	(1985)
11. Buenos Aires (Argen.)	10,728,000	(1987)
12. Rio de Janeiro (Brazil)	10,190,000	(1985)
13. Bombay (India)	10,070,000	(1985)
14. Beijing (China)	9,750,000	(1987)
15. Jakarta (Indonesia)	9,199,000	(1989)

add page 30

Kingdom, Denmark, Ireland, Greece since 1981, Portugal and Spain since 1986. **The European Parliament** consists of 434 members who are elected directly within each of the member countries (seat: Strasbourg and Luxembourg). **The European Economic Community (EEC** or "the Common Market"; H.Q.: Bruxelles), established on 25 March 1957 in Rome with the task of achieving a customs union and to co-ordinate the economic policies of member states, 64 independent developing countries of Africa, the Caribbean and the Pacific are affiliated to the Community. – **The European Coal and Steel Community (ECSC**; H.Q.: Luxembourg) established on 18 April 1951 in Paris with a task of contributing to the economic development and rising standard of living in member countries by establishing a common market for coal, coke, iron ore and steel. – **The European Atomic Energy Community (EAEC,** "Euratom"; H.Q.: Bruxelles) founded in Rome on 25 March 1957 to promote the nuclear energy industry and nuclear research.

The European Free Trade Association **(EFTA**; H.Q.: Genève) was set up in Stockholm on 3 May 1960. Its task was to eliminate tariffs and quantitative restrictions on the import and export of goods between member countries. Members: Austria, Iceland, Norway, Portugal, Sweden and Switzerland; Finland since 1985.

The Organization for Economic Co-operation and Development (OECD; H.Q.: Paris) was set up on 30 Sept. 1961 to further economic growth, rises in the standard of living, to contribute to economic co-operation between member and non-member countries and to contribute to the expansion of world trade. Member countries are: Australia, Austria, Belgium, Canada, Denmark, the Federal Republic of Germany, Finland, France, Greece, Iceland, Ireland, Italy, Japan, Luxembourg, the Netherlands, New Zealand, Norway, Portugal, Spain, Sweden, Switzerland, Turkey, the United Kingdom and the U.S.A.; associated member Yugoslavia.

The Council for Mutual Economic Assistance (CMEA; H.Q.: Moskva) was established on 8 Jan. 1949 by the socialist countries to coordinate economic planning, the implementation of joint provisions for the expansion of industry and agriculture on the basis of an international socialist division of labour, specialization and co-operation in production, the construction of fuel and power and transport systems and the exchange of scientific and technological knowledge. This international socialist organization is based on the principle of a voluntary choice of criteria and on mutual collaboration. Member countries: Bulgaria, Czechoslovakia, Hungary, Poland, Romania, the Union of Soviet Socialist Republics; since 1950 – the German Democratic Republic, 1962 – Mongolia, 1972 – Cuba and 1978 – Vietnam (10 members). Albania withdrew in 1961. Observers: Yugoslavia, the Democratic People's Republic of Korea, Laos, Angola; China has not taken part since 1961. Special status of co-operation: Finland, Iraq, Mexico. **The International Bank for Economic Cooperation** (H.Q.: Moskva) came into being in 1963; it is used by member countries of CMEA for accountancy purposes in trade and economic development.

The Organization of American States (OAS; Secretariat: Washington) was formed at a conference in Bogotá on 30 April 1948 to work towards international peace, to promote American solidarity and to coordinate economic, social, scientific, technological and cultural policies. Membership: 32 independent countries (Cuba was expelled in 1962 after U.N. intervention). **The Inter-American Development Bank (IDB**; H.Q.: Washington) was established in 1960 by 25 Latin American countries (excluding Cuba), Canada, the U.S.A., European states and Japan.

The Latin American Integration Association (ALADI = LAIA; H.Q.: Montevideo) was established in August 1980 to replace LAFTA (in 1960). Instead of across-the-board tariff cuts, the treaty envisaged an area of economic preferences, comprising a regional tariff preference for goods originating in member states. Members: Argentina, Bolivia, Brazil, Chile, Colombia, Ecuador, Mexico, Paraguay, Peru, Uruguay, Venezuela. The Andean Group (Grupo Andino) is an association of Bolivia, Chile (withdrew 1977), Colombia, Ecuador, Peru, Venezuela. Its aims are economic control and the regulation of foreign investments. The Latin American Economic System (SELA; secretariat: Caracas) to allow regional co-operation in economic and social progress of 26 Latin American countries, including Cuba.

The Caribbean Community (CARICOM) and the **Central American Common Market (CACM)** – 13 small island countries in the Caribbean (incl. Belize and Guyana) have been associated since 1973 for the purposes of coordinating foreign trade and economic development and restricting the influence of foreign business in the economic life of member countries; observers Dominican Rep., Haiti, Surinam. H.Q.: Georgetown.

The Organization of African Unity (OAU; H.Q. Addis Abeba) was established on 20 May 1963. Its chief aims are the furtherance of African unity and solidarity, the coordination of the political, economic, cultural, health, scientific and defence policies; the elimination of colonialism in Africa, common defence and the independence of the member countries as well as the development of international collaboration according to the Charter of the U.N. There were 50 members in 1984. **The African Bank of Development** (H.Q.: Abidjan) was founded in 1963 to contribute to economic and social development of member countries. **The Arab League** (H.Q.: Tunis) was founded in Cairo on 22 March 1945 with the purpose of promoting collaboration and unity in political, economic, military, financial and cultural matters. Original members: Egypt, Iraq, Jordan, Lebanon, Saudi Arabia, Syria, Yemen. There were 21 Arab member countries, and the Palestine Liberation Organization in 1984.

The Arab Monetary Fund (H.Q.: Abu Zaby) was founded in 1976, 21 members.

The Asian Development Bank (ADB; H.Q.: Manila) was founded 1966; its aims are to raise funds from private and public sources for development purposes in the region. There are 31 member countries within the ESCAP region and 14 others.

The Association of South East Asian Nations (ASEAN; H.Q.: Krung Thep), came into being in 1967 to stimulate the economic growth, social progress and cultural development of this region. Members: Brunei, Indonesia, Malaysia, the Philippines, Singapore and Thailand.

The Organization of Petroleum Exporting Countries (OPEC; H.Q.: Wien), was established in 1960 as an association of the developing countries that extract and export petroleum to protect their interests particularly against the international oil monopolies. Members: Algeria, Ecuador, Gabon, Indonesia, Iran, Iraq, Kuwait, Libya, Nigeria, Qatar, Saudi Arabia, Syria, the United Arab Emirates and Venezuela.

map 5

EUROPE

Europe lies in the temperate belt of the northern hemisphere, and although it is connected to the western side of Asia it is regarded as a separate continent for both historical and cultural reasons. Its name derives from the Accadian word "ereb", meaning "evening twilight or sunset", i.e. "the land where the sun sets", and the ancient Greeks adapted this Semitic word to the form in which it has come down to us.

Europe covers an **area of 10,382,000 sq.km**, which is 7.0% of the world's land surface (including the European part of the U.S.S.R.). It has **701 mn. inhabitants** (1988) and a population density of 67.5 persons per sq.km.

Geographical position: northernmost point of the mainland: Cape Nordkinn in Norway 71°08′ N.Lat. (of the entire continent: Cape Mys Fligeli on O. Rudol'fa island in Zeml'a Franca Iosifa (Fr. Joseph Land) 81°51′ N.Lat.); southernmost point: Punta Marroqui in Spain in the Strait of Gibraltar 35°59′ N.Lat. (island Gávdhos off the southern coast of Crete 34°48′ N.Lat.); westernmost point: Cabo da Roca in Portugal 9°29′ W.Long. (Tearaght Island off the west coast of Ireland 10°39′ W.Long.); easternmost point: the eastern foothills of the Pol'arnyj Ural in the U.S.S.R. 67°20′ E.Long. The eastern continental boundary between Europe and Asia is over 3,500 km long and leads along the eastern foothills of the Ural Mts. (Ural'skije Gory), further along the river Emba to the Caspian Sea, from there along the Kuma-Manyč Depression (along the rivers Kuma and Manyč) to the mouth of the river Don on the Sea of Azov (Azovskoje More).

Europe's coastline, the longest of all the continents, is extremely varied and measures 37,900 km (excl. the coastlines of all large and small offshore islands). Largest peninsulas: Scandinavia (area 774,000, sq.km), Iberian (581,400 sq.km), Balkan (496,700 sq.km), Appennine (251,000 sq.km). Islands are situated mainly to the North-West, where the largest are Great Britain (area 216,325 sq.km) and Iceland (102,829 sq.km); further to the North Novaja Zeml'a (81,375 sq.km) and Svalbard (62,050 sq.km), and in the South in the Mediterranean Sea there are Sicily (25,426 sq.km), Sardinia (23,813 sq.km), Corsica (8,681 sq.km) and Crete (8,259 sq.km).

The land surface of Europe varies considerably, although it has the lowest average height (340 m) of all the continents. Plains rising no higher than 200 m make up 57% of the total area of the continent. The distribution of lowland and mountain regions is determined by both geological structure and geomorphological evolution. The oldest core of the continent is the lowlands of Eastern Europe ("Fennosarmatia") with the vast East European Plain. The lowest point is the Caspian Sea (−28 m below sea level). To the East rises the longest mountain system, the Ural Mountains (Ural'skije Gory, 1,894 m) stretching over 2,500 km. The Scandinavian mountains (2,472 m) and their numerous glaciers date from the Caledonian age with typical deep fjords. The Central European Plain, which bears the marks of glaciation, and the German-Bohemian ranges (1,602 m) date from the Hercynical age, like the French Massif Central (1,886 m). The highest and most typical European mountains, the Alps (Mt. Blanc, 4,807 m), arose during the Tertiary folding as did the Carpathian Mts. (2,655 m) and the Dinara (2,751 m). Most of the Southern European peninsulas are mountainous, the highest ranges (of Tertiary age) are the Pyrenees (3,404 m) and the Appennines (2,914 m). This is a volcanic region (Etna 3,340 m), with earthquakes.

Europe's relatively moist climate has resulted in a dense **network of rivers.** The mean annual discharge is 2,560 cub.m and roughly 80% of its rivers drain into the marginal seas of the Atlantic Ocean. About 20% drain into the Caspian Sea, which has no outlet and is fed by Europe's longest river, the Volga (length 3,531 km, river basin 1,360,000 sq.km, mean annual flow 8,220 cub.m per sec.). The Eastern European rivers are at their fullest in spring and early summer and at their lowest in autumn and winter. The Central and Northern European rivers are at their fullest in spring and their lowest in early autumn. The Western European rivers, however, are at their greatest flow in winter, and at their smallest in the summer. The Southern European rivers are filled mostly by rain water in winter and some of them dry up completely in summer. The rivers of the high mountain regions have their maximum discharge (as much as 85%) in summer. The majority of **European lakes** are of glacial origin and the largest is Lake Ladoga (Ladožskoje Oz., 18,390 sq.km).

Europe spreads across 4 **climatic belts** in the Northern hemisphere. In the Far North there is the Arctic and Subarctic zone (Svalbard, Novaja Zeml'a and the northern shores of the U.S.S.R.). The main part of the continent lies in the belt of temperate climate. Western Europe has the oceanic type with prevailing westerly winds (mild winters and summers); Central Europe has a transitional climate (the summer is warm with precipitation, the winter has permanent snow cover) and Eastern Europe has the continental type (long cold winters and hot summers). Highest absolute temperature: Sevilla (Spain) 47.8°C; lowest: Ust'-Cil'ma (U.S.S.R.) −69°C, maximum rainfall Crkvice (Yugoslavia) 4,624 mm a year; minimum Almeria (Spain) 218 mm.

Mean January and July temperatures in °C (annual rainfall in mm) are as follows: Vardö −5.0 and 9.1 (597), Reykjavík −1.2 and 10.9 (870), Bergen 1.7 and 16.3 (2,002), Stockholm −2.9 and 17.8 (543), Perm' −15.1 and 18.1 (570), Aberdeen 3.3 and 13.5 (748), Hamburg −0.3 and 17.0 (734), Warszawa −3.6 and 18.9 (531), Moskva −10.5 and 18.3 (694), London 4.1 and 17.5 (638), Paris 3.6 and 19.3 (645), Davos −7.0 and 12.1 (959), Praha −0.8 and 19.9 (491), Budapest −2.3 and 20.9 (647), Genova 7.5 and 24.4 (1184), Dubrovnik 9.0 and 24.5 (1391), Madrid 4.4 and 23.6 (419), Valletta 12.8 and 25.5 (513), Athinai 8.8 and 26.5 (402).

The soil, **flora and fauna** vary with the climatic conditions. From North to South there are the following soil and vegetation zones: tundra (moss, lichen), taiga with coniferous trees, mixed broad-leaved and coniferous forest, broad-leaved woodland of the temperate belt, tree steppe, (dry grasses), semi-desert (in the Caspian region), evergreen maquis and broad-leaved Mediterranean forest. Alpine flora varies according to the altitude at which it is growing. Europe has widespread cultivated steppe with fertile arable soil. The fauna includes reindeer, wolf, brown bear, lynx, fox, deer, hare, hedgehog, various species of birds, reptiles, amphibious animals, fishes and insects.

Map of Western Europe

Grid references
A 1 — 30° — Denmark Str. — Rifstangi — 3 — 10° — 4 — 0° — 5 — 10°
60°

Iceland region
Reykjavík — Askja 1510 — 2119 — Iceland — Arctic Circle — 3921
1491 — Hvannadalshnúkur
3970

Norwegian Sea / North Sea region
B — 3062 — NORWEGIAN SEA — Lofoten
Faeroe Is.
Shetland Is. — Trondheim — 2472 — Glittertinden
I. of Lewis — Orkney Is. — Bergen — Oslo
Hebrides — Duncansby Hd. — Lindesnes — Skagerrak — 725 — Göteborg
Ben Nevis — Grampian Mts. — NORTH — Vänern 44 — 376
1343 — Glasgow — SEA — Jylland
50° — Pennines — 878 — 14 — København
5080 — Tearaght L. 1041 — IRELAND — Eyjа — Kiel — Sjælland
St. George's Chan. — Dublin — Hamburg — Szc.
33 — 1085 — GREAT BRITAIN
CELTIC — Land's End — London — Amsterdam — Central — Berlin
SEA — English Channel — Str. of Dover — Rotterdam — 1142
C — Channel Is. — Le Havre — Bruxelles 694 — Praha
5483 — Brest — Pte. du Raz — Normandie — Ardennes — Frankfurt a.M. — Bohemia — 1456
Bretagne — Plain — Main
Bay — Nantes — of France — Strasbourg — Danube — 1493
5100 — of — Massif — Jura — Bern — 3797 — S
Bordeaux — Puy de Sancy — 4807 — 1274 — 4049 — Grossglockner
Biscay — 1886 — Mt. Blanc — Lyon — Milano — Venezia — Trieste
Central — Les Écrins — APPENN
40° — C. de Finisterre — 4103 — A — Rijeka
La Coruña — 2848 — Pyrenees — G. du — Marseille — Genova
Cord. Cantábrica — Pico de Aneto
Porto — 3404 — IBERIAN — Sist. Central — LIGURIAN — 2710 — Como Grande
C. da Roca — Duero — 2316 — Madrid (Tajo) — Ebro — Mte. Cinto — SEA — 2914 — ADRIATI
5053 — Lisboa — 2592 — Barcelona — Corse — Roma
D — PENINSULA — Valencia — (Corsica) — Vesuvio
Sa. Morena — Islas Baleares — Sardegna — 1277
Pta. Marroquí — Sa. Nevada — Ibiza — Menorca — (Sardinia) — 1634 — 3830 — Napoli
Sevilla — 3478 — Mallorca — TYRRHENIAN
Mulhacén — Almería — 2887 — SEA
Tánger — Str. of Gibraltar — Str. of Bonifacio — Cagliari
1:25 000 000 — MEDITERRA — Messina
0 200 400 500 Km — Alger 2308 — 3340 — C. Pe
0 100 200 300 400 Mi — Atlas Tellien — R. Ben Sekka — Etna
4 — Plateau of the Shotts — 0° — Tunis — Sicilia
Dj. Chélia — (Sicily)
2328 — 10° — Malta — N 6

Map labels

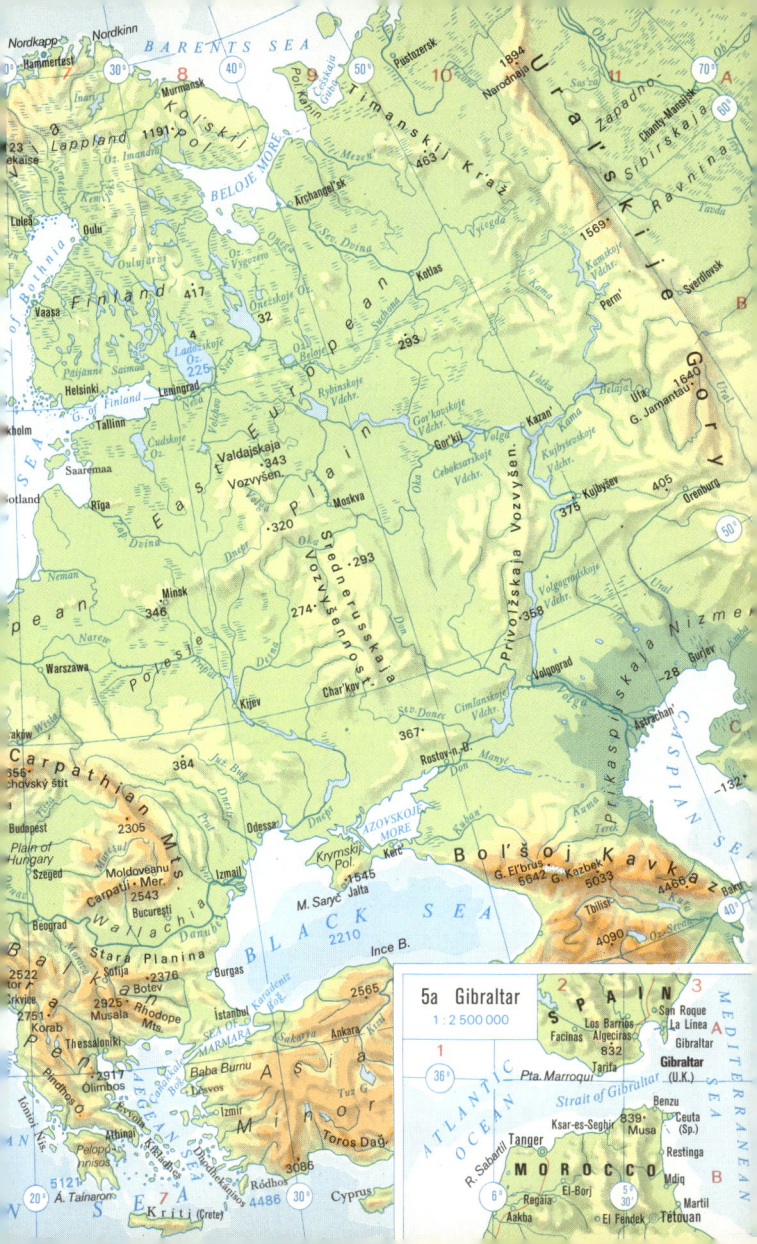

Seas & Oceans: BARENTS SEA, BELOJE MORE, Sea of Bothnia, Gulf of Finland, BLACK SEA, AZOVSKOJE MORE, Sea of Marmara, AEGEAN SEA, MEDITERRANEAN, CASPIAN SEA, ATLANTIC OCEAN

Places / Features (north to south, west to east):
Nordkapp, Nordkinn, Hammerfest, Murmansk, Pustozersk, 1894 Narodnaja, Ural'skije Gory, Zapadno-Sibirskaja Ravnina, Chanty-Mansijsk
Lappland, Kol'skij pol., 1191, Po-luostrov Kanin, Timanskij kraž, 463, Sos-va, 60°
Inari, Oz. Imandra, Pol. Kanin, Mezen, 1569, Tavda
Luleå, Oulu, Archangel'sk, Vyčegda, Kama, Sverdlovsk
Vaasa, Oulujärvi, 417, Kotlas, Kamskoje Vdchr., B
Finland, Oz. Vygozero, Suchona, Perm'
stockholm, Päijänne, Saimaa, Onežskoje Oz., 293, Vjatka
Helsinki, Ladožskoje Oz. 225, East European Plain, Belaja, 1640, Ufa, G. Jamantau
Tallinn, Leningrad, Rybinskoje Vdchr., Gor'kij, Kazan', Kujbyševskoje Vdchr.
Saaremaa, Čudskoje Oz., Valdajskaja Vozvyšen. 343, Gor'kij, Volga, Čeboksarskoje Vdchr., Kujbyšev, 405, Orenburg, 50°
Rīga, Zapadnaja Dvina, 320, Moskva, Oka, 375, Ural
Neman, Dnepr, Srednerusskaja Vozvyšennost', 293, Sura, Penza
Minsk, 346, 274, Volgogradskoje Vdchr., 358, Privolžskaja Vozvyšen.
Warszawa, Narew, Poles'je, Desna, Volgograd, Prikaspijskaja Nizmen., -28, Gur'jev
Kijev, Char'kov, Sev. Donec, C
akow, Wisła, 384, Odessa, Izmail, Rostov-n.-D., Don, Manyč, Kuma, -132
Carpathian Mts., 356, čhovský štít, Plain of Hungary, Krymskij Pol., Kerč, Azov, Astrachan', 40°
Budapest, 2305, M. Saryč, Jalta, 1545, Bol'šoj Kavkaz, G. El'brus 5642, G. Kazbek 5033, 4466, Baku
Carpati - Mer., Moldoveanu 2543, București, Tbilisi, 4090
Szeged, Wallachia, Dunărea
Beograd, Stara Planina, Burgas, Ince B., 2565, Ankara, 2210
2522, Sofija, Botev 2376, İstanbul, Kandilli tepe, Toros Dağı 3086, Cyprus, 30°
Skopje, 2751, Korab, 2925, Rhodope Mts., Baba Burnu, Davos, İzmir, Tuz Gölü, Asia Minor
Thessaloniki, 2917, Olimbos, Pindhos, Peloponnisos, Athínai, 5121, A. Taínaron, 20°, Ródhos, Kríti (Crete), 4486, E, F, 30°

5a Gibraltar

1 : 2 500 000

SPAIN — San Roque, La Línea, Los Barrios, Algeciras, Facinas, 832, **Gibraltar (U.K.)**
Pta. Marroquí, Tarifa, Strait of Gibraltar
ATLANTIC OCEAN — MEDITERRANEAN
Tanger, Ksar-es-Seghir, Benzú, Ceuta (Sp.), 839 Musa, Restinga, Mdiq
MOROCCO — R. Sabarií, Martil, Tétouan, El Fendek, Aakba, Ragaia, El-Borj

LONGEST RIVERS

Name	Length in km	River basin in sq.km
Volga	3,531	1,360,000
Danube /Donau, Dunaj, Duna, Dunav, Dunărea/	2,850	817,000
Ural	2,428	231,000
Dnepr	2,201	503,000
Kama	2,032	522,000
Don	1,870	423,000
Pečora	1,809	322,000
Oka	1,480	245,000
Belaja	1,420	142,000
V'atka	1,367	129,000
Dnestr	1,352	72,000
Rhine /Rhein, Rhin, Rijn/	1,326	224,400
Severnaja Dvina (-Suchona)	1,302	367,000
Desna	1,187	89,000
Labe /Elbe/	1,165	144,055
Vyčegda	1,070	123,000
Wisła	1,047	194,424
Loire	1,020	115,000
Zapadnaja Dvina	1,020	88,000
Tisa /Tisza/	997	157,000
Meuse /Maas/	950	49,000

LARGEST LAKES

Name	Area in sq.km	Greatest Depth in m	Altitude in m
Ladožskoje Oz.	18,390	225	4
Onežskoje Oz.	9,616	120	32
Vänern	5,585	93	44
Saimaa	4,400	58	76
Čudskoje Oz. -Pskovskoje Oz.	3,650	14	30
Vättern	1,912	120	88
IJsselmeer	1,250	6	0
Oz. Vygozero	1,159	40	29
Mälaren	1,140	64	1
Oz. Beloje	1,125	11	110
Päijänne	1,065	93	78
Inari	1,000	60	114
Oz. Il'men'	982	11	18
Oulujärvi	980	38	124
Oz. Topozero	910	56	109
Kallavesi	900	102	85
Oz. Imandra	880	67	126
Pielinen	850	48	94
Balaton	591	11	106
L. Geneva /Genfer See/	582	310	372

LARGEST ISLANDS

Name	Area in sq.km	Name	Area in sq.km	Name	Area in sq.km
Great Britain	216,325	Novaja Zeml'a (South I.)	33,275	Crete /Kríti/	8,259
Iceland	102,820	Sicily /Sicilia/	25,426	Sjælland	7,019
Ireland	83,849	Sardinia /Sardegna/	23,813	O. Kolgujev	5,250
Novaja Zeml'a (North I.)	48,100	Nordaustlandet	14,530	Évvoia	3,654
Vestspitzbergen	39,044	Corsica /Corse/	8,681	Mallorca	3,411

HIGHEST MOUNTAINS

Name (Country)	Height in m	Name (Country)	Height in m
Mont Blanc /Mte. Bianco/ (Fr.-It.)	4,807	La Meije (Fr.)	3,987
Dufourspitze /Mte. Rosa/ (Switz.-It.)	4,634	Eiger (Switz.)	3,970
Dom (Switz.)	4,545	Mt. Pelvoux (Fr.)	3,946
Weisshorn (Switz.)	4,506	Ortles (It.)	3,899
Matterhorn /Mte. Cervino/ (Switz.-It.)	4,478	Monte Viso (It.)	3,841
Dent Blanche (Switz.)	4,357	Grossglockner (Aust.)	3,797
Grand Combin (Switz.)	4,314	Wildspitze (Aust.)	3,774
Finsteraarhorn (Switz.)	4,274	Grossvenediger (Aust.)	3,674
Aletschhorn (Switz.)	4,195	Tödi (Switz.)	3,614
Jungfrau (Switz.)	4,158	Adamello (It.)	3,554
Les Ecrins (Fr.)	4,103	Mulhacén (Sp.)	3,478
Gran Paradiso (It.)	4,061	Pico de Aneto (Sp.)	3,404
Piz Bernina (Switz.)	4,049	Monte Perdido (Sp.)	3,355

ACTIVE VOLCANOES

Name (Country)	Altitude in m	Latest eruption
Etna (Sicilia, It.)	3,340	1986
Beerenberg (Jan Mayen, Nor.)	2,278	1971
Askja (Iceland)	1,510	1961
Hekla (Iceland)	1,491	1981
Vesuvio (It.)	1,277	1949
Pico Gorda (Azores, Port.)	1,021	1968
Stromboli (Ie. Eolie, It.)	926	1975

FAMOUS NATIONAL PARKS

Name (Country)	Area in sq.km
Hohe Tauern (Austria)	10,000
Pečoro-Ilyčskij Zap. (U.S.S.R.)	7,213
Hardangervidda (Nor.)	3,430
Lake District N.P. (U.K.)	2,251
North Wales (Snowdonia) N.P. (U.K.)	2,188
Šumava-Böhmerwald (Czech.-F.R.Ger.)	1,860
Bialowieski P.N. (Pol.-U.S.S.R.)	1,292

map 6

EUROPE

Country	Area in sq.km	Population year 1988	Density per sq.km	Capital
Albania	28,748	3,143,000	109	Tiranë
Andorra	468	49,000	105	Andorra la Vella
Austria	83,853	7,605,000	90	Wien
Belgium	30,521	9,925,000	325	Bruxelles/ Brussel
Bulgaria	110,912	8,995,000	81	Sofija
Czechoslovakia	127,899	15,624,021	122	Praha
Denmark	43,075	5,129,516	119	København
Faeroe Islands (Den.)	1,399	46,950	34	Tórshavn
Finland	338,145	4,955,000	15	Helsinki / Helsingfors
France	543,998	55,874,000	103	Paris
German Democratic Republic[+]	108,333	16,340,000	151	Berlin
Germany, Federal Republic of	248,229	59,303,900	239	Bonn
Gibraltar (U.K.)	6.5	29,692	4,568	Gibraltar
Greece	131,957	10,013,000	76	Athínai
Hungary	93,036	10,596,000	114	Budapest
Iceland	102,829	249,000	2.4	Reykjavík
Ireland	70,283	3,538,000	50	Dublin
Italy	301,278	57,476,000	191	Roma
Liechtenstein	160	28,000	175	Vaduz
Luxembourg	2,586	377,000	146	Luxembourg
Malta	316	345,636	1,094	Valletta
Monaco	1.95	27,850	14,282	Monaco
Netherlands	41,548	14,757,948	355	Amsterdam
Norway	323,878	4,195,661	13	Oslo
Poland	312,683	37,862,063	121	Warszawa
Portugal (incl. Azores, Madeira)	91,985	10,408,000	113	Lisboa
Romania	237,500	23,048,000	97	București
San Marino	60.6	22,746	375	San Marino
Spain (incl. Canary Is.)	504,783	39,085,000	77	Madrid
Svalbard (Nor.)	62,422	3,942[1]	0.06	Longyearbyen
Sweden	449,964	8,436,486	19	Stockholm
Switzerland	41,293	6,566,900	159	Bern
Turkey – European part	23,764	5,800,000	244	Ankara
Union of Soviet Socialist Republics	22,274,900	285,940,000	13	Moskva
U.S.S.R. – European part	5,433,900	204,590,000	38	Moskva
United Kingdom[*]	244,872	57,077,000	233	London
Vatican City, State of	0.44	766	1,741	Città del Vaticano
West Berlin[+]	480	2,016,100[1]	4,200	Berlin (West)
Yugoslavia	255,804	23,558,928	92	Beograd

*) incl. Isle of Man and Channel Is.   [1] year 1987   +) since 3 October 1990 part of FRG

13.7 % of the world's population live in Europe, **701 million people,** with a population density of 68 persons per sq.km (1988), which makes it the most densely inhabited continent. The most densely populated countries (leaving aside small countries like Monaco, Gibraltar, West Berlin and the Vatican City) are the Netherlands, Belgium, the Federal Republic of Germany, the United Kingdom and Italy. The Scandinavian countries, however, have a low population density. Europe has a low rate of **population growth** – 0.35% in the years 1980–85, birth rate 18.9 per 1,000, death rate 9.8 per 1,000. In 1980–85 the average life expectancy was 70 years (men) and 76.6 (women).

European languages are of three main Indo-European types: Slavonic, Germanic, and Romance. But there are other language groups: Celtic, Semitic, Finno-Ugric, etc. The main European nationalities are Russians, Germans, Italians, English, French, Ukrainians, Spanish and Poles.

Conurbations are typical features of all industrial areas, in particular in Central England, the Netherlands, the Rhine and Ruhr regions of the Federal Republic of Germany. Saxony in the German Democratic Republic, Upper Silesia in Poland, the Donbas region of the U.S.S.R. and the Po Valley in Italy. Europe has 33 cities with a population over one million and 71.5% of all inhabitants live in towns.

Economically Europe is the world's most advanced continent. It looks back on a tradition of industrial development and intensive plant and livestock farming. The extraction of coal, oil, natural gas, iron ore, bauxite, nickel, mercury, magnesite, phosphates and potassium salts is of world-wide importance. But Europe's main and most important industry is engineering. Europe has a highly developed transport network and is the continent with the greatest volume of foreign trade.

A 1
2
3
4
5
60°
30°
20°
10°
0°
10°
ICELAND
Akureyri
Reykjavík
Seydisfjördur
Arctic Circle
NORWEGIAN SEA
B
Thorshavn
Faeroe Is. (Den.)
Shetland Is. (U. K.)
ATLANTIC OCEAN
Hebrides
Thurso
Orkney Is. (U. K.)
Molde
Trondheim
Dombås
Bergen
Hamar
Oslo
Stavanger
Skien
Fredrikstad
Vänern
Skagerrak
Kattegat
Frederikshavn
Göteborg
Ålborg
Århus
København
Esbjerg
DENMARK
Malmö
Kiel
UNITED KINGDOM
Aberdeen
GLASGOW
Londonderry
Edinburgh
NORTH SEA
Sligo
Galway
Belfast
Newcastle u. Tyne
IRISH SEA
Limerick
IRELAND
DUBLIN
LEEDS
Liverpool
Kingston u. Hull
Cork
Manchester
BIRMINGHAM
CELTIC SEA
Cardiff
Bristol
Plymouth
LONDON
Dover
Portsmouth
AMSTERDAM
's-Gravenhage
NETHERLANDS
HAMBURG
BREMEN
Rostock
FEDERAL
BERLIN
HANNOVER
Magdeburg
ESSEN
LEIPZIG
KÖLN (Cologne)
REP.
Bonn
DRESDEN
FRANKFURT a. M.
English Ch.
Channel Is. (U. K.)
Calais
BRUXELLES (Brussel)
BELGIUM
C
Brest
Caen
Le Havre
LUXEMBOURG
Luxembourg
Seine
Reims
PARIS
Le Mans
St.-Nazaire
Loire
Orléans
Nantes
Strasbourg
Nürnberg
Plzeň
CZECH
STUTTGART
OF GERMANY
Rhein
Donau
Linz
MÜNCHEN (Munich)
Bay of Biscay
La Rochelle
FRANCE
Dijon
Zürich
Bern
LIECHT.
Vaduz
Innsbruck
AUSTRIA
La Coruña
Limoges
Genève (Geneva)
SWITZERLAND
Lyon
Bordeaux
Udine
Ljubljana
Gijón
Vigo
León
Bilbao
Garonne
TORINO (Turin)
MILANO
Venezia (Venice)
Trieste
Toulouse
Rhône
Porto
Duero
Valladolid
Ebro
40°
SPAIN
GENOVA (Genoa)
Bologna
Pula
Coimbra
MARSEILLE
Nice
MONACO
Monaco
SAN MARINO
San Marino
ANDORRA
Andorra
Toulon
Livorno
Firenze
ADRIATIC
PORTUGAL
LISBOA (Lisbon)
ZARAGOZA
G. du Lion
Corse (Fr.)
Bastia
MADRID
Tajo
BARCELONA
VATICAN C.
Ajaccio
Pescara
Guadiana
VALENCIA
Sassari
ROMA (Rome)
ITALY
Córdoba
Turia
Menorca
TYRRHENIAN SEA
Islas Baleares
D
SEVILLA
Guadalquivir
Palma
Mallorca
NAPOLI (Naples)
Faro
Ibiza
Cádiz
Alicante
Cagliari
Sardegna (It.)
MÁLAGA
MEDITERRANEAN
Str. of Gibraltar
Gibraltar (U. K.)
Almería
Cartagena
Tanger
Ceuta (Sp.)
PALERMO
Messina
1 : 25 000 000
0 200 400 600 Km
0 100 200 300 400 Mi
ALGER
Bejaïa
Annaba
Bizerte
Sicilia
Catania
Constantine
TUNIS
TUNISIA
Siracusa
Safi
10°
4
0°
5
10°
6
MOROCCO
ALGERIA
Djelfa
Biskra
MALTA
Valletta
MARRAKECH
Sfax

BARENTS SEA
BELOJE MORE
UNION OF SOVIET SOCIALIST REPUBLICS
FINLAND
ROMANIA
BULGARIA
GREECE
TURKEY
ALBANIA
Murmansk
Kirovsk
Apatity
Gremicha
Kandalakša
Pečenga
Muonio
Kemi
Taivalkoski
Kalevala
Kem'
Belomorsk
Onega
Archangel'sk
Mezen'
Narjan-Mar
Pečora
Uchta
Ber'ozovo
Serginskij
Chanty-Mansijsk
Surgut
Luleå
Oulu
Iisalmi
Medvežjegorsk
Joensuu
Vaasa
Kuopio
Mikkeli
Petrozavodsk
Tampere
Pori
Kotka
Vyborg
Turku
Helsinki
Espoo
Tallinn
LENINGRAD
Volchov
Narva
Novgorod
Pärnu
Pskov
Riga
Daugavpils
Šiauliai
Polock
Vitebsk
Smolensk
Kaunas
VILNIUS
MINSK
Kaliningrad
Olsztyn
Grodno
Białystok
Mogil'ov
Gomel'
Soligorsk
Pinsk
Brest
WARSZAWA
(Warsaw)
Lublin
Korosten'
KIJEV
L'VOV
Ternopol'
Vinnica
Užgorod
Černovcy
Košice
KRAKÓW
Miskolc
Debrecen
Cluj-Napoca
Iași
Szeged
Oradea
Timișoara
Subotica
BEOGRAD
(Belgrade)
Craiova
Ploiești
Galați
BUCUREȘTI
(Bucharest)
Izmail
Constanța
Vidin
Kruševac
Niš
Pleven
Ruse
Varna
Burgas
SOFIJA
(Sofia)
Plovdiv
Skopje
ISTANBUL
Alexandroúpolis
Thessaloníki
BURSA
Balıkesir
Lárisa
Tríkala
Lamía
ATHÍNAI
(Athens)
Pátrai
Kalámai
IZMIR
Denizli
Ródhos
Iráklion
Kriti
AEGEAN SEA
Rybinsk
JAROSLAVL'
Kalinin
Vladimir
Ivanovo
Kostroma
Vologda
Belozorsk
Konoša
Kotlas
Syktyvkar
Šarja
Kirov
Joškar-Ola
KAZAN'
GOR'KIJ
MOSKVA
(Moscow)
R'AZAN'
TULA
Br'ansk
Or'ol
Kursk
Mičurinsk
Tambov
VORONEŽ
Saransk
PENZA
SARATOV
Syzran'
ULJANOVSK
KUJBYŠEV
Vol'sk
Aleksandrov Gaj
VOLGOGRAD
CHAR'KOV
Poltava
DNEPROPETROVSK
ZAPOROŽJE
LUGANSK
DONECK
ROSTOV-n.-D.
MARIUPOL'
Melitopol'
Nikolajev
KIŠIN'OV
ODESSA
Cherson
Simferopol'
Sevastopol'
Jalta
Kerč'
AZOVSKOJE M.
KRASNODAR
Novorossijsk
Armavir
Stavropol'
Kislovodsk
Nal'čik
Ordžonikidze
Groznyj
Machačkala
Suchumi
Kutaisi
TBILISI
Gandža
BAKU
ASTRACHAN'
Gurjev
Makat
Fort Ševčenko
Ševčenko
CASPIAN SEA
BLACK SEA
Solikamsk
Berezniki
PERM'
SVERDLOVSK
ČEL'ABINSK
IŽEVSK
Naber. Čelny
UFA
Magnitogorsk
Sterlitamak
Išimbaj
Sibaj
ORENBURG
Orsk
Buzuluk
Ural'sk
Akt'ubinsk
Serov
Ivdel'
Polunočnoje
Tobol'sk
T'umen'
Šadrinsk
Tavda
Pečora
Vyčegda
Sev. Dvina
Suchona
Kama
Volga
Oka
Don
Sev. Donec
Dnepr
Dnestr
Desna
Prip'at'
Zap. Dvina
Neman
Dunărea
Prut
Ural
Emba
Kuma
Terek
Rybinskoje Vdchr.
Gor'kovskoje Vdchr.
Kujbyševskoje Vdchr.
Saratovskoje Vdchr.
Volgogradskoje Vdchr.
Ciml'anskoje Vdchr.
Ladožskoje Oz.
Onežskoje Oz.
Čudskoje Oz.
Češskaja G.
6 a Channel Islands
1 : 2 500 000
C. de la Hague
Alderney
Casquets
St. Annes
English Channel
Pas de la Déroute
St. Sampson
St. Peter Port
Guernsey
Sark
Channel Islands
(U. K.)
Jersey
St. Mary
Rozel
St. Aubin
St. Helier
Roches Douvres
Barnouic
ATLANTIC OCEAN
Cherbourg
St.-Pierre-Église
Barfleur
Diélette
Bricquebec
Valognes
St. Sauveur le V.
Barneville-Carteret
La Haye-du-Puits
Lessay
Carentan
Périers
Coutances
Montmartin-s.-M.
FRANCE

UNITED KINGDOM

The United Kingdom of Great Britain and Northern Ireland, area 244,103 sq.km (with the Channel Islands and the Isle of Man 244,872 sq.km), **population 57,077,000** (mid-year 1988), **constitutional monarchy** (Queen Elizabeth II since 6 February 1952). – Currency: £1 = 100 pence.

Geographical position. The United Kingdom occupies the major part of the British Isles off the north-west coast of Europe. It is separated from the continent by the North Sea and the English Channel, which, at its narrowest point, the Strait of Dover, is only 34 km wide. The largest island is Great Britain, 216,325 sq.km; it is separated by the Irish Sea from Ireland, the northern part of which belongs to the United Kingdom. The islands of the Outer and Inner Hebrides stretch along the indented west coast of Scotland. The Orkney Islands and the Shetland Islands form the northernmost part of the British Isles. The Isle of Wight, the Isles of Scilly, and the Channel Islands are to be found off the south coast of England, the Isle of Man and Anglesey in the Irish Sea.

Geology. Up to the Pleistocene Era the British Isles formed part of the European continental plate. Its geological structure and topography developed in the same way as that of the continent. Caledonian and Hercynian foldings affected the islands in the Paleozoic Era. The Caledonian folding left its mark upon Scotland, the northern part of Ireland, England and Wales; the southern parts of the islands were shaped in the Hercynian movements with the hills running predominantly in a north-south direction. The old rocks have since been gradually eroded into rolling plains with hills of rounded shapes. The newer Alpine folding caused numerous faults, along with rift valleys and horsts have formed. The south-eastern part of Great Britain is taken up by the London Basin, formed of sediments and fringed by striking ridges of high ground. The Pleistocene ice sheets and ice caps covered the entire British Isles north of the Thames valley. To this day the land bears numerous marks of glacial activity: moraines, corries, glacial lakes, etc. The subsidence of the continent gave rise to many islands and river estuaries forming deep inlets along the coastline.

Hills and mountains. The most mountainous part of the United Kingdom is Scotland. The Scottish Highlands comprise the North West Highlands and the Grampian Mountains with Ben Nevis, 1,343 m, the highest mountain peak in the United Kingdom. The fertile Central Lowlands extend southward and are enclosed by the hilly Southern Uplands. The border between England and Scotland runs along the Cheviot Hills and the lower reaches of the River Tweed.

The main ranges in England – the Pennines (Cross Fell, 893 m) and the Cumbrian Mountains with Scafell Pike, 978 m, England's highest peak – run in a north-south direction. The Cotswolds rise in the south-west and two rolling uplands, Dartmoor and Exmoor, are in the far south-west. The remaining land consists, for the most part, of either hilly or low-lying country, as in the Midlands. In Wales the highest mountain, at 1,085 m above sea-level, is Snowdon in the Cambrian Mountains. The highest point of Northern Ireland is Slieve Donard, 852 m.

Rivers. The British rivers are short with a strong flow of water throughout the year. The estuaries serve as natural harbours, and some ships have direct access to the hinterland on those rivers with reliable high tides. The sources of the rivers are divided by low watersheds, which facilitated the construction of a wide network of canals. The longest rivers are the Severn (354 km) and the Thames (338 km) with the Thames Barrier below London. Most of the **lakes** are of glacial origin and are to be found in large numbers in Scotland, the Lake District, and in Northern Ireland. Best known are Lough Neagh (396 sq.km), Lough Erne, Loch Lomond and Loch Ness.

Climate. The climate is oceanic with moderate temperatures and abundant precipitation. The temperature is modified in summer and in winter by the Gulf Stream flowing in a north-easterly direction along the west coast. The mean annual temperature in the period 1951–80 in England and Wales was 9.4°C (January 3.6°C, July 15.6°C), Scotland 8.0°C (3.0°C, 13.4°C), Northern Ireland 8.5 (3.5°C, 13.9°C). The prevailing south-westerly winds bring moisture from the Atlantic Ocean. The long-term average precipitation (1941–70) was 912 mm in England and Wales, 1,431 mm in Scotland and 1,095 mm in Northern Ireland. Rainfall is at its highest in November and December and at its lowest in April.

Administrative units. The United Kingdom is composed of four countries, England, Scotland, Wales and Northern Ireland. The main pattern of local government is the division into counties – Scotland has had regions since 1975 – within which there are district authorities. The Channel Islands and the Isle of Man enjoy a degree of autonomy.

System of Government. The monarch (King or Queen) is the head of state, succession following the hereditary principle. The Sovereign is the head of the judiciary, the commander-in-chief of all the armed forces and the temporal 'governor' of the established Church of England. The United Kingdom is governed, in the name of the Queen, by Her Majesty's Government, headed by the Prime Minister. The Government exercises executive power and is responsible to Parliament for its activities.

The supreme organ of state is Parliament composed of the House of Commons and the House of Lords, a law-making body which controls the activities of the Government. All British citizens aged 18 and over have the franchise. General elections are held a minimum of every five years. One Member is returned to the House of Commons for each of the 650 constituencies on the principle of a simple majority.

The political system is based on two major parties, one forming the Government and the other the Opposition. The majority party, at present, is the Conservative Party (with Mrs M. Thatcher as Prime Minister) and the Opposition is formed by the Labour Party.

Population (1988). The estimate population on 30 June 1988 was 57,065,400 persons, of which: 48.6% were male and 51.4% female. England had a population of 47,536,300, Wales 2,857,000, Scotland 5,094,000 and Northern Ireland 1,578,100. The United Kingdom has a high population **density**, 234 persons per sq.km, but they are distributed unevenly: England 365 persons per sq.km, Scotland 65, Wales 138 and Northern Ireland 117. 78.4% are English, 8.9% Scots, 4.0% Irish, 1.3% Welsh. In 1985 92.5% of the population lived in towns. London, **the capital**, is the main administrative, economic, cultural and political centre of country. The City of Inner London had 2,493.6 thousands inhab., Outer London 4,241.8 and the Greater London 6,735.4 including 32 boroughs.

There has been a steady decline in the birth rate from 18.8 per 1,000 in 1964 to 12.9 per 1,000 in 1984. Despite the decline in mortality (11.4 per 1,000) the natural population increase of 1.5 per thousand is very low and a further decline is expected in coming years. The United Kingdom is a country with a very low rate of infant

map 7

mortality, 9.6 per thousand (England and Wales 9.5 per thousand, Scotland 10.3 per thousand, Northern Ireland 10.5 per thousand) and had average life expectancy. In the period 1980–82 men reached an average age of 70.8 years, women 76.9 years. Those aged 0–14 years make up 19.5% of the population, the age group 15–64 years makes up 59.9% and those aged 65 years and over make up 20.6%. There is a considerable migration to and from the United Kingdom. Since the first half of the 20th century the immigration from Commonwealth countries has been rising but is now regulated by several Immigration Acts. In 1984 172,000 people came to the U.K. from outside Europe and 136,000 persons emigrated mainly to Commonwealth countries.

County districts in the United Kingdom (estimate, 30 June 1988)

London	6,735,400	Wigan	307,600	Bolton	263,600
Birmingham	993,700	Coventry	306,200	Walsall	262,300
Leeds	709,600	Dudley	304,300	Plymouth	258,100
Glasgow	703,200	Belfast	299,600	Rotherham	251,800
Sheffield	528,300	Sefton	297,600	Wolverhampton	249,400
Liverpool	469,600	Sandwell	296,300	Kingston upon Hull	247,000
Bradford	464,100	Sunderland	296,100	Stoke-on-Trent	246,800
Manchester	445,900	Doncaster	291,600	Salford	235,600
Edinburgh	433,500	Stockport	290,900	Barnsley	220,900
Bristol	377,700	Cardiff	283,900	Oldham	219,500
Kirklees	375,300	Newcastle upon Tyne	279,600	Thameside	216,800
Wirral	334,800	Leicester	278,600	Trafford	215,800
Wakefield	311,600	Nottingham	273,500	Derby	215,400

The official language is English, together with Welsh in Wales. The Scottish form of Gaelic survives in Scotland, while in Northern Ireland a few people still speak Irish Gaelic.

English is the official language in the Channel Is., with the exception of Jersey, where Norman French (patois) is widely spoken. Manx, the language used on official occasions on the Isle of Man, belongs to the Celtic languages.

Education (1983/84). School attendance is compulsory from the age of 5 to 16 and is free of charge. Primary schools are coeducational but secondary and independent schools are often single sex. The great majority of schools, attended by over 95% of school children, are publically maintained. Children between the age of 2 and 5 attend 1,260 nurseries or play groups. There are 25,326 primary and 5,328 secondary schools attended by 9.7 mn. pupils with a teaching staff of 552,500. There were 300,593 full-time and 36,319 part-time students at universities, of which 39.6% were women students and 9.6% overseas students. Among the 46 universities (including the Open University) are some of the oldest in the world (Oxford, Cambridge, St. Andrews, Aberdeen, Edinburgh and Glasgow). The universities are autonomous institutions with their own forms of government, but receive grants from the University Grants Committee.

Health Services (1983). Medical care is provided free of charge under the National Health Service. In the United Kingdom there were 28,663 physicians, i.e. 1 to 1,967 inhabitants. Total health service staff and practitioners were 1,057,154. There were 430,915 hospital beds (1984). It is also possible to obtain private medical care.

Religion (1980). 87.8% were Christians (57.0% Anglicans, 13.0% Roman Catholics). The majority of the population are nominally members of the established Church of England or the Church of Scotland or of the Free Churches.

The economy (data for 1985). The United Kingdom is one of the most highly developed countries in the world. It holds an important position in the fields of international trade, seafaring, banking, and insurance. Apart from industry and trade, important sources of revenue derive from foreign investments, air and sea transport, financial insurance and banking transactions and tourism. Important industries such as steel and the energy industries (coal, gas, electricity, oil), rail, road haulage and air transport, the post office and the majority of ports are in public ownership. The economically active population numbers 27,325,000 persons, i.e. 48.4% of all inhabitants (female 40.0%, unemployed 12.0%). In 1984 total employees 21,155,000, 1.6% of these were engaged in agriculture, forestry and fishery, 33.7% were in industry and construction, 64.7% were in services. **Industry** (1984). The United Kingdom was the first country to develop factory production, and industry is the most important sector of the British economy. Together with the construction and fuel and power industries it produces 33.7% of the gross national product and employs 32.2% of the economically active population. The most important industry is manufacturing, which contributes 24.4% to the GNP (27.6% of the labour force). In recent years the most successful industries have been engineering, chemical, coal and oil processing.

Mining (1984). The United Kingdom suffers a shortage of mineral raw materials with the exception of coal. The main coal mining regions are in Central and North-west England (Lancashire, South and West Yorkshire, Derbyshire, Nottinghamshire, Durham, Northumberland), Central Scotland (Clydeside) and South Wales (Bristol Channel). The run-down of the coal mining industry – 49.5 mn. tonnes – is being reversed with heavy investments. As a consequence of the world energy crisis there has been increasing local production of crude petroleum, 125.9 mn. tonnes and natural gas 1,492,539 TJ, chiefly in the North Sea oil fields (oil: Argyll, Forties, Piper; natural gas: Frigg Leman Bank, West Sole, Hewett, Indefatigable, Viking). Total crude petroleum – tested reserves in the UK Continental Shelf are 2,033 mn. tonnes and natural gas tested reserves 739,000 mn. cub.m. Ore mining, once of considerable importance, is steadily decreasing. Mining (1982) of: iron ore produces 134,160 tonnes (Fe metal content) in Cumbria, Lancashire and Staffordshire, tin ore 4,176 tonnes (Sn metal content) in Cornwall and lead ore 3,240 tonnes (Pb metal content) in Clwyd, Durham and Derbyshire. Salt is mined in Cheshire, potash in Cleveland, as well as china and potter's clay.

Industrial production. Metallurgy (1985, in tonnes). The United Kingdom is one of the world's largest steel producing nations. Output of crude steel totalled 15.7 mn., pig iron 10.5 mn., coke 3.2 mn. The biggest steel works are run by the British Steel Corporation; the main centres of steel production are Sheffield, Swansea, Port Talbot, Teesside, the counties of Lincolnshire, Lancashire, Cheshire and the Greater Glasgow region. The British non-ferrous metal processing and fabricating industry is also very important (1984, in tonnes): virgin aluminium 287,900 and 143,900 of secondary metal (refineries at Kinlochleven, Foyers, Fort William, Dolgarrog, Resolven); refined virgin copper 69,400, secondary metal 67,400; refined lead 331,300 (Northfleet); zinc 85,600 (Avonmouth), refined nickel 22,300.

North Sea / Atlantic Ocean — Scotland

- Shetland (Yell, Unst, Fetlar, Mainland, St. Magnus B., Sumburgh Hd., Fair I.)
- Orkney Islands (Westray, Rousay, Sanday, Stronsay, Mainland, S. Ronaldsay, Pentland Firth, Dunnet Hd., Duncansby Hd.)
- Kinnaird's Hd., Buchan Ness, Aberdeen
- Outer Hebrides (Butt of Lewis, Lewis, North Uist, Benbecula, South Uist, Barra, Bárra Hd., St. Kilda)
- The Minch, Little Minch, Sd. of Harris
- North Rona, C. Wrath
- Inner Hebrides — Skye, Rhum, Eigg, Coll, Tiree, Mull, Colonsay, Jura, Islay, Passage of Tiree, Fair Hd., Malin Hd.
- North West Highlands — Ben More 998, Ben Wyvis 1045, Ben Hope, Ben Macdhui 1311 M.t.s., Ben Attow, Ben Nevis 1343, Inverness
- Grampians — Ben Lawers 1214, Ben More 966, Lochnagar 1148, Ochil Hills, Ben Lomond
- Firth of Tay, Firth of Forth, Dundee, Edinburgh 535, Glasgow, Clyde, Firth of Clyde
- Southern Uplands — Lammermuir Hs., Cheviot Hills 816, Berwick-upon-Tweed
- Moray Firth, Dornoch Firth

NORTH SEA
ATLANTIC OCEAN

ATLANTIC
IRISH SEA
CELTIC SEA
English Channel
Bristol Channel
St. George's Channel
Strait of Dover
Ireland
Central Plain
Britain
Pennines
Cambrian Mts.
Cumbrian Mts.
Cotswolds
North Downs
South Downs
The Weald
Erris Hd.
Mullet Pen.
Achill I.
Clare I.
Inishbofin
Nephin 807
Mweelrea 819
Aran Is.
Loop Hd.
Blasket Is.
Tearaght I.
Valencia I.
Brandon Mt. 953
Carrauntoohil 1041
Caha Mts. 707
Mizen Hd.
Limerick
Galty Mts. 920
Waterford
Cork
Cork Hr.
St. Bloom Mts. 529
Wicklow Mts.
Lugnaquillia Mtn. 926
Mt. Leinster 796
Dublin
Wexford Hr.
Carnsore Pt.
Mourne Mts.
St. Donard 852
Belfast
Iron Mts. 667
Donegal B.
Sligo B.
Galway B.
Dundalk B.
Dundrum B.
Lough Neagh
Mull of Galloway
St. Bees Hd.
Snaefell 620
I. of Man
Scafell Pikes 978
Whernside 737
North York Moors 454
Vale of York
Middlesbrough
Flamborough Hd.
Kingston upon Hull
Spurn Hd.
Leeds
Goole
Sheffield
The Peaks 636
Liverpool
Formby Pt.
Cheshire Plain
Lincoln
The Wash
The Fens
Norwich
Breckland
Lowestoft
Cambridge
The Naze
Birmingham
The Wrekin 407
Gt. Ormes Hd.
Carmel Hd.
Anglesey
Menai Str.
Caernarvon B.
Snowdon 1085
Cader Idris 892
Plynlimon 752
Cardigan Bay
Tremadoc B.
Brecon Beacons 886
Swansea
Cardiff
St. David's Hd.
Milford Haven
St. Brides B.
Carmarthen B.
Oxford
Chiltern Hs. 280
London
North Foreland
Dover
Leith Hill 294
Bristol
Salisbury Plain
Southampton
Brighton
Beachy Hd.
Dungeness
I. of Wight 239
The Needles
Spithead
Exmoor
Dunkery Beacon 520
Hartland Pt.
High Willhays 621
Dartmoor
Bodmin Moor
Plymouth
Start Pt.
Lyme Bay
I. of Portland
Land's End
Is. of Scilly
Lizard Pt.
Falmouth B.
Channel Is.
Alderney
Guernsey
Jersey
C. de la Hague
Cherbourg
Baie de la Seine
Le Havre
Rouen
Calais
Boulogne-s.-M.
1 : 6 000 000
0 50 100 150 Km
0 20 40 60 80 100 Mi

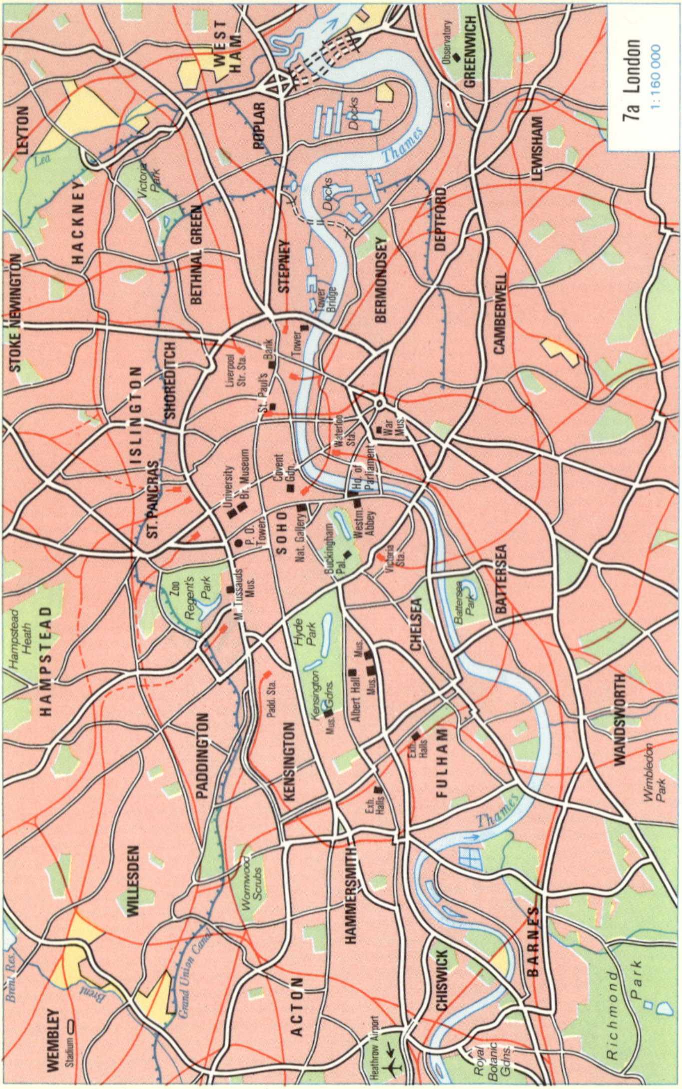
7a London
1:160 000
STOKE NEWINGTON
LEYTON
HACKNEY
Lea
Victoria Park
WEST HAM
POPLAR
Docks
Thames
GREENWICH
Observatory
LEWISHAM
DEPTFORD
BETHNAL GREEN
STEPNEY
Tower Bridge
BERMONDSEY
CAMBERWELL
ISLINGTON
SHOREDITCH
Liverpool Str. Sta.
Bank
Tower
St. Paul's
Waterloo Sta.
War Mus.
ST. PANCRAS
University
Br. Museum
Covent Gdn.
Hs. of Parliament
SOHO
P. O. Tower
Nat. Gallery
Westm. Abbey
Buckingham Pal.
Victoria Sta.
Zoo
Regent's Park
M. Tussauds Mus.
Hyde Park
CHELSEA
Battersea Park
BATTERSEA
HAMPSTEAD
Hampstead Heath
Padd. Sta.
Kensington Gdns.
Mus.
Albert Hall
PADDINGTON
KENSINGTON
Exh. Halls
FULHAM
WANDSWORTH
Wimbledon Park
WILLESDEN
Wormwood Scrubs
HAMMERSMITH
Grand Union Canal
Brent Res.
Brent
WEMBLEY
Stadium
ACTON
CHISWICK
BARNES
Richmond Park
Heathrow Airport
Royal Botanic Gdns.

map 8

Engineering (1984): The United Kingdom is an important producer of transport equipment (London, Birmingham, Coventry, Manchester, Nottingham, Wolverhampton, Glasgow, Newcastle upon Tyne) 908,906 passenger cars, 224,825 commercial vehicles, of which 157,963 light commercial vehicles; 16,499 buses and coaches (of which 1,688 were double-deckers), 56 ships over 100 GRT (shipyards on Clydeside, Tyneside, Wearside, Merseyside, Teesside and at Barrow-in-Furness), civil and military aircraft (Yeovil, Bristol, Gloucester, Coventry, Luton, Derby, Manchester, Bedford). Engineering industries include the production of textile machinery (Bradford, Halifax, Keighley), industrial plants and electrical and electronic engineering (Manchester, Rugby, Newcastle upon Tyne, Stafford). In the **chemicals industry** (1984) (Birmingham, Glasgow, Newcastle upon Tyne, Wilton, Aberdeen) fast growth has been recorded in organic chemicals, the production of all synthetic resins 1.44 mn. tonnes, pharmaceutical chemicals. The production of sulphuric acid amounted to 2.65 mn. tonnes, phosphates 0.41 mn. tonnes (1983), mixed fertilizers 3.08 mn. tonnes, synthetic rubber 240,400 tonnes (Hythe).

The textile industry (1984) produced traditional wool 37,000 tonnes, woollen fabrics 90.7 mn. sq.m (London, Huddersfield, Halifax, Bradford), cotton (single yarn) 38,000 tonnes and 265 mn. m cotton (woven cloth, Lancashire) and new man-made fibres 383 mn. m and fabrics (Wilton, Drighlington, Little Heath, Coventry). The linen industry is centred on Northern Ireland and along the east coast of Scotland (Dundee, Abroath, Montrose). Jute products (Dundee). Macclesfield is the centre of the silk industry and Nottingham and Leicester produce hosiery and knitwear. Footwear production is centred on the Rossendale Valley, Leicester and Norwich 128 mn. pairs. The principal manufacturing centres of the clothing industry are London, Leeds and Manchester. The glass industry is centred in Glasgow, London, Birmingham and Sunderland. Cement production 13.48 mn. tonnes occurs along the Medway and the Humber. The paper industry produced 3.59 mn. tonnes of paper and board, of which 235,700 tonnes newsprint.

The food, drink and tobacco industries have, in recent years, been subject to mergers amongst leading firms. Production (1984): 60,105,000 hl beer (London, Burton-upon-Trent, Birmingham, Edinburgh) and alcoholic spirits 2,986,000 hl mainly of Scotch whisky and gin. The tobacco industry (93.4 billion cigarettes) is centred in Bristol, Nottingham, Liverpool, London and Manchester. The cocoa, chocolate and sugar confectionary industry is located in Yorkshire, Bristol and Nottingham.

Energy (1984). The output capacity of electric power stations was 66,431,000 kW (1983). Electric energy output 266.65 billion kWh; 79.4% in thermal power stations, 18.6% in nuclear power stations, 2% in hydro-electric power stations. Of the total power output (1980) petroleum accounted for 37.7%, coal 36.9%, natural gas 21.4%, nuclear power 4.1% and hydro-electric power 0.6%. Thermal power stations are situated on the coalfields, in the vicinity of the big cities and along the lower reaches of the Trent, Aire, Calder, Thames. The largest nuclear power stations are Hunterston B, Hartlepool, Heysham, Torness (each of 1,320 MW capacity), Dungeness B (1,200 MW), Wylfa (840 MW), Hinkley Point B (800 MW). The largest refineries are situated at Shell Haven, Stanlow, the Isle of Grain, Coryton, Fawley, Llandarcy, Grangemouth, Milford Haven.

Agriculture (1984). Agriculture, forestry and fisheries provided about 2.1% of the GNP and occupy a mere 1.6% of the economically active population. The United Kingdom continues to be dependent on imported food, although home agriculture output is gradually increasing. 75.7% of the land was used for agricultural purposes (arable and under permanent culture 28.9%, meadows and pastures 46.8%). Forests 8.9%. Agriculture specializes in **animal husbandry**: cattle breeding 13,213,000 head (of this 3,281,000 dairy cows), sheep 34,802,000 head, pigs 7,689,000 head, poultry 129,436,000. The United Kingdom is one of the world's leading milk producers (15,900 mn.l with an average of 4,846 l per dairy cow per year). Nearly all the eggs consumed in the United Kingdom are home produced, a total of 12,288 mn. Livestock is raised in Scotland, Northern Ireland, in the South and South-west of England. The main corn growing region is the eastern half of England and the east coast of Scotland. **Crops** (yields): barley 11.03 mn. tonnes (5.39 tonnes per hectare), wheat 14.98 mn. tonnes (7.58 tonnes per hectare), oats 0.55 mn. tonnes (4.67 tonnes per hectare); other crops: potatoes 7.40 mn. tonnes (36.18 tonnes per hectare); vegetables: cabbages, carrots, onions, green peas, etc.; sugar beet 9.02 mn. tonnes (44.0 tonnes per hectare). British agriculture is highly mechanized. The fish catch is relatively small 713,800 tonnes and the high demand is covered by imports. The main fishing ports are Grimsby, Kingston upon Hull, Fleetwood, North Shields, Milford Haven, Lowestoft, Great Yarmouth, Aberdeen, Stornoway.

Transport (1984). Transport is an important modern sector which together with communications contributes 7.1% to the GNP and employs 6.2% of the economically active population. Freight traffic (173,200 mn. tonnes/km) is carried mainly by road 61.7%, railway 7.3% and coastal shipping 24.7%. Pipeline transport is growing at 6.0%. There are 346,872km of roads, of which 2,794km are motorways, 12,422km are trunk roads and 34,717km are principal roads. There were 16.06 mn. licensed private cars in the United Kingdom, 116,000 public road passenger vehicles, and 1.23 mn. motorcycles. Road transport carried 92.4% of passenger transport. The railway network measures 16,816km, of which 3,735km were electrified. Only 7.0% of travellers used rail transport. Britain's railways link up with the European railway system via the cross-Channel ferries and in future a railway tunnel (Eurotunnel) under the Channel. Inland transport uses 1,023km of navigable waterways and canals. The British merchant fleet is one of the largest in the world (3.2% of the world list). It has 777 vessels over 500 GRT with a total tonnage of 14.31 mn. GRT (of this 276 tankers are of 7.46 mn. GRT). The British merchant fleet transported 24% of the U.K.'s exports and re-exports and 22% of imports. The biggest port is the Port of London handling roughly 46.9 mn. tonnes of goods a year. Other ports include Liverpool, Manchester, the oil port of Milford Haven (30.7 mn. tonnes of crude petroleum), Southampton and Grangemouth; there is also a transoceanic passenger terminal at Southampton; most Channel traffic is handled at Dover; there is a coal port at Newcastle upon Tyne, iron ore is handled at Teesside and the main fishing port is at Kingston upon Hull. 51.2 mn. passengers used air transport on domestic and overseas routes. The biggest of the 40 civil airports with scheduled flights (1985) are London-Heathrow and Gatwick, then Manchester, Glasgow, Aberdeen, Luton. British Airways is the largest U.K. air transport operator.

Foreign trade (1985). Foreign trade continues to be an important factor in the British economy, even if the importance of the United Kingdom as an economic power has declined. London remains one of the most important centres of international trade and finance. The pattern of foreign trade is such that imports usually exceed exports; exports were valued at £ 78,331 million, imports £ 84,790 million. The main items of export (1984) consists of over 66.2% of manufactured goods (mainly machinery, transport equipment and chemical products) and 21.8% of mineral fuels. Other items include food, beverages and tobacco (6.7%), crude materials (2.7%). Manufactured goods form 67.2% of imports and crude materials

page 43

Map of Scotland

NORTH — **UNITED KI**[NGDOM]

S c o t l a[nd]

Locations (labels visible on map)

- Shetland Is.
  - Yell I.
  - Mainland
  - Lerwick
- Orkney Is.
  - Mainland
  - Hoy
  - Kirkwall
- Outer Hebrides
  - N. Uist
  - S. Uist
  - Stornoway
- Inner Hebrides
  - Skye
  - Rhum
  - Eigg
  - Coll
  - Tiree
  - Mull
  - Islay
  - Arran
- Duncansby Hd.
- Thurso
- Wick
- Pentland Firth
- Moray Firth
- Elgin
- Inverness
- Dingwall
- R. Shin
- L. Ness
- Aviemore
- Kyle of Lochalsh
- Mallaig
- Fort William
- Pitlochry
- Perth
- Crianlarich
- Stirling
- Dunfermline
- Kirkcaldy
- Firth of Forth
- St. Andrews
- Dundee
- Montrose
- Huntly
- Fraserburgh
- Peterhead
- Aberdeen
- R. Dee
- R. Don
- R. Tay
- Edinburgh
- Galashiels
- Hawick
- Moffat
- Berwick-upon-Tweed
- Alnwick
- Motherwell
- Carstairs
- Hamilton
- GLASGOW
- Paisley
- Coatbridge
- Dumbarton
- Greenock
- Irvine
- Kilmarnock
- Ayr
- R. Clyde
- Firth of Clyde
- Pt. Ellen
- Firth of Lorne
- The Minch
- Little Minch
- Malin Hd.

NORTH ATLANTIC OCEAN

IRISH SEA
CELTIC SEA
St. George's Channel
Bristol Channel
English Channel
Cardigan Bay
Strait of Dover
IRELAND
Northern Ireland
ENGLAND
Wales
UNITED KINGDOM
FRANCE
ATLANTIC
DUBLIN (Baile Átha Cliath)
LONDON
BIRMINGHAM
LEEDS
SHEFFIELD
Belfast
Cork (Corcaigh)
Limerick (Luimneach)
Donegal
Donegal B.
Sligo
Ballina
Castlebar
Westport
Claremorris
Clifden
Galway
Galway B.
Athenry
Loughrea
Aran Is.
Achill I.
Clare I.
Mullet Pen.
Roscommon
Longford
Cavan
Athlone
Mullingar
Tullamore
Birr
Pt. Laoise
Ennis
Nenagh
Thurles
Kilkenny
Carlow
Clonmel
Tipperary
Mallow
Tralee
Killarney
Bantry
Mizen Hd.
Loop Hd.
Slea Hd.
Dingle B.
Valencia I.
Cobh
Youghal
Dungarvan
Waterford
Wexford
Rosslare
Carnsore Pt.
Enniscorthy
Arklow
Wicklow
Bray
Dún Laoghaire
Drogheda
Dundalk
Newry
Armagh
Portadown
Lurgan
Lisburn
Omagh
Newtownabbey
Bangor
L. Neagh
L. Erne
L. Ree
L. Derg
L. Mask
Shannon
Blackwater
Suir
Barrow
Boyne
Mull of Galloway
Isle of Man
Douglas
Maryport
Workington
Penrith
Stockton
Darlington
Hartlepool
Middlesbrough
Whitby
Northallerton
Scarborough
Bridlington
Kendal
Barrow-in-Furness
Heysham
Lancaster
Morecambe B.
Harrogate
York
Bradford
Preston
Blackpool
Burnley
Blackburn
Halifax
Huddersfield
Bolton
Oldham
St. Helens
Liverpool
Salford
Manchester
Barnsley
Doncaster
Rotherham
Scunthorpe
Kingston upon Hull
Grimsby
Birkenhead
Widnes
Stockport
Chester
Stoke-on-T.
Crewe
Mansfield
Lincoln
Newark-u.-T.
Boston
Skegness
The Wash
Holyhead
Anglesey
Colwyn Bay
Bangor
Caernarvon
Wrexham
Pwllheli
Derby
Nottingham
Stafford
Shrewsbury
Walsall
West Bromwich
Wolverhampton
Dudley
Leicester
Nuneaton
Coventry
Corby
Spalding
Peterborough
Ely
King's Lynn
Norwich
Great Yarmouth
Lowestoft
Newtown
Aberystwyth
Craven Arms
Llandrindod Wells
Solihull
Rugby
Northampton
Cambridge
Ipswich
Harwich
Colchester
Worcester
Hereford
Stratford-u.-Av.
Banbury
Bedford
Luton
Harlow
Fishguard
Milford Haven
Pembroke
Carmarthen
Swansea
Merthyr Tydfil
Rhondda
Port Talbot
Cardiff
Newport
Gloucester
Cheltenham
Oxford
St. Albans
Watford
Southend-on-Sea
Margate
Swindon
Slough
Kingswood
Bristol
Bath
Reading
Basildon
Chatham
Canterbury
Dover
Woking
Guildford
Reigate
Tonbridge
Ashford
Folkestone
Basingstoke
Salisbury
Winchester
Havant
Brighton
Hastings
Eastbourne
Newhaven
Worthing
Barnstaple
Taunton
Bridgwater
Yeovil
Southampton
Poole
Dorchester
Bournemouth
Newport
Portsmouth
Isle of Wight
Weymouth
Exeter
Lyme Bay
Torquay
Newton Abbot
Bodmin
Plymouth
St. Austell
Truro
Camborne
Penzance
Land's End
Lizard Pt.
Is. of Scilly
Alderney
Channel Is. (U. K.)
Guernsey
Jersey
Cherbourg
Baie de la Seine
Bayeux
Caen
Le Havre
Fécamp
Dieppe
Rouen
Le Tréport
Abbeville
Boulogne-s.-M.
Calais
Severn
Thames
Trent
Ouse
Wye
Avon
Exe
Dee
Tywi
Nene
Welland
Gt. Ouse
Swale
Wharfe
Aire
Tees
Seine
Solway Fi.
1 : 6 000 000
0 50 100 150 Km
0 20 40 60 80 100 Mi
54°
52°
50°
10°
8°
6°
4°
2°
0°
E
F
G
2
3
4
5
6

ADMINISTRATIVE UNITS

Local authority areas	Area in sq.km	Population in thousands 30 June 1988	Density of population inhab. per sq.km
ENGLAND AND WALES	151,124	50,393.3	333
ENGLAND	130,363	47,536.3	365
Metropolitan counties (admin. centre):			
1 Greater London	1,580	6,735.4	4,263
2 Greater Manchester (Manchester)	1,286	2,577.7	2,004
3 Merseyside (Liverpool)	652	1,448.1	2,221
4 South Yorkshire (Barnsley)	1,560	1,292.7	829
5 Tyne and Wear (Newcastle upon Tyne)	540	1,130.5	2,094
6 West Midlands (Birmingham)	899	2,617.2	2,911
7 West Yorkshire (Wakefield)	2,039	2,056.6	1,009
Non-metropolitan counties (admin. centre):			
8 Avon (Bristol)	1,338	954.3	713
9 Bedfordshire (Bedford)	1,235	530.7	430
10 Berkshire (Reading)	1,256	747.1	595
11 Buckinghamshire (Aylesbury)	1,883	627.3	333
12 Cambridgeshire (Cambridge)	3,409	651.6	191
13 Cheshire (Chester)	2,322	955.8	412
14 Cleveland (Middlesbrough)	583	553.1	949
15 Cornwall and Isles of Scilly (Truro)	3,546	460.6	130
16 Cumbria (Carlisle)	6,809	489.2	72
17 Derbyshire (Matlock)	2,631	924.2	351
18 Devon (Exeter)	6,715	1,021.1	152
19 Dorset (Dorchester)	2,654	655.7	247
20 Durham (Durham)	2,436	596.8	245
21 East Sussex (Lewes)	1,795	712.8	397
22 Essex (Chelmsford)	3,674	1,529.5	416
23 Gloucestershire (Gloucester)	2,638	527.5	200
24 Hampshire (Winchester)	3,772	1,542.9	409
25 Hereford and Worcester (Worcester)	3,927	671.0	171
26 Hertfordshire (Hertford)	1,634	985.9	603
27 Humberside (Kingston upon Hull)	3,512	850.5	242
28 Isle of Wight (Newport)	381	129.8	341
29 Kent (Maidstone)	3,732	1,520.4	407
30 Lancashire (Preston)	3,043	1,381.9	454
31 Leicestershire (Leicester)	2,553	855.5	335
32 Lincolnshire (Lincoln)	5,885	582.6	99
33 Norfolk (Norwich)	5,355	744.3	139
34 Northamptonshire (Northampton)	2,367	570.3	241
35 Northumberland (Morpeth)	5,033	301.4	60
36 North Yorkshire (Northallerton)	8,317	713.1	86
37 Nottinghamshire (Nottingham)	2,164	1,007.7	466
38 Oxfordshire (Oxford)	2,611	579.0	222
39 Shropshire (Shrewsbury)	3,490	400.8	115
40 Somerset (Taunton)	3,458	457.7	132
41 Staffordshire (Stafford)	2,716	1,032.9	380
42 Suffolk (Ipswich)	3,800	638.7	168
43 Surrey (Kingston)	1,655	999.8	604
44 Warwickshire (Warwick)	1,981	484.6	245
45 West Sussex (Chichester)	2,016	703.4	349
46 Wiltshire (Trowbridge)	3,481	557.0	160
WALES	20,761	2,857.0	138
47 Clwyd (Mold)	2,425	407.0	168
48 Dyfed (Carmarthen)	5,765	348.4	60
49 Gwent (Cwmbran)	1,376	445.5	324
50 Gwynedd (Caernarvon)	3,868	239.0	62
51 Mid Glamorgan (Rhondda)	1,019	535.9	526
52 Powys (Llandrindod Wells)	5,077	114.9	23
53 South Glamorgan (Cardiff)	416	403.4	970
54 West Glamorgan (Swansea)	815	362.9	445
SCOTLAND – regions (admin. centre):	78,303[+]	5,094.0	65
55 Borders (Newtown St. Boswells)	1,662	102.6	62
56 Central (Stirling)	2,590	271.6	105
57 Dumfries and Galloway (Dumfries)	6,475	147.5	23
58 Fife (Glenrothes)	1,300	344.7	264

59	Grampian (Aberdeen)	8,550	501.4	59
60	Highland (Inverness)	26,136	201.9	8
61	Lothian (Edinburgh)	1,756	741.1	422
62	Strathclyde (Glasgow)	13,856	2,316.7	167
63	Tayside (Dundee)	7,668	393.7	51
64	Orkney (Kirkwall)	974	19.5	20
65	Shetland (Lerwick)	1,427	22.4	16
66	Western Isles (Stornoway)	2,901	31.0	11
	NORTHERN IRELAND – districts (admin. centre)	13,483	1,578.1	117
1	Antrim (Antrim)	405	47.7	118
2	Ards (Newtownards)	368	64.0	174
3	Armagh (Armagh)	667	49.2	74
4	Ballymena (Ballymena)	634	56.9	90
5	Ballymoney (Ballymoney)	417	23.9	57
6	Banbridge (Banbridge)	441	31.9	72
7	Belfast (Belfast)	130	299.6	2,305
8	Carrickfergus (Carrickfergus)	85	30.0	353
9	Castlereagh (Castlereagh)	84	58.0	690
10	Coleraine (Coleraine)	478	48.1	101
11	Cookstown (Cookstown)	512	27.6	54
12	Craigavon (Portadown)	280	77.2	276
13	Down (Downpatrick)	638	57.0	89
14	Dungannon (Dungannon)	763	43.7	57
15	Fermanagh (Enniskillen)	1,700	50.0	29
16	Larne (Larne)	337	29.0	86
17	Limavady (Limavady)	585	30.0	51
18	Lisburn (Hillsborough)	436	95.5	219
19	Londonderry (Londonderry)	373	98.7	265
20	Magherafelt (Magherafelt)	562	33.1	59
21	Moyle (Ballycastle)	494	17.2	35
22	Newry and Mourne (Newry)	886	87.8	99
23	Newtownabbey (Newtownabbey)	151	72.8	482
24	North Down (Bangor)	72	71.1	988
25	Omagh (Omagh)	1,124	44.9	40
26	Strabane (Strabane)	861	35.2	41
	+ including water area			

for industry 6.2% of imports. The United Kingdom is now less dependent on food imports, which have dropped to 9.9%. Fuels 13.0% form a big portion of imports. British trade with Commonwealth countries has greatly declined in recent years. In the last decade the main trading partners of the United Kingdom have been the EEC countries taking 44.8% of exports, and providing 44.7% of imports, while other countries in Western Europe handled 12.4% of exports and 16.8% of imports. The United States (exports 14.4%, imports 11.9%) and Canada (1.7%, 2.1%) continue to play an important role as do other developed countries 5.2% and 7.1%. Trade with the developing countries represents 10.7% of exports and 10.9% of imports, and to oil exporting countries exports 8.2% and imports 3.6%.

Membership of international organizations. The United Kingdom stands at the head of the Commonwealth, which is a free association of sovereign independent countries. The original dominions and most of the former colonies in the British Empire have retained membership in the Commonwealth after declaring independence. Individual member countries are linked by treaties and agreements on mutual cooperation in political life, economic affairs, finance, education, science, and culture. The British Queen stands at the head of the Commonwealth. The following were 49 member states of the Commonwealth in 1986: America: Antigua and Barbuda, the Bahamas, Barbados, Belize, Canada, Dominica, Grenada, Guyana, Jamaica, Saint Kitts and Nevis, Saint Lucia, Saint Vincent and Grenadine Is., Trinidad and Tobago; Europe: United Kingdom, Malta; Africa: Botswana, Gambia, Ghana, Kenya, Lesotho, Malawi, Mauritius, Nigeria, Seychelles, Sierra Leone, Swaziland, Tanzania, Uganda, Zambia, Zimbabwe; Asia: Bangladesh, Brunei, Cyprus, India, Malaysia, Maldives, Singapore, Srí Lanka; Australia and Oceania: Australia, Fiji, Kiribati, Nauru, New Zealand, Papua New Guinea, Samoa, Solomon Islands, Tonga, Tuvalu, Vanuatu.

The United Kingdom is a founder-member of the United Nations and a permanent member of the Security Council with the right of veto. It takes an active part in NATO. It is a member of the following international organizations: The International Monetary Fund (IMF), the International Bank for Reconstruction and Development (IBRD), the General Agreement on Tariffs and Trade (GATT), the Organization for Economic Co-operation and Development (OECD), the United Nations Conference on Trade and Development (UNCTAD), the European Atomic Energy Community (EAEC or Euratom), the European Coal and Steel Community (ECSC), and others. Since 1973 the United Kingdom has been a member of the European Economic Community (EEC).

THE ISLE OF MAN

572 sq.km, 64,300 inhabitants (1986), **crown dependency of the United Kingdom. Currency:** £ 1 = 100 pence. **Position:** Island in the Irish Sea. **Capital:** Douglas 19,944 inhabitants (1981); other towns: Onchan 7,478, Ramsey 5,818 (1981). **Official language:** English; Manx sometimes used.
Economy: Agriculture: barley, oats, wheat, potatoes. Fish catch (1982): 6,297 tonnes; **animal husbandry** (1984): sheep 135,688 head, cattle 34,062 head, pigs 7,174 head, poultry 75,614. Petroleum refinery; fish processing. Tourism 0.5 mn. visitors annually; airport; railway. The island is the setting of the annual Tourist Trophy motorcycle race.

NORTH SEA
IRISH
Scotland
England
Northern Ireland
Firth of Forth
Firth of Clyde
Firth of Lorn
Sd. of Jura
North Channel
Solway Firth
Morecambe Bay
Liverpool Bay
Dundalk Bay
Dundrum Bay
Luce Bay
Bridlington Bay
Flamborough Hd.
Spurn Hd.
St. Bees Hd.
Spanish Hd.
Mull of Galloway
Mull of Kintyre
Fair Hd.
Carmel Hd.
Menai Str.
Mull
Colonsay
Jura
Islay
Port Ellen
Kintyre
Arran
Brodick
Rathlin Island
Isle of Man
Peel
Ramsey
Douglas
Anglesey
Holyhead
Walney I.
Oban
Inveraray
L. Awe
L. Fyne
Tarbert
Campbeltown
Crianlarich
Loch Lomond
Stirling
Alloa
Perth
Kinross
Cupar
St. Andrews
Glenrothes
Kirkcaldy
Dunfermline
Falkirk
Grangemouth
Musselburgh
Dumbarton
Clydebank
Greenock
GLASGOW
Paisley
Coatbridge
Motherwell
Edinburgh
Haddington
Largs
East Kilbride
Hamilton
Saltcoats
Irvine
Kilmarnock
Troon
Ayr
Cumnock
Carstairs
Lanark
Peebles
Galashiels
Selkirk
Newtown St. Boswells
Duns
Berwick-upon-Tweed
Hawick
Moffat
Girvan
Stranraer
Newton Stewart
Wigtown
Kirkcudbright
Dumfries
Annan
Gretna Green
Alnwick
Morpeth
Ashington
Bedlington
Blyth
Newcastle upon Tyne
Tynemouth
South Shields
Sunderland
Gateshead
Hexham
Consett
Durham
Stanhope
Hartlepool
Redcar
Stockton
Darlington
Middlesbrough
Whitby
Carlisle
Maryport
Workington
Whitehaven
Penrith
Keswick
Appleby
Kendal
Barrow-in-Furness
Morecambe
Lancaster
Heysham
Fleetwood
Blackpool
Preston
Northallerton
Thirsk
Scarborough
Ripon
Norton
Bridlington
Harrogate
York
Skipton
Keighley
Bradford
LEEDS
Burnley
Blackburn
Halifax
Selby
Beverley
Kingston upon Hull
Darwen
Bolton
Bury
Rochdale
Dewsbury
Wakefield
Huddersfield
Southport
Wigan
Salford
Oldham
Ashton-u.-L.
Barnsley
Scunthorpe
Grimsby
Cleethorpes
St. Helens
Stretford
Manchester
Doncaster
Liverpool
Wallasey
Birkenhead
Rhyl
Colwyn Bay
Widnes
Warrington
Stockport
Rotherham
SHEFFIELD
Worksop
Gainsborough
East Retford
Lincoln
Louth
Horncastle
Ballycastle
Ballymoney
Ballymena
Larne
Carrickfergus
Antrim
Newtownabbey
Belfast
Bangor
Newtownards
L. Neagh
Lurgan
Lisburn
Hillsborough
Strangford L.
Portadown
Banbridge
Downpatrick
Newry
Dundalk
Louth
Drogheda
Meath
Balbriggan
DUBLIN
(Baile Átha Cliath)
Dún Laoghaire
Tweed
Teviot
Clyde
Nith
Annan
Coquet
N. Tyne
S. Tyne
Tyne
Wear
Tees
Swale
Ure
Ouse
Wharfe
Aire
Derwent
Don
Trent
Humber
Eden
Windermere
Dee
56°
54°
6°
4°
2°
0°
2°
A
B
1
2
3
4
5

Cardigan Bay
Bristol Channel
English Channel
St. George's Channel
Strait of Dover
Isle of Wight
Lyme Bay
LONDON
BIRMINGHAM
Wales
England
France
1 : 3 500 000
0 20 40 60 80 Km
0 10 20 30 40 50 Mi
52°
50°
6°
4°
2°
0°
Arklow
Gorey
Wexford
Wexford Harbour
Rosslare
Carnsore Pt.
Bardsey I.
Tremadoc Bay
Dolgellau
Tywyn
Machynlleth
Welshpool
Newtown
Aberystwyth
Llandrindod Wells
Builth Wells
Lampeter
Cardigan
Fishguard
St. David's Hd.
St. Brides Bay
Haverfordwest
Milford Haven
Pembroke
Carmarthen
Carmarthen Bay
Llanelli
Swansea
Port Talbot
Porthcawl
Neath
Merthyr Tydfil
Rhondda
Pontypridd
Ebbw Vale
Pontypool
Newport
Caerphilly
Cardiff
Barry
Brecon
Monmouth
Hereford
Leominster
Worcester
Kidderminster
Craven Arms
Shrewsbury
Wolverhampton
Stafford
Dudley
Smethwick
Walsall
West Bromwich
Solihull
Coventry
Redditch
Bromsgrove
Warwick
Royal Leamington Spa
Stratford -u.-Av.
Nuneaton
Rugby
Burton- -u.-T.
Long Eaton
Loughborough
Leicester
Corby
Kettering
Northampton
Banbury
Cheltenham
Gloucester
Cirencester
Oxford
Aylesbury
High Wycombe
Hemel Hempstead
Luton
Hitchin
Bedford
Stevenage
Hertford
St. Albans
Watford
Harlow
Slough
Windsor
Staines
Reading
Newbury
Swindon
Chippenham
Kingswood
Bristol
Bath
Trowbridge
Weston- s.-M.
Wells
Bridgwater
Taunton
Yeovil
Salisbury
Wilton
Andover
Basingstoke
Aldershot
Winchester
Eastleigh
Southampton
Fareham
Gosport
Havant
Portsmouth
Cowes
Newport
Ventnor
The Needles
Bournemouth
Poole
Dorchester
Weymouth
Chichester
Bognor Regis
Worthing
Hove
Brighton
Newhaven
Lewes
Eastbourne
Hastings
Bexhill
Horsham
Crawley
Guildford
Woking
Epsom
Reigate
Tonbridge
Tunbridge Wells
Maidstone
Ashford
Folkestone
Dover
Canterbury
Whitstable
Chatham
Gillingham
Gravesend
Margate
Ramsgate
North Foreland
Southend-on-Sea
Basildon
Brentwood
Chelmsford
Colchester
Clacton-on-Sea
The Naze
Harwich
Felixstowe
Ipswich
Sudbury
Bury St. Edmunds
Stowmarket
Newmarket
Cambridge
Ely
Huntingdon
March
Peterborough
Stamford
Spalding
Wisbech
King's Lynn
East Dereham
Thetford
Norwich
Great Yarmouth
Beccles
Lowestoft
Ilfracombe
Barnstaple
Bideford
Lundy
Hartland Pt.
Okehampton
Exeter
Exmouth
Honiton
Newton Abbot
Torquay
Paignton
Dartmouth
Plymouth
Launceston
Bodmin
Wadebridge
Newquay
St. Austell
Truro
Camborne
Falmouth
Falmouth Bay
St. Ives
Penzance
Mount's Bay
Lizard Pt.
Land's End
Isles of Scilly
Alderney (U. K.)
C. de la Hague
Cherbourg
Barfleur
Boulogne -s.-M.
Étaples
Berck-s.-M.
St.-Valéry-s.-S.
Le Tréport
Dieppe
Neufchâtel-en-B.
Fécamp
Yvetot
Étretat
Severn
Wye
Teme
Avon
Thames
Kennet
Stour
Exe
Taw
Tamar
Tywi
Teifi
Trent
Dove
Nene
Welland
Gt. Ouse
Cam
Waveney
Yare
Bure
Brue
Parrett
Béthune

THE CHANNEL ISLANDS

197 sq.km, 130,000 inhabitants (1983), **crown dependency of the United Kingdom. Currency:** £1 = 100 pence.
Position: Islands in the English Channel off the coast of France. Jersey 116 sq.km, 76,050 inhabitants (1981), administrative centre Saint Helier (28,135 inhab., 1976) and **Guernsey** 63 sq.km, 53,268 inhabitants (1981), administrative centre Saint Peter Port; dependencies of Guernsey: Alderney 8 sq.km, 2,000 inhabitants (1980); Sark 5 sq.km, 420 inhabitants (1984); Brechou 0.3 sq.km; Herm 2 sq.km.; Jethou 0.18 sq.km; Lihou 0.15 sq.km. **Capital:** Saint Peter Port 16,303 inhabitants (1976). **Official language:** English, French on the island of Jersey; Norman French is spoken on the smaller islands.
Economy: Agriculture: potatoes, tomatoes, spring vegetables, flowers; cattle breeding, pigs, poultry. Fish catch (1982): 2,241 tonnes, lobster and crab fishing. Wool and milk processing. Tourism. 3 airports.

ALBANIA

Republika Popullore Socialiste e Shqipërisë, area 28,748 sq.km, population 3,143,000 (1988), **socialist republic** (Chairman of the Presidium of the People's Assembly Ramiz Alia since 1982).
Administrative units: 26 districts (Rrethët). **Capital:** Tiranë 206,100 inhab. (1983); **other towns** (1981, in 1,000 inhab.): Shkodër 65, Durrës 62, Vlorë 61, Elbasan 53, Korçë 53, Berat 33, Fier 29. **Population:** Albanians. **Density** 103 persons per sq.km; average annual rate of population increase 2.4% (1975–82); urban population 35.3% (1980). 60% of inhabitants employed in agriculture (1981). – **Currency:** lek = 100 quindarkas.
Economy: agricultural and industrial country. **Mining** (1983, in 1,000 tonnes, metal content): brown coal 1,700, crude petroleum 3,500 (Qytet Stalin, Patos), chromium 258 (Kam, Bulqizë), copper 15, nickel 9, asphalt. Electricity 2.9 billion kWh (1983). **Industries:** textiles and foodstuffs. **Agriculture** (1983, in 1,000 tonnes): maize (corn) 366, wheat 583, rice, potatoes, sugar beet, cotton, olives, grapes, tobacco; livestock (1983, in 1,000 head): cattle 600, sheep 1,200, goats 700; fish catch 4,000 tonnes; roundwood 2.3 mn. cub.m (1983). – **Communications:** railways 380 km, roads 4,827 km. Merchant shipping 56,000 GRT (1984). – **Exports:** petroleum and petroleum products, ores and metals, cigarettes, fresh and canned fruit and vegetables. **Imports:** machines and equipment, transport equipment.

ANDORRA

Principat d'Andorra – Principauté d'Andorre, area 468 sq.km, population 49,000 (1988), **republic under the joint suzerainty of France and the Bishop of Seo de Urgel** (Spain), headed by two Syndics (Head of Government Josef Pintat Solans since 1986).
Administrative units: 7 villages. **Capital:** Andorra la Vella 15,698 inhab. (1984). **Official languages:** Catalan, Spanish, French. – **Currency:** French franc, Spanish peseta. – **Economy:** mountain agriculture and grazing, cultivation of cereals, vines, tobacco in the valleys; raising of sheep and goats. Tourism is the chief source of inhabitants' incomes.

AUSTRIA

Republik Österreich, area 83,853 sq.km, population 7,605,000 (1988), **neutral federal republic** (President Kurt Waldheim since 1986).

Administrative units: 9 federal countries (Wien, Niederösterreich, Burgenland, Oberösterreich, Salzburg, Steiermark, Kärnten, Tirol, Vorarlberg). **Capital:** Wien (Vienna) 1,501,700 inhab. (1984); **other towns** (1981, in 1,000 inhab.): Graz 243, Linz 200, Salzburg 140, Innsbruck 117, Klagenfurt 87. **Population:** German speaking Austrians 98%, small Croatian, Czech and Slovenian minorities. **Density** 90 persons per sq.km; average annual rate of population increase –0.4%; urban population 55% (1983). 33.2% of inhabitants employed in industry. – **Currency:** schilling = 100 groschen.
Economy: highly developed industrial country with considerable mineral resources. **Principal industries:** metallurgy (Steiermark, Linz), engineering (Steiermark, Wien, W. Neustadt), petroleum refining, energy production, chemicals and electronics. **Mining** (1983, in 1,000 tonnes, metal content): brown coal 3,041, crude petroleum 1,269 (Marchfeld – Matzen, Weinviertel – Mühlberg etc.), natural gas 49,021 TJ, iron ore 1,107 (Steiermark: Erzberg, Radmer), lead 5.7, zinc 22,7, tungsten 1,117 tonnes, antimony 705 tonnes, magnesite 1,006 (Tirol – Hochfilzen, Kärnten – Radenthein, Steiermark – Trieben, Breitenau), salt 530 (Salzkammergut), graphite 40.4. Electricity 42.1 billion kWh (1983), of which 72% hydro-electric power stations. **Production** (1983, in 1,000 tonnes): pig iron 3,333, crude steel 4,410, lead 11, zinc 18.8, refined copper 35, aluminium 482, nitrogenous fertilizers 209, plastics 550, rayon and acetate fibres 11.5, rayon and acetate staple fibres 110, cotton yarn 16, woven cotton fabrics 77 mn. m, cement 4,907, chemical wood pulp 850, paper 1,613, musical instruments (Wien), sugar 464, meat 691, milk 3,650, butter 43, cheese 82, eggs 89, wine 3.7 mn. hl, beer 8.4 mn. hl; 15 billion cigarettes.
Agriculture: principal branch is livestock raising. Land use: arable land 18.3%, meadows and pastures 24.3%, forests 39% (with important hunting grounds in the Alps). **Crops** (1983, in 1,000 tonnes): wheat 1,415, rye 348, barley 1,442, oats, maize (corn) 1,454, potatoes 1,012, sugar beet 1,975, grapes 518, fruit 1,179, vegetables 679; **livestock** (1983, in 1,000 head): cattle 2,546, pigs 3,981, sheep 199, goats, horses, poultry 15,000; roundwood 13.6 mn. cub.m. – **Communications:** railways 5,756 km (1984), of which 3,105 km electrified, roads 11,393 km, motorways 1,137 km (1981), passenger cars 2,468,500 (1984). Navigable waterways 358 km. Civil aviation (1984): 25.6 mn. km flown, 1,514,000 passengers carried. Important tourism 14.5 mn. visitors (1983) – **Exports:** finished products, especially machines, steel, chemicals, textiles, metals, wood, paper, salt, electricity. **Imports:** coal, metals, chemicals, transport equipment, machines, finished electronic products, textile raw materials, foodstuffs. Chief trading partners: Fed. Rep. of Germany, Italy, Switzerland, United Kingdom, France, U.S.S.R.

BELGIUM

Royaume de Belgique – Koninkrijk België, area 30,521 sq.km, population 9,925,000 (1988), **kingdom** (King Baudouin I since 1951).

Administrative units: 9 provinces: **Capital:** Bruxelles – Brussel 138,900 inhab. (1982); with agglomeration 989,877 (1983); **other towns** (1983, in 1,000 inhab.): Antwerpen 491 (with agglom.), Gent 237, Charleroi 216, Liège 207, Brugge 118, Namur 102, Mons 92, Leuven 85, Alost 78, Mechelen 77, Kortrijk 76, Oostende 69. **Population:** Walloons, Flemings. **Density** 323 persons per sq.km; average annual rate of population increase 0.1% (1975–82): urban population 73%. 27.5% of inhabitants employed in industry (1982). – **Currency:** Belgian franc = 100 centimes.
Economy: highly developed industrial country with large concentration of industry and intensive agriculture. **Principal industries:** metallurgy, engineering, chemicals, textiles. **Mining:** coal 6,096,000 tonnes (1983, reg. Borinage, Liège, reg. Campine, Charleroi-Namur), natural gas. Electricity 52.7 billion kWh (1983), of which 40% are nuclear power stations (Mol). **Production** (1983, in 1,000 tonnes): pig iron 8,033, crude steel 10,266 (prov. Liège, Hainaut, Brabant), coke oven coke 5,106, lead 134, zinc 276 (Flône, Balen), refined copper 431, tin 2,214 tonnes (Hoboken), merchant vessels 194,000 GRT (Hoboken, Temse), assembly of passenger cars 972,000 units (Antwerpen, Bruxelles), radio receivers 1,006,000 units, television receivers 766,000, sulphuric acid 1,902, nitric acid 1,445, synthetic nitrogen 495, nitrogenous fertilizers 706[+], phosphorus fertilizers 515[+], plastics 2,246, pharmaceuticals (Bruxelles), capacity of petroleum refineries 28 mn. tonnes (1984, Antwerpen, Gent, Bruxelles), motor spirit 3,943, mineral oils 12,176, cement 5,724, paper products 778[+], woven cotton fabrics 51 (Gent and surroundings), woollen – yarn 87, woven fabrics 36 (Verviers), flax industry (Vlaanderen) – sugar 860[+] (Tienen), meat 1,163[+], butter 115[+], milk 4,170[+], cheese 47.5[+], eggs 185[+], beer 14.2 mn. hl (1983); 29.7 billion cigarettes (1983). ([+]Figures for Belgium and Luxembourg combined.)
Agriculture: highly productive with animal production predominating. Land use: arable land 26%, meadows and pastures 21.1%, forests 23%. **Crops** (1983, in 1,000 tonnes): wheat 1,084[+], barley 745, oats 136, potatoes 1,245, sugar beet 5,070[+], fruit; **livestock** (1983, in 1,000 head): cattle 3,115, pigs 5,210; fish catch 48,600 tonnes (1983); roundwood 3[+] mn. cub. m (1983).
Communications (1984): railways 3,741 km, of which 1,907 km electrified, roads 15,305 km, motorways 1,488 km, passenger cars 3,258,000. Navigable rivers and canals 1,956 km. Merchant shipping 2,407,000 GRT. Largest ports: Antwerpen and Gent. Civil aviation 49.6 mn. km flown, 2,032,000 passengers carried. Tourism 6.6 mn. visitors.
Exports: metals, machines and equipment, cars, chemical and pharmaceutical products, textiles etc. **Imports:** raw materials, especially for the power industry, foodstuffs, machines and equipment. Chief trading partners: Fed. Rep. of Germany, France, Netherlands, United Kingdom, Italy.

BULGARIA

Narodna Republika Bǎlgarija, area 110,912 sq.km, population 8,995,000 (1988), **socialist republic** (President Željo Želev since 1990).

Administrative units: 9 regions (okrǎg) incl. the capital. **Capital:** Sofija (Sofia) 1,093,752 inhab. (1984); **other towns** (1982, in 1,000 inhab.): Plovdiv 367, Varna 295, Ruse 178, Burgas 178, Stara Zagora 142, Pleven 136, Sliven 101, Šumen 100, Tolbuhin 99, Pernik 95, Haskovo 88, Jambol 86, Gabrovo 81, Pazardžik 78. **Population:** Bulgarians 92%, Gipsies, Macedonians etc. **Density** 81 persons per sq.km; average annual rate of population increase 0.6% (1975–82); urban population 62.8% (1981). 29.6% of inhabitants employed in agriculture, 28% in industry. – **Currency:** lev = = 100 stotinki.
Economy: industrial and agricultural country. **Principal industries:** metallurgy (Kremikovci, Pernik), engineering (Sofija, Plovdiv, Ruse), chemicals (Sofija, Burgas, Dimitrovgrad, Stara Zagora, Devnja), textiles (Gabrovo, Sofija), foodstuffs.
Mining (1983, in 1,000 tonnes, metal content): brown coal 32,124 (Marica-East, Dimitrovgrad, Pernik, Bobovdol); crude petroleum 300, natural gas, iron ore 254 (Kremikovci), lead 95, zinc 68, copper 80 (Sredna Gora Mts.), manganese 121, molybdenum 100 tonnes, silver 25 tonnes, uranium, pyrites 680, salt 87. Electricity 42.9 billion kWh (1983), of which 11% are hydro-electric and 25% nuclear power stations (near Kozoduj). **Production** (1983, in 1,000 tonnes): pig iron 1,632, crude steel 2,820, copper smelted 60, lead 116, zinc 93, vessels 159,000 GRT (1984, Varna, Ruse), sulphuric acid 861, nitric acid 977, nitrogenous fertilizers 813, phosphorus fertilizers 244, soda ash 1,245, plastics and resins 270, capacity of petroleum refineries 15 mn. tonnes (1984), motor spirit 1,800, oils 9,430, cement 5,644, cotton yarn 85, woven fabrics – cotton 307 mn. m, woollen 49 mn. m, rayon and acetate 37 mn. m – synthetic staple fibre 42, leather shoes 18 mn. pairs, meat 717, milk 2,080, cheese 176, eggs 146, wine 464, canned vegetables 300, beer 5.5 mn. hl (1983); 91.3 billion cigarettes (1983).
Agriculture: vegetable production predominates. Land use: arable land 34.4%, meadows and pastures 18.3%, forests 34.7%. **Crops** (1983, in 1,000 tonnes): wheat 3,600, barley 1,046, maize (corn) 3,101, rice, potatoes 428, cotton -seed 12, sugar beet 749, sunflower seeds 448, soya beans 84, fruit 2,030, grapes 1,034, strawberries 14, vegetables 1,690, tomatoes 658, legumes, roses (Kazanlǎk), tobacco 118, walnuts 24; **livestock** (1983, in 1,000 head): cattle 1,783, buffaloes 40, horses 119, asses 347, pigs 3,810, sheep 10,761, goats 502; poultry 41,000, silkworms 200 tonnes, wool 17,700 tonnes, honey 8,638 tonnes; fish catch 121,100 tonnes (1983); roundwood 4.8 mn. cub.m (1983).
Communications: railways 4,278 km, of which 2,053 km electrified (1984), roads 33,253 km (1984), passenger cars 500,000 (1980). Navigable waterways 471 km. Merchant shipping 1,283,000 GRT (1984). Chief ports: Varna and Burgas. Civil aviation: 12.7 mn. km flown, 1,800,000 passengers carried. Tourism 5,771,000 visitors (1983).
Exports: machines and equipment, foodstuffs (fresh and canned fruit and vegetables), rose oil, wine, cigarettes, tobacco, chemical products and textiles, furs. **Imports:** petroleum, fuels and raw materials, machines, consumer goods. Chief trading partners: (1984): the socialist countries 76%, of which the U.S.S.R. 57.5%, German Dem. Rep., Poland, Czechoslovakia and Fed. Rep. of Germany.

10a Shetland Is.
Herma Ness
Haroldswick
Unst
Yell
Fetlar
St. Magnus Bay
Voe
Whalsay
Mainland
Foula
Lerwick
Bressay
Sumburgh Hd.
Tolob
ATLANTIC OCEAN
North Rona
C. Wrath
Butt of Lewis
Orkney Islands
Westray
Eday
Sanday
Rousay
Stronsay
Shapinsay
Mainland
Kirkwall
Stromness
Hoy
Scapa Flow
South Ronaldsay
Pentland Firth
Dunnet Hd.
Duncansby Hd.
Thurso
Tongue
Wick
NORTH SEA
The Minch
Lewis
Stornoway
Outer Hebrides
Tarbert
Harris
Sd. of Harris
Little Minch
North Uist
Benbecula
South Uist
Lochboisdale
Barra
Castlebay
Barra Hd.
Skye
Uig
Portree
Raasay
Kyle of Lochalsh
Loch Shin
Helmsdale
Lairg
Dornoch
Dornoch Firth
Ullapool
Gairloch
Loch Maree
Moray Firth
Dingwall
Elgin
Buckie
Banff
Fraserburgh
Kinnaird Hd.
Nairn
Forres
Keith
Deveron
Huntly
Peterhead
Beauly
Inverness
Findhorn
Loch Ness
Spey
Don
Inverurie
Fort Augustus
Aviemore
Aberdeen
Newtonmore
Ballater
Dee
Stonehaven
Rhum
Mallaig
Eigg
Oich
L. Lochy
N. Esk
S. Esk
Fort William
L. Ericht
Pitlochry
Montrose
Coll
Loch Linnhe
L. Rannoch
Forfar
Tiree
Passage of Tiree
Tobermory
Mull
L. Tay
Tay
Arbroath
Dundee
Iona
Oban
Crianlarich
Earn
Perth
Firth of Tay
St. Andrews
Cupar
Firth of Lorn
L. Awe
Inveraray
Kinross
Glenrothes
Loch Lomond
Alloa
Kirkcaldy
Firth of Forth
Colonsay
Stirling
Inner Hebrides
Jura
Sd. of Jura
L. Fyne
Dumbarton
Falkirk
Dunfermline
Clydebank
Grangemouth
Musselburgh
Greenock
GLASGOW
Edinburgh
Haddington
Islay
Tarbert
Largs
Paisley
Coatbridge
Motherwell
Berwick-upon-Tweed
East Kilbride
Hamilton
Carstairs
Duns
Saltcoats
Clyde
Peebles
Galashiels
Tweed
Port Ellen
Kintyre
Arran
Brodick
Irvine
Kilmarnock
Lanark
Newtown St. Boswells
Troon
Selkirk
Teviot
Cumnock
Hawick
Ayr
Firth of Clyde
Malin Hd.
Campbeltown
Rathlin I.
Fair Hd.
Moffat
Donegal
IRELAND
Buncrana
Lough Foyle
Mull of Kintyre
Girvan
Nith
Annan
N. Tyne
Coleraine
Ballycastle
Limavady
Ballymoney
Londonderry
Bann
Dumfries
Northern Ireland
Annan
Gretna Green
S. Tyne
Strabane
Maghera
Ballymena
Larne
Newton Stewart
Carlisle
North Channel
Foyle
Magherafelt
Antrim
Carrickfergus
Stranraer
Wigtown
Kirkcudbright
Solway Firth
Eden
Newtownabbey
Maryport
Penrith
Cookstown
Lough Neagh
Belfast
Bangor
Luce Bay
England
Omagh
Lisburn
Newtownards
Mull of Galloway
Workington
Keswick
Appleby
Whitehaven
Mourne
Scotland

Map of Ireland

Scale 1 : 3 500 000

Provinces and Counties

- Donegal
- Northern Ireland
- Leitrim
- Sligo
- Mayo
- Cavan
- Monaghan
- Louth
- Roscommon
- Longford
- Meath
- Galway
- Westmeath
- Dublin
- Offaly
- Kildare
- Wicklow
- Clare
- Tipperary
- Laois
- Carlow
- Wexford
- Limerick
- Kilkenny
- Kerry
- Cork
- Waterford

Cities and Towns

Gweedore, Buncrana, Coleraine, Ballycastle, Tory I., Letterkenny, Limavady, Ballymoney, Londonderry, Lifford, Strabane, Maghera, Ballymena, Larne, Killybegs, Magherafelt, Antrim, Carrickfergus, Donegal, Omagh, Cookstown, Newtownabbey, Belfast, Bangor, Ballyshannon, Dungannon, Lurgan, Lisburn, Newtownards, Enniskillen, Portadown, Hillsborough, Armagh, Banbridge, Downpatrick, Easky, Sligo, Monaghan, Newry, Belmullet, Ballina, Boyle, Dundalk, Castlebar, Carrick-on-Shannon, Cavan, Kingscourt, Westport, Claremorris, Castlerea, Longford, Drogheda, Clifden, Roscommon, Navan, Balbriggan, Tuam, Mullingar, Trim, Ballinasloe, Athlone, Dublin (Baile Átha Cliath), Galway, Athenry, Dún Laoghaire, Loughrea, Tullamore, Naas, Droichead Nua, Bray, Ennistymon, Gort, Birr, Kildare, Ennis, Nenagh, Roscrea, Port Laoise, Wicklow, Kilkee, Kilrush, Thurles, Athy, Carlow, Arklow, Listowel, Limerick (Luimneach), Tipperary, Kilkenny, Gorey, Tralee, Newcastle West, Cashel, Enniscorthy, Dingle, Clonmel, Wexford, Rosslare, Killarney, Mallow, Fermoy, Waterford, Tramore, Cahirciveen, Kenmare, Macroom, Dungarvan, Carnsore Pt., Bantry, Bandon, Cork (Corcaigh), Youghal, Skibbereen, Clonakilty, Cobh

Physical Features

- Atlantic Ocean
- Irish Sea
- North Channel
- St. George's Channel
- Malin Hd.
- Lough Swilly
- Lough Foyle
- Rathlin I.
- Fair Hd.
- Mull of Kintyre
- Aran Island
- Finn
- Mourne
- Belfast L.
- Strangford L.
- Lough Neagh
- Blackwater
- Upper L. Erne
- Lower L. Erne
- Dundrum Bay
- Erris Hd.
- Mullet Peninsula
- Donegal Bay
- Sligo Bay
- Dundalk Bay
- Achill Island
- Clare Island
- L. Conn
- Inishbofin
- Clew Bay
- L. Mask
- Boyne
- Lough Corrib
- Aran Islands
- Galway Bay
- Shannon
- Liffey
- Lough Derg
- Barrow
- Slaney
- Loop Hd.
- Nore
- Suir
- Wexford Harbour
- Dingle Bay
- Blackwater
- Hook Hd.
- Kenmare River
- Lee
- Bear I.
- Bantry Bay
- Cork Harbour
- Mizen Hd.
- Clear I.
- St. David's Hd.

Scotland
Colonsay, Jura, Islay, Sky of Jura, Port Ellen, Campbeltown, Kintyre

map 10

CZECHOSLOVAKIA

Česká a Slovenská Federativní Republika, area 127,899 sq.km, population 15,624,027 (1988), **federal republic** (President Václav Havel since 1989).

Administrative units: 2 socialist federal republics – the Czech Socialist Republic (7 regions, the capital of the ČSSR Praha with the status of a region), the Slovak Socialist Republic (3 regions, the capital of SSR Bratislava with the status of a region). **Capital:** Praha (Prague) 1,193,513 inhab. (1986); **other towns** (1986, in 1,000 inhab.): Bratislava 417, Brno 386, Ostrava 328, Košice 222, Plzeň 175, Olomouc 106, Ústí n. Labem 104, Liberec 101, Hradec Králové 100, České Budějovice 94, Pardubice 94, Havířov 92, Žilina 92, Gottwaldov 86, Nitra 85, Prešov 83, Banská Bystrica 78, Karviná 75, Kladno 73, Trnava 70, Most 65, Frýdek-Místek 63, Martin 62. **Population:** Czechs 63.4%, Slovaks 31.3%, Hungarians 4%, Poles, Germans. **Density** 121 persons per sq.km; average annual rate of population increase 0.34% (1980–84); urban population 64% (1981). 37.4% of inhabitants employed in industry, 12.4% in agriculture (1985). – **Currency:** koruna (Kčs) = = 100 halers.
Economy: advanced industrial and agricultural country. **Principal industries:** mineral mining, machinery, metallurgy, foodstuffs, textiles and wood-working. **Mining** (1983, in 1,000 tonnes, metal content): coal 26,437 (Ostrava – Karviná), brown coal 102,416 (Chomutov, Most, Sokolov), crude petroleum 93. natural gas 20,100 TJ, iron ore 507, copper 10, lead 2.7, tin 226 tonnes, mercury 144 tonnes, antimony 0.8 tonne, silver 40 tonnes, magnesite (Slovenské rudohorie), uranium (Českomoravská vrchovina, Příbram), salt 77, graphite 27, kaolin and glass sands. Electricity 80.6 billion kWh (1985), of which 5% are hydro-electric and 14.6% nuclear power stations (Jaslovské Bohunice, Dukovany).
Production (1983, in 1,000 tonnes): pig iron 9,466, crude steel 15,024, coke oven coke 10,340 (Ostrava, Třinec, Kladno, Košice), aluminium 36.1 (Žiar nad Hronom), smelted copper 25.7 (Krompachy), lead 21; engineering – Praha, Plzeň ("Škoda" Works), Brno, north-western Slovakia (1983, in 1,000 units): metal cutting machines 35.4, passenger cars 177.5 (Mladá Boleslav), lorries 43.2 (Kopřivnice), motorcycles 136, tractors 34, electric locomotives 148 units, television receivers 415; chemical industry – Záluží, Ostrava vicinity, Elbeland, Bratislava, south-western Slovakia (1983, in 1,000 tonnes): sulphuric acid 1,244, nitrogenous fertilizers 591, phosphorus fertilizers 326, plastics and resins 1,006, synthetic rubber 67.2 (Kralupy nad Vltavou), capacity of petroleum refineries 23 mn. tonnes (1984) – pipeline for the import of Soviet petroleum; motor spirit 1,500, oils 11,470, cement 10,498, paper 934 (Štětí, Větřní, Ružomberok); textile industry uses mainly imported raw materials (northern and north-eastern Bohemia, northern Moravia, Žilina, Ružomberok), cotton yarn 140, woven fabrics – cotton 585 mn. m, linen 105 mn. m, woollen 61.7 mn. m, silk 140,000m, rayon 50.7 mn. m – synthetic fibres 112, shoes 128 mn. pairs (Gottwaldov), glass (northern Bohemia), porcelain (Karlovy Vary), ceramics (Horní Bříza near Plzeň), costume jewellery (Jablonec n. N.), musical instruments (Kraslice, Hradec Králové, Krnov); food industry: sugar 836 (Elbeland), meat 1,382, milk 6,496, condensed milk 147, butter 149, cheese 188, eggs 275, malt, beer 24.9 mn. hl (Plzeň, České Budějovice), wine 127; 25 billion cigarettes.
Agriculture: arable land 37.4%, meadows and pastures 12.8%, forests 35.8%. **Crops** (1983, in 1,000 tonnes): wheat 5,820, rye 751, barley 3,276, maize (corn) 722, oats 410, potatoes 3,177, flax 99, hemp, rapeseed 300, sunflower 40, sugar beet 6,041, hops 12 (Žatec region), fruit 939, grapes 317 (Malé Karpaty, southern Moravia), vegetables 1,194; **livestock** (1983, in 1,000 head): 5,190, pigs 7,070, sheep 1,041, goats, horses; poultry 50,977; fish catch 19,525 tonnes (1983); roundwood 18.9 mn. cub.m (1983).
Communications (1985): railways 13,130km, of which 3,507km electrified, roads 73,809km, passenger cars 2,639,600 (1984). Navigable waterways 483km. Merchant shipping 184,000 GRT (1984). Civil aviation (1984): 21.6mn. km flown, 911,000 passengers carried. Tourism 4.6 mn. visitors (1983).
Exports: machines, equipment, machine tools and transport equipment (cutting machines, cars, power stations and other plant equipment, electromotors), fuels (coal, coke), raw materials, hops, malt, beer, glass, porcelain, wood, shoes, textiles.
Imports: fuels (petroleum, natural gas, coal) and raw materials (iron ores, non-ferrous metals, machines and equipment, consumer goods, foodstuffs (cereals, fruit, vegetables), textile raw materials. Chief trading partners: U.S.S.R., German Dem. Rep., Poland, Hungary, Fed. Rep. of Germany, Yugoslavia, Bulgaria, Austria, Romania.

DENMARK

Kongeriget Danmark, area 43,075 sq.km, population 5,129,516 (1988), **kingdom** (Queen Margrethe II. Alexandrina Ingrid Thorhildur since 1972).

Administrative units: 15 districts (Ämter) and 2 cities (København and Frederiksberg). The autonomous Faeroe Islands (Faerderne) and Greenland belong to Denmark. **Capital:** København (Copenhagen) 638,163 inhab. (1984), with Frederiksberg and agglom. 1,372,019 inhab. (1983); **other towns** (1983, in 1,000 inhab.): Århus 249, Odense 171, Ålborg 155, Esbjerg 80, Randers 62, Helsingør 56, Herning 56, Kolding 56. **Population:** Danes. **Density** 119 persons per sq.km; average annual rate of population increase 0.2% (1975–82); urban population 85% (1983). 18.6% of inhabitants employed in industry (1983). – **Currency:** Danish krone = 100 öre.
Economy: advanced industrial and agricultural country. **Principal industries:** metal-working and engineering (especially shipbuilding, electrical and radio engineering), foodstuffs, chemicals, paper and textiles. København is the chief industrial centre. **Mining:** petroleum mining under the sea near the west coast 2.1 mn. tonnes (1983), lignite, salt 452,000 tonnes (1983), sulphur. Electricity 22.2 billion kWh (1983), 100% thermal power stations. **Production** (1983, in 1,000 tonnes): crude steel 492, vessels 525,000 GRT (København and others), cement 1,556, nitrogenous fertilizers 202.5, meat 1,408, milk 5,427, butter 131, cheese 251, eggs 81, fish flour 430, sugar 376, beer 11 mn. hl, 9.8 billion cigarettes. **Agriculture** is highly developed with intensive animal production. Arable land 61.6%, meadows and pastures 5.7%, forests 11.4%. **Crops** (1983, in 1,000 tonnes): barley 4,450, wheat 1,577, oats 83, rye 321, potatoes 870, sugar beet 2,632; **livestock** (1983, in 1,000 head): cattle 2,900, pigs 9,289, poultry 15,000; fish catch 1,862,100 tonnes (1983); roundwood 3 mn. cub.m (1983).

page 54

Communications (1984); railways 2,448 km, roads 70,170 km, motorways 549 km, passenger cars 1,450,400 (1984). Merchant shipping: 5,211,000 GRT (1984). Chief port København. Civil aviation (1984): 41.3 mn. km flown, 4,126,000 passengers carried.
Exports: industrial products 70% (machinery, transport equipment, vessels, chemical products), agricultural products 30% (meat, live animals, butter, milk products, eggs, fish products). **Imports** fuels and raw materials, machines, equipment and transport equipment. Chief trading partners: Fed. Rep. of Germany, United Kingdom, Sweden, U.S.A.

FAEROE ISLANDS
Faerderne, area 1,399 sq.km, population 46,950 (1988), **autonomous region of Denmark.**
Capital: Thorshavn 13,951

FINLAND

Suomen Tasavalta – Republiken Finland, area 338,145 sq.km, population 4,955,000 (1988), **republic** (President Mauno Henrik Koivisto since 1982).

Administrative units: 12 regions (Läänı), of which islands Ahvenanmaa (Åland) are an autonomous province. **Capital:** Helsinki 484,471 inhab. (1984); **other towns** (1983) in 1,000 inhab.): Tampere 168, Turku 163, Espoo 149, Vantaa 139, Oulu 96, Lahti 95, Pori 79, Kuopio 78, Jyväskyla 65, Kotka 60. **Population:** Finns 93.2%, Swedes 6.6%. **Density** 14 persons per sq.km; average annual rate of population increase 0.5% (1975–82); urban population 63% (1982). 25% of inhabitants employed in industry (1980) – **Currency:** markka = 100 penni.
Economy: developed industrial and agricultural country with modern industry, intensive agriculture and forestry. Large resources of water power. **Chief industries:** wood working, chemical wood pulp and paper manufacturing (Lahti, Kuopio, Kotka, Kemi, Oulu and others), metallurgy, shipbuilding, engineering (Helsinki, Turku, Tampere), foodstuffs and textiles. **Mining** (1983, in 1,000 tonnes, metal content): iron ore 555, chromium 91, copper 37.7 (Ylöjärvi), lead 2.1, zinc 56.3 (Kisko), nickel 5.3 (Leppävirta), cobalt 930 tonnes, vanadium 3,359 tonnes, mercury 65 tonnes, gold 784 kg (Haveri), silver 30 tonnes, pyrites 449. Electricity 40.2 billion kWh (1983), of which hydro-electric power stations 26%, nuclear 17%. **Production** (1983, in 1,000 tonnes): pig iron 1,957, crude steel 2,416 (Tampere, Imatra, Raahe), copper-smelted 70.1, -refined 55.4 (Harjavalta), zinc 128, vessels 317,000 GRT (Raahe, Vaasa, Pori), sulphuric acid 1,145 (Harjavalta), nitrogenous fertilizers 293, phosphorus fertilizers 191.7, capacity of petroleum refineries 12 mn. tonnes (1984, Naantali), motor spirit 2.4 mn. tonnes, oils 6.2 mn. tonnes, cement 1,979; wood-working and paper industry – Lahti, Kuopio, Kemi, Kotka, Oulu and others (1983, in 1,000 tonnes): chemical wood pulp 4,195, paper products 4,775, plywood 580,000 cub.m, sawnwood 7,995,000 cub.m; textile industry (Tampere, Turku, Pori): rayon and acetate staple fibre 57.6, glass industry (Riihimäki, Lahti), porcelain (Helsinki); food industry: meat 331, milk 3,173, cheese 78, butter 70, eggs 83; 8.4 billion cigarettes.
Agriculture: arable land 7.6%, meadows and pastures 0.5%, forests 69.2% – the chief natural wealth of the country. **Crops** (1983, in 1,000 tonnes): cereals 3,865 (barley 1,764, oats 1,407, wheat), hay 2,057, potatoes 804, sugar beet 955; **livestock** (1983, in 1,000 head): cattle 1,800, pigs 1,500, sheep; poultry 8,000, raising of reindeer 205 and fur animals; fish catch 157,100 tonnes (1983); roundwood 38 mn. cub.m (1963). – **Communications** (1984): railways 5,998 km, roads 63,909 km, motorways 205 km, passenger cars 1,474,000. Navigable waterways 6,057 km. Merchant shipping 2,168,000 GRT (1984). Chief port Helsinki. Civil aviation (1984): 37 mn. km flown, 2,991,000 passengers carried. Tourism 451,000 visitors (1983).
Exports: wood-working and paper industry products, machines and equipment, iron and steel, chemical and food products.
Imports: raw materials, semi-finished products, fuels. Chief trading partners: U.S.S.R., Sweden, United Kingdom, Fed. Rep. of Germany.

FRANCE

République Française, area 543,998 sq.km, population 55,874,000 (1988), **republic** (President François Maurice Mitterrand since 1981, re-elected 1988).
Administrative units: The Republic of France comprises 96 metropolitan departments which make up 22 administrative regions. **Overseas departments:** Guadeloupe, Martinique, Guiana, Réunion, St. Pierre et Miquelon, Mayotte; overseas territories New Caledonia, the Wallis and Futuna islands, and French Polynesia. **Capital:** Paris 2,166,449 inhab. (1982, with agglom. 9,650,000 inhab.); **other towns** (in 1,000 inhab.): Marseille 879, Lyon 418, Toulouse 354, Nice 338, Strasbourg 252, Nantes 247, Bordeaux 211, Saint-Étienne 206, Montpellier 201, Le Havre 199, Rennes 192, Reims 182, Toulon 181, Lille 174, Brest 160, Grenoble 159, Clermont-Ferrand 151, Le Mans 150, Dijon 146, Limoges 144. **Population:** French 90%, Italians, Spaniards, Algerians, Portuguese and others. **Density** 102 persons per sq.km; average annual rate of population increase 0.4% (1975–82); urban population 78% (1982). 33.9% of inhabitants employed in industry, 7.5% in agriculture (1983). – **Currency:** French franc = 100 centimes.
Economy: highly developed industrial and agricultural country. With its high concentration of industrial plants France belongs to the leading group of industrial countries in the world. Industry has an insufficient fuel and power base and has to import coal, coke and petroleum. **Chief industries:** mineral mining, metallurgy, engineering, energy production, chemicals, electrical and radio engineering, ship and aircraft building, textile and food industries.
Mining (1983, in 1,000 tonnes, metal content): coal 18,649 (Nord, Pas-de-Calais, reg. Lorraine), lignite 2,606, crude petroleum 1,660 (reg. Aquitaine, Paris Basin, reg. Alsace), natural gas 379,000 TJ (Lacq, Saint Marcet), iron ore 5,174 (Metz--Thionville and Briey-Longwy areas), bauxite 1,660 (Brignoles, Bédarieux, Les Baux), lead 1.5, zinc 34, tungsten 1,243 tonnes, antimony, gold 2,040 kg, silver 1,107 tonnes, uranium 3,529 tonnes (Mts. du Forez-Bois Noirs), salt 5,686, potassium salt 1,651 (at Mulhouse), phosphates. Electricity 283.4 billion kWh (1983), of which 7% hydro-electric power stations (Alps, Massif Central and Pyrenees) and 34.3% nuclear power stations (Chinon, Marcoule, Fessenheim, Blayais).

page 55

Map: Iberian Peninsula (Spain and Portugal) and Northern Morocco

Scale: 1 : 8 000 000
0 50 100 150 200 Km
0 25 50 75 100 125 Mi

Grid references: E (top), F, G, H (bottom); columns 1, 2, 3

Atlantic Ocean / Bay of Biscay (North coast, E1–E3)
- Estaca de Bares, Ortigueira, Vivero, Ribadeo, Luarca, Avilés, Gijón, Llanes, Torrelavega, Santander, Bilbao, Bayonne, Biarritz, Bordeaux, Arcachon, Dax
- C. de Finisterre, La Coruña, El Ferrol del Caud., Santiago de Compostela, Noya, Pontevedra, Vigo
- Oviedo, Cangas de Nar., Sama de Langreo, Mieres, Reinosa, Baracaldo, Vitoria, Irún, San Sebastián, Pamplona, Sangüesa, Jaca

Northern Spain (F1–F3)
- Lugo, Monforte de Lem., Ponferrada, León, Astorga, Benavente, Palencia, Miranda de Ebro, Burgos, Lerma, Logroño, Tudela, Alagón, Zaragoza, Calatayud
- Orense, Verín, Chaves, Braga, Vila Real, Bragança
- Valladolid, Zamora, Medina del Campo, Aranda de Duero, Soria, Almazán, Sigüenza
- Porto, Vila Nova de G., Ovar, Aveiro, Lamego, Viseu, Guarda
- Salamanca, Ciudad Rodrigo, Béjar, Ávila, Segovia, S. Lorenzo de El Escorial, Móstoles, Madrid, Alcalá de Hen., Guadalajara, Getafe, Aranjuez, Cuenca, Teruel

Central / Southern Spain and Portugal (G1–G3)
- Figueira da F., Coimbra, Leiria, Torres Novas, Santarém, Amadora, Lisboa (Lisbon), Almada, Barreiro, Setúbal
- Covilhã, Castelo Branco, Abrantes, Portalegre, Elvas, Évora, Beja, Moura, Sines, Portimão, Lagos, C. de S. Vicente, Vila Real de Sto. Ant., Ayamonte, Faro
- Plasencia, Alcántara, Cáceres, Trujillo, Mérida, Badajoz, Don Benito, Zafra, Fregenal de la Sa., Minas de Riotinto, Huelva
- Talavera de la R., Toledo, Alcázar de S. Juan, Villarrobledo, Requena, Albacete, Hellín, Villena, Cieza, Elche, Orihuela, Murcia, Cartagena, Lorca, Águilas
- Ciudad Real, Almadén, Puertollano, Valdepeñas, Manzanares, Peñarroya Pueblonuevo, Pozoblanco, Andújar, Linares, Úbeda, Jaén, Córdoba, Écija, Pte. Genil, Lucena, Baza, Guadix, Almería, C. de Gata
- Sevilla, Utrera, Jerez de la Frontera, Cádiz, Golfo de Cádiz, Loja, Antequera, Ronda, Marbella, Málaga, Nerja, Motril, Adra, Granada
- Algeciras, La Línea, Gibraltar (U.K.), Pta. Marroquí

Morocco (H1–H3)
- Strait of Gibraltar, I. de Alborán (Sp.), Ceuta (Sp.), Tánger, Asilah, Tétouan, Larache, Chechaouene, Al-Hoceima, Melilla (Sp.), Nador, Ksar-el-Kebir, Ouezzane, Sidi-Kacem, Rabat, Meknès, Fès, Sefrou, Taourirt, Oued Sebou, Oued Moulouya
- Casablanca, Mohammedia

Inset: 11a Azores (A–B)
- Corvo, Rosário, Flores, Sta. Cruz das Flores
- Atlantic

Numbered regions (Portugal — provinces/districts, approximate):
1. (near Ovar / Aveiro)
2. (Beja / Baixo Alentejo)
3. (Minho)
4. (Trás-os-Montes)
5. (Douro)
6. (Figueira da Foz / Coimbra area)
9. (Guarda / Viseu)
10. (Leiria)
11. (Lisboa)
12. (Portalegre)
13. (Braga / Porto)
14. (Santarém)
15. (Setúbal)
16. (Viana do Castelo)
17. (Vila Real)
18. (Viseu)

Numbered regions (Spain — provinces, approximate):
1. Córdoba
2. Zaragoza
3. Asturias / Oviedo
6. Cantabria
7. Toledo / Ciudad Real
8. Palencia
10. Cáceres
12. La Rioja / Burgos
13. Madrid
14. Murcia
15. Navarra
17. Vizcaya

map 11

Production (1983, in 1,000 tonnes): pig iron 2,207, crude steel 7,219, aluminium 59, copper – smelted 17, refined 50 – vessels 362,000 GRT (Rostock, Wismar), passenger cars 188,000 units (Eisenach, Zwickau), radio receivers 975,000 units, television receivers 667,000 units, sulphuric acid 926, soda ash 887, caustic soda 687, fertilizers: nitrogenous 698, phosphorus 315; synthetic rubber 161 (Schkopau), plastics and resins 1,045, photographic materials (Wolfen), electrochemistry (Bitterfeld): capacity of petroleum refineries 26.6 mn. tonnes (1984), pipeline for the import of Soviet petroleum, motor spirit 4 mn. tonnes, oils 15 mn. tonnes, cement 11.8 mn. tonnes, chemical wood pulp 170 (Premnitz), paper 1,154. Textile industry mainly in Saxony, Thuringia (1983, in 1,000 tonnes): yarn – cotton 134.7, woollen 76.4 – woven fabrics – cotton 298 mn. sq.m, woollen 39 mn. sq.m, rayon and acetate 48.6 mn. sq.m – fibres – rayon and acetate 35, synthetic 82 – staple fibre – rayon and acetate 131, synthetic 150 – shoes 87 mn. pairs. Food industry (1983, in 1,000 tonnes): meat 1,746, milk 8,208, butter 266, cheese 225, eggs 350, sugar 750, beer 25.3 mn. hl (1983); 27.4 billion cigarettes (1983). Glass industry (Jena), porcelain (Meissen), printing (Leipzig, Gotha).
Agriculture: mainly cultivation of cereals and potatoes. Land use: arable land 46.5%, meadows and pastures 11.4%, forests 27.3%. **Crops** (1983, in 1,000 tonnes): wheat 3,470, barley 3,900, rye 2,064, oats 500, potatoes 7,500, flax, sugar beet 6,400, rapeseed 303, vegetables 1,278, tobacco; **livestock** (1983, in 1,000 head): cattle 5,690, pigs 12,107, sheep 2,198; poultry 51,000, honey 39,000 tonnes; fish catch 239,900 tonnes (1983); roundwood 10.9 mn. cub.m (1983). – **Communications** (1983): railways 14,226 km, of which 2,321 km are electrified, roads 47,261 km, passenger cars 3,157,100. Navigable waterways 2,319 km. Merchant shipping 1,422,000 GRT (1984). Chief ports: Rostock, Wismar, Stralsund. Civil aviation: 1,359,000 passengers carried. Tourism 1.5 mn. visitors (1983).
Exports: machines and equipment, transport equipment, precision instruments, optics and electronics, chemical products, dyes, photo materials, brown coal, potassium salts and consumer goods. **Imports:** petroleum, ores and other raw materials, foodstuffs. Chief trading partners: U.S.S.R., Czechoslovakia, Fed. Rep. of Germany, Hungary, Poland, Bulgaria, Romania, West Berlin.

GERMANY, FEDERAL REPUBLIC OF

Bundesrepublik Deutschland, area 248,229 sq.km, population 59,303,900 (1988), **federal republic** (President Dr Richard von Weizsäcker since 1984).

Administrative units: 10 federal countries (Schleswig-Holstein, Hamburg, Niedersachsen, Bremen, Nordrhein-Westfalen, Hessen, Rheinland-Pfalz, Baden-Württemberg, Bayern /Bavaria/, Saarland). **Capital:** Bonn 289,688 inhab. (1984); **other towns** (1984, in 1,000 inhab.: Hamburg 1,606, München (Munich) 1,283, Köln (Cologne) 997, Essen 635, Frankfurt am Main 614, Dortmund 600, Düsseldorf 576, Stuttgart 562, Duisburg 578, Hannover 544, Bremen 540, Nürnberg 473, Bochum 414, Wuppertal 393, Bielefeld 307, Mannheim 302, Gelsenkirchen 296, Münster 273, Karlsruhe 271, Wiesbaden 268, Mönchengladbach 260, Braunschweig 255, Kiel 248, Augsburg 246, Aachen 245, Oberhausen 228, Krefeld 227. **Population:** Germans. **Density** 238 persons per sq.km, average annual rate of population increase –0.2% (1983); urban population 85%. 42% of inhabitants employed in industry. There were 4.5 mn. foreign workers in 1983. – **Currency:** Deutsche mark = 100 pfennigs.
Economy: highly developed industrial country with advanced agriculture. The Fed. Rep. of Germany belongs economically among the most advanced countries of the world, ranking fourth in value of production, after the U.S.A., the U.S.S.R. and Japan, and it holds a decisive position in the EEC. **Industry:** the 50 largest firms produce more than 50% of the total industrial output. **Principal industries:** mining, metallurgy, engineering (shipbuilding, manufacture of motor vehicles, electrotechnical), chemicals, building, textiles and food processing. The production of optical instruments, watches, toys, musical instruments and jewellery is important, too. The principal economic region is the Ruhr agglomeration with more than one third of total industrial production in the country, followed by the Saarland, Siegerland, Peine-Salzgitter and metropolitan agglomerations. **Mining** (1983, in 1,000 tonnes, metal content): coal 89,620 (the Ruhr Basin, Aachen, Saarland), brown coal 124,335 (reg. Ville near Köln), crude petroleum 4,116 (Emsland, Hannover region, smaller resources near Hamburg and in Bayern, extensive pipeline network from abroad; Ingolstadt is a major centre of petroleum industry, natural gas 634,733 TJ (Emsland, Niedersachsen, Rehden, Hengstlage; gas pipeline from Netherlands resources in Groningen to Hamburg), iron ore 280 (Peine, Salzgitter, Siegen and Amberg), lead 23, zinc 92.6 (Harz, Sauerland), copper 1.2, gold 9,296 kg (1980), silver 40 tonnes, uranium 40 tonnes (Schwarzwald), kaolin 1,969, salt 6,862 (Schwäbisch Hall, Berchtesgaden), potassium salt 2,985 (valleys of the Leine and Werra rivers), pyrites 480, sulphur. Electricity 372 billion kWh (1983), of which 4% are hydro-electric and 12% nuclear power stations (Biblis, Neckarwestheim, Brunsbüttel, Würgassen, Stade.
Production: metallurgy (1983, in 1,000 tonnes): pig iron 26,633, crude steel 35,728 (most plants in the Ruhr Basin - Duisburg, Oberhausen, Bochum, Gelsenkirchen, in Niedersachsen - Peine, Salzgitter, in the Saarland and elsewhere), lead 365 (Braubach, Nordenham), zinc – primary 247, secondary 314 (Datteln, Harlingerode), aluminium – primary 743.4, secondary 38 (Töging, Rheinfelden), copper – smelted 159, refined 420 (Hamburg, Lünen), magnesium 638 tonnes, tin 562 tonnes (1981, Essen), coke oven coke 23 mn. tonnes.
Engineering: the Ruhr Basin (Düsseldorf, Wuppertal, Köln), Hamburg, Bremen, Solingen, Stuttgart and others (1983, in 1,000 units): motor vehicles – passenger 3,875 (Wolfsburg – "Volkswagen", Rüsselsheim, Bochum – "Opel", Köln – "Ford", Stuttgart – "Mercedes", München – "BMW"), commercial 260 – locomotives (München, Essen, Düsseldorf), carriages (Köln, Braunschweig), tractors 119 (Hannover, Kassel), vessels 528,000 GRT (Hamburg, Bremen, Emden, Kiel), printing

add page 58

Industry: manufacturing is concentrated in the Paris Basin and the territory of the lower Seine, the North, East, Lyon district, Atlantic ports and Marseille. A major part of metallurgy is situated near the resources: reg. Lorraine (from Longwy to Nancy), Nord (Dunkerque, Valenciennes and others), centre (Le Creusot, Saint-Étienne). The main concentration of engineering is to be found around Paris, Lille and its surroundings and Lyon. Chemical industry: in the coal and metallurgical regions, Paris region, petroleum processing in the ports. Textile industry: reg. Alsace, Lille and vicinity, Lyon.

Production (1983, in 1,000 tonnes): pig iron 14,304, crude steel 17,612, coke oven coke 8,458, aluminium 523 (Saint-Jean-de-Maurienne, Noguères), zinc 286, lead 174, refined copper 62.4, magnesium 11,075 tonnes, synthetic nitrogen 2,016 (1980), nitric acid, sulphuric acid 4,243, hydrochloric acid 242.5, nitrogenous fertilizers 1,600, caustic soda 1,393, soda ash 1,560 (1980), phosphorus fertilizers 1,230, synthetic rubber 512, plastics and resins 2,877; capacity of petroleum refineries 109.6 mn. tonnes (1984), oil pipelines network 102,540 km (1978), naphtha 3,127, motor spirit 16,046, oils 44,946, cosmetics and pharmaceuticals (Paris, Lyon), tyres 47.3 mn. units, motor vehicles – pasenger 3,359,000 (Paris, Le Mans, Rennes, Flins, Sochaux), – commercial 457,000 (Lyon-Vénissieux) – ships 229,000 GRT (shipyards Saint-Nazaire, La Ciotat, Dunkerque), aircraft (Paris, Toulouse, Bordeaux), locomotives, carriages, railway equipment (Le Creusot, Lille, Belfort), agricultural machines (Vierzon, Beauvais, Saint-Dizier), radio receivers 2,498,000 units, television receivers 1,956,000, cement 24,504, chemical wood pulp 1,361, paper 5,041, yarn – cotton 199, woollen 107.9, jute 3.3 – woven fabrics -cotton 128, -woollen 76, -silk 606 tonnes – jute 2.8 – rayon and acetate – fibres 8.4, staple fibre 29.6 – synthetic – fibres 63.6, staple fibre 144 – sugar 3,875, meat 5,568, milk 35,150, condensed milk 125, butter 645, cheese 1,200, eggs 900, canned fish 98, wine 6,000 (second world producer, reg. Languedoc, Bordeaux, reg. Bourgogne, reg. Champagne), alcoholic spirits (Cognac, Fécamp, reg. Armagnac, Isère), beer 22.1 mn. hl (1983); 62.1 billion cigarettes (1983).

Agriculture: France has many large agricultural establishments, although small and medium-sized farms predominate. Animal production exceeds vegetable production. Land use: arable land 31.5%, meadows and pastures 23.3%, forests 26.7%; tractors 1,535,000 (1983), combine harvesters 148,000 (1983). **Crops** (1983, in 1,000 tonnes): wheat 24,781 (Paris Basin, reg. Picardie), barley 8,865, oats 1,469, rye, maize (corn) 10,143 (reg. Aquitaine, Paris Basin), rice (Camargue), sorghum, potatoes 5,325, flax 31, sugar beet 23,955 (second world producer, Nord, Paris Basin), rapeseed 969, olives, sunflower seed 837, hops, fruit 11,914, apples 1,950, grapes 8,550 (second world producer, principal vine-growing region from the lower Rhône to the Pyrenees and Gironde), strawberries 90, vegetables 7,104, tomatoes 870, tobacco 37; **livestock** (1983, in 1,000 head): cattle 23,656, sheep 12,103, goats 1,243, pigs 11,709, horses 312, asses, mules; poultry 187,000, wool 11,000 tonnes, honey 19,000 tonnes; fish catch 784,000 tonnes (1983), roundwood 39.8 cub.m (1983).

Communications (1984): railways 34,688 km, of which 11,335 km are electrified, roads 781,869 km, of which 32,869 km are national and 345,000 km departmental roads; motorways 4,514 km, cars 19.3 mn. (1982). Navigable waterways 8,500 km, of which canals take up 4,575 km. Merchant shipping 8,945,000 GRT (1984). Chief ports: Marseille (second largest European port, 92 mn. tonnes of freight in 1982), Le Havre, Dunkerque, Rouen, Nantes, Bordeaux. Civil aviation (1984): 270.4 mn. km flown, 23,646,000 passengers carried. Tourism 33.6 mn. visitors (1983).

Exports: machines, cars, aircraft, raw materials and semi-finished products (iron, ores), textile and chemical products, agricultural products, wine and others. **Imports:** fuels (petroleum, coal), finished products and equipment, agricultural products (fruit, early vegetables), raw materials and semi-finished products (cotton, wool, rubber), consumer goods. Chief trading partners: Fed. Rep. of Germany, Italy, Belgium-Luxembourg, United Kingdom, U.S.A., Netherlands.

GERMANY, FEDERAL REPUBLIC OF
(former German democratic republic)

Area 108,333 sq.km, population 16,340,000 (1988). Since 3 October 1990 part of Federal republic of Germany.

Administrative units: 15 regions (Bezirke), **the capital** Berlin 1,185,533 inhab. (1984) also has the status of a region; **other towns** (1983, in 1,000 inhab.): Leipzig 559, Dresden 523, Karl-Marx-Stadt 319, Magdeburg 289, Rostock 241, Halle 236, Erfurt 214, Potsdam 136, Gera 130, Schwerin 123, Cottbus 121, Zwickau 120, Jena 107, Dessau 104, Stralsund 75, Weimar 63, Gotha 58. **Population:** Germans (over 99%). Density 154 persons per sq.km; average annual rate of population increase only 0.7%; urban population 76.5%. 38% of inhabitants employed in industry. – **Currency:** Mark of the DDR = 100 pfennigs.

Economy: highly developed industrial country with intensive agriculture. **Principal industries:** engineering (Saxony, Thuringia, Magdeburg, Berlin with surroundings), electrotechnical (Berlin), chemicals (region of brown coal deposits, Leuna), electronics, precision mechanics and optics (Jena), textiles. **Mining** (1983, in 1,000 tonnes, metal content): brown coal 277,968 (leading world producer, Thuringian-Saxon Basin – Leipzig, Halle, Merseburg; Lower-Lusatian Basin – Senftenberg, Spremberg), natural gas 145,028 TJ, copper 12 (Harz), nickel 2.2, tin 1,800 tonnes, silver 45 tonnes, uranium (Aue), potassium salt 3,430 and salt 2,907 (Stassfurt, Halberstadt, Bleicherode, valleys of the Werra and Unstrut). Limited mining of coal, iron ore, lead, zinc, tungsten. Electricity 105 billion kWh (1983), of which 88% are thermal and 10% nuclear power stations (at Rheinsberg, Lubmin).

machines (Augsburg, Offenbach), textile machines (Mönchengladbach, Esslingen), agricultural machines (Mannheim, Hannover), precision engineering (München, Kassel, Göttingen), watches (Schwarzwald), radio receivers 3,292 (1983), television receivers 4,705 (1983).
Chemical industry in the lower Rhine zone (Köln–Leverkusen–Ruhr Basin), southern zone (from Mannheim-Ludwigshafen to Frankfurt am Main). Production (1983, in 1,000 tonnes): acids: sulphuric 4,340, hydrochloric 900, nitrogenous 2,626; soda ash 1,218, caustic soda 3,350 (second world producer), synthetic nitrogen 1,703, chlorine 2,848, fertilizers: nitrogenous 746, phosphorus 552, potash 2,275, plastics and resins 7,031, synthetic rubber 432, dyes (Frankfurt am Main), pharmaceuticals and photo materials (Leverkusen), synthetic fibres 332; capacity of petroleum refineries 105 mn. tonnes (1984, Ruhr Basin, Karlsruhe, Ingolstadt, Hamburg, Bremen, Emden, Missburg/Hannover), naphtha 6,825, motor spirit 19,913, fuel oils 50,849, tyres 37.9 mn. units. Production of cement 30.5 mn. tonnes (1983). **Chemical wood pulp and paper industry** (1983, 1,000 tonnes): chemical wood pulp 576, newsprint 654, paper and paper products 7,619. **Textile industry** in the Rhineland (from Aachen, Krefeld to Bielefeld, Bonn), Münster, Osnabrück, south-west zone (Esslingen, Reutlingen), Augsburg, Kempten, Hof (1983, in 1,000 tonnes): yarn – cotton 181.4, woollen 46.4, flax and hemp 3.4, jute 3.4, woven fabrics (in mn. sq.m) – cotton 881, woollen 79.2, rayon and acetate 320.9, footwear (Pirmasens, Stuttgart), sale of furs (Frankfurt am Main). Glass industry (Ruhr Basin, Saarland), optics, photographic apparatus (München, Stuttgart), ceramics (München), musical instruments (Trossingen, Mittenwald), jewellery (Pforzheim), toys, **Food industry:** mainly in large cities and surroundings (1983, in 1,000 tonnes): meat 4,694, milk 26,141, condensed milk 538, butter 627, cheese 848, margarine 606, eggs 800, honey 14, wheat flour 2,280, sugar 3,150 (Braunschweig), wine, beer 91.4 mn. hl (second world producer, Bayern – München, Nürnberg): 156 billion cigarettes, 1.6 billion cigars.
Agriculture: is very intensive. 80% of the food supply derives from domestic agricultural resources. Animal production predominates (^{3}/$_4$ of agricultural production). Land use: arable land 31%, meadows and pastures 19.1%, forests 29.5%. High average hectare yields, extensive use of synthetic fertilizers. Tractors 1,471,681 (1983), combine harvesters 165,500 (1983). **Crops** (1983, in 1,000 tonnes): wheat 8,998 (Rhineland and Danubeland), barley 8,914, rye 1,599 (North German Lowlands), oats 2,068, maize (corn) 934, potatoes 6,088, sugar beet 16,500 (surroundings of Braunschweig and Köln), rapeseed 580, fruit 4,386, grapes 1,739 (cultivation of fruit and viniculture – middle Rhineland, valleys of the Mosel, Main, Neckar and others), vegetables 6,088, hops 37 (leading world producer, Danubeland), flax, tobacco; **livestock** (1983, in 1,000 head): cattle 15,098, pigs 22,478, horses 369, sheep 1,172, goats; poultry 80,000, fish catch 305,600 tonnes; roundwood 29.5 mn. cub.m.
Communications (1984): railways 30,808 km, of which 11,571 km are electrified, roads 267,050 km, motorways 8,080 km, passenger cars 25,217,800. Navigable waterways 4,354 km (river transport – the Rhein and the North German canal system), the largest river port Duisburg. Merchant shipping 6,242,000 GRT (1984). Chief ports: Hamburg (turnover 58.9 mn. tonnes in 1981), Bremen, Wilhelmshaven, Emden, Lübeck. Civil aviation (1984): 215.3 mn. km flown, 14,052,000 passengers carried. Tourism 11.3 mn. visitors (1983).
Foreign trade: the Fed. Rep. of Germany is the second most important trading country in the world. – **Exports:** machines of all kinds, cars, chemical and electrotechnical products, iron and steel, textiles, products of precision mechanics, coal, metals. **Imports:** finished products (machines, motor vehicles, electrotechnical products, textile and clothes, paper and paper products, semi-finished products (non-ferrous metals, fuel and lubricating oils), raw materials (petroleum, iron ore, cotton, wool), foodstuffs (fruit, vegetables, meat, coffee, tobacco). Chief trading partners: France, Netherlands, Italy, Belgium-Luxembourg, United Kingdom, U.S.A., Switzerland, Austria.

GIBRALTAR

Dominion of Gibraltar, area 6.5 sq.km, population 29,692 (1988), **British territory** since 1704, with **extended internal autonomy** according to the 1969 Constitution. Security, foreign affairs and defence fall within the competence of the British Governor (Sir William Jackson). – **Currency:** Gibraltar pound = 100 pence. **Importance:** British naval and air base of great strategic importance, also a merchant port. Transit trade, fishing, food processing. Tourism 66,000 visitors (1983).

GREECE

Eliniki Dimokratia, area 131,957 sq.km, population 10,013,000 (1988), **republic** (President Constantine Karamanlis since 1990).

Administrative units: 12 provinces, 52 prefectures (Nomói). One of these is the monastic state of Mount Áthos (Áyion Óros), area 336 sq.km, 1,472 inhab. in 1981 on the Khalkidhiki Peninsula. **Capital:** Athínai (Athens) 885,737 inhab. (1981), Greater Athínai with agglomeration 3,027,331 inhab.; **other towns** (census 1981, in 1,000 inhab.): Thessaloniki (Salonica) 406, Pátrai 142, Lárisa 103, Iráklion 102, Vólos 71, Kaválla 56, Khaniá 48, Khalkís 45, Ioánnina 44. **Population:** Greeks 95%, Turks, Albanians. **Density** 75 persons per sq.km; average annual rate of population increase 1.1% (1975–82); urban population 63% (1981). 35% of inhabitants employed in agriculture (1983), 15% in industry. – **Currency:** drachma = 100 lepta. **Economy:** industrial and agricultural country with heavy foreign investments (Philips, Pirelli, Benz, Péchiney and others). **Principal industries:** textiles, food processing, chemicals and mining. Heavy industry is only developing. **Mining** (1983, in 1,000 tonnes, metal content): brown coal 30,336 (Ptolemaís, Alivérion, Megalópolis), crude petroleum 1,332, iron ore 572 (Khalkidhiki), manganese 2.6, chromium 15 (reg. Thessalía, Kozáni), lead 19.4, zinc 21.4, nickel 15.0 (Larimna), silver 50 tonnes, bauxite 2,387 (Elevsis, Distomon), magnesite 937.7 (island Évvoia), salt 133, pyrites 144, emery (island Náxos), marble. Electricity 22 billion kWh (1983). **Production** (1983, in 1,000 tonnes): crude steel 755, aluminium 157.9 (Distomon); capacity of petroleum refineries 18 mn. tonnes (1984 – Thessaloníki, Athíni), petroleum products 11.7 mn. tonnes; sulphuric acid 988, phosphorus fertilizers 194, cement 14,124, cotton yarn 118, woollen yarn 14, carpets (Thessaloníki, Athíni), sugar 326, meat 530, milk 690, cheese 196, eggs 125, canned food, raisins 145, wine 530, olive oil 259; 26.2 billion cigarettes (1983).

1 : 8 000 000
0 50 100 150 200 Km
0 25 50 75 100 125 Mi
NORTH SEA
UNITED KINGDOM
Gr. Yarmouth
Lowestoft
DENMARK
Grenen
Hjørring
Frederikshavn
Læsø
Thisted
Ålborg
Limfj.
Jylland
Kattegat
Holstebro
Viborg
Herning
Randers
Århus
Horsens
Vejle
Kolding
Esbjerg
Ribe
Odense
Fyn
Nyborg
Kalundborg
Åbenrå
Svendborg
Sylt
North Frisian Is.
København (Copenhagen)
Roskilde
Sjælland
Korsør
Næstved
Nakskov
Lolland
Møn
Falster
Nykøbing Falster
Rødby
Gedser
Helsingør
The Sound
Göteborg
Borås
Varberg
Halmstad
Hässleholm
Helsingborg
Lund
Malmö
Trelleborg
Ätran
Nissan
Lagan
FEDERAL REPUBLIC OF GERMANY
Flensburg
Schleswig
Kieler B.
Kiel
Fehmarn
Mecklenburger B.
Zingst
Stralsund
Greifswald
Neumünster
Deutsche B.
Ostfriesische In.
Lübeck
Rostock
Wismar
Cuxhaven
Hamburg
Schwerin
Neubrandenburg
Neustrelitz
Wilhelmshaven
Emden
Bremerhaven
Lüneburg
Elbe
Oldenburg
Bremen
Weser
Verden
Uelzen
Wittenberge
Celle
Aller
Neuruppin
Stendal
Eberswalde
Ems
Mittellandkanal
Hannover
Braunschweig
Wolfsburg
Berlin
Osnabrück
Hildesheim
Brandenburg
Potsdam
Münster
Bielefeld
Salzgitter
Magdeburg
Essen
Dortmund
Duisburg
Wittenberg
Bernburg
Dessau
Göttingen
Halle
Düsseldorf
Wuppertal
Kassel
Nordhausen
Merseburg
Leipzig
Riesa
Köln (Cologne)
Siegen
Erfurt
Marburg a. d. L.
Gotha
Weimar
Jena
Gera
Chemnitz
Bonn
Neuwied
Giessen
Koblenz
Fulda
Suhl
Zwickau
Teplice
Limburg
Plauen
Most
Wiesbaden
Frankfurt a. M.
Hanau
Hof
Ohře
Mosel
Schweinfurt
Offenbach
Cheb
Karlovy Vary
Trier
Mainz
Darmstadt
Bayreuth
Worms
Main
Bamberg
Mariánské Lázně
Ludwigshafen
Mannheim
Würzburg
Kaiserslautern
Heidelberg
Fürth
Amberg
Plzeň
Saarbrücken
Heilbronn
Nürnberg
Cham
Klatovy
Karlsruhe
Pforzheim
Stuttgart
Ingolstadt
Regensburg
Baden-Baden
Göppingen
Straubing
Esslingen
Passau
Tübingen
Ulm
Augsburg
Landshut
Donau
Isar
Lech
Inn
Freiburg
Memmingen
München (Munich)
Tuttlingen
Rosenheim
Bodensee
Kempten
NETHERLANDS
Waddeneilanden
Waddenzee
Groningen
Den Helder
Leeuwarden
Assen
IJsselmeer
Meppel
Emmen
Alkmaar
Zwolle
Haarlem
Amsterdam
Enschede
Leiden
's-Gravenhage
Utrecht
Apeldoorn
Rotterdam
Rijn
Arnhem
Maas
Vlissingen
Dordrecht
Nijmegen
Rhein
Zeebrugge
Breda
Tilburg
Oostende
Eindhoven
BELGIUM
Brugge
Schelde
Antwerpen (Anvers)
Dunkerque
Kortrijk
Gent (Gand)
Mechelen
Leuven
Roubaix
Lille
Maastricht
Valenciennes
Mons
Bruxelles (Brussel)
Aachen
Arras
Maubeuge
Charleroi
Namur
Liège
St. Quentin
Bastogne
LUXEMBOURG
Luxembourg
Esch-s.-A.
FRANCE
Amiens
Charleville-Mézières
Laon
Sedan
Compiègne
Reims
Marne
Verdun
Thionville
Épernay
Châlons-s.-Marne
Metz
Meuse
Bar-le-Duc
St.-Dizier
Nancy
Troyes
Strasbourg
Sens
Seine
Chaumont
St.-Dié
Auxerre
Colmar
Épinal
Rhine
Montbard
Mulhouse
Saône
Belfort
Vesoul
Yonne
Dijon
Besancon
Doubs
Nevers
Autun
Le Creusot
Dole
Chalon-s.-Saône
Loire
Moulins
Roanne
Thiers
Lyon
Rhône
Vienne
Annecy
Chamonix-Mt. Blanc
SWITZERLAND
Basel
Winterthur
Aare
Zürich
St. Gallen
Bregenz
Neuchâtel
Biel
Luzern
Zug
LIECHTENSTEIN
Vaduz
Fribourg
Bern
Schwyz
Chur
St. Moritz
Brig
Aosta
Lugano
AUSTRIA
Salzburg
Bad Ischl
Kufstein
Bischofshofen
Innsbruck
Landeck
Lienz
Drau
Villach
ITALY
Merano
Bolzano
Adige
Piave
Sondrio
Trento
Belluno
Udine
Ljubljana
CZ
Wels
Čes.
Kap
Saßnitz
A
B
D
1
2
3
4°
8°
12°
48°
52°
56°

12a The Ruhr Basin

1 : 2 000 000

FEDERAL REPUBLIC OF GERMANY

1. Baden-Württemberg
2. Bayern
3. Berlin
4. Brandenburg
5. Bremen
6. Hamburg
7. Hessen
8. Mecklenburg-Vorpommern
9. Niedersachsen
10. Nordrhein-Westfalen
11. Rheinland-Pfalz
12. Saarland
13. Sachsen
14. Sachsen-Anhalt
15. Schleswig-Holstein
16. Thüringen

AUSTRIA

1. Burgenland
2. Kärnten
3. Niederösterreich
4. Oberösterreich
5. Salzburg
6. Steiermark
7. Tirol
8. Vorarlberg
9. Wien

CZECHOSLOVAKIA

1. Středočeský
2. Jihočeský
3. Západočeský
4. Severočeský
5. Východočeský
6. Jihomoravský
7. Severomoravský
8. Západoslovenský
9. Stredoslovenský
10. Východoslovenský

POLAND

49 Districts (województw)

The seat of the districts is underlined

Agriculture: arable land 22%, meadows and pastures 39.8%, forests 19.8%. **Crops** (1983, in 1, 000 tonnes): wheat 2,026, barley 572, maize (corn) 1,622, rice, potatoes 809, cotton -seed 275, -lint 140, sugar beet 2,560, olives 1,052, groundnuts, sesame, fruit 3,636 – watermelons 660, oranges 550, lemons 165, grapes 1,600, figs, vegetables 3,849, tomatoes 1,970, tobacco 115, walnuts 21; **livestock** (1983, in 1,000 head): cattle 850, sheep 8,400, goats 4,630, pigs 1,400 horses 97, asses 220, mules, buffaloes; poultry 36,000; silkworms, honey 12,500 tonnes, wool 5,150 tonnes; fish catch 100,000 tonnes (1983); roundwood 2.8 mn. cub.m (1983).
Communications (1984): railways 2,479km, roads 61,613km, passenger cars 1,151,000. Merchant shipping 35,059,000 GRT. Chief port is Athínai-Piraiévs. Corinth canal: length 6,345m, depth 7 m, width at level 24.6m, at bottom 21m, opened in 1893. Civil aviation: 47.5 mn. km flown, 6,878,000 passengers carried. Tourism 4.8 mn. visitors. **Exports:** iron and steel, fresh and dried fruit, aluminium, chemical products, tobacco, cotton. **Imports:** industrial and consumer goods, raw materials, foodstuffs, fuels and oils. Chief trading partners: Fed. Rep. of Germany, Italy, U.S.A., France, United Kingdom.

HUNGARY

Magyar Köztársaság, area 93,036 sq.km, population 10,596,000 (1988), **republic** (Provisional Head of State Arpád Göncz since 1990).
Administrative units: 19 counties (megye), and the **capital** – Budapest 2,064,374 inhab. (1984); **other towns** (1984, in 1,000 inhab.): Miskolc 211, Debrecen 206, Szeged 176, Pécs 174, Györ 128, Nyíregyháza 114, Székesfehérvár 109, Kecskemét 101, Szombathely 86, Szolnok 79, Tatabánya 78, Kaposvár 74, Békéscsaba 70, Eger 64, Veszprém 62, Zalaegerszeg 60, Salgótarján 50. **Population:** Hungarians 98%, Serbs, Croats, Slovenians, Germans, Slovaks. **Density** 114 persons per sq.km; average annual rate of population increase 0.2% (1975–81); urban population 54% (1981). 13.5% of inhabitants employed in agriculture, 50.6% in industry. – **Currency:** forint = 100 fillers.
Economy: industrial and agricultural country. **Principal industries:** engineering, metallurgy, chemicals, textiles and food processing. Half the industrial production occurs in Budapest. Shortage of energy resources. **Mining** (1983, in 1,000 tonnes, metal content): coal 2,832 (Pécs, Komló), brown coal 22,392 (Salgótarján, Tatabánya, Gyöngyös), crude petroleum 2,004 (Nagylengyel, Algyö, Demjén, Szolnok), natural gas 248,517 TJ (Karcag, Szolnok), bauxite 2,917 (Iszkaszentgyörgy, Gúttamási, Halimba), iron ore 96, manganese 23.3, uranium (Pécs), copper, lead, zinc. Electricity 25.7 billion kWh (1983), 14% nuclear power stations. **Production** (1983, in 1,000 tonnes): pig iron 2,047 and crude steel 3,617 (Dunaújváros, Miskolc-Diósgyör, Özd), aluminium 74.4 (Ajka, Várpalota, Tatabánya), refined copper 12, engineering (Györ, Eger, Debrecen, Pécs, Miskolc) – lorries 13,200 units, buses 11,800 units (Budapest), railway carriages (Györ), – television receivers 363,000 units, cutting machines, sulphuric acid 606, nitric acid 1,076, nitrogenous fertilizers 700 (Leninvárois); capacity of petroleum refineries 11 mn. tonnes (1984), oil pipeline for the import of Soviet petroleum, photochemical (Vác) and pharmaceutical products (Debrecen, Tiszavasvári), cement 4,248, textile industry (Szeged, Vác, Sopron) – woven fabrics – cotton 280 mn. sq.m, – woollen 23 mn. sq.m, – rayon and acetate 36 mn. sq.m, yarn – cotton 56.4, – woollen 10.8, synthetic fibres 9.6, artificial fibres 6.1, leather shoes 43.5 mn. pairs, food industry (Debrecen, Szeged) – meat 1,664, milk 2,800, butter 32.7, cheese 80, eggs 215, Hungarian salami for export, sugar 478, wine 640 (Tokaj), beer 7.8 mn. hl (1983); 25.7 billion cigarettes.
Agriculture: vegetable production and cereals predominate; important viniculture, cultivation of fruit and vegetables. Land use: arable land 54.3%, meadows and pastures 13.9%, forests 17.6%. **Crops** (1983, in 1,000 tonnes): wheat 5,985, maize (corn) 7,600, barley 1,000, rye, rice, potatoes 1,506, flax 10, hemp 11, sugar beet 4,800, sunflower seed 638, soya beans, hops, fruit 2,581, grapes 1,000, vegetables 1,766, walnuts 12; **livestock** (1983, in 1,000 head): cattle 1,922, pigs 9,035, sheep 3,180, horses 112; poultry 63,000, honey 15,000 tonnes; fish catch 43,900 tonnes (1983) roundwood 6.4 mn. cub.m (1983).
Communications (1984): railways 7,830km, of which 1,903km electrified, roads 29,633km, passenger cars 1,344,000. Navigable waterways 1,373km (1984). Civil aviation: 17.6 mn. km flown, 1,039,000 passengers carried. Tourism 6.8 mn. visitors (1983).
Exports: machines and industrial equipment, transport equipment, chemical products, bauxite, aluminium, foodstuffs (meat, smoked meat products, canned fruits, wine, fruit, vegetables). **Imports:** fuels (petroleum, natural gas), raw materials, semi-finished products, machines and equipment, cars, industrial consumer goods. Chief trading partners: U.S.S.R. 30%, socialist countries 21% (mainly German Dem. Rep., Czechoslovakia, Yugoslavia), Fed. Rep. of Germany, Austria.

ICELAND

Lýdveldid Ísland, area 102,829 sq.km, population 249,000 (1988), **republic** (President Mrs Vigdís Finnbogadottir since 1980).

Administrative units: 7 districts. **Capital:** Reykjavík 86,092 inhab. (1982); **other towns** (in 1,000 inhab.): Akureyri 14, Kópavogur 14, Hafnarfjördur 12. **Population:** Icelandic. **Density** 2 persons per sq.km; average annual rate of population increase 1.1% (1975–82); urban population 87% (1981). – **Currency:** Icelandic króna = 100 aurars.
Economy: agricultural country without raw material resources. The economy is based on fishing – catch 839,200 tonnes (1983) – whaling, raising of sheep 748,000 head (1983), cattle 64,000 (1983). Electricity 3.8 billion kWh (1983), of which 97% are hydro-electric power stations; hot springs. **Industry:** fish processing, canning, freezing plants, production of aluminium and textiles. – **Communications:** roads 11,619km (1984). Merchant shipping 179,000 GRT (1984). – **Exports:** fresh and canned fish 68%, aluminium, diatomite, woollen products. **Imports:** industrial products, fuels and foodstuffs. Chief trading partners: U.S.A., United Kingdom, Fed. Rep. of Germany, U.S.S.R.

map 13

IRELAND

Éire, area 70,283 sq.km, population 3,538,000 (1988), **republic** (President Dr Padraig Ohlrighile/ Dr Patrick J. Hillery since 1976).

Administrative units: 4 provinces (27 counties). **Capital:** Dublin (Baile Átha Cliath) 525,882 inhab. (census 1981); **other towns** (1981, in 1,000 inhab.): Cork 136, Limerick 61, Dún Laoghaire 54. **Population:** Irish. **Density** 51 persons per sq.km; average annual rate of population increase 1.3% (1975–1982); urban population 58% (1981). 19.3% of inhabitants employed in agriculture, 31% in industry. – **Currency:** Irish pound = 100 pence.
Economy: industrial and agricultural country. **Principal industries:** mining of minerals, metallurgy, engineering, chemicals, textiles and food processing. Centres of industry: Dublin, Cork, Cobh. **Mining** (1983, in 1,000 tonnes, metal content): coal, peat (Timahoe), natural gas 87,000 TJ, zinc 186, lead 33.6 (Tynagh), silver 20 tonnes. Electricity 11.2 billion kWh (1983). **Production** (1983, in 1,000 tonnes): cement 1,486, woven fabrics – cotton 36 mn. sq.m, woollen 2.7 mn. sq.m, rayon and acetate 48.3 mn. sq.m, sugar 203, meat 601, milk 5,490, butter 150, cheese 53, eggs 34, beer 4 mn. hl ("Guinness"), alcoholic spirits; 7.5 billion cigarettes (1983). **Agriculture** – animal production predominates. Land use: arable land 13.8%, meadows and pastures 69%, forests 4.6%. **Crops** (1983, in 1,000 tonnes): wheat 350, oats 103, barley 1,437, potatoes 800, sugar beet 1,520; **livestock** (1983, in 1,000 head): cattle 6,771, sheep 3,480, pigs 1,145; poultry 8,000; fish catch 203,400 tonnes (1983).
Communications: railways 1,944 km (1984), roads 89,579 km, passenger cars 716,800 (1984). Navigable waterways 1,040 km. Merchant shipping 221,000 GRT (1984). Chief ports: Dublin, Cobh. Civil aviation (1984): 20.5 mn. km flown, 1,838,000 passengers carried. Tourism 2.3 mn. visitors (1983).
Exports: meat, live cattle, machines, textiles, chemicals, pharmaceuticals, beverages. Chief trading partners: United Kingdom (34% of export and 43% of import in 1984), Fed. Rep. of Germany, U.S.A., France, Netherlands.

ITALY

Repubblica Italiana, area 301,278 sq.km, population 57,476,000 (1988), **republic** (President Dr Francesco Cossiga since 1985).

Administrative units: 20 regions (95 provinces). **Capital:** Roma (Rome) 2,826,733 inhab. (1984); **other towns** (1984, in 1,000 inhab.): Milano 1,536, Napoli (Naples) 1,207, Torino (Turin) 1,050, Genova 738, Palermo 716, Bologna 442, Firenze (Florence) 436, Catania 378, Bari 368, Venezia (Venice) 338, Messina 266, Verona 261, Taranto 244, Trieste 244, Padova 229, Cagliari 224, Brescia 202, Modena 178, Parma 177, Reggio di Calabria 177, Livorno 176, Prato 160, Foggia 158, Salerno 156, Ferrara 146, Ravenna 137, Pescara 132, Reggio n.Emilia 130. **Population:** Italians 98%. **Density** 190 persons per sq.km; average annual rate of population increase 0.4% (1975–81); urban population 70% (1981). 9.5% of inhabitants employed in agriculture, 36.3% in industry (1983). – **Currency:** Italian lira.
Economy: highly developed industrial and agricultural country, economically the most advanced in southern Europe. There is considerable difference between the advanced industrial North with its large modern plants and the under-developed agricultural South. **Principal industries:** engineering, hydroenergetics, electrometallurgy, electrotechnics, electronics, chemistry, textiles and food processing. **Mining** (1983, in 1,000 tonnes, metal content): lignite 1,908, crude petroleum 2,196 (Gela, Ragusa), natural gas 500,835 TJ (The Po plain and others), manganese 2,200 tonnes, lead 12.5, zinc 21 (Iglesias), mercury 159 tonnes (1982, Monte Amiata, Grosseto), copper, bauxite 14, silver 73 tonnes, uranium (Piemonte Alps, Novazza), salt 3,454 (Sicilia), potassium salts 140 (Sicilia), pyrites 646 (Grosseto), sulphur 8 (Sicilia), marble, magnesite, asbestos 139, fluorite 173, barytes 180, graphite, kaolin. Electricity 182.9 billion kWh (1983), of which 27% are hydro-electric, nuclear power stations 4% (Caorso, Trino, Garigliano, Latina). **Production** (1983, in 1,000 tonnes): metallurgy: pig iron 10,519 (Trieste, Napoli, Piombino, Aosta), crude steel 21,810 (reg. Lombardia – Milano, reg. Liguria – Genova, reg. Piemonte – Torino; Taranto and others), lead 40 (Sardegna, La Spezia), zinc 156 (Monteponi), cadmium 500 tonnes, aluminium 473.7 (Marghera near Venezia), magnesium 9,799 tonnes. **Engineering** (1983, in 1,000 units): vessels 241,000 GRT (1984, Genova, La Spezia, Livorno, Napoli, Palermo), electric locomotives 209 units, railway carriages 2,940 units (Torino, Pinerolo, Vado Ligure), aircraft (Torino, Varese), passenger cars 1,395 ("Fiat" – Torino, 71% of production, "Alfa Romeo" – Milano, "Lancia" – Torino, "Ferrari" – Maranello), bicycles 1,978 (Milano), motorcycles 780, tractors 84 (Torino), precision mechanics (microtechnics, photo and cinema apparatus – Milano, Torino), spectacles, electrotechnical apparatus (Milano, Roma, Torino), radio receivers, television receivers 1,615, calculating machines, typewriters 439 ("Olivetti" – Ivrea).
Chemical industry (Lombardia, 1983, in 1,000 tonnes): acid – sulphuric 2,339, hydrochloric, nitric 1,021 – caustic soda 1,009, synthetic nitrogen 1,134, nitrogenous fertilizers 1,081 (Novara, Merano), phosphorus fertilizers 434, potash fertilizers 125, coke oven coke 6,450, pharmaceuticals, dyes (Milano and surroundings), plastics and resins 2,436 (Ferrara, Castellanza), synthetic fibres 536, synthetic rubber 233, capacity of petroleum refineries 145.3 mn. tonnes, oil pipeline network 3,266 km, gas pipelines 14,270 km, motor spirit 14.5 mn. tonnes, oils 49.6 mn. tonnes; production of cement 39.8 mn. tonnes, sheet and crystal glass (Marghera near Venezia, Milano), chandeliers (Murano), chemical wood pulp 148, paper and paper products 4,065, furniture (Cantù, Lissone), musical instruments (Emilia-Romagna, Marche, Milano).
Textile industry – cotton processing (The Po Plain, Lombardia), wool processing (reg. Piemonte – Biella), silk processing (reg. Lombardia – Como), flax processing (Lombardia and Piemonte). Production (1983, in 1,000 tonnes): cotton yarn 217, woven fabrics -cotton 206, -woollen 154 (1982), -silk 16, -jute 11, rayon and acetate fibres 4.2 (1981), non-cellulosic staple fibre 313, shoes 500 mn. pairs (Vigevano).
Food industry (1983, in 1,000 tonnes): sugar 1,360, meat 3,606, milk 10,650, butter 76, cheese 636, eggs 640, production of spaghetti etc., sweets, canned fish and foodstuffs, olive oil 874 (leading world producer), wine 8,000 (leading world producer, "Chianti", "Barbero", "Cinzano", "Martini" etc.); beer 10 mn. hl; 73.6 billion cigarettes.

page 63

SWITZERLAND
AUSTRIA
YUGOSLAVIA
FRANCE
ITALY
TUNISIA
ALGERIA
MONACO
SAN MARINO
MALTA
VATICAN C.
Fribourg
Thun
Chur
Rhein
Inn
Lausanne
Montreux
Sion
Brig
L. Geneva
Rhône
Lugano
L. Maggiore
L. di Como
St. Moritz
Sondrio
Merano
Adige
Bolzano
Lienz
Drau
Villach
Klagenfurt
Graz
Mur
Zalaeger
Nagyk
Maribor
Drava
Varaždin
Jesenice
Kranj
Celje
Sava
Ljubljana
ZAGREB
Postojna
Sisak
Kupa
Karlovac
Una
Rijeka
Crikvenica
Opatija
Istrije
Kvarner
O. Krk
O. Cres
O. Pag
Pula
Bihać
Gospić
Banja
Zadar
Dugi O.
Knin
Šibenik
Split
Trogir
O. Hvar
O. Vis
O. K
O. B
O. Pal
Chamonix-Mt. Blanc
Aosta
Biella
Busto Arsizio
Como
Bergamo
L. di Garda
Monza
Novara
MILANO (Milan)
Pavia
Brescia
Cremona
Verona
Vicenza
Trento
Belluno
Pordenone
Udine
Gorizia
Piave
Treviso
Padova
G. di Trieste
Trieste
Koper
Venezia (Venice)
G. di Venezia
Mantova
Po
TORINO (Turin)
Briançon
Asti
Alessandria
Bormida
Piacenza
Parma
Reggio n. Emilia
Ferrara
V. di Comacchio
GENOVA (Genoa)
Cuneo
Savona
Modena
Bologna
Ravenna
Cesena
Forlì
Rimini
La Spezia
Carrara
Pistoia
Prato
San Marino
Pesaro
Fano
San Remo
Nice
Monaco
Imperia
Golfo di Genova
Viareggio
Lucca
Pisa
Firenze (Florence)
Cannes
LIGURIAN SEA
Livorno
Arezzo
Siena
Ancona
Macerata
C. Corse
Portoferraio
Piombino
Perugia
Foligno
Ascoli Piceno
Spoleto
Bastia
Calvi
I. d'Elba
Grosseto
Orbetello
Terni
Teramo
Pescara
Corte
Corse
Viterbo
L'Aquila
Chieti
Ajaccio
Taravo
Rieti
Tevere
Civitavecchia
Tivoli
Avezzano
Vasto
ROMA (Rome)
Sartène
Porto-Vecchio
Frosinone
Campobasso
San Severo
St. of Bonifacio
La Maddalena
Latina
Foggia
Manfredonia
Barletta
Pto. Torres
Sassari
Olbia
Gaeta
Caserta
Benevento
Cerignola
Ofanto
Andria
Alghero
NAPOLI (Naples)
Avellino
Mate
Nuoro
Tirso
Sardegna
Salerno
G. di Salerno
Potenza
Torre del Greco
I. di Capri
Castellammare di St.
Oristano
Tortoli
TYRRHENIAN SEA
ADRIATIC
Agri
Sapri
Lauria
Castrovillari
Iglesias
Carbonia
Cagliari
G. di Cagliari
C. Teulada
Paola
Cos
Lamezia Terme
I. Stromboli
I. di Ustica
Is. Eolie
I. Lipari
Messina
Stretto di Messina
Palmi
Locri
Reggio di Ca
C. Spartive
MEDITERRANEAN SEA
Trapani
PALERMO
Barcellona
Ie. Egadi
Alcamo
Cefalù
Marsala
Sicilia
Acireale
Catania
Sciacca
Enna
Caltanissetta
Agrigento
Salso
Gela
Siracusa
Licata
Ragusa
C. Passero
R. Ben Sekka
Bizerte
Menzel Bourguiba
Annaba
El Kala
Tabarka
Mateur
TUNIS
Golfe de Tunis
R. Addar
Strait of Sicily
Kelibia
Béja
Oued Medjerda
Hammam Lif
I. di Pantelleria (It.)
1 : 8 000 000
0 50 100 150 200 Km
0 25 50 75 100 125 Mi
El Kairouan
Sousse
Monastir
Valletta
8°
12°
16°
44°
40°
36°
A
B
C
D
1
2
3

ITALY Regions (20)

1 Abruzzi	11 Molise
2 Basilicata	12 Piemonte
3 Calabria	13 Puglia
4 Campania	14 Sardegna
5 Emilia-Romagna	15 Sicilia
6 Friuli-Venezia Giulia	16 Toscana
7 Lazio	17 Trentino-Alto Adige
8 Liguria	18 Umbria
9 Lombardia	19 Valle d'Aosta
10 Marche	20 Veneto

YUGOSLAVIA Socialist Republics (6)

1 Bosna i Hercegovina
2 Crna Gora
3 Hrvatska
4 Makedonija
5 Slovenija
6 Srbija
 a) Kosovo
 b) Vojvodina

13 a Plain of Po 1 : 4 500 000

Agriculture: arable land 31,4%, meadows and pastures 17%, forests 21%. Number of tractors 1,169,513 (1983).
Crops (1983, in 1,000 tonnes): wheat 8,514 (The Po Plain), barley 1,174, oats 307, rye, maize (corn) 6,900 (Veneto and Lombardia), rice 1,060 (Piemonte and Lombardia), potatoes 2,828, flax, hemp, cotton, sugar beet 10,000 (Po delta, Emilia-Romagna), sunflower seed 140, olives 4,212 (leading world producer, Puglia, Calabria), fruit 21,277 – oranges 1,945 (Sicilia), tangerines 400, lemons 770 (second world producer), almonds 175, figs 71, apples 1,990, pears 1,235 (leading world producer), peaches 1,700 (second world producer), apricots 157 (second world producer), grapes 12,255 (leading world producer, Veneto, Puglia, Piemonte, Sicilia), sweet chestnuts 70, walnuts 49 – vegetables 13,503, water-melons 780, tomatoes 4,550, strawberries 150, tobacco 141. **Livestock** (1983, in 1,000 head): cattle 9,127, horses 271, asses 123, mules, buffaloes 110, sheep 9,256, goats 1,031, pigs 9,132; poultry 110,000; wool 7,370 tonnes, raising of silkworms (20 tonnes of cocoons); fish catch 478,000 tonnes (1983); roundwood 8.7 mn. cub.m (1983).
Communications (1984): railways 19,793km, of which 10,175km are electrified (1983), roads 299,849km, motorways 5,901km, passenger cars 20,388,600 (1983). Navigable waterways 1,366km, of which 322km are canals. Merchant shipping 9,158,000 GRT (1984). Chief ports: Genova, Trieste, Augusta, Taranto, Venezia. Civil aviation (1984): 132.6 mn. km flown, 12,594,000 passengers carried. Important tourism, 22.1 mn. visitors (1983).
Exports: machines and equipment, cars, tractors, chemical products (plastics, pharmaceuticals, fertilizers), metals, products of precision mechanics (calculating machines and typewriters), metallurgical products, textiles, shoes, rubber products, wine, fresh fruit, vegetables.
Imports: raw materials and semi-finished products, fuels, machines and equipment, metals, cars, agricultural products (cereals), meat, wool, cotton, rubber, cattle, sugar, coffee etc.). Chief trading partners: Fed. Rep. of Germany, France, U.S.A., United Kingdom, Switzerland, Saudi Arabia, Libya, Belgium-Luxembourg.

LIECHTENSTEIN

Fürstentum Liechtenstein, area **160 sq.km**, population **28,000** (1988), **principality** (Head of State Prince Mike Adam since 1984).
Administrative units: 11 villages. **Capital:** Vaduz 4,896 inhab. (1984). – **Currency:** Swiss franc, customs union with Switzerland. – **Economy:** agriculture (cereals, potatoes), livestock raising. Textiles and other industries. Tourism. Chief sources of revenue are the numerous registered foreign firms and postage stamps.

LUXEMBOURG

Grand-Duché de Luxembourg – Grousherzogdem Lezebuurg, area **2,586 sq.km**, population **377,000** (1988), **grand duchy** (Grand Duke Jean since 1964).

Administrative units: 12 cantons. **Capital:** Luxembourg (Lezeburg) 78,924 inhab. (census 1981). **Density** 142 persons per sq.km; average annual rate of population increase –0.1% (1975–82); urban population 67% (1981). 41% of inhabitants employed in industry (1982). **The official language** is French, but the inhabitants speak mainly Luxemburgish (German dialect). – **Currency:** Luxembourg franc = 100 centimes.
Economy: advanced industrial country. Metallurgy is the principal industry. Financial centre of Western Europe. Electricity 437 mn. kWh (1983). **Production** (1983, in 1,000 tonnes): pig iron 2,316, crude steel 3,294. **Agriculture:** cultivation of cereals. **Crops** (1983, in 1,000 tonnes): wheat 19, barley 35, potatoes 17, fruit and vines 18; raising of cattle 224,645 head and pigs 71,957 head, poultry. – **Communications** (1984): railways 270km, roads 2,885km, passenger cars 145,800. –
Exports: steel, plastics, textiles and others. Chief trading partners: Fed. Rep. of Germany, Belgium, France. Customs union with Belgium.

MALTA

Republika Ta Malta, Republic of Malta, area **316 sq.km**, population **345,636** (1988), **republic, member of the Commonwealth** (President Vincent Tabone since 1989).

Administrative units: 6 regions. **Capital:** Valletta 14,096 inhab. (1983). **Population:** Maltese of Italian-Arabic descent. **Density** 1,212 persons per sq.km; average annual rate of population increase 1.8% (1975–81); urban population over 94%. – **Currency:** Maltese pound = 100 pence.
Economy: cultivation of wheat, potatoes, vines, tomatoes, fruit, citrus fruit; livestock (1983, in 1,000 head): cattle 15, sheep 5, goats 7, pigs 5; poultry 1 mn. Electricity 675 mn. kWh (1983). Manual production of lace on Gozo I. (Ghawdex). Naval base. – **Communications** (1984): roads 1,324km, passenger cars 80,300. Merchant shipping 1,366,000 GRT. Civil aviation: 5.1 mn. km flown, 364,000 passengers carried. Tourism 491,000 visitors (1983). – **Exports:** domestic manufactures. Chief trading partners: Fed. Rep. of Germany, United Kingdom, Italy.

MONACO

Principauté de Monaco, area **1.95 sq.km**, population **27,850** (1988), **principality** (Prince Rainier III since 1949).
The state consists of 3 joint urban districts: Monaco, Monte Carlo and La Condamine. **Capital:** Monaco 1,649 inhab. (1982). Tourist centre on the French Riviera. – **Currency:** French franc. Customs union with France. Chief sources of revenue are tourism and gambling.

NETHERLANDS

Kóninkrijk der Nederlanden, area 41,548 sq.km, population 14,757,948 (1988), kingdom (Queen Beatrix Wilhelmina Armgard since 1980).

Administrative units: 13 provinces; autonomous state Netherlands Antilles. **Capital:** Amsterdam 676,439 inhab. (1984, with agglomeration 994,062 inhab.); **other towns** (1984, in 1,000 inhab.): Rotterdam 555 (with agglom. 1,025), 's-Gravenhage 445 (the seat of the Royal Court and Government), Utrecht 230, Eindhoven 193, Groningen 168, Tilburg 154, Haarlem 153, Nijmegen 147, Enschede 145, Arnhem 128, Breda 119, Maastricht 113, Dordrecht 107. **Population:** Dutch, small number of Frisians in the North. **Density** 349 persons per sq.km is the highest in Europe (excluding miniature countries); average annual rate of population increase 0.7% (1975–82); urban population 76% (1981). 28% of inhabitants employed in industry, in agriculture 4.7% (1983). – **Currency:** guilden = 100 cents.
Economy: highly developed industrial and agricultural country. **Principal industries:** engineering (especially shipbuilding), electrotechnics, metallurgy, chemistry, textiles and food processing. **Mining** (1983, in 1,000 tonnes): crude petroleum 2,592 (Coevorden-Schoonebeek, Rijswijk), natural gas 2,690,966 TJ (Groningen surroundings – Slochteren, Delfzijl, North Sea shelf, Ameland I., Zuidwal), salt 3,084 (Hengelo, Delfzijl). Electricity 59.7 billion kWh (1983), of which 96% are thermal and 4% nuclear power stations (Borsele, Dodewaard). **Production** (1983, in 1,000 tonnes): pig iron 3,744, crude steel 4,488 (IJmuiden), coke oven coke 2,126, zinc 188 (Budel), aluminium 294 (Delfzijl), lead 9.6, vessels 190,000 GRT (shipyards Amsterdam, Rotterdam), passenger cars 105,600 units (Eindhoven, Born), electrotechnics ("Philips" in Eindhoven, vacuum tubes, radio receivers, telephones), nitrogenous fertilizers 1,659 (IJmuiden), phosphorus fertilizers 403, sulphuric acid 1,436, synthetic rubber 196, soda ash 417, plastics and resins 2,777; capacity of petroleum refineries 78.6 mn. tonnes (1984, near Rotterdam, Amsterdam), naphtha 8 mn. tonnes, motor spirit 9.2 mn. tonnes, fuel oils 30.5 mn. tonnes, cement 3,108, paper and paperboard 1,567, production of porcelain and ceramics (Delft, Maastricht), yarn – cotton 9.1, woollen 6.5 – woven fabrics – cotton 14.8 (reg. Twente), woollen 2.7 mn. sq.m (Tilburg) – synthetic fibres 33.6, sugar 815, meat 2,085, milk 13,200, condensed milk 537, cheese 488 (Edam, Gouda, Hoorn), butter 271, margarine 235, eggs 650, canned fish 19, chocolate and cocoa (Amsterdam, Bussum, Weesp, Zaandam), beer 17.3 mn. hl (1983), alcoholic spirits (curaçao – Amsterdam, gin); 46.3 billion cigarettes (1983), production of quinine (Amsterdam), diamond cutting and polishing (Amsterdam).
Agriculture is highly productive. There is a shortage of land which is partly overcome by the reclamation of polders from the sea. Cereal yields are among the highest in the world. Land use: arable land 22.3%, meadows and pastures 30.6%, forests 7.9%. **Crops** (1983, in 1,000 tonnes): wheat 1,043 (leading world yield per ha 7,037kg), barley 177, potatoes 5,457, flax, sugar beet 5,600, fruit 523, vegetables 2,835, tomatoes 463, important cultivation of flowers (hyacinths, tulips etc); **livestock** (1983, in 1,000 head): cattle 5,390, pigs 10,590, sheep 750, poultry 90,000; fish catch 503,300 tonnes (1983); roundwood 900,000 cub.m.
Communications (1984): railways 2,852km, of which 1,796km electrified, roads 53,848km, motorways 1,889km, passenger cars 4,772,000. Navigable waterways and canals 4,384km. Highly developed sea transport and trade. Chief ports: Rotterdam (the world's largest port, turnover of cargo 246 mn. tonnes, 1982), Amsterdam. Merchant shipping 4,586,000 GRT (1984). Civil aviation (1984): 118.4 mn. km flown, 5,655,000 passengers carried. Tourism 2,992,000 visitors (1983). **Exports:** foodstuffs (dairy products, eggs, meat), machines and transport equipment, petroleum products, chemicals, electrotechnical goods, manufactured products, flowers. **Imports:** raw materials (petroleum, metals, tropical fruit), machines and equipment, cars, and others. Chief trading partners: Fed. Rep. of Germany, Belgium and Luxembourg, France, United Kingdom, Italy.

NORWAY

Kongeriket Norge, area 323,878 sq.km, population 4,195,661 (1988), kingdom (King Olav V since 1957).

Administrative units: 19 counties (fylker), overseas territories in Europe: Svalbard, Bjørnøya and Jan Mayen; in the Antarctica: island Bouvetøya. **Capital:** Oslo 447,257 inhab. (1984); **other towns** (1984, in 1,000 inhab.): Bergen 207, Trondheim 134, Stavanger 93, Bærum 82, Kristiansand 62, Drammen 51, Tromsø 46. **Population:** Norwegians 97.5%, Lapps, Finns. **Density** 13 persons per sq.km; average annual rate of population increase 0.4% (1975–82); urban population 53% (1981). 28% of inhabitants employed in industry (1983). – **Currency:** Norwegian krone = 100 øre.
Economy: developed industrial and agricultural country. Large resources of hydro-electricity and timber. **Principal industries:** mining of minerals, shipbuilding, electrometallurgy, radioelectronics, wood and paper processing, fishery. **Mining** (1983, in 1,000 tonnes, metal content): coal 480 (Svalbard), crude petroleum 30.6 mn. tonnes (North Sea shelf – Ekofisk, Statfjord), natural gas 1,031,867 TJ (Frigg, Cod, Heimdal, Odin, Troll, Statfjord), iron ore 2,307 (Fossdalen, Rana), copper 22.6, lead 4,100 tonnes, zinc 32.3, titanium, pyrites 357 (Løkken, Sulitjelma). Electricity 106.2 billion kWh (1983), almost 100% from hydro-electric power stations. **Production** (1983, in 1,000 tonnes): pig iron 1,624, crude steel 903 (Stavanger, Arendal, Rana), copper – smelted 26, refined 28.6, zinc 90.7, nickel 28, aluminium – primary 713 (Kristiansand, Tyssedal, Odda, Sunndalsøra, Årdal, Eydehamn) – magnesium 29.8, vessels 97,000 GRT (shipyards in Oslo, Bergen, Frederikstad), sulphuric acid 440 (chemical industry – Rjukan, Notodden, Odda), capacity of petroleum refineries 12.8 mn. tonnes (1984), petroleum products 7.1 mn. tonnes, cement 1,666, chemical wood pulp 645, paper and paper products 1,390, rayon and acetate staple fibre 20 (textile industry in Bergen, Oslo, Sandnes), meat 204, milk 2,017, butter 26, cheese 66, eggs 51.
Agriculture: intensive animal production predominates. Land use: arable land 2.6%, meadows and pastures 0.3%, forests 25.7%. **Crops** (1983, in 1,000 tonnes): cereals 1,081 (barley 569, oats), potatoes 470; **livestock** (1983, in 1,000 head): cattle 975, sheep 2,272, pigs 705; raising of fur animals (foxes and minks), reindeer in the North (174,300 head in 1980); fish catch 2,822,300 tonnes (1983); whaling; roundwood 9.6 mn. cub.m (1983).
Communications (1984): railways 4,242km, of which 2,443km electrified, roads 71,842km, passenger cars 1,428,700.

HUNGARY:
19 counties and capital district

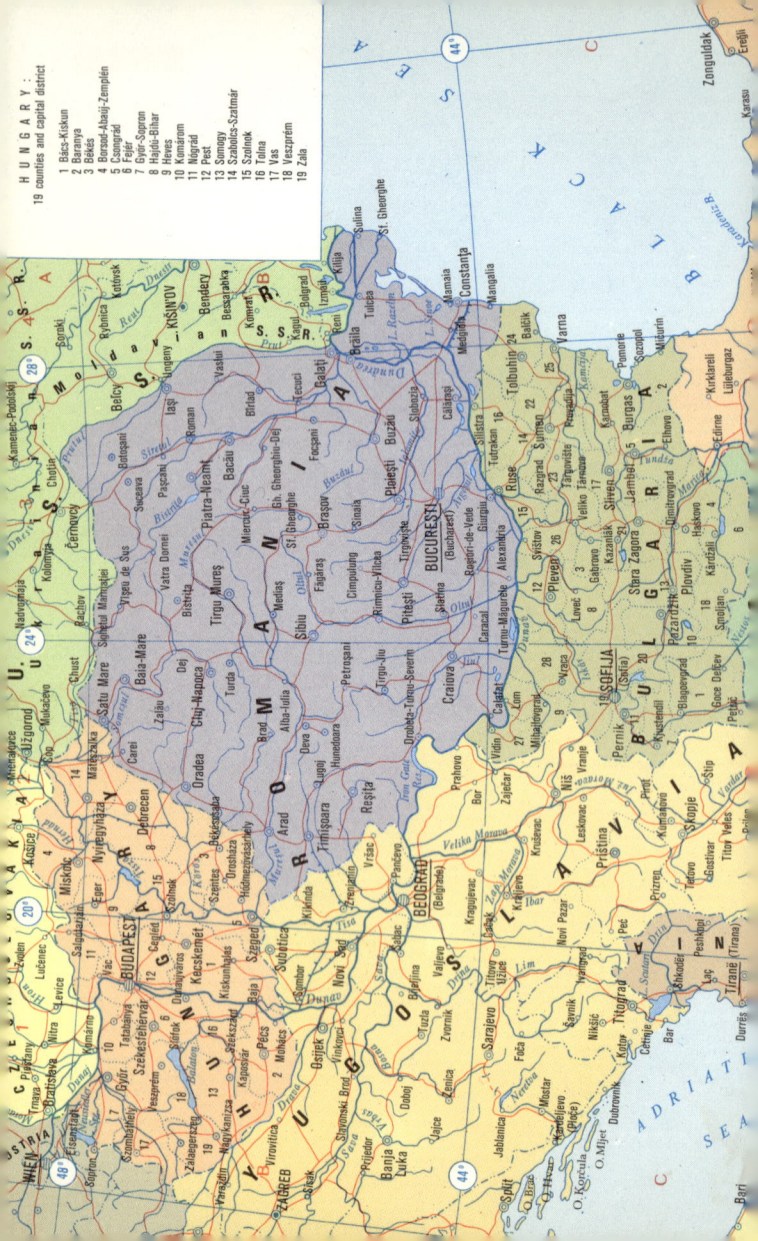

1 Bács-Kiskun
2 Baranya
3 Békés
4 Borsod-Abaúj-Zemplén
5 Csongrád
6 Fejér
7 Győr-Sopron
8 Hajdú-Bihar
9 Heves
10 Komárom
11 Nógrád
12 Pest
13 Somogy
14 Szabolcs-Szatmár
15 Szolnok
16 Tolna
17 Vas
18 Veszprém
19 Zala

BULGARIA : 28 districts

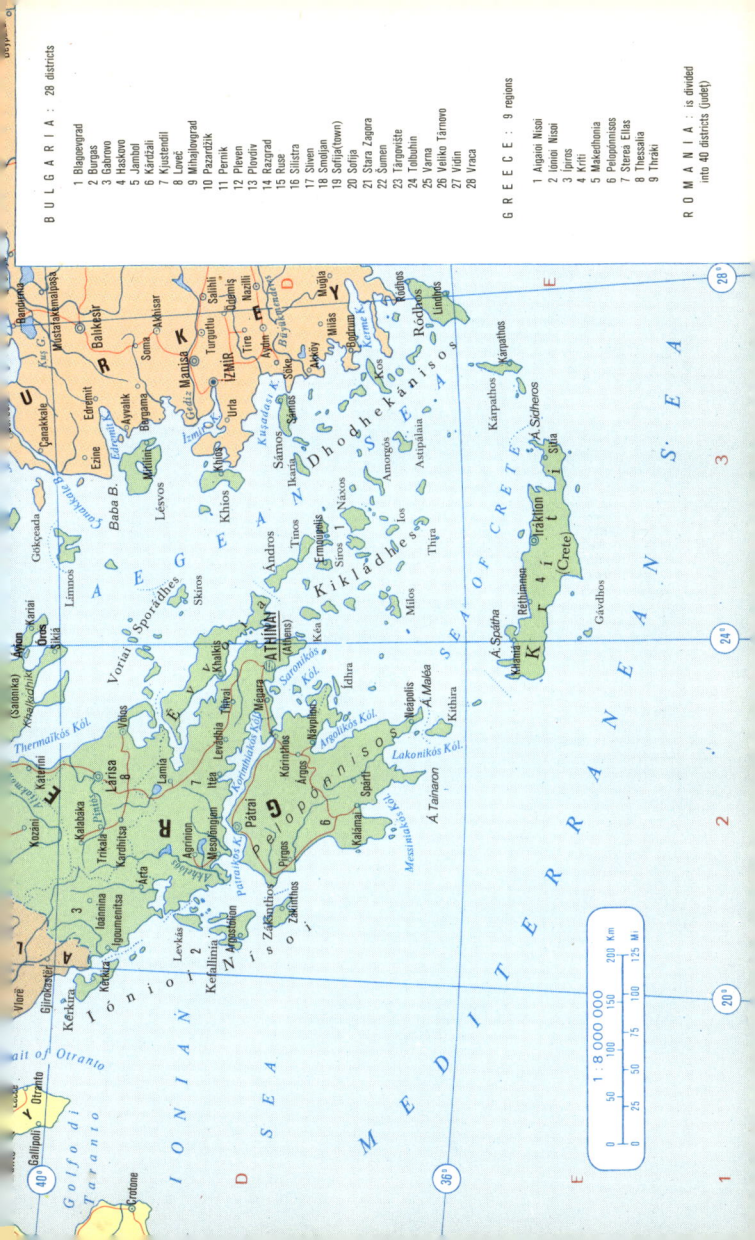

1 Blagoevgrad
2 Burgas
3 Gabrovo
4 Haskovo
5 Jambol
6 Kărdžali
7 Kjustendil
8 Loveč
9 Mihajlovgrad
10 Pazardžik
11 Pernik
12 Pleven
13 Plovdiv
14 Razgrad
15 Ruse
16 Silistra
17 Sliven
18 Smoljan
19 Sofija (town)
20 Sofija
21 Stara Zagora
22 Šumen
23 Tărgovište
24 Tolbuhin
25 Varna
26 Veliko Tărnovo
27 Vidin
28 Vraca

GREECE : 9 regions

1 Aigaion Nisoi
2 Iónioi Nísoi
3 Ípyros
4 Kríti
5 Makethonía
6 Pelopónnisos
7 Steréa Ellás
8 Thessalía
9 Thráki

ROMANIA : is divided into 40 districts (judeţ)

Merchant shipping 17,663,000 GRT (1984). Chief ports: Narvik, Oslo, Bergen. Civil aviation (1984): 59 mn. km flown, 6,114,000 passengers carried. Tourism 1.3 mn. visitors (1983). – **Exports:** petroleum and products, machines and equipment, vessels, non-ferrous metals, fish and fish products, iron, paper. **Imports:** fuels, ores, machines, cars and others. Chief trading partners: United Kingdom, Fed. Rep. of Germany, Sweden, Netherlands, U.S.A., Denmark.

POLAND

Rzeczpospolita Polska, area 312,683 sq.km, population 37,862,063 (1988), republic (President Gen. Wojciech Jaruzelski since 1989).

Administrative units: 49 provinces (województwa). **Capital:** Warszawa (Warsaw) 1,649,000 inhab. (1985); **other towns** (1983, in 1,000 inhab.): Łódź 848, Kraków 735, Wrocław 631, Poznań 571, Gdańsk 465, Szczecin 389, Katowice 361, Bydgoszcz 358, Lublin 320, Sosnowiec 252, Bytom 238, Częstochowa 244, Gdynia 240, Białystok 240, Gliwice 211, Radom 201. **Population:** Poles 98.5%, Ukrainians, Byelorussians, Germans. Density 119 persons per sq.km; average annual rate of population increase 0.9% (1975–82); urban population 59.8% (1983). 28% of inhabitants employed in agriculture, 25% in industry (1983). – **Currency:** złoty = 100 groszy.
Economy: advanced industrial and agricultural country with important mining industry. Industry is concentrated chiefly in the south-west part of the country and the Kraków region. **Principal industries:** mineral mining, engineering (Poznań, Wrocław, Katowice, Kraków, Kielce), chemical (Upper Silesian region, Łódź, Poznań), textile (cotton processing – Łódź, wool processing – the South), food processing. Metallurgy plays an important role. **Mining** (1983, in 1,000 tonnes, metal content): coal 191,092 (Upper and Lower Silesian Basins in the vicinity of Katowice, Bytom, Zabrže, Lublin Basin), brown coal 42,532 (Turoszów Basin – Bogatynia, Konin, Bełchatów), crude petroleum 252 (Krosno), natural gas 166,151 TJ (Lubaczów, Przemyśl), iron ore, copper 393 (Bolesławiec, Polkowice, Lubin), lead 47 and zinc 189 (Olkusz, Bytom, Chrzanów), nickel 2.1, silver 678 tonnes, cadmium, magnesite 16, salt 4,326 (Wapno, Inowrocław, Kłodawa), sulphur 4,999 (leading world producer, Tarnobrzeg/Machów, Jeziórko, Grzybów), kaolin. Electricity 125.8 billion kWh (1983), of which 93% are thermal power stations. **Production** (1983, in 1,000 tonnes): pig iron 9,372 and crude steel 16,236 (Silesia, Kraków-Nowa Huta, Częstochowa, Katowice, Warszawa), zinc 170 and lead 81 (Silesia), copper – smelted 320, – refined 348 (Katowice), aluminium 44 (Skawina, Konin), locomotives, railway carriages, agricultural machines, tractors 55,500 units, passenger cars 270,200 units (Warszawa), vessels 320,000 GRT (Gdańsk, Szczecin, Gdynia), radio 2.1 mn. and television receivers 566,500 units, suphuric acid 2,786, nitric acid 2,065, soda ash 808, nitrogenous fertilizers 1,342, phosphorus fertilizers 872, plastics and resins 525, synthetic rubber 120 (Oświęcim), coke oven coke 17,580; capacity of petroleum refineries 19.5 mn. tonnes (1984, Płock, Gdańsk), pipeline for the import of Soviet petroleum, motor spirit 2.4 mn. tonnes, fuel oils 7.5 mn. tonnes, pharmaceuticals (Warszawa), cement 16,200, chemical wood pulp 664, paper 1,026, yarn – cotton 177, woollen 81 – woven fabrics – cotton 744 mn. m, woollen 148 mn. m, linen 80 mn. m, silk 1 mn. m – rayon and acetate – fibres 19.5, staple fibre 51.9, woven fabrics 58.3 mn. m – synthetic – fibres 80.3, staple fibre 49.1; meat 2,281, milk 16,496, butter 280, cheese 401, eggs 423, sugar 2,141, beer 10.3 mn. hl; 82.8 billion cigarettes (1983).
Agriculture: private holdings predominate, vegetable production concentrates on cereals and potatoes. Land use: arable land 46.5%, meadows and pastures 13.0%, forests 27.8%. Tractors 757,000 (1983). **Crops** (1983, in 1,000 tonnes): rye 8,781 (second world producer), wheat 5,165, barley 3,262, oats 2,377, maize (corn), potatoes 34,473 (third world producer), flax 20 (second world producer), hemp 10, sugar beet 16,358, rapeseed 555, hops, fruit 2,572, tomatoes 513, strawberries 191, vegetables 4,373, tobacco 35; **livestock** (1983, in 1,000 head): cattle 11,269, pigs 15,587, sheep 4,103, horses 1,600, poultry 61,000; wool 6,900 tonnes, honey 20,873 tonnes; fish catch 735,100 tonnes (1983); roundwood 24.7 mn. cub.m (1983).
Communications (1984): railways 24,353km, of which 8,307km electrified, roads 253,976km, passenger cars 3,425,800. Navigable waterways 2,977km, important river port Koźle on the Odra. Merchant shipping 3,267,000 GRT (1984). Chief ports: Szczecin, Gdańsk, Gdynia. Civil aviation (1984): 23 mn. km flown, 1,596,000 passengers carried. Tourism 1.9 mn. visitors (1983).
Exports: coal, coke oven coke, iron and steel, copper, sulphur, cars, vessels, engineering, chemicals, textiles and food products. **Imports:** petroleum, natural gas, raw materials (iron ore, cotton), foodstuffs, machines and transport equipment, industrial consumer goods. Chief trading partners: socialist countries 50% of turnover (chiefly U.S.S.R., German Dem. Rep., Czechoslovakia), Fed. Rep. of Germany, United Kingdom, France.

PORTUGAL

República Portuguesa, area 91,985 sq.km, population 10,408,000 (1988), republic (President Dr Mário Alberto Nobre Lopes Soares since 1986).

Administrative units: 22 districts (distrito), of which 3 on Azores and 1 on Madeira (both autonomous territories). **Capital:** Lisboa (Lisbon) 807,200 inhab. (1981); **other towns** (1981, in 1,000 inhab.): Porto 327, Amadora 96, Setúbal 78, Coimbra 75, Vila Nova de Gaia 63, Braga 63, Barreiro 51, Funchal 44. **Population:** Portuguese. Density 111 persons per sq.km; average annual rate of population increase 0.9% (1975–82) urban population 29.7% (1981), 24% of inhabitants employed in agriculture, 36.8% in industry (1983). – **Currency:** escudo = 100 centavos.
Economy: agricultural and industrial country, having good raw material resources. **Mining** (1983, in 1,000 tonnes metal content): tungsten 1.4 (Panasqueira), tin 347 tonnes, uranium 10 tonnes, gold 211 kg, silver, iron ore, manganese, pyrites 262, sulphur, copper, salt 508, marble 370, tantalum and niobium. Electricity 18.2 billion kWh (1983). **Production** (1983, in 1,000 tonnes): pig iron 432, crude steel 384, vessels 36,000 GRT, cement 5,988, chemical wood pulp 950, woven cotton fabrics 70.4, traditional textile industry – embroidery, lace – canned fish 43.3, wine 795 (Porto), beer 4 mn. hl; 15.6 billion cigarettes; further data for 1983: meat 481, milk 800, butter 3.7, cheese 33, eggs 70.

Agriculture: arable land 38.6%, meadows and pastures 5.8%, forests 39.5%. **Crops** (1983, in 1,000 tonnes): cereals 1,087 (chiefly wheat and maize), rice 100, potatoes 954, sugar beet, olives 110, fruit 1,615 – grapes 1,150, oranges 80, lemons 20, bananas – vegetables 1,551, tomatoes 500, sweet chestnuts 19; **livestock** (1983, in 1,000 head): cattle 990, sheep 5,220, goats 750, pigs 3,480, asses 180, mules; poultry 18,000; fish catch 246,500 tonnes (1983); roundwood 8.3 mn. cub.m, cork 125,100 tonnes (1982, leading world producer).
Communications: railways 3,614 km (1983), of which 458 km are electrified, roads 18,849 km (1984), passenger cars 1,517,600 (1983). Navigable waterways 124 km (1984). Merchant shipping 1,571,000 GRT (1984). Chief port: Lisboa. Civil aviation (1984): 37.3 mn. km flown, 2,330,000 passengers carried. Tourism 3,714,000 visitors (1983).
Exports: woven cotton fabrics and textile products, wine, canned fish and tomatoes, cork. **Imports:** industrial products, transport equipment, metals, petroleum, chemicals and foodstuffs. Chief trading partners: United Kingdom, Fed. Rep. of Germany, France, U.S.A., Netherlands, Italy.

Azores
Area 2,247 sq.km, **population** 243,400 (1981), mountainous volcanic islands in the Atlantic Ocean (the largest São Miguel 747 sq.km). **Capital:** Ponta Delgada 54,600 inhab. **Economy:** cultivation of maize, wheat, bananas and vines; raising of cattle and pigs, fish catch and whaling. Roads 1,657 km (1980), sea and air transport.

ROMANIA

România, area 237,500 sq.km, population 23,048,000 (1988), **republic** (President Ion Iliescu since 1990).

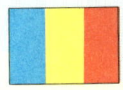

Administrative units: 40 districts including capital district București. **Capital:** București (Bucharest) 1,961,189 inhab. (1984): **other towns** (1983, in 1,000 inhab.): Brașov 331, Constanța 316, Iași 306, Timișoara 303, Cluj-Napoca 301, Galați 285, Craiova 260, Ploiești 230, Brăila 225, Oradea 206, Arad 184, Sibiu 172, Bacău 166, Tîrgu Mureș 155, Pitești 150, Baia Mare 130, Buzău 127, Satu Mare 125, Piatra Neamț 103, Reșița 102, Drobeta-Turnu Severin 92, Hunedoara 87.
Population: Romanians 88%, Hungarians 7.9%, Germans 1.6%, Gipsies 1.1%. **Density** 96 persons per sq.km, average annual rate of population increase 0.8% (1971–83); urban population 49.6% (1980). 44.6% of inhabitants employed in agriculture, 28% in industry (1983). **Currency:** leu = 100 bani.
Economy: industrial and agricultural country. **Principal industries:** engineering, mining, metallurgy, chemical, textiles and food processing. Industry is concentrated in the south of the country. 50% of Romanian industry is located at București and in the petroleum extraction region near Ploiești. **Mining** (1983, in 1,000 tonnes, metal content): crude petroleum 11,600 (Ploiești, Pitești, Ticleni, Moinești), oil pipelines to București and ports, natural gas 1.6 mn. TJ (Transylvanian Depression, Bacău Region), brown coal 35,998 (Rovinari), coal 7,793 (Petroșani, Reșița), iron ore 510 (Munții Poiana Ruscăi, Ocna de Fier), manganese 78, lead 28.5, bauxite 420 (Roșia), gold (Munții Apuseni), silver 28 tonnes, salt 4,596, pyrites 930, graphite 12.5. Electricity 70.3 billion kWh (1983), of which 14% are hydro-electric power stations. **Production** (1983, in 1,000 tonnes): pig iron 8,190, crude steel 12,593 (Galați, Hunedoara, Reșița, Roman), coke oven coke 4,268, aluminium 244 (Oradea, Slatina), lead 49 (Baia-Mare), zinc 42, tractors 82,700 units (Brașov), motor vehicles – commercial 40,800 (1980, Brașov), passenger 90,000 units (Pitești) – locomotives and carriages (Craiova), agricultural machines, petroleum mining and processing equipment (Ploiești, București), vessels 263,000 GRT (Galați, Constanța), radio 542,000 and television receivers 390,000 units, sulphuric acid 1,941, nitrogenous – 2,091 and phosphorus fertilizers 733, șoda ash 788, synthetic rubber 147, plastics and resins 633; capacity of petroleum refineries 30.9 mn. tonnes (1980), motor spirit 5,102, oils 14,400, cement 13,027, chemical wood pulp 565. Textile industry (București, Arad, Timișoara, Brașov and others – 1983, in 1,000 tonnes): yarn – cotton 171, woollen 79 – woven fabrics – cotton 709 mn. sq.m, woollen 144 mn. sq.m, silk 1 mn. sq.m – rayon and acetate staple fibre 64, synthetic fibres 171, shoes 114 mn. pairs; food industry (1983, in 1,000 tonnes): meat 1,612, milk 3,134, butter 47, cheese 125, eggs 347, sugar 556, canned fruit and vegetables 447, vegetable oil 371, wine 1,000, beer 9.9 mn. hl (1983); 36 billion cigarettes (1983).
Agriculture: vegetable production is predominant. Land use: arable land 41.6%, meadows and pastures 18.7%, forests 26.7%. **Crops** (1983, in 1,000 tonnes): wheat 5,250, barley 2,192, maize (corn) 11,982, rice 50, potatoes 6,100, linseed 41, hemp 20, sugar beet 4,819, sunflower seed 705, soya beans 280, castor beans 5, fruit 3,677 (apples 755, peaches 85, plums 665, grapes 1,710), vegetables 5,130 (tomatoes 2,000, onions 356, chillies 279), walnuts 40, tobacco 37; **livestock** (1983, in 1,000 head): cattle 6,010, horses 600, buffaloes 220, sheep 16,921, goats 513, pigs 12,000; poultry 111,000; wool 23,000 tonnes, raising of silkworms (120 tonnes of cocoons), honey 15,000 tonnes; fish catch 242,500 tonnes (1983); roundwood 23 mn. cub.m (1983).
Communications (1984): railways 11,106 km, of which 2,868 km are electrified; roads 73,369 km. Navigable waterways – primarily the Danube – 1,659 km. Merchant shipping 2,667,000 GRT (1984). Chief port Constanța. Civil aviation (1984): 19.5 mn. km flown, 1,163,000 passengers carried. Tourism 5.8 mn. visitors (1983).
Exports: machines, chemical products, minerals and metals, foodstuffs. **Imports:** machines and industrial equipment, raw materials, electrotechnical and chemical products, consumer goods. Chief trading partners: U.S.S.R., Fed. Rep. of Germany, German Dem. Rep., Poland, Iran, Italy, China, U.S.A., Czechoslovakia.

SAN MARINO

Repubblica di San Marino, area 60.6 sq.km, population 22,746 (1988), **republic** (headed by two Captains-Regents, appointed every 6 months).

Capital: San Marino 4,516 inhab. (1983); Italian **currency**, customs union with Italy. **The official language** is Italian. **Economy:** agriculture (wheat, maize, vines, fruit); tourism (3 mn. visitors yearly) and postage stamps are the chief sources of revenue.

15a Iceland 1 : 10 000 000

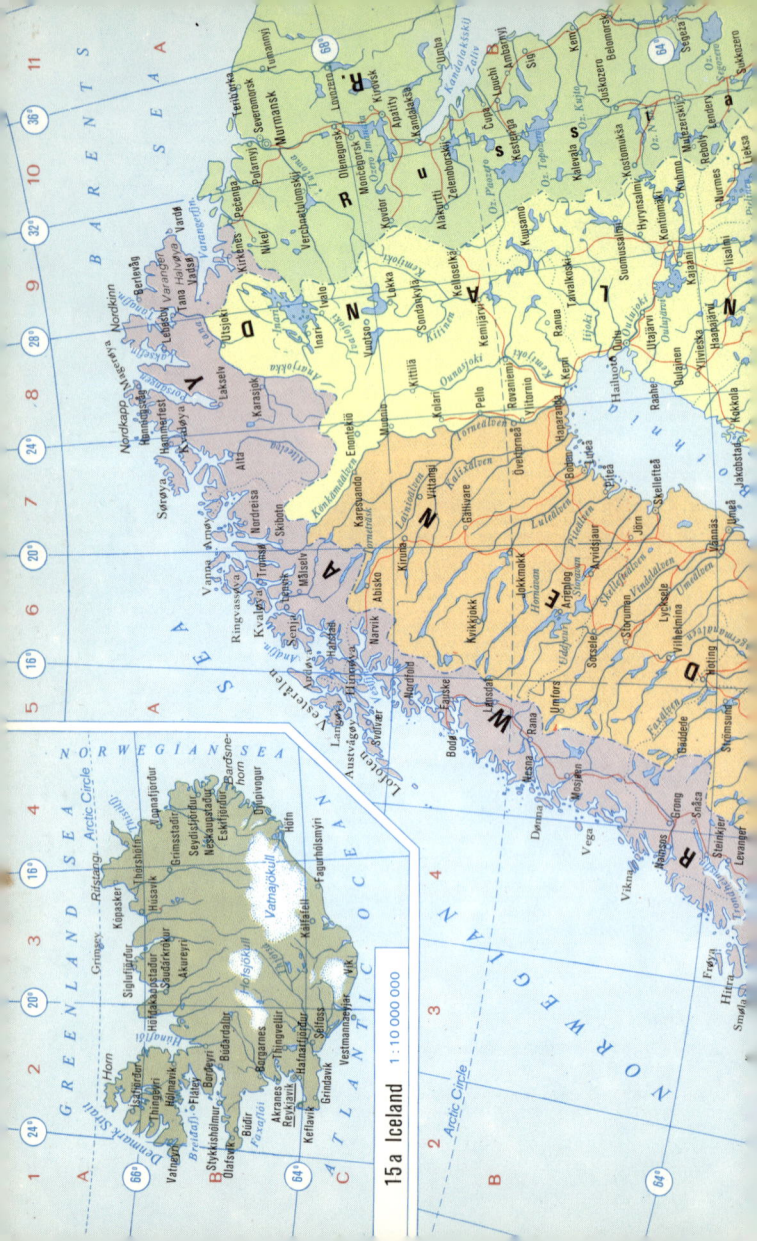

N O R W A Y
S W E D E N
F I N L A N D
D E N M A R K
P O L A N D
U. S. S. R.
R. S. F. S. R.
Estonian S.S.R.
Latvian S.S.R.
Lithuanian S.S.R.
Byelorussian S.S.R.
FEDERAL REP. OF GERMANY
NETHERLANDS
NORTH SEA
BALTIC SEA
Gulf of Finland
Gulf of Bothnia
Skagerrak
Kattegat
Rižskij Zaliv
Ladožskoje Ozero
Gotland
Öland
Bornholm
Hiiumaa
Saaremaa
Ahvenanmaa (Åland)
OSLO
STOCKHOLM
HELSINKI
LENINGRAD
Tallinn
RIGA
VILNIUS
MINSK
København (Copenhagen)
Göteborg
Bergen
Stavanger
Kristiansand
Malmö
Helsingborg
Uppsala
Västerås
Örebro
Norrköping
Linköping
Jönköping
Turku
Tampere
Vantaa
Espoo
Tartu
Pskov
Novgorod
Daugavpils
Kaunas
Klaipėda
Liepāja
Kaliningrad
Gdańsk
Gdynia
Szczecin
Rostock
Kiel
Århus
Ålborg
Odense
1 : 10 000 000
0 50 100 150 200 250 Km
0 50 100 150 Mi
60°
56°
12°
16°
20°
24°
28°

SPAIN

Estado Español, area 504,783 sq.km, population 39,085,000 (1988), including Balearic and Canary Is., **kingdom** (King Juan Carlos I since 1975).

Administrative units: 17 regions (50 provinces – continental Spain, Balearic Is., Canary Is., North African settlements – towns Ceuta and Melilla, islands Islas Chafarinas, Peñón de Vélez de la Gomera, Peñón de Alhucemas). **Capital:** Madrid 3,272,000 inhab. (1982); **other towns** (census 1981, in 1,000 inhab.): Barcelona 1,755, Valencia 752, Sevilla 654, Zaragoza 591, Málaga 503, Bilbao 433, Las Palmas de G. Can. 366, Valladolid 330, Palma de Mallorca 304, Hospitalet 294, Murcia 289, Córdoba 285, Granada 262, Vigo 259, Gijon 256, Alicante 251, La Coruña 232, Badalona 228, Santa Cruz de Tenerife 191, Oviedo 190, Sabadell 185, Pamplona 183, Santander 180, Jerez de la Frontera 176, San Sebastian 176, Cartagena 173, Salamanca 167, Elche 165, Cádiz 158, Tarrasa 156, Burgos 153, Almería 141, Huelva 128, León 127.

Population: Spaniards 75%, Catalans, Basques, Galicians. **Density** 77 persons per sq.km; average annual rate of population increase 0.9% (1975–82); urban population 75% (1981). 15.1% of inhabitants employed in agriculture, 18% in industry (1980). – **Currency:** peseta = 100 centimos.

Economy: industrial and agricultural country with considerable raw material resources. Heavy foreign investments have encouraged the rapid development of industry in the last few years. Developed industries: mineral mining, metallurgy, engineering, production of motor vehicles, electrotechnics, the chemical and textile industries. **Mining** (1983, in 1,000 tonnes, metal content): coal 15,800 (Asturia, Castilla-León), brown coal 23,850 (Teruel), crude petroleum 2,977 (Ayoluengo), iron ore 3,652 (prov. Vizcaya, Asturia, Oviedo), copper 54.8 (Minas de Ríotinto, Cangas de Onís), lead 82 (Sierra Morena), zinc 175.8 (Reocín), tungsten 352 tonnes, mercury 1,619 tonnes (second world producer, Almadén, Mieres), tin 444 tonnes, antimony 489 tonnes, titanium, gold 5,434 kg, silver 177 tonnes, magnesite 597, bauxite 51, uranium 150 tonnes (Ciudad Rodrigo), tantalum and niobium 59 tonnes – 1982), salt 3,158, potassium salt 773 (Suria), pyrites 2,306 (prov. Huelva), kaolin 698. Electricity 115.4 billion kWh (1983), of which 28% are hydro-electric and 21.5% nuclear power stations (Zorita, Santa Maria de Garoña, Vandellós).

Production: Metallurgy (1983, in 1,000 tonnes): pig iron 5,681, crude steel 13,262 (San Vicente de Baracaldo, Avilés, Mieres, Santander, Sagunto), coke oven coke 4,150, aluminium 395 (Valladolid), copper – smelted 118, refined 159 (Minas de Ríotinto, Córdoba), lead 130 (Cartagena), zinc 190 (Avilés), tin 3,762 tonnes (Villagarcía de Arosa). **Engineering** predominantly in large cities: locomotives (Barcelona), passenger cars 1,136,000 units (1983, Madrid, Barcelona, Zaragoza), aircraft (Madrid and vicinity, Sevilla), tractors 17,484 (1983), vessels 669,900 GRT (1983, El Ferrol del Caudillo, Cartagena), weapons (Reinosa, Toledo), television receivers 818,000 (1981). **Chemical industry** (Cataluña, Barcelona and vicinity, Asturia, Madrid, Valladolid, Zaragoza – 1983, in 1,000 tonnes): acid -sulphuric 2,995, -nitric 1,055, -hydrochloric 135, caustic soda 458, soda ash 500, fertilizers -nitrogenous 858, -phosphorus 410, potash 656; synthetic rubber 51, plastics and resins 1,175; capacity of petroleum refineries 76 mn. tonnes (1984, Tarragona, Bilbao, Cartagena, Puertollano), motor spirit 5.7 mn. tonnes, fuel oils 30 mn. tonnes; cement 31 mn. tonnes, chemical wood pulp 1,093, paper 2,639. **Textile industry** (chiefly Barcelona and vicinity, 1983, in 1,000 tonnes): yarn (1981) – cotton 102, woollen 31.8 – woven fabrics (1981) – cotton 101, woollen 15.5 – artificial fibres 10.5, synthetic fibres 66. **Food industry** (1983, in 1,000 tonnes): sugar 1,318, meat 2,785, milk 6,250, cheese 141, butter 13, eggs 719, olive oil 268 (second world producer), wine 3,157 (Jerez, Málaga, Sherry), beer 19.3 mn. hl (1981), canned fish 92.3; 44 billion cigarettes, 1 billion cigars (1983). Glass industry (Bilbao, Santander), ceramics.

Agriculture is extensive, not very productive. Vegetable production predominates; large output of cereals, fruit and viniculture are of importance. Irrigation in dry areas. Land use: arable land 30.8%, meadows and pastures 21.2%, forests 30.8%. **Crops** (1983, in 1,000 tonnes): wheat 4,330 (Castilla, Andalucia), barley 6,571, maize (corn) 1,788 (Galicia), rye 247, rice 223, oats 470, rice 223, potatoes 5,098, sweet potatoes, cotton – seed 63, -lint 35; sugar beet 9,132 (provinces Valladolid, Burgos, León), sugarcane 302, pulses 314, sunflower seed 674, olives 1,297 (second world producer), soya beans, hops, fruit 11,998; oranges 1,895 (Valencia), tangerines 1,113 (second world producer), lemons 522, almonds 160, dates 12, figs, bananas 461 (Canary Is.), grapes 5,046 (Mediterranean coast, Castilla-La Mancha and Andalucía), peaches, apricots 161, sweet chestnuts 19; vegetables 8,566: tomatoes 2,258, watermelons 554, melons 668, onions 957, garlic 203; tobacco 42, alfalfa 20. **Animal production** is extensive (1983, in 1,000 head): cattle 5,070, horses 250, asses 177, mules 169, sheep 17,000, goats 2,500, pigs 11,700, poultry 54,000; wool (merinos) 11,360 tonnes, honey 9,500 tonnes, raising of silkworms; fish catch 1,250,000 tonnes (1983), roundwood 14.8 mn. cub.m (1983), cork 110,715 tonnes (1980).

Communications (1984): railways 15,083 km, of which 6,394 km are electrified, roads 149,553 km, motorways 2,018 km, passenger cars 8,874,400. Navigable waterways – only the Guadalquivir 103 km. Merchant shipping 7,005,000 GRT (1984). Chief ports: Barcelona, Bilbao, Cartagena, Valencia. Civil aviation (1984): 156.5 mn. km flown, 14,284,000 passengers carried. Tourism 25.6 mn. visitors (1983).

Exports: transport equipment, petroleum products, metals, food products (citrus fruit, wine, olive oil, canned fish), engineering products, chemicals, textiles, shoes and hides. **Imports:** petroleum, chemical products, machines and equipment, iron and steel, foodstuffs (cereals, sugar and others). Chief trading partners: France, Fed. Rep. of Germany, United Kingdom, U.S.A., Italy, Netherlands, Saudi Arabia.

SVALBARD

Area 62,422 sq.km, **population** 3,942 (1987), **autonomous territory of Norway**, including the islands of Jan Mayen and Bjørnéya. **Capital:** Longyearbyen.

Economy: mining of coal 480,000 tonnes (1983), exported to Norway and the U.S.S.R.; petroleum prospecting is in progress. Fishing station. **Jan Mayen**, area 372 sq.km, inhabited by radio and meteorological staff.

map 16

SWEDEN

Konungariket Sverige, area 449,964 sq.km, population 8,436,486 (1988), **kingdom** (King Carl XVI Gustaf since 1973).

Administrative units: 24 provinces (län). **Capital:** Stockholm 647,121 inhab. (1982, with agglomeration 1,383,481); **other towns** (1982, in 1,000 inhab.): Göteborg 428, Malmö 232, Uppsala 148, Norrköping 119, Västerås 118, Örebro 117, Linköping 113, Jönköping 107, Borås 102, Helsingborg 102, Sundsvall 95, Eskilstuna 90, Gävle 87, Umeå 82, Lund 79, Karlstad 72, Skellefteå 74, Kristianstad 69. **Population:** Swedes 95%, in the North Finns, nomadic Lapps. **Density** 19 persons per sq.km; average annual rate of population increase 0.2% (1975–82); urban population 88% (1981). 30% of inhabitants employed in industry (1983). – **Currency:** Swedish krona = 100 öre.
Economy: highly developed industrial country with intensive, mechanized agriculture. Sweden is one of the economically most advanced countries in the world. Basic natural resources: forests, iron ore, hydro-electric energy. **Chief industries:** engineering (electrotechnics, shipbuilding), wood processing and paper industry, mineral mining, energy production. Metallurgy, the chemical industry and food processing are also highly developed. **Mining** (1983, in 1,000 tonnes, metal content): iron ore 8,442 (Kiruna, Gällivare), copper 64 (Boliden, Aitik), lead 78 (Laisvall), zinc 203 (Ämmeberg), tungsten 301 tonnes, silver 171 tonnes, gold 3,199 kg (Boliden), uranium, pyrites 430. Electricity 109.6 billion kWh (1983), of which 59% hydro-electric and 37% nuclear power stations (Ringhals, Oskarshamn).
Production (1983, in 1,000 tonnes): pig iron 2,016, crude steel 4,212 (Borlänge, Luleå, Oxelösund, Sandviken), aluminium, primary 81.6 (Kubikenborg), copper – smelted 101.8, refined 63 (Rönnskär, Helsingborg), lead 30 (Landskrona), electrotechnics (Västerås), motor vehicles – passenger 280,800 units ("Volvo"), commercial 45,600 (Göteborg, Trollhättan, Södertälje) – weapons (Bofors), aircraft (Malmö, Linköping), vessels 292,000 GRT (Göteborg, Malmö, Landskrona), sulphuric acid 884, nitric acid 407, plastics and resins 520, explosives; capacity of petroleum refineries 20.6 mn. tonnes (1984), motor spirit 2,500, fuel oils 10,250, cement 2,232, sawnwood 11.5 mn. cub.m, chemical wood pulp 6,444 (Husum, Örnsköldsvik, Karlsborg), paper and paper products 5,000, matches (Jönköping), leather industry (Örebro, Kumla), ornamental glass (prov. Kronoberg), woven cotton fabrics 8.4 (Borås), rayon and acetate staple fibre 39.3, meat 556, milk 3,766, butter 73, eggs 115, cheese 119; 10.4 billion cigarettes (1983).
Agriculture: predominantly animal production. Land use: arable 6.6%, meadows and pastures 1.8%, forests 58.7%. **Crops** (1983, in 1,000 tonnes): wheat 1,721, barley 2,026, oats 1,268, rye, potatoes 958, sugar beet 1,922, rapeseed 365; **livestock** (1983, in 1,000 head): cattle 1,932, sheep 435, pigs 2,620; poultry 13,000; fish catch 265,500 tonnes (1983); roundwood 53.3 mn. cub.m (1983).
Communications (1984): railways 12,101 km, of which 7,595 km are electrified, roads 98,418 km, motorways 1,352 km, passenger cars 3,081,000 (1983). Navigable waterways 1,165 km. Merchant shipping 3,520,000 GRT (1984). Chief ports: Göteborg, Luleå, Stockholm, Helsingborg. Civil aviation (1984): 78.8 mn. km flown, 7,335,000 passengers carried. Tourism 3.4 mn. visitors (1983).
Exports: engineering and metal products, cars, paper, chemical wood pulp, wood and wood products, iron and steel. **Imports:** petroleum, fuels, machines and transport equipment, metals, foodstuffs, chemicals. Chief trading partners: Fed. Rep. of Germany, United Kingdom, Norway, Denmark, U.S.A., Finland.

SWITZERLAND

Schweizerische Eidgenossenschaft – Confédération Suisse – Confederazione Svizzera – Confederaziun Svizra, area 41,293 sq.km, population 6,566,900 (1988), **federal republic** (President Arnold Koller since 1990).

Administrative units: 26 cantons. **Capital:** Bern 143,070 inhab. (1983); **other towns** (1983, in 1,000 inhab.): Zürich 363, Basel 180, Genève (Geneva) 158, Lausanne 127, Winterthur 86, St. Gallen 74, Luzern 62. **Official languages:** German (65% of inhabitants), French (18%), Italian (10%), Romansch (1%). **Density** 156 persons per sq.km; average annual rate of population increase –0.1% (1975–80); urban population 59% (1981). 38% of inhabitants employed in industry. – **Currency:** franc = 100 rappen.
Economy: highly developed industrial country and a leading financial and banking centre. **Principal industries:** precision engineering (watches, electrical and optical apparatus), the chemical and textile industries, food processing. Chief industrial centres: Zürich, Basel. **Mining:** salt 317,000 tonnes (1983). Electricity 51.8 billion kWh (1983), of which 70% hydro-electric and 28% nuclear power stations (Beznau, Mühleberg). **Production** (1983, in 1,000 tonnes): crude steel 855, aluminium 76 (canton Valais), watches 52 mn. pieces (cantons: Neuchâtel, Bern and Solothurn; Genève, Schaffhausen), geodetic apparatus (Genève), electrical apparatus (Basel, Baden), electrochemical products (canton Valais), dyes and pharmaceuticals (Basel), cement 4,138, paper and paper products 705 (Jura, Alp region), cotton yarn 53, woven cotton fabrics 109 mn. m (eastern Switzerland), wool processing (Solothurn, canton Thurgau), woven silk fabrics 16.3 mn. m (Zürich, Basel), synthetic fibres 30.5, shoes 7.5 mn. pairs, meat 447, milk 3,733, cheese 130, butter 39, eggs 44,7, chocolate, wine 161, beer 4.2 mn. hl (1983); 25.7 billion cigarettes (1983).
Agriculture: predominantly livestock, chiefly cattle raising. Land use: arable 9.6%, meadows and pastures 39.3%, forests 25.5%. **Crops** (1983, in 1,000 tonnes): cereals 888, potatoes 711, sugar beet 832, fruit 751, grapes 209, vegetables; **livestock** (1983, in 1,000 head): cattle 1,919, pigs 2,166, sheep 349; poultry 6,000; roundwood 4.3 mn. cub.m (1983).
Communications (1984): railways 5,064 km (all electrified), roads 69,775 km, motorways 1,258 km (1981): passenger cars 2,552,100. Navigable waterways 21 km, river port Basel. Merchant shipping 319,000 GRT (1984). Civil aviation (1984): 103.6 mn. km flown, 6,254,000 passengers carried. Tourism 9.2 mn. visitors (1983).

page 75

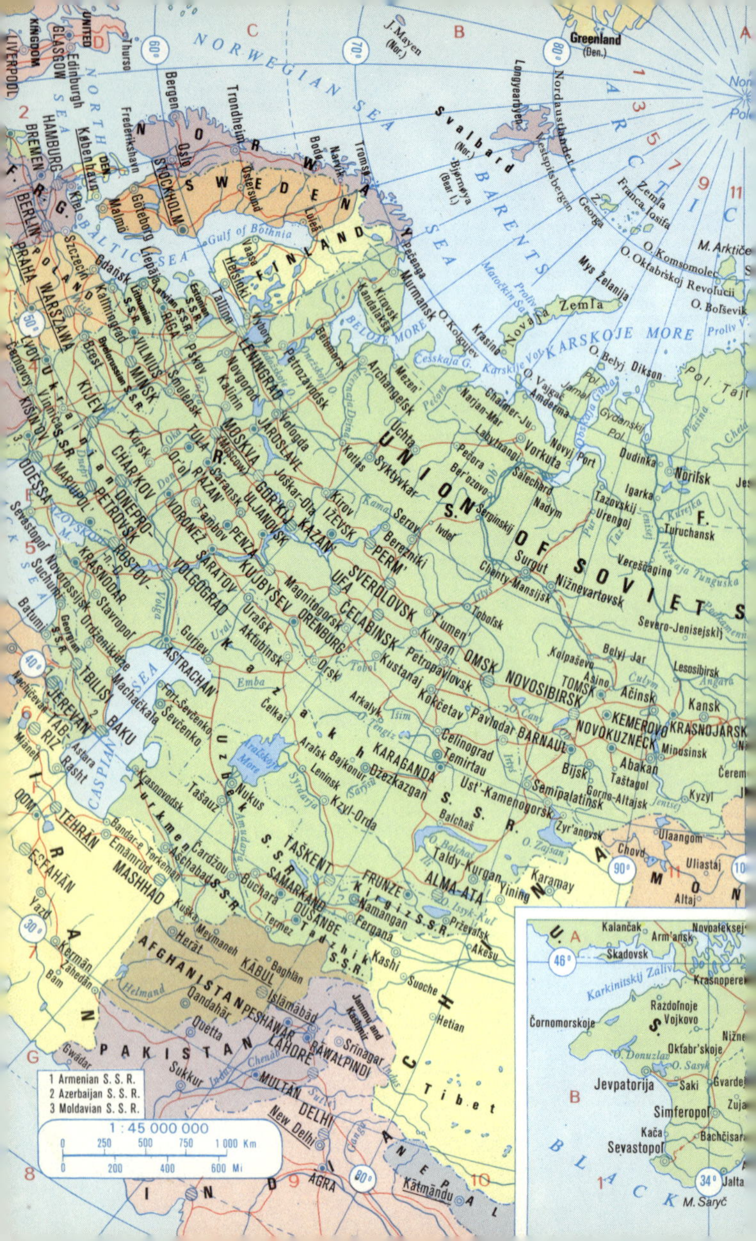

NORWEGIAN SEA
NORTH SEA
BALTIC SEA
Gulf of Bothnia
BARENTS SEA
ARCTIC
BELOJE MORE
KARSKOJE MORE
CASPIAN SEA
Aral'skoje More
BLACK SEA
AZOVSKOJE M.
Greenland (Den.)
J. Mayen (Nor.)
Svalbard (Nor.)
Bjørnøya (Bear I.)
Longyearbyen
Nordaustlandet
Vestspitsbergen
Zemla Franca Iosifa
Novaja Zemla
M. Arktičeskij
O. Komsomolec
O. Oktabr'skoj Revolucii
O. Bol'ševik
Mys Želanija
O. Kolgujev
O. Belyj
O. Vajgač
UNITED KINGDOM
LIVERPOOL
GLASGOW
Edinburgh
Thurso
NORWAY
Bergen
Oslo
Trondheim
Bodø
Narvik
Tromsø
SWEDEN
STOCKHOLM
Göteborg
Malmö
Östersund
Luleå
FINLAND
Helsinki
Vaasa
DENMARK
København
Frederikshavn
F. R. G.
HAMBURG
BREMEN
Kiel
BERLIN
PRAHA
POLAND
WARSZAWA
Szczecin
Gdańsk
Kaliningrad
Lithuanian S.S.R.
Latvian S.S.R.
Estonian S.S.R.
Liepāja
RIGA
Tallinn
VILNIUS
MINSK
Belorussian S.S.R.
Brest
LVOV
Černovcy
KIŠIN'OV
Ukrainian S.S.R.
KIJEV
Vinnica
ODESSA
Sevastopol'
Mariupol'
DNEPROPETROVSK
CHAR'KOV
LENINGRAD
Vyborg
Pskov
Novgorod
Smolensk
Kalinin
Petrozavodsk
Belomorsk
Kandalakša
Kirovsk
Murmansk
Pečenga
Archangelsk
Mezen'
MOSKVA (Moscow)
TULA
Kursk
Or'ol
RAZAN'
VORONEŽ
JAROSLAVL
Vologda
Kotlas
GOR'KIJ
Joškar-Ola
Saransk
Tambov
PENZA
ULJANOVSK
KAZAN'
KIROV
IŽEVSK
PERM'
Syktyvkar
Uchta
Pečora
Narjan-Mar
Vorkuta
Amderma
Labytnangi
Salechard
Chalmer-Ju
Ber'ozovo
Ivdel'
Serov
Berezniki
SVERDLOVSK
UFA
KUJBYŠEV
SARATOV
VOLGOGRAD
ROSTOV-NA-DONU
KRASNODAR
Novorossijsk
Stavropol'
Ordžonikidze
Suchumi
Batumi
Georgian S.S.R.
TBILISI
JEREVAN
BAKU
Machačkala
ASTRACHAN'
Gurjev
Ural'sk
Aktubinsk
ORENBURG
Magnitogorsk
ČELABINSK
Orsk
Kurgan
T'umen'
Tobol'sk
OMSK
Petropavlovsk
Kustanaj
Kokčetav
Celinograd
Temirtau
KARAGANDA
Džezkazgan
Pavlodar
Semipalatinsk
Ust'-Kamenogorsk
Zyr'anovsk
Balchaš
Taldy-Kurgan
ALMA-ATA
FRUNZE
Kirgiz S.S.R.
Prževal'sk
Namangan
Fergana
TAŠKENT
SAMARKAND
DUŠANBE
Tadzhik S.S.R.
Termez
Buchara
Čardžou
Ašchabad
Turkmen S.S.R.
Krasnovodsk
Tašauz
Nukus
Uzbek S.S.R.
Kazakh S.S.R.
Arkalyk
Celkar
Aral'sk
Bajkonur
Leninsk
Kzyl-Orda
Fort-Ševčenko
Ševčenko
Surgut
Nižnevartovsk
Chanty-Mansijsk
Kolpaševo
TOMSK
Asino
Belyj Jar
NOVOSIBIRSK
BARNAUL
Bijsk
Gorno-Altajsk
KEMEROVO
NOVOKUZNECK
Ačinsk
KRASNOJARSK
Kansk
Lesosibirsk
Abakan
Minusinsk
Taštagol
Kyzyl
Čeremchovo
Severo-Jenisejskij
Norilsk
Dudinka
Igarka
Tazovskij
Urengoj
Nadym
Novyj Port
Turuchansk
Vereščagino
Dikson
Serginskij
Gydanskij Pol.
Jamal Pol.
UNION OF SOVIET SOCIALIST REPUBLICS
Ob
Irtyš
Jenisej
Volga
Ural
Emba
Amudarja
Syrdarja
Tobol
Išim
Dnepr
Don
Kama
Pečora
Ulaangom
Uliastaj
Chovd
Altaj
MONGOLIA
CHINA
Karamay
Yining
Kashi
Akesu
Suoche
Hetian
Tibet
IRAN
TEHRĀN
QOM
Rasht
Tabriz
Astara
Bandar-e Torkeman
Emāmrūd
MASHHAD
EṢFAHĀN
Yazd
Kermān
Zāhedān
Bam
AFGHANISTAN
KĀBUL
Herāt
Meymaneh
Kuška
Baghlān
Qandahār
Helmand
PAKISTAN
ISLĀMĀBĀD
PESHĀWAR
RĀWALPINDI
LAHORE
Quetta
MULTĀN
Sukkur
Gwādar
Jammu and Kashmir
Srinagar
Indus
INDIA
DELHI
New Delhi
ĀGRA
Ganga
NEPAL
Kātmāndu
1 Armenian S. S. R.
2 Azerbaijan S. S. R.
3 Moldavian S. S. R.
1 : 45 000 000
0 250 500 750 1 000 Km
0 200 400 600 Mi
Kalančak
Arm'ansk
Novoalekseevka
Skadovsk
Krasnoperekopsk
Karkinitskij Zaliv
Razdol'noje
Vojkovo
Černomorskoje
Oktabr'skoje
O. Donuzlav
O. Sasyk
Jevpatorija
Saki
Gvardejskoje
Simferopol'
Zuja
Kača
Bachčisaraj
Sevastopol'
Jalta
M. Saryč
BLACK SEA

16a Crimea
1 : 6 000 000

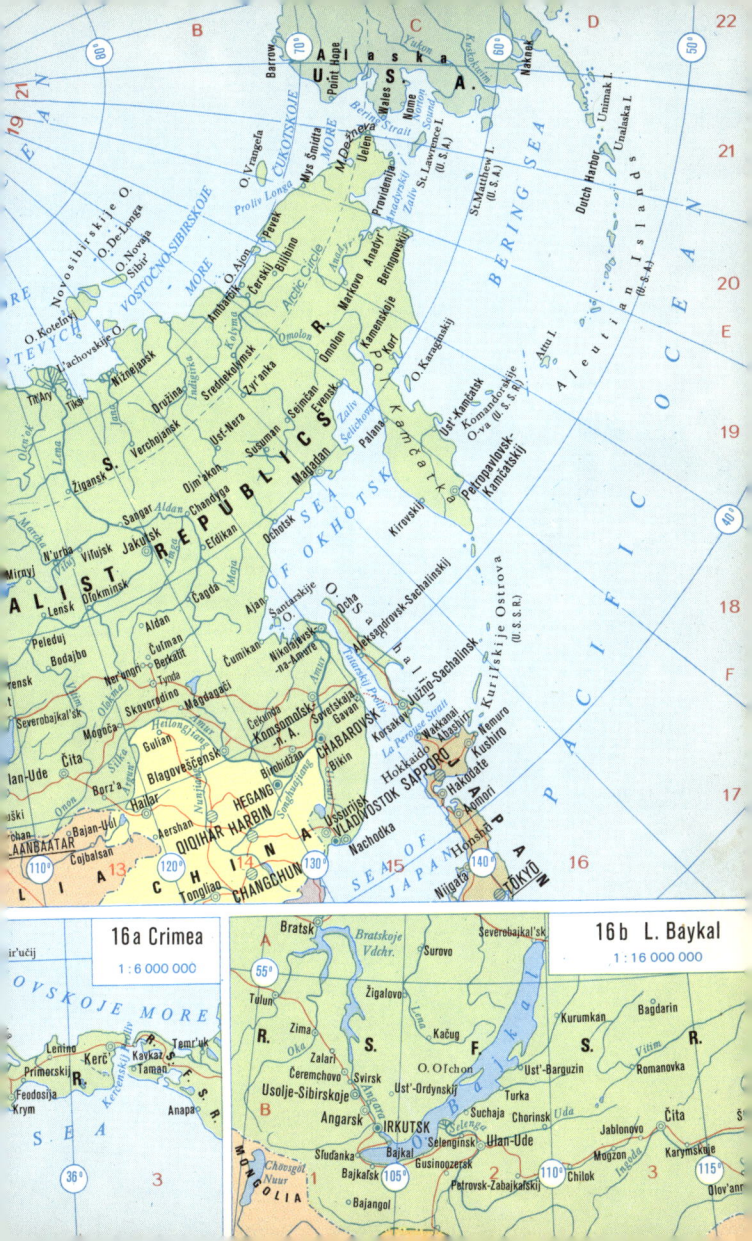

16b L. Baykal
1 : 16 000 000

Exports: machines and apparatus, watches, chemical products (dyes, pharmaceuticals), textiles, foodstuffs (dried and condensed milk, cheese, chocolate). **Imports:** machines, transport equipment, fuels (petroleum), raw materials for the textile and food industries. Chief trading partners: Fed. Rep. of Germany, France, U.S.A., Italy, United Kingdom.

VATICAN CITY, STATE OF
Stato della Città del Vaticano, area **0.44 sq.km**, population **766** (1988), **papal state** (Pope John Paul II [Karol Wojtyla] since 1978).

The smallest state in the world due to the area; religious and political centre of the Roman Catholic Church, seat of the Pope, Cardinals and the highest ecclesiastical officials. **Official languages** are Latin and Italian. – **Currency:** Italian lira. Revenue from tourism and postage stamps.

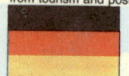

GERMANY, FEDERAL REPUBLIC OF
(former West-Berlin)

Area **480 sq.km**, population **2,016,100** (1987). Since 3 October 1990 part of Federal republic of Germany.

Density 3,862 persons per sq.km. After the Second World War Berlin was divided into 4 sectors on the basis of the Potsdam Agreement (1945). West Berlin consisted of 3 sectors under the control of the U.S.A., the United Kingdom and France. West Berlin contains the **administrative districts** of Kreuzberg, Neukölln, Schöneberg, Steglitz, Tempelhof, Zehlendorf, Charlottenburg, Spandau, Tiergarten, Wilmersdorf, Wedding, Reinickendorf.

Economy: highly developed industries, dependent on imported raw materials. Leading industries: electrotechnical, engineering and textiles. The extensive exchange of goods between West Berlin and Fed. Rep. of Germany is dependent upon specific autobahns and air corridors for transport across the territory of the German Dem. Rep.

YUGOSLAVIA

Socialistička Federativna Republika Jugoslavija, area **255,804 sq.km**, population **23,558,928** (1988), **socialist federal republic** (President of the State Presidency Borislav Jović since 1990).

Administrative units: 6 socialist republics – Bosna i Hercegovina, Crna Gora, Hrvatska, Makedonija, Slovenija, Srbija (2 autonomous regions of Vojvodina and Kosovo). **Capital:** Beograd (Belgrade) 1,145,000 inhab. (1981 with agglomeration 1,455,046 inhab.); **other towns** (1981, in 1,000 inhab.): Zagreb 763, Sarajevo 448, Skopje 406, Ljubljana 303, Novi Sad 170, Split 169, Niš 161, Rijeka 158, Banja Luka 124, Maribor 105, Osijek 104, Subotica 100, Titograd 96, Kragujevac 87, Bitola 81, Zrenjanin 81, Pančevo 70, Priština 70. **Population:** Serbs, Croats, Slovenians, Montenegrians. **Density** 91 persons per sq.km; average annual rate of population increase 0.9% (1975–82); urban population 46% (1981). 33.8% of inhabitants employed in agriculture, 38% in industry (1983). **Currency:** dinar.

Economy: developed industrial and agricultural country. Rich resources of raw materials, forests and hydro-electric energy. **Principal industries:** mining of minerals, engineering, metallurgy, textiles, wood-working and food processing. Manufacturing of motor vehicles, shipbuilding, electrotechnics, radioelectronics and the chemical industry are under development. **Mining** (1983, in 1,000 tonnes, metal content): coal 392, lignite 58,188 (Slovenija – Trbovlje, Zagorje; Srbija), crude petroleum 4,128 (Lendava, Gojilo, Kloštar), natural gas 104,569 TJ, iron ore 1,756 (Ljubija, Vareš), manganese 9.6 (Drača), copper 128.6 (Bor, Majdanpek, Raška), lead 114.6 and zinc 87.8 (Mežica, Crna), antimony 1,360 tonnes, gold 3,732kg, silver 124 tonnes, bauxite 3,501 (Rovinj, Mostar, Titograd), magnesite 308 (Štip), pyrites 810, salt 425, asbestos 11. Electricity 71.6 billion kWh (1983), of which 44% are hydro-electric power stations and 5% nuclear power stations.

Production (1983, in 1,000 tonnes): pig iron 3,096, crude steel 4,135 (Zenica), coke oven coke 3,440, copper -smelted 153, -refined 122 (Bor), lead 98 (Mežica), zinc 87 (Celje), aluminium 284 (Lozovac, Kidričevo), motor vehicles – commercial 16,400 units, passenger 220,000 (Maribor, Kragujevac) – tractors 55,900 (Kruševac), agricultural machines (Subotica, Novi Sad), railway carriages (Kraljevo), locomotives (Slavonski Brod), vessels 243,000 GRT (Rijeka, Split, Trogir), electrotechnics (Beograd), sulphuric acid 1,300 (Bor), nitric acid 741, nitrogenous fertilizers 410, phosphorus fertilizers 383 (Kosovska Mitrovica); capacity of petroleum refineries 15.5 mn. tonnes (1984, Rijeka, Beograd, Sisak), motor spirit 2,497, fuel oils 8,902, cement 9,588, yarn – cotton 120, woollen 51 – woven fabrics – cotton 379 mn. sq.m, woollen 96.7 mn. sq.m, silk 34.9 mn. – rayon and acetate staple fibre 58, woven rayon and acetate fabrics 34.9 mn. sq.m, leather shoes 80.1 mn. pairs, chemical wood pulp 531, paper and paper products 1,116, sugar 722, meat 1,433, milk 4,550, butter 14, cheese 156, eggs 239, wine 720, beer 12.4 mn. hl (1983), alcoholic spirits; 58.5 billion cigarettes (1983).

Agriculture: arable land 27.8%, meadows and pastures 24.9%, forests 36.5%. **Crops** (1983, in 1,000 tonnes): maize (corn) 10,688, wheat 5,519, barley 670, oats 248, rice, potatoes 2,580, hemp, sugar beet 5,700, sunflower seed 135, sesame, olives, soya beans 220, hops, fruit 3,797; apples 589, plums 1,038 (second world producer), grapes 1,629 (Dalmacija, Danubeland); pulses 217, vegetables 2,935, tomatoes 475, watermelons 622, tobacco 77 (Bosna i Hercegovina, Makedonija), walnuts 37; **livestock** (1983, in 1,000 head): cattle 5,351, buffaloes 60, horses 505, asses, sheep 7,452, pigs 8,370, poultry 68,000; wool 6,004 tonnes, honey 5,540 tonnes; fish catch 79,800 tonnes; roundwood 15.4 mn. cub.m (1983).

Communications (1984): railways 9,279km, of which 3,462km are electrified, roads 116,602km, motorways 714km, passenger cars 2,874,000. Navigable waterways 2,001km. Merchant shipping 2,682,000 GRT (1984). Chief ports: Rijeka, Split, Dubrovnik. Civil aviation (1984): 29.8 mn. km flown, 2,944,000 passengers carried. Important tourism 5.9 mn. visitors (1983).

Exports: ores and non-ferrous metals, machines and equipment, transport equipment (vessels, cars, railway carriages), foodstuffs (meat, canned fish, fruit, wine), electrotechnical products, furniture, textiles and leather goods. **Imports:** machinery, transport and industrial equipment, fuels (petroleum), chemicals, raw materials and semi-finished products, foodstuffs. Chief trading partners: U.S.S.R., Italy, Fed. Rep. of Germany, Czechoslovakia, U.S.A.

UNION OF SOVIET SOCIALIST REPUBLICS

Soyuz Sovyetskikh Sotsialisticheskikh Respublik, area 22,274,900 sq.km, (22,402,200 sq.km incl. Beloje More 90,000 sq.km and Azovskoje More 37,300 sq.km); of this, the European part has approx. 5,443,900 sq.km and the Asiatic part about 16,831,000 sq.km; **population 285,940,000** (1988), **Union of Soviet Socialist Republics** (President Mikhail Sergeievich Gorbachev since 1990).

Administrative units: 15 federal Soviet Socialist Republics (S.S.R.) divided into 3,201 districts and 630 urban districts (1983). In addition to this, some of the republics include Autonomous Soviet Socialist Republics (A.S.S.R., 20), Autonomous Regions (8), Autonomous Areas (only in the Russian Soviet Federal Socialist Republics, 10,) Territories and Regions. **Capital:** Moskva (Moscow) 8,642,000 inhab. (1984); **other towns** (1984, in 1,000 inhab.): Leningrad 4,832, Kijev 2,411, Taškent 1,985, Char'kov 1,536, Minsk 1,442, Gor'kij 1,392, Novosibirsk 1,386, Sverdlovsk 1,288, Kujbyšev 1,251, Baku 1,166, Dnepropetrovsk 1,140, Tbilisi 1,140, Jerevan 1,114, Odessa 1,113, Omsk 1,094, Čel'abinsk 1,086, Doneck 1,064, Perm' 1,049, Ufa 1,048, Alma-Ata 1,046, Kazan' 1,039, Rostov-na-Donu 983, Volgograd 969, Saratov 894, Riga 875, Krasnojarsk 860, Zaporožje 844, Voronež 841, Lvov 728, Krivoj Rog 680, Jaroslavl' 623, Karaganda 608, Kišin'ov 605, Ustinov 603, Krasnodar 603, Vladivostok 591, Irkutsk 590, Frunze, 590, Toljatti 576, Novokuzneck 572, Chabarovsk 569, Barnaul 567, Dušanbe 539, Vilnius 535, Tula 529, Uljanovsk 524, Penza 522, Ždanov 520, Samarkand 515, Orenburg 513, Kemerovo 495, Vorošilovgrad 485, R'azan' 483, Astrachan' 481, Ivanovo 474, Nikolajev 474, Tomsk 459, Tallinn 454, Makejevka 446, Kalinin 433, Gomel' 432, Lipeck 422, Magnitogorsk 419.

Population: the most numerous nationalities at the 1979 census were 197.4 mn. Russians, 42.3 mn. Ukrainians, 12.5 mn. Uzbeks, 9.5 mn. Byelorussians, 6.9 mn. Tatars, 6.6 mn. Kazakhs, 5.5 mn. Azerbaijanians, 4.2 mn. Armenians, 3.6 mn. Georgians, 2,9 mn. Lithuanians, 3 mn. Moldavians, 1.8 mn. Jews, 2.9 mn. Tadzhiks, 1.9 mn. Germans, 1.7 mn. Chuvashes, 1.9 mn. Kirghizians, 2 mn. Turkmenians, 1.4 mn. Latvians, 1.2 mn. Mordovians, 1.4 mn. Bashkirs, 1.2 mn. Poles. **Density** 12.4 persons per sq.km; average annual rate of population increase 0.98%; urban population 65% (1984). 14.5% of the economically active inhabitants employed in agriculture. – **Currency:** rouble = 100 kopeks.

Economy: well-developed industrial and agricultural country. It produces about 20% of the total world industrial output and holds the leading position in many branches of mining and processing: mining of crude petroleum, natural gas, peat, iron ore, manganese, nickel, chromium, mercury, asbestos, potash, magnesite; in the production of pig iron and crude steel, coke oven coke, cement, bricks, cotton and woollen yarn, woven woollen and linen fabrics, milk, butter, flour etc. The U.S.S.R. is the second greatest producer in the world of lignite and brown coal, copper, zinc, tungsten, vanadium, diamonds and phosphates. The size of the cultivated area is the largest in the world, and the U.S.S.R. is the world's leading producer of wheat, barley, rye, oats, potatoes, sunflower seed, flax fibre, sugar beet, roundwood and it has the largest sheep population. The U.S.S.R. is the second greatest producer in the world of hemp, cotton lint, cattle and pigs, fish catch and honey. Arable land constitutes 10%, meadows and pastures 17% and forests 41% of the total land area.

Agriculture: (1983, in 1,000 tonnes) – **crops:** wheat 82,000 (Ukraine, Plain of Kuban', a district called the Black Earth Central Zone – Tambov, Voronež, Kursk; North Kazakhstan), barley 54,000 (southern European Russia), maize (corn) 14,000 (Ukraine, North Caucasia, Moldavia), rye 13,500 (central European Russia), oats 16,000 (western Siberia, central European Russia), rice 2,500 (Central Asian republics), millet 2,200, sorghum 180, potatoes 83,060 (European Russia, Byelorussia), sunflower seed 5,040 (southern European Russia), linseed 220, flax fibre 699 (Byelorussia, Baltic shore, central European Russia), hemp 30, cotton seed 5,694, -lint 2,716 (Uzbekistan); sugar beet 81,813 (Ukraine), tomatoes 7,250, grapes 6,443 (Moldavia, Transcaucasia, Central Asia), oranges 345 (Georgia), tea 150 (Georgia), tobacco 377. **Livestock** (1983, in 1,000 head): horses 5,601, asses 344, cattle 117,186, buffaloes 320, camels 240, pigs 73,671, sheep 142,182, goats 6,340, poultry 1,044,000. **Production** (1983): eggs 4,116,000 tonnes, cowhides 752,000 tonnes, sheepskins 126,000 tonnes, wool-grease 454,000 tonnes, honey 190,000 tonnes. Fish catch 9,756,800 tonnes (second world catch). Roundwood 356 mn. cub.m (leading world producer).

Mining (1983, in 1,000 tonnes, metal content): coal 486,812 – Donbas Basin (Doneck and Vorošilovgrad region), Kuzbas Basin (Kemerovo region), Karaganda (Ekibastuz), lignite and brown coal 154,774 peat, combustible shale, crude petroleum 616,343 (the Ural-Volga area – Tatar A.S.S.R., Bashkir A.S.S.R., Kujbyšev region; T'umen' region in western Siberia, Baku etc.), international oil pipelines supply Czechoslovakia, Hungary, German Dem. Republic and Poland; natural gas 18,637.8 PJ (T'umen' region, Doneck-Dnepr district, North Caucasia, Volga Basin, an extensive gas pipeline system supplies industrial regions in the U.S.S.R. and in a number of European countries (Czechoslovakia, German Dem. Republic, Fed. Rep. of Germany, Austria, Italy, France, Yugoslavia), uranium, iron ore 133,563 (Fe content – Krivoj Rog, Kursk, the Ural Mts.), manganese 2,957 (Nikopol', Čiatura), copper 1,180 (Kazakhstan, the Ural Mts.), bauxite 4,600 (the Ural Mts., Kazakhstan, eastern Siberia), zinc 805 (Kazakhstan, Kuzbas Basin, North Caucasia), lead 435 (Kazakhstan, North Caucasia, the Ural Mts.), nickel 170 (northern Siberia, the Ural Mts., Kol'skij Pol. – Kola Peninsula), chromium 977 (the Ural Mts., Kazakhstan), tin 17, antimony 9,200 tonnes (Kazakhstan, Central Asia), molybdenum 11,100 tonnes (Transcaucasia, Central Asia, eastern Siberia), tungsten 9,100 tonnes (Kazakhstan, Central Asia, eastern Siberia), vanadium 9,500 tonnes (the Ural Mts., Kazakhstan), mercury 2,206 tonnes (Central Asia), asbestos 2,250 (the Ural Mts.), mica (eastern Siberia), gold 267,500 kg (eastern Siberia, the Ural Mts.), silver 1,465 tonnes (Kuzbas Basin, Central Asia), platinum (the Ural Mts., northern Siberia), diamonds 11 mn. carats (Yakut A.S.S.R., the Ural Mts.), magnesite 2,500 (the Ural Mts.), cobalt, phosphates 27,000 (Kola Pen., Kazakhstan), sulphur 1,800 (the Ural Mts., Ukraine), potash 9,300 (the Ural Mts., Byelorussia, Turkmenistan), salt 16,178.

Electricity 1,418 billion kWh, of which 180 billion kWh hydro-electric power stations. Largest power station (in mn. kWh): Reftinsk 3.8, Kostroma 3.6, Krivoj Rog 3 (thermal), Krasnojarsk 6, Bratsk 4.6, Sajano-Šušenskaja 6.4 (hydro-electric), Sosnovyj Bor 4, Novovoronežskaja 2.5 (nuclear).

Metallurgy: iron – Doneck-Dnepr district (Krivoj Rog), the Ural Mts.; non-ferrous metals – the Ural Mts., Kazakhstan, North Caucasia, Kola Peninsula. Production (1983, in 1,000 tonnes): pig iron 110,000, crude steel 153,000, aluminium 1,790, copper 1,450, lead 525, zinc 785, coke oven coke 86,000.

page 79

17a Ural Region 1:10 000 000

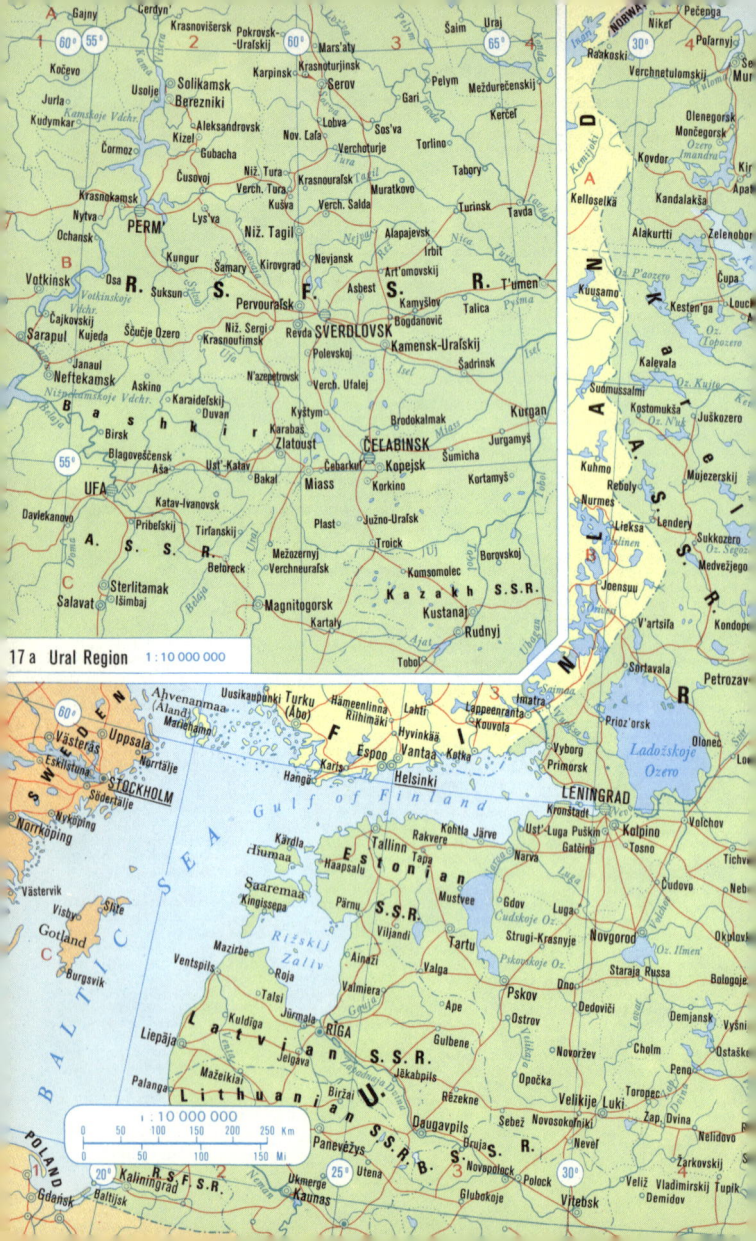

O. Kolguje
Bugrino
Nosovaj
5
40°
6
45°
7
50°
8
55°
9
Chorej-Ver
Kanin Nos
Andeg
Charlovka
Poluo. Kanin
Narjan-Mar
Oksino
R.
Indiga
Sapkina
Laja
Gremicha
Šojna
Velikovisočnoje
Arctic Circle
Adz'vavom
Kolva
A
ľskij
MORE
(WHITE SEA)
Češskaja Guba
Zacharvan'
Usinsk
Volonga
Novyj Bor
Ust'-Usa
Krasnoščel'je
Ponoj
Čiža
Niž'n'aja Peša
Pečora
Usa
Okun'ov Nos
Mutnyj Materik
ostrov
Mezenskaja Guba
Nes'
Pečora
Kojda
65°
Kuzomen'
Strel'na
BELOJE
Mezen'
Safonovo
Cil'ma
Ust'-Cil'ma
Ščeljajur
Iž'ma
Peza
Myla
Kadžerom
Verchn'aja Zolotica
Karjepolje
Kuloj
Mezen'
Irajoľ
Iž'ma
Dvinskaja Guba
Mezen'
Lešukonskoje
Vožgora
Kedvavom
Patrakejevka
Pinega
Pušlachta
Archangel'sk
Severodvinsk
Novodvinsk
Pinega
Ust'-Pinega
Šilega
Karpogory
Važgort
K
o
m
i
Sosnogorsk
Uchta
Jarega
Troicko-Pečorsk
Mezen'
Onežskaja Guba
Vendenga
Koslan
Meščura
S.
S.
R.
Voj-Vož
B
Onega
Kodino
N'uchča
Vaška
A.
S.
Vožajol'
Malošujka
Jemeck
S.
Pinega
Železnodorožnyj
Pomozdino
Vyčegda
Jemca
Bereznik
Mikun'
Ajkino
Vym'
Storoževsk
Onega
Plesec k
Puksoozero
Oksovskij
Severnaja Dvina
Verchn'aja Tojma
Jarensk
Žešart
Syktyvkar
Ust'-Kulom
Šalakuša
Šenkursk
Vyčegda
n
Lopydino
Kon'ovo
Vaga
Krasnoborsk
Kor'ažma
a
N'andoma
i
Kotlas
Vizinga
Sysola
Gajny
Vodla
Kargopol'
s
Kiz'oma
Kojgorodok
Kažym
Oz. Lača
Luza
60°
Konoša
Vel'sk
Oktabr'skij
Velikij Ust'ug
Luza
Objačevo
Vytegra
Verchovažje
Pin'ug
Lesnoj
Rudničnyj
Kirs
Kama
Oz. Vože
Vaga
N'uksenica
Kičmengskij Gorodok
Oparino
Letka
Čarozero
Vožega
Nagorsk
V'atka
Oz. Beloje
Nikol'sk
Muraši
Rosľatino
Maloma
Tot'ma
Charovsk
Omutninsk
Beloz'orsk
Kirillov
Slobodskoj
Sukhona
Sokol
Oz. Kubenskoje
R.
Kirovo-Čepeck
Udmurt A.S.S.R.
Glazov
Vochma
Kirov
Zujevka
Čerepovec
Vologda
Soligalič
Kologriv
Černovskoje
S.
F.
S.
Koteľnič
Šarja
Uni
Čuchloma
Leninskoje
C
Manturovo
Pošechonje-Volodarsk
Buj
Nolinsk
Vesjegonsk
Galič
Unža
Vetluga
Rybinskoje Vdchr.
Danilov
Makarjev
Šachunja
Sovetsk
Kil'mez
Rybinsk
Jaransk
Uržum
IŽEVSK
Kostroma
V'atka
Sonkovo
Volga
Vetluga
Možga
Bežeck
JAROSLAVL'
Nerechta
Kinešma
Vetlužskij
A. S. S. R.
Malmyž
Uglič
Gor'kovskoje Vdchr.
Kašin
Kaľazin
Rostov
Ivanovo
Vičuga
Joškar-Ola
V'atskije Pol'any
Sem'onov
Mari
Naber.-Čelny
Teikovo
Šuja
Koz'modemjansk
Tatar A.S.S.R.
Kimry
Pereslavl'-Zalesskij
Zavolžje
Novočeboksarsk
Dubna
Bor
Volga
KAZAN'
Kan. Im. Moskvy
Aleksandrov
Kovrov
GOR'KIJ
Čeboksary
Kujbyševskoje Vdchr.
Nižnekamsk
Dzeržinsk
Zelenodoľsk
Klin
Vladimir
Kstovo
Čeboksarskoje Vdchr.
Zagorsk
Chuvash
Čistopol'
Puškino
Kanaš
Zelenograd
Pavlovo
Sergač
55°
8
Mytišči
Oka
Sumerľa
Gus'-Chrustaľnyj
A.S.S.R.
MOSKVA
(Moscow)
Orechovo-Zujevo
Murom
Arzamas
Sura
40°
6
45°
7
50°
D
Buinsk
Nurlat
Melenki
Vyksa
Lukojanov
Alatyr
Možajsk
Podoľsk
Jegorjevsk

map 17

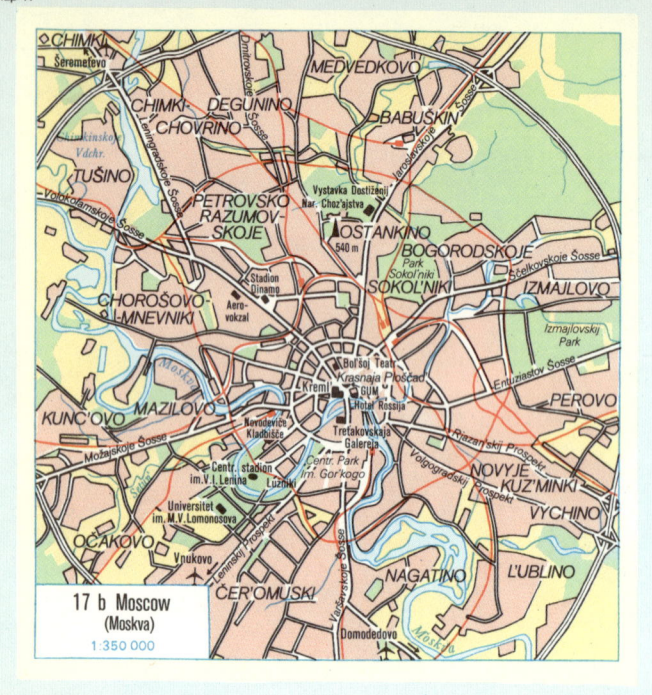

Engineering (1983, in 1,000 units): metal-working machines 190 (Moskva, Leningrad), motor vehicles – passenger 1,315 (Toljatti, Ustinov, Moskva, Gor'kij), commercial 1,307 (Moskva, Brežnev), buses 85.1 (L'vov) – locomotives 1.8 (Vorošilovgrad, Char'kov, Kolomna), railway carriages 60.3 (Nižnij Tagil, Ždanov), tractors 564.0 (Volgograd, Char'kov, Minsk), grain combines 118 (Rostov-na-Donu), shipbuilding (Leningrad, Nikolajev, Cherson), radio receivers 9,297, television receivers 8,578, refrigerators 5,700).
Chemical industry – Moskva and surroundings, the Ural Mts., Doneck-Dnepr district, Leningrad, Gor'kij, regions near raw material deposits. Production (1983, in 1,000 tonnes): sulphuric acid 24,700, synthetic resins and plastics 4,419, caustic soda 2,853, nitrogenous fertilizers 11,481, phosphate fertilizers 6,560, chemical wood pulp 7,913.
Building industry – Moskva and surroundings, Leningrad, Char'kov, Krivoj Rog, Volgograd, Kujbyšev, the Ural Mts. Production (1983): cement 128 mn. tonnes, bricks 42 billion pieces. **Wood and paper industry:** production of furniture – Moskva, Ivanovo, Leningrad, Riga, Užgorod, Kijev; paper 5.7 mn. tonnes, of which 1.4 mn. tonnes newsprint.
Textile industry: cotton yarn 1.6 mn. tonnes, woollen yarn 447,100 tonnes; woven fabrics – cotton 8,029 mn. sq.m, woollen 911 mn. sq.m, silk 56.6 mn. sq.m, linen 753 mn. sq.m. Leather footwear 745 mn. pairs. **Food industry** – in cities and agricultural production regions (1983, in 1,000 tonnes): meat 16,196, milk 96,000, butter 1,455, cheese 1,622, flour 43,000, sugar 12,400, margarine 1,483, wine 34.4 mn. hl, beer 63 mn. hl; 364 billion cigarettes.
Communications (1983): railways 143,690 km, roads 973,000 km, of which hard surfaced 773,000 km, motor vehicles – passenger 9.6 mn., commercial 8.3 mn. Navigable waterways 138,931 km. Merchant shipping 24.5 mn. GRT. Chief ports: Novorossijsk, Odessa (with Iljičovsk), Leningrad, Nachodka, Astrachan', Archangel'sk, Murmansk, Baku. Civil aviation 109.5 mn. passengers carried. Length of oil and oil products pipelines 76,225 km, gas pipelines 155,095 km. Tourism 6,777,000 visitors (1983).
Foreign trade: with 120 countries (1983). Total turnover 127.5 billion roubles, of which exports 67,9 billion, imports 59.6 billion roubles. – **Exports:** fuels, raw materials, ores 60.8%; machines, equipment and transport equipment 12,9%; chemical products, building materials and other products 17.9%; agricultural raw materials and their products, consumer goods. **Imports:** machines, industrial and transport equipment 38%, raw materials, rolled iron, food materials, foodstuffs and consumer goods. Chief trading partners: German Dem. Rep., Czechoslovakia, Bulgaria, Poland, Hungary, Fed. Rep. of Germany, Finland, Yugoslavia, Italy, France, Romania, Japan.

map 18

RUSSIAN SOVIET FEDERAL SOCIALIST REPUBLIC (R.S.F.S.R.), Rossiskaya Sovietskaya Federativnaya Sotsialisticheskaya Respublika, **area 17,075,400 sq.km, population 143,078,000** (1985); 16 Autonomous Soviet Socialist Republics (A.S.S.R.): Bashkir A.S.S.R., Buryat A.S.S.R., Checheno-Ingush A.S.S.R., Chuvash A.S.S.R., Daghestan A.S.S.R., Kabardino-Balkar A.S.S.R., Kalmyk A.S.S.R., Karelian A.S.S.R., Komi A.S.S.R., Mari A.S.S.R., Mordovian A.S.S.R., North Ossetian A.S.S.R., Tatar A.S.S.R., Tuva A.S.S.R., Udmurt A.S.S.R., Yakut A.S.S.R.; **capital:** Moskva 8,642,000 inhab. (1984). **Population:** more than 100 nationalities live there; the most numerous are (1980): Russians 82.6%, Tatars 3.7%. – **Economy:** the R.S.F.S.R. produces about two thirds of the total industrial and one half of the agricultural output of the Soviet Union. 90% of the total coal and 80% of petroleum reserves are found here as well as 60% of iron ore, 80% of peat, 90% of wood, 70% of hydro-electric resources, the majority of precious ores and gems. About 60% of the total cultivated area of the U.S.S.R. lies here.

UKRAINE, Ukrainska Radyanska Sotsialistichna Respublika (Ukrainian S.S.R.), **area 603,700 sq.km, population 50,843,000** (1985); **capital:** Kijev 2,411,000 inhab. (1984). **Population** (1980): Ukrainians 73.6%, Russians 21.1%. – **Economy:** raw materials, high quality coal, iron and manganese ores, petroleum, chemical raw materials, important metallurgical, engineering and chemical production, intensive agriculture (sugar beet, wheat, maize [corn]).

BYELORUSSIA, Belaruskaya Sovietskaya Sotsialistychnaya Respublika, **area 207,600 sq.km, population 9,941,000** (1985); **capital:** Minsk 1,442,000 inhab. (1984). **Population** (1980): Byelorussians 79.4%, Russians 11.9%, Poles 4.2%. – **Economy:** raw materials – forest products, peat, phosphides; engineering and food industry, cultivation of potatoes and flax; cattle breeding.

AZERBAIJAN, Azerbaijchan Soviet Sotsialistik Republikasy, **area 86,600 sq.km, population 6,614,000** (1985), 1 autonomous republic – Nakhichevan A.S.S.R.; **capital:** Baku 1,166,000 inhab. (1984). **Population** (1980): Azerbaijanis 78.1%, Russians 7.9%, Armenians 7.9%. – **Economy:** important mining of petroleum, chemical, engineering, textile and food industries, cultivation of cotton, subtropical products and sheep breeding.

GEORGIA, Sakartvelos Sabchota Sotsialisturi Respublica, **area 69,700 sq.km, population 5,203,000** (1985), 2 autonomous republics – Abkhaz A.S.S.R. and Adzhar A.S.S.R.; **capital:** Tbilisi 1,140,000 inhab. (1984). **Population** (1980): Georgians 68.8%, Armenians 9.0%, Russians 7.4%. – **Economy:** mineral resources – manganese ore and coal, metallurgical, engineering, textile and food industries. Main crops: tea, tobacco, cotton, citrus fruit, grapes.

ARMENIA, Haikakan Sovetakan Sotsialistakan Respublika, **area 29,800 sq.km, population 3,320,000 inhab.** (1985); **capital:** Jerevan 1,114,000 inhab. (1984). **Population** (1980): Armenians 89.7%, Azerbaijanis 5.3%, Russians 2.3%. **Economy:** mining and processing of copper ore, engineering, chemical and food industries; cultivation of cotton, vines, fruit.

MOLDAVIA, Respublika Sovietike Sochialiste Moldovenyaske, **area 33,700 sq.km, population 4,105,000** (1985); **capital:** Kišin'ov 605,000 inhab. (1984). **Population** (1980): Moldavians 63.9%, Ukrainians 14.2%, Russians 12.8%, Gagauzians 3.5%. – **Economy:** cultivation of vines, fruit, sugar beet, tobacco, cereals. Food industry.

ESTONIA, Eesti Nõukogude Sotsialistik Vabariik, **area 45,100 sq.km, population 1,529,000** (1985); **capital:** Tallinn 454,000 inhab. (1984). **Population** (1980): Estonians 64.9%, Russians 27.4%. – **Economy:** mining of combustible shales and peat; engineering, textile industry, production of cement. Cultivation of potatoes, flax, barley, fodder crops. Cattle breeding.

LATVIA, Latvijas Padomju Socialistiska Republika, **area 63,700 sq.km, population 2,604,000** (1985); **capital:** Riga 875,000 inhab. (1984). **Population** (1980): Latvians 53.7%, Russians 32.8%, Byelorussians 4.5%. – **Economy:** mining of peat; engineering (electrotechnical), food industry. Cultivation of flax, sugar beet, potatoes; livestock breeding.

LITHUANIA, Lietuvos Tarybu Socialistine Respublika, **area 65,200 sq.km, population 3,572,000** (1985); **capital:** Vilnius 535,000 inhab. (1984). **Population** (1980): Lithuanians 80%, Russians 8.9%, Poles 7.3%, Byelorussians 1.7%. – **Economy:** mining of peat, engineering and food industry. Cultivation of flax and potatoes; livestock breeding.

KAZAKHSTAN, Kazak Soviettik Sotzialistik Respublikasy, **area 2,717,300 sq.km, population 15,858,000** (1985); **capital:** Alma-Ata 1,046,000 inhab. (1984). **Population** (1980): Kazakhs 36%, Russians 40%. – **Economy:** mining and metallurgy of non-ferrous metals, extraction of coal and petroleum. Cultivation of wheat, fruit, cattle breeding.

TURKMENISTAN, Tiurkmenostan Soviet Sotsialistik Respublikasy, **area 488,100 sq.km, population 3,197,000** (1985); **capital:** Ašchabad 356,000 inhab. (1984). **Population** (1980): Turkmenians 68.4%, Russians 12.6%, Uzbeks 8.5%. – **Economy:** extraction and processing of petroleum, mining of sulphur, textile industry. Deserts and dry steppes cover about 90% of the land area; cultivation of cotton and rice on irrigated land. Karakul sheep breeding.

UZBEKISTAN, Ozbekistan Soviet Sotsialistik Respublikasy, **area 447,400 sq.km, population 17,989,000** (1985); 1 autonomous republic – Karakalpak A.S.S.R.; **capital:** Taškent 1,985,000 inhab. (1984). **population:** (1980): Uzbeks 68.7%, Russians 10.8%, Tatars 4.2%, Kazakhs 4%. – **Economy:** mining of petroleum, coal, copper, sulphur; heavy engineering, chemical, textile and food industries. Cultivation of cotton and breeding of Karakul sheep.

TADZHIKISTAN, Respublikai Sovieth Sotsialistii Tojokiston, **area 143,100 sq.km, population 4,500,000** (1985); **capital:** Dušanbe 539,000 inhab. (1984). **Population** (1980): Tadzhiks 58.8%, Uzbeks 22.9%, Russians 11.9%. – **Economy:** mining of coal, petroleum, polymetallic ores; processing of agricultural products. Cultivation of cotton, rice, fruit and vines; sheep breeding.

KIRGIZIA, Kyrgyz Sovietik Sotsialistik Respublikasy, **area 198,500 sq.km, population 3,976,000** (1985); **capital:** Frunze 590,000 inhab. (1984). **Population** (1980): Kirghizians 47.9%, Russians 25.9%. – **Economy:** mining of petroleum, coal, mercury, non-ferrous metals; engineering. Cultivation of cotton, sugar beet, fruit; cattle and sheep breeding.

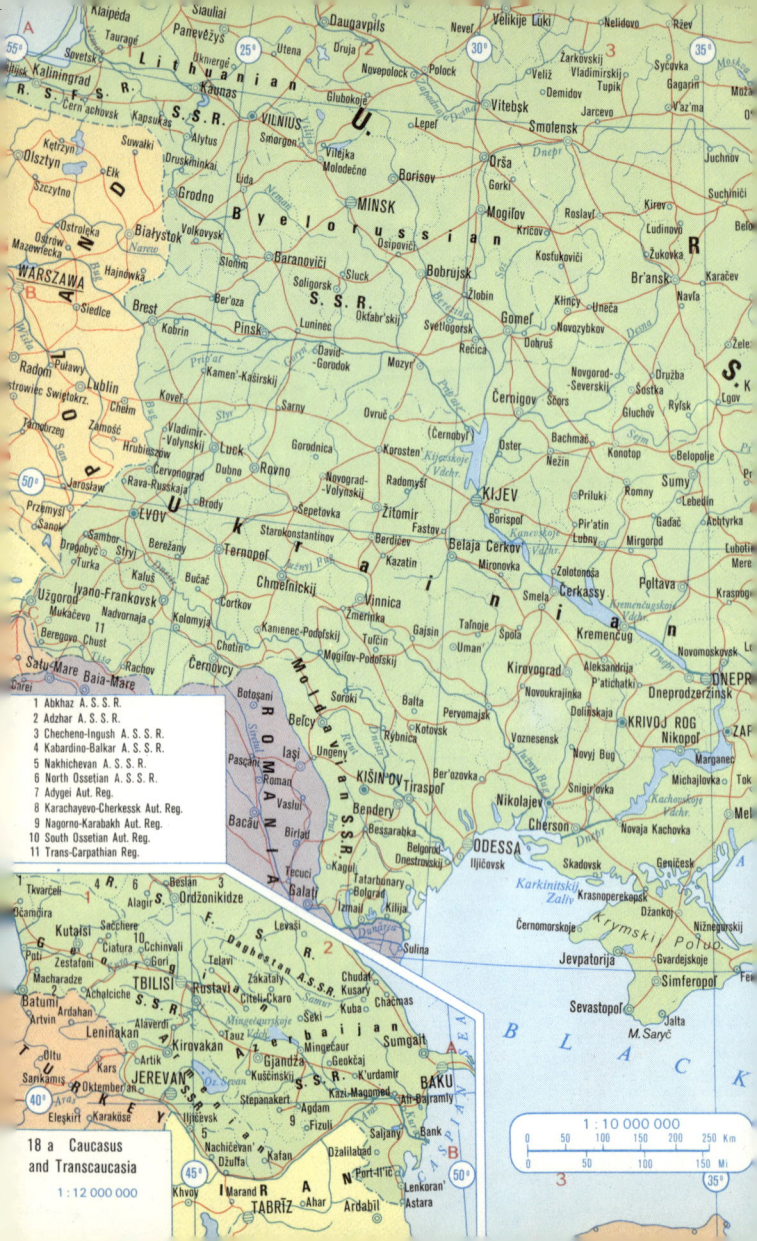

1. Abkhaz A.S.S.R.
2. Adzhar A.S.S.R.
3. Checheno-Ingush A.S.S.R.
4. Kabardino-Balkar A.S.S.R.
5. Nakhichevan A.S.S.R.
6. North Ossetian A.S.S.R.
7. Adygei Aut. Reg.
8. Karachayevo-Cherkessk Aut. Reg.
9. Nagorno-Karabakh Aut. Reg.
10. South Ossetian Aut. Reg.
11. Trans-Carpathian Reg.

18 a Caucasus and Transcaucasia
1 : 12 000 000

1 : 10 000 000

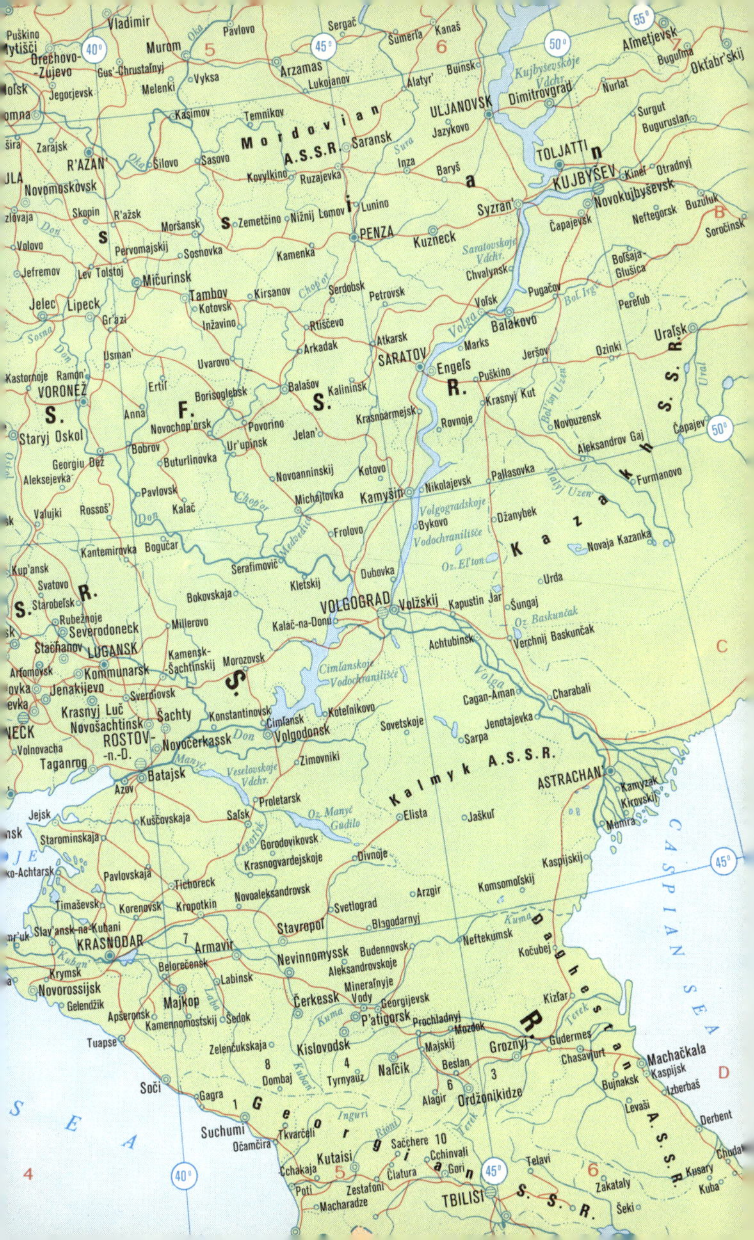

Puškino
Mytišči
Vladimir
Pavlovo
Sergač
Šumerľa
Kanaš
Aľmetjevsk
Orechovo-Zujevo
Murom
Oka
Arzamas
Lukojanov
Alatyr'
Buinsk
Kujbyševskoje Vdchr.
Bugulma
Okťabr'skij
Gus'-Chrustaľnyj
Melenki
Vyksa
Jegorjevsk
Dimitrovgrad
Nurlat
ULJANOVSK
Kasimov
Temnikov
Mordovian A.S.S.R.
Saransk
Jazykovo
Surgut
Buguruslan
Zarajsk
R'AZAN'
Šilovo
Sasovo
Sura
Inza
TOLJATTI
Novomoskovsk
Kovylkino
Ruzajevka
Baryš
KUJBYŠEV
Kineľ
Otradnyj
Novokujbyševsk
Skopin
R'ažsk
Zemetčino
Nižnij Lomov
Lunino
Syzran'
Neftegorsk
Buzuluk
Don
Moršansk
PENZA
Kuzneck
Čapajevsk
Soročinsk
Volovo
Pervomajskij
Sosnovka
Kamenka
Saratovskoje Vdchr.
Jefremov
Lev Tolstoj
Mičurinsk
Chvalynsk
Boľšaja-Glušica
Serdobsk
Chop'or
Tambov
Kirsanov
Petrovsk
Pugačov
Boľ. Irgiz
Jelec
Lipeck
Kotovsk
Voľsk
Pereľub
Gr'azi
Inžavino
Rtiščevo
Balakovo
Sosna
Arkadak
Atkarsk
Volga
Uraľsk
Usman'
Uvarovo
SARATOV
Marks
Jeršov
Ozinki
Kastornoje
Ramon'
Engeľs
Ertiľ
Borisoglebsk
Balašov
Kalininsk
Puškino
VORONEŽ
Krasnyj Kut
Ural
Boľšoj Uzen'
Anna
Povorino
Krasnoarmejsk
Rovnoje
Novouzensk
Čapajev
Staryj Oskol
Novochop'orsk
Jelan'
Bobrov
Ur'upinsk
Aleksandrov Gaj
Georgiu Dež
Buturlinovka
Novoanninskij
Kotovo
Furmanovo
Aleksejevka
Pavlovsk
Michajlovka
Kamyšin
Nikolajevsk
Pallasovka
Malyj Uzen'
Valujki
Rossoš'
Kalač
Volgogradskoje Vodochranilišče
Bykovo
Džanybek
Frolovo
Medvedica
Kantemirovka
Bogučar
Novaja Kazanka
Kup'ansk
Serafimovič
Oz. El'ton
Svatovo
Kletskij
Dubovka
Urda
Starobeľsk
Bokovskaja
VOLGOGRAD
Volžskij
Kapustin Jar
Šungaj
Rubežnoje
Kalač-na-Donu
Oz. Baskunčak
Severodoneck
Millerovo
Verchnij Baskunčak
Stachanov
LUGANSK
Achtubinsk
Kamensk-Šachtinskij
Morozovsk
Artomovsk
Kommunarsk
Cimlanskoje Vodochranilišče
Jenakijevo
Sverdlovsk
Charabali
Krasnyj Luč
Šachty
Konstantinovsk
Koteľnikovo
Cagan-Aman
Novošachtinsk
Cimlansk
Sovetskoje
Jenotajevka
ROSTOV-n.-D.
Novočerkassk
Volgodonsk
Sarpa
Volnovacha
Taganrog
Zimovniki
Manyč
Veselovskoje Vdchr.
Kalmyk A.S.S.R.
Batajsk
ASTRACHAN'
Kamyzak
Azov
Proletarsk
Kirovskij
Jejsk
Kuščovskaja
Saľsk
Oz. Manyč Gudilo
Elista
Jaškuľ
Olinja
Starominskaja
Jegorlyk
Gorodovikovsk
Divnoje
Krasnogvardejskoje
Primorsko-Achtarsk
Pavlovskaja
Tichoreck
Kaspijskij
Novoaleksandrovsk
Arzgir
Komsomoľskij
Timaševsk
Korenovsk
Kropotkin
Svetlograd
Kuma
Slav'ansk-na-Kubani
Stavropoľ
Blagodarnyj
Dagestan A.S.S.R.
KRASNODAR
Armavir
Neftekumsk
Kuban'
Nevinnomyssk
Budennovsk
Kočubej
Krymsk
Belorečensk
Aleksandrovskoje
Labinsk
Novorossijsk
Mineraľnyje Vody
Laba
Gelendžik
Majkop
Čerkessk
Georgijevsk
Kizľar
Apšeronsk
Kamennomostskij
Sedok
P'atigorsk
Prochladnyj
Terek
Mozdok
Tuapse
Zelenčukskaja
Kislovodsk
Majskij
Groznyj
Gudermes
Chasavjurt
Machačkala
Kaspijsk
Dombaj
Tyrnyauz
Nalčik
Beslan
Soči
Alagir
Ordžonikidze
Bujnaksk
Izberbaš
Gagra
Inguri
Georgian S.S.R.
Levaši
Suchumi
Rioni
Derbent
Očamčira
Tkvarčeli
Sačchere
Cchinvali
Telavi
Chudat
Kutaisi
Kusary
Cchakaja
Čiatura
Gori
Zakataly
Kuba
Poti
Zestafoni
TBILISI
Macharadze
Šeki
S. F. S. R.
Kazakh S. S. R.
CASPIAN SEA
SEA

ASIA

The Asian continent lies in the northern hemisphere, although in the south-east some Indonesian islands belong to the southern hemisphere. On its western side Asia is linked to Europe, which is in fact a gigantic peninsula of Asia (Eurasia). In the south-west the boundary with Africa runs along the Isthmus of Suez (120 km long) on the Sinai Peninsula. The name "Asia" derives from the Accadian word "Asu", meaning "Land of the East, the Dawn".

Asia covers an **area of 44,410,000 sq.km**, including the islands and takes up 29.7% of the world's land surface, making it the largest continent. It has **3,077 mn. inhabitants** (1988, including the Asian part of the U.S.S.R.), i.e. 60.2% of the world's population with a density of 69 persons per sq.km.

Geographical position — northernmost point of the continent: Cape Mys Čeľuskin (U.S.S.R.) 77°43′ N.Lat. (of the entire continent: Cape Mys Arktičeskij /O. Komsomolec island/ in Severnaja Zemľa 81°16′ N.Lat.); southernmost: Cape Tg. Buru on the Malay Peninsula 1°25′ N.Lat. (island Pulau Roti in the Indonesian Lesser Sunda Is. 11° S.Lat.); westernmost: Cape Baba Burnu in Asia Minor 26°03′ E.Long. and easternmost: Cape Mys Dežneva on the peninsula Čukotskij Poluostrov (U.S.S.R.) 169°40′ W.Long. (O. Ratmanova island in the Diomede Is. in the Bering Strait 169°02′ W.Long).

The coast line of Asia is very varied and is 69,000 km long (excluding the offshore islands). Largest peninsulas: Arabian (area: 2,780,000 sq.km), India (1,850,000 sq.km), Indo-China (1,450,000 sq.km), Asia Minor (580,000 sq.km), Tajmyr (420,000 sq.km), and Kamčatka (275,000 sq.km). There are numerous islands; the largest include: The Greater Sunda Is. (area: 1,548,600 sq.km), the Japanese Is. (377,458 sq.km), the Philippines (297,413 sq.km), the Lesser Sunda Is. (91,860 sq.km) and the Moluccas (Maluku, 74,500 sq.km).

The complex **geological and tectonic structure** of Asia is the main reason for its varied relief. The basic geological structure is formed by Primary continental tables: the Siberian table in the North and the Chinese table in the East, the Indian in the South and the Arabian in the South-West. **The surface.** The vertical features of the Asian continent differ enormously. The average height above sea level is 960 m, i.e. a figure higher than that for any other continent, with the exception of Antarctica. About 26% of Asia is lowland, not higher than 200 m, but 14% of the land is above 2,000 m. Huge mountain ranges cross the continent in two zones which link up in the Pamir in Central Asia (7,719 m). The first zone, a system of folded ranges of the Alpine-Himalayan type, stretches from Asia Minor across Central Asia, around the Pamir and Indo-China as far as Sumatra and Java. This includes: the Armenian Plateau (5,165 m), the Caucasus (Boľ. Kavkaz, 5,642 m), the Iranian Mountains (5,670 m) and the Hindu Kush (7,708 m) which adjoins the Pamir. The Karakoram Range (Godwin Austen, 8,611 m) runs in a south-easterly direction from the Pamir, as well as the mighty range of the Himalayas (11 summits above 8,000 m), with the highest mountain in the world, Mt. Everest (8,848 m). The Kunlunshan (Ulugh Muztagh, 7,723 m) lies to the east of the Pamir. The second zone of mountains stretches in a north-easterly direction from the Pamir as far as the peninsula of Čukotskij Pol.: Tien Shan (7,439 m), Altai (4,506 m), and the lower Sayan Mts., Stanovoj Chr. and Chr. Čerskogo (3,147 m). The Pacific zone of Tertiary mountains lies in eastern Asia, with high volcanic activity (130 volcanoes) and frequent earthquakes. - Greatest plains: Western Siberian (Zapadno-Sibirskaja Nizm.), Indo-Gangetic, Great Plain of China. The Dead Sea (−400 m) is the lowest point and Lake O. Bajkal the deepest crypto-depression (−1,286 m below sea level).

The river system. Over 40% of central and south-west Asia has no outlet to the sea. The Siberian rivers carry most water and flow into the Arctic Ocean (the longest is the Ob'-Irtyš, 5,410 km, which has a drainage basin of 2,975,000 sq.km and a mean annual discharge of 12,600 cub.m per sec). Monsoon rivers are an important source of water for agriculture. They include Asia's longest river, the Yangtze (Changjiang), 5,520 km, drainage basin 1,942,000 sq.km, and a mean annual discharge of 31,000 cub.m per sec). The rivers in the tropical belt, especially on the islands, have ample water throughout the year. The largest among the many **lakes** is the Caspian Sea covering 371,000 sq.km (depth 1,025 m), −28 m below sea level.

Large parts of Asia have a continental **climate;** the very low winter temperatures and hot inland summers cause oscillations in the atmospheric circulation. The north of Asia is influenced by the cold Arctic air and has heavy frosts. The lowest absolute temperature, −78°C, was measured at Ojm'akon in Siberia. Almost two thirds of Asia lie in the temperate belt and the Asian Plateau is a region of extreme drought. The south of Asia has a tropical climate: the south-west is dry with high temperatures; the highest absolute temperature, 53°C, was measured at Jacobābād in Pakistan; in south-east, in particular on the islands, it is hot and damp with only minor variations in temperature. The monsoon rains are a life-giving force bringing an average precipitation of 2,500 mm per year. Maximum rainfall was recorded at Cherrapunji (India) 11,013 mm a year and the minimum at Al-'Aqabah (Jordan) 24 mm annually.

Mean January and July temperatures in °C (and annual rainfall in mm) are as follows: Verchojansk −48.9 and 15.3 (142), Sapporo −6.2 and 19.4 (1,063), Beijing −4.7 and 25.6 (610), Ulaanbaatar −26.7 and 17.2 (101), Alma-Ata −7.4 and 23.3 (575), İstanbul 5.6 and 23.1 (679), Baghdād 9.6 and 34.7 (156), Tehrān 2.1 and 29.7 (250), Multān 13.5 and 36.1 (161), Bombay 23.8 and 27.4 (1,878), Calcutta 19.6 and 28.9 (1,625), Cherrapunji 11.7 and 20.4 (11,013), Hong Kong 15.6 and 27.9 (2,177), Tōkyō 3.2 and 25.0 (1,575), Manila 24.6 and 26.9 (2,123), Krung Thep 26.1 and 28.6 (1,420), Ar-Riyāḍ 14.4 and 33.8 (82), Aden 25.4 and 32.5 (41), Colombo 26.2 and 27.2 (2,236), Singapore 26.1 and 27.4 (2,413), Jakarta 25.9 and 26.5 (1,784), Kupang 26.8 and 25.3 (1,458).

The vegetation of Asia falls into two zones. First, the extensive Holarctic realm in the north, west and south-west which includes, from north to south, tundra with woodland, typical taiga with coniferous forest, mixed forest, broad-leaved deciduous forest, the Sino-Japanese region of evergreen plants, Central Asian wooded steppe, grassland steppe, semi-desert with scrub, Mediterranean evergreen maquis, and the North-African-Indian desert region with xerophilous scrub. Second, the smaller Paleo-tropical realm in the south and south-east of Asia, which includes semi-desert with sparse thorn forest, dry deciduous tropical forest and grassland savanna in India and monsoon tropophilous woodland, subtropical forest, evergreen tropical rain forest and mangrove swamp, etc., in India and Southeastern Asia. — **The fauna** belongs to two zoogeographical realms: the larger is Palearctic and poorer in species (e.g. polar bear, ermine, reindeer, wolf, tiger, stag, sheep, forest and water fowl, pheasant, vulture, bustard, numerous rodents, fresh water fish, insects, etc.). The smaller Indo-Malaysian is richer in species and older in evolution (e.g. monkeys, rare orangutans, Indian elephant, rhinoceros, buffalo, leopard, tiger, tapir, pheasant, peacock, python, crocodile, flying gurnard, and large numbers of insects and other fishes).

LONGEST RIVERS

Name	Length in km	River Basin in sq.km
Changjiang /Yangtze/	5,520	1,942,000
Ob' (-Irtyš)	5,410	2,975,000
Huanghe /Yellow/	4,845	772,000
Mekong /Lancangjiang/	4,500	810,000
Irtyš	4,422	1,595,680
Amur (-Šilka, -Onon)	4,416	1,855,000
Lena	4,400	2,490,000
Jenisej	4,092	2,580,000
Indus /Sindh/	3,190	960,000
Syrdarja (-Naryn)	3,019	219,000
Nižn'aja Tunguska (-Nepa)	2,989	473,000
Brahmaputra /Yaluzangbujiang/	2,960	935,000
Salween /Nujiang/	2,820	325,000
Euphrates /Al-Furāt, Firat/	2,760	765,000
Talimuhe /Tarim/	2,750	1,210,000
Ganga - Padma /Ganges/	2,700	1,125,000
Vil'uj	2,650	454,000
Amudarja (-P'andž)	2,620	227,000
Kolyma	2,513	647,000

LARGEST LAKES

Name	Area in sq.km	Greatest Depth in m	Altitude in m
Caspian Sea[+]	371,000	1,025	−28
Aral'skoje More[+]	64,115	67	53
O. Bajkal	31,500	1,620	455
O. Balchaš	18,200	26	340
D.-y. Orümiyeh[+]	7,500	15	1,275
O.Issyk-Kul'[+]	6,280	702	1,609
Tônlé Sab	5,700	10	15
O. Tajmyr	4,560	26	6
Qinghai /Kukunuoer/[+]	4,460	38	3,250
O. Chanka	4,200	10	68
Hongzehu	3,780	.	3
Dongtinghu	3,750	.	25
Van Gölü[+]	3,738	25	1,662
Uvs- Nuur[+]	3,350	.	759
Poyanghu	3,150	.	15
Chövsgöl Nuur	2,620	.	1,645
Luobubo /Lop Nor/[+]	2,600	.	780
Dead Sea[+]	980	399	−400

[+]Salt Lake

LARGEST ISLANDS

Name	Area in sq.km	Name	Area in sq.km	Name	Area in sq.km
Borneo (Kalimantan)	746,546	Mindanao	98,692	Hainandao	33,670
Sumatera	433,800	Hokkaidō	78,073	Timor	33,615
Honshū	227,414	Sachalin	76,400	Seram	18,625
Sulawesi (Celebes)	179,416	Sri Lanka (Ceylon)	65,607	Shikoku	18,256
Jawa (Java)	126,700	Kyūshū	36,554	Halmahera	17,800
Luzon	106,983	Taiwan	35,961	Flores	15,600

HIGHEST MOUNTAINS

Name (Country)	Height in m	Name (Country)	Height in m
Mt. Everest /Sagarmatha, Zhumulangmafeng/ (Nepal, China)	8,848	Himālchūli (Nepal)	7,893
Godwin Austen /Qogir/ /K2/ (China-Pakistan)	8,611	Nuptse (Nepal)	7,855
Kānchenjunga (Nepal-India)	8,586	Masherbrum (Pak.)	7,821
Lhotse (Nepal-China)	8,516	Nandā Devī (India)	7,816
Makālu (Nepal-China)	8,463	Rakaposhi (Pak.)	7,789
Lhotse-Shar (Nepal-China)	8,430	Distegil Sar (Pak.)	7,785
Cho Oyu (China-Nepal)	8,201	Batura (Pak.)	7,785
Dhaulāgiri (Nepal)	8,167	Kāmēt (India-China)	7,756
Manāslu (Nepal)	8,163	Namuchabawashan (China)	7,755
Nānga Parbat (Pak.)	8,125	Ulugh Muztagh (China)	7,723
Annapūrna (Nepal)	8,091	Gonggeershan (China)	7,719
Gasherbrum (Pak.-China)	8,068	Tirich Mīr (Pak.)	7,708
Phalchan Kangrī /Broad Pk./ (Pak.-China)	8,047	Pik Kommunizma (U.S.S.R.)	7,495
Xixabangma (China)	8,013	Nowshāk (Afghan.)	7,492
		Pik Pobedy (U.S.S.R.)	7,439

ACTIVE VOLCANOES

Name (Country)	Altitude in m	Latest eruption
V. Kľučevskaja Sopka (U.S.S.R.)	4,750	1984
Gunung Kerintji (Indon.)	3,805	1968
Gunung Rinjani (Indon.)	3,726	1966
Gunung Semeru (Indon.)	3,676	1981
Korjakskaja Sopka (U.S.S.R.)	3,456	1957
Gunung Slamet (Indon.)	3,428	1967
Galunggung (Indon.)	2,830	1982

FAMOUS NATIONAL PARKS

Name (Country)	Area in sq.km
Kronockij Zap. (U.S.S.R.)	9,770
Altajskij Zap. (U.S.S.R.)	8,638
Issik-Kulskij Zap. (U.S.S.R.)	7,816
Taman Negara (Malaysia)	4,360
Gunung Leuser (Indon.)	4,165
Sagarmatha (Mt. Everest, Nepal)	1,243
Fuji-Hakone (Jap.)	948

ARCTIC OCEAN
NORWEGIAN SEA
BARENTS SEA
NORTH SEA
British Is.
London
Scandinavia
Svalbard
Spitsbergen
Vestspitsbergen
Zemľa Fr. Iosifa
M. Fligeli
M. Arktičeskij
Severnaja Zemľa
M. Čeľuskin
MORE LAPTEVYCH
Nordkinn
Murmansk
Koľskij Pol.
Novaja Zemľa
KARSKOJE MORE
Dikson
Pol. Tajmyr
G. of Bothnia
BALTIC SEA
Oslo
Stockholm
Helsinki
Riga
Leningrad
Berlin
Praha
Warszawa
Wien
Alps
4807
Carpathian Mts.
2655
București
Istanbul
Kijev
Srednerusskaja Vozvyš.
Moskva
Volga
Dnepr
Don
Volgograd
Astrachan'
Kama
Ural
Uraľskije Gory
1894
Narodnaja
1640
Pečora
Ob
Salechard
Pol. Jamal
Dudinka
1701
Kamen'
Sredne-Sibirskoje Ploskogo
Nižn. Tunguska
Podkam. Tunguska
Jenisej
Lena
Zapadno-Sibirskaja Ravnina
SIB
Irtyš
Tobol
Išim
Omsk
Novosibirsk
O. Bajkal
455
Sayan Mts.
3491
Irkutsk
G. Munku Sardyk
G. Belucha
4506
Altai
Changajn Nu.
Ulaanba
BLACK SEA
Ankara
Asia Minor
Toros Dağ.
Cyprus
Boľ. Kavkaz
5642
G. El'brus
Baku
Büyük Ağri D.
5165
-28
CASPIAN SEA
-132
Plato Ust Urt
Araľskoje More
53
Syrdarja
Amudarja
Emba
O. Balchaš
Ili
Zhuangaerp.
Turanskaja Nizmen
Kyzylkum
Karakumy
Aschabad
Taškent
Alma-Ata
O. Issyk-Kuľ
Tien Shan
7439
Pik Pobedy
Pik Kommunizma
7495
Pamir
-154
Tulufanwadi
Lop Nur
Tarim Pendi
5934
Qiliansh.
Qinghai
MEDIT. S.
Suez Canal
Sinai Pen.
Bayrūt
Dead S.
-400
Euphrates
Tigris
Mesopotamia
Baghdād
Q.-ye Damāvand
Tehrān
5670
Alborz
Dasht-e Kavīr
Zagros
Plateau of Iran
4420
7708
Hindu Kush
Kābul
Godwin Austen
8611
Karakoram Ra.
Nanga Parbat
8125
Kunlunshan
Ulugh Muztagh
7723
TIBET
Tongtianhe
Huanghe
An-Nafūd
Arabian Pen.
Tropic of Cancer
Ar-Riyāḍ
Persian Gulf
Dubayy
J. ash-Shām
3018
G. of Oman
Ra's al-Hadd
Ar-Rab' al-Khālī
Hadūr Shu'ayb
3760
Adan
RED SEA
Helmand
Jacobābād
Indus
Sutlej
Karāchi
Thar Desert
Delhi
Indo-Gangetic Plain
Ganga
Himalayas
8167
Dhaulāgiri
Mt. Everest
8848
Lhasa
Brahmaputra
Gonggash
7590
INDIA
Narmada
Calcutta
Cherrapunji
3053
Salween
Irrawaddy
ARABIAN SEA
Gulf of Aden
R. Asir
Suqutrā
Somali Pen.
R. Hafūn
Bombay
West Ghāts
Godāvari
Krishna
Deccan
East Ghāts
Madras
Bay of Bengal
Rangoon
Andaman Is.
ANDAMAN SEA
Krung
Phnum
G. of Thai
Malay
5824
5803
Lakshadweep
2695
C. Comorin
Maldives
Sri Lanka
Colombo
2524
Pidurutalagala
3835
Nicobar Is.
Str. of Malacca
Sumat
Kep. Mentawai
G. Kerin
Equator
INDIAN OCEAN
Chagos Is.
Madagascar
1 : 65 000 000
0 300 600 900 1 200 1 500 Km
0 200 400 600 800 1 000 Mi

19a Hong Kong and Macau
1 : 2 000 000

19b Malay Peninsula
1 : 15 000 000

1. Johor
2. Kedah
3. Kelantan
4. Melaka
5. Negeri Sembilan
6. Pahang
7. Perak
8. Perlis
9. Pinang
10. Selangor
11. Terengganu

19c Cyprus
1 : 4 500 000

Attila Line since 27.7.1976

map 19

ASIA

Country	Area in sq.km	Population year 1988	Density per sq.km	Capital
Afghanistan	652,090	15,513,000	24	Kābul
Bahrain	688	430,000	625	Al-Manāmah
Bangladesh	143,998	104,532,000	726	Dacca
Bhutan	47,000	1,451,000	31	Thimbu
Brunei	5,765	241,000	42	B. S. Begawan
Burma / Myanma	676,552	39,966,000	59	Rangoon
China (incl. Taiwan)	9,596,961	1,103,983,000	115	Beijing
Cyprus	9,251	687,000	74	Levkosia/Nicosia
Egypt-Sinai Peninsula	58,824	200,493[1]	3.4	Al-Qāhirah
Ghaza	378	656,000[2]	1,735	
Hong Kong (U.K.)	1,071	5,681,000	5,304	Victoria
India	3,287,590	796,596,000	242	New Delhi
Indonesia (incl. East Timor)	2,027,087	174,951,000	86	Jakarta
Iran	1,648,100	52,522,000	32	Tehrān
Iraq	438,446	17,250,000	39	Baghdād
Israel	20,770	4,478,000[3]	216	Yerushalayim
Japan	377,815	122,613,000	25	Tōkyō
Jordan	97,740	3,943,000	40	'Ammān
Kampuchea	181,035	7,869,000	43	Phnum Pénh
Korea, Democratic People's Rep.of	120,538	21,902,000	182	P'yŏngyang
Korea, Republic of	99,022	41,975,000	424	Sŏul
Kuwait	17,818	1,958,000	110	Al-Kuwayt
Laos	236,800	3,875,000	16	Viangchan
Lebanon	10,452	2,828,000	271	Bayrūt
Macau (Port.)	16.9	444,000	26,272	Macau
Malaysia	329,749	16,921,000	51	Kuala Lumpur
Maldives	298	202,000	678	Male
Mongolia	1,566,500	2,092,000	1.3	Ulaanbaatar
Nepal	147,181	18,234,000	124	Kātmāndu
Oman	212,457	1,377,000	6.5	Masqat
Pakistan	803,942	105,409,000	131	Islāmābād
Philippines	297,413	58,721,307	197	Manila
Qatar	11,437	369,000[1]	32	Ad-Dawhah
Saudi Arabia	2,153,168	14,016,000	6.5	Ar-Riyād
Singapore	620	2,670,000[3]	4,306	Singapore
Sri Lanka	65,610	16,587,000	253	Colombo
Syria	185,180	11,338,000	61	Dimashq
Taiwan (China)	36,174	19,672,000	544	T'aipei
Thailand	514,121	54,536,000	106	Krung Thep
Turkey	779,452	52,422,000	67	Ankara
U.S.S.R. – Asiatic part	16,831,000	81,350,000	4.8	Moskva
United Arab Emirates	83,657	1,501,000	18	Abu Zaby
Vietnam	332,560	64,227,000	193	Ha-Nôi
Yemen	531,869	11,109,000	21	San'á

[1]) year 1986, [2]) year 1987, [3]) year 1989

Asia has a **population of 3,077 mn.** (1988), which is roughly 60% of the total population of the world, with a density of 69 persons per sq.km. Its geographical distribution is very uneven. Large desert regions, tundra and forest zones are almost uninhabited. The fertile agricultural lands of China, India, Bangladesh and elsewhere, and the industrial areas of Japan, are among the most densely populated regions in the world. Extreme density of population is found in the smallest countries: Macau 24,500, Hong Kong 5,334, Singapore 4,285; among other countries: Bangladesh 685, Bahrain 630, Maldives 606, Rep. of Korea 418 and Japan 320 (1985).

The average **population increase** is highest (1980–85) in Qatar 6.8%, United Arab Emirates 6.1% and Kuwait 5.5%. The highest birth rate is in Yemen (48.6 per 1,000), Afghanistan (48.4 per 1,000), the highest death rate in Afghanistan (27.3 per 1,000), Kampuchea (19.7 per 1,000). The average life expectancy in southern Asia is 53 years and 68 years in eastern Asia (1980–85). There are several hundred nations and nationalities in Asia. The country with the highest population is China. Asia has an ancient tradition of urban settlement. The highest percentages of urban dwelling are in Japan (76%) and Israel 90%). There are (incl. the U.S.S.R.) more than 90 **towns** and urban agglomerations with over 1 mn. people. The largest are: Sŏul, Tōkyō, Bombay, Jakarta, Shanghai, Tehrān, Beijing, Tiajin, Karāchi, Delhi.

Economy: Asia is an important source of raw materials, primarily petroleum, ores, textile raw materials, skins and hides, oil-producing crops and fruit. In the majority of Asian countries agriculture remains the most important industry. 55.5% of the working population worked in agriculture, tilling 455 mn. hectares of arable land (1983). Not quite one third of the world total of arable land is in Asia, which is far less than its share of the world's population. Industry is located unevenly on the continent, and in the majority of countries industrial production is in its infancy. Exceptions to this include Japan, a leading industrial world power, Israel and the Republic of Korea.

page 90

AFGHANISTAN

De Afghanistan Democrateek Jamhuriat, area 652,090 sq.km, population 15,513,000 (1988), **republic** (President Maj.-Gen. Najibullah since 1987).

Administrative units: 28 provinces. **Capital:** Kábul 913,164 inhab. (1982, with agglom. 1,127,417); **other towns** (1982, in 1,000 inhab.): Qandahár 198, Herát 155, Mazár-e Sharif 115. **Population:** Afghans 60%, Tadzhiks 25–30%, Uzbeks etc. Average annual rate of population increase 2.6% (1973–83); urban population 17.0% (1983). 77% of the economically active inhabitants engaged in agriculture (1981). – **Currency:** afgháni = 100 puls.
Economy: predominantly agricultural country. Arable land 12.4% of the land area. **Agriculture** (1983, in 1,000 tonnes): wheat 3,750, rice 650, barley 450, maize (corn) 1,000, millet, sesame, cotton – seed 30, – lint 15; sugar beet 20, vegetables, fruit, grapes 510, raisins 88; livestock (1983, in 1,000 head): cattle 3,800, sheep 20,000 (of which more than one third are karakul sheep), camels 250, goats 3,000; hides and skins, wool; roundwood 6.7 mn. cub.m (1983). **Mining** (1983): coal, natural gas 99,482 TJ, salt 10,000 tonnes. Textile and food industries. – **Communications:** roads 18,752 km. Civil aviation: 3.8 mn. km flown, 220,000 passengers carried (1984). – **Exports:** natural gas, karakul skins, sheep, wool, cotton, carpets, raisins, fruit. Chief trading partners: U.S.S.R., India, Japan, Pakistan, the United Kingdom.

BAHRAIN

Dowlat al-Bahrain, area 688 sq.km, population 430,000 (1988), **emirate** (Amir Shaikh Isa bin Sulman Al-Khalifa since 1961).
Capital: Al-Manámah 108,684 inhabitants (1981). – **Currency:** Bahrain dinar = 1,000 fils.
Economy (1983, in 1,000 tonnes): dates 43, pearl fishery, fish catch 6.8; mining of petroleum 2,049, natural gas 125,860 TJ, petroleum refineries, production of aluminium 171.7, motor spirit 653, jet fuel 1,269; electricity 2,026 mn. kWh (1983). – **Communications:** roads 700 km, passenger cars 60,100. – **Exports:** petroleum and petroleum products, aluminium, dates, pearls. Chief trading partners: United Kingdom, Japan, U.S.A., Fed. Rep. of Germany, Saudi Arabia.

BANGLADESH

People's Republic of Bangladesh, area 143,998 sq.km, population 104,532,000 (1988), **republic, member of the Commonwealth** (President Lieut.-Gen. Hossain Mohammad Ershad since 1983).
Administrative units: 21 districts. **Capital:** Dacca 3,458,602 inhab. (1981); **other towns** (in 1,000 inhab.): Chittagong 1,388, Khulna 623, Nárayanganj 298, Rájsháhí 171. **Population:** Bengals. **Density** 685 persons per sq.km; average annual rate of population increase 2.4% (1973–83); urban population 17% (1983). 83% of the economically active inhabitants engaged in agriculture (1983). – **Currency:** taka = 100 poisha.
Economy (1983): predominantly an agricultural country. Arable land 63.5% of the land area. **Agriculture – crops** (in 1,000 tonnes): rice 21,700, wheat 1,095, sugarcane 7,307, jute 908, bananas 678, teá 45, tobacco 52, vegetables, pineapples 160; **livestock** (in 1,000 head): cattle 36,000, buffaloes 1,700, sheep 1,090, goats 12,000; fish catch 728,500 tonnes. **Mining:** coal, crude petroleum, natural gas 78,800 TJ, salt 249,000 tonnes. Electricity: 3,758 mn. kWh. **Production** (1983): jute fabrics 1,235 mn. sq.m, sugar 178,000 tonnes. Textile and food industries. – **Communications** (1983): railways 4,473 km, roads 22,471 km. Merchant shipping 367,000 GRT. Civil aviation: 11.5 mn. km flown. **Exports:** jute and jute products, hides and skins, tea. Chief trading partners: U.S.A., Japan, Singapore, United Kingdom, China.

BHUTAN

Druk-yul, area 47,000 sq.km, population 1,451,000 (1988), **monarchy** (King Jigme Singhye Wangchuck since 1972).
Capital: Thimbu 20,000 inhab. (1981), winter seat Paro. – **Currency:** ngultrum = 100 chetrums.
Economy: arable land 2%, meadows and permanent crops 4.6%, forests 69.4%. Agriculture in the valleys (1983, in 1,000 tonnes): rice 60, maize (corn) 83, millet, barley; cattle raising in the mountains (1983, in 1,000 head): cattle 312, sheep 43, horses. Mining of coal, handicrafts. – **Exports:** wood, rice, coal, animal products.

BRUNEI

The Sultanate of Brunei, area 5,765 sq.km, population 241,400 (1988), **sultanate, member of the Commonwealth** (Sultan Hasan al Bolkiah Muizzaddin Waddaulah since 1967).
Capital: Bandar Seri Begawan 49,902 inhab. (1981). **Population:** Malays 65%, Chinese, Dayaks and others. Average annual rate of population increase 5.6% (1973–83). – **Currency:** Brunei dollar = 100 cents.
Economy (1983, in 1,000 tonnes): rice 10, bananas 5, coconuts, natural rubber, rare timber; raising of buffaloes 15,000 head, pigs 15,000 head. Fish catch 3,100 tonnes. **Mining** of petroleum 8.1 mn. tonnes, natural gas 339,499 TJ (1983). Petrochemical industry. – **Communications:** roads 1,474 km, passenger cars 62,500 (1983). – **Exports:** petroleum and petroleum products 95%, natural gas, natural rubber, rare timber.

BURMA / MYANMAR

Pyidaungsu Myanma Naingngandaw, area 676,552 sq.km, population 39,966,000 (1988), **federal republic** (Head of State Gen. Saw Maung since 1988).
Administrative units: 7 states and 7 provinces. **Capital:** Rangoon 2,458,712 inhab. (1983); **other towns** (in 1,000

1	BAHRAIN	7	KUWAIT
2	BANGLADESH	8	LEBANON
3	BHUTAN	9	QATAR
4	DEM. PEOPLE'S REP. OF KOREA	10	REP. OF KOREA
5	ISRAEL	11	SINGAPORE
6	JORDAN	12	SYRIA
		13	UNITED ARAB EMIRATES

1 : 65 000 000

0 300 600 900 1 200 1 500 Km
0 200 400 600 800 1 000 Mi

20 a Southern India and Sri Lanka   1 : 15 000 000

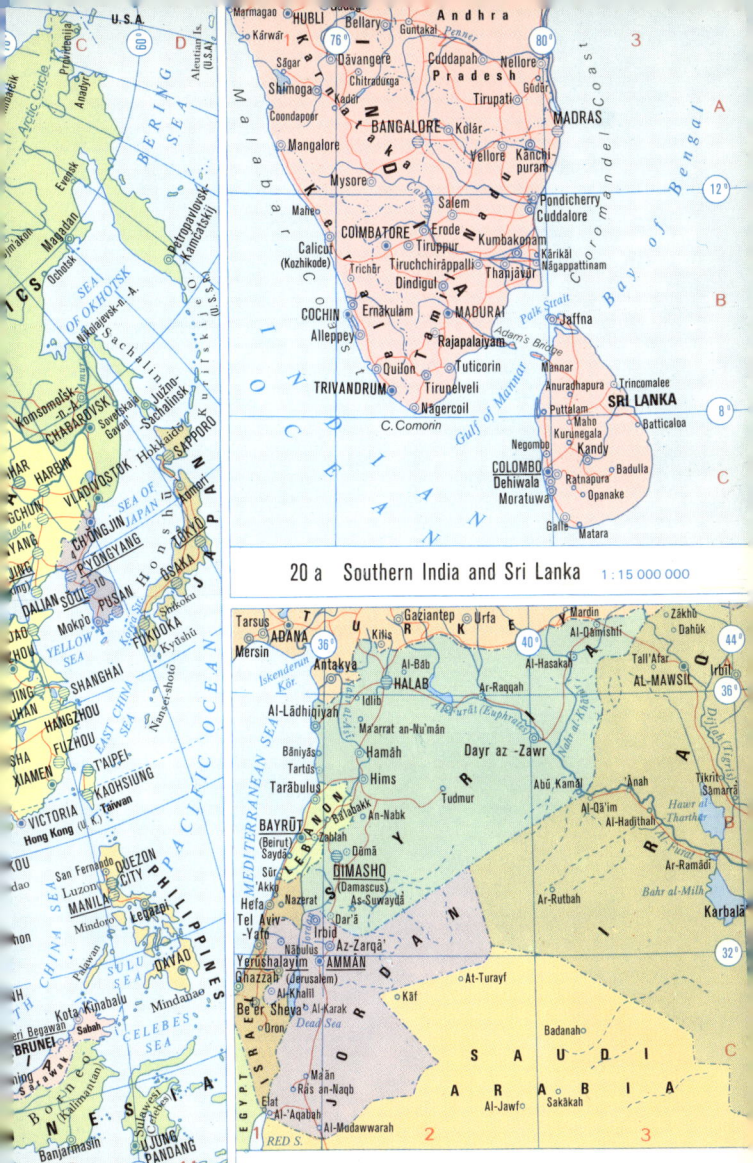

20 b Levantine Countries   1 : 12 500 000

inhab.): Mandalay 533, Bassein 336, Henzada 284, Pegu 260, Myingyan 220, Moulmein 220. **Population:** Burmese, minorities: Karens, Shans, Kachins and others. **Density** 56 persons per sq.km; average annual rate of population increase 2% (1973–83); urban population 29% (1983). 50% of the economically active inhabitants engaged in agriculture (1983). – **Currency:** kyat = 100 pyas.
Economy: predominantly an agricultural country with extraction industry. Arable land 14.9%, forests 47.5% of the land area. **Agriculture** (1983, in 1,000 tonnes): rice 14,500, millet 119, sugarcane 3,135, groundnuts 691, cotton, jute 45, vegetables, fruit, tobacco 55, teak, natural rubber 16; livestock (1983, in 1,000 head): cattle 9,400, buffaloes 2,150, pigs 2,900, sheep 260, goats 770, fish catch 585,800 tonnes. **Mining** (1983, in 1,000 tonnes): crude petroleum 1,493, natural gas 18,563 TJ, lead, zinc, copper, nickel, silver 16 tonnes, tungsten 738 tonnes, tin 1.6, salt, precious stones. Food and textile industries. Production of woven cotton fabrics 91 mn. m; electricity 1,872 mn. kWh.
Communications (1982): railways 4,473 km, roads 22,471 km, passenger cars 47,800. Civil aviation: 6.7 mn. km flown, 515,000 passengers carried. – **Exports:** rice, teak, ores, vegetable oil, natural rubber, cotton, jute. Chief trading partners: Japan, Singapore, Indonesia, United Kingdom, Fed. Rep. of Germany, China, India.

CHINA

Zhonghua Renmin Gonghe Guo – People's Republic of China, area (including Taiwan) **9,596,961 sq.km, population 1,103,983,000** (1988), **people's republic** (Head of State and Chairman of the State Council Yang Zhangkun since 1988).

Administrative units: 23 provinces (incl. Taiwan), 5 autonomous regions, 3 self-administrated municipalities. **Capital:** Beijing 5,760,000 mn. inhab. (1984, with agglom. 9.29 mn. – 1982); other towns (1984, in 1,000 inhab.): Shanghai 6,880 (with agglom. 11,860), Tianjin 5,300 (with agglom. 7,790), Shenyang 4,130, Wuhan 3,340, Guangzhou 3,220, Chongqing 2,730, Harbin 2,590, Chengdu 2,540, Xi'an 2,280, Nanjing 2,210, Taiyuan 1,840, Changchun 1,810, Dalian 1,590, Kunming 1,480, Lanzhou 1,460, Jinan 1,390. **Population:** about 93% Chinese (Han), minorities Chuang, Uighur, Hui, Yi, Tibetans, Mongolians and others. **Density** 110 persons per sq.km; average annual rate of population increase 1.5% (1973–83); urban population 21% (1983). 57% of the economically active inhabitants work in agriculture. – **Currency:** renminbi juan = 10 chiao = 100 fen.
Economy: agricultural and industrial country. The main industrial region is eastern China (40% of industrial production – provinces Jiangsu, Anhui, Zhejiang, Fujian and self-administrated city of Shanghai). Large raw material resources and heavy industry in north-east China (provinces Liaoning, Jilin, Heilongjiang). **Agriculture** (1983): arable land 11%, meadows and pastures 29.8%, forests 14% of the land area. There are two or three harvests annually in the east and south-east of China: **Crops** (in 1,000 tonnes): rice 172,184 (leading world producer), wheat 81,392 (second world producer), millet 7,004 (second world producer), sorghum 8,369, barley 3,400, maize (corn) 64,135 (second world producer), oats 800, sweet potatoes 95,700 (leading world producer), potatoes 50,033 (second world producer), beans 1,745, peas 2,000, sugarcane 37,941, sugar beet 9,182, cotton – lint 4,637 – seed 9,282 (leading world producer), jute 1,019 (second world producer), flax, hemp, sisal, ramie, soya beans 9,770, sesame 350 (second world producer), coconuts 63, palm kernels 50, palm oil 200, tung oil 62 (leading world producer), rapeseed 4,288 (leading world producer), groundnuts 4,036 (second world producer), tea 429 (second world producer), tobacco 1,523 (leading world producer), oranges 1,203, tangerines 269, grapefruit 157, lemons 99, pineapples 295, mangoes 353, grapes 264, bananas 480, apples 2,740, pears 2,098 (leading world producer), tomatoes 4,559, walnuts 120, chestnuts 230, spices, vegetables 85.9 mn. tonnes. **Livestock** (in 1,000 head): horses 10,981 (leading world population), cattle 57,450, buffaloes 18,750 (second world population), camels 610, pigs 305,580 (highest world population), sheep 106,568, goats 75,397, asses 8,999, mules 4,464, chickens 1,144,000 (highest world population), silkworms. **Production** (in 1,000 tonnes): eggs 3,614, cattle hides 89, goatskins 60, wool 194, raw silk 38 (leading world producer), honey 125 (second world producer); fish catch 5,213,300 tonnes, roundwood 231.7 mn. cub.m, natural rubber 165.
Mining (1983, in 1,000 tonnes): coal 688,000 (leading world producer – provinces Shǎnxī, Shaanxī, Hebei, Liaoning), crude petroleum 106,068 (Heilongjiang, Shandong, northern China, north-west China), uranium, natural gas 475,162 TJ (provinces Hebei, Hubei), combustible shale (Liaoning), iron ore 56,834, manganese 479, antimony 10, cobalt, bauxite 1,500, copper 200, lead 160, magnesite 2,000, mercury 700, molybdenum 2.0, nickel, gold 59,097 kg, silver 78 tonnes, tin 17, tungsten 12.5 (leading world producer – provinces Jiangxi, Guangdong, Hunan), zinc 160, phosphates 12,500, potash, sulphur 200, asbestos 110, graphite 185 (second world producer), vanadium, salt 15,876. Electricity 351.44 billion kWh.
Production (1983, in 1,000 tonnes): pig iron 37,385, crude steel 40,136, cement 105,864, fertilizers 13,790, metal-working machines 120,000 units, motor vehicles 240,000 units, locomotives 486, woven cotton fabrics 17,968 sq.m, silk fabrics 1,092 mn. sq.m, newsprint 400, sugar raw 4,100, meat 16,862, cow milk 6,052, buffalo milk 1,500, butter 40.5, cheese 115.3.
Communications (1983): railways 51,100 km, roads 890,000 km, motor vehicles 2.8 mn. (of which 240,000 passenger cars. Merchant shipping 9,300,000 GRT. Civil aviation: 87.6 mn. km flown, 5 mn. passengers carried. Tourism 9.5 mn. visitors (1983). – **Exports:** rice, soya beans, cotton, fruit, tea, meat and meat products, eggs, sugar, edible oils, tung oil, silk; chemical and textile products, raw materials for the power industry, ores – especially tungsten and ore concentrates. Chief trading partners: Japan, Hong Kong, Fed. Rep. of Germany, U.S.A., U.S.S.R.

TAIWAN

Ta Chunghwa Min-Kuo, area **36,174 sq.km,** population **19,672,000** (1988), part of China under the control of the Kuomintang Nationalist Party (President Lee Teng Hui since 1988).

Capital: T'aipei 2,271,000 inhab. (1981); other towns (in 1,000 inhab.): Kaohsiung 1,227, T'aichung 607, T'ainan 595, T'aipeihsien 403; urban population 94.2%. – **Currency:** New Taiwan dollar = 100 cents.
Economy: arable land 8.9%, forests 64.5% of the land area. **Agriculture** (1982, in 1,000 tonnes): rice 2,483, sugarcane 8,275, manioc, soya beans, sweet potatoes 741, pineapples 145, bananas 203, tea 24; livestock (1983, in 1,000 head):

cattle 130, pigs 5,888, silkworms; fish catch 930,582 tonnes. **Mining** (in 1,000 tonnes): coal 2,384, crude petroleum, gold 223 kg, silver 2,232 kg, salt 262. Electricity 45,517 mn. kWh (1983). **Industry:** textile and chemical industries, electrical machinery, shipbuilding, engineering. **Production:** woven cotton fabrics 822 mn.m, sugar, cement. **Communications** (1982): railways 3,409 km, roads 17,522 km, passenger cars 619,500; merchant shipping 2,225,000 GRT. – **Exports:** textile products, plastic products, television and radio receivers, synthetic fibres.

CYPRUS

Kypriaki Dimokratia – Kıbrıs Cumhuriyeti, area 9,251 sq.km, population 687,000 (1988), **republic, member of the Commonwealth** (President George Vassiliou since 1988).

Administrative units: Since 27 July 1976 Cyprus has been divided into two parts: southern with Greek and northern with Turkish speaking population by Attila Line. **Capital:** Levkosia (Nicosia) 180,000 inhab. (1982); **other towns** (in 1,000 inhab.): Lemesós 107.2, Ammókhostos 39.4. **Population:** Cyprian Greeks 80%, Cyprian Turks 18%, Armenians, Englishmen and others. **Density** 72 persons per sq.km; average annual rate of population increase 1.4% (1980–83); urban population 43% (1983). 32.9% of the economically active inhabitants engaged in agriculture. – **Currency:** Cyprian pound = 100 cents.

Economy: Mediterranean agriculture and extraction of raw materials. Arable land and permanent crops 47%. **Agriculture:** crops (1983, in 1,000 tonnes): grapes 200, oranges 140, lemons 47, grapefruit 87, olives 12, wheat 10, vegetables, early potatoes, tobacco; livestock (1983, in 1,000 head): cattle 43, pigs 200, sheep 500, goats 360, fish catch 2,100 tonnes. **Mining** (1983, in 1,000 tonnes): pyrites Fe 47, copper 1.1, chromium, asbestos 17, sulphur. **Production:** wine 450,000 hl, olive oil 3,000 tonnes, raisins, cigarettes 3.3 mn.

Communications: roads 10,950 km, passenger cars 110,600. Civil aviation: 10.2 mn. km flown, 536,000 passengers carried (1984). Merchant shipping 6,728,000 GRT (1984). Tourism 621,000 visitors (1983). – **Exports:** citrus fruit, potatoes, tobacco and cigarettes, wine, copper and concentrates, pyrites. Chief trading partners: United Kingdom, Fed. Rep. of Germany, Greece, Italy, U.S.A.

INDIA

Bharat, area 3,287,590 sq.km, population 796,596,000 (1988), **federal republic, member of the Commonwealth** (President Ramaswamy Venkataraman since 1987).

Administrative units: 23 federal states and 8 territories. **Capital:** New Delhi 273,036 inhab. (census 1981); **other towns** (in 1,000 inhab., [+]with agglom.): Bombay 8,243 ([+]9,950), Delhi 4,865 ([+]5,228), Calcutta 3,292 ([+]9,194), Madras 3,266 ([+]4,277), Bangalore 2,483 ([+]2,914), Hyderābād 2,142 ([+]2,566), Ahmadābād 2,025 ([+]2,515), Kānpur 1,531 ([+]1,875), Nāgpur 1,215 ([+]1,298), Pune 1,203 ([+]1,685), Jaipur 967 ([+]1,006), Lucknow 896 ([+]1,060), Indore 827, Madurai 818, Surat 776, Patna 774, Howrah 742, Baroda 734, Āgra 724, Vārānasi 705. **Population:** Hindustani, Bihari, Marathi, Bengali, Santhali, Telugu and others. **Density** 229 persons per sq.km; average annual rate of population increase 2.3% (1973–83); urban population 24% (1983). 60.9% of the economically active inhabitants engaged in agriculture (1983). – **Currency:** Indian rupee = 100 paise.

Economy: agricultural and industrial country; arable land 50.2%, meadows and pastures 3.7%, forests 20.5%. **Agriculture. Crops** (1983, in 1,000 tonnes): rice 90,000 (second world producer), wheat 42,502, millet 10,050 (leading world producer), sorghum 12,000 (second world producer), maize (corn) 7,300, sugarcane 189,129 (second world producer), potatoes 10,108; important legumens: peas 330, lentils 550, soya beans 730, groundnuts 7,300 (leading world producer), chick-peas 5,092 (leading world producer), sesame 590 (leading world producer), coconuts 3,900, copra 350, cotton – seed 2,540, – lint 1,260, linseed 476, jute 1,590 (leading world producer), hemp 60, tea 595 (leading world producer), coffee 130, oranges 1,200, lemons 500, bananas 4,500 (second world producer) pineapples 660, apples 920, cashew nuts 200, tobacco 594, vegetables 43.1 mn. tonnes – tomatoes 780. **Animal production** (1983, in 1,000 head): horses 900, cattle 182,000 (highest world population), buffaloes 63,000 (highest world population), camels 1,050, pigs 8,600, sheep 41,700, goats 78,000 (highest world population), silkworms; cattle hides 810,000 tonnes (second world producer), goatskins 72,900 tonnes (leading world producer), grease wool 37,000 tonnes, raw silk 2,650 tonnes. Fish catch 2,520,000 tonnes (1983). Roundwood 228.3 mn. cub.m. Natural rubber 170,000 tonnes.

Mining (1983, in 1,000 tonnes, metal content): coal 133,349 (West Bengal – Rānīganj and Bihār), brown coal 7,347, crude petroleum 25,148 (Mahārāshtra), natural gas 106,575 TJ, uranium, iron ore 24,359 (Bihār, Orissa, Madhya Pradesh), manganese 488.3, lead 20.7, zinc 40.4, chromium 108, copper 46.9, gold 2,156 kg, mica 16.0 (second world producer – Bihār-Hazāribāgh, Andhra Pradesh, Rājasthān), asbestos 23, bauxite 1,929, magnesite 436, salt 9,979, phosphates 241, diamonds. Electricity 147,952 mn. kWh. **Industry.** Important textile and food industries, metal-working. **Production** (1983, in 1,000 tonnes): pig iron 9,087, crude steel 11,030, coke oven coke 11,610, motor vehicles – commercial 106,400, – passenger 45,000 units; merchant vessels 95,000 GRT, radio receivers 1.23 mn. units, cement 25,422, naphtha 3,474, motor spirit 1,880, jet fuel 1,163, sulphuric acid 2,388, soda ash 744, nitrogenous fertilizers 3,358, phosphate fertilizers 373, superphosphates 222, woven fabrics – cotton 8,632 mn. m, – silk, jute 2,916 mn. sq.m – of cellulosic fibres 899 mn. m – of non-cellulosic fibres 683 mn. m, woven woollen fabrics, sugar 6,635, flour 2,475, meat 958, cow milk 14,000, buffalo milk 20,000, butter 740 (second world producer), cheese; cigarettes 86,850 mn.

Communications (1983): railways 61,240 km, roads 1,604,000 km, motor vehicles – passenger 1,351,000, commercial 1,450,800. Merchant shipping 6,415,000 GRT. Civil aviation: 98.3 mn. km flown, 9,165,000 passengers carried. Tourism 1,305,000 visitors (1983). – **Exports:** woven cotton fabrics and products, jute and jute products, tea, hides, skins and furs, spices, fruit, vegetables, tobacco, sugar, iron ore and concentrates, handicraft products. Chief trading partners: U.S.A., United Kingdom, U.S.S.R., Japan, Fed. Rep. of Germany.

BULG.
İSTANBUL
Karadeniz Boğ.
B L A C K S E A
25°
30°
35°
40°
45°
1
2
3
4
Zonguldak
Ordžonikidze
Kutaisi
Poti
Batumi
SEA OF MARMARA
Ereğli
Kastamonu
A
Bandırma
İzmit
Adapazarı
Karabük
Samsun
U.
Çanakkale Boğ.
Çanakkale
BURSA
Sakarya
Çankırı
Merzifon
Trabzon
TBILISI
Edremit
Balıkesir
Çorum
Amasya
Ordu
Giresun
Rize
Çoruh
Kura
Leninakan
Eskişehir
Kırıkkale
Kelkit
Lésvos
Khios
T
Zile
Tokat
Kars
Manisa
Akhisar
Kütahya
ANKARA
Yozgat
Sivas
Erzincan
Erzurum
Aras
Gediz
Uşak
İZMİR
U
Kırşehir
Kızıl
Fırat (Euphrates)
Karaköse
Sámos
Aydın
Nazilli
Afyon
R
Tuz G.
K
Elâziğ
E
Y
Murat
Van G.
Khvoy
B
İsparta
Aksaray
Kayseri
Denizli
Burdur
Konya
Malatya
Muğla
Ereğli
Niğde
Bitlis
Tatvan
Van
Dhodhekánisos
Beyşehir G.
Seyhan
Maraş
Diyarbakır
Batman
Karaman
Tarsus
Kurtalan
Orūmīyeh
Antalya
Göksu
Dicle (Tigris)
Antalya Kör.
Mersin
ADANA
Gaziantep
Fırat
Urfa
Mardin
Cizre
Iráklion
E
Ródhos
Birecik
Al-Qāmishlī
İskenderun Kör.
İskenderun
35°
Kríti
HALAB
Ar-Raqqah
Dijlah
Irbil
Al-Lādhiqīyah
B. al-Asad
Al-Furāt
A
AL-MAWSIL
Levkosia
Ammókhostos
CYPRUS
Bāniyās
Hamāh
R
Dayr az-Zawr
KIRKŪK
Lemesós
Hims
Tarābulus
Tudmur
MEDITERRANEAN SEA
LEBANON
Y
Al-Qā'im
Tikrīt
BAYRŪT
An-Nabk
Abū Kamāl
Sāmarrā'
Zahlah
Al-Hadīthah
Al-Kāzimīyah
Saydā
S
Ar-Ramādī
BAGH
C
Hefa
DIMASHQ (Damascus)
Ar-Rutbah
Dar'ā
N
Karbalā'
I
R
Tel Aviv-Yafo
AMMĀN
A
Al-Hillah
A
AL-ISKANDARĪYAH (Alexandria)
Matrūh
Dumyāt
D
An-Najaf
Jordan
Būr Sa'īd
Ghazzah
Yerūshalayim (Jerusalem)
Al-'Alamayn
Al-'Arīsh
R
Dead Sea
Tantā
Suez Canal
O
Badanah
30°
AL-JĪZAH
Al-Ismā'īlīyah
ISRAEL
Oron
As-Samāwah
As-Suways (Suez)
J
Ma'ān
Al-Fayyūm
AL-QĀHIRAH (Cairo)
Elat
Ra's an-Naqb
E
G
Banī Suwayf
Abū Zanīmah
Al-'Aqabah
Al-Jawf
Sakākah
Al-Bawītī
Y
T
D
P
S
A
U
D
I
Al-Minyā
At-Tūr
Tabūk
Mallawī
Nile
Ras Gharib
G. of Suez
Nabq
Ash-Sharmah
Al-Qa
A
R
Qasr al-Farāfirah
Asyūt
RED SEA
Al-Ghurdaqah
A
Taymā'
Būr Safājah
Qubā
Hā'il
Sawhāj

Elhovo
BULGARIA
Mičurin
B L A C K S E A
İnce B.
Sinop
Kırklareli
1
2
3
30°
35
Ayancık
Edirne
Karadeniz Boğ.
Lüleburgaz
Zonguldak
Bartın
Bafra
Samsun
GREECE
Ereğli
Kastamonu
Çorlu
İSTANBUL
Kızıl
Çarşamba
Ordu
Tirebolu
Tekirdağ
Karabük
Tosya
İskilip
Merzifon
Alexandroúpolis
Keşan
T
İzmit (Kocaeli)
Adapazarı
Düzce
Giresun
SEA OF MARMARA
Kelkit
Amasya
Bolu
Çankırı
Gümüşhane
Gökçeada
Gelibolu
Mudanya
Gemlik
Göynük
Çorum
Bandırma
Sakarya
Beypazarı
Zile
Yeşil
Şebinkarahisar
40°
BURSA
Bilecik
ANKARA
Kalecik
Sungurlu
Tokat
Çanakkale Boğ.
Ezine
Edremit
Balıkesir
U
Eskişehir
Yozgat
Sivas
Zara
Erzincan
Tavşanlı
Kırıkkale
Fırat
Baba B.
Soma
Sivrihisar
Polatlı
İliç
Lésvos
Bergama
Kütahya
Kulu
Şarkişla
Divriği
R
Kırşehir
Akhisar
Emirdağ
Kızıl
Bünyan
Arapkir
Keban G.
Manisa
Gediz
Şereflikoçhisar
K
Pınarbaşı
Khios
Uşak
Afyon
Tuz G.
Salihli
Cihanbeyli
Keban
Ödemiş
Çivril
Nevşehir
Kayseri
Köyyeri
Malatya
İZMİR
Dinar
Akşehir
Aksaray
B
Tire
Nazilli
Ilgın
Saimbeyli
Elbistan
Sámos
Söke
Büyükmenderes
Niğde
Adıyaman
Aydın
Eğridir
Beyşehir G.
Konya
Akköy
Denizli
Burdur
Isparta
Beyşehir
Ulukışla
Seyhan
Maraş
Besni
Fırat (Euphrates)
Milâs
Bucak
Ereğli
Kozan
Dhodhekánisos
Bodrum
Muğla
Antalya
Karaman
Osmaniye
Gaziantep
Urfa
Tarsus
Ceyhan
Birecik
Manavgat
Göksu
Mersin
ADANA
İskenderun
Kilis
Fethiye
Kemer
Alanya
Erdemli
S Y R I
Ródhos
Antalya Kör.
Silifke
İskenderun Kör.
HALAB
Kaş
Finike
Anamur
Al-Bāb
E
Ródhos
Lindhos
Antakya
Kárpathos
MEDITERRANEAN SEA
Al-Lādhiqīyah
Idlib

CASPIAN SEA
Zaliv Kara-Bogaz-Gol
S. S. R.
Kizyl-Kaja
Tašauz
Urgenč
Amudarja
Leninabad
Navoi
Kattakurgan
Zeravšan
Dargan-Ata
Buchara
Kagan
SAMARKAND
Sachrisabz
Karši
Kamaši
DUŠANBE
Denau
Kurgan-T'ube
Čardžou
Kerki
Termez
Sumgait
BAKU
Magomed
Ali-Bajramly
Krasnovodsk
Nebit-Dag
Kizyl-Arvat
Bacharden
Aščabad
Tedžen
Mary
Bajram-Ali
Iolotan'
Murgab
Sandykači
Tachta-Bazar
Kuška
Astara
Gasan-Kuli
Atrak
Bojnūrd
Shīrvān
Qūchān
MASHHAD
Ardabīl
Bandar-e Anzalī
Rasht
Safīd
Tonekābon
Bandar-e Torkeman
Gorgān
Bābol
Sārī
Emāmrūd
Sabzevār
Neyshābūr
Torbat-e Heydarīyeh
Qazvīn
Abhar
Shar
TEHRĀN
KARAJ
Rey
Semnān
Garmsar
Kāshmar
Qareh Su
QOM
Daryācheh-ye Namak
Jandaq
Ferdows
Tabas
Arāk
Borūjerd
Kāshān
Golpāyegān
Ardestān
Bīrjand
ESFAHĀN
Nā'īn
Ardakān
Dezfūl
Chamgordan
Shūshtar
Masjed Soleymān
Qomisheh
Shūrāb
Yazd
Bāfq
Naft-e Safīd
Īzad Khvāst
Ābādeh
Zarand
Rāmhormoz
Deh Bīd
Anār
Kermān
Bandar-e Khomeynī
Behbehān
Gachsārān
Rafsanjān
Ābādān
SHĪRĀZ
Daryācheh-ye Bakhtegān
Sa'īdābād
Bam
Kāzerūn
J.-ye Khārk
Neyrīz
Halīl
Al-Kuwayt
Būshehr
Fasā
Kahnūj
Jahrom
Mand
Kangān
Lār
Bandar 'Abbās
Nāy Band
Qeshm
Hāmūn-e-Jaz Mūriān
Bandar-e Lengeh
Strait of Hormuz
Persian Gulf
Al-Jubayl
Al-Qatīf
Ad-Dammām
Abqaiq
BAHRAIN
Al-Manāmah
Al-Mubarraz
Al-Hufūf
QATAR
Ad-Dawhah
Al-Khasab
OMAN
Ra's al-Khaymah
'Ujmān
Ash-Shāriqah
Dubayy
Al-Fujayrah
Jāsk
Gulf of Oman
Suhār
Al-'Ayn
Al-Buraymī
Abū-Zaby
Tarīf
Habshān
UNITED ARAB EMIRATES
Masqat
Matrah
Tropic of Cancer
'Ibrī
Nazwā
Sūr
Ra's al-Hadd
Fahūd
ARABIAN SEA
Al-Maşīrah
Ra's ad Daqm
OMAN
Khuriyā Muriyā
Şalālah
Mirbāt
Zāhedān
Mīrjāveh
Khāsh
Īrānshahr
Sūrān
Bampūr
Chāh Bahār
Gwādar
Shūsf
Hāmūn Sāberī
Zābol
Daryācheh-ye Sīstān
IRAN
AFGHANISTAN
Shebergān
Mazār-e Sharīf
Sar-e Pol
Meymaneh
Morghāb
Bāmīān
Qal'eh-ye Now
Harīrūd
Chaghcharān
Herāt
Ghūrīān
Farāh
Tarīn-Kowt
Mūs'a Qal'eh
Qalāt
Gereshk
Lashkar Gāh
Qandahār
Chaman
Khāsh
Helmand
Zaranj
Nushki
Chāgai
Dālbandin
Nok Kundi
Hāmūn-i-Māshkel
Khārān
PAKISTAN
Bazdār
Turbat
Pasni
Ormāra
50°
55°
60°
65°
40°
35°
30°
25°
20°
1 : 18 000 000
0 100 200 300 400 Km
0 50 100 150 200 250 Mi
Artvin
Oltu
Kars
Sarıkamış
Aras
Erzurum
Eleşkirt
Karaköse
Doğubayazıt
Mākū
Hınıs
Malazgirt
Erciş
Muradiye
Khvoy
Muş
Tatvan
Van
Bitlis
Van Gölü
Kurtalan
Siirt
Hakkâri
Batman
Cizre
Nusaybin
Zākhū
Dahūk
Al-Qāmishlī
IRAQ
Rawāndūz
IRAN
Turkey
1 : 12 500 000

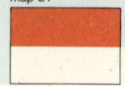

INDONESIA

Republik Indonesia, area 2,027,087 sq.km (incl. East Timor), **population 174,951,000** (1988), **republic** (President Gen. I. Suharto since 1967).

Administrative units: 27 provinces, in 1976 annexed East Timor. **Capital:** Jakarta 7,636,000 inhab. (1983); **other towns** (1980, in 1,000 inhab.): Surabaya 2,028, Bandung 1,463, Medan 1,379, Semarang 1,027, Palembang 787, Ujung Pandang 709, Malang 512, Padang 481, Surakarta 470, Yogyakarta 399, Banjarmasin 381, Pontianak 305, Balikpapan 281. **Population:** Malay Indonesians (over 140 ethnic groups; most numerous are the Javanese and the Chinese among the minorities). **Density** 82 persons per sq. km; average annual rate of population increase 2.3% (1973–83); urban population 24% (1983). 56.5% of the economically active inhabitants engaged in agriculture (1983). – **Currency:** Indonesian rupiah = 100 sen.
Economy: agricultural country, and mining of minerals. Arable land and permanent crops 10.2%, meadows and pastures 6.3%, forests 63.9% of the land area. **Agriculture: Crops** (1983, in 1,000 tonnes): rice 34,300, manioc 19,770, sweet potatoes 2,120 (second world producer), soya beans 590, groundnuts 760, sugarcane 24,531, sisal, cotton, coconuts 11,100 (leading world producer), copra 1,070 (second world producer), palm kernels 154, palm oil 950 (second world producer), sesame, fruit, tea 110, coffee 233, tobacco 122; **livestock** (1983, in 1,000 head): cattle 6,600, buffaloes 2,500, pigs 3,600, sheep 4,300, goats 7,900, horses 660; fish catch 2,112,200 tonnes (1983). Natural rubber 920,000 tonnes (second world producer), roundwood 122.2 mn. cub.m.
Mining (1983, in 1,000 tonnes, metal content): coal 486, crude petroleum 65,971, natural gas 689,582 TJ, tin 26.5 (second greatest producer in the world), nickel 31, manganese, bauxite 778, gold 259 kg, diamonds 27,000 carats, phosphates, salt 698. Electricity 15,280 mn. kWh. **Industry:** Important processing of tin, petroleum refineries, food and textile industries. Production (1983, in 1,000 tonnes): tin 28 (second world producer), motor spirit 1,597, jet fuel 355, naphthas 865, nitrogenous fertilizers 1,077, phosphate fertilizers 368, sugar 1,759; 91,463 mn. cigarettes; radio 1.1 mn. and television receivers 517,000 units.
Communications (1983): railways 6,877 km, roads 128,900 km, motor vehicles – passenger 791,000, commercial 791,500; merchant shipping 1,857,000 GRT; civil aviation: 117.6 mn. km flown, 6,494,000 passengers carried. Tourism 626,000 visitors (1983). – **Exports:** petroleum and petroleum products, natural gas, wood, natural rubber, palm oil, coffee, tin concentrates, tea, tobacco, spices. Chief trading partners: Japan, U.S.A., Fed. Rep. of Germany, Australia.

IRAN

Jomhori-e-Islami-e-Irân, area 1,648,100 sq.km, population 52,522,000 (1988), **republic** (President Hojatoleslam Ali Akbar Hashemi Rafsanjani since 1989).
Administrative units: 21 provinces (ostán), 2 governorates (farmándár). **Capital:** Tehrân 5,734,199 inhab. (with agglom., 1982); **other towns** (in 1,000 inhab.): Mashhad 1,120, Esfahán 927, Shírâz 880, Tabríz 852, Bakhtarân 531, Karaj 526, Ahvâz 471, Qom 424. **Population:** two thirds are Iranian Persians; Azerbaijanis, Kurds, Arabs. **Density** 27 persons per sq.km; average annual rate of population increase 3.1% (1973–83); urban population 53%. 36.3% of the economically active inhabitants engaged in agriculture (1983). – **Currency:** rial = 100 dinars.
Economy: agricultural and industrial country with important mining of petroleum. Arable land and land under permanent crops 10%, forests 10.9% of the land area. **Agriculture: Crops**: (1983, in 1,000 tonnes): wheat 6,669, barley 1,413, rice 1,400, millet 27, sorghum 10, maize (corn) 55, potatoes 800, peas 34, lentils 29, groundnuts 100, soya beans 96, sunflower, sesame, olives, castor beans, cotton – seed 170, –lint 90; sugar beet 2,340, sugarcane 1,600, vegetables, tea 22, oranges 72, lemons 36, apricots 55, grapes 1,600, raisins 52, almonds 52, dates 302, hazelnuts, pistachios 35 (leading world producer), tomatoes 407, onion 253; **livestock** (1983, in 1,000 head): horses 350, cattle 8,600, sheep 34,500, goats 13,800, asses 1,800, cattle hides 41,139 tonnes, sheepskins 38,886 tonnes, grease wool 16,000 tonnes, eggs 200,000 tonnes.
Mining (1983, in 1,000 tonnes, metal content): coal, crude petroleum 123,119 (chiefly in south-west Iran), natural gas 264,000 TJ, iron ore 340, manganese, copper 48.5, lead 26, zinc 39.9, bauxite, magnesite, sulphur 50, salt 753. Electricity 29,900 mn. kWh, (of which 19% hydro-energy). The most developed **industries** are petrochemical and chemical, textile, leather, and food processing. Production (1983, in 1,000 tonnes): naphtha 430, motor spirit 3,400 (of which aviation spirit 60), jet fuel 490, coke oven coke 300, sulphuric acid 108, phosphate fertilizers 3.9, nitrogenous fertilizers 23.6, cement 10,665, woven cotton fabrics 118 mn. m, woven woollen fabrics 16 mn. m, non-cellulosic continuous fibres 18, meat 726, sugar 600, flour 2,517, milk 1,786.
Communications (1983): railways 4,567 km, roads 63,115 km, motor vehicles – passenger 079,133, commercial 405,994. Merchant shipping 2,106,000 GRT (1983). Civil aviation: 28.6 mn. km flown, 4,088,000 passengers carried. Tourism 100,000 visitors (1983). – **Exports:** petroleum and petroleum products, cotton and cotton goods, carpets, dates, raisins, skins, pistachios. Chief trading partners: countries of CMEA 60%, Japan, Fed. Rep. of Germany, United Kingdom, U.S.A., Italy, France, Netherlands, India.

IRAQ

al Jumhouriya al'Iraqia, area 438,446 sq.km, population 17,250,000 (1988), **republic** (President Saddam Hussein at-Takriti since 1979).
Administrative units: 15 governorates (liwa), 3 autonomous regions. **Capital:** Baghdâd 3,200,000 inhab. (with agglom. 1983); **other towns** (1980, in 1,000 inhab.): Al-Basrah 720, Al-Mawsil (Mosul) 570, Kirkûk 570, An-Najaf 190, Al-Hillah 140, Irbil 110, Karbalá 110. – **Population:** about 80% Arabic speaking Iraqis, 15% Kurds, 2% Turks. Average annual rate of population increase 3.6% (1973–83); urban population 69% (1983). 38% of the economically active inhabitants engaged in agriculture. – **Currency:** Iraqi dinar = 1,000 fils.

page 98

Economy: agricultural country with developing industry. Arable land 12% and forests 3.5% of the land area. **Agriculture** (1983, in 1,000 tonnes): rice 200, wheat 1,000, barley 900, cotton – lint 5, – seed 10, almonds 700, sesame, olives, oranges 140, lemons; livestock (1983, in 1,000 head): cattle 3,000, buffaloes 240, camels 250, sheep 12,000, goats 3,800; grease wool 17,500 tonnes; fish catch 26,200 tonnes. **Mining** (1983, in 1,000 tonnes): crude petroleum 46,819 (Kirkūk, Al-Mawsil), natural gas 17,000 TJ, sulphur 300, salt 72. Electricity 13,700 mn. kWh (1983). Petrochemical, textile and food **industries. Production** (1983, in 1,000 tonnes): naphtha 460, motor spirit 1,300, fuel oil 360, nitrogenous fertilizers 14, phosphate fertilizers 86, sulphuric acid, woven cotton fabrics; 7,900 mn. cigarettes, sugar, canned fruit and vegetables, vegetable oils.
Communications: railways 1,589 km, roads 15,123 km, motor vehicles – passenger 345,900, commercial 206,300 (1982). Merchant shipping 1,074,000 GRT (1983). Civil aviation: 1.4 mn. km flown, 435,000 passengers carried. Tourism 1,673,000 visitors (1983). – **Exports:** petroleum and petroleum products, dates, skins, wool. Chief trading partners: France, Fed. Rep. of Germany, United Kingdom, Italy, U.S.S.R., Brazil, Japan.

ISRAEL

Medinat Israel, area 20,770 sq.km, population 4,478,000 (1989), **republic** (President Chaim Herzog since 1983).
Administrative units: 6 districts (mechnusa). **Capital:** Yerûshalayim (Jerusalem) 428,668 inhab. (1983); **other towns** (1982, in 1,000 inhab.): Tel Aviv-Yafo 327 (with agglom. 1,555), Hefa (Haifa) 226, Holon 133, Bat Yam 129. **Population:** Jews 83%, Arabs 15%. **Density** 204 persons per sq.km; average annual rate of population increase 2.3% (1973–83); urban population 90% (1983). 6.2% of the economically active inhabitants engaged in agriculture. – **Currency:** shekel.
Economy: industrial and agricultural country. Arable land 16.8%, meadows and pastures 39.4%, forests 5.6% of the land area. **Agriculture** (1983, in 1,000 tonnes): wheat 335, potatoes 210, sugar beet, oranges 857, tangerines, grapefruit 450 (second world producer), bananas 66, peaches, cotton, vegetables, grapes 88; livestock (1983, in 1,000 head): cattle 330, sheep 240, goats 115; eggs 100,800 tonnes. Fish catch 22,400 tonnes. **Mining** (1983, in 1,000 tonnes): crude petroleum, natural gas 2,297 TJ, salt 203, phosphates 1,966, potash salt 1,000. Electricity 14,578 mn. kWh. Engineering and electronics, chemical, textile and food **industries.** Diamond polishing. **Production** (1983, in 1,000 tonnes): motor spirit 1,107, jet fuel 520, nitrogenous fertilizers 81.6, phosphate fertilizers 100, potash fertilizers 955.8; meat 210, cheese 62, butter, margarine; 6,373 mn. cigarettes; wine 328,000 hl.
Communications: railways 827 km, roads 11,950 km, motor vehicles – passenger 599,300, commercial 113,100. Merchant shipping 563,000 GRT (1983). Civil aviation: 34.9 mn. km flown, 1,669,000 passengers carried. Tourism 1,093,000 visitors (1983). – **Exports:** polished gems, citrus fruit, products of engineering, chemical and textile industries. Chief trade with U.S.A.

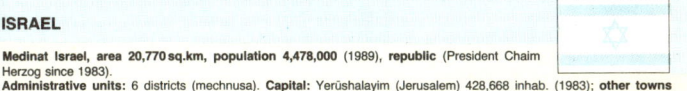

JAPAN

Nippon (or **Nihon**), **area 377,815 sq.km, population 122,613,000** (1988), **empire** (Emperor Akihito since 1989).

Administrative units: 47 prefectures. **Capital:** Tōkyō 8,361,054 inhab. (with agglom. 11,746,190 – 1983); **other towns** (in 1,000 inhab.): Yokohama 2,899, Ōsaka 2,624, Nagoya 2,100, Sapporo 1,496, Kyōto 1,484, Kōbe 1,394, Fukuoka 1,138, Kawasaki 1,066, Kitakyūshū 1,065, Hiroshima 908, Sakai 810, Chiba 766, Sendai 669, Okayama 555, Kumamoto 527, Kagoshima 519, Amagasaki 509, Hamamatsu 504, Higashiōsaka 502, Funabashi 494, Shizuoka 464, Sagamihara 463, Niigata 461, Nagasaki 449, Himeji 449, Yokosuka 429, Matsuyama 418, Matsudo 416, Kanazawa 415, Kurashiki 412, Gifu 409, Nishinomiya 405, Hachioji 405, Wakayama 404, Toyonaka 399. **Population:** Japanese, 674,680 Koreans, 63,160 Chinese, 15,000 Ainu (1983). **Density** 320 persons per sq.km; average annual rate of population increase 0.9% (1973–83); urban population 76% (1983). 9.2% of the economically active inhabitants engaged in agriculture and 34.8% in industry (1983). – **Currency:** yen = 100 sen.
Economy: economically highly developed industrial and agricultural country. Arable land 13%, forests 67% of the land area. **Agriculture: Crops:** (1983, in 1,000 tonnes): rice 12,958, wheat 747, barley 380, oats, maize (corn), soya beans 217, groundnuts 51, beans 93, sugarcane 2,400, sugar beet 3,412, potatoes 3,700, sweet potatoes 1,400, hemp, flax, vegetables 14,925 (tomatoes 900, onions 1,200), fruit – apples 1,001, pears 534, oranges 360, tangerines 3,767 (leading world producer), grapes 324, strawberries 196, sweet chestnuts 59, tobacco 138; **livestock** (1983, in 1,000 head): cattle 4,590, pigs 10,273, poultry 297,000, raising of silkworms; eggs 2,085,000 tonnes, raw silk 13,000 tonnes (second world producer); fish catch 11,250,000 tonnes (largest world catch). Roundwood 32.8 mn. cub.m (1983).
Mining (1983, in 1,000 tonnes, metal content): coal 17,062, crude petroleum 418, natural gas 89,685 TJ, uranium, iron ore 185, pyrites 551, copper 46, lead 47, zinc 255.7, chromium 11, tin 600 tonnes, manganese 19.9, tungsten 474 tonnes, gold 3,139 kg, silver 307 tonnes, molybdenum 95 tonnes, mercury, salt 921. Electricity 602,357 mn. kWh, of which hydro-energy 15%, nuclear energy 13.5% (1983).
Industry: one of the chief producers in the world in metallurgy (Kitakyūshū, Muroran), electronic machinery, many branches of the engineering (Ōsaka, Yokohama, Kōbe, Nagasaki, Hiroshima), chemical (Kōbe, Tōkyō, Ōsaka) and textile industries. **Production** (1983, in 1,000 tonnes): coke oven coke 46,675, pig iron 72,900 (second world producer), crude steel 97,200 (second world producer), aluminium 1,096.2, copper 1,075, lead 241, zinc 701 (second world producer), magnesium 19,038 tonnes, radio receivers 13.3 mn., television receivers 13.3 mn. (leading world producer), merchant vessels 9,408,000 GRT (leading world producer), of which tankers 698,000 GRT, motor vehicles – passenger 7,152,000 (leading world producer), – commercial 3,897,000 (leading world producer), cement 80,890, naphtha 8,328, motor spirit 26,428, jet fuel 3,597, tyres 123 mn., sulphuric acid 6,662, hydrochloric acid 561.1, nitric acid 540, caustic soda 2,778, nitrogenous fertilizers 1,076, phosphate fertilizers 647, woven cotton fabrics 2,079 mn. sq.m, woven silk fabrics 121.8 mn. sq.m (second world producer), woven woollen fabrics 301 mn. sq.m, synthetic fabrics

INDIA	
States:	7 Mizoram
1 Haryana	Union Territories:
2 Manipur	8 Chandigarh
3 Meghalaya	9 Dādra and Nagar Haveli
4 Nāgaland	10 Damān and Diu
5 Tripura	11 Pondichery
6 West Bengal	

1 : 25 000 000

22 a Plain of Bengal
1 : 15 000 000

3,218 mn. sq.m, cotton yarn 438, woollen yarn 110, non-cellulosic staple and tow 750 (second world producer), newsprint 2,562, milk 7,042, butter 75, meat 3,208, beer 50,534,000hl, wine 402,000hl, sugar 476, flour 4,356; 306,320 mn. cigarettes.
Communications (1983): railways 26,889 km, of which about 50% are electrified; roads 1,088,300 km, motor vehicles – passenger 26.4 mn., commercial 15.7 mn. Merchant shipping 40,752,000 GRT (1984 world's second largest fleet). Civil aviation: 377.1 mn. km flown, 46,554,000 passengers carried. Tourism 1.67 mn. visitors.
Exports: 55% machines and equipment – cars, vessels, products of heavy engineering, radio and television receivers, 14% metals and metal products, textile products – cotton and silk fabrics and others, chemical products. Chief trading partners: U.S.A., Saudi Arabia, Australia, Canada, Indonesia, Iran, Fed. Rep. of Germany, Hong Kong, Republic of Korea, China.

JORDAN

Al Mamlaka at Urduniya al Hashemiyah, area 97,740 sq.km (incl. the territory occupied by Israel), **population** 3,943,000 (1988), **kingdom** (King Hussein Ibn Talal since 1952).
Administrative units: 8 districts (liwa) and the Desert Area. **Capital:** Ammān 744,000 inhab. (1983); **other towns** (in 1,000 inhab.): Az-Zarqā 256, Irbid 131.2. – **Currency:** Jordan dinar = 1,000 fils.
Economy: developing agricultural country with nomadic cattle raising. Arable land and permanent crops 14.1% of the land area. **Agriculture** (1983, in 1,000 tonnes): wheat 120, barley 28, lentils 8.4, olives 30, grapes 28, oranges 26, dates, vegetables 1,260, tomatoes 210; livestock (1983, in 1,000 head): cattle 40, camels 15, sheep 1,000, goats 500. **Mining:** phosphates 4.75 mn. tonnes, potash salt, salt, sulphur. Electricity 1,918 mn. kWh (1983). Processing of fruit and vegetables, chemical and textile industries. – **Communications** (1982): railways 544 km, roads 5,227 km, passenger cars 147,200 (1983). Civil aviation: 25.1 mn. km flown, 1.5 mn. passengers carried. Tourism 1.7 mn. visitors (1983). **Exports:** phosphates, citrus and fruit, vegetables, olive oil, chemical products. Chief trading partners: Saudi Arabia, U.S.A., Fed. Rep. of Germany and other EEC countries, Iraq.

KAMPUCHEA

Roat Kampuchea, area 181,035 sq.km, **population** 7,869,000 (1988), **republic** (President of the Council of State Heng Samrin since 1979).
Administrative units: 4 self-administered cities and 17 provinces. **Capital:** Phnum Pénh 650,000 inhab. (1985). – **Currency:** riel = 100 sen.
Economy: agricultural country. Arable land 16.8%, forests 74% of the land area. **Agriculture** (1983, in 1,000 tonnes): rice 1,700, maize (corn) 60, sweet potatoes 25, soya beans, groundnuts 6, sugarcane 181, cotton, sesame, bananas 82, coconuts 33, pineapples 7, oranges 30, spices, tobacco; livestock (1983, in 1,000 head): cattle 1,148, pigs 717; fish catch 63,800 tonnes (1983). Natural rubber 8,000 tonnes (1983), teak and other timber – roundwood 5.1 mn. cub.m. Electricity 129.7 mn. kWh (1983). Developing chemical, textile and food industries. – **Communications:** railways 272 km, roads 15,029 km, passenger cars 38,300. Civil aviation: 800,000 km flown, 113,000 passengers carried. – **Exports:** rice, natural rubber, rare timber, pepper, fruit, vegetables. Chief trading partners: U.S.S.R., Vietnam.

KOREA, DEMOCRATIC PEOPLE'S REPUBLIC OF

Chosun Minchu-chui Inmin Konghwa-guk, area 120,538 sq.km, **population** 21,902,000 (1988), **people's democratic republic** (Chairman of the Presidium of the Supreme People's Assembly Kim Il Sung since 1972).
Administrative units: 2 statutory cities and 9 provinces. **Capital:** P'yŏngyang 1,283,000 inhab. (1981); **other towns** (in 1,000 inhab.): Hamhŭng 775, Ch'ŏngjin 520, Wŏnsan 500, Sinŭiju 420, Kaesŏng 420. **Population:** Koreans. Density 169 persons per sq.km; 44.1% of the economically active inhabitants engaged in agriculture. – **Currency:** won = 100 yun.
Economy: agricultural and industrial country. Arable land 18.6%. **Agriculture** (1983, in 1,000 tonnes): rice 5,200, wheat 500, barley 420, maize (corn) 2,500, millet 475, sorghum 160, potatoes 1,650, sweet potatoes 400, soya beans 380, tobacco 50, fruit, vegetables; livestock (1983, in 1,000 head): cattle 1,000, pigs 2,500, sheep 330, silkworms; fish catch 1.6 mn. tonnes. Raw silk 3,150 tonnes. **Mining** (1983, in 1,000 tonnes, metal content): coal 38,000, iron ore 3,200, tungsten 500 tonnes, graphite 25, magnesite 1,850, lead 95, silver 45 tonnes, gold 5,000 kg, zinc 140, salt 572, phosphates. Electricity 28,200 mn. kWh (1983). – **Production** (1983): pig iron 3.1 mn. tonnes, crude steel 3.6 mn. tonnes, cement 8 mn. tonnes, nitrogenous fertilizers 608,000 tonnes, tractors, textile and food industries. – **Communications:** railways 11,000 km, roads 21,000 km. Merchant shipping 439,000 GRT (1983). – **Exports:** ores, coal, graphite, fish, industrial and agricultural products. Chief trading partners: U.S.S.R., China.

KOREA, REPUBLIC OF

Han Kook, area 99,022 sq.km, **population** 42,975,000 (1988), **republic** (President Roh Taewoo since 1988).
Administrative units: 4 statutory cities and 9 provinces. **Capital:** Sŏul 9,501,414 inhab. (1984, with agglom 11.46 mn.); **other towns** (1983, in 1,000 inhab.): Pusan 3,395, Taegu 1,959, Inch'ŏn 1,220, Kwangju 843, Taejŏn 800, Ulsan 510, Masan 424, Songnam 417, Suwŏn 374. **Population:** Koreans. Density 418 persons per sq.km; urban population 62% (1983). 35.6% of the economically active inhabitants engaged in agriculture. – **Currency:** won = 100 chon.
Economy: industrial and agricultural country with advanced consumer industries. Arable land 22.3%, forests 66.7% of the land area. **Agriculture** (1983, in 1,000 tonnes): rice 7,608, wheat 112, barley 815, sweet potatoes 1,012, potatoes 469, soya beans 233, maize (corn) 101, pulses 52, sesame 43, vegetables 8,868, fruit 1,467, tobacco 101; livestock (1983, in 1,000 head): cattle 1,754, pigs 2,183, goats 251, poultry 48 mn., silkworms; fish catch 2,400,400 tonnes. Raw silk 2,500 tonnes.

Mining (1983, in 1,000 tonnes, metal content): coal 18,945, iron ore 331, tungsten 2.29, graphite 33.3, gold 2,224 kg, lead 10, manganese, molybdenum 142 tonnes, silver 49 tonnes, tin, zinc 57, salt 853. Electricity 53,047 mn. kWh (1983). **Production** (1983, in 1,000 tonnes): pig iron 8,024, crude steel 5,062, cement 21,282, shipbuilding 2,515,000 GRT, radio 6,719,000 and television receivers 7,641,000 units, sulphuric acid 1,610, hydrochloric acid 50.9, nitrogenous 580.3 and phosphate fertilizers 457.5, woven fabrics – cotton 442 mn. sq.m – silk 19.6 mn. sq.m, non-cellulosic staple and tow 327, newsprint 232; meat 679, milk 712, eggs 295.
Communications (1983): railways 3,135 km, roads 53,935 km, passenger cars 381,000, commercial vehicles 391,400. Merchant shipping 6,771,000 GRT. Civil aviation: 72.1 mn. km flown, 5,097,000 passengers carried (1983). Tourism 1.2 mn. visitors (1983). – **Exports:** machinery and electronic machinery, ships, chemical products, fish and fish products, textile, ores. Chief trading partners: U.S.A. 30%, Japan almost 30%, Saudi Arabia, United Kingdom, Fed. Rep. of Germany.

KUWAIT

Dowlat al Kuwayt, area 17,818 sq.km, population 1,958,000 (1988), **emirate** (Emir Shaikh Jabir al-Ahmad al-Jabir al-Sabah since 1978).
Capital: Al-Kuwayt 181,800 (1980, with agglom. 1.1 mn.) inhab. – **Currency:** Kuwait dinar = 1,000 fils.
Economy: based on mining and the processing of petroleum and natural gas. **Agriculture.** Arable land only 1,000 ha; livestock (1983, in 1,000 head): cattle 18, camels 5, sheep 550, goats 300, fish catch 4,100 tonnes. **Mining** (1983): crude petroleum 53,545,000 tonnes, natural gas 90,000 TJ (both incl. one nalf of the former Neutral Zone production). Electricity 12,831 mn. kWh. Petrochemical industry. **Production** (1983, in 1,000 tonnes): naphtha 2,444, motor spirit 1,174, jet fuel 1,016, distillate fuel oils 6,127. – **Communications:** roads 920 km, passenger cars 519,500. Merchant shipping 2,551,000 GRT (1983). Civil aviation: 26.1 mn. km flown, 1,498,000 passengers carried (1983). – **Exports:** petroleum and petroleum products almost 95%. Chief trading partners: Japan, United Kingdom, Fed. Rep. of Germany and other EEC countries, U.S.A.

LAOS

Sa Thalanalath Pasathipatay Pasason Lao, area 236,800 sq.km, population 3,875,000 (1988), **people's democratic republic** (President Phoumi Vongvichit since 1986).
Administrative units: 16 provinces (khueng). **Capital:** Viangchan (Vientiane) 300,000 inhab. (1983); **other towns** (in 1,000 inhab.): Savannakhet 60, Pakxé 50, Louangphrabang 48. – **Currency:** kip = 10 bi = 100 att.
Economy: developing agricultural country. Arable land 3.7%, forests 54.9%. **Agriculture** (1983, in 1,000 tonnes): rice 1,002, maize (corn) 39, sweet potatoes 35, potatoes 44, manioc 74, groundnuts, coffee 4, cotton, tobacco 4, rare timber, roundwood 3.9 mn. cub.m, natural fibre; livestock (1983, in 1,000 head): cattle 490, buffaloes 910, pigs 1,300; fish catch 20,000 tonnes (1983).
Mining: tin 600 tonnes (1983). Electricity 1,250 mn. kWh (1983). Handicraft production. – **Communications:** roads 10,200 km (1981). – **Exports:** coffee, tin, timber, rice, cotton, tobacco.

LEBANON

al-Jumhouriya al-Lubnaniya, area 10,452 sq.km, population 2,828,000 (1988), **republic** (President Elias Hravi since 1989).
Administrative units: 5 provinces (mohafazat). **Capital:** Bayrūt 750,000 inhab. (1983), **other towns** (in 1,000 inhab): Tarābulus 195, Zahlah 68, Saydā 35. – **Currency:** Lebanese pound = 100 piastres.
Economy: arable land 33.5%. **Agriculture** of Mediterranean type (1983, in 1,000 tonnes): grapes 172, oranges 205, tangerines 30, lemons 76, olives 20, vegetables 418, cereals 31; livestock (1983, in 1,000 head): cattle 50, sheep 140, goats 440; fish catch 1,400 tonnes (1983). Electricity 1,220 mn. kWh (1983). Food **industry**, production of carpets and jewellery. Processing of imported petroleum. – **Communications** (1980): railways 417 km, roads 7,350 km. Merchant shipping 458,000 GRT (1983). Civil aviation: 28.3 mn. km flown, 411,000 passengers carried (1983). **Exports:** jewellery, textile products, fruit, vegetables, skins, wool, olive oil.

MALAYSIA

Persekutuan Tanah Malaysia, Federation of Malaysia, area 329,749 sq.km, population 16,921,000 (1988), **federation, member of the Commonwealth** (Supreme Head of State Sultan Azlan Muhibbuddin Shah ibni Al-Marthum Sultan Yussuff Izzuddin Shah since 1988).
Administrative units: Peninsular Malaysia: 11 states and 1 capital district, Sabah, Sarawak. **Capital:** Kuala Lumpur 937,875 inhab.; **other towns** (census 1980, in 1,000 inhab): Petaling Jaya 373, Ipoh 301, Pinang (George Town) 251, Johore Baharu 250, Kuala Terengganu 187, Kota Baharu 171, Butterworth 161, Kuantan 137, Seremban 136, Sandakan 118, Kuching 74 (Sarawak), Kota Kinabalu 60 (Sabah). **Population:** mainly Malays (55%) and Chinese (35%). **Density** 47 persons per sq.km; average annual rate of population increase: 2.4%; (1973–83) urban population 31% (1983). 45.4% of the economically active inhabitants engaged in agriculture. – **Currency:** Malaysian ringgit = 100 sen.
Economy: plantational agriculture and mining industry. Arable land 13.2%, forests 66.7%. **Agriculture** (1983, in 1,000 tonnes): rice 2,000, maize (corn), sweet potatoes 69, coconuts 1,200, copra 204, palm kernels 840 (leading world producer), palm oil 3,000 (leading world producer), groundnuts, manioc 305, bananas 475, fruit 880, pineapples 160, sugarcane 1,000, coffee, cocoa beans 55, tea, cashew nuts 735 tonnes, pepper; livestock (1983, in 1,000 head): cattle 600, buffaloes 300, pigs 2,100, goats 350, poultry 59 mn.; fish catch 741,000 tonnes. Natural rubber 1,530,000 tonnes (leading world producer), roundwood 41.9 mn. cub.m, rare timber.

23 a Java
1 : 15 000 000

1 : 25 000 000

23 b Philippines
1 : 15 000 000

Mining (1983, in 1,000 tonnes metal content): crude petroleum 18,972, natural gas 13,320 TJ, iron ore 64, bauxite 502, copper 29, manganese, tin 41.4 (leading world producer), antimony 180 tonnes, tungsten 25 tonnes, gold 185 kg. Electricity 12,135 mn. kWh. **Industry:** processing of tin, petroleum and agricultural products. **Production** (1983, in 1,000 tonnes): tin 53,338 tonnes (leading world producer), naphtha 110, motor spirit 935, jet fuel 360, woven cotton fabrics 241 mn. sq.m, sugar 75, meat 240.
Communications (1982): railways 2,375 km, roads 38,900 km, motor vehicles – passenger 1,332,000, commercial 350,000. Merchant shipping 1,475,000 GRT (1983). Civil aviation: 44.3 mn. km flown, 5,685,000 passengers carried (1983). Tourism 1,050,000 visitors. – **Exports:** natural rubber, tin, petroleum and petroleum products, wood, palm oil, copra. Chief trading partners: Japan, U.S.A., Singapore, United Kingdom, Fed. Rep. of Germany, Australia.

MALDIVES

Divehi Jumhuriya, **area** 298 sq.km, **population** 202,000 (1988), **republic** (President Maumoon Abdul Gayoom since 1978).
Capital: Male 45,000 inhab. (1982). – **Currency:** Maldive rupee = 100 laaris. – **Economy:** coconuts 9,000 tonnes, copra 1,000 tonnes, sweet potatoes, fruit; fish catch 38,500 tonnes. – **Exports:** coconuts, copra, fish.

MONGOLIA

Bügd Nayramdakh Mongol Ard Uls, **area** 1,566,500 sq.km, **population** 2,092,000 (1988), **people's democratic republic** (Chairman of the Presidium of the People's Great Khural Dr Jambyn Batmunkh since 1984).
Administrative units: 18 provinces (aimag) and 3 self-administered cities. **Capital:** Ulaanbaatar 435,400 inhab. (1982); **other towns** (1981, in 1,000 inhab.): Darchan 56, Erdenet 39. **Density** 1.2 person per sq.km. – **Currency:** tugrik = = 100 möngö.
Economy: agricultural and industrial country with nomadic cattle raising and processing of agricultural products. Arable land only 0.8%, meadows and pastures 78.8%. **Agriculture** (1983, in 1,000 tonnes): wheat 650, barley 90; livestock (1983, in 1,000 head): horses 2,028, cattle 2,396, camels 570, sheep 14,955, goats 4,802; hides 11,500 tonnes, sheepskins 15,600 tonnes. Electricity 1,975 mn. kWh (1983). Food industry (1983, in 1,000 tonnes): milk 170, meat 255, butter 8, cheese 3. – **Communications** (1983): railways 1,585 km, roads 29,018 km. Airport Ulaanbaatar. – **Exports:** hides and skins, wool, meat. Chief trading partners: U.S.S.R. (80%), China.

NEPAL

Sri Nepala Sarkar, **area** 147,181 sq.km, **population** 18,234,000 (1988), **kingdom** (King Mahárájádhirája Birendra Bir Bikram Sháh Dev since 1972).
Administrative units: 14 zones. **Capital:** Kätmåndu 393,494 inhab. (1981); **other towns:** Birâtnagar 93,544, Lalitpur 59,000 inhab. – **Currency:** Nepalese rupee = 100 pice.
Economy: agriculture, home crafts and industrial processing of agricultural products in new plants. **Agriculture** (1983, in 1,000 tonnes): rice 2,744, wheat 657, maize (corn) 768, millet 113, jute 40; livestock (1983, in 1,000 head): cattle 6,980, buffaloes 4,460, pigs 365, sheep 2,480, goats 2,650; roundwood 14.4 mn. cub.m. Electricity 257 mn. kWh (1983). – **Communications** (1983): railways 63 km, roads 5,270 km. – **Exports:** rice, jute, wood.

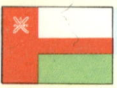

OMAN

Sultanate of Oman, **area** 212, 457 sq.km, **population** 1,377,000 (1988), **sultanate** (Sultan Qaboos bin Said since 1970).
Capital: Masqat (Muscat) 30,000 inhab. (1983, with agglom. 100,000); **other towns:** Sur 30,000, Naswa 25,000 inhab. – **Currency:** Oman rial = 1,000 baiza.
Economy. Agriculture (1983, in 1,000 tonnes): dates 75, cereals 3, fruit, lemons 13, tobacco; livestock (1983, in 1,000 head): cattle 150, sheep 140, goats 250, camels 8. Fish catch 108,000 tonnes. Electricity 1,402 mn. kWh (1983). **Mining** (1983): crude petroleum 18,685,000 tonnes, natural gas. – **Communications:** roads 1,911 km (1983). – **Exports:** petroleum, dates, citrus fruit, tobacco, fish, pearls. Chief trading partners: Japan, Fed. Rep. of Germany, U.S.A.

PAKISTAN

Islami Jumhouryat-e-Pakistan, **area** 803,942 sq.km, **population** 105,409,000 (1988), excluding the territory of „Free Kashmir" (Azad Kashmir, 79,900 sq.km), **republic, member of the Commonwealth** (President Ghulam Ishaq Khan since 1988).
Administrative units: 6 provinces. **Capital:** Islâmâbâd 204,364 inhab. (census 1981); **other towns** (in 1,000 inhab.): Karâchi 5,180, Lahore 2,953, Faisalâbâd 1,104, Rāwalpindi 794, Hyderâbâd 751, Multân 722, Gujrânwâla 659, Peshâwar 566, Siâlkot 302, Sargodha 291, Quetta 291. **Population:** Punjabi, Sindhi, Urdu etc. **Density** 120 persons per sq.km. Average annual rate of population increase 3% (1973–83); urban population 29% (1983). 52% of the economically active inhabitants engaged in agriculture. – **Currency:** Pakistani rupee = 100 paisa.
Economy: agricultural and industrial country. Arable land 25% of the land area. **Agriculture. Crops** (1983, in 1,000 tonnes) wheat 12,414, rice 5,210, maize (corn) 1,000, barley 185, millet 270, sorghum 235, chick-peas 491, sugarcane 32,534,

groundnuts 84, sesame 12, cotton – seed 1,040, – lint 520, dates 218; **livestock** (1983, in 1,000 head): horses 448, cattle 16,157, buffaloes 12,483, sheep 23,531, goats 27,716, asses 2,626; grease wool 42,700 tonnes, cattle hides 83,468 tonnes. Fish catch 343,400 tonnes. Roundwood 19.1 mn. cub.m. **Mining** (1983, in 1,000 tonnes, metal content): coal 1,855, crude petroleum 588, natural gas 318,984 TJ, chromium 2, antimony, magnesite, manganese, sulphur, salt 544, graphite, mica. Electricity 19.6 billion kWh (1983). Food, textile and leather **industries. Production** (1983, in 1,000 tonnes): cow milk 2,353, buffalo milk 6,902, butter 224, meat 949; 38,199 mn. cigarettes, woven cotton fabrics 370 mn m.
Communications (1982): railways 8,823 km, roads 57,494 km, motor vehicles – passenger 339,800, commercial 140,800 (1983). Merchant shipping 507,000 GRT. Civil aviation: 47.3 mn. km flown, 3,642,000 passengers carried (1983). Tourism 365,000 visitors (1983). – **Exports:** cotton and cotton products 60%, rice 20%, woollen and jute products. Chief trading partners: U.S.A., Japan, Fed. Rep. of Germany, United Kingdom, Saudi Arabia.

PHILIPPINES

Republika ng Pilipinas – Republic of the Philippines – República de Filipinas, area 297,413 sq.km, population 58,721,307 (1988), **republic** (President Mrs Corazon Aquino since 1986).

Administrative units: 73 provinces. **Capital:** Manila 1,630,485 inhab. (1980, with agglom. 6.8 mn.); **other towns** (in 1,000 inhab., +with agglom.): Quezon City 1,166, Davao+ 611, Cebu+ 600, Caloocan 471, Makati 372, Zamboanga+ 344, Pasay 266, Pasig 269, Bacolod 267. – **Population:** Filipino; chief tribes: Visay, Tagal, Igorot. **Density** 183 persons per sq.km; average annual rate of population increase 2.7% (1973–83); urban population 39% (1983). 44% of the economically active inhabitants engaged in agriculture. – **Currency:** Philippine peso = 100 centavos.
Economy: plantational agriculture with developing industry. Arable land 26%, forests 41% of the land area. **Agriculture. Crops:** (1983, in 1,000 tonnes): rice 8,150, maize (corn) 3,385, manioc 2,300, sweet potatoes 1,050, sugarcane 21,467, coconuts 9,200 (second world producer), copra 1,930 (leading world producer), palm kernels 2.7, palm oil 13.4, abaca, bananas 4,200, pineapples 1,300 (second world producer), coffee 160, tobacco 45, vegetables 2,114; **livestock** (1983, in 1,000 head): horses 300, cattle 1,938, buffaloes 2,946, pigs 7,980, goats 1,859, poultry 72 mn.; fish catch 1,836,900 tonnes. Roundwood 35.8 mn. cub.m; natural rubber 80,000 tonnes (1983). **Mining** (1983, in 1,000 tonnes, metal content): coal 1,020, brown coal, crude petroleum 731, uranium, iron ore, manganese, chromium 89, copper 208, nickel 14.4, silver, zinc, gold 25,397 kg, salt 382. Electricity 20,761 mn. kWh (1983). **Production** (1983, in 1,000 tonnes): cement 4,560, television receivers 190,000 units, motor vehicles – passenger 42,996, commercial 26,004 units, merchant vessels 260,000 GRT, woven cotton fabrics 156 mn. m, meat 830, sugar 2,578; 57,812 mn. cigarettes.
Communications: railways 1,069 km, roads 119,220 km, motor vehicles – passenger 367,000, commercial 556,000. Merchant shipping 3,441,000 GRT (1984). Civil aviation: 50.9 mn. km flown, 4,394,000, passengers carried (1983). Tourism 848,000 visitors (1983). – **Exports:** electrotechnical goods, sugar, coconuts, copra, coconut oil, abaca, copper concentrates, pineapples, bananas, wood. Chief trading partners: U.S.A., Japan, Fed. Rep. of Germany, Saudi Arabia.

QATAR

Dawlat Qatar, area 11,437 sq.km, population 369,000 (1986), **monarchy** (Amir Shaikh Khalifa bin Hamad Al-Thani since 1972).
Capital: Ad-Dawhah (Doha) 209,000 inhab. (1982). – **Currency:** Qatar riyal = 100 dirhams.
Economy: agriculture in oases (1983): dates, citrus fruit, extensive cattle raising (cattle 10,000, camels 6,000, sheep 53,000 head), fish catch 2,100 tonnes, pearl fishery. **Mining** (1983, in 1,000 tonnes): crude petroleum 14,540, natural gas 210,400 TJ. Electricity 3,105 mn. kWh (1983). **Production** (1983, in 1,000 tonnes): motor spirit 130, jet fuel 61. – **Communications:** roads 1,700 km, cars 136,800 (1982). Port Ad-Dawhah. – **Exports:** petroleum, dates. Chief trading partners: Japan, United Kingdom, Fed. Rep. of Germany, U.S.A.

SAUDI ARABIA

al-Mamlaka al-'Arabiya as-Sa'udiya, area 2,153,168 sq.km, population 14,016,000 (1988), **kingdom** (King Fahd ibn Abdul-Aziz since 1982).

Administrative units: 5 regions. **Capital:** Ar-Riyād 1,250,000 inhab. (1980), **other towns** (in 1,000 inhab.): Jiddah 1,300, Makkah (Mecca) 550, At-Tā'if 300, Al-Madīnah (Medina) 290. – **Population:** mainly Arabs, minorities: Iranians, Ludas and others. Average annual rate of population increase 4.7% (1973–83); urban population 68% (1981). 58% of the economically active inhabitants engaged in agriculture (1983). – **Currency:** Saudi rial = 100 halala.
Economy: the country with the largest resources of petroleum in the world (about 15,000 mn. tonnes) and large-scale extraction. Arable land 0.5% and pastures 39.5% of the land area. Cultivation of cereals and fruit in the oases, nomadic raising of cattle on pastures. **Agriculture** (1983, in 1,000 tonnes): dates 440, wheat 72, barley 12, maize (corn), millet 7, sorghum 87, oranges 26; **livestock** (1983, in 1,000 head): cattle 500, camels 160, sheep 3,500, goats 2,300. **Mining** (1983, in 1,000 tonnes): crude petroleum 252,707 (along the shore of the Persian Gulf and offshore wells), natural gas 50,000 TJ, Saudi Arabia participates with Kuwait in petroleum and natural gas extraction in the former Neutral Zone. Iron ore, pyrites, gold, phosphates. Electricity 32,000 mn. kWh (1983). **Production** (1983, in 1,000 tonnes): naphtha 1,100, motor spirit 3,300, jet fuel 91, distillate fuel oils 9,500.
Communications: railways 1,248 km, roads 20,134 km, motor vehicles – passenger 1,250,000, commercial 150,000 (1983). Merchant shipping 3,863,000 GRT. Civil aviation: 112.3 mn. km flown, 11.4 mn. passengers carried. – **Exports:** petroleum and petroleum products (one of the largest petroleum ports in the world is Ra's At-Tannūrah), dates, oranges. Chief trading partners: Japan, U.S.A., Fed. Rep. of Germany, Italy, United Kingdom.

C H I N A :

Autonomous regions:
1 Guangxi Zhuangzu Z.
2 Nei Mongol Z.
3 Ningxia Huizu Z.
4 Xinjiang Uygur Z.
   (Sinkiang)
5 Xizang Z. (Tibet)

Provinces:
6 Anhui
7 Fujian
8 Gansu
9 Guangdong
10 Guizhou
11 Hebei
12 Heilongjiang
13 Henan
14 Hubei
15 Hunan
16 Jiangsu
17 Jiangxi
18 Jilin
19 Liaoning
19a Hainan
20 Qinghai
21 Shaanxi
22 Shandong
23 Shanxi
24 Sichuan
25 Taiwan
26 Yunnan
27 Zhejiang

Municipalities:
28 Beijing
29 Shanghai
30 Tianjin

1 : 25 000 000

S.
R.
Ulan-Ude
Čita
Romanovka
Sretensk
Mogoča
Gulian
Mangui
Huma
Šimanovsk
Svobodnyj
Belogorsk
Blagoveščensk
Urgal
Komsomol'sk-na-Amure
Novoburejskij
Obluč'e
Birobidžan
CHABAROVSK
Petrovsk-Zabajkal'skij
Chilok
Aginskoje
Olov'annaja
Borz'a
Šilka
Ergun Zuoqi
Heihe
Nenjiang
Jiayin
Nižneleninskoje
Qianjin
Bikin
Altanbulag
Darchan
Čarüngol
ULAANBAATAR
Öndörchaan
Dzuunmod
Sümber
Mandalgov'
Sajnšand
Manzhouli
Bajan-Uul
Čojbalsan
Kerulen
Tamsagbulag
Džargalant
Baruun Urt
Hailar
Xiguituqi
Hulunchi
Butehaqi
QIQIHAR
Aershan
Wulanhaote
Tailai
Baicheng
Taoan
Beian
YICHUN
Hailun
HEGANG
JIAMUSI
Shuangyashan
Hurao
Dalnerečensk
Dalnegorsk
Anda
Songhuajiang
HARBIN
JIXI
Chanka
Arsenjev
Ussurijsk
VLADIVOSTOK
Nachodka
MUDANJIANG
JILIN
Dunhua
Yanji
CHANGCHUN
Tongliao
Siping
Jus Hua
Abagnar Qi
Linxi
Erlian
Shuangliao
LIAOYUAN
FUSHUN
SHENYANG
(Mukden)
BENXI
Chifeng
Duolun
JINZHOU
ANSHAN
DANDONG
Baiyunebo
Wuyuan
HOHHOT
Jining
ZHANGJIAKOU
Chengde
TANGSHAN
Linhe
BAOTOU
DATONG
BEIJING
(Peking)
BAODING
TIANJIN
CANGZHOU
DALIAN
Yantai
Weihai
Wuhai
Dongsheng
Ningwu
Shizuishan
TAIYUAN
Yulin
SHIJIAZHUANG
ZIBO
Weifang
QINGDAO
Jiaoxian
Wuzhong
Suide
Fenyang
Yuci
HANDAN
JINAN
Yan'an
Changzhi
Anyang
Jingyuan
Qingyang
Linfen
Hancheng
XINXIANG
Jining
Linyi
Shijiusuo
Lianyungang
Pingliang
Yuncheng
KAIFENG
Tongchuan
LUOYANG
ZHENGZHOU
XUZHOU
Yancheng
Tianshui
Baoji
XI'AN
Huaiyin
BANGBU
Luohe
NANJING
Nantong
Hanzhong
Nanyang
Guanghua
Huaihe
HUAINAN
HEFEI
Wuhu
WUXI
SHANGHAI
Guangyuan
Ankang
Xiangfan
XINYANG
SUZHOU
Shaoxing
NINGBO
Daxian
Wanxian
Fengjie
Yichang
WUHAN
Anqing
HANGZHOU
Nanchong
Shashi
Huangshi
Jiujiang
JINGDEZHEN
JINHUA
Linhai
Hechuan
CHONGQING
Dongtinghu
Changde
YUEYANG
Poyanghu
WENZHOU
CHANGSHA
Shangrao
Luzhou
Yiyang
NANCHANG
Fuzhou
Jianou
Zunyi
Zhijiang
Xiangtan
Zhuzhou
Ji'an
FUZHOU
Bijie
HENGYANG
Nanping
Sanming
GUIYANG
Shaoyang
Quanzhou
Anshun
Duyun
Lingling
Ganzhou
XIAMEN
Dushan
Guilin
Chezhou
Meixian
Shaoguan
Yishan
LIUZHOU
Chaoan
Baise
Wuzhou
GUANGZHOU
(Canton)
SHANTOU
NANNING
Xijiang
Foshan
NEW KOWLOON
Yulin
Maoming
Macau
(Port.)
VICTORIA
Hong Kong
(U.K.)
Dongshaqundao
(China)
Pingxiang
HA-NOI
Hon-Gai
Beihai
ZHANJIANG
HAI-PHONG
HAIKOU
Nam-Dinh
Thanh-Hoa
Vinh
Gulf of Tonkin
Hainandao
Yaxian
VIETNAM
SOUTH CHINA SEA
T'AIPEI
Hsinchu
T'AICHUNG
Chiai
Taiwan
T'AINAN
KAOHSIUNG
Taiwan Strait
Bashi Ch.
Luzon Strait
Batan Is.
Balintang Ch.
Babuyan Is.
PHILIPPINES
Laoag
Tuguegarao
Ilagan
Luzon
Tropic of Cancer
Nansei-shotō (Ryukyu Is.) (Jap.)
Sakishima-shotō
Okinawa-jima
Naha
Satsunan-shotō
EAST CHINA SEA
PACIFIC OCEAN
YELLOW SEA
Bo Hai
SEA OF JAPAN
DEM. PEOP. REP. OF KOREA
CH'ŎNGJIN
Kimch'aek
HAMHŬNG
Hŭngnam
SINŬIJU
WŎNSAN
P'YŎNGYANG
Ch'unch'ŏn
Haeju
INCH'ŎN
SŎUL
REP. OF KOREA
TAEGU
ULSAN
TAEJŎN
PUSAN
KWANGJU
Masan
Mokp'o
Korea Strait
Tsushima-kaikyō
Cheju
Cheju-do
Shimonoseki
KITAKYUSHU
FUKUOKA
Nagasaki
KUMAMOTO
KAGOSHIMA
JAPAN
Mongolia
China
110°
120°
130°
50°
40°
30°
20°

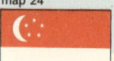

SINGAPORE

Republik Singapura – Republic of Singapore, area 620 sq.km, population 2,670,000 (1989), **republic, member of the Commonwealth** (President Wee Kim Wee since 1985).
Capital: Singapore 2,529,100 inhab. (1984). – **Population:** about 77% Chinese, 15% Malays, Indians, Pakistanis. **Density** 4,285 persons per sq.km; average annual rate of population increase 1.3% (1973–83); urban population 100%. 1.9% of the economically active inhabitants engaged in agriculture (1983). – **Currency:** Singapore dollar = = 100 cents.
Economy: important transit port, processing of Malayan tin (the largest tin smelting plant in Asia), shipyards, petrochemical industry, processing of natural rubber, textile industry. Arable land 10.5% of the land area. **Agriculture:** sweet potatoes, manioc, coconuts, natural rubber; raising of pigs 1,300,000 head (1983); fish catch 19,500 tonnes (1983). Electricity 8,626 mn. kWh (1983). **Production** (1983, in 1,000 tonnes): vessels 39,000 GRT, naphtha 3,550, motor spirit 2,325, jet fuel 2,125, distillate fuel oils 7,050.
Communications (1984): railways 25.8 km, roads 2,569 km, passenger cars 223,116. Merchant shipping 6,512,000 GRT (1983). Civil aviation: 75.6 mn. km flown, 4,792,000 passengers carried (1984). Tourism 2,854,000 visitors (1983). – **Exports:** petroleum products, machinery products, textiles, transit from Malaysia (natural rubber, tin, iron ore, copra). Chief trading partners: U.S.A., Malaysia, Japan, Hong Kong, United Kingdom, Australia.

SRI LANKA

Janarajaya Srī Lanka, area 65,610 sq.km, population 16,587,000 (1988), **republic, member of the Commonwealth** (President Ranasinghe Premadasa since 1989).
Administrative units: 9 provinces. **Capital:** Colombo 623,000 inhab. (1983); **other towns** (in 1,000 inhab.): Dehiwala-Mt. Lavinia 181, Moratuwa 137, Jaffna 128. – **Population:** about 74% Sinhalese, 13% Ceylon and Indian Tamils, 7% Moors etc. **Density** 241 persons per sq.km; average annual rate of population increase 1.7%; urban population 26% (1983). 52% of the economically active inhabitants engaged in agriculture. – **Currency:** Sri Lanka rupee = 100 cents.
Economy: tropical fruit growing on plantations and mineral mining. Arable land 15.6%, land under permanent crops 17.1%, forests 36.3% of the land area. **Agriculture** (1983, in 1,000 tonnes): rice 2,200, sweet potatoes 160, tea 175, coconuts 2,300, copra 145, natural rubber 135, cocoa beans 3; **livestock** (1983, in 1,000 head): cattle 1,700, buffaloes 880, pigs 80, sheep 28; fish catch 222,000 tonnes. Roundwood 8.4 mn. cub.m. **Mining:** graphite 5,870 tonnes (1983), gem stones, salt 128. Electricity 2,114 mn. kWh (1983). Chemical, textile and food **industries.**
Communications (1983): railways 1,453 km, roads 31,150 km, motor vehicles – passenger 136,900, commercial 109,600. Merchant shipping 746,000 GRT. Civil aviation: 13.1 mn. km flown, 681,000 passengers carried (1983). Tourism 338,000 visitors (1983). **Exports:** tea (60% of exports), textiles, natural rubber, coconuts, copra, graphite, gem stones, cocoa beans. Chief trading partners: Japan, U.S.A., Iraq, Saudi Arabia, United Kingdom.

SYRIA

al Jamhouriya al-'Arabiya as Souriya, area 185,180 sq.km, population 11,338,000 (1988), **republic** (President Gen. Hafez al-Assad since 1971).
Administrative units: 14 districts (mohafaza). **Capital:** Dimashq (Damascus) 1,251,028 inhab. (census 1981); **other towns** (in 1,000 inhab): Halab (Aleppo) 977, Hims 355, Al-Lādhiqīyah 197, Hamāh 177, Dayr az-Zawr 87, Ar-Raqqah 87. – **Population:** Syrian Arabs, minorities: Kurds 5%, Armenians, Cherkese. **Density** 60 persons per sq.km; average annual rate of population increase 3.3% (1973–83); urban population 48%. 46% of the economically active inhabitants engaged in agriculture (1983). – **Currency:** Syrian pound = 100 piastres.
Economy: agricultural and industrial country. Arable land 28.2%, meadows and pastures 45.2% of the land area. **Agriculture** (1983, in 1,000 tonnes): wheat 1,612, barley 1,043, potatoes 300, cotton – seed 335, – lint 18, legumens, vegetables 3,294. Mediterranean products – chiefly olives 235, oranges 55, lemons 12, grapes 389, tobacco 14; **livestock** (1983, in 1,000 head): cattle 800, sheep 11,000, goats 1,100; fish catch 3,800 tonnes (1983). **Mining** (1983, in 1,000 tonnes): crude petroleum 9,359, natural gas 2,960 TJ, natural asphalt, phosphates 1,231, salt 88. Electricity 6,175 mn. kWh (1983). **Industry:** petrochemical, textile and food industries. **Production** (1983, in 1,000 tonnes): woven cotton fabrics 374, motor spirit 474, jet fuel 200, disillate fuel oils 2,095.
Communications (1982): railways 2,086 km, roads 18,850 km, motor vehicles – passenger 127,300, commercial 108,700. Civil aviation: 8.8 mn. km flown, 464,000 passengers carried (1983). – **Exports:** petroleum, cotton, fruit and vegetables, cereals, hides and skins, furs, phosphates. Chief trading partners: U.S.S.R., Italy, United Kingdom, France, Greece.

THAILAND

Prathes Thai (Muang-Thai), area 514,121 sq.km, population 54,536,000 (1988), **monarchy** (King Bhumibol Adulyadej since 1946).
Administrative units: 72 provinces (changwad). **Capital:** Krung Thep (Bangkok) 5,468,286 inhab. (1983, with Thon Buri); **other towns** (census 1980, in 1,000 inhab.): Chiang Mai 100, Hat Yai 98, Khon Kaen 94, Nakhon Ratchasima 89, Nakhon Sawan 89, Udon Thani 81, Phitsanulok 73. – **Population:** Thais 85% (chiefly Siamese and Lao), Chinese, Malays etc. **Density** 100 persons per sq.km; average annual rate of population increase 2.3% (1973–83); urban population 18% (1983). 74% of the economically active inhabitants engaged in agriculture. – **Currency:** baht = 100 satang.
Economy: agricultural country with few industries. Arable land 31.6%, forests 30.7% of the land area. Rice is cultivated on 65–70% of the arable land. **Agriculture** (1983, in 1,000 tonnes): rice 18,535, maize (corn) 3,552, sorghum 327, sweet potatoes 355, manioc 17,000, sugarcane 24,407, groundnuts 157, sesame 26, jute 234, cotton – seed 87, lint 44, bananas

2,035, pineapples 1,439 (leading world producer), oranges 57, coconuts 800, palm kernels 12.4, tobacco 92; **livestock** (1983, in 1,000 head): cattle 4,600, buffaloes 6,150, pigs 3,800; fish catch 2,250,000 tonnes (1983); roundwood 40.4 mn. cub.m; natural rubber 570,000 tonnes. **Mining** (1983, in 1,000 tonnes, metal content): brown coal 2,250, crude petroleum, natural gas 56,972 TJ, iron ore 23, tungsten 563 tonnes, tin 19.9, antimony 1,236 tonnes, manganese 2.3, gem stones. Electricity 18,875 mn. kWh. **Industry:** food processing, textile and food industries. **Production** (1983, in 1,000 tonnes): pig iron 12, crude steel 244, tin 18.6, woven cotton fabrics 800, sugar 2,550, meat 771; 28,941 mn. cigarettes.
Communications (1982): railways 3,735 km, roads 44,200 km, motor vehicles – passenger 511,200, commercial 351,500. Merchant shipping 567,000 GRT (1983). Civil aviation: 57.7 mn. km flown, 3,671,000 passengers carried (1983). Tourism 2,154,000 visitors (1983). – **Exports:** rice 15%, maize (corn), manioc, textiles, natural rubber, tin, jute, wood. Chief trading partners: Japan, U.S.A., Singapore, Fed. Rep. of Germany, United Kingdom, Saudi Arabia.

TURKEY

Türkiye Cumhuriyeti, area 779,452 sq.km, population 52,422,000 (1988), of which the Asiatic part 755,688 sq.km and population 46,622,000, **republic** (President Turgut Özal since 1989).

Administrative units: 67 provinces (iller). **Capital:** Ankara 1,981,300 inhab. (1983, with agglom. 3.4 mn. 1985); **other towns** (in 1,000 inhab., *with agglom. 1985): İstanbul 2,903, İzmir 832 (*2,300), Adana 637, Bursa 510, Gaziantep 421, Konya 385, Eskişehir 340, Kayseri 332, Diyarbakır 282, Mersin 262, Erzurum 207. – **Population:** over 90% Turks, about 7% Kurds, Arabs etc. **Density** 66 persons per sq.km, in the Asiatic part 54 persons per sq.km; average annual rate of population increase 2.2% (1973–83); urban population 45% (1983). 50% of the economically active inhabitants engaged in agriculture (1983). – **Currency:** Turkish Lira = 100 kuruş.
Economy: agricultural and industrial country with great regional differences. Arable land 32.5%, meadows and pastures 12.4%, forests 25.9% of the land area. **Agriculture. Crops** (1983, in 1,000 tonnes): wheat 16,400, barley 5,600, maize (corn) 1,375, rye 430, rice 325, oats 330, potatoes 3,080, beans 166, lentils 450, peas, sugar beet 12,000, sunflower 725, groundnuts 65, sesame 12, chick-peas 250, cotton – seed 800, lint 520 – olives 450, figs, raisins 300 (second world producer), oranges 701, tangerines 232, lemons 330, grapes 3,400, apples 1,700, pears 344, almonds 35; hazelnuts 370 (leading world producer), walnuts 121 (second world producer), pistachios, 20, chestnuts 60, tomatoes 3,700, dry onions 1,040, tobacco 225. **Livestock** (1983, in 1,000 head): horses 770, cattle 17,100, buffaloes 808, camels 10, sheep 49,636, goats 18,213, asses 1,300; cattlehides 70,000 tonnes, sheepskins 67,000 tonnes, grease wool 64,000 tonnes, mohair; fish catch 567,300 tonnes (1983), roundwood 19.2 mn. cub.m.
Mining (1983, in 1,000 tonnes, metal content): coal 4,110, brown coal 17,000, crude petroleum 2,203, uranium, chromium 135, iron ore 2,207, manganese, lead 6.3, zinc, mercury 127 tonnes, antimony 1,089 tonnes, cobalt, copper 25, magnesite 719, sulphur, bauxite 296, asbestos, marble, salt 1,261, phosphates 50. Electricity 27,321 mn. kWh (1983). **Industry:** food, tobacco and textile industries. **Production** (1983, in 1,000 tonnes): pig iron 2,645, crude steel 2,479, cement 13,595, sulphuric acid 338, nitrogenous fertilizers 783.1, phosphate fertilizers 621.5, motor spirit 1,917, jet fuel 283, naphtha 893, distillate fuel oils 4,582, motor vehicles, merchant vessels 74,000 GRT, radio receivers 188,000, television receivers 603,000, woven cotton fabrics 234 mn. m, woven woollen fabrics 8 mn. m, carpets, meat 943, sugar 1,654, milk 3,700, cheese 133.5, butter 125, olive oil 70, flour 1,582, wine 370,000 hl, beer 3.2 mn. hl; 61,500 mn. cigarettes.
Communications (1983): railways 8,373 km, roads 60,712 km, motor vehicles – passenger 856,400, commercial 342,500. Merchant shipping 3,125,000 GRT (1983). Civil aviation: 25.1 mn. km flown, 2.2 mn. passengers carried (1983). Tourism 1.2 mn. visitors (1983). – **Exports:** fruit and raisins, cotton and textiles, cotton fabrics, tobacco and tobacco products, fruit (hazelnuts, raisins etc.), animal products (cattle, wool, hides), carpets, clothing. Chief trading partners: Iran, Fed. Rep. of Germany, Iraq, U.S.A., Italy, United Kingdom, Switzerland.

UNITED ARAB EMIRATES

Dawlat al-Imārāt al-'Arabīya al Muttahida, area 83,657 sq.km, population 1,501,000 (1988), **federation of emirates** (President Sheikh Zayed bin Sultan al Nahyan since 1971).
Administrative units: 7 emirates. **Capital:** Abu Zaby 242,975 inhab., census 1980); **other towns:** Dubayy 267,702, Ash-Shāriqah 125,149. – **Population:** average annual rate of population increase 11.3% (1973–83); urban population 79%. – **Currency:** dirham = 100 fils.
The economy is based on petroleum and natural gas extraction. Cultivation of vegetables. Arable land covers only 15,000 ha. Fish catch 73,100 tonnes (1983), pearl fishery. **Mining** (1983, in 1,000 tonnes): crude petroleum 53,640 (of which more than two thirds emirate Abu Zaby), natural gas 542,200 TJ. Electricity 7,900 mn. kWh. **Production** (1983, in 1,000 tonnes): motor spirit 370, naphtha 250, distillate fuel oils 280. – **Exports:** petroleum and petroleum products, dry fish, pearls. Chief trading partners: Japan, U.S.A., United Kingdom, Fed. Rep. of Germany, France, Italy, Bahrain.

VIETNAM

Công Hòa Xã Hôi Chu Nghĩa Viêt Nam, area 332,560 sq.km, population 64,227,000 (1988), **socialist republic** (Chairman of the State Council Vo Chi Cong since 1987).
Administrative units: 3 self-administrated cities, 37 provinces. **Capital:** Ha-Noi 2,570,909 inhab. (census 1979); **other towns** (in 1,000 inhab.): Thanh-phô Hô Chi Minh (Saigon) 3,120, Hai-Phong 1,279, Da-Nang 620, Can-Tho 183, Nha-Trang 173, Hue 166, Nam-Dinh 161. – **Population:** Vietnamese 84%, other nationalities Thai, Khmer, Meo etc. **Density** 180 persons per sq.km; average annual rate of population increase 2.7% (1973–83); urban population 20%. 69% of the economically active inhabitants engaged in agriculture. – **Currency:** dông = 10 liao = 100 xu.

MONGOLIA
Nei Mongol Zizhiqu
Heilongjiang
Jilin
Liaoning
Hebei
Shandong
Jiangsu
Anhui
Zhejiang
Wulanhaote
Tailai
Anda
Suihua
JIAMU
Yilan
Mulan
Songhuajiang
HARBIN
Baicheng
Jus Hua
Taoan
Dalai
Nenjiang
Shuangcheng
Shangzhi
Fuyu
Jarud Qi
Tongyu
Yushu
MUDANJIANG
Abagnar Qi
Nong'an
Shulan
Ningan
Balinzuoqi
Linxi
Bairin Youqi
Dalai Nur
CHANGCHUN
Lafa
Mudanjiang
Hexigten Qi
Kailu
Tongliao
Xihe
Shuangliao
Huaide
JILIN
Dunhua
Siping
LIAOYUAN
Huadian
Songhuahu
Kulunqi
Duolun
Faku
Yanji
Weichang
Chifeng
Laohahe
FUXIN
Kaiyuan
Liaohe
Hailong
Xinmin
Tieling
Fusong
Helong
Guyuan
Luanhe
Beipiao
Musan
Fengning
Longhua
Chaoyang
SHENYANG
(Mukden)
FUSHUN
Tonghua
Linjiang
ZHANGJIAKOU
Chengde
Heishan
Liaoyang
Hyesan
Jianping
Xuanhua
Luanping
Lingyuan
JINZHOU
BENXI
Ji'an
Kanggye
Huailai
Jinxi
ANSHAN
Kuancheng
Yingkou
Kuandian
Kilchu
Shunyi
Fengcheng
Amnok-kang
Yalujiang
Kimch'aek
BEIJING
(Peking)
Tongxian
Zunhua
Liaodongwan
Gaiping
Sakchu
Hŭich'ŏn
Pukch'ŏng
Shanhaiguan
DANDONG
SINŬIJU
HAMHŬNG
Iwŏn
Qinhuangdao
Gushan
Anju
TANGSHAN
Fuxian
Hŭngnam
Tanggu
Xinjin
Chengzituan
Korea Bay
Kowŏn
BAODING
TIANJIN
(Tientsin)
Jinxian
P'YŎNGYANG
WŎNSAN
Tongjosŏn-man
Dingxian
Hejian
Bo Hai
T'ongch'ŏn
CANGZHOU
DALIAN
NAMP'O
Nanyunhe
Kosŏng
Songnim
Sariwŏn
Kansŏng
P'yŏnggang
Hengshui
Penglai
Haeju
Kaesŏng
Huimin
Dezhou
Laizhouwan
Ongjin
Ch'unch'ŏn
Kangnŭng
Linqing
Huanghe
Yantai
Weihai
INCH'ŎN
SŎUL
Wŏnju
Samch'ŏk
JINAN
ZIBO
Yidu
Laiyang
Wendeng
Suwŏn
Liaocheng
Tai'an
Weifang
Haiyang
Ch'ŏnan
Ch'ungju
Jiaoxian
Ch'ŏngju
Zhucheng
Andong
Jining
Yanzhou
Yishui
TAEJŎN
QINGDAO
Changhang
Iri
TAEGU
P'ohang
Juxian
Kunsan
Nanyanghu
Chŏnju
Kyŏngju
Zaozhuang
Linyi
YELLOW SEA
Chinju
Masan
ULSAN
Weishanhu
Shijiusuo
Peixian
Lianyungang
KWANGJU
PUSAN
Donghai
Mokp'o
Sunch'ŏn
XUZHOU
Guanhe
Yŏsu
Korea Strait
Suxian
Shuyang
Chin-do
Izuhara
Tsushima
Suqian
Yunhe
Grand Canal
Huaiyin
Funing
Tsushima-kaikyo
Hongzehu
Yancheng
Cheju
Huaihe
BANGBU
Gaoyou
Cheju-do
FUKUOKA
Gaoyouhu
Dongtai
Gotō-rettō
HUAINAN
Yangzhou
Sasebo
HEFEI
Taizhou
Rugao
NANJING
Nagasaki
Liuan
Zhenjiang
Nantong
Chaohu
Amakusa-shotō
Maanshan
Changzhou
Shucheng
Changjiang
WUXI
Chongming
Yixing
SUZHOU
Wuhu
Tongling
SHANGHAI
KAGOSHIMA
Guichi
Taihu
Jiaxing
Huzhou
EAST CHINA SEA
Anqing
Yupanyang
HANGZHOU
Qimen
Shaoxing
Tunxi
Shexian
NINGBO
Zhoushanqundao
Xiangshan
Linhai
Shangrao
Lishui
Nansei-shotō
(Ryukyu Is.)
(Jap.)
DEM. PEOPLE'S REP. OF KOREA
REP. OF KOREA
1 : 12 500 000
0 100 200 300 Km
0 50 100 150 200 Mi
115°
120°
125°
45°
40°
35°
30°
A
B
C
D
E
1
2
3
4
27
28
29
30

25 a Taiwan (Formosa) 1 : 12 500 000

Economy: agricultural country with developing industrial production. Arable land 18%, forests 31% of the land area.
Agriculture. Crops (1983, in 1,000 tonnes): rice 11,500, maize (corn) 420, sweet potatoes 1,700, potatoes 500, manioc 2,700, soya beans 107, groundnuts 87, sugarcane 4,600, jute 38, cotton, vegetables 2,839, fruit 3,107 (oranges 95, pineapples 380), tea 28, coffee 9, tobacco 32; **livestock** (1983, in 1,000 head): cattle 2,000, buffaloes 2,390, pigs 10,787; raw silk 300 tonnes; fish catch 710; roundwood 23.7 mn. cub.m, natural rubber 43,000 tonnes. **Mining** (1983, in 1,000 tonnes): coal 6,000, iron ore, molybdenum, tin, gold, phosphates 200, salt 889. Electricity 4,200 mn. kWh (1983). **Industry:** textile and food industries, processing of phosphates. **Production:** phosphate fertilizers 35,000 tonnes (1983), woven cotton fabrics 287 mn. m, cement 910,000 tonnes.
Communications: railways 3,216km, main roads 60,000km, motor vehicles – passenger 170,000; merchant shipping 358,400 GRT. – **Exports:** natural rubber, fruit, tea, fish, wood, vegetables, minerals. Chief trading partners: U.S.S.R. and CMEA countries, Japan, South-eastern Asia countries.

YEMEN

al Jamhuriya al Yamaniya, **area** 531,869 sq.km, **population** 11,109,000 (1988), republic (President Ali Abdullah Saleh since 1990).

Administrative units: 8 provinces (liwa). **Capital:** San'ā' 440,000 inhab. (1984); **other towns:** Ta'izz 220,000, Al-Hudaydah 140,000. – **Population:** Arabs, minorities of other Asian and African nationals. Density 21 persons per sq.km; urban population 18%. 73% of the economically active inhabitants engaged in agriculture. – **Currency:** Yemeni riyal = = 100 fils.
Economy: developing agricultural country. Arable land 14%, meadows and pastures 36%. **Agriculture** (1983, in 1,000 tonnes): wheat 27, barley 10, sorghum 248, maize 32, potatoes 140, coffee 4, cotton 5, grapes 59, dates 84; **livestock** (in 1,000 head): cattle 950, camels 108, sheep 3,150, goats 7,500, fish catch 22,200 tonnes. **Mining** of salt. – **Communications:** main roads 2,170km, chief port Al-Hudaydah. **Exports:** cotton, coffee, hides and skins, fish.

Including the part of former Democratic (or South) Yemen since 22. May 1990.

Administrative units: 6 governorates (muchafaz). **Ports:** Adan (Aden) 343,000 inhab. (1980); **other towns:** Al-Mukallā 100,000. – **Population:** Arabs, small number of Indians and Somalis. Density 7 persons per sq.km; average annual rate of population increase 2.2% (1973–83): urban population 37% (1983). 57% of the economically active inhabitants engaged in agriculture. – **Currency:** Yemeni dinar (YD) = 1,000 fils.
Economy: nomadic raising of cattle, petrochemical industry, major transit port. Arable land only 0.6% of the land area.
Agriculture (1983, in 1,000 tonnes): wheat 15, millet 80, cotton, dates 44; livestock (1983, in 1,000 head): cattle 120, sheep 1,000, goats 1,350, camels 100; fish catch 74,000 tonnes (1983). Electricity 280 mn. kWh (1983). **Production** (1983, in 1,000 tonnes): motor spirit 200, jet fuel 160, distillate fuel oils 480. – **Communications:** roads 1,152km, rough tracks 10,270km, motor vehicles – passenger 17,800, commercial 19,400 (1981). Adan is an important naval and air base and a major transit port. – **Exports:** petroleum products, cotton.

BRITISH TERRITORY:

HONG KONG

Crown Colony of Hong Kong, area 1,071 sq.km, **population** 5,681,000 (1988), British Dependent Territory (Governor Sir David Wilson since 1987).
Capital: Victoria 633,138 inhab. (census 1981): **other towns** (in 1,000 inhab.): New Kowloon 1,651, Kowloon 799, Tsuen Wan 720, Sha Tin 625, Tuen Mun 547. **Density** 5,229 persons per sq.km; average annual rate of population increase 2.5% (1973–83); urban population 92%. – **Currency:** Hong Kong dollar = 100 cents.
Economy: important industrial and trading centre, naval and air base. **Agriculture:** arable land and permanent crops 8% of the land area. Crop of rice 4,000 tonnes, raising of pigs and poultry. Fish catch 188,800 tonnes (1983). Textile, clothing and leather **industries,** shipbuilding, electronics, chemical and printing industries. Electricity 16,482 mn. kWh. **Production** (1983): radio receivers 47,986,000 units, television receivers 368,000 units, woven cotton fabrics 642 mn. sq.m, woven silk fabrics 1.6 mn. sq.m, clocks and watches, plastic products, toys.
Communications: railways 73km, roads 1,237km, passenger cars 33,000. Merchant shipping 5,784,000 GRT. Tourism 2,137,000 visitors (1983). – **Exports:** textile products and clothing, electronic products, cameras, watches, fish, metalware. Chief trading partners: U.S.A., China, Japan, Singapore, Fed. Rep. of Germany, United Kingdom.

PORTUGUESE TERRITORY:

MACAU

Provincia de Macau, **area** 16.9 sq.km, **population** 444,000 (1988). Portuguese territory (Gov. Carlos Melancia). **Capital:** Macau 276,673 inhab. (1980). – **Currency:** pataca = 100 avos. **Economy:** fish catch 7,000 tonnes (1983). **Industry:** clothing, knitwear, porcelain ware. Transit merchant port. Tourism 673,000 visitors. – **Exports:** textiles, clothing, fish.

AFRICA

Africa lies on both sides of the Equator, with the larger part in the northern hemisphere. The name Africa is derived from a Berber tribe, the Afrigi (or Afridi), who lived in the territory of today's Tunisia. The Latin name "Africa" was applied to a Roman province extending over the area previously under the control of Carthage.

Africa covers an **area** of **30,329,000 sq.km**, i.e. 20.3% of the land surface of the Earth and is the second largest continent. It has **610 million inhabitants** (1988), and a population density 20.1 persons per sq.km. **Geographical position**: northernmost point: Cape Râs Ben Sekka (Tunisia) 37°21' N.Lat.; southernmost point: Cape Agulhas (South Africa) 34°52' S. Lat.; westernmost point: Cape Pointe des Almadies 17°38' W.Long. (4 km northwest of Cap Vert); easternmost point: Cape Râs Hafûn 51°23' E.Long. Africa is joined to Asia by the Isthmus of Suez (120 km long), and it is separated from Europe by the Strait of Gibraltar (14 km wide). The coast of Africa, 30,500 km in length, has little articulation. The largest peninsula is the Somali Pen. (area 850,000 sq.km). The principal islands are Madagascar (area 587,041 sq.km) and the small Mascarene Is. (4,555 sq.km) in the Indian Ocean; off the northwest coast in the Atlantic Ocean lie the Canary Is. (7,273 sq.km) and the Cape Verde Is. (4,033 sq.km).

Orographically, Africa is divided into 3 main regions: the Atlas Mts., the African Tableland and the East African Highlands. The Atlas Mts. stretch over 2,000 km in north-west Africa (highest peak: Jbel Tubqâl, 4,165 m) adjoined by the Plateau of the Shotts and its salt lakes. To the south of the Atlas Mts. lie the extensive Sahara-Sudanese plains and plateau (average height 200–500 m). The Sahara is the world's largest desert (7,820,000 sq.km); it is a rock (hamada), gravel (reg, serir) and sand desert with dunes (ergs), with the barren Mountains of Ahaggar (3,005 m), Tibesti (Emi Koussi, 3,415 m), Aïr (2,310 m) and Dârfûr (3,088 m) in its centre. South-west of the Sahara lie the Upper Guinean Highlands (1,948 m) and the Adamaoua Highlands (2,679 m). In Central Africa a vast tectonic depression formed the Congo Basin (3 million sq.km). Its centre is 300–500 m high, and the border ridges are between 500 and 1,000 m. The Lower Guinean Highlands (2,620 m) rise at its western border. South of the Luanda-Katanga Plateau lies the synclinal Kalahari Basin, a plain (average height 950 m) and to the west, along the coast, the Namib Desert, 1,500 km in length. South Africa comprises the Karroo Plateau, the Cape Mts. (2,326 m) and the Drakensberg Mountains, which are South Africa's highest at Thabana-Ntlenyana 3,482 m. The Ethiopian Highlands (average altitude 2,500 m) are the eastern continuation of the Saharan-Arabian Tableland (highest point: Ras Dashen, 4,620 m). The Assal Depression in the Afar Pan by the Red Sea is the lowest point in Africa, −173 m below sea level. The East African Plateau has the most varied forms: tectonic rifts (e.g. the Great Rift Valley), mountain ridges (Ruwenzori, Ngaliema, 5,119 m), volcanoes, craters (Ngorongoro, 3,648 m) and plateau. Africa's highest mountain stands here; the volcanic Kilimanjaro with its three conical peaks, Uhuru, 5,895 m being the highest.

Africa's **rivers** were formed more recently. The network of rivers and drainage is highly irregular. The average volume of water flow per year is 4,657 cubic km. Almost one third of Africa lacks any form of drainage, especially the Sahara. More than one third of Africa drains into the Atlantic Ocean. Africa's major river is the Congo (Zaïre), 4,835 km in length with a river basin of 3,822,000 sq.km, the mean discharge is 41,400 cub.m per second. The Niger reaches the Gulf of Guinea through the Niger delta; its length is 4,160 km, the river basin occupies 2,092,000 sq.km. Africa's longest river is the Nile (length: 6,671 km, river basin 2,881,000 sq.km, mean discharge 1,600 cubic m per second). It forms a vast delta (25,000 sq.km) as it flows into the Mediterranean Sea. The greatest river in South Africa is the Zambezi. Most of the great African **lakes** are of tectonic origin, the largest being Lake Victoria (68,800 sq.km) and the deepest Lake Tanganyika (1,470 m, its bottom lying 697 m below sea level).

In view of its position Africa is the warmest continent. The climatic differences between regions are conditioned by pressure systems on the mainland and the adjacent ocean. Four **climatic zones** can be distinguished: the equatorial zone (Congo Basin and the coast of the Gulf of Guinea) has a hot wet climate all year; the zone of equatorial monsoons affects one third of Africa (up to 15° N.Lat. and 18° S.Lat.) with hot wet summers and warm dry winters; the zone of tropical trade-winds (Sahara and Kalahari deserts) to the north and the south of the continent suffers extreme drought; the subtropical (Mediterranean) zone has hot dry summers and temperate rainy winters. The maximum absolute temperature is found at Al-Azîzîyah (Libya) 58 °C; the highest average annual temperature, 34.4 °C was recorded in Dalol (Ethiopia) and the lowest, −15 °C, in the Atlas Mts. Maximum rainfall in Africa was measured at C. Debunja (Cameroon): 10,470 mm, while Aswân (Egypt) is the driest place (0.5 mm).

Mean January and July temperatures in °C (annual precipitation in mm): Alger 10.3 and 24.4 (746), Al-Qâhirah 13.8 and 28.4 (25), Al-Khurtûm 22.5 and 30.8 (168), Tombouctou 22.6 and 31.5 (230), Conakry 26.5 and 25.6 (4,349), Kumasi 25.2 and 24.2 (1,530), Douala 27.3 and 24.8 (4,439), Mesewa 25.5 and 34.5 (181), Mombasa 27.8 and 23.9 (1,197), Kisangani 25.5 and 24.2 (1,530), Lusaka 20.6 and 15.5 (837), Windhoek 23.5 and 14.0 (386), Antananarivo 21.3 and 14.7 (1359), Pretoria 21.0 and 10.3 (748), Cape Town 22.7 and 18.4 (644).

In terms of its **flora**, Africa is divided into two regions: the Holarctic realm in the north and the Sahara desert and the larger, the Paleotropical, south of the Sahara. Tropical evergreen rain forests in the wettest regions are bordered to the north, east and south by grass savannas (covering 35% of the land) and gallery woods in the river valleys, grass and scrub semi-deserts and deserts (xerophilous and succulent scrub). The north has Mediterranean evergreen scrub and dry forests. The flora of the Cape region is related to that of south-west Australia. The **fauna** of Africa is mostly found in the Ethiopian region. The savannas are inhabited by antelopes, elephants, giraffes, hippopotami, rhinoceroses, zebras, wildebeests, lions, leopards, hyenas, monkeys, crocodiles, ostriches, waterfowl (flamingos, pelicans, cranes, herons, etc), vultures and insects (termites, locusts); the forests by gorillas, chimpanzees, vervets, buffaloes, parrots, beetles and butterflies. Madagascar has fauna of the Tertiery era: lemurs, running-birds, iguanas, etc. Africa has a number of extensive National Parks and wildlife reservations where the animals and the environment are protected. The best-known are: Etosha Pan (69,153 sq.km), Kafue (22,400 sq.km), Salonga, Tsavo, Serengeti, Virunga, Kruger N.P., Kalahari-Gemsbok, Wankie, Ngorongoro, Selous, Southern N.P., Gorongoza etc.

Africa takes up 20.3% of the area of the world, and in 1988 **610 million people** lived on the continent, i.e. 11.9 % of the world's population. With 20 persons per sq.km Africa is the least densely populated continent. The unevenness of settlement is most striking in a comparison between the density of population in the Nile valley (over 500 persons per sq.km) and that in desert areas where there is less than 1 person per sq.km. Apart from certain islands, the greatest density of population is found in Rwanda, Burundi and Nigeria, and the lowest (1 person per sq.km) in Botswana, Mauritania, Namibia and the Western Sahara. From 1980–85 the average annual

26a Nile Delta Suez Canal
1 : 5 000 000

26b Canary Islands 1:10 000 000

Canary Islands
- La Caldera 2423
- Garatia
- Sta. Cruz de la Palma
- La Palma
- Tenerife
- Fuerteventura
- Lanzarote
- Arrecife
- La Laguna
- Pto. de la Cruz
- Sta. Cruz de Ten.
- Pto. del Rosario
- Gomera
- Pico de Teide 3718
- S. Sebastián-de la Gom.
- Las Palmas
- Valverde
- Arucas
- Hierro
- Gran Canaria
- Tarfaya
- MOROCCO
- WEST. Sahara

Main map features

Mediterranean / Asia Minor region
- 5121, Kriti, Cyprus, RANEAN SEA, Syrian Desert

North Africa
- Qattara Depr. -133
- Al-Qāhirah
- Sinai Pen. 2642
- Dead Sea -400
- Western Desert
- Libyan Desert
- J. al-'Uwaynāt 1934
- Aswān
- L. Nasser
- Nubian Desert
- Ennedi 1450
- Dārfūr 3088
- Al-Fāshir
- Eastern Desert

Red Sea / Horn of Africa
- 3039
- 2780 Mesewa
- Hadūr Shu'ayb 3760
- Arabian Pen.
- Al-Khurtūm
- Asmera
- Ras Dashen 4620
- Dalol -116
- Assal Depr. -155
- Ethiopian
- Djibouti
- Adan (Aden)
- Bāb el Mandeb
- Suquṭrā
- Addis Abeba
- Batu 4307
- Highlands
- Rās Asir
- Dante
- Rās Hafūn
- Gulf of Aden
- Somali Pen.
- 5824

East Africa / Great Lakes
- 1400
- Bahr al-'Arab
- Bahr al-Jabal
- Sobat
- Bomu
- Uele
- Aruwimi
- Kisangani
- Ngalema
- Stanley Falls 5119
- L. Albert
- L. Kyoga
- Mt. Elgon 4321
- L. Turkana
- Mt. Kenya/Kirinyaga 5199
- L. Edward
- Karisimbi 4507
- Nairobi
- L. Kivu
- L. Victoria
- Kilimanjaro-Uhuru 5895
- Bujumbura 1134
- Mt. Meru 4567
- Mombasa
- Pemba I.
- Masai Steppe
- Zanzibar I.
- L. Tanganyika 1470 / 773
- Lukuga
- Dar es-Salaam
- Mafia I.
- L. Rukwa 2961
- Lomami
- Sankuru

Indian Ocean islands
- Seychelles Is.
- Amirante Is.
- Mahé I.
- 5477
- Aldabra Is.
- Providence I.
- Agalega Is.
- Gr. Comore
- Comores Is.
- C. d'Ambre
- Maromokotro 2876
- Mascarene Is.
- Rodrigues
- Réunion 3069
- Mauritius
- Antananarivo 2643
- L. Europa
- C. Ste. Marie
- Madagascar
- 6400

Southern Africa
- Likasi
- Katanga
- L. Mwero
- L. Bangweulu
- C. Delgado
- L. Nyasa (Malawi) 785 / 473
- Lusaka
- L. Cabora Bassa
- Sapitwa 3000
- Maramba
- Kafue
- Harare 2596
- Chinde
- L. Kariba
- Victoria Falls
- Maun
- Makgadikgadi Pans
- Kahari Desert
- Plateau
- Mozambique Channel
- Pretoria
- Vaal
- Tugela Falls
- Thabana-Ntlenyana 3482
- Maputo
- Drakensberg
- Mts.
- Gt. Karroo 2326
- Orange
- Agulhas

Scale
1:50 000 000
0 — 250 — 500 — 750 — 1 000 — 1 250 Km
0 — 200 — 400 — 600 — 800 Mi

ATLANTIC OCEAN · Is Selvagens · INDIAN OCEAN · Equator · Tropic of Capricorn

LONGEST RIVERS

Name	Length in km	River Basin in sq.km
Nile – Kagera	6,671	2,881,000
Congo (Zaïre) – Lualaba	4,835	3,822,000
Niger	4,160	2,092,000
Zambeze (Zambezi)	2,660	1,450,000
Ubangi – Uele	2,280	770,000
Kasai (Kwa, Cassai)	2,200	875,000
Shebele	1,950	.
Al-Bahr al-Azraq /Blue Nile/ – Abay	1,900	324,500
Volta – Volta Noire	1,900	440,000
Orange	1,860	1,020,000
Okavango (Cubango)	1,800	785,000
Luvua – Luapula	1,800	.
Juba	1,650	200,000
Limpopo – Krokodil	1,600	440,000
Lomani	1,500	110,000
Benue (Benoué)	1,450	319,000
Chari – Ouham	1,450	880,000
Sénégal – Bafing	1,430	450,000
Cuando	1,400	.
Kwango (Cuango)	1,400	.
Aruwimi – Ituri	1,300	116,100

LARGEST LAKES

Name	Area in sq.km	Greatest Depth in m	Altitude in m
L. Victoria (Ukerewe)	68,800	125	1,134
L.Tanganyika	32,880	1,470	773
L. Nyasa (Malawi)	28,480	785	473
L. Chad	20,700	4-7	240
L. Turkana[+] /L. Rudolf/	8,560	404	375
Chott Melrhir[+]	6,700	.	-30
Chott Djerid[+]	5,700	.	16
L. Albert	5,345	57	619
L. Mweru	4,920	18	917
L. Tana	3,630	72	1,830
L. Bangweulu	2,850	4	1,067
L. Kivu	2,650	496	1,455
L. Rukwa	2,640	4	793
L. Kyoga	2,600	5	1,033
B. al-Manzilah	2,600	.	2
L. Mai-Ndombe	2,320	15	340
L. Edward	2,150	117	914
Chott ech Chergui[+]	2,000	.	940
B. al-Burullus	1,930	.	2
L. Chilwa	1,240	.	600
L. Abaya	1,162	13	1,285

[+]salt lake

LARGEST ISLANDS

Name	Area in sq.km	Name	Area in sq.km	Name	Area in sq.km
Madagascar	587,041	Mauritius	1,865	Jarbah (Î.d. Djerba)	1,050
Suquṭrā (Socotra)	3,579	Fuerteventura	1,722	São Tiago	991
Réunion	2,510	Zanzibar I.	1,658	Pemba	984
Bioko	2,017	Gran Canaria	1,376	Dahlak Kebir I.	900
Tenerife	1,946	Njazidja (Gde. Comore)	1,148	São Tomé	836

HIGHEST MOUNTAINS

Name (Country)	Height in m	Name (Country)	Height in m	Name (Country)	Height in m
Kilimanjaro-Uhuru (Tanz.)	5,895	Mt. Elgon (Kenya-Ugan.)	4,321	Lesatima (Kenya)	3,994
Mt. Kenya /Kirinyaga (Ken.)	5,199	Batu (Eth.)	4,307	Amba Ferit (Eth.)	3,975
Kilimanjaro-Mawenzi (Tanz.)	5,149	Abuye Meda (Eth.)	4,305	Mt. Kinangop (Kenya)	3,906
Ngaliema (Margherita) (Ugan.-Zaïre)	5,119	Guna (Eth.)	4,231	Jbel Tignüsti (Mor.)	3,825
Ras Deshen (Eth.)	4,620	Guge (Eth.)	4,200	Ari n'Ayachi (Mor.)	3,737
Mt. Meru (Tanz.)	4,567	Abune Yosef (Eth.)	4,190	Gurag (Eth.)	3,719
Buahit (Eth.)	4,510	Jbel Tubqāl (Mor.)	4,165	Loolmalassin (Tanz.)	3,648
V. Karisimbi (Rwanda-Zaïre)	4,507	Birhan (Eth.)	4,154	Thabana-Ntlenyana (Les.)	3,482
Talo (Eth.)	4,413	Muhavura (Ugan.)	4,113	Emi Koussi (Chad)	3,415
		Irhil M'goun (Mor.)	4,071	Ngorongoro-Oldeani (Tanz.)	3,188

ACTIVE VOLCANOES

Name (Country)	Altitude in m	Latest eruption
Mt. Cameroun/Fako (Cameroon)	4,070	1982
Pico de Teide (Canary Is.)	3,718	1909
Nyiragongo (Zaïre)	3,470	1977
Nyamulagira (Zaïre)	3,056	1984
Ol Doinyo Lengai (Tanzania)	2,878	1960
Pico (Cape Verde Is.)	2,829	1951
Piton de la Foumaise (Réunion)	2,631	1983
La Caldera (Canary Is.)	2,423	1971

LARGEST NATIONAL PARKS

Name (Country)	Area in sq.km
Kafue (Zambia)	22,400
Salonga (Zaïre)	22,300
Tsavo (Kenya)	20,800
Kalahari-Gemsbok (Botsw., S.-A.)	18,550
Kruger (South Africa)	18,170
Southern N.P. (Sudan)	16,000
Serengeti (Tanzania)	14,500
Wankie (Zimbabwe)	13,353
Ruaha (Tanzania)	11,500

map 27

AFRICA

Country	Area in sq.km	Population year 1988	Density per sq.km	Capital
Algeria	2,381,741	23,841,000	10	Alger
Angola	1,246,700	9,481,000	7.6	Luanda
Benin	112,622	4,446,000	39	Porto-Novo
Botswana	600,372	1,212,000	2.0	Gaborone
Burkina	274,200	8,798,000	32	Ouagadougou
Burundi	27,834	5,149,000	185	Bujumbura
Cameroon	475,442	10,822,000[1]	23	Yaoundé
Canary Islands (prov. of Spain)	7,237	1,442,962[1]	198	Madrid
Cape Verde	4,033	358,000	89	Praia
Central African Republic	622,984	2,771,000	4.5	Bangui
Chad	1,284,000	5,401,000	4.2	Ndjamena
Comoros	2,236	487,000	218	Njazidja (Moroni)
Congo	342,000	1,888,000	5.5	Brazzaville
Djibouti	23,200	456,000[1]	20	Djibouti
Egypt	1,001,449	51,897,000	52	Al-Qâhirah
Equatorial Guinea	28,051	420,000	15	Malabo
Ethiopia	1,221,900	47,882,000	39	Addis Abeba
Gabon	267,667	1,206,000	4.5	Libreville
Gambia	11,295	812,000	72	Banjul
Ghana	238,537	14,130,000	59	Accra
Guinea	245,857	5,071,000	21	Conakry
Guinea-Bissau	36,125	945,000	26	Bissau
Ivory Coast/Côté d'Ivoire	322,464	11,612,000	36	Yamoussoukro/Abidjan
Kenya	582,646	23,882,000	41	Nairobi
Lesotho	30,355	1,679,000	55	Maseru
Liberia	111,369	2,508,000	23	Monrovia
Libya	1,759,540	4,232,000	2.4	Tarābulus
Madagascar	587,041	11,238,000	19	Antananarivo
Madeira (autonomous reg. of Port.)	794	269,500[1]	339	Lisboa
Malawi	118,484	7,755,000	65	Lilongwe
Mali	1,240,192	8,918,000	7.2	Bamako
Mauritania	1,032,455	1,916,000	1.9	Nouakchott
Mauritius and dependencies	2,045	1,077,000	527	Port Louis
Morocco	458,730	23,910,000	52	Rabat
Mozambique	799,380	14,932,000	19	Maputo
Namibia	824,295	1,761,000	2.1	Windhoek
Niger	1,266,995	7,250,000	5.7	Niamey
Nigeria	923,768	104,957,000	114	Abuja, Lagos
Réunion (Fr.)	2,510	575,000	229	Saint-Denis
Rwanda	26,338	6,755,000	256	Kigali
Saint Helena and deps. (U.K.)	314	6,879[1]	22	Jamestown
São Tomé and Principe	964	115,600	120	São Tomé
Senegal	196,722	6,881,919	35	Dakar
Seychelles and dependencies	453	66,626	147	Victoria
Sierra Leone	71,740	3,946,000	55	Freetown
Somalia	637,657	7,106,000	11	Muqdisho
South Africa	1,221,037	33,747,000	28	Pretoria, Cape Town
Spanish North Africa	33	127,336[1]	3,859	–
Sudan	2,505,813	23,797,000	9.5	Al-Khurtūm
Suqutrā/Socotra (Yemen)	3,626	16,000[1]	4.4	–
Swaziland	17,363	737,000	42	Mbabane
Tanzania	945,087	23,997,000	25	Dar es-Salaam
Togo	56,785	3,247,000	57	Lomé
Tunisia	163,610	7,809,000	48	Túnis
Uganda	241,139	17,189,000	71	Kampala
Western Sahara	266,769	175,000	0.7	El-Aaiún
Zaïre	2,345,409	33,458,000	14	Kinshasa
Zambia	752,614	7,531,000	10	Lusaka
Zimbabwe	390,580	8,878,000	23	Harare

[1] year 1984, [2] year 1982, [3] year 1981

population increase in Africa was 2.92%, the birth rate was 45.9, and the death rate 16.6 per 1,000. Relatively few persons live in towns, in 1980 the figure was only 32%. Africa has 16 cities with over one million inhabitants.

Africa's **economy** is typical of that of developing countries. With the exception of the Republic of South Africa, which is an advanced industrial and agricultural country, **agriculture** predominates in the economy of most African countries with the stress on the production of plantation crops. Plant production takes precedence over livestock breeding. Africa produces a major share in the world production of oil crops (groundnuts, palm kernels, palm oil), cocoa, sisal,

page 119

Map of Northwest Africa and Adjacent Atlantic

Grid References
- A, B, C, D, E, F, G (rows)
- 1, 2, 3, 4, 5 (columns)
- Longitude: 30°, 20°, 10°, 0°, 10°
- Latitude markers: 30°, 20°, 10°, 0°, 10°, 20°
- Tropic of Cancer
- Tropic of Capricorn

Countries and Territories
- SPAIN
- MOROCCO
- Western Sahara
- MAURITANIA
- ALGERIA
- TUNISIA
- LIBYA
- MALI
- NIGER
- SENEGAL
- GAMBIA
- GUINEA-BISSAU
- GUINEA
- SIERRA LEONE
- LIBERIA
- IVORY COAST
- BURKINA FASO
- GHANA
- TOGO
- BENIN
- NIGERIA
- CAMEROON
- EQ. GUINEA
- SÃO TOMÉ AND PRÍNCIPE
- GABON
- Cabinda (Ang.)
- Madeira (Port.)
- Is. Canarias (Spain)
- CAPE VERDE

Cities
- Tanger, Tétouan, Gibraltar (U.K.), Ceuta
- CASABLANCA, RABAT, FÈS, Safi
- MARRAKECH, Agadir, Sidi Ifni
- Santa Cruz de T., Las Palmas
- Tarfaya, El Aaiún, Dachla
- Tlemcen, ALGER, Annaba
- Djelfa, Batna, Touggourt
- Gabès, Misrāta, Ghudāmis
- Béchar, Tindouf, Adrar
- Fdérik, Atar, Taoudenni
- Tamanrasset, Djanet, Ghāt
- Nouadhibou, Nouakchott
- Tombouctou, Gao, Bilma
- St.-Louis, DAKAR, Praia
- Thiès, Banjul, BISSAU
- Kayes, BAMAKO
- Bobo-Dioulasso, Ouagadougou
- Kankan, CONAKRY, Freetown
- Monrovia, ABIDJAN, Yamoussoukro
- Kumasi, ACCRA, Lomé, Porto Novo
- Sekondi-Takoradi
- Niamey, Zinder, Agadez
- Sokoto, Kaduna, KANO, Nguru, Maiduguri
- Parakou, Ilorin, Jos, Abuja
- IBADAN, LAGOS, Enugu
- Port Harcourt, Malabo, Bioko, Bata
- DOUALA, YAOUNDÉ
- Príncipe, São Tomé, Pagalu (Equat. Gui.)
- Libreville, Port-Gentil
- Pointe-Noire, Brazzaville
- Soyo, LUANDA
- Lobito, Benguela, Namibe
- Swakopmund, Walvisbaai
- Ascension (U.K.)
- Saint Helena (U.K.), Jamestown
- Bight of Benin
- Gulf of Guinea
- ATLANTIC OCEAN

Scale
1 : 50 000 000
0 — 250 — 500 — 750 — 1 000 — 1 250 Km
0 — 200 — 400 — 600 — 800 Mi

27a Tunisia and East Algeria
1 : 15 000 000

dates and spices. It also possesses great wealth in its forests, especially in the wet equatorial parts of the continent and has rich sources of water power, which are still underdeveloped. The enormous wealth of mineral resources has only been partly prospected. **Mining** is fairly widespread. Africa leads world production in diamonds, gold, platinum, and contributes an important share in uranium, copper, manganese, chromium, cobalt, vanadium, bauxite, antimony and phosphates. The only **industry** that is to be found practically in all African countries is the food industry. **Transport and foreign trade** are of immense importance for the economic development of the continent.

ALGERIA

Al Jumhuriya al Jazaïriya ad-Dimuqratiya ash-Shabiya – République Algérienne Démocratique et Populaire, area 2,381,741 sq.km, population 23,841,000 (1988), democratic people's republic (President Bendjedid Chadli since 1979).

Administrative units: 48 departments. **Capital:** Alger 1,721,607 inhab. (1983); **other towns** (1983, in 1,000 inhab.): Oran (Ouahran) 663, Constantine 449, Annaba 348, Blida 191, Sétif 187, Sidi bel Abbès 147, Tlemcen 146, Skikda 141, Béjaia 124, Batna 123, Ech Chéliff 119. – **Currency:** Algerian dinar = 100 centimes.
Economy: agricultural country with developing industry, especially mining. **Agriculture : crops** (1983, in 1,000 tonnes): wheat 810, barley, potatoes 610, grapes 350, oranges 230, tangerines 120, lemons, olives 120, olive oil 12, dates 210, figs, fruit, tomatoes 310, tobacco, sugar beet 93; **livestock** (1983, in 1,000 head): cattle 1,400, sheep 13,750, goats 2,780, camels 154, horses, mules 207, asses; poultry 20,000, eggs 21,000 tonnes; fish catch 70,000 tonnes; cork oak 15,000 tonnes, alfalfa. **Mining** (1983, in 1,000 tonnes, metal content): crude petroleum 31,788 (Hassi Messaoud, Edjeleh, Ohanet); natural gas 515,700 TJ (Hassi R'Mel), iron ore 1,966, zinc, lead, mercury 345 tonnes (Ras el Ma), silver, salt 150, phosphates 893, pyrites. Electricity 8,520 mn. kWh (1983). **Industry:** food processing (canning plants, oil processing plants, mills), construction of metallurgy (Annaba), new plants for machinery and chemical industries, petroleum processing. **Production** (1983, in 1,000 tonnes): meat 186, milk 540, wine 264, cement 4,776. – **Communications:** railways 3,900 km, roads 102,000 km. Merchant shipping 1,372,000 GRT. – **Exports:** petroleum, natural gas, wine, fruit.

ANGOLA

República Popular de Angola, area 1,246,700 sq.km, population 9,487,000 (1988), republic (President José Eduardo Dos Santos since 1979).

Administrative units: 16 districts. **Capital:** Luanda 1,200,000 inhab. (with agglom. 1982); **other towns** (1982, in 1,000 inhab.): Lobito, 135, Huambo 110, Benguela 60, Cabinda 50. – **Currency:** kwanza = 100 lwei.
Economy: agriculture (1983, in 1,000 tonnes): coffee 27, sisal 20, maize (corn) 275, millet, manioc, cotton, groundnuts, palm oil, sugarcane, bananas, pineapples, tobacco; **livestock** (1983, in 1,000 head): cattle 3,300, goats 950, sheep; fish catch 112,400 tonnes (1983); roundwood 9 mn. cub.m (1983). **Mining** (1983, in 1,000 tonnes): crude petroleum 8,304, diamonds 1,200,000 carats, salt 41. – **Communications:** railways 2,900 km, roads 72,300 km. – **Exports:** petroleum, diamonds, coffee, etc.

BENIN

République populaire du Benin, area 112,622 sq.km, population 4,446,000 (1988), republic (President Gen, Mathieu Kérékou since 1972).

Administrative units: 6 departments. **Capital:** Porto-Novo 131,989 inhabs., Cotonou (seat of president and government) 215,000 inhab. (1982); **other towns** (in 1,000 inhab.): Parakou, 61, Abomey 50, Natitingou 32. – **Currency:** CFA franc = 100 centimes. – **Economy:** developing agricultural country. **Agriculture** (1983, in 1,000 tonnes): maize, manioc 600, coffee, bananas, palm kernels 75, palm oil 34, groundnuts 50, cotton; **livestock** (1983, in 1,000 head): cattle 880, sheep 1,080, goats 1,000; fish catch 21,100 tonnes. – **Communications:** railways 579 km, roads 7,200 km. – **Exports:** palm kernels and oil.

BOTSWANA

Republic of Botswana, area 600,372 sq.km, population 1,212,000 (1988), republic, member of the Commonwealth (President Dr Quett Ketumile Jonny Masire since 1980).

Administrative units: 9 districts. **Capital:** Gaborone 72,200 inhab. (1983); **other towns** (1982, in 1,000 inhab.): Francistown 32, Selebi-Pikwe 29, Serowe 24, Kanye 22. – **Currency:** pula = 100 thebe. – **Economy:** livestock rearing (1983, in 1,000 head): cattle 3,050, sheep 160, goats 670; cultivation of millet, sorghum and maize (corn). **Mining** (1983, in 1,000 tonnes, metal content): nickel 18,200 tonnes, copper 20.3, gold, diamonds 11 mn. carats, coal 395. – **Communications:** railways 716 km, roads 8,026 km. – **Exports:** diamonds, meat, nickel.

BURUNDI

République du Burundi – Republica y'u Burundi, area 27,834 sq.km, population 5,149,000 (1988), republic (President Major Pierre Buyoya since 1987).

Administrative units: 10 districts. **Capital:** Bujumbura 160,000 inhab. (1982). **Density** 170 persons per sq.km. – **Currency:** Burundi franc = 100 centimes. – **Economy:** developing agricultural country with livestock rearing. **Agriculture** (1983, in 1,000 tonnes): coffee 30, maize (corn), sorghum, manioc 500, sweet potatoes 502, bananas 970, groundnuts, tea, cotton; **livestock** (1983, in 1,000 head): cattle 560, sheep 310, goats 760; fish catch 12,000 tonnes in Lake Tanganyika. – **Communications:** roads 5,144 km. – **Exports:** coffee, tea, cotton, hides etc.

CAMEROON

République Unie du Cameroun, area 475,442 sq.km, population 10,822,000 (1987), **republic** (President Paul Biya since 1982).
Administrative units: 10 provinces. **Capital:** Yaoundé 488,000 inhab. (1983); **other towns** (1983, in 1,000 inhab.): Douala 713, Nkongsamba 97, Maroua 95, Garoua 88. – **Currency:** CFA franc = 100 centimes.
Economy: developing agricultural country. **Agriculture** (1983, in 1,000 tonnes): cocoa beans 90, coffee 115, bananas 58, groundnuts 100, palm oil 100, cotton; **livestock** (1983, in 1,000 head): cattle 3,000, sheep 2,190, goats 2,400, pigs 1,200; fish catch 84,300 tonnes; roundwood 9.9 mn. cub.m, rubber 17,600 tonnes. **Mining:** crude petroleum 5.6 mn. tonnes, tin, gold, titanium. – **Communications:** railways 1,172 km, roads 63,781 km. – **Exports:** petroleum, coffee, cocoa, wood.

CAPE VERDE

República do Cabo Verde, area 4,033 sq.km, population 358,000 (1988) **republic** (President Aristides Pereira since 1975).
Capital: Praia 40,000 inhab. (1982). – **Currency:** Cape Verde escudo = 100 centavos. – **Economy:** maize (corn), sweet potatoes, manioc, sugarcane, groundnuts, bananas, coffee; fishing. Important naval station.

CENTRAL AFRICAN REPUBLIC

Area 622,984 sq.km, population 2,771,000 (1988), **republic** (President André Kolingba since 1986).
Administrative units: 14 prefectures. **Capital:** Bangui 387,143 inhab. (1981). – **Currency:** CFA franc = 100 centimes.
Economy: chiefly agriculture; **crops** (1983, in 1,000 tonnes): cotton lint 13, coffee 18, maize (corn), rice, millet, manioc 800, sweet potatoes, groundnuts, sesame; **livestock** (1983, in 1,000 head): cattle 1,500, goats 960; roundwood. **Mining:** diamonds 295,000 carats, gold. – **Communications:** roads 22,600 km. – **Exports:** diamonds, wood, cotton etc.

CHAD

République du Tchad, area 1,284,000 sq.km, population 5,401,000 (1988), **republic** (President Hissène Habré since 1982).
Administrative units: 14 prefectures. **Capital:** Ndjamena 303,000 inhab. (1980). – **Currency:** CFA franc = 100 centimes.
Economy: backward agricultural country. **Agriculture:** cotton lint, maize (corn), rice, millet, manioc, sweet potatoes, groundnuts, sugarcane, dates, sesame, tobacco; **livestock** (1983, in 1,000 head): cattle 3,600, sheep 2,300, goats 2,100, camels; roundwood; fish catch 110,000 tonnes (1983). – **Communications:** roads 40,000 km. – **Exports:** cotton, cattle, meat.

COMOROS

République fédérale et islamique des Comores, area 2,236 sq.km, population 487,000 (1988), **republic** (President Mohammed Djohar since 1990).
Capital: Njazidja (Moroni) 16,000 inhab. (1982). **Density** 199 persons per sq.km. **Currency:** CFA franc = 100 centimes. – **Production for export:** vanilla, ylang-ylang, cloves, sisal, coconuts, copra, cinnamon, essential oils.

CONGO

République populaire du Congo, area 342,000 sq.km, population 1,888,000 (1988), **republic** (President Colonel Denis Sassou-Nguesso since 1979).
Administrative units: 9 regions. **Capital:** Brazzaville 422,402 inhab. (1980, with agglom.); **other towns:** Pointe-Noire 185,105 inhab. – **Currency:** CFA franc = 100 centimes.
Economy: agricultural country. **Agriculture** (1983, in 1,000 tonnes): manioc 600, maize (corn), sweet potatoes, coffee, cocoa beans, palm oil 15, groundnuts 15, sugarcane, bananas; fish catch 31,900 tonnes; roundwood 2.2 mn. cub.m. **Mining** (1983, in 1,000 tonnes, metal content): crude petroleum 4,236, lead, zinc, gold, copper. – **Communications:** railways 802 km, roads 12,000 km, navigable waterways 5,000 km. – **Exports:** petroleum, wood, coffee, cocoa.

DJIBOUTI

République de Djibouti, area 23,200 sq.km, population 456,000 (1987), **republic** (President Hasan Gouled Aptidon since 1977).
Capital: Djibouti 120,000 inhab. (1983). – **Currency:** Djibouti franc = 100 centimes. – **Economy:** coffee grown for export; **livestock** (1983, in 1,000 head): goats 540, sheep, camels 52. – **Communications:** railways 90 km, roads 1,875 km.

EGYPT

Al-Jumhūrīya Misr al-'Arabīya, area 1,001, 449 sq.km, population 51, 897,000 (1988), **republic** (President Muhammad Hosnī Mubarak since 1981).
Administrative units: 25 governorates. **Capital:** Al-Qāhirah (Cairo) 6,780,000 inhab. (1980) with agglom. 9,750,000 (1982);

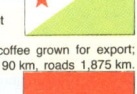

PORTUGAL
SEVILLA
Córdoba
SPAIN
Cartagena
Faro
Cádiz
MÁLAGA
Str. of Gibraltar
Gibraltar (U.K.)
MED
ALGER
Blida
ORAN
(Ouahran)
O. Chéliff
Tizi-Ouzou
Tanger
Ceuta (Sp.)
Larache
Tétouan
Melilla (Sp.)
Ech Chéliff
Tagdempt
Kenitra
Ksar-el-Kebir
Sidi bel Abbès
RABAT
Taza
OUJDA
Tlemcen
Saïda
Djelfa
CASABLANCA
(Dar-el-Beida)
FÈS
Meknès
O. Moulouya
Laghouat
El-Jadida
Oued Zem
Safi
Khouribga
Midelt
Bou Arfa
Aïn Sefra
Hassi R'Mel
MARRAKECH
Beni-Mellal
Figuig
Ghardaïa
Essaouira
Ksar-es-Souk
Ouarzazate
Béchar
Abadla
Agadir
Taroudant
O. Drâa
MOROCCO
El Goléa
Tiznit
Béni Abbès
Sidi Ifni
Madeira
(Port.)
Funchal
Is. Canarias
(Sp.)
La Palma
Sta. Cruz de T.
Lanzarote
Tenerife
Gomera
Fuerteventura
Hierro
Las Palmas
Gran Canaria
Tarfaya
El Aaiún
O. Daoura
Tabelbala
O. Saoura
Timimoun
Sba
O. Mya
Tindouf
ALGERIA
Adrar
Aoulef
In Salah
Reggane
O. Irharhar
ATLANTIC OCEAN
C. Bojador
Semara
Bu Craa
Western Sahara
Bir Mogrein
Guelta Zemmur
Dachla
MAURITANIA
Fdérik
Zouîrât
Uad Aîui
Taoudenni
Tamanrasset
O. Tamanrasset
C. Blanc
Nouadhibou
Atar
Akjoujt
Tessalit
Tidjikdja
Tichit
Araouane
Nouakchott
Qualâta
Rosso
Tombouctou
Bourem
Podor
Kaédi
Kiffa
Néma
'Ayoûn el 'Atroûs
Sénégal
C. Vert
St-Louis
Gao
Ménaka
O. Azaouak
N
Thiès
Linguère
Ansongo
SENEGAL
Diourbel
Nioro du Sahel
Nara
Hombori
DAKAR
Kaolack
Ambidédi
Kayes
MALI
Mopti
Tahoua
Tambacounda
Dori
Tillabéry
GAMBIA
Birni Nkonni
Banjul
Gambie
Niger
Ségou
Kaya
Niamey
Ziguinchor
Kita
San
Bani
Dosso
BAMAKO
Koulikoro
Doura
BURKINA FASO
Sokoto
GUINEA-BISSAU
Bissau
Mâdina do Boé
Labé
Siguiri
Bougouni
Koudougou
Ouagadougou
Gusau
GUINEA
Boké
Fria
Dabola
Sikasso
Bobo-Dioulasso
Kandi
Mamou
Kindia
Kankan
Bolgatanga
White Volta
Natitingou
Yelwa
CONAKRY
SIERRA LEONE
Korhogo
Ferkéssédougou
Black Volta
Komoé
Parakou
Minna
Makeni
Kissidougou
IVORY COAST
Tamale
Bassari
Freetown
Bo
Pendembu
Touba
Man
Zuénoula
Bouaké
GHANA
Bittta
TOGO
BENIN
OGBOMOSHO
Ilorin
Oyo
Oshogbo
Yekepa
Lake Volta
IBADAN
Iwo
Ife
Ikerre
Robertsport
LIBERIA
Daloa
Gawso
Kumasi
COTONOU
LAGOS
Monrovia
Yamoussoukro
Asamankese
Lomé
Porto Novo
Benin City
Sassandra
Buchanan
ABIDJAN
Tema
Bight of Benin
Greenville
ACCRA
Harper
Tabou
Sassandra
Sekondi-Takoradi
Port Harcourt
C. Palmas
Gulf of Guinea
NIGERIA
1 : 25 000 000
0 200 400 600 Km
0 100 200 300 400 Mi
20°
10°
0°
30°
A
B
C
D
1
2
3

towns (1980, in 1,000 inhab.): Kumasi 476, Tema 346, Sekondi-Takoradi 226, Tamale 196, Asamankese 135, Bolgatanga 110, Cape Coast 86. – **Currency:** cedi = 100 pesewas.
Economy: based on agriculture specialized in products for export. Rich resources of raw materials. **Agriculture** (1983, in 1,000 tonnes): cocoa beans 160 (Ashanti region), maize (corn) 260, millet, rice, manioc 1,500, sugarcane, groundnuts, palm kernels 30, palm oil 25, coconuts 160, copra 7, coffee, oranges 35, lemons, pineapples, bananas, tomatoes 165; **livestock** (1983, in 1,000 head): cattle 800, sheep 2,000, goats 2,000, pigs 375; poultry 13,000; fish catch 228,000 tonnes (1983); roundwood 9.8 mn. cub.m (1983), natural rubber 3,000 tonnes. **Mining** (1983, in 1,000 tonnes, metal content): manganese 83, gold 8,602 kg, diamonds 369,000 carats, bauxite 70, salt. Electricity 2,589 mn. kWh (1983), of this 99% hydro-electric power stations (on the R. Volta at Akosombo). – **Communications:** railways 960 km, roads 47,190 km. Merchant shipping 186,000 GRT (1984). River transport on the R. Volta. – **Exports:** cocoa, gold, wood, diamonds, manganese.

GUINEA

République de Guinée, area 245,857 sq.km, population 5,071,000 (1988), **republic** (President Brig.-Gen. Lansana Conté since 1984).

Administrative units: 34 regions. **Capital:** Conakry 763,000 inhab. (1980): **other towns** (1980, in 1,000 inhab.): Labé 253, Kankan 229, Kindia 150. – **Currency:** Guinean franc = 100 centimes. **Economy:** agricultural products for export, mineral mining. **Agriculture** (1983, in 1,000 tonnes): rice 300, maize (corn), manioc 640, sisal, groundnuts 75, palm oil 45, coffee, bananas 110, pineapples, tobacco; **livestock** (1983, in 1,000 head): cattle 1,900, sheep 450, goats 440; roundwood 3.6 mn. cub.m (1983). **Mining** (1983, in 1,000 tonnes, metal content): bauxite 12,986 (second world producer, deposits Boké, Fria), diamonds 45,000 carats. Electricity 499 mn. kWh. **Industry:** production of aluminium, food processing. – **Communications:** railways 1,100 km, roads 30,000 km. – **Exports:** bauxite and aluminium 96%, coffee, groundnuts, diamonds, bananas, pineapples etc.

GUINEA-BISSAU

República da Guiné-Bissau, area 36,125 sq.km, population 945,000 (1988), **republic** (Head of State Chairman of the State Council Maj. João Bernardo Vieira since 1980).

Capital: Bissau 110,000 inhab. (1981). – **Currency:** Guinean peso = 100 centavos. – **Economy:** agricultural country. **Agriculture** (1983, in 1,000 tonnes): rice, groundnuts 30, palm kernels 5, palm oil, coconuts 25; roundwood 500,000 cub.m (1983).

IVORY COAST / CÔTE D'IVOIRE

République de Côte d'Ivoire, area 322,464 sq.km, population 11,612,000 (1988), **republic** (President Félix Houphouet-Boigny since 1960).

Administrative units: 34 departments. **Capitals:** Abidjan 1,600,000 inhab. (with agglom.; 1983) and Yamoussoukro 80,000 inhab. (1983); **other towns** (1983, in 1,000 inhab.): Bouaké 275, Korhogo 125, Man 110, Daloa 100, Grand Bassam 65. – **Currency:** CFA franc = 100 centimes. **Economy:** agricultural country, export products grown on plantations. **Agriculture** (1983, in 1,000 tonnes): millet, sorghum, rice 430, manioc 800, sugarcane 2,500, cotton lint 66, sesame, palm oil 133, coconuts 161, copra 23, groundnuts, coffee 225, cocoa beans 400 (leading world producer), bananas 150, pineapples 350; **livestock** (1983, in 1,000 head): cattle 780, sheep 1,380; fish catch 94,000 tonnes; roundwood 11.8 mn. cub.m (1983), natural rubber 30,500 tonnes (1983). **Mining** (1983, in 1,000 tonnes): crude petroleum 1,158. Electricity 1,932 mn. kWh (1983). **Processing** of agricultural products. – **Communications:** railways 665 km, roads 46,400 km. – **Exports:** cocoa, coffee, wood, bananas.

KENYA

Jamhuri ya Kenya, area 582,646 sq.km, population 23,882,000 (1988), **republic, member of the Commonwealth** (President Daniel Arap Moi since 1978).

Administrative units: 8 provinces. **Capital:** Nairobi 1,334,000 inhab. (with agglom., 1983), **other towns** (1983, in 1,000 inhab.): Mombasa 504, Kisumu 189, Nakuru 120. Average annual rate of population increase 4.1%. – **Currency:** Kenyan shilling = 100 cents.
Economy: agricultural country with developing livestock production. **Agriculture** (1983, in 1,000 tonnes): maize (corn) 2,000, wheat, barley, rice, millet, manioc, sweet potatoes; on plantations: cotton, sisal 51, sugarcane, pyrethrum 11 (leading world producer), groundnuts, sesame, palm oil, copra, coffee 90, tea 112, pineapples 160, bananas 140; **livestock** (1983, in 1,000 head): cattle 11,500, sheep 6,500, goats 8,000, camels 620; poultry; fish catch 97,500 tonnes (1983);

add page 126

other towns (1976, in 1,000 inhab.): Al-Iskandarīyah (Alexandria) 2,415 (1978), Al-Jīzah 1,247, Shubrā al Khaymah 394, Al-Mahallah al Kubrā 293, Tantā 285, Būr Saʿīd (Port Said) 263, Al-Mansūrah 258, Asyūt 214, Az-Zaqāzīq 203, As-Suways (Suez) 194, Damanhūr 189. – **Currency:** Egyptian pound = 100 piastres. **Economy:** agricultural and industrial country; cultivated land only 2.8% in the Nile delta and valley. **Agriculture: crops** (1983, in 1,000 tonnes): wheat 1,996, maize (corn) 3,510, barley, rice 2,440, potatoes 1,150, sweet potatoes, sugarcane 9,000, cotton-seed 685, -lint 410; groundnuts, sesame, fruit: oranges 1,250, tangerines, lemons, grapes 310, bananas 140, dates 440 (leading world producer), figs-vegetables; tomatoes 2,500, onions 660, water-melons 1,200; **livestock** (1983, in 1,000 head): cattle 1,826, buffaloes 2,393, camels 80, asses 1,775, sheep 1,394, goats 1,498, poultry 28,000; fish catch 140,000 tonnes. **Mining** (1983, in 1,000 tonnes, metal content): crude petroleum 36,036 (Gulf of Suez region), natural gas 59,320 TJ, iron ore 2,064, phosphates 647, titanium, salt 918. Electricity 23 billion kWh (1983), of this 48% hydro-electric power stations; chief Aswān dam on the R. Nile. Most developed **industries:** textiles and food processing. **Production** (1983, in 1,000 tonnes): pig iron 196, crude steel 125, cement 4,080, nitrogenous fertilizers 646, cotton yarn 229, meat 507, milk 650, sugar 812; 44 billion cigarettes. – **Communications:** mainly along the Nile valley and Suez Canal zone; railways 4,385 km, roads 10,708 km, navigable waterways 3,100 km. Merchant shipping 779,000 GRT. **Suez Canal:** opened in 1869, length Būr Saʿīd–As-Suways 161 km, width on level 70–125 m, depth 11–12 m, passage permitted to vessels up to 10.36 m draught. Civil aviation (1984): 35.3 mn. t. flown and 2,786,000 passengers carried. – **Tourism:** 1,498,000 visitors (1983). – **Exports:** petroleum, cotton, fruit, rice.

EQUATORIAL GUINEA

República de Guinea Ecuatorial, area 28,051 sq.km, population 420,000 (1988), **republic** (President Lieut.-Col. Theodoro Obiango Nguema Mbasogo since 1979).

Administrative units: 2 provinces. **Capital:** Malabo 80,000 inhab. – **Currency:** ekuele = 100 centimos. **Agriculture:** manioc, sweet potatoes, palm oil, coffee, cocoa beans; roundwood. – **Exports:** coffee, cocoa, wood.

ETHIOPIA

Hybretesebawit Itjopja, area 1,221,900 sq.km, population 47,882,000 (1988), **republic** (President Lieut.-Col. Menghistu Haile Mariam since 1987).

Administrative units: 14 provinces. **Capital:** Addis Abeba 1,408,068 inhab. (1982); **other towns** (1982, in 1000 inhab.): Asmera 474, Dire Dawa 92, Gonder 86, Dese 83, Nazret 81. – **Currency:** birr = 100 cents. **Economy:** agricultural country with predominantly livestock production. **Agriculture** (1983, in 1,000 tonnes): wheat 950, barley 1,200, maize (corn) 1,600, millet, sorghum 1400, potatoes 1,600, cotton lint 27, flax, groundnuts, sesame 36, castor beans 12, coffee 204, bananas, legumes, tobacco; **livestock** (1983, in 1,000 head): cattle 26,300, sheep 23,400, goats 17,240, camels 1,010, horses 1,560, mules 1,460, asses 3,905; poultry 55,000; roundwood 29.8 mn. cub.m (1983). **Mining** (1983): gold 435 kg, platinum, salt 124,000 tonnes. **Production** (1983, in 1,000 tonnes): meat 540, milk 610. – **Communications:** railways 1,000 km, roads 23,158 km. – **Exports:** coffee, hides, skins, oil seeds, meat.

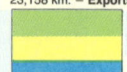

GABON

République Gabonaise, area 267,667 sq.km, population 1,206,000 (1988), **republic** (President Omar Bongo since 1967).

Administrative units: 9 provinces. **Capital:** Libreville 350,000 inhab. (with agglom., 1982); **other towns** (1982, in 1,000 inhab.): Port-Gentil 164, Franceville 75, Lambaréné 24. – **Currency:** CFA franc = 100 centimes. **Economy:** agricultural country with mining and wood processing industries. Forests cover 75% of the land area. **Crops:** rice, manioc, coffee, cocoa beans, bananas; roundwood 2.6 mn. cub.m (1983). **Mining** (1983, in 1,000 tonnes, metal content): crude petroleum 7,476, natural gas 6,000 TJ, manganese 947, uranium 1,042 tonnes, gold. – **Communications:** railways 410 km, roads 7,174 km. – **Exports:** petroleum (80%), wood, manganese, uranium, cocoa, coffee.

GAMBIA

Republic of Gambia, area 11,295 sq.km, population 812,000 (1988), **republic, member of the Commonwealth** (President Al Hadji Sir Dawda Kairaba Jawara since 1970).
Capital: Banjul 50,000 inhab. (1983). – **Currency:** dalasi = 100 bututs. – **Economy:** agriculture specialized mainly in growing groundnuts (106,000 tonnes), rice, millet, cotton, palm kernels and oil, cattle. – **Communications:** roads 3,083 km, goods transport on the R. Gambia. – **Exports:** groundnuts and groundnut oil.

GHANA

Republic of Ghana, area 238,537 sq.km, population 14,130,000 (1988), **republic, member of the Commonwealth** (Chairman of the Provisional National Defence Council Flight-Lieutenant Jerry John Rawlings since 1982).
Administrative units: 10 regions. **Capital:** Accra 1,176,000 inhab. (1980, with agglomeration 1,575,000); other

roundwood 29.3 mn. cub.m (1983). **Mining** gold, niobium, salt, soda. Electricity 2,166 mn. kWh (1983). **Industries:** processing of agricultural products, canning plants, processing of petroleum, fertilizers and textiles. **Production** (1983, in 1,000 tonnes): cement 1,280, sugar 355, milk 1,300. – **Communications:** railways 2,730 km, roads 53,500 km. – **Exports:** coffee, tea, petroleum products, sisal etc.

LESOTHO

Kingdom of Lesotho – 'Muso oa Lesotho, area **30,355 sq.km**, population **1,679,000** (1988), **kingdom, member of the Commonwealth** (King Moshoeshoe II since 1966).
Administrative units: 10 districts. **Capital:** Maseru 75,000 inhab. (1981). – **Currency:** maluti = 100 licente. – **Economy:** developing agriculture and livestock rearing. **Agriculture:** wheat, maize (corn), sorghum, **livestock** (1983, in 1,000 head): cattle 640, sheep 1,690, goats 1,000, wool 5,000 tonnes. **Mining** of diamonds. – **Exports:** wool, livestock, diamonds.

LIBERIA

Republic of Liberia, area **111,369 sq.km**, population **2,508,000** (1988) **republic** (President Gen. Samuel Kanyon Doe since 1980).
Administrative units: 9 provinces. **Capital:** Monrovia 306,500 inhab. (1981). – **Currency:** Liberian dollar = 100 cents. **Economy:** agricultural country with a relatively developed mining industry. **Agriculture** (1983, in 1,000 tonnes): rice 250, manioc 300, palm kernels 8, palm oil 30, coffee 10, bananas 78, pineapples; roundwood 4.6 mn. cub.m (1983), natural rubber 76,000 tonnes. **Mining** (1983, in 1,000 tonnes): iron ore 9,671 (metal content), gold 479 kg, diamonds 462,000 carats. – **Communications:** railways 520 km, roads 10,219 km. Merchant shipping 62,025,000 GRT (1984, first place in the world). – **Exports:** iron ore, natural rubber, diamonds, wood, coffee.

LIBYA

Al-Jamahiriyah Al-Arabiya Al-Libya Al-Shabiya Al-Ishtirakiya, area **1,759,540 sq.km**, population **4,232,000** (1988), **republic** (Secretary General – Gen. Muammar al-Qadhafi since 1969).
Administrative units: 10 provinces. **Capital:** Tarābulus (Tripoli) 989,000 inhab. (1982); **other towns** (1982, in 1,000 inhab.): Banghāzī 650, Misrātah 285, Zāwiyat al-Baydā 96, Tubruq 72. – **Currency:** Libyan dinar = 1000 dirhams. **Economy:** developing agricultural country with major petroleum mining. Arable land 1.2% only on the coast and in the oases, unproductive land 91.1%. **Agriculture** (1983, in 1,000 tonnes): barley 195, olives 104, olive oil 16, dates 96, figs, agrums, tobacco, alfalfa; raising of livestock: sheep 4,800,000, goats, camels. **Mining** (1983, in 1,000 tonnes): crude petroleum 49,368, deposits Sarīr, Zaltan, Jālū etc.; pipelines to the coast; natural gas 384,500 TJ, salt. – **Communications:** roads 13,800 km. Merchant shipping 855,000 GRT (1984). – **Exports:** petroleum 93%.

MADAGASCAR

République démocratique de Madagascar – Repoblika demokratika Malagasy, area **587,041 sq.km**, population **11,238,000** (1988), **republic**, (President Capt. Didier Ratsiraka since 1975).
Administrative units: 6 provinces. **Capital:** Antananarivo 800,000 inhab. (1982); **other towns** (1982, in 1,000 inhab.): Fianarantsoa 350, Antsirabe 300, Toamasina 200, Mahajanga 90. – **Currency:** Malagasy franc = 100 centimes. **Economy:** developing agricultural country. **Agriculture** (1983, in 1,000 tonnes): rice 2,147, maize (corn), sweet potatoes 492, manioc 1,726, cotton, sisal 13, sugarcane 1,464, groundnuts, coconuts, oranges 56, bananas 297, pineapples, pepper 2.9, vanilla 3.3, cloves, coffee 81, tobacco; **livestock** (1983, in 1,000 head): cattle 10,322, pigs 1,300, sheep 630, goats 1,750, poultry 18,000; fish catch 54,500 tonnes; roundwood 6.3 mn. cub.m. **Mining** (1983, in 1,000 tonnes, metal content): chromium 12, gold, ilmenite, graphite 15.4, salt 30, mica. – **Communications:** railways 884 km, roads 40,000 km. – **Exports:** coffee, cloves, vanilla, sugar, chromium.

MALAWI

Republic of Malawi, area **118,484 sq.km**, population **7,755,000** (1988), **member of the Commonwealth** (President Dr Hastings Kamuzu Banda since 1966).
Administrative units: 3 regions. **Capital:** Lilongwe 103,000 inhab. (1981); **other towns** (1981, in 1,000 inhab.): Blantyre 229, Zomba 25. – **Currency:** Malawi-kwacha = 100 tambals. – **Economy:** developing agricultural country. **Agriculture** (1983, in 1,000 tonnes): maize (corn) 1,500, rice, sorghum, manioc, sweet potatoes, cotton, tobacco 72, sugarcane 1,830, groundnuts 180, tung oil, tea 38, bananas; **livestock** (1983, in 1,000 head): cattle 900, goats 750; inland fish catch 58,400 tonnes. **Deposits** of coal, iron ore, gold, uranium, bauxite and asbestos. – **Communications:** railways 789 km, roads 16,500 km. – **Exports:** tobacco, tea, groundnuts, cotton.

MALI

République du Mali, area **1,240,192 sq.km**, population **8,918,000** (1988), **republic** (President Gen. Moussa Traoré since 1968).
Administrative units: 6 regions. **Capital:** Bamako 570,000 inhab. (1981, with agglomeration); **other towns** (in 1,000

MAURITANIA
SENEGAL
GAMBIA
GUINEA-BISSAU
GUINEA
SIERRA LEONE
LIBERIA
ATLANTIC OCEAN
Nouamrhar
Akjoujt
Talorza
Nouakchott
Tidjikdja
Tîchît
Moudjéria
Boutilimit
Mederdra
Aleg
Tamchaket
Qualâta
Rosso
Bogué
Podor
Dagana
Kiffa
'Ayoûn el 'Atroûs
Néma
Kaédi
Mbout
Timbédra
St.-Louis
Louga
Linguère
Matam
Kébémer
DAKAR
Thiès
Rufisque
C. Vert
Touba
Diourbel
Sélibaby
Bakel
Sénégal
Nioro du Sahel
Ballé
Nara
Sandaré
Ambidédi
Kidira
Kayes
Guinguinéo
Kaolack
Diéma
Sokolo
Mourdiah
Koungheul
Banjul
Niono
Didiéni
Bafoulabé
Sadiola
Maka
Tambacounda
Banamba
Brikama
Basse Santa Su
Toukoto
Ségou
Kolda
Vélingara
Gambie
Kita
Niger
Ziguinchor
Kati
Koulikoro
Farim
Kédougou
Satadougou
Canchungo
Bissau
Koundara
Bafing
BAMAKO
Géba
Bafatá
Niagassola
Korodougou
Gaoual
Bolama
Madina do Boé
Kangaré
Siguiri
Sangarédi
Labé
Dinguiraye
Bougouni
Sikasso
Arq. dos Bijagós
Boké
Pita
Télimélé
Kamsar
Dalaba
Dabola
Kouroussa
Boffa
Fria
Mamou
Baoulé
Kankan
Kindia
Faranah
Milo
Tingréla
Dubréka
CONAKRY
Kabala
Boundiali
Odienné
Port Loko
Makeni
Kérouané
Korhogo
Kissidougou
Pepel
Lunsar
Sefadu
Sewa
Freetown
Rokel
Macenta
Beyla
Moyamba
Bo
Pendembu
Voinjama
Touba
Mankono
Kenema
Nzérékoré
Séguéla
Bonthe
Yekepa
Man
Zuénoula
Zimi
Bendaja
St. Paul
Sanniquellie
Bomi Hills
Gbarnga
Ganta
Daloa
Robertsport
Bong
Toulépleu
Monrovia
Harbel
Guiglo
Nzi
Marshall
Cestos
Buchanan
Tchien
Taï
Soubré
Sassandra
Greenville
Cavalla
Grand Cess
Tabou
San-Pédro
Harper
C. Palmas
1 : 12 500 000
0 100 200 300 Km
0 50 100 150 200 Mi
16°
12°
8°
4°
1
2
3
4
A
B
C
D
E

map 29

NAMIBIA

Republic of Namibia, area 824,295 sq.km, population 1,761,000 (1988), (President Samuel Nujoma since 1990).
Administrative units: 5 bantustans. **Capital:** Windhoek 88,700 inhab. – **Currency:** South African rand = 100 cents. – **Economy:** livestock (1983, in 1,000 head): cattle 1,900, sheep 5,500 (4 mn. karakul sheep), goats 2,200; fish catch 341,000 tonnes (1983). **Mining** (1983, in 1,000 tonnes, metal content): diamonds 963,000 carats, tin 800 tonnes, zinc 39.2, lead 33.8, copper 52.1, pyrites 202, silver 110 tonnes, uranium 3,719 tonnes, salt 137. – **Communications:** railways 2,600 km, roads 34,915 km.

NIGER

République du Niger, area 1,266,995 sq.km, population 7,250,000 (1988), republic (Head of State, President of Supreme Military Council Col. Ali Seybou since 1987).
Administrative units: 7 departments. **Capital:** Niamey 399,100 inhab. (1983). – **Currency:** CFA franc = 100 centimes. – **Economy:** developing agricultural country with animal production predominating. **Agriculture** (1983, in 1,000 tonnes): millet 1,325, sorghum, rice, manioc, cotton, sugarcane, groundnuts 74, dates; **livestock** (1983, in 1,000 head): cattle 3,521, sheep 3,448, goats 7,478, horses 283, asses 501, camels 410. **Mining** (1983): uranium 4,265 tonnes, tin. – **Communications:** roads 8,547 km, river transport on the R. Niger. – **Exports:** uranium (over 75%), groundnuts, cattle.

NIGERIA

Federal Republic of Nigeria, area 923,768 sq.km, population 104,957,000 (1988), federal republic, member of the Commonwealth (President Maj.-Gen. Ibrahim Babangida since 1985).
Administrative units: 19 states. **Capital:** Abuja 80,000 inhab. (1982) and Lagos 1,404,000 inhab. (1982, with agglom. 3.7 mn. inhab.); **other towns** (1982, in 1,000 inhab.): Ibadan 1,009, Ogbomosho 514, Kano 475, Oshogbo 336, Ilorin 335, Abeokuta 301, Port Harcourt 289, Ilesha 267, Zaria 267, Onitsha 262, Iwo 255, Ado-Ekiti 253, Kaduna 238, Mushin 234, Maiduguri 225. **Density** 103 persons per sq.km. – **Currency:** naira = 100 kobo. **Economy:** agricultural country with rapidly developing industry. **Agriculture** (1983, in 1,000 tonnes): maize (corn) 1,600, rice 1,000, millet 2,300, sorghum 2,660, manioc 9,950, sweet potatoes 260, cotton -seed 30, -lint 15; sugarcane 1,150, coconuts 90, palm kernels 360, palm oil 710, groundnuts 450, sesame 75, coffee, cocoa beans 150, tropical fruit 2,470, vegetables 3,600, tomatoes, tobacco 15; **livestock** (1983, in 1,000 head): cattle 12,300, sheep 12,850, goats 26,300, pigs 1,300, asses 700, poultry 150,000, eggs 235,000 tonnes; fish catch 515,200 tonnes (1983); roundwood 85.8 mn. cub.m, natural rubber 49,000 tonnes (1983). **Mining** (1983, in 1,000 tonnes): crude petroleum 61,150 (deposits in the Niger delta), natural gas 220,000 TJ, coal 40, tin 1,535 tonnes, columbite 182 tonnes (1982). Electricity 8,500 mn. kWh (1983), of this 60% hydro-electric power stations. **Production** (1983, in 1,000 tonnes): food processing of domestic agricultural production; beer 4 mn. hl, meat 826, milk 357; 10 billion cigarettes, cement 3,600, woven cotton fabrics 423 mn. sq.m. – **Communications:** railways 4,300 km, roads 115,000 km. Merchant shipping 442,000 GRT (1984), river transport. – **Exports:** petroleum 98%, cocoa, rubber, tin, palm kernels, groundnut oil.

RWANDA

République rwandaise – Republica y'u Rwanda, area 26,338 sq.km, population 6,755,000 (1988), republic (President Gen. Juvénal Habyalimana since 1973).
Administrative units: 10 prefectures. **Capital:** Kigali 155,000 inhab. (1981). – **Currency:** Rwanda franc = 100 centimes. – **Economy:** developing agricultural country. **Agriculture** (1983): coffee 28,000 tonnes, sorghum, potatoes, manioc, sweet potatoes, groundnuts, tea, tobacco; **livestock:** cattle 652,000 head, sheep and goats; roundwood 5.2 mn. cub.m (1983). – **Exports:** coffee, tin, tea, tungsten.

SÃO TOMÉ AND PRINCIPE

República democrática de São Tomé e Principe, area 964 sq.km, population 115,600 (1988), republic (President Dr Manuel Pinto da Costa since 1975).
Capital: São Tomé 17,000 inhab. (1979). – **Currency:** dobra = 100 centavos. – **Economy:** agriculture (1983): coffee, cocoa beans 8,000 tonnes, coconuts 42,000 tonnes, copra, palm oil, spice.

add page 130

inhab): Ségou 79, Mopti 65, Sikasso 57. – **Currency:** Mali franc = 100 centimes. – **Economy:** agricultural country with predominating livestock production. **Agriculture** (1983, in 1,000 tonnes): rice 122, maize (corn), millet, manioc, sweet potatoes, cotton -seed 65, -lint 43, groundnuts 70; **livestock** (1983, in 1,000 head): cattle 5,400, sheep 6,450, goats 7,500, horses 140, asses 425, camels 240, poultry 14,000; inland fish catch 33,000 tonnes. **Mining** (1983, in 1,000 tonnes): gold 404 kg, salt 6.– **Communications:** railways 645 km, roads 18,600 km, river transport on the R. Niger. – **Exports:** livestock, cotton, groundnuts, fish.

MAURITANIA

République Islamique de Mauritanie, area 1,032,455 sq.km, population 1,916,000 (1988), **republic** (President Col. Maaouya Ould Sidi Mohamed Taya since 1989).

Administrative units: 12 regions and 1 capital district. **Capital:** Nouakchott 150,000 inhab. (1982). – **Currency:** ouguiya = 5 khoums. – **Economy:** agricultural country with predominating livestock production. **Agriculture:** growing of millet, maize (corn), rice, dates 11,000 tonnes (1983), gum arabic; **livestock** (1983, in 1,000 head): cattle 1,500, sheep 5,000, goats 3,000, camels 750; fish catch 53,800 tonnes (1983). **Mining:** iron ore 4,183,000 tonnes (1983, metal content), copper, ilmenite. – **Communications:** railways 652 km, roads 7,800 km. – **Exports:** iron ore 65%, fish, cattle, gum arabic.

MAURITIUS AND DEPENDENCIES

Area 2,045 sq.km, population 1,077,000 (1988), **independent state, member of the Commonwealth** (Prime Minister Aneerood Jugnauth since 1984).

Dependencies: Agaloga Is., Cargados-Carajos Shoals, Rodrigues Island (109 sq.km) is now part of Mauritius.
Administrative units: 9 districts. **Capital:** Port Louis 147,386 inhab. (1981, with agglomeration 415,000 inhab.): **other towns** (in 1,000 inhab.): Beau-Bassin 87, Curepipe 57. **Density** 499 persons per sq.km. – **Currency:** Mauritius rupee = 100 cents.
Economy: agricultural country with monocultural cultivation of sugarcane – 5,500,000 tonnes in 1983; coconuts, copra, coffee, tea, bananas, vanilla, tobacco. Mining of salt. Food industry (sugar 567,000 tonnes in 1983), petroleum refinery.– **Communications:** roads 2,000 km. – **Exports:** sugar 60%, tea etc.

MOROCCO

al-Mamlaka al-Maghrebia, area 458,730 sq.km, population 23,910,000 (1988), **kingdom** (King Hassan II since 1961).

Administrative units: 31 provinces and 2 urban prefectures. **Capital:** Rabat 841,000 inhab. (1983, with agglomeration); **other towns** (1983, in 1,000 inhab.): Casablanca (Dar-el-Beida) 2,500 (with agglom.), Fès 562, Marrakech 548, Meknès 486, Oujda 470, Kenitra 450, Tétouan 371, Tanger 304, Safi 256. – **Currency:** dirham = 100 centimes.
Economy: agricultural country with a relatively developed mining industry. **Agriculture** (1983, in 1,000 tonnes): wheat 1,971, barley 1,228, maize (corn), rice, potatoes, cotton, sugar beet 2,400, groundnuts, olives 250, olive oil 25, oranges 691, tangerines 245, lemons, grapes 200, dates 66, figs, tomatoes 390, tobacco; **livestock** (1983, in 1,000 head): cattle 3,000, sheep 15,000, goats 6,270, asses 1,550, horses 315, camels 240, poultry 25,000; fish catch 439,000 tonnes; roundwood 1.7 mn. cub.m (1983). **Mining** (1983, in 1,000 tonnes, metal content): coal 816, natural gas, iron ore 153, manganese 37, copper 23, lead 102, zinc 7, cobalt 700 tonnes (1982), antimony 988 tonnes, silver 88 tonnes, phosphates 20,106 (deposits Khouribga and Youssoufia), pyrites, fluorite. Electricity 6,010 mn. kWh (1983). **Industry:** developed food processing (mills, oil presses, sugar refineries; fish, fruit and vegetable canning plants). Traditional textile industry; developing chemical and construction industries; processing of petroleum. **Production** (1983, in 1,000 tonnes): meat 297, milk 800, wine 83, cement 3,852. – **Communications:** railways 1,786 km, roads 25,700 km. Tourism 1,877,000 visitors (1983). – **Exports:** phosphates, citrus fruit, canned fish etc.

MOZAMBIQUE

República Popular de Moçambique, area 799,380 sq.km, population 14,932,000 (1988), **people's republic** (President Joaquim Alberto Chissano since 1986).

Administrative units: 11 districts. **Capital:** Maputo 785,500 inhab. (1982): **other towns** (1980, in 1,000 inhab.): Beira 350, Quelimane 184, Nampula 126 (1970). – **Currency:** Metical = 100 centavos.
Economy: developing agricultural country. **Agriculture** (1983, in 1,000 tonnes): maize (corn) 200, rice 30, sugarcane 1,000, cotton -seed 35, -lint 17, sisal 4, groundnuts 60, coconuts 400, copra 65, cashew nuts 70, tea 15, citrus fruit, bananas: **livestock** (1983, in 1,000 head): cattle 1,440, goats; roundwood 14.7 mn. cub.m (1983). **Mining:** coal 380,000 tonnes (1983), salt, beryllium, fluorite. Electricity 6,426 mn. kWh, of this 90% from hydroelectric power stations. – **Communications:** railways 3,843 km, roads 39,173 km. – **Exports:** cashew nuts, sugar, cotton, tea, wood.

map 30

SENEGAL

République du Sénégal, area 196,722 sq.km, population 6,881,919 (1988), republic (President Abdou Diouf since 1981).
Administrative units: 10 regions. **Capital:** Dakar 1,048,000 inhab. (with agglom. 1980); **other towns** (1979, in 1,000 inhab.): Thiès 127, Kaolack 116, Saint-Louis 97, Ziguinchor 79. — **Currency:** CFA franc = 100 centimes.
Economy: agricultural country, cultivates chiefly groundnuts. **Agriculture** (1983, in 1,000 tonnes): groundnuts 650, millet 352, rice 70, oranges, bananas; **livestock** (1983, in 1,000 head): cattle 2,250, sheep 2,100, goats 1,050, fish catch 212,900 tonnes; roundwood 3.9 mn. cub.m (1983). **Mining** (1983, in 1,000 tonnes): phosphates 1,397, salt 170. — **Communications:** railways 1,400 km, roads 14,500 km, river transport. — **Exports:** groundnut oil, phosphates.

SEYCHELLES AND DEPENDENCIES

Republic of Seychelles, area 453 sq.km, population 66,626 (1988), republic, member of the Commonwealth (President F. Albert René since 1977).
Capital: Victoria 23,000 inhab. (1982). — **Currency:** Seychelles rupee = 100 cents. — **Economy:** coconuts, copra, cinnamon, vanilla; cattle and pig breeding, fish catch. Mining of phosphates and sea salt.

SIERRA LEONE

Republic of Sierra Leone, area 71,740 sq.km, population 3,946,000 (1988), republic, member of the Commonwealth (President Joseph Momoh since 1985).
Administrative units: 3 provinces and capital district. **Capital:** Freetown 300,000 inhab. (1980). — **Currency:** leone = 100 cents. — **Economy:** developing agricultural country with important mineral mining. **Agriculture** (1983, in 1,000 tonnes): rice 609, maize (corn) millet, manioc, sweet potatoes, palm kernels 30, palm oil 45, groundnuts, piassaba, coffee 19, cocoa beans, citrus fruit 67; fish catch 53,000 tonnes; roundwood 8.1 mn. cub.m. **Mining** (1983, in 1,000 tonnes, metal content): iron ore 190, chromium, diamonds 345,000 carats, bauxite 600, rutile 47.7. — **Communications:** railways 597 km, roads 8,000 km. — **Exports:** diamonds, coffee, cocoa, rutile, bauxite, iron ore.

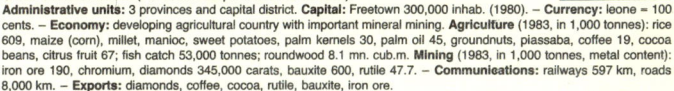

SOMALIA

Al-Jumhouriya As-Somaliya Al-Domocradia, area 637,657 sq.km, population 7,106,000 (1988), republic (President Maj.-Gen. Mohammed Siyad Barre since 1980).

Administrative units: 8 regions. **Capital:** Muqdisho 500,000 inhab. (1981); **other towns** (1981, in 1,000 inhab): Hargeysa 90, Kismaayo 70, Berbera 65, Marka 60. — **Currency:** Somalian shilling = 100 centimes.
Economy: agricultural country. **Agriculture** (1983, in 1,000 tonnes): maize (corn), sorghum, cotton, sugarcane 480, groundnuts, sesame, bananas 80; fish catch 15,500 tonnes (1983); collection of gum arabic; **livestock** (1983, in 1,000 head): cattle 4,050, sheep 10,400, goats 16,900, camels 5,650 (leading world population). — **Communications:** roads 19,380 km. — **Exports:** cattle, meat, bananas.

SOUTH AFRICA

Republiek van Suid-Africa – Republic of South Africa, area 1,221,037 sq.km, population 33,747,000 (1988), republic (President Frederik Willem de Klerk since 1989).
Administrative units: 4 provinces, 8 bantustans. **Capital:** Pretoria: 739,043 inhab. (1980); Cape Town (legislative capital 213,830 inhab.; with agglom. 1,500,000); **other towns** (1980, in 1,000 inhab.): Johannesburg 1,726 (3,500 with agglomeration), Durban 961 (+Pinetown), Port Elizabeth 492, Vereeniging 448 (+Vanderbijlpark, Sasolburg), Germiston 222, Benoni 207, Bloemfontein 198, Pietermaritzburg 192, Springs 174. — **Currency:** rand = 100 cents.
Economy: highly developed industrial and agricultural country with enormous mineral wealth, economically the most important country of Africa. **Agriculture** (1983, in 1,000 tonnes): wheat 1,770, maize (corn) 3,910, sorghum 195, potatoes 900, cotton -seed 50, -lint 27; sugarcane 13,370, sunflower seeds 202, groundnuts 92, soya beans, oranges 483, lemons 48, grapefruits 108, bananas 115, pineapples 237, grapes 1,200, fruit, tobacco 38; **livestock** (1983, in 1,000 head): cattle 13,086, goats 5,950, sheep 31,750, pigs 1,450, horses, eggs 180,000 tonnes; fish catch 600,000 tonnes, whaling; roundwood 20.5 mn. cub.m. **Mining:** in a number of branches leading world output (1983, in 1,000 tonnes): coal 139,557, iron ore 10,459, manganese 1,154 (second world producer), chromium 703 (second world producer), copper 211, tin 2,668 tonnes, zinc 110, nickel 20.5, antimony 6,302 tonnes, lead 80, rutile 47, vanadium 8,074 tonnes (second world producer), zircon 125, gold 679,527 kg (leading world producer), silver 173 tonnes, platinum 75,000 kg (leading world producer), magnesite 21, uranium 9,600 tonnes (leading world producer), diamonds 10,311,400 carats, salt 727, phosphates 2,742, pyrites 1,475, sulphur, mica, asbestos 211. Electricity 108,961 mn. kWh (1982). **Principal industries:** iron metallurgy, machinery, shipbuilding, chemical, construction, textiles and foodstuffs. **Production:** (1983, in 1,000 tonnes): pig iron 5,208, coke 1,795, crude steel 7,068, copper 192, aluminium 163, nitrogenous fertilizers 397, phosphate fertilizers 420, synthetic rubber 27.5, cement 7,908, paper 896, cotton yarn 40.8, woven cotton fabrics 148 mn. sq.m., meat 1,096, butter 19, milk 2,600, beer 11.6 mn. hl, wine 9.2 mn. hl; 31.1 billion tobacco products. — **Communications:** railways 23,400 km, roads 229,372 km. Merchant shipping 712,000 GRT (1984). — **Exports:** diamonds, food products, metals, minerals, textiles, machines.

page 131

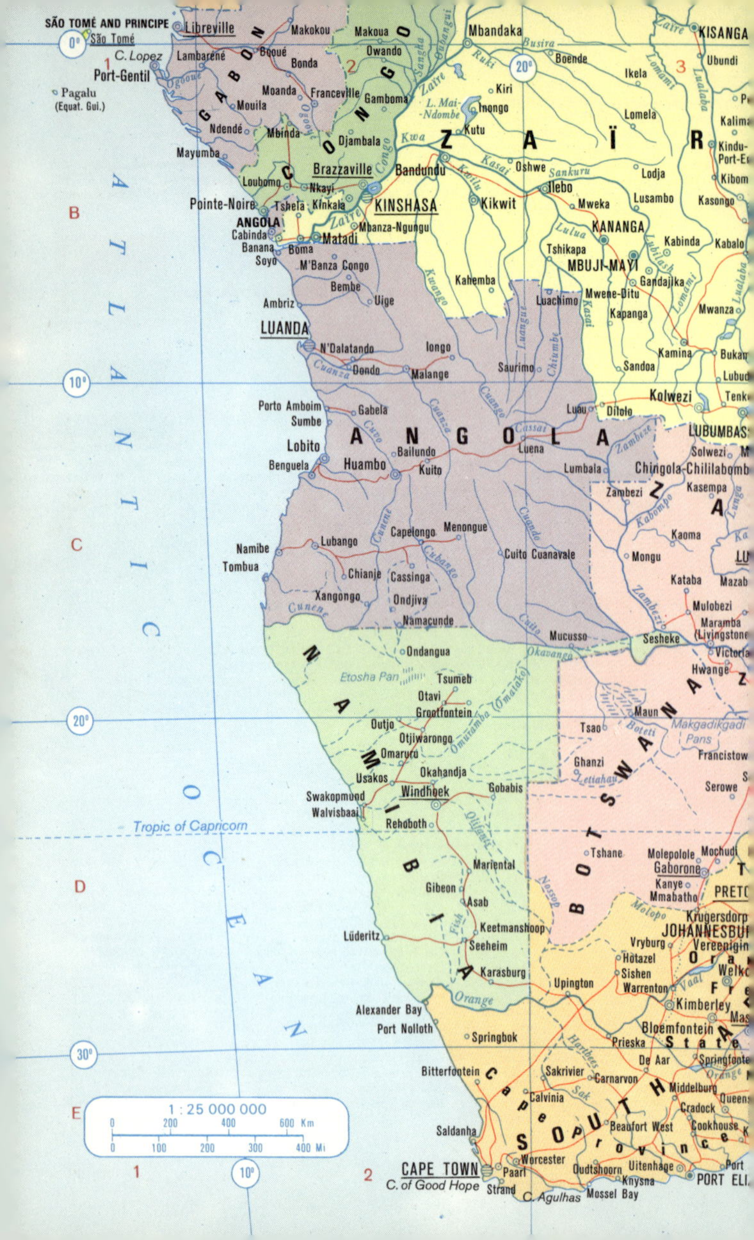

30a Mauritius, Réunion
1 : 7 500 000

SUDAN

Jamhuryat es-Sudan, area 2,505,813 sq.km, population 23,797,000 (1988), **republic** (Head of State Gen. Oumar Hassan Ahmad Bashir since 1989).
Administrative units: 9 regions and 19 provinces. **Capital:** Al-Khurtūm (Khartoum) 557,000 inhab. (1983); **other towns** (1983, in 1,000 inhab.): Umm Durmân (Omdurman) 613, Al-Khurtūm Bahrī 341, Būr Sūdān (Port Sudan) 204, Kassalā 143, Wad Madanī 141, Al-Ubayyid 140. – **Currency:** Sudanese pound = 100 piastres.
Economy: developing agricultural country. **Agriculture** (1983, in 1,000 tonnes: millet 314, sorghum 1,819, wheat, rice, cotton -seed 379,-lint 201; sugarcane 4,000, groundnuts 900, sesame 235, dates 139, bananas 92, grapes 56, tomatoes 154; **livestock** (1983, in 1,000 head): cattle 19,550, sheep 19,500, goats 12,900, camels 2,730 (second world population), asses 688; roundwood 38.2 mn. cub.m, gum arabic 43,918 tonnes (90% of world production). **Mining:** iron ore, gold, chromium, manganese, salt. – **Communications:** railways 5,503 km, roads 23,042 km. – **Exports:** cotton, livestock, groundnuts, sesame, gum arabic.

SWAZILAND

Kingdom of Swaziland – Umbuso wake Ngwane, area 17,363 sq.km, population 737,000 (1988), **constitutional monarchy, member of the Commonwealth** (King Mswati III since 1986).
Administrative units: 4 districts. **Capital:** Mbabane 29,875 inhab. (1981). – **Currency:** lilangeni = 100 cents. – **Economy:** developing agricultural country. **Agriculture** (1983, in 1,000 tonnes): maize (corn), rice, cotton, sugarcane 3,486, citrus fruit, bananas, tobacco, cattle and goat breeding. **Mining:** coal, tin, asbestos. – **Exports:** sugar, fruit, asbestos etc.

TANZANIA

United Republic of Tanzania, area 945,087 sq.km, population 23,997,000 (1988), **republic, union of Tanganyika and Zanzibar, member of the Commonwealth** (President Ali Hassan Mwinyi since 1985).
Administrative units: 22 regions. **Capitals:** Dar-es-Salaam 851,522 inhab. (1978); legislative capital Dodoma 158,577 inhab. (1978); **other towns** (1978, in 1,000 inhab.): Musoma 219, Zanzibar 111. – **Currency:** Tanzanian shilling = 100 cents.
Economy: agricultural country. **Agriculture** (1983, in 1,000 tonnes): maize (corn) 2,000, rice 400, millet, sorghum, manioc 6,800, sweet potatoes 307, potatoes, cotton -seed 109, -lint 57; sisal 82 (second world producer), sugarcane 1,320, coconuts 320, copra 29, palm kernels 5.4, cashew nuts 35, groundnuts, pyrethrum 1.0, coffee 48, tea 18, bananas 820, pineapples 50, tobacco 18, cloves 8,000 tonnes (leading world producer, Zanzibar and Pemba islands); **livestock** (1983, in 1,000 head): cattle 13,446, sheep 4,020, goats 6,031, asses; fish catch 272,500 tonnes; roundwood 39.8 mn. cub.m (1983). **Mining** (1983): gold, diamonds 250,000 carats, salt, mica – **Communications:** railways 3,550 km, roads 45,638 km. – **Exports:** coffee, cotton, sisal, diamonds, tea, cloves etc.

TOGO

République Togolaise, area 56,785 sq.km, population 3,247,000 (1988), **republic** (President Gen. Gnassingbe Eyadema since 1967).
Administrative units: 5 regions. **Capital:** Lomé 240,000 inhab. (1980). – **Currency:** CFA franc = 100 centimes. – **Economy:** developing agricultural country. **Agriculture** (1983, in 1,000 tonnes): millet, maize (corn), manioc 400, cotton, coconuts, copra, palm oil 14, groundnuts, coffee 10, cocoa beans 10, bananas; raising of cattle, sheep, goats, pigs; fish catch 14,600 tonnes. **Mining** (in 1,000 tonnes): phosphates 2,081 (1983), deposits of iron ore and bauxite. – **Communications:** railways 516 km, roads 8,057 km. – **Exports:** phosphates, cocoa, coffee.

TUNISIA

Al-Jumhuriya at-Tunisiya, area 163,610 sq.km, population 7,809,000 (1988), **republic** (President Zine El Abidine Ben Ali since 1987).
Administrative units: 21 governorates. **Capital:** Tunis 596,654 inhab. (1984); **other towns** (1984, in 1,000 inhab.): Sfax 232, Ariana 99, Bizerte 95, Djerba 92, Gabès 92. – **Currency:** Tunisian dinar = 1,000 millimes.
Economy: agricultural country with developed mining industry. **Agriculture** (1983, in 1,000 tonnes): wheat 618, barley, potatoes, olives 600, olive oil 132, oranges 81, tangerines 34, lemons 22, dates 77, fruit, almonds, grapes 105, tomatoes 360, tobacco; **livestock** (1983, in 1,000 head): cattle 560, sheep 5,100, camels 175, asses; fish catch 67,100 tonnes; cork 5.9, alfalfa 59,000 tonnes. **Mining** (1983, in 1,000 tonnes): crude petroleum 5,578, natural gas 17,540 TJ, iron ore 169, lead 4.9, zinc 7.5, silver, salt 375, phosphates 5,924. – **Communications:** railways 2,032 km, roads 23,695 km. – **Exports:** petroleum, phosphates, olive oil, wine, fruit.

UGANDA

Republic of Uganda, area 241,139 sq.km, population 17,189,000 (1988), **republic, member of the Commonwealth** (President Yoweri Museweni since 1986).
Administrative units: 4 regions. **Capital:** Kampala 458,423 inhab.; **other towns** (1982, in 1,000 inhab.): Jinja 55, Bugembe 48. – **Currency:** Uganda shilling = 100 cents. – **Economy:** developing agricultural country. **Agriculture** (1983, in 1,000 tonnes): maize (corn) 450, millet 600, sorghum 470, manioc 1,650, sweet potatoes 760, cottonseed 95, groundnuts 100, sesame 38, tea 4, bananas 450; **livestock** (1983, in 1,000 head): cattle 5,100, sheep 1,080, goats; fish

catch 172,000 tonnes; roundwood 26.3 mn. cub.m. **Mining** (1983, tonnes metal content): tin 30, tungsten 14, salt 27,000. – **Communications:** railways 1,300 km, roads 27,544 km. – **Exports:** coffee, cotton, tea.

BURKINA FASO (Upper Volta)

République de Burkina Faso, area 274,200 sq.km, population 8,798,000 (1988), **republic** (Head of State Capt. Blaise Compaoré since 1987).
Administrative units: 11 departments. **Capital:** Ouagadougou 235,000 inhab. (1982). – **Currency:** CFA franc = 100 centimes. – **Economy:** developing agricultural country. **Agriculture** (1983, in 1,000 tonnes): maize (corn), millet 300, sorghum 600, rice 37, manioc, cotton -seed 50, -lint 29; sugarcane 330, groundnuts 77, sesame, tobacco; **livestock** (1983, in 1,000 head): cattle 2,950, sheep 2,000, goats 2,500.- **Communications:** railways 517 km, roads 18,000 km.

WESTERN SAHARA

Area 266,769 sq.km, population 175,000 (1988). **The territory occupied by Morocco. Capital:** El Aaiún 30,000 inhab. (1980). – **Economy:** large supplies phosphates (mining 440,000 tonnes in 1978) and deposits of gold and uranium.

ZAÏRE

République du Zaïre, area 2,345,409 sq.km, population 33,458,000 (1988), **republic** (President Gen. Mobutu Sese Seko since 1965).
Administrative units: 8 regions and capital district. **Capital:** Kinshasa 3,682,000 inhab. (1980); **other towns** (1985, in 1,000 inhab.): Kananga 938, Lubumbashi 765, Mbuji-Mayi 625, Kisangani 557, Bukavu 418, Kikwit 346, Mbandaka 294, Matadi 216, Likasi 172 (1976). – **Currency:** zaïre = 100 makuta.
Economy: agricultural country with developed mining industry and metallurgy. **Agriculture** (1983, in 1,000 tonnes): maize (corn) 668, rice 258, manioc 14,600, sweet potatoes 310, potatoes 206, cotton seed 50, sisal, sugarcane 740, palm oil 140, groundnuts 370, coffee 50, tea 4, cocoa beans, pineapples 153, tobacco; **livestock** (1983, in 1,000 head): cattle 1,300, sheep 760, goats 2,900, pigs 750; fish catch 102,000 tonnes; roundwood 31.3 mn. cub.m, natural rubber 24,000 tonnes. **Mining** (1983, in 1,000 tonnes, metal content): crude petroleum 1,212, copper 535, zinc 75, tin 2.1, cobalt 11,300 tonnes (leading world producer), tungsten 170 tonnes, cadmium, niobium, tantalum, gold 1,866 kg, silver 62 tonnes, diamonds 11,438,000 carats (leading world producer). Electricity 4,213 mn. kWh (1983). **Production** (1983, in 1,000 tonnes): copper 227, zinc 62.5, cement 400. – **Communications:** railways 5,254 km, roads 145,000 km, navigable waterways 16,400 km. – **Exports:** copper, petroleum, coffee, diamonds, cobalt, palm oil, wood etc.

ZAMBIA

Republic of Zambia, area 752,614 sq.km, population 7,531,000 (1988), **republic, member of the Commonwealth** (President Dr Kenneth David Kaunda since 1964).
Administrative units: 9 provinces. **Capital:** Lusaka 538,500 inhab. (1980); **other towns** (1980, in 1,000 inhab.): Kitwe-Kalulushi 374, Ndola 282, Chingola-Chililabombwe 208, Mufulira 150. – **Currency:** kwacha = 100 ngwee.
Economy: chiefly mining and metallurgy of non-ferrous metals. **Agriculture** (1983, in 1,000 tonnes): maize (corn) 935,000 tonnes, sugarcane 1 mn. tonnes, manioc, groundnuts, tobacco; **livestock** (1983, in 1,000 head): cattle 2,380, goats, poultry 18,000; fish catch 67,200 tonnes; roundwood 9 mn. cub.m. **Mining** (1983, in 1,000 tonnes, metal content): coal 456, copper 576, lead 14.8, zinc 38, manganese, tin, cobalt 2,400 tonnes, gold 316 kg, silver 29 tonnes. Electricity 10,071 mn. kWh (1983). – **Communications:** railways 2,189 km, roads 37,068 km. – **Exports:** copper 90%, zinc, cobalt, lead, maize etc.

ZIMBABWE

Republic of Zimbabwe, area 390,580 sq.km, population 8,878,000 (1988), **republic, member of the Commonwealth** (President Dr Robert Gabriel Mugabe since 1988).
Administrative units: 8 provinces. **Capital:** Harare (Salisbury) 656,000 inhab. (1982); **other towns** (1982, in 1,000 inhab.): Bulawayo 414, Chitungwiza 173, Gweru 79, Mutare 70, Kwekwe 58. – **Currency:** Zimbabwe dollar = 100 cents. **Economy:** developed agriculture and mining industry. **Agriculture** (1983, in 1,000 tonnes): maize (corn) 1,023, wheat, millet, cotton seed 101, sugarcane 3,700, groundnuts 32, tea, citrus fruit, bananas, tobacco 99; **livestock** (1983, in 1,000 head): cattle 5,350, sheep 455, goats 1,000; roundwood 6.7 mn. cub.m (1983). **Mining** (1983, in 1,000 tonnes, metal content): coal 2,391, iron ore 554, chromium 144, copper, tin, nickel, tungsten, gold 14,090 kg, silver, antimony, magnesite, emeralds, phosphates, pyrites, asbestos 153. Electricity 4,426 mn. kWh (1983). – **Communications:** railways 3,470 km, roads 78,800 km. – **Exports:** tobacco, asbestos, gold, copper, chromium, sugar.

BRITISH TERRITORIES:
SAINT HELENA AND DEPENDENCIES – British colony and 5 dependencies. Saint Helena – **area 314 sq.km, population 6,879** (1987). **Capital:** Jamestown 1,862 inhab. – **Currency:** English pound = 100 pence. – **Dependencies:** Ascension, Tristan da Cunha and volcanic islands.

FRENCH TERRITORY:
RÉUNION – **Area 2,510 sq.km, population 575,000** (1988). **French overseas department. Capital:** Saint-Denis 104,603 inhab. (1982). – **Currency:** CFA franc = 100 centimes. – **Economy:** sugar 223,700 tonnes, vanilla, oil of geranium, rum.

31a U.S.A. Pacific Coast
1 : 15 000 000

Greenland
Gunnbjørns Field 3734
Mt. Forel 3383
Iceland
Disko
Davis Strait
Arctic Circle
Nûk (Godthåb)
Uummannarsuaq (K. Farvel)
BAFFIN SEA
2414
Baffin Island
2591
C. Dyer
Foxe Basin
Southampton I.
Hudson Strait
C. Chidley
Ungava B.
Ivujivik
Ungava Pen.
1676
LABRADOR SEA
4316
Hudson Bay
258
Labrador Peninsula
Plateau
Churchill
1128
L. Mistassini
James B.
Albany
Shield
C. Charles
I. of Newfoundland
St. John's
C. Race
G. of St. Lawrence
Cabot Str.
C. Breton I.
1268
Québec
Nova Scotia
C. Sable
St. Lawrence
Ottawa
183
L. Superior
393
1629
L. Huron
L. Ontario
75
Niagara Fs.
Hudson
L. Michigan
Appalachian Mountains
New York
L. Erie
Washington
Chicago
Ohio
St. Louis
Mississippi
Lowlands
Mt. Mitchell 2037
Lowlands
C. Hatteras
Bermuda
Atlantic
Mexico Plain
New Orleans
Florida
C. Canaveral
Miami
Bahamas
C. Sable
Str. of Florida
Gulf of Mexico
5203
La Habana
Cuba
P. Duarte 3175
Hispaniola
Puerto Rico
8648
Guadeloupe
Dominica
Martinique
St. Lucia
Barbados
Greater Antilles
Grenada
Tobago
Trinidad
Lesser Antilles
Jamaica
7535
5630
CARIBBEAN SEA
Yucatán Str.
C. Catoche
Golfo de Campeche
Yucatán
Isthmus of Tehuantepec
V. Tajumulco 4220
Guatemala
Coco
Managua
L. de Nicaragua
6488
Chirripó 3837
Panama Canal
Isthmus of Panama
Pta. Mariato
Pta. Gallinas
L. de Maracaibo
Caracas
P. Cristóbal Colón 5775
Cord. de Mérida 5007
P. Bolívar 5493
Magdalena
Orinoco
Georgetown
SOUTH AMERICA
Equator
Amazonas
ATLANTIC OCEAN
5819
6995
Tropic of Cancer
Azores
EUROPE
Iberian Pen.
6321
1 : 50 000 000
0 250 500 750 1 000 1 250 Km
0 200 400 600 800 Mi
30° 60° 50° 40° 30° 20° 10° 50° 90° 70° 60°
15 B 16 17 C 18 D 19 E
F G H I
11 12 13 14 15

NORTH AMERICA

The physical geography of the North American continent includes Central America, the islands of the Caribbean Sea and Greenland. It is the largest continent in the western hemisphere. The original term "the New World" (Mundus Novus) was replaced, in the first half of the 16th century, by the name America, after the Florentine Amerigo Vespucci, an Italian seafarer who took part in Columbus's expeditions in the late 15th century.

North America covers an **area of 24,360,000 sq.km**, i.e. 16.3% of the land area of the world; it has **416 mn. inhabitants** (1988), i.e. 8.1% of the world's population and a population density of 17.1 persons per sq.km. **Geographical position:** northernmost point: on the mainland – Cape Murchison on the Boothia Peninsula 71°50′ N.Lat., of the entire continent – cape K. Morris Jesup 83°40′ N.Lat. in Greenland; southernmost point: cape Punta Mariato on the Peninsula de Azuero in Panama 7°12′ N.Lat.; easternmost point: on the mainland – Cape Charles 55°40′ W.Long. in Labrador, in Greenland cape Nordostrundingen 11°39′ W.Long.; westernmost point: on the mainland – Cape Prince of Wales on the Seward Peninsula in Alaska 168°05′ W.Long. (here America comes within 75 km of Asia), of the entire continent – Cape Wrangell on the Aleutian island of Attu 172°27′ E.Long. The American continent reaches its maximum length between Point Barrow (Alaska) and Punta Mariato (Panama) a total length of roughly 8,700 km; its width from the most westerly point of Alaska as far as Canso on the peninsula of Nova Scotia (Canada) measures 5,950 km; and the narrowest point is on the Isthmus of Panama, a mere 48 km.

Geological evolution gave North America highly varied contours, an uneven coastline and large numbers of islands (mostly of continental origin). North America has the longest coastline of all continents, reaching a length of 75,600 km. 1 km of shore corresponds to 320 sq.km on the continent. **Islands and peninsulas** makes up 25.4% of the area of the continent. The islands – 4,160,000 sq.km in area – are concentrated chiefly in the Arctic region. There lies Greenland, the largest island in the world (2,175,600 sq.km), and also the vast Canadian Arctic Archipelago (area: 1,405,000 sq.km) with the two largest islands Baffin I. (507,414 sq.km) and Victoria I. (217,274 sq.km). The second island region is that of the Caribbean Sea with the Greater (207,700 sq.km) and the Lesser Antilles (14,200 sq.km). The Aleutian Is. (37,850 sq.km) stretch northwest in the Pacific Ocean, together with the Alexander Archipelago (36,780 sq.km) and Queen Charlotte Is. (9,600 sq.km). The largest peninsula is Labrador (1,320,000 sq.km).

The surface of North America is divided in a north-south direction by the mountains of the Cordilleras with high plateaux between the ranges in the west of the continent, by the vast Great Plains and the Central Lowlands, the alluvial Mississippi Lowlands (1,000 km long and 80–100 km wide) in the interior of the continent, and by the eastern ranges (the Laurentin Plateu and the Appalachian Mts.), which line the coastal plain on the Atlantic Ocean and the Gulf of Mexico. The highest mountain of the continent is Mt. McKinley/Denali (6,194 m) in the Alaska Range in the Pacific Mountain System, which includes the Cascade Range (4,391 m) and the Sierra Nevada (Mt. Whitney, 4,418 m). The lowest point is Death Valley (–86 m) on the western edge of the Great Basin in California. The Rocky Mts. (Mt. Elbert, 4,398 m) enclose the Great Basin without outlet to the sea. The geologically younger Cordilleras in Central America have a number of volcanoes (V. Citlaltépetl 5,699 m), many of them active, and this is also a region of frequent earthquakes. The Laurentin Plateau, known as the Canadian Shield (comprising half of Canada) is geologically the oldest part of the continent; it is considerably worn down by glaciers, with a vast number of shallow valleys, rivers, streams and lakes. In the east of the continent the Paleozoic Appalachian Mts. reach the height of 2,037 m.

The river system, especially in the North of the continent, was greatly affected by Quaternary glaciation. The annual mean discharge is 7,130 cub.km. Most of the river basins drain into the Atlantic Ocean through the mouth of the third longest river in the world, the Mississippi-Missouri (length 6,212 km, draining an area of 3,250,000 sq.km with an average annual flow 19,800 cub.m per second) and the St. Lawrence (3,058 km), which flows from the Great Lakes. Both of these are very important shipping routes. The Mackenzie, the longest river of Canada (4,240 km, drainage area 1,813,000 sq.km) drains into the Arctic Ocean, and in the West, the Colorado (with the famous Grand Canyon), the Columbia and the Fraser flow into the Pacific Ocean. The longest river in Alaska is the Yukon (3,185 km), which drains into the Bering Sea. The northern rivers have an ample supply of water from glaciers and snow-fall throughout the year, but they freeze up in winter. On the other hand, the rivers in the Central Basins of the South-West of the United States and Mexico often dry up in summer. The Great Lakes, the largest fresh water **lakes** in the world, covering an area of 246,515 sq.km, are of glacial and tectonic origin.

North America stretches across 3 **climatic zones** in the northern hemisphere. In the far North, on the Arctic islands and in Greenland there is the polar-Arctic-climate (mean annual temperature between 0°C and –20°C, precipitation c. 200 mm). The central part of the continent has an extreme climate (with great differences in temperature in summer and winter). A transitional zone of subtropical climate is found around the Gulf of Mexico (sufficient rainfall), in northern Mexico and southern California – U.S.A. (little rainfall). The climate of the Central American mainland and the islands in the Caribbean Sea is tropical, oceanic. In winter, blizzards blow from the North across the open continent, the temperature drops by about 20°C and in summer tornadoes and hurricanes strike the South-east of the continent and especially the islands. The highest temperature, 57°C, was measured in Death Valley and the lowest, at Fort Good Hope, was –78.2°C. Mean January and July temperatures in °C (and annual precipitation in mm): Barrow –26.4 and 4.5 (112), Dawson –29.4 and 15.6 (321), Cambridge Bay –30.7 and 9.6 (170), Úpernavik –21.8 and 4.9 (230), Prince Rupert 1.7 and 13.4 (2,417), Churchill –28.3 and 12.1 (405), Winnipeg –18.7 and 19.9 (535), St. John's –4.5 and 15.3 (1,348), Montréal –9.2 and 21.5 (1,061), New York 0.1 and 24.6 (1,076), Chicago –3.3 and 23.9 (843), Salt Lake City –2.6 and 24.7 (353), San Francisco 10.2 and 14.7 (528), Miami 19.2 and 27.4 (1,518), México 11.0 and 15.6 (765), Kingston 24.7 and 27.6 (802), Colón 26.2 and 26.7 (3,680).

There are four **natural vegetation** regions in North America, the Holarctic in the North and the neo-tropical in the South. From North to South we can find arctic deserts, tundra, North Canadian coniferous forest, a zone of Pacific forests, Laurentinian and South Atlantic mixed forest, grassland, steppe, shrub with cacti and thorn bushes, Central American coniferous forest and tropical swamp forest, savanna and tropical rain forest. There are also two zones of **animal life:** the neo-arctic (e.g. elk, "wapiti" stag, grizzly bear, racoon, beaver, puma, wild turkey, waterfowl, etc.) and the neo-tropical (e.g. jaguar, armadillo, tapir, porcupine, alligator, parrots, humming birds, etc.). Buffaloes exist only in reservations. Great attention is being paid to conservation; national parks, monuments and reservations have been established, the largest being Wood Buffalo N.P. in Canada (44,807 sq.km) and Yellowstone N.P. in the U.S.A.

LONGEST RIVERS

Name	Length in km	River Basin in sq.km
Mississippi-Missouri	6,212	3,250,000
Mackenzie-Athabasca	4,240	1,813,000
Yukon	3,185	848,400
St. Lawrence	3,058	1,260,000
Rio Grande/Bravo del Norte	3,023	580,000
Nelson-Saskatchewan	2,575	1,250,000
Arkansas	2,334	416,000
Colorado	2,334	590,000
Ohio-Allegheny	2,102	525,700
Columbia	1,954	668,000
Saskatchewan	1,940	336,700
Peace	1,923	303,000
Snake	1,671	382,300
Red	1,638	214,500
Churchill	1,609	410,000
Canadian	1,458	.
Tennessee	1,387	105,950
Fraser	1,368	232,800
Kuskokwim	1,287	126,900
Ottawa	1,271	.

LARGEST ISLANDS

Name	Area in sq.km
Greenland	2,175,600
Baffin I.	507,414
Victoria I.	217,274
Ellesmere I.	196,221
Cuba	110,922
Newfoundland	108,852
Hispaniola	77,218
Banks I.	70,023
Devon I.	55,243
Axel Heiberg I.	43,175
Melville I.	42,146
Southampton I.	41,221
Prince of Wales I.	33,336
Vancouver I.	31,282
Somerset I.	24,784
Bathurst I.	16,041
Prince Patrick I.	15,847
King William I.	13,110
Ellef Ringnes I.	11,294
Jamaica	11,424

LARGEST LAKES

Name	Area in sq.km	Greatest Depth in m	Altitude in m	Name	Area in sq.km	Greatest Depth in m	Altitude in m
L. Superior	82,414	393	183	Reindeer L.	6,651	.	337
L. Huron	59,596	226	176	Nettilling L.	5,542	.	30
L. Michigan	58,016	281	176	L. Winnipegosis	5,374	12	253
Great Bear Lake	31,328	137	157	L. Nipigon	4,848	123	261
Great Slave Lake	28,570	187	158	L. Manitoba	4,660	7	248
L. Erie	25,745	64	174	Great Salt Lake	4,365	16	1,283
L. Winnipeg	24,388	21	217	Lake of the Woods	4,349	21	323
L. Ontario	19,553	237	75	Dubawnt L.	3,833	.	236
Lago de Nicaragua	8,430	70	34	L. Melville	3,069	.	tidal
L.Athabasca	7,935	91	213	Wollaston L.	2,681	.	398

HIGHEST MOUNTAINS

Name (Country)	Height in m	Name (Country)	Height in m	Name (Country)	Height in m
Denali/Mt. McKinley (U.S.A.)	6,194	Mt. Bona (U.S.A.)	5,029	Mt. Shasta (U.S.A.)	4,316
Mt. Logan (Can.)	5,951	Mt. Sanford (U.S.A.)	4,940	Mt. Kennedy (Can.)	4,238
V. Citlaltépetl (Mex.)	5,699	Mt. Wood (Can.)	4,842	V. Tajumulco (Guat.)	4,220
Mt. St. Elias (Can.-U.S.A.)	5,489	Mt. Vancouver (Can.-U.S.A.)	4,785	Mt. Waddington (Can.)	4,042
Mt. Foraker (U.S.A.)	5,303	Toluca/Zinantecatl (Mex.)	4,577	Mt. Robson (Can.)	3,954
Ixtaciluatl (Mex.)	5,286	Mt. Whitney (U.S.A.)	4,418	Chirripó (Costa Rica)	3,837
Mt. Lucania (Can.)	5,227	Mt. Elbert (U.S.A.)	4,398	Mt. Columbia (Can.)	3,747
Mt. Blackburn (U.S.A.)	5,036	Mt. Rainier (U.S.A.)	4,391	Gunnbjørns Fjeld (Green.)	3,734

ACTIVE VOLCANOES

Name (Country)	Altitude in m	Latest eruption
V. Popocatépetl (Mex.)	5,452	1932
Mt. Wrangell (Alaska, U.S.A.)	4,268	1907
V. Acatenango (Guat.)	3,976	1972
V. de Colima (Mex.)	3,885	1983
V.Fuego (Guat.)	3,835	1980
V.Santiaguito (Guat.)	3,768	1983
V. Irazú (Costa Rica)	3,432	1967
Shishaldin V. (Alaska, U.S.A.)	2,857	1981
Mt. St. Helens (U.S.A.)	2,549	1982
V. El Chichón (Mex.)	2,225	1983

FAMOUS NATIONAL PARKS

Name (Country)	Area in sq.km
Wood Buffalo (Can.)	44,807
Wrangell-St. Elias (U.S.A., Alaska)	33,717
Gates of the Arctic (U.S.A., Alaska)	30,345
Denali/Mt.McKinley (U.S.A., Alaska)	19,015
Katmai N.M. (U.S.A., Alaska)	14,886
Yellowstone (U.S.A.)	8,985
Jasper (Can.)	6,760
Everglades (U.S.A.)	5,660
Grand Canyon (U.S.A.)	4,930
Banff (Can.)	4,126

32 a New York   1 : 900 000

ICELAND
Reykjavík
IRELAND
SPAIN
PORTUGAL
Greenland
(Denmark)
Arctic Circle
Ammassalik
Disko
Qeqertarssuaq
(Godhavn)
Nûk
(Godthåb)
Qaqortoq
(Julianehåb)
Uummannarsuaq
(K.Farvel)
Davis Strait
Frobisher Bay
Port Burwell
Hudson Strait
LABRADOR SEA
ATLANTIC OCEAN
Azores
(Port.)
Kuujjuaq
Schefferville
Goose Bay
I. of Newfoundland
Channel Port-aux-Basques
St. John's
C. Race
Ft. George
Sept-Îles
G. of St. Lawrence
St.-Pierre-et Miquelon
(Fr.)
Sydney
Halifax
Moosonee
Chicoutimi-Jonquière
Cochrane
Québec
St. John
Augusta
Sault Ste. Marie
MONTRÉAL
Ottawa
TORONTO
BOSTON
Albany
Buffalo
NEW YORK
DETROIT
CLEVELAND
PHILADELPHIA
WASHINGTON
BALTIMORE
CHICAGO
Cincinnati
Richmond
Norfolk
C. Hatteras
Hamilton
Bermuda
(U.K.)
Tropic of Cancer
Nashville-Davidson
Charlotte
MEMPHIS
Birmingham
Atlanta
Charleston
Savannah
Mobile
Montgomery
JACKSONVILLE
NEW ORLEANS
Tampa
Miami
BAHAMAS
Nassau
Strs. of Florida
Turks and Caicos Is. (U.K.)
Gd. Turk
DOMINICAN REP.
STO. DOMINGO
San Juan
Virgin Is. (U.K.)
ST. CHRISTOPHER NEVIS
ANTIGUA AND BARBUDA
Guadeloupe (Fr.)
DOMINICA
Martinique (Fr.)
ST. LUCIA
BARBADOS
ST. VINCENT AND GRENADINES
GRENADA
Port of Spain
TRINIDAD AND TOBAGO
Gulf of Mexico
LA HABANA
CUBA
Santiago de C.
PORT-AU-PRINCE
HAITI
Puerto Rico
(U.S.A.)
Virgin Is.
(U.S.A.)
Greater Antilles
Lesser Antilles
Yucatán Str.
Mérida
Campeche
Cayman Is.
(U.K.)
JAMAICA
Kingston
CARIBBEAN SEA
BELIZE
Belmopan
Pto. Barrios
GUATEMALA
HONDURAS
TEGUCIGALPA
S. Salvador
EL SALVADOR
NICARAGUA
MANAGUA
COSTA RICA
San José
Colón
Canal Zone
Panama
PANAMA
BARRANQUILLA
Sta. Marta
CARTAGENA
MARACAIBO
Neth. Antilles
Barquisimeto
CARACAS
Orinoco
VENEZUELA
COLOMBIA
San Cristóbal
MEDELLÍN
Georgetown
GUYANA
Paramaribo
SURINAM
Cayenne
French Guiana
Macapá
BRAZIL
1 : 50 000 000
0 250 500 750 1 000 1 250 Km
0 200 400 600 800 Mi

NORTH AMERICA

Country	Area in sq.km	Population year 1988	Density per sq.km	Capital
Anguilla (U.K.)	96	6,700[1]	70	The Valley
Antigua and Barbuda	442	82,400[1]	186	Saint John's
Bahamas	13,935	245,000	18	Nassau
Barbados	431	254,600	591	Bridgetown
Belize	22,965	176,500	7.7	Belmopan
Bermuda (U.K.)	53.5	57,800	1,080	Hamilton
Canada	9,976,139	25,949,600	2.5	Ottawa
Cayman Islands (U.K.)	260	24,800	95	Georgetown
Costa Rica	51,100	2,851,000	56	San José
Cuba	110,861	10,402,400	94	La Habana
Dominica	751	94,191[1]	125	Roseau
Dominican Republic	48,734	6,867,368	141	Santo Domingo
El Salvador	21,393	5,107,000	239	San Salvador
Greenland (Denmark)	2,175,600*)	55,000	0.03	Nuuk
Grenada	344	104,000[1]	302	Saint George's
Guadeloupe and Depend. (Fr.)	1,780	338,000	190	Basse-Terre
Guatemala	108,889	8,681,000	80	Guatemala
Haiti	27,750	5,523,000	199	Port-au-Prince
Honduras	112,088	4,802,000	43	Tegucigalpa
Jamaica	10,991	2,358,000	215	Kingston
Martinique (Fr.)	1,102	335,000	304	Fort-de-France
Mexico	1,972,546	82,734,454	42	Ciudad de México
Montserrat (U.K.)	106	13,200[1]	125	Plymouth
Nicaragua	129,350	3,622,000	28	Managua
Panama (incl. Canal Zone)	77,326	2,321,000	30	Panama
Puerto Rico (U.S.A.)	8,897	3,606,000	405	San Juan
Saint Christopher and Nevis	262	49,000	187	Basseterre
Saint Lucia	616	146,600	238	Castries
Saint Pierre et Miquelon (Fr.)	242	6,400	26	Saint-Pierre
Saint Vincent and Grenadines	389	113,600	292	Kingstown
Turks and Caicos Islands (U.K.)	430	10,800	25	Grand Turk
United States of America	9,372,614**)	247,083,000	26	Washington
Virgin Islands (U.K.)	153	13,246[1]	87	Road Town
Virgin Islands (U.S.A.)	344	106,500[1]	310	Charlotte Amalie

*) exclud. ice 341,700 sq.km, **) with the area of Great Lakes 9,519,617 sq.km, [1] year 1987

Today's **racial and ethnic composition** of the inhabitants of North America (incl. Central America) is the consequence of an intermingling of races and nationalities that began after the discovery of the continent. The population can be divided into five groups: 1. the original inhabitants – Indians and Eskimos, 2. inhabitants of European origin (immigrants and their descendants), 3. inhabitants of African origin (Negroes and their descendants), 4. mixed races between Indians, Whites and Negroes, 5. a small number of immigrants from Asia. In 1988 the total **number of inhabitants** was 416 million, not quite 66% living in the U.S.A. and Canada (of this: 96,000 Eskimos, over 3/4 million Indians and more than 28 million Negroes and mixed races) and 34% in Mexico and the countries and islands of Central America (where Indians, Negroes and mixed races predominate. Population density per sq.km is highest, with 136 persons, on the islands of the Caribbean Sea (Barbados 588), 42 persons in Central America and lowest in North America, with 13 persons per sq.km. Between 1975 and 1985 **the population** of the continent **increased at the high rate of 1.8%** (Honduras 3.45%, the U.S.A. only 0.97%), resulting from a high birth rate of 26.8 per thousand (e.g. Honduras 43.9 per thousand in 1980–85) and a decreasing death rate of 8.5 per thousand (e.g. Haiti 14.2, Jamaica 5.6 per thousand). The annual migration inflow amounts to 600,000 persons. There has been a remarkable growth in the number of inhabitants of towns and conurbations. Urban populations are highest in North America 77.2% (Canada 78.5%, the United States 76.5% in 1983), lower in Central America 59.2% (Mexico 67%), and least on the islands in the Greater Antilles 50% (Cuba 65.5%, Haiti only 25%). North America had 12 cities with a population of over a million (without agglomeration) and 33 cities with more than 500,000 inhabitants in 1983.

Economy: The United States is economically the strongest and technologically the most advanced country in the western world. It produces about 35% of the entire industrial production and roughly 20% of the agricultural production of the world, excluding the socialist countries, and handles almost one fifth of world trade. Canada, too, is a highly developed industrial and agricultural country with an important ore mining industry and very considerable agricultural output. The most developed country of Latin America is Mexico with its important mineral resources. Monoculture on plantations is the predominant form of agriculture in Central America.

CANADA

Area 9,976,139 sq.km, population 25,949,600 (1988), independent federal state, member of the Commonwealth (Prime Minister Martin Brian Mulroney since 1985, Governor-General Raymon John Hnatyshyn since 1990).

Administrative units: 10 provinces and 2 territories (see table). **Capital:** Ottawa 295,163 inhab. (census 1981, with agglom. 737,600 inhab.); **other towns** (1981, in 1,000 inhab. and with agglom. 1983 in brackets): Montréal 980 (2,862),

Toronto 599 (3,067[+]), Calgary 593 (635), Winnipeg 565 (601), North York[+] 560, Edmonton 532 (699), Scarborough[+] 443, Vancouver 414 (1,311), Mississauga[+] 315, Hamilton 306 (548), Etobicoke[+] 299, Laval[+] 268, London 254 (287), Windsor 192 (245), Québec 166 (580), Regina 163 (168), York[+] 141, Saskatoon 154, Brampton[+] 149, Kitchener 140 (294), Burnaby 136, Saint Catharines 125 (304), Longueuil 124, Oshawa 118, Halifax 115 (281), Burlington 115, Thunder Bay 112, East York[+] 102, Richmond 96, Montréal-Nord[+] 95, Sudbury 92 (150), Nepean 85, Saint John's 84 (155), Sault Sainte Marie 83, Saint John 81 (114). **Population** (1981, in 1,000): British Canadians 9,674, French Canadians 6,439, Indians 332 (1984), Eskimos 28; Germans 1,142, Italians 748, Ukrainians 530, Dutch 408, Chinese 289, Scandinavian 283, Poles 254 and others. **Density** more than 2.5 persons per sq.km; average annual rate of population increase 1.1%, birth rate 15.1 per 1,000 and death rate 7.3 per 1,000 (1980–85). Immigration: 121,147 (1982). Urban population 75.7% (1981). Economically active inhabitants 12.68 mn. of which only 4.3% worked in advanced agriculture, 28.4% in industry, 6.1% in transport and 61.2% in services (1984). – **Currency:** Canadian dollar = 100 cents.

Province	Area in sq.km	Population in 1,000 (census 1986)	Density per sq.km	Capital (population in 1,000, 1986)
Alberta	661,185	2,375.3	3.6	Edmonton (574.0)
British Columbia	948,596	2,889.2	3.1	Victoria (66.3)
Manitoba	650,086	1,071.2	1.7	Winnipeg (594.6)
New Brunswick	73,437	710.4	9.7	Fredericton (44.4)
Newfoundland	404,517	568.3	1.4	St. John's (96.2)
Nova Scotia	55,491	873.2	15.7	Halifax (113.6)
Ontario	1,068,582	9,113.5	8.5	Toronto (612.3)
Prince Edward Island	5,657	126.6	22.4	Charlottetown (15.8)
Québec	1,540,680	6,540.3	4.3	Québec (164.6)
Saskatchewan	651,902	1,010.2	1.6	Regina (175.1)
Northwest Territories	3,379,682	52.2	0.02	Yellowknife (11.8)
Yukon Territory	536,324	23.5	0.04	Whitehorse (15.2)
CANADA	**9,976,139[+]**	**25,354.1**	**2.5**	**Ottawa (300.8)**

[+] including interior water areas

Economy: highly advanced industrial country. Canada's contribution to industrial production of non-socialist countries is roughly 3%, to the total turnover of foreign trade is 3.5% and it is the third largest in agricultural production. In 1983/84 Canada had the highest output of uranium (28.8% of world output), zinc (19.3%) and newsprint (32.9%), sulphur recovered as by-product (25.7%); it held second place in the output of nickel (24.7%), asbestos, platinum, cobalt, titanium, potash salt, gypsum; in the production of wood pulp, nickel; third place in the output of natural gas, tungsten, gold, production of aluminium, zinc, paper and paperboard, sawnwood, electric energy. – **Principal industries:** metallurgy, mining of fuels and ores, electricity, processing of fuels, engineering, food processing, wood-working, paper and textile industry.
Mining (1984, in 1,000 tonnes metal content): coal 32,064 (Alberta, Nova Scotia), brown coal 25,344 (Saskatchewan), crude petroleum 70,586 (Alberta, Saskatchewan, Brit. Columbia), natural gasoline 3,457, natural gas 2,969.2 PJ (Alberta, above all, Medicine Hat), iron ore 25,050 (Québec – Schefferville, Gagnon; Newfoundland – Labrador City Wabush), nickel 174.2 (Ontario – Sudbury, Falconbridge; Manitoba – Thompson, Lynn Lake), asbestos 838 (Québec – Thetford Mines, Asbestos; Ontario – Matheson), uranium 11,170 tonnes (Ontario – Elliot Lake; Saskatchewan – Key Lake, Uranium City), gold 83,450 kg (Ontario – Chemlo; Kirkland L., Porcupine, Red Lake; Québec – Val-d'Or, Malartic; Northwest Territories – Yellowknife; Yukon – region Klondike), silver 1,169 tonnes (British Columbia – Kimberley; Ontario – Timmins, Gowganda; Yukon – Faro), platinum 12,820 kg (Ontario – Sudbury; Manitoba – Thompson), cobalt 2,325 tonnes (Ontario – Cobalt, Lac Preissac), lead 307 (British Columbia – Kimberley, Slocan; Yukon – Faro, Mayo), zinc 1,207 (Ontario – Timmins; Québec – Mattagami, Amos; Manitoba – Flin Flon; British Columbia – Kimberley, Nelson, Remac; Yukon – Faro, Elsa; Northwest Ter. – Pine Point), copper 712 (Manitoba – Sherridon; Ontario – Manitouwadge, Copper Cliff; Québec – Noranda, Chibougamau; British Columbia – Highland Valley, Merritt), molybdenum 10,965 tonnes (British Columbia – Peachland, Revelstoke), tungsten 3,432 tonnes (Yukon – Tungsten), tin 216 tonnes, niobium 4,985 tonnes, columbite 3,086 tonnes (1982, Québec – Oka), salt 10,190 (largest Pugwash – Nova Scotia; Goderich, Sarnia – Ontario), potash salt 7,484 (Saskatchewan), gypsum 8,439, sulphur recovered as by-product 6,602 (Alberta 90%).
Industrial production – some branches belong to the largest in the world: production of paper and chemical wood pulp, newsprint, motor spirit and oils, electric energy, aluminium, nickel, zinc, sawnwood. In the South-east of Canada the engineering, metallurgy, textiles, chemical and food industries predominate; in the South-west of the country timber and paper industry, metallurgy of non-ferrous metals (especially aluminium), and engineering. Ontario is the most industrialized province – providing 60% of industrial production value.
Metallurgy (1984, in 1,000 tonnes): pig iron 9,704 and crude steel 14,568 (largest steel plants Hamilton), aluminium 1,295 (6.7% of world production; Arvida, Kitimat, Baie-Comeau, Tomago, Shawinigan), zinc 638 (10% of world production; Trail, Flin Flon, Timmins), lead 252 (Trail, Belldune Point); copper -smelted 440 (Noranda, Montréal, Flin Flon), -refined 504 (Montréal, Copper Cliff, Murdochville), cadmium 1,602 tonnes (Flin Flon, Trail). Processing of cobalt – Lynn Lake, Sudbury, Fort Saskatchewan; nickel 104 (15% of world production, Thompson, Bécancour, Sudbury); uranium – Port Hope in Ontario.
Engineering (1984): production of motor vehicles – passenger 1,033,000 units, – commercial 808,800 (Windsor, Oshawa, Toronto, Hamilton, St. Thomas) – aircraft (Toronto, Milton, Montréal, Vancouver); railway carriages and locomotives (Trenton, Montréal, London, Rivière-du-Loup, Winnipeg); vessels (Montréal, Sorel, Halifax, Victoria); electrotechnical industry (Toronto, Montréal, Ottawa, Trois-Rivières, Hamilton) – 705,000 radio and 444,000 television receivers (1980); machine tools, mining, textiles, agricultural machines (Toronto, Montréal, Vancouver, Winnipeg, Québec).

33 a Vancouver Area
1 : 10 000 000

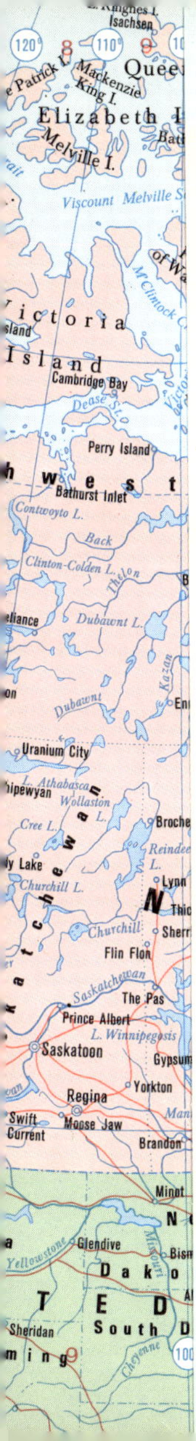

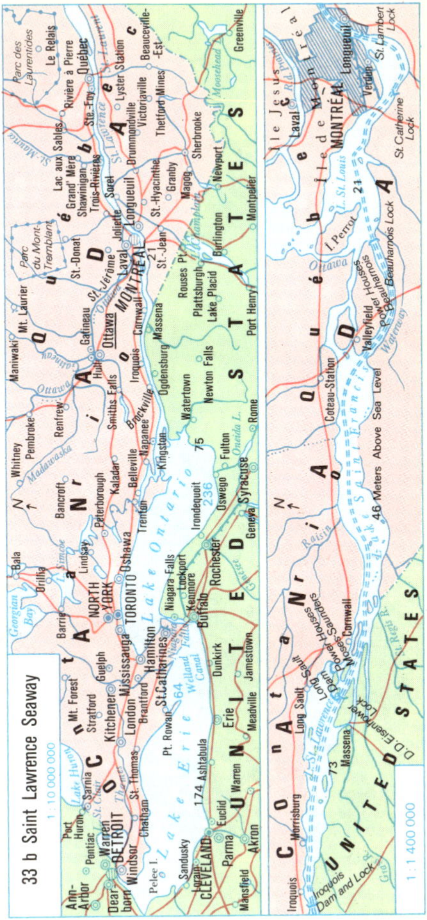

33 b Saint Lawrence Seaway
1:10 000 000

1:1 400 000

add page 146

Chemical industry – chief production centres: Sarnia, Welland, Trail, Ft. Saskatchewan, Calgary, Brandon, Redwater etc. Production (1984, in 1,000 tonnes): sulphur 6,620, sulphuric acid 4,043; fertilizers – nitrogenous 2,371, – phosphatic 655, – potash 7,154, organic chemicals 1,082, synthetic rubber 217, plastics 893. Capacity of petroleum refineries 108 mn. tonnes (largest Montréal, Sarnia, Québec, Edmonton, Vancouver, Regina, Calgary, Ft. McMurray, Winnipeg, Toronto, Halifax, Point Tupper, St. John etc.); production: motor spirit 23,965, jet fuels 3,403, kerosene 1,780, distilled fuel oils 20,115, residual fuel oils 8,261, gas (by cokeries) 45,453 TJ, liquefied petroleum gas 6,943, asphalt 2,664 (all 1984).

Wood and paper industry (1984, 1,000 tonnes): roundwood 141.5 mn. cub.m, sawnwood 48.1 mn. cub.m, newsprint 9,013, mechanical wood pulp 8,800, chemical wood pulp 11,099, (second world producer), other paper and paperboard 4,807. Largest paper mills include Thunder Bay, Port Alberni, Kapuskasing, Campbell River, Hull, Corner Brook, St. John; wood processing plants: Vancouver, Prince George, Edmonton, Merritt, La Sarre and Ottawa. – **The textile industry** (Québec, Ontario – production 1981): cotton fabrics 289 mn. sq.m, woollen fabrics 29 mn. sq.m; synthetic fibres 65,900 tonnes.

The food industry is concentrated in large cities and ports. Production (1984, in 1,000 tonnes): meat 2,446, milk 8,200, cheese 229, butter 112, flour 1,710, sugar 1,135, beer 23.3 mn. hl, soft drinks 17 mn. hl, wine 55. **Production** of cement 8.6 mn. tonnes (Ontario, Québec), tyres 25 mn. units; 61.6 billion cigarettes.

Electricity (1983, +1984): installed capacity of electric power stations 89.8 mn. kW (of which 56.8% were hydroelectric power stations, 10.1% nuclear power stations), produced +437,990 mn. kWh (production of nuclear power stations +52,701 mn. kWh). Largest power stations: hydro-electric – La Grande 5,328 MW (Québec), Churchill Falls 5,225 MW (Labrador), Mica 2,610 MW, Bennett (Peace R.) and Revelstoke (Brit. Columbia), Manicouagane – Riv. aux Outardes, Beauharnois (Québec), Niagara-Queenston (Ontario) etc., nuclear – Bruce-Tiverton 2,984 MW and Pickering-Toronto 2,572 MW (Ontario) and others.

Agriculture: arable land 5.1%, meadows and pastures 2.6%, forests 35.4% of the land area. In 1983 658,000 tractors and 161,950 combine harvesters were in use. Only 446,000 people work in the advanced, highly mechanized system of agriculture. **Animal production** predominates (1984, in 1,000 head): cattle 12,284 (dairy cows+ 1,728. Alberta, Saskatchewan, Québec+, Ontario+), pigs 10,760 (Ontario, Québec), sheep 791 (Alberta, Ontario), horses 380, poultry 93 mn. (Ontario, Québec, Brit. Columbia); (in 1000 head): eggs 328, honey 44, fresh hides 106, fish, frozen 236. Fish catch 1,337,300 tonnes. Hunting of fur animals. – **Vegetable production:** mostly cultivation of cereals and fodder (Edmonton – Regina – Winnipeg). **Crops** (1984, in 1,000 tonnes): wheat 21,200 (Saskatchewan 60%), barley 10,252 (Alberta 55%), oats 2,670 (Alberta 38%, third world producer), maize (corn) 7,024, rye 664, potatoes 2,728, linseed 676 (second world producer), rapeseed 3,246 (second world producer), soya beans 934 (Ontario), pulses 230, vegetables 1,858 and fruit 717 (Ontario, British Columbia, Québec) sugar beet 932 (Alberta), tobacco 90.

Communications (1982): railways 72,678 km mostly electrified, freight 196 billion tonnes/km; roads 928,258 km, of which 712,319 km were surfaced and 7,820 km of the Trans-Canada Highway: St John's – Victoria; motor vehicles in use 14.1 mn., of which 10.7 mn. passenger cars. Civil aviation: 324.7 mn. km flown and 19.4 mn. passengers carried (1984). Largest airports: Montréal, Ottawa and Vancouver. Naval transport: merchant shipping 3,449,000 GRT (1984, of which over vessels 2.1 mn. GRT) including vessels for inland navigation with a gross tonnage of 4.8 mn., annual freight turnover in ports 186 mn. tonnes (1982). Almost 65% of merchant shipping operates on the 3,650 km long "great inland waterway" from the St. Lawrence to Great Lakes. Largest ports: Vancouver, Port-Cartier, Montréal, Thunder Bay, Sept-Îles, St. John, Québec, Hamilton etc. Length of pipelines 36,500 km (1983). Tourism 12.9 mn. visitors.

Foreign trade (1983) – **Exports** Canadian share in world export is 4.1%): transport equipment 31%, ores and other raw materials 15% (ores 3.2%, wood 4.5%), industrial products 15.4% (paper 5.6%), fuels 14.1% (petroleum and products 5.8%), cereals 6.6%; above all to the U.S.A. 72.6%, Japan 5.1%, the United Kingdom 2.7%, U.S.S.R. 2.1%, China, Fed. Rep. of Germany, the Netherlands, France, Italy, Belgium. – **Imports** (Canadian share in world import is 3.2%): machines 50.8% (transport equipment 25.7%), industrial products 12.3%, mineral fuels 6.8%, chemicals 6.6%, food and fruit 6%; above all from the U.S.A. 71.6%, Japan 5.9%, the United Kingdom 2.4%, Fed. Rep. of Germany, Mexico, Venezuela, France, Italy, Hong Kong etc.

UNITED STATES OF AMERICA

United States of America (U.S.A.), **area 9,372,614 sq.km, population 247,083,000** (1988), **census population** 1 April 1980 **226,545,825** (including armed forces overseas 227.66 mn.) **federal republic** (President George Herbert Walker Bush since 1989).

Administrative units: 50 federal states and 1 federal district (the capital). To the continental U.S.A. belong overseas territories: 1. one self-governing federal state: the Commonwealth of Puerto Rico; 2 territories: American Samoa, Guam, Midway Is., Virgin Is.; 3. the United Nations Trust Territory of the Pacific Is.: the Commonwealth of the Northern Mariana Is., Republic of the Marshall Is., Republic of Palau, the Federated States of Micronesia.
Capital: Washington 623,000 inhab. (1984, with agglomeration 3.4 mn.); **other towns** (in 1000 inhab., 1984, with agglom. in brackets): New York 7,165 (17,807), Los Angeles 3,097 (12,373), Chicago 2,992 (8,035), Houston 1,706 (3,566), Philadelphia 1,647 (5,755), Detroit 1,089 (4,577), Dallas 974 (3,348), San Diego 960 (2,064), Phoenix 853 (1,715), San Antonio 843 (1,138), Baltimore 764 (2,245), San Francisco 713 (5,685), Indianapolis 710 (1,195), San Jose 686, Memphis 648 (935), Milwaukee 621 (1,568), Jacksonville 578 (795), Boston 571 (4,027), Columbus 566 (1,279), New Orleans 559 (1,319), Cleveland 546 (2,788), Denver 505 (1,791), Seattle 488 (2,208), El Paso 464 (526), Nashville-Davidson 462 (890), Kansas City 440 (1,477), Oklahoma City 443 (963), St. Louis 429 (2,398), Atlanta 426 (2,380), Fort Worth 413 (2,372), Pittsburgh 402 (2,372), Austin 397 (645), Long Beach 380, Tulsa 374 (726), Miami 373 (2,799), Honolulu 373 (805), Cincinnati 370 (1,673), Portland 366 (1,341), Tuscon 365 (531), Minneapolis 358 (2,231), Oakland 353 (1,863), Albuquerque 351 (449), Toledo 344 (611), Buffalo 339 (1,205), Omaha 334

map 34

State (abbv.)	Area in sq.km	Population in 1,000 (1988)	Density per sq.km	Capital (population in 1,000, 1986, 1987) +
Alabama (AL)	133,667	4,102	31	Montgomery (194)
Alaska (AK)	1,528,775	524	0.3	Juneau (25) +
Arizona (AZ)	295,024	3,489	12	Phoenix (894)
Arkansas (AR)	137,539	2,395	17	Little Rock (181)
California (CA)	411,015	28,314	69	Sacramento (324)
Colorado (CO)	269,998	3,301	12	Denver (505)
Connecticut (CT)	12,973	3,233	249	Hartford (138)
Delaware (DE)	5,328	660	124	Dover (25) *)
District of Columbia (DC)	174	617	3,546	Washington (626)
Florida (FL)	151,670	12,335	81	Tallahassee (119)
Georgia (GA)	152,489	6,324	42	Atlanta (422)
Hawaii (HI)	16,706	1,098	66	Honolulu (372)
Idaho (ID)	216,413	1,003	4.6	Boise (108)
Illinois (IL)	146,076	11,614	80	Springfield (100)
Indiana (IN)	93,994	5,556	59	Indianapolis (720)
Iowa (IA)	145,791	2,834	19	Des Moines (192)
Kansas (KS)	213,064	2,495	12	Topeka (119)
Kentucky (KY)	104,623	3,727	36	Frankfort (27) *)
Louisiana (LA)	125,675	4,408	35	Baton Rouge (241)
Maine (ME)	86,027	1,205	14	Augusta (23) *)
Maryland (MD)	27,394	4,622	169	Annapolis (33)
Massachusetts (MA)	21,386	5,889	275	Boston (574)
Michigan (MI)	150,779	9,240	61	Lansing (129)
Minnesota (MN)	217,736	4,307	20	Saint Paul (264)
Mississippi (MS)	123,584	2,620	21	Jackson (208)
Missouri (MO)	180,487	5,141	28	Jefferson City (34) *)
Montana (MT)	381,073	805	2.1	Helena (25)
Nebraska (NE)	200,018	1,602	8	Lincoln (183)
Nevada (NV)	286,299	1,054	3.7	Carson City (37) +
New Hampshire (NH)	24,097	1,085	45	Concord (36) +
New Jersey (NJ)	20,295	7,721	380	Trenton (93) *)
New Mexico (NM)	315,115	1,507	4.8	Santa Fe (56)
New York (NY)	128,402	17,909	139	Albany (101)
North Carolina (NC)	136,198	6,489	48	Raleigh (180)
North Dakota (ND)	183,022	667	3.6	Bismarck (46) *)
Ohio (OH)	106,765	10,855	102	Columbus (566)
Oklahoma (OK)	181,090	3,242	18	Oklahoma City (446)
Oregon (OR)	251,181	2,767	11	Salem (95) +
Pennsylvania (PA)	117,412	12,001	102	Harrisburg (53) *)
Rhode Island (RI)	3,144	993	316	Providence (157)
South Carolina (SC)	80,432	3,470	43	Columbia (93)
South Dakota (SD)	199,552	713	3.6	Pierre (14) *)
Tennessee (TN)	109,412	4,895	45	Nashville-Davidson (474)
Texas (TX)	692,407	16,841	24	Austin (467)
Utah (UT)	219,932	1,690	7.7	Salt Lake City (158)
Vermont (VT)	24,887	557	22	Montpelier (9) *)
Virginia (VA)	105,716	6,015	57	Richmond (218)
Washington (WA)	176,617	4,648	26	Olympia (29) *)
West Virginia (WV)	62,629	1,876	30	Charleston (59)
Wisconsin (WI)	145,439	4,855	33	Madison (171)
Wyoming (WY)	253,597	479	1.9	Cheyenne (51)
UNITED STATES OF AMERICA (U.S.A.)	9,372,614**)	245,807	26	Washington (626)

*) year 1982, **) including Great Lake area 9,536,535 sq.km

(607), Charlotte 331 (647), Newark 320 (1,882), Sacramento 304 (1,220), Louisville 290 (963), Virginia Beach 285, Wichita 283 (429), Birmingham 280 (895), Norfolk 280 (1,026), Tampa 275 (1,811) and further 121 cities with a population of more than 100,000. The share of the urban population was 76.2%.
Census population on 1 April 1980 was 226,545,825 inhabitants (excluding 995,546 inhab. overseas), of whom 188,340,790 were Whites, 26,488,218 Negroes and 11,716,817 other races (of whom 1,420,200 were Indians, 806,000 Chinese, 774,700 Filipino (on Hawaii 132,075), 701,000 Japanese (on Hawaii 239,734), in Alaska 78,480 were Indians, Aleutians and Eskimos; on Hawaii 118,251 were Hawaiians). The total population comprised 48.5% males and 51.5% females; 73.7% were urban and 26.3% were rural. The average annual rate of population increase was 0.88% (1980–85). The age composition was (1983): 0–14 years 22.1%, 15–64 years 66.3%, older than 65 years 11.6%. In 1983 the birth rate was 15.7 per 1,000, death rate 8.7 per 1,000, and infant mortality 10.6 per 1,000. The number of immigrants was 3.1 mn. in 1975–81, in 1981 it was 435,700 (15% from Europe, 36% from Asia, 12% from Mexico, 30% from America. There were 108.4 mn. economically active inhabitants in 1984, of which only 1.8% were in agriculture, 33.2% in industry and 65% in services. – **Currency:** US dollar = 100 cents.

CANADA
British Columbia
Alberta
Saskatchewan
Manitoba
Washington
Oregon
Idaho
Montana
Wyoming
North Dakota
South Dakota
Nebraska
Kansas
Nevada
Utah
Colorado
California
PACIFIC OCEAN
Vancouver
Vancouver I.
C. Flattery
Victoria
Squamish
Burnaby
Hope
Bellingham
Kelowna
Penticton
Revelstoke
Columbia
Procter
Trail
Cranbrook
Michel
CALGARY
Bassano
Bow
Red Deer
Hanna
Lethbridge
Medicine Hat
Orion
Milk
Biggar
Kindersley
Leader
South Saskatchewan
Saskatoon
Watrous
Swift Current
Watson
Sturgis
Big Quill Lake
Yorkton
Melville
Regina
Moose Jaw
Qu'Appelle
Weyburn
Mankota
Arena
Lake Winnipegosis
Minitonas
Winnipegosis
Dauphin
Birtle
L. Manitoba
Gladstone
Brandon
Assiniboine
Alida
Deloraine
Carman
Portage-la-Prairie
WINNIPEG
Red
Emerson
Lake Winnipeg
Gypsumville
Hodgson
Victoria Beach
Beaver
Moclips
Aberdeen
Seattle
Everett
Bellevue
Olympia
Tacoma
Astoria
Republic
Sandpoint
Grand Coulee
Moses Lake
Spokane
Coeur d'Alene
Yakima
Lind
Pasco
Snake
Walla Walla
Tillamook
Vancouver
Columbia
Portland
The Dalles
Toledo
Salem
Corvallis
Eugene
Coos Bay
Pendleton
Baker
Bend
Seneca
Burns
Roseburg
Chemult
Grants Pass
Crater Lake
Medford
Klamath Falls
Lakeview
C. Mendocino
Kootenai
Rexford
Clark Fork
Moscow
Lewiston
Salmon
New Meadows
Nampa
Boise
Mackay
Hailey
Snake
Twin Falls
Idaho Falls
Pocatello
Mc Cammon
Kalispell
Flathead L.
Shelby
Marias
Augusta
Missoula
Great Falls
Havre
Missouri
Fort Peck
Fort Peck Lake
Opheim
Helena
Anaconda
Butte
Darby
Three Forks
Bozeman
Yellowstone
Billings
Gardiner
Brockway
Glendive
Terry
Miles City
Bighorn
Crow Agency
Powder
West Yellowstone
Cody
Yellowstone L.
Sheridan
Gillette
Lander
Casper
Edgemont
Granger
Rock Springs
Walcott
Laramie
Cheyenne
Flaxton
Minot
Surrey
Souris
Devils Lake
Warren
Grand Forks
Lake Sakakawea
Dickinson
Bismarck
Jamestown
Valley City
Mahnomen
Moorhead
Fargo
Sheyenne
Fergus Falls
Wahpeton
Little Missouri
Aberdeen
Faith
Belle Fourche
Rapid City
Cheyenne
Pierre
Huron
James
Watertown
White
Wood
Mitchell
Pipestone
Sioux Falls
Yankton
Le Mars
Crawford
Niobrara
Scottsbluff
Alliance
Thedford
Norfolk
Sioux City
North Platte
Sidney
Fremont
Omaha
Grand Island
Lincoln
South Platte
Holdrege
Hastings
Beatrice
Republican
Colby
Manhattan
Eureka
Klamath
Weed
Alturas
Redding
Sacramento
Vya
Winnemucca
Humboldt
Elko
Wells
Lovelock
Pyramid L.
Ft. Bragg
Ukiah
Chico
Yuba City
Squaw Valley
Reno
Hazen
Santa Rosa
Vallejo
Sacramento
Carson City
L. Tahoe
Austin
Berkeley
Oakland
Stockton
SAN FRANCISCO
SAN JOSE
Sunnyvale
Merced
S. Joaquin
Salinas
Bishop
Luning
Ruth
Rioche
Great Salt Lake
Lakeside
Logan
Ogden
Wendover
Salt Lake City
Utah L.
Provo
Eureka
Hiawatha
Sevier
Green
Craig
Grand Junction
Fort Collins
Greeley
Brush
DENVER
Lakewood
Aurora
Limon
Colorado Springs

34 a Panama Canal
1 : 1 000 000

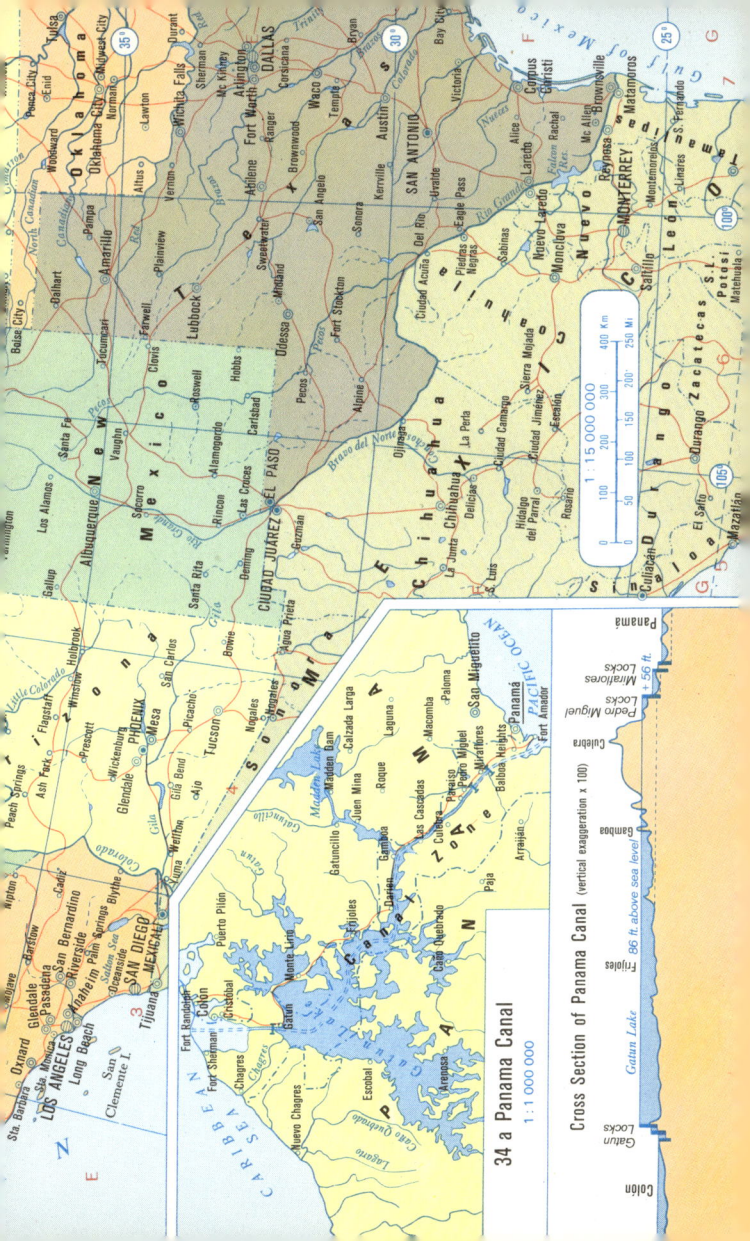

Cross Section of Panama Canal (vertical exaggeration x 100)

1 : 15 000 000

Economy: developments in science, research and technology have created the most advanced industrial and agricultural country in the western world. The total volume of the gross domestic product reached 3,276,000 mn. dollars in 1983 (the gross domestic product per capita 13,968 dollars). The US share in the industrial production of all countries (excepting socialist) amounted to 35% and in agricultural production to 20%. The United States of America occupied the leading position (share in world production in 1984): — in mining: first place — mica (69%), bentonite (50%), molybdenum ore (49%), natural gasoline (37%), phosphates (33%), kaolin (31%), salt (22%); second place — sulphur (30%), natural gas (29%), coal (26%), talc (16%), uranium (15%), copper (13%); — in industrial production: first place — petroleum coke (78%), kraft paperboard (69%), chemical wood pulp (48%), magnesium (48%), jet fuel (46%), motor spirit (42%), aviation spirit (40%), paper (33%), tyres (28%), electric energy (27%), passenger cars (26%), beer (24%), lead (20%), cigarettes (20%), fuel oils (19%), copper-refined (16%), roundwood (15%); second place — aluminium (29%); — in agricultural production: first place — soya beans (56%), grapefruits (52%), corn (43%), sorghum (31%), margarine (30%), poultry meat (25%), beef meat (25%), cheese (19%), lemons (16%), tomatoes (14%); — second place: hops (21%), cotton-lint (16%), eggs (14%), milk (14%), tobacco (13%), pork meat (12%), wheat flour (10%), barley, peaches etc.

Industry: these industries hold a leading position in the U.S.A.: energy, mining of fuels and ores, metallurgy, engineering (especially transport and electrotechnical), nuclear industry, chemical industry (above all, petrochemistry and electrochemistry), production of plastics and artificial fibres.

Mining (1984, in 1,000 tonnes): coal and anthracite 750,262 (highest quality coking coal and anthracite — the Appalachians district, Pennsylvania, West Virginia, Kentucky, Illinois, Ohio), brown coal 57,262 (North and South Dakota, New Mexico), crude petroleum 438,127 (Texas 30%, Alaska 20%, Louisiana, California, Oklahoma) — verified deposits 3,775 mn. tonnes (1985), natural gasoline 10.7 mn. tonnes, natural gas 17,181 PJ (Texas 35%, Louisiana 33%, Oklahoma, New Mexico) — verified deposits 5,578 billion cub.m (1985), iron ore 33,640 (region around Lake Superior 80%: Minnesota, Wisconsin), copper ore 1,091 (Arizona 60%, Utah, New Mexico), lead ore 333 (Missouri, Idaho, Utah), zinc ore 278 (Tennessee, New York, Idaho, Colorado), molybdenum ore 47,021 tonnes (Colorado, Arizona, New Mexico), bauxite 856 (Arkansas, Alabama, Georgia), mercury 864 tonnes (California, Nevada, Idaho), gold 64,035 kg (South Dakota, Utah, Nevada, Arizona), silver 1,382 tonnes (Idaho, Arizona, Colorado, Montana), vanadium 1 (Colorado, Utah), tungsten 1,203 tonnes (California, Colorado), nickel ore 13.2, antimony ore, asbestos (California, Vermont), uranium 5,722 tonnes (New Mexico, Wyoming, Utah, Colorado), sulphur — native 11,523 (Texas, Louisiana, California), natural phosphates 49,197 (Florida, Idaho, Tennessee, Montana), kaolin 6,534, bentonite 2,862, mica 146 (North Carolina, Alabama, New Mexico), potassium salt 1,564 (New Mexico, California, Utah), salt 35,544 (Louisiana, Texas, Ohio, New York), asphalt 2,662 (Texas, Utah, Alabama), barytes 703, borate minerals 1,240, gypsum 13,000, pyrites 676 (1982, Tennessee, Colorado), ilmenite 239 (1982, Florida, New Jersey, New York), talc 1,061.

Energy production (1984): capacity of all electric power stations 675 mn. kW, of which hydro-electric power plants 79 mn. kW (11.7%) and nuclear 68 mn. kW (10%). Electricity 2,472 billion kWh (1984), of which nuclear 294 billion kWh and hydro-electric 334 billion kWh (1983). Some of the largest thermal power plants: e.g. Monroe, Pittsburg (Cal.), Paradise, Johnsonville, Sammis, Stuart, Gavin, Houston etc.; largest hydro-electric power plants: e.g. the Grand Coulee 6,494 MW, John Day, Chief Joseph, Niagara Falls System, Raccoon Mt., Ludington, The Dalles, Hoover, St. Lawrence Power System, Castaic, Glen Canyon; largest nuclear power plants: e.g. Browns Ferry, McGuire, Trojan, La Salle, Salem, Susquehanna, Peach Bottom, San Onofre, Zion. Production of gas (by cokeries) 260,371 TJ (1984). **Metallurgy:** production (1984, in 1,000 tonnes): pig iron 47,090 and crude steel 83,940 (13% of the world production, Pennsylvania, Indiana, Ohio, the Appalachians district — Pittsburgh, Youngstown, Chicago, Cleveland, Bethlehem, Sparrows Point), steel products 79,200 (especially Pittsburgh, Chicago, Youngstown, Steubenville, Trenton), aluminium 5,705 (Rockdale, Bellingham, Evansville, Massena), copper - smelted 1,014, -refined 1,516 (Anaconda, Morenci, Garfield, Carteret, El Paso), lead 978 (El Paso, East Helena, Herculaneum, Omaha), zinc 331 (Josephtown, Anaconda, Corpus Christi), cadmium 1,682 tonnes, magnesium 188 (Freeport, Albany, Henderson), uranium processing (Bluewater, Moab, Uravan, Shirley Basin).

Engineering — production (1984): motor vehicles — passenger 7.62 mn., — commercial 3.1 mn., road tractors 156,600 units (Detroit, Cleveland, Kenosha, San Francisco, Toledo, Kansas City), seeders 492,807 and combine harvesters 11,296 units, locomotives and railway carriages (Chicago, Erie, Greenville), aircraft (Los Angeles, Wichita, New York, Fort Worth, Columbus), vessels 286,000 GRT (1982, Baltimore, Boston, Norfolk, Pascagoula, San Diego, San Francisco), machinery equipment, machines and apparatus (Chicago, New York, Cleveland, Philadelphia, Boston, Los Angeles, Worcester, St. Louis, Detroit, Houston, radio 9.8 mn. and television receivers 13.4 mn. (95% colour), (Los Angeles, Rochester, New York etc.), refrigerators 7.5 mn., washing machines 5 mn. units. The rocket and astronautical industries are concentrated on the Pacific coast (San Diego, Los Angeles, San Jose, Seattle), in Texas (Fort Worth, Dallas, Houston), Florida (Orlando), on the Atlantic coast (New York, Philadelphia, Hartford, Boston) and around the Great Lakes (Chicago, Detroit, Buffalo, Cleveland, Cincinnati etc.

Chemical industry (1984, in 1,000 tonnes): sulphuric acid 36,217, nitrogenous fertilizers 9,682, plastics 15,505, synthetic rubber 2,219. Sulphur (as by-product) 5,214. Petroleum refineries have an annual capacity of 771 mn. tonnes (Houston, Beaumont, Port Arthur, Baton Rouge, Philadelphia, Toledo, Chicago, Tulsa, Los Angeles, San Francisco, New York and others). Leading world producer (in 1,000 tonnes): motor spirit 277,887, jet fuels 53,356 and fuel oils 184,989. Production of tyres 209.4 mn. units (Akron). **The timber and paper industries** (1984) are concentrated in the states of Washington, Oregon, California, Montana and in the South- and North-east of the U.S.A. Roundwood 435.3 mn. cub.m, sawnwood 77.4 mn. cub.m. **Production** (1984, in 1,000 tonnes): chemical wood pulp 39,037, mechanical wood pulp 5,023, newsprint 5,121, other paper 16,348, kraft paperboard 33,901. Production of cement 70.8 mn. tonnes (states of California, Texas, Pennsylvania, New York).

The textile and clothing industries are concentrated in the East of the U.S.A. from the southern state of Alabama to the north-eastern state of Maine. Production (1983): cotton -fibres 1,064 mn. tonnes, -fabrics 3,505 mn. m, woollen-fibres 58,800 tonnes, -fabrics 120 mn. sq. m, 60.7 mn. m, 42,800 tonnes, linen fabrics, silk fabrics, synthetic fibres 1.29 mn. tonnes. Footwear 344.3 mn. pairs, rubber footwear 76.2 mn. pairs. Rubber (reclaimed) 72.7 mn.tonnes.

Food industry (1984, in 1,000 tonnes): meat 25,627 (of which poultry 7,479), milk 61,436, cheese 2,042, butter 508, margarine 2,920, soya bean oil 4,931, wheat flour 13,584, sugar 8,434, canned fish 407, beer 228.9 mn. hl, alcoholic beverages 14.4 mn. hl, wine 25.73 mn. hl; 699 billion cigarettes, 3.7 billion cigars.

Agriculture: arable land covers 187,895,000 ha (i.e. 20.5% of the area of the country), permanent crops 2,034,000 ha. (0.2%), meadows and pastures 26.4%, forests 28.9%; irrigated land 19.8 mn. ha (1983, i.e. 10.6% of the arable land), 4.3 mn. inhabitants engaged in agriculture (1984, i.e. 1.8% of the total population) and 1.95 mn. persons work in advanced agricultural production (i.e. 1.8% of economically active inhabitants). In 1983 4.55 mn. tractors and 676,000 harvester-threshers were used on highly mechanized and specialized farms. The number of farms declined from 6.3 mn. in 1940 to 2,370,000 in 1983. – **Animal production** predominates in the region of the Great Lakes and in California (Wisconsin, Minnesota, New York, Pennsylvania, Ohio etc.), pasture cattle-farming on the prairies (Texas, Iowa, Nebraska, Montana).
Livestock (1984, in 1,000 head): cattle 114,040 (dairy cows 11,204), pigs 55,819 (Iowa, Illinois, Indiana, Minnesota), sheep 11,411 (Texas, California, Colorado, Utah, Wyoming), horses 10,300, poultry 394 mn. production (1984, in 1,000 tonnes): eggs 4,035, honey 96, fresh hides 1,073 (sheepskins 20.7). Fish catch 4.14 mn. tonnes (1983). **Vegetable production:** the world's largest corn-growing region, known as the "corn-belt", runs through the Mid-West (from the Great Lakes along the Canadian frontier to the Great Plains), the Mississippi Lowlands to the Appalachian Mts. Wheat, barley, soya beans, fodder plants, sugar beet, potatoes and vegetables are all grown there. **Crops** (1984, in 1,000 tonnes): maize (corn) 194,475 (Iowa, Illinois, Indiana, Nebraska, Minnesota), wheat 70,638 (Kansas, North Dakota, Oklahoma, Montana, Washington), oats 6,850 (Minnesota, North Dakota, Iowa), barley 12,988 (North Dakota, California, Montana, Idaho), rice 6,216 (Arkansas, Texas, California, Louisiana), sorghum 21,994 (Kansas, Texas, Nebraska, Montana), potatoes 16,404 (Idaho, Washington, Oregon, Maine, California), sweet potatoes 589, pulses 1,164, soya beans 50,643 (Illinois, Iowa, Montana, Indiana, Ohio), groundnuts 2,008, linseed 178, sunflower seed 1,699, cotton -seed 4,811, -lint 2,894 (Texas, California, Mississippi, Arizona), vegetables 28,073 (California, Texas, Ohio, Florida), tomatoes 8,165 (California, Ohio etc.), fruit 22,743 (California, Washington, New York, Michigan, Florida), apples 3,729, peaches 1,365; grapes 4,644 (California), raisins 280, sugarcane 25,427 (Hawaii, Louisiana, Florida), sugar beet 20,146 (California, Idaho, Colorado etc.), oranges (+ tangerines) 6,566 (+446) — lemons 787 — grapefruits 1,945 (California, Florida, Texas, Arizona); pineapples 544 (Hawaii), almonds 417 (37% of the world crops), walnuts 191, tobacco 791 (North Carolina, Kentucky, Virginia, South Carolina, Georgia); hops 25.5, strawberries 447.
Communications (1982): length of railways, decreasing, 265,542 km, carried 17.8 billion passenger-km and 1,340 billion tonnes-km freight; surfaced roads 6,364,955 km (of which 1,332,252 km highways and 687,430 km federal highways); passenger cars 130,053,000 and commercial vehicles (incl. buses) 38,554,000 (1984), 30% of all automobiles in the world. Petroleum pipelines 343,880 km, inter-state gas pipelines 437,500 km, other gas pipelines 1.6 mn. km (1983). Civil aviation (1984); leading world position: 15,831 airports (of which 4,805 public), civil aircraft 264,866, length of air-routes 489,619 km, flown 4,825 mn. km, passengers carried 331.4 mn., recorded 479 billion passenger-km and 10.1 billion tonnes-km. Largest airports: Chicago, New York, Atlanta, Los Angeles, Dallas, Denver, Santa Ana, San Francisco, Phoenix. Sea-going merchant vessels (1984) 752 (of 1,000 grosstonnes or over) with tonnage of 24.4 mn. GRT, of which 274 tankers of 16.16 mn. GRT, 24 bulk carriers 1.1 mn. GRT. US exports and imports carried on dry cargo and tanker vessels in the year 1983 totalled 630 mn. tonnes, of which 36.7 mn. tonnes or 5.8% were carried in US flag vessels. Largest ports: New Orleans, New York, Houston, Corpus Christi, Baton Rouge, Norfolk, Tampa, Baltimore, Los Angeles, Beaumont, Philadelphia; inland ports: Duluth, Pittsburgh, Chicago, St. Louis, Toledo, Cincinnati, Detroit. Tourism 21.7 mn. visitors (1983).
The foreign trade of the U.S.A. reached a total turnover of 470,416 mn. dollars in 1983 (i.e. 12.6% of the world turnover), of which exports amounted to 200,538 (11%) and imports to 269,878 (14%) mn. dollars. – **Exports:** machines, machinery equipment, transport vehicles (especially cars and aircraft), metal products and others 50.6%, agricultural products 14.6%, chemicals 14.5%, raw materials (ores, coal etc.) 4.2%, foodstuffs and tobacco products 5.6%. Exports mainly to Canada 18.6%, Japan 10.8%, United Kingdom 5.2%, Mexico 4.6%, Fed. Rep. of Germany 4.2%, Netherlands 3.8%, Saudi Arabia, France, Rep. of Korea etc. – **Imports:** machines, apparatus, industrial products 31.5%, crude petroleum and fuels 22.2%, consumer goods 15.9%, foodstuffs and tropical fruit 7.5%, passenger cars 9.3% etc. Imports came mostly from Canada 19.2%, Japan 16.2%, Mexico 6.3%, Fed. Rep. of Germany 4.9%, United Kingdom 4.8%, Rep. of Korea 2.9%, Hong Kong 2.5%, France 2.4%, Italy, Indonesia, Brazil, Venezuela etc.

PUERTO RICO

Commonwealth of Puerto Rico, area **8,897 sq.km,** population **3,606,000** (1988), **self-governing federal state of the United States of America** (since 25 July 1952).
Capital: San Juan 434,849 inhabitants (census 1980, with agglom. 820,442 inhab.); **other towns** (1980, in 1,000 inhab.): Bayamón 196, Ponce 189, Carolina 166, Caguas 118, Mayagüez 96, Arecibo 87, Guaynabo 81. **Density** 368 persons per sq.km; average annual rate of population increase 1.6%, birth rate 19.8 per 1,000, death rate 6.5 per 1,000 (1980–85); urban population 67.1%. – **Currency:** US dollar = 100 cents.
Agriculture: arable land 15%, meadows and pastures 37.5%, forests 21%; crops (1983, in 1,000 tonnes): sugarcane 1,287, bananas 99, pineapples 36, citrus fruit 37, coffee 15, high quality tobacco 1.4; cattle 585,000, pigs 206,000, poultry 6.2 mn. head; milk 384, eggs 20; fish catch 2.54 mn. tonnes. **Production** (1983, in 1,000 tonnes): sugar 101, cement 855, petroleum refineries (largest: Guayanilla, Bayamón and Ponce), motor spirit 2,441, oils 3,870, chemicals, cigars, textiles, electric machinery and equipment, pharmaceuticals, spirits. Electricity (1983) 12.1 billion kWh (of which 96% thermal). – **Communications** (1982): roads 16,827 km, cars 1,164,000. Tourism 1.56 mn. visitors. – **Exports:** sugar, tobacco, textiles, chemicals, spirits.

BAHAMAS

The Commonwealth of the Bahamas, area **13,935 sq.km,** population **245,000** (1988), **member of the Commonwealth** (Prime Minister Lynden Oscar Pindling since 1973).
Nearly 700 islands (largest Andros I. 4,145 sq.km). **Capital:** Nassau 135,437 inhab. (1985). **Population:** Negroes, mestizos 85%, Whites 15%. Average annual rate of population increase 1.9%. **Currency:** Bahamian dollar = 100 cents. **Economy:** chiefly tourism – 1.84 mn. visitors (1982); sugarcane 228,000 tonnes, rum, pineapples, sisal, roundwood, mining of salt 684,000 tonnes, fish catch, light industry. Electricity (1983) 905 mn. kWh. – **Exports:** crabs, salt, wood, rum.

CANADA
Manitoba
Ontario
Québec
New Brunswick
Maine
N.H.
Vermont
New York
Mass.
R.I.
Conn.
Pennsylvania
N.J.
Del.
Maryland
West Virginia
Ohio
Indiana
Illinois
Michigan
Wisconsin
Minnesota
Iowa
N.D.
S.D.
Nebr.
OCEAN
Lake Superior
Lake Michigan
Lake Huron
Lake Erie
Lake Ontario
Georgian Bay
Lake Winnipeg
L. of the Woods
L. Nipigon
Lac Mistassini
James B.
Delaware Bay
WINNIPEG
Thunder Bay
Duluth
Minneapolis
St. Paul
MILWAUKEE
CHICAGO
DETROIT
TORONTO
NORTH YORK
MONTRÉAL
Québec
Ottawa
CLEVELAND
COLUMBUS
INDIANAPOLIS
PHILADELPHIA
BALTIMORE
WASHINGTON
NEW YORK
BOSTON
Pittsburgh
Buffalo
Cincinnati
Des Moines
Sudbury
Sault Sainte Marie
Manitoulin I.
I. Royale
Long I.
95°
90°
85°
80°
75°
70°
65°
50°
45°
40°

Oklahoma
Arkansas
Tennessee
Mississippi
Alabama
Georgia
South Carolina
Carolina
Louisiana
Texas
Florida
ATLANTIC
BAHAMAS
CUBA
Gulf of Mexico
MEMPHIS
Little Rock
Nashville-Davidson
Knoxville
Chattanooga
Birmingham
Montgomery
Atlanta
Jackson
Shreveport
DALLAS
HOUSTON
NEW ORLEANS
Baton Rouge
Mobile
Tallahassee
JACKSONVILLE
Orlando
Tampa
St. Petersburg
Miami
Savannah
Charleston
Columbia
Charlotte
Greensboro
Winston-Salem
Wilmington
LA HABANA
Nassau
Grand Bahama
Andros I.
Eleuthera
Straits of Florida
Tropic of Cancer
Mississippi
Tennessee
Cumberland
35 a Hawaiian Is.
1 : 15 000 000
Kauai
Oahu
Honolulu
Molokai
Lanai
Kahoolawe
Maui
Hawaii
PACIFIC OCEAN
1 : 15 000 000
0 100 200 300 400 Km
0 50 100 150 200 250 Mi

BARBADOS

Area 431 sq.km, population 254,600 (1988), sovereign state, member of the Commonwealth (Prime Minister Erskine Sandiford since 1989, Gov.-Gen. Hugh W. Springer).
Capital: Bridgetown 7,552 inhab. (1980, with agglomeration 99,953). **Population:** Negroes 89%. Density 588 persons per sq.km. – **Currency:** Barbadosian dollar = 100 cents.
Economy (1983, in 1,000 tonnes): 45% of island area covered by sugarcane plantations, crops 805, vegetables 12.5; most important products: sugar 83, world-famous rum, electrical goods. Fish catch 3,480 tonnes. Tourism 385,000 visitors (1982). – **Exports:** sugar (45%), rum, electrical goods, chemicals, fish.

BELIZE

Area 22,965 sq.km, population 176,500 (1988), sovereign state, member of the Commonwealth (Prime Minister George Price since 1989).
Capital: Belmopan 2,935 inhab. (1980), **largest town** and harbour Belize 39,771 inhab. **Currency:** Belize dollar = 100 cents. **Economy** (1983, in 1,000 tonnes): sugarcane 1,150, sugar 116, citrus fruit 70, bananas 18, maize 22, coconuts, fishing, hardwoods 118,000 cub.m. – **Exports:** sugar, canned fruit, wood, chicle, fish. Trading partner: U.S.A.

COSTA RICA

República de Costa Rica, area 51,100 sq.km, population 2,851,000 (1988), republic (President Oscar Arias Sánchez since 1986).
Administrative units: 7 provinces. **Capital:** San José 277,754 inhab. (1984, with agglom. 766,960); **other towns** (in 1,000 inhab.): Limón 55, Alajuela 43, Puntarenas 36, Heredia 30, Cartago 29. Average annual rate of population increase 2.6% (1980–85). – **Currency:** colón = 100 centimos.
Economy (1983, in 1,000 tonnes): high quality coffee 126, bananas 1,021, sugarcane 2,560, cocoa beans 5, rice 242, maize 95, cotton-seed 10, oranges 78, coconuts 27, palm oil 24, sugar 200, cattle 2.3 mn. head, poultry 6 mn. head; rare hardwoods 2.6 mn. cub.m; fish catch 10,900 tonnes. Gold 933kg. Cement 0.8 mn. tonnes. Electricity 2,700 mn. kWh (85% hydro energy). – **Communications** (1981): railways 1,285km, roads 28,525km. – **Exports** (1982): coffee 29%, bananas 24%, meat, medicaments, sugar, cocoa. Chief trade with: U.S.A. (40%), Fed Rep. of Germany, Guatemala, Venezuela, Mexico.

CUBA

República de Cuba, area 110,861 sq.km, population 10,402,400 (1988), republic (President Dr Fidel Castro Ruz since 1976).

Administrative units: 14 provinces. **Capital:** La Habana 1,924,886 inhab. (census 1981); **other towns** (in 1,000 inhab.): Santiago de Cuba 345, Camagüey 245, Holguín 186, Santa Clara 172, Guantánamo 167, Cienfuegos 103, Bayamo 101, Matanzas 99, Pinar del Río 95. **Population:** Creoles 72%, mulattoes 15%, Negroes 12%. Urban population 70%. 21.5% inhabitants employed in agriculture (1983). – **Currency:** Cuban peso 100 centavos.
Economy: monocultural agriculture, mineral mining and industry developing. **Agriculture** (1983): (crops in 1,000 tonnes): sugarcane 66,000 (7.5% of world crops), tobacco 37, citrus fruit 616, bananas 185, pineapples 16, coffee 26, rice 490, manioc 335, maize 96, vegetables 503, potatoes 222, sweet potatoes 332; eggs 115; **livestock** (1983, in 1,000 head): cattle 6,305, pigs 2,100, horses 820, sheep 370, poultry 24 mn.; fish catch 198,500 tonnes. – **Mining** (1983, in 1,000 tonnes, metal content): nickel 39.3 (6.3% of world output), manganese 28, chromium 8, copper 2.7, crude petroleum 742, marble 14, limestone 5,118, salt 180. **Industrial production** (1983, in 1,000 tonnes): sugar 7,480 (7.6% of world production), meat 317, milk 1,109; 16.8 billion cigarettes, 333 mn. cigars; woven cotton fabrics 170 mn. sq.m, silk fabrics 14 mn. sq.m, sulphuric acid 356. Electricity 11,551 mn. kWh. – **Communications** (1982): railways 14,872km, roads 33,200km. Merchant shipping 959,000 GRT. – **Exports** (1983): sugar (75% of turnover), nickel ores, fruit, tobacco and tobacco products, fish. Chief trading partners: U.S.S.R. (70%), Japan, German Dem. Rep., China, Bulgaria, Czechoslovakia.

DOMINICA

The Commonwealth of Dominica, area, 751 sq.km, population 94,191 (1987), member of the Commonwealth (President Clarence Augustus Seignoret since 1984).
Capital: Roseau 8,346 inhab. (1981). **Population:** Negroes 74%. **Currency:** Eastern Caribbean dollar = 100 cents.
Economy (1983, in 1,000 tonnes): bananas 37, cocoa beans 3.5, citrus fruit 13, coconuts 15. Forests 42% of the area. Fisch catch. – **Exports:** coconut oil, laurel oil, bananas, citrus fruit. Trade with: United Kingdom, U.S.A., Jamaica.

DOMINICAN REPUBLIC

República Dominicana, area 48,734 sq.km, population 6,867,368 (1988), republic (President Dr Joaquín Balaguer since 1986).

Administrative units: 26 provinces and 1 national district. **Capital:** Santo Domingo 1,318,172 inhab. (census 1981, with agglomeration 1.6 mn. inhab.) – oldest town in America established by Europeans in 1496; **other towns** (in

1,000 inhab.); Santiago de los Caballeros 279, La Romana 92, San Pedro d. Mac. 79, San Francisco d. Mac. 65, San Cristóbal 59, Concepción d. l. Vega 52. **Population:** mullattoes 68%, Creoles 20% and Negroes 12%. Average annual rate of population increase 2.3% (1980–85). 54% of inhabitants engaged in agriculture (1983). – **Currency:** peso = 100 centavos. **Economy: Agriculture** (1983, in 1,000 tonnes): sugarcane 11,520, coffee 68, cocoa beans 45, tropical fruit 1,370 (of which citrus fruit 74, avocadoes and mangoes 320, bananas 320), tobacco 34, cattle 2 mn. head, poultry 9 mn. head; fish catch 13,170 tonnes. **Mining and industry** (1983, in 1,000 tonnes): nickel 20.2, gold 11,618 kg, salt 46; production of sugar 1,219; 3.6 billion cigarettes. Electricity: 3,400 mn. kWh. **Communications:** railways 1,076 km, roads 17,227 km. – **Exports:** sugar (43%), coffee and cocoa (21%), tropical fruit. Chief trade with: U.S.A., Venezuela, Mexico.

EL SALVADOR

República de El Salvador, area 21,393 sq.km, population 5,107,000 (1988), republic (President Alfredo Cristiani since 1989).
Administrative units: 14 departments. **Capital:** San Salvador 445,150 inhab. (1983); **other towns** (1980, in 1,000 inhab.): Santa Ana 121, San Miguel 80, Mejicanos 78, Delgado 59. **Population:** mestizos 70%, Indians 15%, Creoles 11%. 48% of inhabitants engaged in agriculture (1983). – **Currency:** colón = 100 centavos.
Economy (1983, in 1,000 tonnes): good quality coffee 155, maize (corn) 444, cotton -seed 60, -lint 41; sugarcane 2,984, citrus fruit 122, bananas 55; raising of cattle 0.95 mn. head, poultry 4.9 mn. head; fish catch 13,490 tonnes; roundwood 4.5 mn. cub.m, balsam gum (the world's principal source). **Production** (1,000 tonnes): sugar 234, cement 320, textiles, paper; gold 93 kg. Electricity 1,610 mn. kWh. **Communications:** railways 602 km, roads 12,235 km. – **Exports** (1982): coffee (29%), cotton, textile yarn, textiles, fish. Chief trade with: Guatemala, U.S.A., Fed. Rep. of Germany, Venezuela.

GRENADA

Area 344 sq.km (including part of Grenadine Is. with area 33 sq.km), **population 104,000** (1987), **member of the Commonwealth** (Prime Minister Nicholas Brathwaite since 1990).
Capital: Saint George's 31,000 inhab. **Population:** Negroes 55%, mestizos 38%. **Density** 326 persons per sq.km. – **Currency:** Eastern Caribbean dollar = 100 cents. **Economy:** spices, mainly nutmeg and mace, cloves and vanilla; bananas 14,000 tonnes, cocoa beans 3,000 tonnes, coconuts, good quality cotton. – **Exports:** cocoa (45%), spices, bananas.

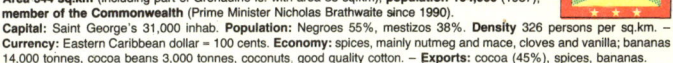

GUATEMALA

República de Guatemala, area 108,889 sq.km, population 8,681,000 (1988), republic (President Vinicio Cerezo Arévalo since 1986).

Administrative units: 22 departments. **Capital:** Guatemala 754,243 inhab. (1981); **other towns** (in 1,000 inhab.); Escuintla 77, Quezaltenango 74, Pto.Barrios 53, Retalhuleu 49. **Population:** Indians 65%, mestizos 30%. 53% of inhabitants engaged in agriculture (1983). – **Currency:** quetzal = 100 centavos.
Economy: (1983, in 1,000 tonnes): coffee 153, bananas 675, sugarcane 6,624, cotton -seed 76, -lint 48; maize (corn) 1,046, chicle 900 tonnes; cattle 2.2 mn. head, pigs 806,000, sheep 657,000, poultry 14.8 mn.; rare hardwoods 6.8 mn. cub.m; mining (1983): crude petroleum 0.6 mn. tonnes, antimony; production of sugar 536,000 tonnes. Electricity 1,705 mn. kWh. – **Communications** (1981): railways 946 km, roads 17,465 km. – **Exports:** coffee (28%), cotton, bananas, sugar, chicle, essential oils. Chief trade with: U.S.A., El Salvador, Fed. Rep. of Germany, Japan.

HAITI

République d'Haïti, area 27,750 sq.km, population 5,523,000 (1988), republic (Provisional President Ertha Pascal-Trouillot since 1990).
Administrative units: 9 departments. **Capital:** Port-au-Prince 684,284 inhab. (1982). **Population:** Negroes 60%, mulattoes 30% and Creoles 10%. 65% of inhabitants engaged in agriculture. – **Currency:** gourde = 100 centimos.
Economy (1983, in 1,000 tonnes): high quality coffee 35, sugarcane 3,000, bananas 230, mangoes 340, rice 113, maize (corn) 180; breeding of pigs 0.6 mn. head, cattle 1.3 mn., goats 1.1 mn., mining of bauxite 431,000 tonnes; roundwood 5.6 mn. cub.m. – **Exports:** coffee (30%), bauxite, sugar, fruit. Chief trade with: U.S.A. (65%), France, Canada.

HONDURAS

República de Honduras, area 112,088 sq.km, population 4,802,000 (1988), republic (President Francisco Callejas since 1990).
Administrative units: 18 departments. **Capital:** Tegucigalpa 508,000 inhab. (1983); **other towns** (in 1,000 inhab.): San Pedro Sula 398, El Progreso 105, La Ceiba 61, Choluteca 54, Puerto Cortés 40. Average annual rate of population increase 3.4% (1980–85). – **Currency:** lempira = 100 centavos.
Economy: Agriculture (1983, in 1,000 tonnes): bananas 1,186, sugarcane 3,195, coffee 87, maize (corn) 458, palm kernels, citrus fruit; cattle 2.7 mn. head, pigs 409,000, poultry 5.2 mn. head. **Mining** (1983, in 1,000 tonnes): lead 19.3, zinc 38, silver 78 tonnes, salt 32; production of sugar 213; roundwood 5.2 mn. cub.m. Electricity 1,150 mn. kWh. – **Communications** (1983): railways 1,268 km, roads 9,718 km. – **Exports:** bananas (35%), coffee (25%), wood, meat, ores. Chief trade with: U.S.A. (47%), Trinidad, Japan, Guatemala.

MEXICO:

States:

1 Aguascalientes	9 Durango	18 Nuevo León	27 Tamaulipas
2 Baja California Norte	10 Guanajuato	19 Oaxaca	28 Tlaxcala
3 Baja California Sur	11 Guerrero	20 Puebla	29 Veracruz
4 Campeche	12 Hidalgo	21 Querétaro	30 Yucatán
5 Chiapas	13 Jalisco	22 Quintana Roo	31 Zacatecas
6 Chihuahua	14 México	23 San Luis Potosí	Distrito Federal
7 Coahuila	15 Michoacán	24 Sinaloa	(México)
8 Colima	16 Morelos	25 Sonora	
	17 Nayarit	26 Tabasco	

1 : 25 000 000

Economy (1983, in 1,000 tonnes: cotton -seed 119, -lint 80; coffee 48, sugarcane 2,911, maize (corn) 218, rice 171, oranges 55, pineapples 37, bananas 128; cattle 2.1 mn. head, poultry 5 mn. head. **Mining:** gold 1,444 kg, silver 2,000 kg. Sugar 249,000 tonnes, meat 88,000 tonnes. – **Communications:** railways 344 km, roads 24,748 km. – **Exports:** coffee (40%), cotton (23%), sugar, meat. Chief trade with Mexico, Fed. Rep. of Germany, U.S.S.R., Costa Rica, Japan.

PANAMA

República de Panamá, **area 77,326 sq.km** (incl. Canal Zone), **population 2,321,000** (1988), **republic** (President Guillermo Endara since 1990).
Administrative units: 10 provinces. **Capital:** Panamá 388,600 inhab. (1980, with agglom. 645,000); **other towns** (in 1,000 inhab.): San Miguelito 158, Colón 60, David 51, La Chorrera 37. **Population:** mestizos 60%, Whites 15%, Indians 10%, Negroes, mulattoes. Average annual rate of population increase 2.2% (1980–85). – **Currency:** balboa = 100 centesimos.
Economy (1983, in 1,000 tonnes): bananas 1,100, maize (corn) 69, rice 198, oranges 65, coconuts 23, sugarcane 2,094; sugar 188; cattle 1.5 mn. head, poultry 6 mn. head; fish catch 166,100 tonnes. Roundwood 2.1 mn. cub.m – forests cover 53% of the land area. Electricity: 2,700 mn. kWh. – **Communications** (1984): railways 185 km, roads 8,862 km, petroleum pipeline 130 km. Merchant shipping 37,244,000 GRT (third place in world; tankers 7,920,000 and ore vessels 14,558,000 GRT). – **Exports:** bananas (25%), fish, sugar, petroleum products. Chief trade with: U.S.A. (42%), Venezuela, Mexico, Japan.
CANAL ZONE, area 746 sq.km, population 38,750 (1982), **territory of Panama** rented to the U.S.A. till 2000. **The Panama Canal** was built in 1903–14, length 81.6 km, depth 12.5–13.7 m, 6 locks lifting ships to 26 m above sea-level. In 1984 11,230 ships passed through the canal with a cargo of 140.5 mn. tonnes (of which 78.3 mn. tonnes from the Atlantic to the Pacific Ocean and 62.2 mn. tonnes from the Pacific to the Atlantic Ocean). Railways 77 km.

ANTIGUA AND BARBUDA

Area 442 sq.km, population 82,400 (1987), **sovereign state, member of the Commonwealth** (Prime Minister Vere C. Bird since 1981).

Islands: Antigua (280 sq.km), Barbuda (160 sq.km) and Redonda (2 sq.km). **Capital:** St. John's 18,000 inhab. (1980). **Economy:** sugarcane, cotton. **Production:** sugar, rum, spirits. Tourism 64,400 visitors (1981).

SAINT CHRISTOPHER AND NEVIS

Area 262 sq.km, population 49,000 (1988), **member of the Commonwealth** (Prime Minister Dr Kennedy Alphonse Simmonds since 1980).

Islands: St. Christopher 168 sq.km, Nevis 93 sq.km. **Capital:** Basseterre 15,726 inhab. **Population:** Negroes, mestizos. – **Currency:** Eastern Caribbean dollar = 100 cents.
Economy (1983, in 1,000 tonnes): sugarcane 315, cotton, coconuts 3, copra, sugar 30, salt. Tourism. – **Exports:** salt, cotton, copra.

SAINT LUCIA

Area 616 sq.km, population 146,600 (1988), **member of the Commonwealth** (Prime Minister John G. M. Compton since 1985).

Capital: Castries 47,000 inhab. (1982). **Population:** Negroes 65%, mestizos 20%, Indos. **Density** 190 persons per sq.km. – **Currency:** Eastern Caribbean dollar = 100 cents.
Economy (1983, in 1,000 tonnes): bananas 61, mangoes 45, coconuts 30, copra 5, cocoa beans, citrus fruit and citrus juices, ginger. Tourism 87,610 visitors. – **Exports:** bananas, copra, juices.

SAINT VINCENT AND GRENADINES

Area 389 sq.km, population 113,600 (1988), **member of the Commonwealth** (Prime Minister James Fitz Allen Mitchell since 1985).

Capital: Kingstown 24,764 inhab. (1982). **Population:** Negroes and mulattoes 75%, mestizos 15%. – **Currency:** Eastern Caribbean dollar = 100 cents.
Economy (1983, in 1,000 tonnes): world producer of arrowroot (used in pharmacy), bananas 33, coconuts 21, copra, nutmeg, ginger and other spices. – **Exports:** arrowroot, bananas, spices.

add page 158

map 36

JAMAICA

Area 10,991 sq.km, population 2,358,000 (1988), **member of the Commonwealth** (Prime Minister Michael Manley since 1989, Gen.-Governor Florizel A. Glasspole).

Capital: Kingston 100,637 inhab. (1982, with agglom. 565,487); **other towns** (in 1,000 inhab.): Spanish Town 81, Portmore 67, Montego Bay 60. **Population:** Negroes and mulattoes 97%. Only 19% of inhabitants engaged in agriculture (1982). – **Currency:** Jamaica dollar = 100 cents.
Agriculture (1983, in tonnes): sugarcane 2,655, bananas 160, citrus fruit 79, coconuts 112, Jamaica pepper 3,790 tonnes; cattle 315,000 head, poultry 5 mn. head. **Mining** (1983, in 1,000 tonnes): bauxite 7,672 (10% of world production); **production:** aluminium 1.73 mn. tonnes, cement 240, sugar 198, world-famous rum 186,000 hl, light industry. Electricity: 2,350 mn. kWh. – **Communications:** railways 328km, roads 4,737km. Tourism 408,000 visitors. – **Exports** (1983): aluminium (47%), bauxite (18%), sugar, rum, bananas.

MEXICO

Estados Unidos Mexicanos, area 1,972,546 sq.km, population 82,954,454 (1988), **federal republic** (President Carlos Salinas de Gortari since 1988).
Administrative units: 31 federal states and 1 federal district. **Capital:** México 9,373,353 inhab. (census 1980; with agglom. 15.7 mn., 1983); **other towns** (1980, in 1,000 inhab.): Guadalajara 2,245, Monterrey 1,916, Netzahualcoyotl 1,341, Puebla 836, Léon 656, Ciudad Juárez 567, Culiacán 560, Mexicali 511, Tijuana 461, Mérida 425, Acapulco 409, Chihuahua 407, San Luis Potosí 407, Torreón 364, Aguacalientes 359, Toluca 357, Morelia 353, Hermosillo 340, Saltillo 322, Durango 321, Veracruz 305, Querétaro 294, Tampico 268, Villahermosa 251, Mazatlán 250, Irapuato 246, Matamoros 239, Cuernavaca 232, Celaya 219, Jalapa 213, Reynosa 211, Nuevo Laredo 203, Coatzacoalcos 186, Cd. Obregón 182 and further 24 cities with more than 100,000 inhabitants. **Population:** mestizos 55%, Indians 30%, Whites and Creoles 15%. **Density** 40 persons per sq.km (1985); average annual rate of population increase 2.7%, birth rate 34 per 1,000, death rate 7.1 per 1,000 (1980–85); urban population 66.5% (1982). Economically active 21.8 mn., 33.5% engaged in agriculture (1983). – **Currency:** Mexican peso = 100 centavos.
Economy: agricultural and industrial country with important mineral mining, among the most developed countries in Latin America. **Agriculture:** arable land covers 12.3% (of this: 5.3 mn. ha irrigated), meadows and pastures 38.7% and forests 25% of the land area (1983). **Crops** (1983, in 1,000 tonnes): cereals 15,740 (of this: wheat 3,697, rice 655, barley 533, maize (corn) 13,928, sorghum 6,367 (10% of world production), potatoes 910, beans 1427 (11% of world production), soya beans 880, groundnuts 51, sesame 99 (states Michoacán, Guerrero, Oaxaca), cotton -seed 350, -lint 220; coconuts 825, copra 145, olives 44, palm kernels 8.5, vegetables 2,580 (tomatoes 1,090), sugarcane 36,000, fruit 7,028 (oranges and tangerines 1,710, lemons 580, avocadoes 448, mangoes 665, pineapples 410, bananas 1,624, grapes 480), coffee 240 (states Veracruz, Chiapas, Oaxaca), cocoa beans 43, tobacco 66. **Livestock** (1983, in million head): cattle 33.9 (dairy cows 9.1), pigs 18.9, sheep 6.5, horses 5.7 (9% of world production), mules and asses 6.4, goats 10.4, poultry 219 (turkeys 14.2); eggs 660,200 tonnes, honey 70,000 tonnes, cowhides 101,000 tonnes; fish catch 1.1 mn. tonnes. Roundwood 19.8 mn. cub.m (1983), chicle 1.500 tonnes.
Mining (1983, in 1,000 tonnes, metal content): crude petroleum 138,577 (deposits 6,800 mn. tonnes, along the Gulf of Mexico: states Veracruz, Chiapas, Tabasco), natural gasoline 410, natural gas 1,048 PJ, silver 1,911 tonnes (first place, 14.1% of world output, states Hidalgo, Chihuahua), lead 167 and zinc 257 (Chihuahua, Nuevo León, Hidalgo): coal 7,830, iron ore 5,306 (states Durango, Colima), copper 206, manganese 133, molybdenum 5.9, gold 6,930kg, antimony 2.5, mercury 221 tonnes, graphite 44.3, mica 1,560 tonnes, bismuth 606 tonnes, tungsten 71 tonnes, barytes 350, fluorite 605, sulphur 1,602, natural phosphates 210, salt 5,703. **Production** (1983, in 1,000 tonnes): pig iron 4,968, crude steel 6,727, lead 153, zinc 174, aluminium 40, copper 81; cars 284,100 units, tyres 8.7 mn. units, tractors 15,714 units, sulphuric acid 2,996, synthetic rubber 132, motor spirit 15,118, kerosene 1,828, jet fuels 1,288, fuel oils 30,960 (capacity of petroleum refineries 67.6 mn. tonnes), nitrogenous fertilizers 1,045, chemical wood pulp 405, paper 1,937, woven cotton fabrics 477 mn. sq.km, cement 17,363; 46.8 billion cigarettes, beer 24.1 mn. hl, soft drinks 52 mn. hl, wine 502,900 hl, meat 1,648, flour 2,435, sugar 2,920, oils of vegetable origin 769, milk 7,300, cheese 101, canned fish 69. Electricity (1983): capacity 21.9 mn. kWh, production 82,343 mn. kWh. – **Communications** (1983): railways 25,645km, roads 216,100km (of which 10,283km Panamerican Highway), motor vehicles – passenger 5.2 and commercial 1.9 mn. units. Merchant shipping 1,475,102 GRT. Civil aviation – 182 mn. km flown, 14.6 mn. passengers carried. Tourism 4.7 mn. visitors. – **Exports** (1983): crude petroleum and petroleum products (72%), chemicals, coffee, metals, natural gas, fruit, vegetables, fish and canned fish, sugar, cotton. Chief trading partners: U.S.A. (58%), Japan, Spain, France, Brazil, United Kingdom, Canada.

NICARAGUA

República de Nicaragua, area 129,350 sq.km, population 3,622,000 (1988), **republic** (President Mrs. Violetal Barrios Chamorro since 1990).
Administrative units: 16 departments. **Capital:** Managua 627,000 inhab. (1981), **other towns** (in 1,000 inhab.): León 122, Granada 88, Masaya 65, Chinandega 54. **Population:** mestizos 70%, Whites, Indians 6%. Average annual rate of population increase 3.3% (1980–85). – **Currency:** cordóba = 100 centavos.

page 158

SOUTH AMERICA

The larger part of the South American continent lies in the Southern Hemisphere where it is isolated from the other continents, save North America to which it is linked by the narrow Isthmus of Panama (width 48 km). Christopher Columbus is generally recognized as one of the first explorers to have reached South America, and on his third expedition (1498–1500), he discovered Trinidad and the mouth of the Orinoco; in 1499 a Spanish expedition led by Alonso de Ojeda reached the mouth of the Amazonas (Amazon), and in 1500 the Portuguese P.A. Cabral reached the shores of Brazil.

South America is the fourth largest continent; it measures **17,843,000 sq.km**, has **285 mn. inhabitants** (1988) but with a density of only 16 persons per sq.km. **Geographical position**: northernmost point: Punta Gallinas 12°27′ N.Lat.; southernmost point – on the mainland: Cape Froward 53°54′ S.Lat., on the Peninsula of Brunswick, of the entire continent – Is. Diego Ramirez 56°32′ S.Lat. in Drake Passage; easternmost point: C.Branco 34°45′ W.Long.; westernmost point: Cape Punta Pariñas 81°22′ W.Long., incl. Galapagos Is. 92°01′ W. Long. The maximum length of the South American continent is 7,350 km, as far as Cape Horn 7,550 km, and its maximum width is 5,170 km.

The topography of South America has few distinguishing horizontal features. The coastline is 28,700 km long and islands make up but 1% of the area of the continent. The largest islands include Tierra del Fuego (71,500 sq.km) and the Falkland Is. (11,961 sq.km) in the South Atlantic Ocean, the Chilean Islands of Western Patagonia (18,000 sq.km) and the Galapagos Is. (7,844 sq.km) to the West of Ecuador in the Pacific Ocean, Ilha de Marajó (42,000 sq.km) and the Ilha Caviana (5,000 sq.km) in the mouth of the Amazonas and Trinidad in the Atlantic Ocean (4,827 km).

The vertical features of the continent are most striking in the West where the Andes rise to nearly 7,000 m, but otherwise low-lying land prevails. Lowlands not higher than 300 m make up more than 50% of the land area, and higher plateaus only 15%. The simple shape of the continent is due to its geological structure and geomorphological evolution. Above the geologically old depressions in the Pacific Ocean, from west of the Isthmus of Panama as far as the southern point of the continent, Tertiary and Quaternary folding raised the narrow strip of high mountain ranges of the South American Cordilleras, called the Andes, to a length of some 9,000 km. They are divided into 30 main ranges, of which the most important are: the north and north-western Andes reaching their highest point in P. Cristóbal Colón (5,775 m), the Ecuadorian Andes with the extinct crater of Chimborazo (6,297 m), the Peruvian Andes with the highest peaks Nevado de Huascarán (6,768 m) and Nudo Coropuna (6,425 m). In the Bolivian Cordillera Real, Nev. Ancohuma reaches the height of 6,550 m. The highest point of the continent, Aconcagua (6,959 m) rises in the Argentinian-Chilean Cordilleras, and the strongly glaciated Patagonian Cordilleras rise to 4,058 m on San Valentin. The core of the continent is formed by the vast, ancient Brazilian-Guyanian shield, which is composed of the oldest rocks and effusive plutonic rock, deeply eroded and denuded, which reach their highest point in the Brazilian peak of Pico de Neblina (3,014 m). Between these two main units, the Andes and the shield, stretch extensive lowlands: those of the Orinoco, the Amazonas and the Rio de La Plata where the basins of the great rivers form terraces and plains with slopes and plateaux – chapadas – at the watersheds. The lowest point is Salinas Chicas (−40 m) on the Valdés peninsula (Argentina). Volcanic activity in the Andes dates back to the end of the Tertiary period and it continues even now. There are some 40 inactive volcanoes and roughly 50 active ones (the highest: V. Guallatiri, 6,060 m, Lascar, 5,900 m and Cotopaxi, 5,897 m). The Chile-Peru Trench (8,066 m) off the west coast of the continent is the epicentre of powerful earthquakes.

The river network is one of the densest in the world. The annual mean discharge amounts to 7,904 cub.km. Almost 88% of the land drains into the Atlantic Ocean, where the Amazonas (Amazon), the longest river in the world, has its mouth (on the Ucayali-Apurímac: length 7,025 km, drainage area 7,050,000 sq.km, annual discharge 3,800 cub.km, maximum flow 225,000 cub.m per sec., minimum 115,000 cub.m per sec.). The Amazonas has 20 tributaries longer than 1,500 km. Other major rivers include the Paraná, Madeira, Orinoco, São Francisco, Paraguay and Magdalena. There are few **lakes**, the largest being L. Maracaibo (14,343 sq.km), Lagoa dos Patos (10,145 sq.km), and L. Titicaca (6,850 sq.km). The Andes are characterized by valleys that have no outlet to the sea, extensive salt swamps – salars (Salar de Uyuni) and, in the South, lakes of glacial origin.

The main part of South America belongs to zones with tropical and subtropical **climates**, while the narrower South belongs to the temperate zone. Everywhere the climate changes with altitude, as do the natural and cultivated forms of vegetation. The highest annual mean temperature was measured at Maracaibo (Venezuela) 28.9°C, the lowest at Cristo Redentor in the Paso de Bermejo (Argentina) −1.8°C; absolute maximum temperature – Rivadavia 48.9°C (Argentina), minimum – Sarmiento (−33°C). Highest annual mean precipitation – Buenaventura 7,155 mm, lowest – Arica 0.8 mm. Mean January and July temperatures in °C (and annual rainfall in mm): Maracaibo 26.7 and 29.5 (577), Bogotá 14.2 and 13.9 (1,059), Quito 13.1 and 12.9 (1,246), Manaus 25.9 and 26.9 (2,001), Recife 27.1 and 24.2 (1,498), Lima 21.7 and 15.6 (41), Cuzco 13.6 and 10.3 (813), La Paz 11.6 and 8.7 (574), Arica 27.1 and 19.3 (0.8), Goiás 23.6 and 22.5 (1,646), Rio de Janeiro 25.4 and 20.2 (1,076), São Paulo 27.7 and 21.2 (1,361), Asunción 28.8 and 18.2 (1,344), Córdoba 23.2 and 10.8 (707), Buenos Aires 29.5 and 14.5 (1,008), Santiago 29.4 and 14.5 (351), Sarmiento 17.7 and 3.6 (142), Punta Arenas 10.8 and 2.0 (366).

The natural vegetation of the neotropical region: the largest evergreen rain forests in the world (Hylea), scrub steppe, savanna (llanos), Xerophilous Chaco woodlands, pampas, deserts with cacti, Andean desert (punas and paramos), Antarctic flora. The neotropical zone contains some **animal life**: pumas, jaguars, tapirs, mountain llamas, guanaco, vicuñas, alpaca, ant-eaters, sloths, armadillos, howler, chatter monkeys, etc. It has the richest bird life in the world, more than 3,500 species, including Harpie eagles, condors, toucans with brilliant plumage, humming-birds, parrots, as well as the largest snakes in the world – anacondas, rattle snakes, caymans – large numbers of insects and big fishes – piraibas, pirañas, multi-coloured aquarium fishes, etc.

The oldest **inhabitants** of South America are Indians. The inflow of White Europeans began in the 16th century and later Black Africans (and fewer Asians) arrived, which led to a marked intermingling of races: mestizos – Indian and White, mulattoes – Negro and White, and zamboes – Indian and Negro. In 1988 there were 285 mn. inhabitants, i.e. 5.6% of the world's population, of which 50.4% lived in Brazil, 11.4% in Argentina and 10.7% in Colombia. At almost 2.5% there is a high natural increase of population. Over 70% of the inhabitants live in towns (Uruguay 83.5%, Argentina 83%) and there has been a rapid expansion of the metropolises, usually the capital cities. There are 19 towns with over a million inhabitants (largest: São Paulo, Rio de Janeiro, Buenos Aires, Lima, Bogotá) and 18 towns with more than 500,000 inhabitants.

CARIBBEAN SEA
5630
Martinique
Lesser Antilles
Grenada
Tobago
Trinidad
ATLANTIC OCEAN
5414
Panama Canal
Isthmus of Panama
G. de Panamá
Pta. Gallinas
P. Cristóbal Colón
5775
L. de Maracaibo
Caracas
Cord. de Mérida
P. Bolívar
5007
Apure
Orinoco
Llanos
Georgetown
Paramaribo
C. Orange
Salto Angel
Mt. Roraima
2810
Guiana Highlands
Cordillera Occidental
Cordillera Central
Cordillera Oriental
Cauca
Magdalena
5493
Bogotá
Meta
Nev. del Huila
5750
Guaviare
Vaupés
Pico da Neblina
3014
Branco
Caviana Is.
Macapá
I. de Marajó
Equator
Belém
Cotopaxi
5897
Caquetá
Japurá
Negro
Amazonas
Manaus
6297
Sangay 5230
Chimborazo
Putumayo
Iquitos
Tefé
Purus
Juruá
Tapajós
Xingu
Iriri
Tocantins
Marañón
Pta. Pariñas
Ucayali
Selvas
Madeira
Parnaíba
São Francisco
Cach. Paulo Afonso
Nev. de Huascarán
6768
6632
Co. Yerupaja
Lima
Apurímac
Teles Pires
Juruena
Guaporé
Mamoré
Beni
Brazilian Highlands
Planalto do Mato Grosso
Araguaia
Sa. Geral de Goiás
1850
Salvador
Nev. Auzangate
6384
L. Titicaca
N. Coropuna
6425
6550
Nev. Ancohuma
5672
Ubinas
La Paz
1995
Brasília
1678
6866
Arica
6060
V. Guallatiri
L. de Poopó
Corumbá
Paranaíba
Salar de Uyuni
Grande
P. d. Bandeira
2890
Agulhas Negras
2787
Tietê
Paraná
Paraguay
Gran Chaco
Andes
Des. de Atacama
8066
Tropic of Capricorn
V. Lascar
5990
V. Llullaillaco
6723
6880
Ojos del Salado
6872
Co. Bonete
Rivadavia
Pilcomayo
Bermejo
Asunción
São Paulo
Rio de Janeiro
Saltos do Iguaçu
Sa. do Mar
2000
I. San Félix
I. San Ambrosio
550
Salado
Entre Ríos
Uruguay
6380
Sa. de Córdoba
Córdoba
2884
Lagoa dos Patos
Porto Alegre
Aconcagua
6959
Islas Juan Fernández
Santiago
I. Rób. Crusoe
I. A. Selkirk
V. Maipo
5323
Buenos Aires
Lagoa Mirim
Montevideo
Río de la Plata
658
PACIFIC OCEAN
4709
Pampas
V. Lanín
3776
Negro
Colorado
Bahía Blanca
2661
V. Osorno
5021
G. S. Matías
Pen. Valdés
-40
Chubut
I. de Chiloé
Arch. de los Chonos
Patagonia
Sarmiento
G. S. Jorge
5585
San Valentín
4058
C. Tres Puntas
6212
I. Wellington
Str. of Magellan
Falkland Is.
West Falkland
East Falkland
Pta. Arenas
Tierra del Fuego
C. Froward
2469
Drake Pas.
C. Horn
Is. D. Ramírez
5840
South Georgia
1 : 50 000 000
0 250 500 750 1 000 1 250 Km
0 200 400 600 800 Mi

CARIBBEAN SEA
ATLANTIC OCEAN
PACIFIC OCEAN
Martinique (Fr.)
ST. LUCIA
Neth. Antilles
ST. VINCENT A. GR.
GRENADA
Port of Spain
TRINIDAD AND TOBAGO
Sta. Marta
MARACAIBO
CARACAS
VALENCIA
Barquisimeto
VENEZUELA
S. Cristóbal
Pto. Carreño
Ciudad Bolívar
Pto. Ayacucho
Orinoco
Georgetown
GUYANA
Paramaribo
SURINAM
Cayenne
French Guiana
MEDELLÍN
Bucaramanga
BOGOTÁ
COLOMBIA
CALI
Neiva
Pasto
Mitú
Meta
Magdalena
Boa Vista
Branco
Macapá
Equator
I. de Marajó
Óbidos
Negro
Japurá
Putumayo
Arica
Napo
ECUADOR
Iquitos
Leticia
Fonte Boa
Tefé
MANAUS
Amazonas
Santarém
BELÉM
SÃO LUÍS
Parnaíba
FORTALEZA
Codó
Teresina
Macau
Natal
João Pessoa
RECIFE
MACEIÓ
Aracaju
SALVADOR
Ilhéus
Crato
Juázeiro
Paulistana
Carolina
Parnaíba
Marabá
Tocantins
Xingú
Tapajós
Madeira
Purus
Juruá
Manicoré
Barra do-São Manuel
Eirunepé
Marañón
Ucayali
PERU
Rio Branco
Pôrto Velho
Guajará-Mirim
Rondônia
BRAZIL
Pôrto Nacional
Araguaia
São Francisco
Huánuco
Cerro de Pasco
Callao
LIMA
Cuzco
Ica
Cobija
BOLIVIA
Trinidad
Guaporé
Mato Grosso
Cuiabá
BRASÍLIA
GOIÂNIA
Pirapora
Montes Claros
L. Titicaca
LA PAZ
Cochabamba
Arequipa
Puno
Mollendo
Oruro
Santa Cruz d. l. S.
Sucre
Arica
Pisagua
Iquique
L. de Poopó
Potosí
Corumbá
Campo Grande
Uberaba
BELO HORIZONTE
Vitória
CAMPINAS
RIO DE JANEIRO
Niterói
SÃO PAULO
Santos
CURITIBA
Florianópolis
PÔRTO ALEGRE
Paraná
Paraguay
Pilcomayo
PARAGUAY
Asunción
Formosa
Resistencia
Tropic of Capricorn
Antofagasta
Salta
Saladо
S. M. DE TUCUMÁN
Copiapó
I. San Ambrosio (Chile)
La Serena
CHILE
ARGENTINA
CÓRDOBA
Santa Fe
Uruguay
Lag. dos Patos
URUGUAY
Rio Grande
Mendoza
ROSARIO
Valparaíso
Islas Juan Fernández (Chile)
SANTIAGO
BUENOS AIRES
LA PLATA
MONTEVIDEO
Río de la Plata
Talca
Talcahuano
Concepción
Zapala
Mar del Plata
Bahía Blanca
Colorado
Negro
Valdivia
Puerto Montt
San Carlos-d. Bar.
G. S. Matías
I. de Chiloé
Chubut
Rawson
Pto. Aisén
Comodoro Rivadavia
Colonia-Las Heras
G. S. Jorge
Puerto Deseado
I. Wellington
Falkland Is. (U. K.)
Stanley
Río Gallegos
Strait of Magellan
Punta Arenas
Tierra del Fuego
Ushuaia
Drake Passage
South Georgia (U. K.)
1 : 50 000 000
0 250 500 750 1 000 1 250 Km
0 200 400 600 800 Mi
10° 0° 20° 30° 40°
90° 80° 70° 60° 50° 40° 30°
1 2 3 4 5 6 7
A B C D E F G H

LONGEST RIVERS

Name	Length in km	River basin in sq.km
Amazonas (-Ucayali-Apurímac)	7,025	7,050,000
Paraná (-Grande)	4,380	4,250,000
Madeira (-Mamoré)	4,100	1,360,000
Purus	3,380	1,100,000
Juruá	3,285	
Tocantins (-Araguaia)	3,100	1,180,000
São Francisco	2,900	631,670
Japurá (-Caquetá)	2,820	
Orinoco	2,740	1,085,000
Tocantins	2,700	840,000
Araguaia	2,630	340,000
Paraguay	2,550	1,150,000
Uruguay (-Canoas)	2,200	420,000
Xingú	2,100	450,000
Ucayali (-Apurímac)	1,980	375,000
Tapajós	1,950	460,000
Parnaíba do Norte	1,720	

HIGHEST MOUNTAINS

Name (Country)	Height in m
Aconcagua (Arg.)	6,959
Ojos del Salado (Arg.-Chile)	6,880
Co. Bonete (Arg.)	6,872
Mte. Pissis (Arg.)	6,779
Co. Mercedario (Arg.)	6,770
Nev. de Huascarán (Peru)	6,768
V. Llullaillaco[+] (Chile-Arg.)	6,723
Nev. Cachi (Arg.)	6,720
Co. Yerupaja (Peru)	6,632
Nev. Ancohuma (Bol.)	6,550
Nev. Sajama (Bol.)	6,542
Nev. Illampú (Bol.)	6,485
Nudo Coropuna[+] (Peru)	6,425
Nev. Auzangate (Peru)	6,384
Chimborazo (Ecuador)	6,297
P. Cristóbal Colón (Col.)	5,775
[+] inactive volcano	

LARGEST LAKES

Name	Area sq.km	Altitude in m
Lago de Maracaibo	14,343	Sea level
Lagoa dos Patos	10,145	Sea level
Salar de Uyuni	10,000	3,660
Lago Titicaca	6,850	3,812
Lagoa Mirim	2,965	1
Lago de Poopó	2,530	3,690
Lago Buenos Aires	2,400	217
Lago Argentino	1,415	187

LARGEST ISLANDS

Name	Area in sq.km
Tierra del Fuego	71,500
Ilha de Marajó	42,000
Isla de Chiloé	8,394
Wellington	6,750
East Falkland	6,682
West Falkland	5,258
Trinidad	4,827
Isla Isabela	4,278

ACTIVE VOLCANOES

Name (Country)	Altitude in m	Latest eruption
V. Guallatiri (Chile)	6,060	1960
Lascar (Chile)	5,990	1968
Cotopaxi (Ecuador)	5,897	1975
Ubinas (Peru)	5,672	1969
Nev. del Ruíz (Col.)	5,380	1986
Sangay (Ecuador)	5,230	1981
Puracé (Col.)	4,756	1977
Reventador (Ecuador)	3,485	1976
V. Osorno (Chile)	2,661	1980

FAMOUS NATIONAL PARKS

Name (Country)	Area in sq.km
P. da Neblina (Braz.-Ven.)	35,600
Jaú (Braz., Amazonas)	27,720
Manu (Peru)	15,328
Nahuel Huapi (Argentina)	7,850
Def. del Chaco (Paraguay)	7,800
Galápagos (Ecuador)	6,912
Los Glaciares (Argentina)	6,430
Iguaçú (Braz.-Arg.)	2,530

SOUTH AMERICA

Country	Area in sq.km	Population year 1988	Density per sq.km	Capital
Argentina	2,780,092	31,965,000	12	Buenos Aires
Aruba (Neth.)	193	62,500	324	Oranjestad
Bolivia	1,098,581	6,993,000	6.4	Sucre, La Paz
Brazil	8,511,965	144,428,000	17	Brasília
Chile	757,402	12,748,209	17	Santiago
Colombia	1,141,748	30,241,000	26	Bogotá
Ecuador	283,561	10,204,000	36	Quito
Falkland Islands (U.K.)	12,173	3,800	0.2	Stanley
French Guiana (Fr.)	91,000	90,500	1.0	Cayenne
Guyana	214,969	1,006,000	4.7	Georgetown
Netherlands Antilles	800	189,500	237	Willemstad
Paraguay	406,752	4,039,000	10	Asunción
Peru	1,285,216	21,255,900	17	Lima
Surinam	163,265	415,000	2.5	Paramaribo
Trinidad and Tobago	5,128	1,243,000	242	Port of Spain
Uruguay	177,508	3,059,545	17	Montevideo
Venezuela	912,050	18,751,389	21	Caracas

South America has two distinct types of **economy:** one typical of the developing countries and the other typical of advanced, more industrialized countries, like Brazil, Argentina, Venezuela. The economies of countries with highly specialized industries fluctuate in accordance with world economics. Agriculture takes the form of monoculture on plantations: the most important crops are corn, manioc, sugarcane, soya beans, wheat, sunflower seed, coffee, bananas, oranges, while cattle breeding and sheep rearing are also important. The mining industry is highly developed and extremely important, but most of the products are exported as raw materials. Manufacturing is developing slowly as yet and plays only an insignificant part. The continent is densely covered in forests (53.4% of the total area) and it has the richest sources of water power in the world 617,600 MW (especially Brazil, 35%), but so far it has been put to limited use, for only in recent decades have major dams and hydro power-stations been built, mainly in Brazil. **Transport and foreign trade** are of exceptional importance to the economic development of South America.

ARGENTINA

República Argentina, area 2,780,092 sq.km, population 31,965,000 (1988), **federal republic** (President Carlos Saúl Menem since 1989).

Administrative units: 22 provinces, 1 federal district and 1 national territory. **Capital:** Buenos Aires 2,908,100 inhab. (1980, [+]metropolitan area Gran Buenos Aires 9,710,000 inhab.); **other towns** (1980 census, in 1,000 inhab.): Córdoba 989, Rosario 954, La Matanza[+] 947, Morón[+] 597, La Plata 560, Lomas de Zamora[+] 509, Gen. Sarmiento[+] 501, S.M.d. Tucumán 497, Lanús[+] 466, Quilmes[+] 442, Gen. San Martín[+] 384, Mar del Plata 384, Santa Fe 375, Tres de Febrero[+] 340, Almirante Brown[+] 333, Avellaneda[+] 331, San Juan 291, Vicente López[+] 290, San Isidro[+] 287, Merlo[+] 283, Salta 266, Bahia Blanca 221, Corrientes 180, Resistencia 175, Paraná 160, Sgo. del Estero 148, Mendoza 118. **Population:** Argentinians (only 36,000 Indians). **Density** 11 persons per sq.km (1985); average annual rate of population increase 1.6%; urban population 83%. 12% of inhabitants employed in agriculture (1984). – **Currency:** Austral = 1,000 Pesos.
Economy: agricultural and industrial country. **Agriculture:** 13.2% of the land area covered by arable land, 52% meadows and pastures, 22% forests; irrigated land 1.62 mn. ha. **Crops** (1983, in 1,000 tonnes): wheat 11,700, maize (corn) 8,840, barley 171, oats 538, sorghum 8,250, rice 277, potatoes 2,013, sugarcane 15,794, soya beans 3,750, groundnuts 230, sunflower 2,300, flax (seed) 670 (28% of world crop – leading world producer), cotton -seed 202, -lint 111; olives 108, vegetables 2,561, fruit 6,471 (citrus fruit 1,454, grapes 3,555), tea 41, yerba maté tea 146, tobacco 74. **Livestock** (1983, in million head): cattle 53.7 (dairy cows 3.1), pigs 3.8, sheep 31, horses 3.1, poultry 48.1; fish catch 416,360 tonnes; production (1983, in 1,000 tonnes): meat 3,214, milk 5,730, eggs 306, tung oil 15, grease wool 104, cowhides 333, sheepskins 35.6. Roundwood: 10.4 mn. cub.m, quebracho 111,000 tonnes.
Mining (1983, in 1,000 tonnes, metal content): crude petroleum 25,220, natural gas 456.5 PJ, coal 518, iron ore 389.8, zinc 36.6, lead 32, silver 78 tonnes, gold 727 kg, uranium 180 tonnes, salt 1,095, beryllium, mica. Electricity: 42,998 mn. kWh (of this 5,054 nuclear). **Industry:** food processing predominates, light industry and metallurgy are important. **Production** (1983, in 1,000 tonnes): pig iron 972, crude steel 2,892, lead 39, zinc 27.6, aluminium 141, motor spirit 5,628, cement 5,868, sulphuric acid 264; fibres – cotton 83, paper 887, sunflower oil 468, flour 2,678, sugar 1,635, cheese 230, wine 25,1 mn. hl, 28.3 billion cigarettes.
Communications (1983): railways 36,185 km, roads 229,600 km (4,835 Panamerican Highway), passenger cars 3.6 mn. Merchant shipping 2,470,000 GRT. Civil aviation (1984): 70.8 mn. km flown and 5.1 mn. passengers carried. – **Exports** (1982): cereals (wheat, maize etc.) and animal (meat, hides, wool) products predominate, flour, foodstuffs (65% of turnover), machines, chemicals, leather, raw materials. Chief trading partners: U.S.A., U.S.S.R., Brazil, Japan, F.R. of Germany.

BOLIVIA

República de Bolivia, area 1,098,581 sq.km, population 6,993,000 (1988), **republic** (President Jaime Paz Zamora since 1989).

Administrative units: 9 departments. **Capital:** La Paz 881,404 (seat of the government) and Sucre 79,941 inhab. **other towns** (1982, in 1,000 inhab.): Santa Cruz de la Sierra 377, Cochabamba 282, Oruro 132, Potosí 103. **Population:** Indians 65%, mestizos 30% and Creoles. 48% of inhabitants engaged in agriculture (1983); average annual rate of population increase 2.7%. – **Currency:** Boliviano.
Economy: principal branch – mineral **mining** (1983, in 1,000 tonnes, metal content): antimony 10.5 (prime world producer, Potosí), tin 25.3 (Oruro, Potosí), tungsten 2,410 tonnes (Atocha), crude petroleum 1,090, natural gas 88.5 PJ, zinc 48, lead 12.4, silver 158 tonnes, gold 1,545 kg. **Agriculture: crops** (1983, in 1,000 tonnes): maize 338, rice 61, manioc 180, potatoes 305, sugarcane 2,590, bananas 151, citrus fruit 132, coffee 18; sugar 249; **livestock** (1983, in million head): cattle 4.2, pigs 1.7, sheep 9.2, llamas and alpacas 1.9, poultry 10. Electricity 1,698 kWh (1983). – **Communications** (1983): railways 3,774 km, roads 40,969 km. – **Exports** (1982): tin (50%), base metal ores, natural gas etc. Chief trading partners: Argentina, U.S.A., Brazil, Japan, Peru.

BRAZIL

República Federativa do Brazil, area 8,511,965 sq.km, population 144,428,000 (1988), **federal republic** (President Fernando Collor de Mello since 1990).

Administrative units: 23 federal states, 3 federal territories, 1 federal district. **Capital:** Brasília 1,177,393 inhab.; **other towns** (1980, in 1,000 inhab.): São Paulo 8,494 (with agglomeration 12.8 mn.), Rio de Janeiro 5,093 (with agglom. 9.3 mn.), Belo Horizonte 1,782, Salvador 1,507, Fortaleza 1,309, Recife 1,205, Pôrto Alegre 1,126, Nova Iguaçu 1,095, Curitiba 1,026, Belém 934, Goiânia 718, Manaus 635, São Gonçalo 615, Duque de Caxias 576, Campinas 566, Santo

C A R I B B E A N S E A
Pta. Gallinas
Neth. Antilles
Curaçao
Willemstad
Lesser Antilles
GRENADA
St. George's
Toba
Port of Spa
TRINIDA
San Fernand
I. de Margarita
Riohacha
Santa Marta
Ciénaga
Valledupar
Golfo de Venezuela
Punto Fijo
Coro
Cabimas
Puerto Cabello
Maracay
La Guaira
Barcelona-Pto. la Cruz
Carúpano
Cumaná
Barquisimeto
BARRANQUILLA
CARTAGENA
Calamar
MARACAIBO
L. de Maracaibo
Cd. Ojeda
VALENCIA
CARACAS
Maturín
Canal Zone
Colón
PANAMÁ
Panamá
Golfo del Darién
Golfo de Panamá
La Palma
Sincelejo
Magdalena
Valera
Mérida
Acarigua-Araure
Maiquetía
V E N E Z U E L A
El Tigre
Tucupita
Calabozo
Orinoco
Cd. Guayana
Upata
Montería
Turbo
Cauca
Gamarra
Barinas
Apure
San Fernando de A.
Caicara
Cd. Bolívar
Cd. Piar
El Callao
Cúcuta
San Cristóbal
Arauca
Barrancabermeja
Jurado
Bello
Bucaramanga
Caura
MEDELLÍN
Puerto Berrio
Pto. Carreño
Pto. Ayacucho
Quibdó
Itagüí
Sogamoso
Tunja
Meta
Caroní
Manizales
Pereira
Armenia
La Dorada
BOGOTÁ
Tomo
Sucuaro
Sta. Elena de Uairen
Ibagué
Guaviare
Buenaventura
Sevilla
Palmira
Villavicencio
Obando
Esmeralda
Boa Vista
CALI
Neiva
Guaviare
Inírida
Brazo Casiquiare
Orinoco
Roraima
C O L O M B I A
Popayán
Magdalena
San Felipe
Caracaraí
Tumaco
Florencia
Calamar
Vaupés
Içana
Mitú
Pasto
Mocoa
Catrimani
Branco
San Lorenzo
Caquetá
Uaupés
Içana
Esmeraldas
Yarí
Negro
Ibarra
Tapurucuara
Barcelos
QUITO
E C U A D O R
Moura
Caquetá
Vila Bittencourt
Japurá
Maraã
Negro
Manta
Portoviejo
Ambato
Napo
Arica
Riobamba
Salinas
GUAYAQUIL
Tigre
Putumayo
Sto. Antônio-do-Içá
Fonte Boa
Santa Elena
Tefé
Codajás
Machala
Cuenca
Iquitos
Amazonas
Leticia
Coari
Tumbes
Loja
Nauta
Yavari
Benjamin Constant
A m a z o n a
Talara
Borja
Marañón
Carauari
Purus
Sullana
Piura
Ucayali
Jutaí
Juruá
Tapauá
Manicoré
Madeira
Moyobamba
B R
Eirunepé
Chachapoyas
Orellana
Cruzeiro do Sul
Lábrea
Chiclayo
Cajamarca
Purus
Ituxi
Humaitá
Aripu
Pacasmayo
Pôrto Valter
A c r e
Juruá
Roosevelt
Pataz
Huallaga
Pucallpa
Bôca do Acre
Madeira
Pôrto Velho
TRUJILLO
Marañón
Rio Branco
Chimbote
Huaraz
Ucayali
Huánuco
Abunã
Beni
Guajará Mirim
Rondônia
Cerro de Pasco
P E R U
Purus
Mamoré
Paramonga
Huacho
Cobija
Riberalta
R o n d ô n i a
La Oroya
Urubamba
Príncipe da Beira
Vilhena
Callao
Huancayo
Madre de Dios
Puerto Maldonado
Guaporé
LIMA
Huancavelica
Machupicchu
Itonamas
San Martín
P A C I F I C O C E A N
Ayacucho
Cuzco
Santa Ana
Chincha Alta
Pisco
Abancay
Apurímac
Reyes
Trinidad
La Esperanza
Ica
Sicuani
Beni
San Miguel
San Nicolás
El Pico
Chala
Puno
L. Titicaca
San Ignacio
Arequipa
LA PAZ
Grande
Guaqui
B O L I V I
Mollendo
Oruro
Cochabamba
San José de
Tacna
Charaña
Mizque
Santa Cruz-de la Sierra
L. de Poopó
Arica
Sucre
C H I L E
Potosí
Pilcomayo
Camiri
Fortin Ay
Pisagua
Uyuni
Boyuibe
Iquique
Ollagüe
Villa Montes
PARAG
Tupiza
Tarija
Tocopilla
Chuquicamata
1 : 25 000 000
0 200 400 600 Km
0 100 200 300 400 Mi
80°
70°
60°
10°
0°
10°
1 2 3
A B C D E

BRAZIL

States:

1. Acre
2. Alagoas
3. Amazonas
4. Bahia
5. Ceará
6. Espirito Santo
7. Goias
8. Maranhão
9. Mato Grosso
10. Mato Grosso do Sul
11. Minas Gerais
12. Pará
13. Paraiba
14. Paraná
15. Pernambuco
16. Piaui
17. Rio de Janeiro
18. Rio Grande do Norte
19. Rio Grande do Sul
20. Santa Catarina
21. São Paulo
22. Sergipe
23. Rondônia

Federal Territory:

24. Amapá
25. Fernando de Noronha
26. Roraima

Federal District:

27. Distrito Federal

map 38

André 549, Osasco 474, São Luís 450, Santos 417, São Joao d.M. 399, Guarulhos 395, Niterói 386, São Bernardo d.C. 381, Natal 377, Maceió 376, Campos 349, Teresina 339, Jaboatão 331, João Pessoa 330, Londrina 302, Ribeirão Prêto 301, Juiz de Fora 300, Aracaju 293, Campo Grande 283, São José d.C. 268. – **Population:** Brazilians – Whites 62%, mestizoes 28%, Negroes 8% and Indians 2%. **Density** 16 persons per sq.km (1985), average annual rate of population increase 2.3% birth rate 31 per 1,000, death rate 8.4 per 1,000 (1980–85); urban population 68%. Economically active inhabitants 43.5 mn., 36% engaged in agriculture (1983). – **Currency:** cruzado = 100 centavos.
Economy: agricultural and industrial country moving towards the group of countries with a highly developed economy. It has enormous mineral resources – the world's richest deposits of: iron ore, tin, manganese, bauxite, tungsten and precious stones. **Agricultural production** is among the greatest in the world; highly-productive monocultural plantations predominate. Arable land takes up 8.8% of the land area, meadows and pastures 19.2%, forests 67.4%. **Crops** (1983, in 1,000 tonnes): – leading world producer (% of world crops): coffee 1,705 (31%), bananas 6,690 (16%), manioc 22,096 (18%), sisal 188 (49%); – second largest producer in the world: oranges and tangerines 10,095 (22%), cocoa beans 350 (22.5%), soya beans 14,582 (19%); – third largest producer in the world: maize (corn) 20,165, beans 1,592 castor beans 172 (18.5%); other products: wheat 2,273, rice 7,960, potatoes 1,815, sweet potatoes 755, cotton -seed 1,025, -lint 552; coconuts 241, palm kernels 250, vegetables 4,537 (tomatoes 1,590), grapes 673, pineapples 841, tobacco 400, jute 61, natural rubber 33. **Livestock** (1983, in million head): cattle 94 (milk cows 14.7), pigs 34, sheep 17.6, horses 5.2, poultry 457; fish catch 846,000 tonnes. **Production** (1983, in 1,000 tonnes): meat 5,117, milk 10,810, eggs 835, cowhides 322. Roundwood: 220 mn. cub.m (1983).
Mining (1983, in 1,000 tonnes, metal content): iron ore 77,649 (second largest producer in the world, Minas Gerais, Pará), manganese 1,141 (Pará, Amapá), bauxite 7,200 (Pará, Minas Gerais), magnesite 486 (Ceará, Bahia), nickel 15,561 tonnes (Goiás), chromite 122 (Bahia, Minas Gerais, Goiás), tungsten 870 tonnes, tin 13.3 (Rondónia), coal 6,380, crude petroleum 23.2 mn. (1984, Bahia, Alagoas, Sergipe), natural gas 80.8 PJ, gold 53,684 kg (Minas Gerais), diamonds 570,000 carats, precious and semi-precious stones (Minas Gerais, Goiás), uranium 290 tons, zinc 73, mica 2, asbestos 159, niobium 16.8 (leading world producer), graphite 443 (Minas Gerais), phosphate rock 3,208, salt 3,259. **Industrial production** (1983, in 1,000 tonnes): pig iron 12,920, crude steel 14,660, fertilizers 1,590, synthetic rubber 221, 18.2 mn. tyres, cement 20,586, paper 3,320, aluminium 552, zinc 111; motor vehicles: passenger 718,300 and commercial 320,400 units; motor spirit 7,876, fuel oils 29,731; television receivers 1.9 mn. units; flour 4,539, sugar 9,460 (leading world producer), wine 261; 129 billion cigarettes. Electricity (1983): capacity 40.1 mn. kW (of which 85% hydro-electric power stations – e.g. Itaipú, Tucuruí, Paulo Afonso etc.), production 161,970 kWh.
Communications (1983): railways 32,136 km, roads 1,458,000 km (98,100 km hard-surfaced, 8,415 km Panamerican Highway); motor vehicles: – passenger 9.3 mn., – commercial 1.93 mn. Merchant shipping 5.8 mn. GRT. Civil aviation (1984): 225 mn. km flown and 12.9 mn. passengers carried. – **Exports** (1983): agricultural products 36% (coffee, fruit, sugar, cocoa etc.), industrial products 39.5%, iron ore, metals, motor vehicles, machines. Chief trading partners: U.S.A., Japan, Saudi Arabia, Iraq, Venezuela, F.R. of Germany, Netherlands, Argentina.

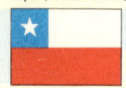

CHILE

República de Chile, area 757,402 sq.km, population 12,748,209 (1988), republic (President Patricio Aylwin Azócar since 1990).

Administrative units: 13 regions. **Capital:** Santiago 4,039,275 inhab.; **other towns** (1982, in 1,000 inhab.): Valparaíso 276, Viña del Mar 259, Concepción 266, Talcahuano 203, Antofagasta 183, Temuco 157, Rancagua 140, Arica 139, Talca 126, Chillán 121, San Bernardo 116, Iquique 110, Puente Alto 105, Valdivia 103. **Population:** Chileans (only 160,000 Indians). **Density** 16 persons per sq.km (1985), average annual rate of population increase 1.7%, urban population 82.4%. 16% of inhabitants engaged in agriculture. – **Currency:** Chilean peso = 100 centesimos.
Economy: developing agricultural and industrial country with important mineral resources. **Agriculture** – crops (1983, in 1,000 tonnes): wheat 810, maize (corn) 512, potatoes 684, sugar beet 1,460, vegetables 1,243, citrus fruit 140, grapes 1,000; **livestock** (1983, in million head): cattle 3.9, sheep 6.4, pigs 1.3, poultry 21.1; fish catch 4,060,000 tonnes; meat 382, milk 910, eggs 61. Roundwood 12.8 mn. cub.m. **Mining** (1983, in 1,000 tonnes, metal content): copper 1,256 (leading world producer – El Teniente, El Salvador and Chuquicamata), coal 1,038, crude petroleum 1,772, natural gas 188 PJ, iron ore 3,602, saltpeter 578, iodine 2,605 tonnes (60% of world output), molybdenum 15.3, gold 17,759 kg, silver 468 tonnes, native sulphur 99, salt 715. **Production** (1983, in 1,000 tonnes): copper -smelted 893, -refined 650; pig iron 538, crude steel 611, cement 1,255, motor spirit 1,165, chemical wood pulp 637, paper 348; sugar 232, wine 575, fish meal 796, fish oil 145, flour 915; cigarettes 7,680 mn. Electricity 12,624 mn. kWh (of which 67% hydro-electric).
Communications (1983): railways 9,287 km, roads 80,060 km. Merchant shipping 487,000 GRT. Civil aviation: 22.5 mn. km flown and 652,000 passengers carried. – **Exports** (1983): copper (49%), raw materials, iron ore, fish, fish meal, roundwood. Chief trading partners: U.S.A., Fed. Rep. of Germany, Japan, Brazil, Argentina, France.

COLOMBIA

República de Colombia, area 1,141,748 sq.km, population 30,241,000 (1988), republic (President César Gaviria Trujillo since 1990).

Administrative units: 23 departments, 4 intendancies, 5 commissaries and 1 Capital District. **Capital:** Bogotá 4,079,848 inhab. (with agglom. 4.58 mn.); **other towns** (1980 census, in 1,000 inhab.): Medellín 1,585, Cali 1,378, Barranquilla 859, Cartagena 435, Cúcuta 426, Bucaramanga 424, Ibagué 297, +Valledupar 263, Pereira 261, Manizales 253, Montería 236, Palmira 231, Pasto 214, Santa Marta 212, Buenaventura 185, +Ciénaga 181, Armenia 179, Bello 165, Neiva 161, +Villavicencio 144, +Tuluá 138, Tunja 135, Barrancabermeja 128, Popayán 115. **Population:** mestizos 50%, mulattoes 18%, Whites and Creoles 25%, Negroes, Indians 450,000. **Density** 26 persons per sq.km, average annual rate of population

page 166

increase 2.2%, birth rate 32.2 per 1,000, death rate 7.9 per 1,000 (1980–85); urban population 70%. 32% of inhabitants engaged in agriculture. – **Currency:** Columbian Peso = 100 centavos.
Economy: developing agricultural and industrial country with mineral mining. **Agriculture** – crops (1983, in 1,000 tonnes): chief products – coffee 798 (second world producer, 14.4% of world crops), bananas 1,280, plantains 2,247, surgarcane 28,000, rice 1,845, maize (corn) 867, sorghum 599, potatoes 2,132, manioc 2,188, soya beans 120, cotton -seed 132, -lint 64; coconuts 56, palm kernels 21.1, vegetables 1,469, citrus fruit 285, pineapples 110, cocoa beans 42, tobacco 47; **livestock** (1983, in million head): cattle 24.2, sheep 2.7, pigs 2.2, horses 1.8, poultry 34.5; fresh hides 74,470 tonnes; fish catch 71,410 tonnes. Forests cover 53% of the land area, roundwood 17 mn. cub.m.
Mining (1983, in 1,000 tonnes, metal content): gold 13,337 kg (dep. Antioquia), coal 5,880, crude petroleum 8,420, natural gas 232 PJ, iron ore 435, platinum 625 kg (1982), precious stones, salt 688, sulphur 30. **Production** (1983, in 1,000 tonnes): motor spirit 2,350, fuel oils 4,383, pig iron 270, crude steel 440, cement 3,480; palm oil 104, sugar 1,391, meat 865, milk 2,647, eggs 165; 21.7 billion cigarettes. Electricity 27,100 mn. kWh (68% hydro-electric). – **Communications** (1983): railways 3,485 km, roads 102,075 km (4,985 km Panamerican Highway), passenger cars 824,000. Merchant shipping 358,900 GRT. Civil aviation (1984): 60.8 mn. km flown and 5.8 mn. passengers carried. – **Exports** (1983): coffee (52%), bananas, cut flowers, petroleum, chemicals, sugar, cotton. Chief trading partners: U.S.A. (30%), Fed. Rep. of Germany, Venezuela, Japan, Italy, Brazil, Spain.

ECUADOR

República del Ecuador, area 283,561 sq.km, population 10,204,000 (1988), **republic** (President Rodrigo Borja Cevallos since 1988).
Administrative units: 20 provinces (inc. Arch. de Colón = Galapagos Is.). **Capital:** Quito 918,800 inhab. (1983); **other towns** (1983, +1981, in 1,000 inhab.): Guayaquil 1,249, Cuenca +144, Machala +114, Esmeraldas +110, Ambato +104, Manta +94. **Population:** mestizos 40%, Indians 40%, Creoles 10%. **Density** 33 persons per sq.km; average annual rate of population increase 3.1%. 38.2% of inhabitants engaged in agriculture. – **Currency:** sucre = 100 centavos.
Economy: agriculture predominates. **Agriculture** – crops (1983, in 1,000 tonnes): bananas 2,770, coffee 81, cocoa beans 58, citrus fruit 441, pineapples 102, sugarcane 5,620, rice 274, potatoes 314, coconuts 63; **livestock** (1983, in million head): cattle 3.3, pigs 3.7, sheep 2.3, poultry 42; fish catch 654,100 tonnes. Roundwood 7.8 mn. cub.m. **Mining** (1983): crude petroleum 11.8 mn. tonnes, gold 2,300 kg. **Production** (1983, in 1,000 tonnes): motor-spirit 985, -oils 2,420; milk 981, sugar 220, palm oil 43; cement 1,265. Electricity 4,289 mn. kWh. – **Communications** (1983): railways 1,121 km, roads 37,980 km. – **Exports** (1982): petroleum (65%), bananas, coffee, cocoa, sugar, fish, balsawood. Chief trading partners: U.S.A. (40%), Fed. Rep. of Germany, Japan, Brazil, Rep. of Korea, Colombia.

GUYANA

Co-operative Republic of Guyana, area 214,969 sq.km, population 1,006,000 (1988), **co-operative republic,** member of the Commonwealth (President Hugh Desmond Hoyte since 1985).
Capital: Georgetown 195,000 inhab. (1982 with agglomeration). **Population:** Indos 51%, Negroes 30%, mestizos 11%, Indians 5%. **Density** 3.7 persons per sq.km (1985). – **Currency:** Guyana dollar = 100 cents.
Economy: forests cover 83% of the land area. **Mining** (1983, in 1,000 tonnes): bauxite 1,791, gold 143 kg, diamonds 17,200 carats. **Agriculture:** (1983, in 1,000 tonnes): rice 246, sugarcane 3,628, coconuts 22; cattle 310,000 head; poultry 14.2 mn. head. **Production** (in 1,000 tonnes): sugar 256, aluminium 73, rum 75,000 hl. – **Exports** (1982): bauxite, sugar, aluminium, rice. Chief trade with United Kingdom, U.S.A., Trinidad – Tobago, Canada, Jamaica.

NETHERLANDS ANTILLES – ARUBA

De Nederlandse Antillen, area 800 sq.km, population 189,500 (1988) – 2 main islands: Curaçao, Bonaire; 3 Leeward Islands: St. Maarten, St. Eustatius, Saba (Prime Minister Maria L. Peters). – **Aruba, area 193 sq.km, population 62,500** (1988), separate state since 1986 (Prime Minister Henny Eman). – **Two autonomous state of the Netherlands.**
Capital: Willemstad 134,118 inhab. Oranjestad 16,326 inhab. – **Currency:** guilder. – **Economy:** processing of petroleum imported from Venezuela; production (1981, in million tonnes): motor spirit 2.1, oils and naphtha 29.1 (capacity of refineries 39 mn. tonnes per year); electricity 2,310 mn. kWh. Tourism. – **Exports** (1981): petroleum products and chemicals (97%), chief trade with U.S.A., Venezuela, Netherlands, Nigeria.

PARAGUAY

República del Paraquay, area 406,752 sq.km, population 4,039,000 (1988), **republic** (President Gen. Andres Rodríguez since 1989).
Administrative units: 20 departments. **Capital:** Asunción 455,517 inhab. (1982, with agglomeration 560,000 inhab.); **other towns** (in 1,000 inhab.): San Lorenzo 75, Fernando d.I.M. 67, Lambaré 62, Encarnación 50. **Population:** Indians (Guaraní) 65%, mestizos 30%; 48% of inhabitants engaged in agriculture. – **Currency:** guaraní = 100 centimos.
Economy: backward agricultural country. **Agriculture:** (1983, in 1,000 tonnes): manioc 2,150, maize 420, rice 75, soya beans 746, cotton -seed 171, -lint 81; castor beans 20, sugarcane 1,700, bananas 315, citrus fruit 360, pineapples 36, coffee 18, tobacco 17; extensive cattle breeding (in million head): cattle 5.6, pigs 1.4, poultry '14. **Production** (1983, in 1,000 tonnes): tung oil 13, orange oil 740 tonnes (70% of world production), cocos oil 16, sugar 95, meat 196; tannin 11, rare hardwoods 6.8 mn. cub.m. Electricity 848 mn. kWh. – **Communications** (1982): railways 634 km, roads 12,930 km. **Exports** (1982): cotton, soya beans, leather, meat, vegetable oils, wood, tannin, essential oils. Chief trading partners: Brazil, Argentina, Fed. Rep. of Germany, U.S.A., Netherlands.

Map of Southern South America

Countries
- BOLIVIA
- PARAGUAY
- ARGENTINA
- CHILE
- URUGUAY

Oceans and Water Bodies
- PACIFIC OCEAN
- ATLANTIC OCEAN
- Tropic of Capricorn
- Río de la Plata
- Bahía Blanca
- Bahía Grande
- Strait of Magellan
- Drake Passage
- G. S. Matías
- G. S. Jorge

Bolivia — Cities
- Uyuni, Camiri, Boyuibe
- Ollagüe, Tupiza, Tarija, Villa Montes
- Chuquicamata

Paraguay — Cities
- Fuerte Olimpo, Puerto Sastre
- Pedro J. Concepción
- San Pedro
- Asunción
- Coronel Oviedo
- Villarrica
- Caazapá
- Encarnación

Chile — Cities
- Tocopilla
- Calama
- Mejillones
- Antofagasta
- Taltal
- Chañaral
- Potrerillos
- Copiapó
- Vallenar
- La Serena
- Coquimbo
- Ovalle
- Illapel
- Viña del Mar
- Valparaíso
- SANTIAGO
- Rancagua
- S. Bernardo
- Talca
- Linares
- Chillán
- Talcahuano
- Lota
- Concepción
- Lebu
- Los Ángeles
- Temuco
- Valdivia
- Osorno
- Puerto Montt
- Ancud
- I. de Chiloé
- Castro
- Arch. de los Chonos
- Puerto Aisén
- Coyhaique
- I. Wellington
- Is. Hanover
- Puerto Natales
- El Turbio
- Punta Arenas
- Puerto Williams

Argentina — Cities
- Humahuaca
- S. Salvador de Jujuy
- Salta
- Embarcación
- Metán
- S. MIGUEL DE TUCUMÁN
- Formosa
- Tinogasta
- Santiago del Estero
- Resistencia
- Corrientes
- Posadas
- Catamarca
- Vichigasta
- Testado
- La Rioja
- Mercedes
- Uruguaiana
- Jáchal
- Cruz d. Eje
- CÓRDOBA
- Santa Fe
- San Juan
- Villa Dolores
- Paraná
- Mendoza
- Villa María
- San Francisco
- Guaymallén
- Godoy Cruz
- San Luis
- Río Cuarto
- ROSARIO
- Pergamino
- BUENOS AIRES
- San Rafael
- Junín
- MORÓN
- LA MATANZA
- LA PLATA
- LOMAS DE ZAM.
- Soitué
- Eduardo Castex
- Las Flores
- Malargüe
- Santa Rosa
- Azul
- Dolores
- Olavarría
- Tandil
- Bahía Blanca
- Lobería
- Necochea
- Mar del Plata
- Zapala
- Neuquén
- Sierra Colorada
- Carmen de Patagones
- San Antonio Oeste
- Viedma
- San Carlos de Bariloche
- Puerto Lobos
- Sacanana
- Pen. Valdés
- Pto. Madryn
- Esquel
- Trelew
- Rawson
- Las Plumas
- Camarones
- Sarmiento
- Comodoro Rivadavia
- Perito Moreno
- Colonia Las Heras
- Pto. Deseado
- Gdor. Gregores
- San Julián
- Calafate
- Sta. Cruz
- Río Gallegos
- Río Grande
- Tierra del Fuego
- Ushuaia

Uruguay — Cities
- Salto
- Rivera
- Paysandú
- Mercedes
- MONTEVIDEO
- Minas
- Ibicuy

Regions
- CHACO
- LA PAMPA
- PATAGONIA
- Tierra del Fuego
- Pen. Valdés

Islands
- I. San Félix (Chile)
- I. San Ambrosio (Chile)
- Islas Juan Fernández (Chile)
- I. de Chiloé
- Arch. de los Chonos
- I. Magdalena
- I. Wellington
- Is. Hanover
- I. Dawson
- I. Hoste
- I. Navarino
- C. Horn
- Falkland Is. (U.K.)
- East Falkland
- West Falkland
- Stanley

Rivers
- Pilcomayo
- Bermejo
- Paraná
- Uruguay
- Colorado
- Río Negro
- Neuquén
- Chubut
- Gubut
- Buenos Aires
- Viedma
- Argentino

Scale 1 : 25 000 000
0   200   400   600 Km
0   100   200   300   400 Mi

Inset Map — Cities
- San Cristo
- Rafaela
- San Francisco
- Sant
- Gálvez
- Casilda
- Firmat
- Pergamino
- Rojas
- Nueve de Julio
- Pehuajó
- Puán
- Saavedra
- Tres A.
- Bahía Blanca
- Punta A.

39 a River Plate Countries, Southern Brazil 1 : 15 000 000

ARGENTINA

Provinces:

1	Buenos Aires	14	Neuquén
2	Catamarca	15	Rio Negro
3	Córdoba	16	Salta
4	Corrientes	17	San Juan
5	Chaco	18	San Luis
6	Chubut	19	Santa Cruz
7	Entre Ríos	20	Santa Fe
8	Formosa	21	Santiago del Estero
9	Jujuy	22	Tucumán
10	La Pampa	23	Federal Capital
11	La Rioja	24	Terr. Nac. de la Tierra del Fuego
12	Mendoza		
13	Misiones		

map 39

PERU

República del Perú, area 1,285,216 sq.km, population 21,255,900 (1988), **republic** (President Alberto Fujimóri since 1990).

Administrative units: 24 departments and 1 constitutional province (Callao). **Capital:** Lima 3,968,972 inhab. (1981, with agglomeration 4.9 mn.); **other towns** (in 1,000 inhab.): Arequipa 447, Callao 441, Trujillo 355, Chiclayo 280, Chimbote 216, Piura 186, Cuzco 182, Iquitos 174, Huancayo 165, Ica 123, Sullana 109. **Population:** Indians 47% (Quechuas, Aymarás, Panos etc.), mestizos 32%, Whites 12%, Negroes and mulattoes. Density 15 persons per sq.km, average annual rate of population increase 2.7%, birth rate 37.3 per 1,000, death rate 10.7 per 1,000 (1980–85); urban population 68.8%. 36% of inhabitants engaged in agriculture. – **Currency:** inti = 100 centimos.
Economy: developing agricultural and industrial country with important mining of minerals. **Agriculture:** only 2.8% of the land is cultivated and of this 38% is irrigated. **Crops** (1983, in 1,000 tonnes): maize 585, rice 798, potatoes 1,290, manioc 361, pulses 89, vegetables 164, cotton -seed 165 and - lint 87, sugarcane 6,664, coffee 91, cocoa 14, citrus fruit 231, avocadoes and mangoes 103; **livestock** (1983, in million head): sheep 14.7, cattle 3.9, pigs 2.1, llamas, alpacas and vicuñas 2.2, horses 0.7, poultry 40; fresh hides 24,740 tonnes, grease wool 5,500 tonnes; fish catch 3.6 mn. tonnes. Forests cover 55% of the land, roundwood 7.8 mn. cub.m.
Mining (1983, in 1,000 tonnes, metal content): iron ore 4,220 (Ica, Arequipa), crude petroleum 8,462, natural gas 101 PJ, copper 336 (Cerro de Pasco, La Oroya), zinc 576 (Junín, 8.3% of world output), lead 213, silver 1,739 tonnes (12.8% of world output), tin 2.4, gold 4,821 kg, vanadium, bismuth 665 tonnes, antimony 713 tonnes, molybdenum 995 tonnes, tungsten 725 tonnes (dep. Áncash). **Production** (1983, in 1,000 tonnes): copper -smelted 296, -refined 191; lead 73, zinc 154, pig iron 113 and crude steel 289, motor spirit 1,517, oils 4,490, cement 2,165, sugar 535, meat 457, fish oil 190, milk 757, eggs 68. Electricity 10,408 mn. kWh (76% hydro-electric).
Communications (1982): railways 2,740 km, the Lima-La Oroya line reaches the highest world altitude 4,829 m at Galero; roads 66,210 km (Panamerican Highway 3,390 km), passenger cars 372,000. Merchant shipping 836,200 GRT. Civil aviation (1984): 24.4 mn. km flown, and 1.6 mn. passengers carried. – **Exports** (1982): metals (copper, zinc, lead etc.) – processed non-ferrous metals (39%), petroleum – petroleum products (27%), silver, coffee, cotton. Chief trading partners: U.S.A., Japan, Brazil, Fed. Rep. of Germany, United Kingdom, Italy, Argentina, Spain.

SURINAM

Republiek van Suriname, area 163,265 sq.km, population 415,000 (1988), **republic** (President Ramsewak Shankar since 1988).
Capital: Paramaribo 67,718 inhab. (with agglomeration 164,879 inhab., census 1980). **Population:** Indos 35%, Creoles 32%, Indonesians (15%), Negroes, Indians. – **Currency:** Surinama guilder = 100 cents.
Economy: forests cover 95% of the land area. **Mining** of bauxite 2,793,000 tonnes (1983), gold 143 kg; production of aluminium 1.2 mn. tonnes; electricity 1,670 mn. kWh (83% hydro). **Agriculture:** (1983, in 1,000 tonnes): rice 278, bananas 42, coconuts 6.5, sugarcane 150; poultry 1 mn. head. – **Exports:** aluminium oxide, aluminium, bauxite, rice, fish. Chief trading partners: U.S.A., Netherlands, Japan, Trinidad and Tobago, Norway.

TRINIDAD AND TOBAGO

Republic of Trinidad and Tobago, area 5,128 sq.km, population 1,243,000 (1988), **republic, member of the Commonwealth** (President Noor Mohammed Hassanali since 1987).
Capital: Port of Spain 65,904 inhab. (census 1980), San Fernando 33,395 inhab. **Population:** Negroes 41%, Indos 41%, mestizos 17%. Density 231 persons per sq.km. – **Currency:** Trinidad and Tobago dollar = 100 cents.
Economy (1983): agriculture with mining of petroleum 8.3 mn. tonnes, natural gas 190 PJ, asphalt 32,000 tonnes (Pitch Lake). **Agriculture:** crops (1983, in 1,000 tonnes): sugarcane 1,006, rice 17, cocoa beans 2.1, coffee 2.2, coconuts 58, copra 9, citrus fruit 18; cattle 76,000 head; poultry 8 mn. head. **Production** (1983): electricity 2,260 mn. kWh, sugar 77,000 tonnes, rum and spirits. **Communications:** roads 7,173 km. – **Exports** (1983): petroleum and petroleum products (83%), chemicals, sugar. Chief trading partners: U.S.A. (52%), United Kingdom, Canada, Japan, Jamaica.

URUGUAY

República Oriental del Uruguay, area 177,508 sq.km, population 3,059,545 (1988), **republic** (President Luis Alberto Lacalle Herrera since 1990).
Administrative units: 19 departments. **Capital:** Montevideo 1,329,899 inhab. (1981); **other towns** (in 1,000 inhab.): Paysandú 82, Salto 85, Mercedes 56, Las Piedras 54, Rivera 52. – **Population:** Whites (descendants of immigrant Spaniards) 90%, mestizos, Indians. **Density** 17 persons per sq.km; average annual rate of population increase 0.7%, urban population 83.5%. – **Currency:** nuevo peso = 100 centésimos.
Economy: agricultural country with extensive animal production. **Agriculture:** arable land 11%, meadows and pastures 82% of the land area. **Livestock** (1983, in million head): cattle 10.1, sheep 21.2, horses 0.53, pigs 0.44, poultry 6.2; grease wool 47,050 tonnes, hides 85,000 tonnes, fish catch 128,440 tonnes. **Crops** (1983, in 1,000 tonnes): wheat 450, rice 323, maize (corn) 104, sorghum 110, potatoes 118, sunflower 34, flax, sugar beet 394, sugarcane 551, citrus fruit 124, grapes 105. **Production** (1983, in 1,000 tonnes): petroleum oils 1,211, sugar 87, wine 85, meat 513, milk 809, production of shoes, clothing, cement 401. Electricity 7,343 mn. kWh. – **Communications** (1983): railways 3,018 km, roads 50,860 km, passenger cars 168,720. Merchant shipping 217,300 GRT. – **Exports** (1983): meat and meat products (26%), wool (18%), cereals, clothing, leather, fish. Chief trading partners: Brazil, Argentina, U.S.A., Nigeria, Fed. Rep. of Germany, Iran, Egypt, U.S.S.R., Mexico.

VENEZUELA

República de Venezuela, area 912,050 sq.km, population 18,751,389 (1988), **federal republic** (President Carlos Andrés Pérez Rodriguez since 1989).

Administrative units: 20 states, 2 federal territories, 1 federal district (the capital) and 1 federal dependency. **Capital:** Caracas 2,070,742 inhab. (1981, with agglom. 4.1 mn. inhab. in 1984); **other towns** (census 1981, in 1,000 inhab.): Maracaibo 920, Valencia 506, Barquisimeto 490, Maracay 348, Barcelona – Pto. l. Cruz 278, San Cristobal 275, Ciudad Guyana 220, Cabimas 175, Maturín 170, Cumaná 163. **Population:** mestizos 55%, Whites 38%, Indians 4%. **Density** 19 persons per sq.km; average annual rate of population increase 3.2%, birth rate 35 per 1,000, death rate 5.6 per 1,000 (1980–85); urban population 78.5%. 16% of inhabitants engaged in agriculture. – **Currency:** bolivar = 100 céntimos.
Economy: agricultural and industrial country with important mining of petroleum. **Agriculture:** arable land 6%, meadows and pastures 19%, forests 42% of the land area. **Crops** (1983, in 1,000 tonnes): rice 450, maize 488, sorghum 364, manioc 325, potatoes 238, sesame (seed) 57, cotton -seed 26, -lint 15; coconuts 101, sugarcane 4,816, bananas 934, oranges 384, pineapples 54, mangoes 111, coffee 59, cocoa beans 14. **Livestock** (1983, in million head): cattle 11.6, pigs 2.6, horses 0.5, poultry 42; fish catch 226,900 tonnes; fresh hides 45,875 tonnes. Roundwood 8 mn. cub.m.
Mining (1983, in 1,000 tonnes): crude petroleum 95,180 (in the Maracaibo Basin and lower reaches of the R. Orinoco) natural gas 1,415 PJ, good quality iron ore 5,928 (Cerro Bolívar, El Pao, Cd. Piar), gold 1,719 kg, diamonds 560,000 carats (of which 75% industrial), salt 361. **Production** (1983, in 1,000 tonnes): motor spirit 7,185, aviation spirit 2,650, oils and other petroleum products 27,745 (capacity of refineries 69,407), pig iron 202, crude steel 2,246, aluminium 335, car assembly 155,000 units; sugar 385, meat 748 and milk 1,518, eggs 138; cement 4,147; 20.2 billion cigarettes. Electricity 41,700 mn. kWh. – **Communications** (1983): railways 268 km, roads 65,780 km, motor vehicles – passenger 1.5 mn., – commercial 0.86 mn. Merchant shipping 973,000 GRT. Civil aviation (1984): 51.8 mn. km flown and 4.5 mn. passengers carried. – **Exports** (1975): petroleum and petroleum products (82%), iron ore, steel, natural gas, aluminium, diamonds, agricultural products. Chief trading partners: U.S.A., Canada, Italy, Japan, Brazil, Netherlands Antilles, Spain.

FALKLAND ISLANDS

Falkland Islands, area 12,173 sq.km, population 3,800 (1988), **British crown colony** to which Argentina lays claim as Islas Malvinas.
Administrative units: East and West Falkland (12,347 sq.km). **Capital:** Stanley 1,200 inhab. (1986). – **Currency:** Falkland pound. – **Economy** (1983): sheep raising 669,000 head, cattle 8,000 head; grease wool 1,500 tonnes, skins, fish catch. – **Exports:** wool, skins. A new airport is sited at Mt. Pleasant on East Falkland.

FRENCH GUIANA

Guyane Française, area 91,000 sq.km, population 90,500 (1988), **French overseas department**.
Capital: Cayenne 38,135 inhab. (1982). – **Currency:** franc = 100 centimes. – **Economy:** forests cover almost 90% of the land area. **Production:** roundwood 51,000 cub.m; gold; crops: sugarcane, bananas, manioc, rice, rum, electricity 65 mn. kWh. – **Exports:** shellfish (74%), wood, essential oils. Trade predominantly to U.S.A., France, Japan.

AUSTRALIA AND OCEANIA

The smallest and least densely inhabited continent on the Earth is Australia with the island world of Oceania. It is very remote from the other continents: 13,000 km from South America and 350 km from Asia. It lies in the southern hemisphere surrounded by the waters of the Pacific and the Indian Oceans. The name derives from the Latin "australis", i.e. "southern" (Terra Australis Incognita). Australia was first discovered by the Dutch explorer W. Jansz, who in 1606 landed on the west coast of the Cape York Peninsula. In the forties of the 17th century Abel Tasman discovered Tasmania, New Zealand (1642), Tonga, Fiji and Bismarck Archipelago. The British seafarer Captain James Cook proved in 1769 that New Zealand consisted of islands, and in 1770 he discovered the eastern shores of Australia, which he named New South Wales. The British were not slow to colonize it. In 1788 the first convict colony was established and in the 19th century settlers came in the wake of the gold rush. The exploration of the inland areas was completed by the end of the century, and by 1884 the British had occupied Papua. On 1 January 1901 the individual British colonies on the Australian continent federated under the name of the Commonwealth of Australia. The colonization of New Zealand began in the first half of the 19th century despite resistance from the native Maoris.
The **area** of Australia is 7,686,848 sq.km (8,910,000 sq.km including Oceania), which has **16,532,000 inhabitants** (with Oceania 26 mn.). **Geographical position:** the northernmost point of the mainland is Cape York 10°41′ S.Lat. (Mata Kawa I. 9°11′ S.Lat.); southernmost point: South East Point 39°07′ S.Lat. (South East Cape 43°39′ S.Lat. – Tasmania); easternmost: Cape Byron 153°39′ E.Long.; westernmost: Steep Point 113°09′ E.Long. Width of the continent 3,200 km, length 4,100 km, length of the coastline 19,700 km. Oceania – the largest island area on Earth – extends in the central and south-western part of the Pacific Ocean: in the North, Kure I. (Midway Is.) 28°25′ N.Lat., in the South, Campbell I. 52°30′ S.Lat., in the East, Isla Sala y Gómez 105°28′ W.Long. and in the West, Pulau Misool I. (Indonesia) 129°43′ E.Long. Largest island: New Guinea (785,000 sq.km). Largest peninsula: Arnhem Land (243,000 sq.km).
The **geological structure** of Australia is very simple; **the surface** has three basic units. First, the Western Australian Hills (the oldest part) which cover one half of the continent, at an average height of 200–500 m rising to 1,524 m on Mt. Liebig in the Macdonnell Ranges; its deserts extend over an area of roughly 1.7 mn. sq.km. Second, the Central Australian Lowlands with the Great Artesian Basin and the Lake Eyre Basin, which has no outlet to the sea; the lowest point on the continent is Lake Eyre (–16 m) in the middle. Third, the Great Dividing Range, known as the Australian Cordilleras, which is the result of Hercynican folding in the East. It reaches its highest point at Mt. Kosciusko, 2,228 m, in the Australian Alps. The mountainous islands of New Zealand are varied in character. In the Southern Alps there are glaciers (Tasman Gl. 156 sq.km); the highest point is Mt. Cook (3,764 m). On North Island there is volcanic activity (Ruapehu, 2,796 m), hot springs and geysers. The islands of Oceania can be divided into two groups:

I N D O N E S
Bali
Lombok
3726
Raba
Ende
Flores
Dili
Vila de Manatuto
Timor
Jawa
Denpasar
Mataram
Sumbawa
Waingapu
Sumba
Kupang
P. Roti
120°
130°
10°
A R A F U R
T I M O R
S E A
Melville I.
Bathurst I.
Darwin
Rum Jungle
Arnhem
Land
Pine Creek
Katherine
Alyangula
Daly
Roper
Victoria
6270
I N D I A N
O C E A N
C. Londonderry
J. Bonaparte Gulf
Ord
776
Wyndham
Kununurra
Birdum
Borroloola
Daly Waters
Victoria River Downs
Newcastle Waters
Yampi Sound
Kimberley Plat.
983
Mt. Ord
Mt. Wells
936
Broome
Derby
Fitzroy Crossing
Halls Creek
Fitzroy
N o r t h e r
Tanami
Tennant Creek
Wallal Downs
20°
Port Hedland
Goldsworthy
Marble Bar
Dampier
Roebourne
Fortescue
North-West C.
Onslow
Deepdale
Tom Price
Mt. Meharry
1251
Paraburdoo
Learmonth
Ashburton
Newman
Great Sandy Desert
L. Mackay
Western
T e r r i t o r
1524
Mt. Liebig
Macdonnell Ranges
Alice Springs
L. Amadeus
Gibson Desert
1219
Simp
L. Mc Leod
Mt. Augustus
1106
Carnarvon
Gascoyne
A U S T R
Musgrave Ranges
Mt. Woodroffe 1440
Kulgera
Finke
-Des
L. Carnegie
Meekatharra
Wiluna
Oodnadatta
Murchison
Cue
Steep Pt.
Sandstone
South
Laverton
Leonora
Great Victoria Desert
L. Eyre
Mullewa
Yalgoo
Magnet
Coober Pedy
Geraldton
Australia
Menzies
L. Barlee
Forrest
L. Torrens
Tarcoola
Dongara
Kalgoorlie-Boulder
Rawlinna
Nullarbor Plain
A u s t r a l
30°
L. Moore
Coolgardie
Kambalda
Eucla
Penong
L. Gairdner
Southern Cross
L. Cowan
Ceduna
Iron Knob
PERTH
Northam
Merredin
Norseman
Great
Australian Bight
Bucklebob
5395
Kwinana
582
Rockingham
Mt. Cooke
Narrogin
Ravensthorpe
Esperance
Port Lincoln
Bunbury
Busselton
Bridgetown
Spencer
1109
Augusta
Bluff Knoll
Albany
Victo
Kanga
I N D I A N
O C E A N
1 : 25 000 000
0 200 400 600 Km
0 100 200 300 400 Mi
40°
130°
B
C
D
E
1
2
3

40 a New Zealand
1 : 25 000 000

AUSTRALIA AND OCEANIA

LARGEST ISLANDS

Name	Area in sq.km
New Guinea	785,000
South I. (New Zealand)	150,461
North I. (New Zealand)	114,688
Tasmania	64,408
Birara (New Britain)	34,750
New Caledonia	16,058
Viti Levu	10,497
Hawaii	10,414
Tombara (New Ireland)	9,842
Bougainville	9,792
Guadalcanal	6,470
Vanua Levu	5,816

HIGHEST MOUNTAINS

Name (Country)	Altitude in m
Puncak Jaya (Irian-Indon.)	5,030
P. Mandala (Irian-Indon.)	4,760
P. Trikora (Irian-Indon.)	4,750
Mt. Wilhelm (Pap.N.Guinea)	4,509
Mauna Kea (Hawaii-U.S.A.)	4,205
Mt. Cook (N.Z.)	3,764
Mt. Tasman (N.Z.)	3,498
Mt. Sefton (N.Z.)	3,157
Mt. Orohena (Tahiti-Fr. Polynesia)	2,235
Mt. Kosciusko (Austr.)	2,228

LARGEST RIVERS

Name	Length in km	River basin in sq.km
Murray-Darling	3,490	1,072,000
Darling (-Barwon)	2,720	710,000
Murrumbidgee	2,160	84,020
Fly	1,150	
Lachlan	1,126	
Cooper Creek (-Thomson)	960	67,500

LARGEST LAKES

Name	Area in sq.km	Altitude in m
L. Eyre	9,500	−16
L. Torrens	5,880	30
L. Gairdner	5,500	110
L. Frome	2,410	80
L. Barlee	1,450	370
L. McLeod	1,300	5
L. Cowan	1,035	380
L. Taupo	606	369

ACTIVE VOLCANOES

Name (Country, Island)	Altitude in m	Latest eruption
Mauna Loa (Hawaii)	4,168	1984
Ruapehu (North I. N.Z.)	2,796	1982
Ulawun (Birara)	2,296	1984
Ngauruhoe (North I. N.Z.)	2,291	1975
Manam (Pap.N.Guinea)	1,830	1984
Kilauea (Hawaii)	1,222	1986

Country	Area in sq.km	Population year 1988	Density per sq.km	Capital
American Samoa (U.S.A.)	197	37,000	188	Pago Pago
Australia	7,686,848	16,532,000	2.2	Canberra
Cook Islands (N.Z.)	237	17,185[1]	72	Avarua
Fed. States of Micronesia (U.S.A.)	721	86,094	119	Kolonia
Fiji	18,376	727,000	40	Suva
French Polynesia (Fr.)	4,198	191,400	46	Papeete
Guam (U.S.A.)	549	126,000[1]	230	Agaña
Hawaii – U.S.A.	16,759	1,098,000	66	Honolulu
Kiribati	868	66,250[1]	76	Tarawa
Marshall Islands (U.S.A.)	181	40,609	224	Uliga
Midway Islands (U.S.A.)	8	2,260[3]	283	–
Nauru	21.4	9,000	421	Yaren
New Caledonia and Depend. (Fr.)	19,058	161,000	8.5	Nouméa
New Zealand	268,675	3,292,300	12	Wellington
Niue Island (N.Z.)	263	2,190	8.3	Alofi
Norfolk Island (Austral.)	36.3	2,367[2]	65	Kingston
Northern Mariana Is. (U.S.A.)	471	20,591	44	Garapan
Palau (U.S.A.)	487	14,106	29	Koror
Papua New Guinea	462,840	3,561,000	7.7	Port Moresby
Pitcairn Islands (U.K.)	37	59	1.6	Adamstown
Samoa	2,842	167,000	59	Apia
Solomon Islands	29,785	299,016	10	Honiara
Tokelau Islands (N.Z.)	12.1	1,780[1]	147	Fale
Tonga	747	116,000	155	Nuku'alofa
Tuvalu	25.8	9,700	376	Vaiaku
Vanuatu	14,763	149,400	10	Vila
Wake Islands (U.S.A.)	7.8	1,640[3]	205	–
Wallis and Futuna (Fr.)	255	15,400	60	Mata Utu

[1] year 1987, [2] year 1986, [3] year 1983

one of low, flat coral islands which arose on the atolls and submarine coral reefs and the other of hilly, volcanic or continental islands. The highest active volcano is Mauna Loa, 4,168 m. Inland New Guinea is mountainous – it contains the highest peak of the continent, Puncak Jaya (5,030 m) – and has swampy lowlands.

Australia lacks a developed **network of rivers.** 54% of the land has no outlet to the sea, 38% drains into the Indian Ocean and 8% into the Pacific Ocean. There is great fluctuation in water level, chiefly in the periodical and seasonal rivers. The mean annual discharge amounts to 610 cub.km. The biggest river is the Murray (-Darling) 3,490 km with a river basin of 1,072,000 sq.km, and a mean annual discharge of 1,900 cub.m per sec. New Zealand and New Guinea have numerous rivers with ample water throughout the year. The most remarkable of the numerous **lakes** is L. Manapouri in New Zealand with an area of 142 sq.km, depth 445 m, and whose bottom is 263 m below sea level.

Climate: Oceania (which, except for the most southerly islands, has a mean annual temperature above 20°C and two fifths of the Australian continent lie within the tropical belt, and three fifths of Australia lie in the subtropical belt – as does the North of New Zealand, which has a generally mild oceanic climate. The warmest place in Australia is Marble Bar with a mean temperature of 34°C, in Oceania Canton I. 28.6°C; Cloncurry (Australia) has absolute maximum temperature at 52.8°C and Lake Tekapo minimum at −15.6°C (New Zealand), in Oceania Canton I. 36.7°C and Honolulu (Hawaiian Is.) 13.9°C. Maximum annual rainfall Ninati 6,350mm (New Guinea), Tully 7,773 mm (Queensland) and world record is held by Waialeale 11,684mm (Kauai in the Hawaiian Is.). Mean January and July temperatures in °C (and annual rainfall in mm) in selected places: Port Moresby 27.6 and 25.8 (1,038), Darwin 28.6 and 25.0 (1,491), Cairns 27.7 and 20.8 (2,253), Broome 29.7 and 21.1 (582), Cloncurry 31.1 and 17.8 (457), Brisbane 25.1 and 14.7 (1,135), Alice Springs 28.6 and 11.7 (252), Perth 23.3 and 13.0 (881), Sydney 21.9 and 11.7 (1,181), Auckland 19.2 and 10.6 (1,247), Dunedin 14.4 and 5.8 (937), Yap 27.1 and 27.6 (3,108), Kanton 28.4 and 28.7 (938), Honolulu 22.1 and 25.4 (697), Banaba 27.8 and 28.1 (1,874), Suva 26.3 and 22.9 (3,240), Papeete 25.7 and 24.1 (1,872).

The fauna and flora have a unique primordial character. Almost 75% of all plants are endemic. This includes eucalyptus forests, scrub-land, acacias with brightly coloured blossom, salt-scrub flora, and in the regions of heavy rainfall, there are tropical rain forests or subtropical forests with typical tree-sized ferns. New Zealand has evergreen broad-leaved forests and characteristic coniferous Kauri. In the drier regions to the East of South Island steppes are the predominant form. Oceania has large numbers of palm trees and forests rich in rare coloured timber varieties. The fauna supports a wide range of marsupials and monotremes, mainly kangaroos, koala bears, phalangers, gliders, wombats and the primitive platypus and the echidna. The largest Australian bird is the brown emu; there are 50 varieties of parrot, black swans, the kookaburra, the New Zealand kiwi, poisonous snakes, the rare Hatteris lizard. In New Guinea we find crocodiles, rare birds of paradise. Nature conservation has a long tradition: Australia's largest National Park is the Kosciusko N.P. (5,800 sq.km) and in New Zealand the Fiordland N.P. (11,200 sq.km).

The original **inhabitants** of Australia – the black Australiands and the New Zealand Maoris – are today greatly reduced in number. On the other hand, in Oceania the original inhabitants form the main part of the population (the Papuas, pygmy tribes, Melanesians, Micronesians, Polynesians and others). The number of Australian Whites is growing (in mn.): 1900 – 3.8, 1950 – 8.3, 1985 – 15.7. The number of New Zealanders has more than trebled between 1900 and 1978, reaching 3.1 mn. 86.2% of the population of Australia and 83.8% of New Zealand reside in towns. The largest towns are Sydney, Melbourne, Brisbane, Adelaide, Perth, Honolulu, Auckland.

AUSTRALIA

The Commonwealth of Australia, area 7,686,848 sq.km, population 16,532,000 (1988), independent member of the Commonwealth (Prime Minister Robert Hawke since 1983, Governor-General Sir William Hayden since 1989).

Administrative units: 6 states (New South Wales, Victoria, Queensland, South Australia, Western Australia, Tasmania), 3 territories (Australian Capital Territory, Northern Territory, Coral Sea Islands Territory). **Capital:** Canberra 255,900 inhab. (1983, with agglomeration); **other towns** (1983, in 1,000 inhab. with agglom.): Sydney 3,333, Melbourne 2,865, Brisbane 1,138, Adelaide 970, Perth 969, Newcastle 414, Wollongong 235, Gold Coast 192, Hobart 174, Geelong 143. **Population:** 99% Whites of European descent of whom 92% British; Aborigines 144,665 (1981). **Density** 2 persons per sq.km (1985); average annual rate of population increase 1.35%, birth rate 16 per 1,000, death rate 7.6 per 1,000 (1980–85), urban population 85.7% (1981). Immigration: 102,860 (1982). – **Currency:** Australian dollar = 100 cents.
Economy: advanced industrial and agricultural country with rich deposits and important mining of minerals, food, metallurgical and chemical industries. **Mining** (1983, in 1,000 tonnes, metal content): coal 97,754 (N.S.Wales, Queensland), brown coal 34,686 (Victoria), iron ore 50,540 (Western Australia – Newman, Tom Price, Goldsworthy etc.), bauxite 22,865 (leading world producer, Weipa), lead 458 and zinc 678 (third world producer, Mt. Isa, Broken Hill), copper 235, tin 10.7, manganese 672, gold 25,825kg, silver 1.02, tungsten 2.1, nickel 82.9, cobalt 2,833 tonnes, zirconium ore 317, rutile 221 and ilmenite 1,158 (leading world producer), crude petroleum 17,655, natural gas 463.3 PJ, salt 5,987, uranium 3,882 tonnes. **Production** (1983, in 1,000 tonnes): pig iron 4,990, crude steel 5,392, copper smelted 172 and refined 200, nickel 46, aluminium 404, lead 239, zinc 293; motor spirit 11,056, jet fuels 1,891 and oils 10,297 with refineries capacity 36 mn. tonnes; cement 5,351, tyres 5.8 mn. units, plastics 715, sulphuric acid 1,734, superphosphates 734, cars 363,000 units, cotton fibres 18.9 and woven fabrics 32 mn. sq.m, 35.4 billion cigarettes; foodstuffs: flour 1,085, meat 2,654, milk 5,685, butter 96,160, sugar 3,075, wine 340, beer 19.7 mn. hl. Electricity (1983): installed capacity of electric power stations 30.2 mn. kW; production 106,287 mn. kWh.
Agriculture is of major importance: sheep rearing, wool production and wheat cultivation. Arable land only 6.1% of the land area, meadows and pastures 58%, forests 14%. **Crops** (1983, in 1,000 tonnes): wheat 22,064, barley 4,937, rice 548, oats 2,270, sorghum 958, potatoes 858, pulses 245, sunflower 104, cotton -seed 164, -lint 101; vegetables 1,178, sugarcane 24,263, grapes 768, citrus fruit 478, pineapples 121, bananas 133, tobacco 13. **Livestock** (1983, in million head): cattle 22.5 (dairy cows 1.8), pigs 2.5, sheep 133.2 (second world producer), poultry 49; (in 1,000 tonnes): grease wool 702 (leading world producer) and scoured wool 424, hides 182, sheep skins 149.8, eggs 197, honey 22.4; fish catch 169; roundwood 16 mn. cub.m (1983)
Communications (1984): railways 40,860 km, roads 885,300 km; motor vehicles – passenger 6.64 mn. and commercial

GUANGZHOU
KAOHSIUNG
VICTORIA
Taiwan (China)
Hong Kong (U. K.)
PHILIPPINES
PHILIPPINE SEA
Northern Marianas Is. (U.S.A.)
Garapan
Guam (U. S. A.)
Agana
Laoag
Luzon
San Fernando
Baguio
Tarlac
QUEZON CITY
MANILA
SOUTH CHINA SEA
Mindoro
Legazpi
Samar
Panay
Iloilo
CEBU
Negros
Palawan
Surigao
Butuan
SULU SEA
Cagayan de Oro
Zamboanga
DAVAO
Mindanao
Kudat
BRUNEI
Kota Kinabalu
Sulu Arch.
Tawau
CELEBES SEA
Borneo
Manado
Selat Makasar
Samarinda
Balikpapan
Majene
Banjarmasin
Sulawesi
Luwuk
Kep. Sula
Galela
Halmahera
Ternate
Maluku
MICRONESIA
Yap
Koror
Palau (U.S.A.)
Federated States of Micronesia (U. S. A.)
Caroline Is.
Sonsorol Is.
Tobi
Truk Is.
Kolonia
Pohnpei
Enewetak
MELANESIA
Manokwari
Biak
P. Yapen
Jayapura
P. Misool
Seram
Buru
Ambon
Kendari
P. Butung
INDONESIA
Nabire
Kokonau
New Guinea (Irian)
UJUNG PANDANG
BANDA SEA
Kep. Aru
Kep. Tanimbar
P. Wetar
Bali
Lombok
Banyuwangi
FLORES SEA
Mataram
Dili
Flores
Timor
Sumbawa
Sumba
Kupang
P. Yos Sudarsa
Merauke
Fly
PAPUA NEW GUINEA
Admiralty Is.
Kavieng
Wewak
Bismarck Arch.
Tombara (New Ireland)
Madang
Birara (New Britain)
Rabaul
Sohano
Bougainville
Lae
Popondetta
New Georgia
SOLOMON
Gulf of Papua
Pt. Moresby
D'Entrecasteaux Is.
Honiara
Louisiade Arch.
ARAFURA SEA
Torres Str.
C. York
Melville I.
TIMOR SEA
Darwin
Pine Creek
Groote Eylandt
Weipa
Great Barrier Reef
Gulf of Carpentaria
Cooktown
Cairns
CORAL SEA
Victoria
Wyndham
Birdum
Borroloola
Northern Territory
Normanton
Croydon
Queensland
Townsville
Bowen
Broome
Derby
Fitzroy
Tennant Creek
Mount Isa
Cloncurry
Flinders
Mackay
Is. Chesterfield (N. Cal.)
Port Hedland
Dampier
Marble Bar
Western Australia
Newman
Ashburton
Georgina
Rockhampton
Paraburdoo
Alice Springs
AUSTRALIA
Barcoo
Fraser I.
Carnarvon
Gascoyne
Meekatharra
L. Amadeus
Cooper Creek
Maryborough
Charleville
Warrego
Murchison
L. Eyre
Oodnadatta
Toowoomba
BRISBANE
Cunnamulla
Gold Coast
Geraldton
Leonora
South Australia
Dirranbandi
Grafton
Coolgardie
Kalgoorlie-Boulder
Bourke
Broken Hill
Northam
PERTH
Eucla
L. Gairdner
Darling
New South Wales
Tamworth
Lord Howe (Austr.)
Bunbury
Penong
Pt. Augusta
Newcastle
Great Australian Bight
Whyalla
Pt. Pirie
Mildura
Bathurst
SYDNEY
Esperance
Albany
Pt. Lincoln
Murray
Wollongong
Spencer G.
ADELAIDE
Albury
Canberra
Kangaroo I.
Victoria
Ballarat
TASMAN SEA
Mt. Gambier
MELBOURNE
Geelong
Bass Str.
Furneaux Gr.
Banks Str.
Burnie
Launceston
Tasmania
Hobart
NEW
Stewart I.
INDIAN OCEAN
1 : 50 000 000
0 250 500 750 1 000 1 250 Km
0 200 400 600 800 Mi
120° 130° 140° 150° 160° 110°
20° 10° 0° 10° 20° 30° 40°
1 2 3 4 5 6
A B C D E F G H

map 41

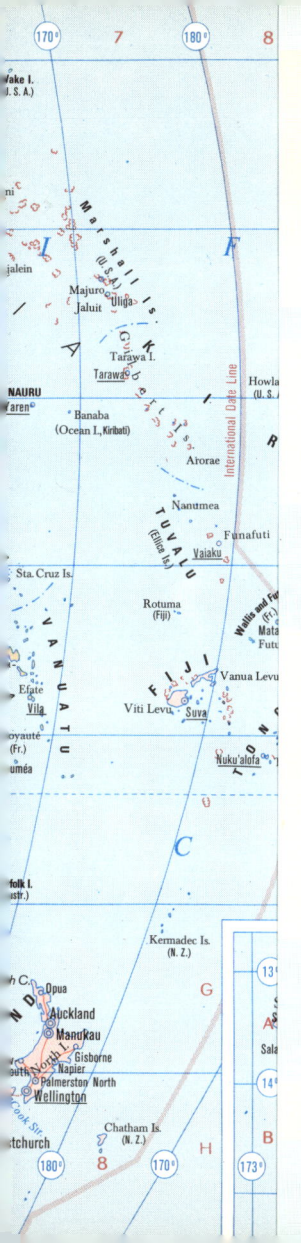

(1983 in 1,000 tonnes): coal 2,180, crude petroleum 631, natural gas 106 PJ, gold 249 kg. **Production** (1983, in 1,000 tonnes): aluminium 218.6, motor spirit 1,255, oils 962, superphosphates 330, paper 718, chemical wood pulp 471, meat 1,334, flour 242, sugar 116, milk 6,774, butter 295, cheese 115, cement 760. Electricity (1983): 25,527 mn. kWh (of which 77% is hydro-electric, 4% geothermal).
Communications (1983): railways 4,418 km, passenger cars 1.4 mn., roads 92,648 km, aviation: 50 mn. km flown. – **Exports** (1983): meat (24%), wool (12%), dairy products (15%, butter-cheese 9.5%), aluminium (4.7%), machines, fish, newsprint, hides etc. Chief trading partners: Japan 16.7%, Australia 16.3%, United Kingdom 10%, Fed. Rep. of Germany, Iran, U.S.S.R., Indonesia, Singapore, Canada.

NEW ZEALAND TERRITORIES:

COOK ISLANDS, area 237 sq.km, population 17,185 (1987), **annexed state with internal self-government; capital:** Avarua (on Rarotonga) 850 inhab. **Economy:** citrus fruit, bananas, coconuts. **Exports:** tropical fruit, juices.
NIUE ISLAND, area 263 sq.km, population 2,290 (1988), annexed state with internal self-government; **capital:** Alofi. **Economy:** coconuts, copra, tropical fruit.
TOKELAU ISLANDS, area 12.1 sq.km, population 1,780 (1987), **overseas territory,** 3 atolls. **Economy:** coconuts.

PAPUA NEW GUINEA

Area 462,840 sq.km, population 3,561,000 (1988), **independent state, member of the Commonwealth** (Prime Minister Rabbie Namaliu, Gov.-Gen. I. Kilage since 1988).
The territory of the state is formed by the eastern part of the island of New Guinea and 2,890 islands and islets; the largest are Birara (New Britain), Tombara, the northern part of Solomon Is. (the largest Bougainville), Admiralty Is. and Louisiade Arch. **Administrative units:** 19 provinces. **Capital:** Port Moresby 144,000 inhab. (1984); **other towns** (in 1,000 inhab.): Lae 62, Rabaul 48, Madang 21, Wewak 20. **Population:** Papuans and Melanesians. – **Currency:** kina = 100 toea.
Economy (1983): **mining:** copper 201,200 tonnes, gold 18,067 kg, silver 47 tonnes, platinum; **Agriculture:** crops (1983, in 1,000 tonnes): sweet potatoes 460, coconuts 750, copra 134, manioc 99, palm oil 84, vegetables 262, bananas 905, sugarcane 324, coffee 54; **livestock** (in 1,000 head): pigs 1,450, poultry 4,000; fishing. Forests cover 72% of the land area; tropical woods 6.8 mn. cub.m. Electricity: production 1,425 mn. kWh. **Communications:** roads 19,538 km, chief airport Port Moresby. – **Exports:** copper (51%), coffee (13%), wood, cocoa, palm – coconut oils. Trade with Australia, Japan.

SAMOA

Mālōtuto'atasi o Samoa, area 2,842 sq.km, population 167,000 (1988), **kingdom** (King Malietoa Tanumafili II since 1963), **member of the Commonwealth.**
Capital: Apia 33,170 inhab. (1981). **Currency:** tala. **Economy:** (1983, in 1,000 tonnes): coconuts 200, copra 23, cocoa, bananas 22, cattle, pigs, fishing. **Exports:** cocoa, copra.

add page 178

1.8 mn. Merchant shipping: 2.17 mn. GRT (of which 984,000 GRT are ore vessels); civil aviation: 196.3 mn. km flown 13.2 mn. passengers carried. – **Exports** (1983): coal 15.4%, wool 8.4%, cereals 7.5%, meat 7.3%, iron ore 7.3%, non-ferrous metals 6.6%, alumina 5.5%, petroleum products, sugar. Chief trading partners: Japan 24%, U.S.A. 14.3%, United Kingdom 6.1%, Fed. Rep. of Germany, New Zealand, Saudi Arabia, Singapore, Rep. of Korea.

AUSTRALIAN OVERSEAS TERRITORIES:

CHRISTMAS ISLAND, area 135 sq.km, population 3,214 (1983), in the Indian Ocean on 10°25′ S.Lat. and 105°40′ E.Long.; **population:** Chinese 56% and Malays 29%. **Seat of administration:** Flying Fish Cove; **economy:** mining and export of phosphates 1,094,000 tonnes (1983): South Point.
COCOS ISLANDS, The Cocos (Keeling) Islands, area 14.2 sq.km, population 555 (1983); 27 coral islands in the Indian Ocean on 12°05′ S.Lat. and 96°53′E.Long. Islands became the part of Western Australia (since 1984). Seat of administration: Home Island; **economy:** coconuts 10,000 tonnes, oil and copra.
NORFOLK ISLAND, area 36.3 sq.km, population 2,367 (1986), in the Pacific Ocean on 29°04′ S. Lat. and 167°57′ E.Long.; **seat of administration:** Kingston; **economy:** vegetables, citrus fruit and especially tourism.

FIJI

Area 18,376 sq.km, population 727,000 (1988), independent state (President Ratu Penaia Kanatabatu Ganilau since 1987).

Administrative units: 4 divisions. 106 of the 844 islands and islets are inhabited; the largest, Viti Levu, 10,497 sq.km and Vanua Levu 5,534 sq.km. **Capital:** Suva 71,255 inhab. – **Currency:** Fiji dollar. **Economy** (1983, in 1,000 tonnes): sugarcane 2,260, sugar 276, coconuts 234, copra 24, rice 16, manioc 96, ginger; raising of cattle and poultry; fishing, mining of gold 960 kg (1981). – **Exports:** sugar, fish, coconut oil.

HAWAIIAN ISLANDS – U.S.A.

State of Hawaiian Islands, area 16,759 sq.km, population 1,098,000 (1988). Since 18 March 1959 50th state of the U.S.A. in the North Pacific Ocean on 20°50′ N.Lat. and 157°40′ W.Long.
The archipelago is formed by more than 20 islands, 7 of which are inhabited. The largest are Hawaii 10,414 sq.km, Maui 1,886 sq.km, Oahu 1,549 sq.km, Kauai 1,427 sq.km. **Capital:** Honolulu 365,048 inhab. (1980, with agglom. 762,565). **Economy:** farming – sugarcane, sugar, pineapples, vegetables, flowers, cattle raising, poultry, fishing; petroleum refinery at Honolulu. – **Communications** (1981): 7,231 km roads (526,000 cars), important air and naval crossroads. Tourism is of great importance 3.93 mn. visitors.

KIRIBATI

Republic of Kiribati, area 868 sq.km, population 66,250 (1987), republic, member of the Commonwealth (President Ieremia Tabai since 1979).

Includes 3 large groups of the Pacific coral islands: Kiribati Is. (Gilbert is.), Phoenix Is. 28 sq.km, Line Is. 595 sq.km (includes the world's largest atoll Kiritimati 359 sq.km) and Banaba (Ocean I.) 5.2 sq.km. **Capital:** Tarawa 17,188 inhab. **Population:** Micronesians. – **Currency:** Australian dollar. – **Economy:** (1983, in 1,000 tonnes): coconuts 77, copra 10, fish catch 24,050 tonnes. **Exports:** copra, fish. Trade with Australia.

NAURU

Republic of Nauru, Naoero, area 21.4 sq.km, population 9,000 (1988), republic, member of the Commonwealth (President Hammer De Roburt since 1972).

Coral island in the Pacific Ocean on 0°32′ S.Lat. and 166°55′ E.Long. **Capital:** Yaren 430 inhab. – **Currency:** Australian dollar = 100 cents. **Economy:** important mining of phosphates 1,684,000 tonnes for exports (1983).

NEW ZEALAND

Area 268,675 sq.km, population 3,292,300 (1988), independent state, member of the Commonwealth (Prime Minister Geoffrey Winston Rusell Palmer since 1989, Governor-General The Most Rev. Sir Paul Alfred Reeves since 1985).

Administrative units: 13 statistical areas, overseas territories. **Capital:** Wellington 135,094 inhab. (census 1981, with agglom. 343,982); **other towns** (1981, in 1,000 inhab., [*] with agglom.): Christchurch 290 ([*]323), Auckland 276 ([*]830), Dunedin 107 ([*]114), Hamilton 98 ([*]160), Invercargill 54. **Population:** New Zealanders and Maoris 282,600 (1982). **Density** 12 persons per sq.km; urban population 83.6%; 8.4% of inhabitants employed in agriculture. – **Currency:** New Zealand dollar = 100 cents.
Economy: advanced agricultural country with important animal production. Arable land covers only 1.8%, meadows and pastures 53% and forests 38% of the land area. **Agriculture:** crops (1983, in 1,000 tonnes): wheat 324, barley 346, maize (corn) 176, potatoes 250, peas 60, vegetables 405, fruit 374 (apples 194); **livestock** (1983, in 1,000 head): sheep 70,263 (6.2% of world population), cattle 7,630 (dairy cows 2,130), pigs 410, poultry 5,600; (in 1,000 tonnes): grease wool 371, hides and skins 177, eggs 57.2, fish catch 141.5, roundwood 10.3 mn. cub.m. **Mining**

SOLOMON ISLANDS

Area 29,785 sq.km, population 299,016 (1988), **independent state, member of the Commonwealth** (Prime Minister Ezekiel Alebua since 1986, Gov.-Gen. George Lepping since 1984).
Administrative units: 4 divisions. **Capital:** Honiara (on Guadalcanal) 22,520 inhab. (1984). **Population:** Melanesians 94%, Polynesians. – **Currency:** Solomon dollar. – **Economy** (1983): forests cover 93% of the land area; roundwood 512,000 cub.m; gold 34 kg; crops (in 1,000 tonnes): coconuts 235, copra 31, sweet potatoes 48, rice, cocoa, palm oil 28; raising of cattle, pigs, poultry; fish catch 47,200 tonnes. – **Exports:** copra, wood, fish, palm oil.

TONGA

Pule'anga Tonga – Kingdom of Tonga, area 747 sq.km, population 116,000 (1988), **kingdom, member of the Commonwealth** (King Taufa'ahau Tupou IV since 1965).
The archipelago called Friendly Is. is formed by 169 islets; 3 chief groups: Tongatapu (257 sq.km), Ha'apai and Vava'u. **Capital:** Nuku'alofa 20,564 inhab. **Currency:** pa'anga. **Economy:** coconuts, copra, citrus fruit, bananas; pigs, poultry.

TUVALU

The Tuvalu Islands, area 25.8 sq.km, population 9,700 (1988), **independent state, member of the Commonwealth** (Prime Minister Dr Tomasi Puapua since 1981, Gov.-Gen. Tupua Leupena).
The archipelago was formerly called Ellice Islands. **Capital:** Vaiaku (Funafuti I.) 826 inhab. **Population:** Polynesians. – **Currency:** Australian dollar. – **Economy:** coconuts, copra, fishing; raising of pigs and poultry.

VANUATU

Ripablik blong Vanuatu, area 14,763 sq.km, population 149,400 (1988), **independent state** (President Fred Timakata since 1989).
The archipelago is formed by 40 islands; the largest are Espiritu Santo, Malekula, Efate, Eromanga. **Capital:** Vila (Efate I.) 14,880 inhab. (1980). **Currency:** vatu. – **Economy:** coconuts 280,000 tonnes, copra 37,000 tonnes, bananas, cocoa, coffee; cattle 115,000 head, pigs; fishing. Deposits: manganese (Efate I.). – **Exports:** copra, fish, wood.

BRITISH TERRITORY:
PITCAIRN ISLANDS – area 37 sq.km, population 59 (1988). **Capital:** Adamstown. **Economy:** tropical fruit, vegetables.

FRENCH TERRITORIES:
FRENCH POLYNESIA – Polynésie Française, area 4,198 sq.km, population 191,400 (1988). **French overseas territory** (High Commissioner: Alain Ohrel). **Administrative units:** 5 district: Îles du Vent 1,250 sq.km (the largest Tahiti 1,042 sq.km) and Îles sous le Vent 490 sq.km called Îles de la Société; Îles Tuamotu and Îles Gambier 948 sq.km, Îles Marquises 1,345 sq.km, Îles Toubouai (Îs. Australes) 165 sq.km. **Capital:** Papeete 65,000 inhab.
Economy: deposits of phosphates (Makatea); crops (1983, in 1,000 tonnes: coconuts 90, copra 15, sugarcane 3, cotton, coffee, tropical fruit; poultry. Fish catch 2,680 tonnes. – **Exports:** copra, vanilla, citrus fruit. Tourism (111,000 visitors) is of importance. The uninhabited island of Clipperton is under the authority of the Governor.
NEW CALEDONIA – Nouvelle-Calédonie, area 19,058 sq.km, population 161,000 (1988), **the Pacific overseas territory; dependencies:** Îles Loyauté (2,072 sq.km), Île des Pins, Îs. Huon, Îs. Bélep, Îs. Chesterfield, Î. Walpole. **Capital:** Nouméa 60,112 inhab. (1983). **Population:** Melanesians (45%), French (36%), Polynesians. **Economy** (1983): important mining of nickel 46,162 tonnes (third world producer), chromium 30,000 tonnes, cobalt; crops: coconuts, coffee, bananas; raising of cattle, pigs. Tourism: 91,780 visitors. **Exports:** nickel and nickel ore (95%), cobalt, coffee, fruit.
WALLIS AND FUTUNA, area 255 sq.km, population 15,400 (1988), **overseas territory; seat of the administration:** Mata Utu (Î. Uvéa) 590 inhab. **Economy:** coconuts 3,000 tonnes, copra, tropical fruit, livestock.

TERRITORIES OF THE UNITED STATES:
AMERICAN SAMOA and dependency, area 197 sq.km, population 37,000 (1988), **unincorporated territory of the U.S.A. Capital:** Pago Pago 2,451 inhab. (on Tutuila), **seat of the Government:** Fagatogo 1,340 inhab. **Economy:** coconuts, bananas, copra, cocoa; fishing tinned fish 90,100 tonnes. – **Exports:** tinned fish, copra.
FEDERATED STATES OF MICRONESIA, area 721 sq.km, population 86,094 (1988), includes atolls of the Caroline Is. in Micronesia. Federated **4 states:** Kosrae, Pohnpei, Truk, Yap (President: Tosiwo Nakayama). **Capital:** Kolonia (Pohnpei I.). **Economy:** coconuts, copra, fruit; fishing.
GUAM, area 549 sq.km, population 126,000 (1987), **unincorporated territory of the U.S.A. – Capital:** Agana 2,199 inhab. **Economy – crops:** maize (corn), bananas, coconuts, citrus fruit, sugarcane; fishing; jet fuel. The air and naval base.
MARSHALL ISLANDS, area 181 sq.km, population 40,609 (1988), **republic** (President Kabua), includes atolls of the northeastern Micronesia. **Capital:** Uliga. **Economy:** coconuts, copra, tropical fruit; fishing.
MIDWAY ISLANDS, area 8 sq.km, population 2,260 (1983), **overseas territory of the U.S.A.** under naval administration.
NORTHERN MARIANA ISLANDS, area 471 sq.km, population 20,591 (1988), **commonwealth, 14 islands** – the largest Saipan, Tinian. **Capital:** Garapan. **Economy:** crops: tropical fruits, coconuts, fishing. Important tourism.
PALAU, area 487 sq.km, population 14,106 (1988), **republic** (President Ngiratkel Etpison since 1988), includes coral islands of Palau Is. **Capital:** Koror. **Economy:** corn, coconuts, copra, fruit; fishing.
WAKE ISLAND, area 7.8 sq.km, population 1,640 (1983), **island under naval administration of the U.S.A.**, air base.

EXPLORATION ROUTES TO THE NORTH POLE REGIONS

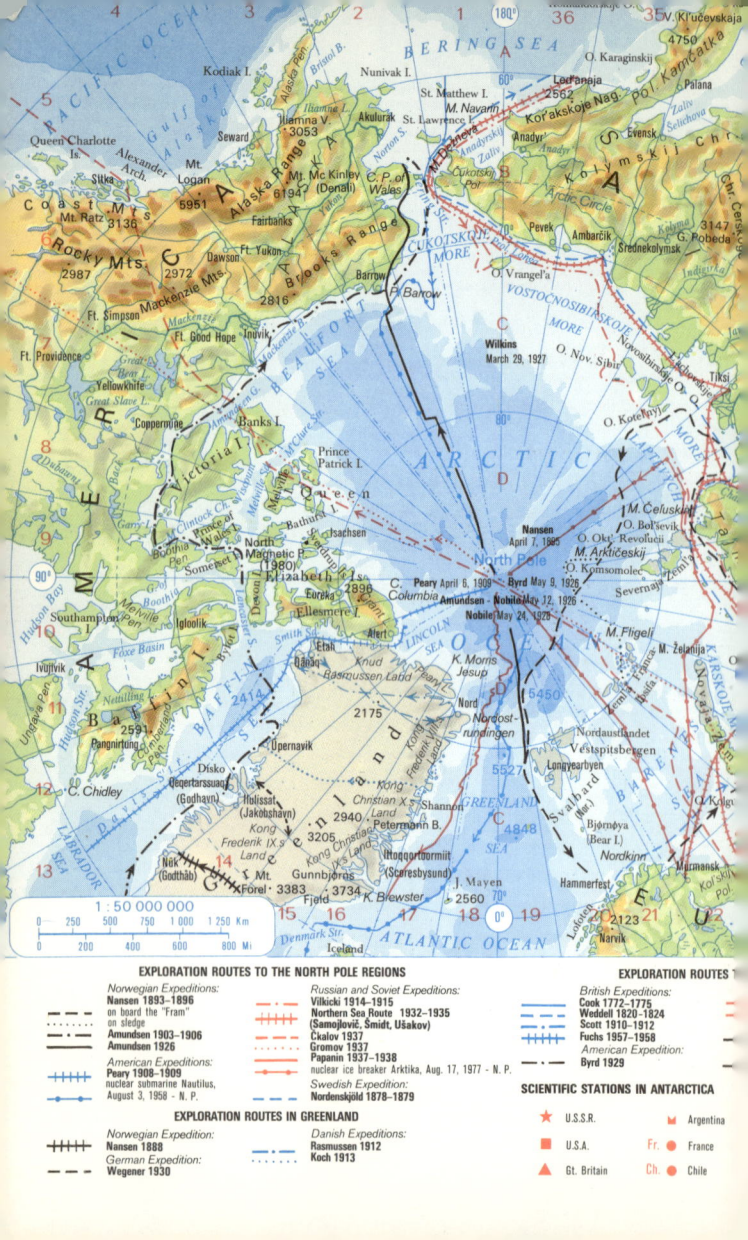

Norwegian Expeditions:
- Nansen 1893–1896 on board the "Fram"
- on sledge
- Amundsen 1903–1906
- Amundsen 1926

American Expeditions:
- Peary 1908–1909
- nuclear submarine Nautilus, August 3, 1958 – N. P.

Russian and Soviet Expeditions:
- Vilkicki 1914–1915
- Northern Sea Route 1932–1935 (Samojlovič, Šmidt, Ušakov)
- Čkalov 1937
- Gromov 1937
- Papanin 1937–1938
- nuclear ice breaker Arktika, Aug. 17, 1977 – N. P.

Swedish Expedition:
- Nordenskjöld 1878–1879

British Expeditions:
- Cook 1772–1775
- Weddell 1820–1824
- Scott 1910–1912
- Fuchs 1957–1958

American Expedition:
- Byrd 1929

EXPLORATION ROUTES IN GREENLAND

Norwegian Expedition:
- Nansen 1888

German Expedition:
- Wegener 1930

Danish Expeditions:
- Rasmussen 1912
- Koch 1913

SCIENTIFIC STATIONS IN ANTARCTICA

- ★ U.S.S.R.
- ■ U.S.A.
- ▲ Gt. Britain
- ◼ Argentina
- Fr. ● France
- Ch. ● Chile

1 : 50 000 000

map 42

bird, though there are large numbers of animals in the sea. As far as **Man** is concerned the region is inhabited only by the staff of the scientific research stations. Great mineral wealth is assumed, but no mining is as yet in progress.

In 1773 Captain James Cook was the first to set eyes on South Georgia and the Sandwich Group during his voyage along the Antarctic Circle. The Russian explorers F. F. Bellingshausen and M. P. Lazarev discovered Peter Ist I. and saw Alexander I. in 1819–21; in 1819 the South Shetland Is. were discovered by W. Smith, but the coast of the Antarctic continent was not discovered until 27 February 1831 when John Biscoe reached the mountainous Enderby Land. J. C. Ross discovered Victoria Land, Ross I. and the Ross Ice Shelf in 1840–43. The first to stand on the continent was C. E. Borchgrevink (1894–95) near Cape Adare. Attempts to reach the South Pole date from the early 20th century; in October 1909 E. Shackleton reached Lat. 88°23′ – 180 km from the Pole, but he was forced to turn back. The first to stand on the Pole was Roald Amundsen on 14 December 1911, and he was followed by R. F. Scott on 18 January 1912. Aerial surveys of Antarctica began in 1928; in the years 1928–30 H. Wilkes explored Palmer Land, on 20 November 1929 R. E. Byrd reached the Pole and he led a total of 5 expeditions until 1947. During expeditions in 1934–38 L. Ellsworth crossed Western Antarctica by plane. The first research stations were set up in 1947, and during the International Geophysical Year 1957–58 alone there were 55 such bases. On 14 December 1958 a Soviet expedition reached a place known as the Pole of Relative Inaccessibility, 82°06′ S.Lat. and 54°58′ E.Long. On 1 December 1959 a treaty was signed for peaceful cooperation in scientific investigation and research and the demilitarization of Antarctica; the treaty came into force on 23 June 1961. Some countries lay claim to territory in Antarctica in the given **sectors** (south of 60° S.Lat.).

AUSTRALIAN ANTARCTIC TERRITORY 45° to 136° E.Long. and 142° to 160° E.Long, an **area** roughly **6.4 mn. sq.km** with Mawson as the largest station; incl. Macquarie Is. 176 sq.km, Heard I. and McDonald I. 258 sq.km.
BRITISH ANTARCTIC TERRITORY 20° to 80° W.Long., since 1962 a colony roughly **388,500 sq.km in area**, incl. the South Orkney Is. 622 sq.km, South Shetland Is. 4,622 sq.km and Graham Land. Argentina has laid claims to a part of the British sector from 25° to 74° W.Long. and Chile to 53° to 90° W.Long. and have set up their own stations.
TERRES AUSTRALES ET ANTARCTIQUES FRANÇAISES, since 6 August 1955 French overseas territory, roughly **395,500 sq.km in area**. Adélie Coast, about 388,500 sq.km with the Dumont d'Urville station from 136° to 142° E.Long; islands in the Indian Ocean: Îles Kerguélen 6,232 sq.km with the Pt-aux-Français research station, Îs. Crozet 476 sq.km, Î. Amsterdam 66 sq.km and Î. St. Paul 7 sq.km.
NORWEGIAN DEPENDENCY 20° W.Long. to 45° E.Long., known as Queen Maud Land. The Dependencies in the Atlantic Ocean; Bouvetøya 59 sq.km, Peter Ist I. 249 sq.km.
NEW ZEALAND ROSS DEPENDENCY between 160° E.Long. and 150° W.Long., an **area of about 414,500 sq.km**, mostly ice shelf (330,000 sq.km) with the Scott Station.
PRINCE EDWARD ISLAND and MARION ISLAND, area 255 sq.km, occupied by South Africa since 1947.
The SECTOR OF THE U.S.A., between 80° and 150° W.Long. has not been officially proclaimed. Of the four American bases in the Antarctic, McMurdo Station is the largest; it has an atomic power station. The Amundsen-Scott Station stands on the South Pole itself.
The **U.S.S.R.** has 6 permanent scientific research bases in Antarctica; the largest of these is Mirnyj.

add page 182

map 42

ARCTIC REGIONS

The Arctic – the northern Arctic polar region – owes its name to the Ancient Greeks, for it lies below the northern constellation of the Great Bear, and the Greek for bear was "Arktos". The boundary of the Arctic region does not run only along the Arctic Circle (66°32' N.Lat.), making it 21.18 mn. sq.km in area; it is defined climatically by the 10°C July isotherm, which roughly coincides with the northern timber line and the range of tundra and taiga. This gives the Arctic an **area of 26.4 mn. sq.km**, of which 18.5 mn. sq.km are ocean and 7.9 mn. sq.km (30%) islands and continent. The point closest to the North Pole is Morris Jesup Cape on Greenland (83°40' N.Lat.). **The largest islands** are Greenland 2,175,600 sq.km and the Canadian Arctic islands 1,403,134 sq.km, of which Baffin I. 507,414 sq.km, Victoria I. 217,274 sq.km, Ellesmere I. 196,221 sq.km lie within the American Arctic; Novaja Zeml'a 82,180 sq.km, Svalbard 62,050 sq.km and Zeml'a Franca-Iosifa 16,100 sq.km are within the European Arctic, and Novosibirskije Ostrova 38,400 sq.km, Severnaja Zeml'a 37,560 sq.km and Ostrov Vrangel'a 7,270 sq.km are in the Asian Arctic. **The Arctic Ocean** proper covers an area of 13,950,000 sq.km with a maximum depth of 5,527 m; in the region of the North Pole it is covered with a thick layer of pack-ice and drift-ice, which extends southwards beyond 70° N.Lat. The depth of the ocean at the North Pole is 4,316 m.

Climate: The inner part of the Arctic Ocean is permanently covered with pack-ice (annual precipitation is 100–300 mm), and such is the intense cold that its effects spread far into the northernmost countries of the world. The warming effect of the ocean and its currents make it possible for the temperature to rise in the short summer on the North Pole to +1 to +3°C, while in the long winter it drops in January to about −35 to −40°C. Extreme winter temperatures spread to subarctic continental Sibir' (Siberia) (Ojm'akon −78°C), Canada (Fort Good Hope −78.2°C) and Greenland (−62°C). The ice shield covers 1,830,000 sq.km of Greenland and 155,000 sq.km of the Canadian Arctic islands. The land that is not icebound has permafrost with tundra **vegetation** (mosses, lichens, perennial plants, dwarf bushes) that passes into subarctic taiga. **Animal life** is limited in species and number (polar bears, polar foxes, hares, reindeer, caribou, waterfowl, etc.), and there are more species in the sea (cod, flatfish, walrus, seal, whale). Along the edge of the Arctic there are only sparse **settlements** of Eskimos, Lapps, Nenets, Yakufs, Chukchi, white immigrants and others, who make a living by fishing, trapping and reindeer farming and the extraction of minerals, which is on the increase. The northernmost settlement is Alert in Canada (82°30' N.Lat.) on Ellesmere I., 3,480 inhabitants live on Svalbard (1984, of these 2,228 Russians) and 502,000 tonnes of coal were mined (1983). Petroleum is being drilled in North Alaska, petroleum and natural gas are also found on the Arctic islands of Canada.

The Vikings, who settled in Iceland 870–930, were the first to explore the Arctic. Eric the Red discovered Greenland in 986, and around 1000 Leif Eriksson reached the American continent near Cape Dyer on Baffin I. Svalbard was discovered in 1194. The Russians explored northern Sibir' (Siberia) in the 17th century, and in 1648 S. Dezhnyov circumnavigated the eastern point of Asia. The North-East passage along the northern coast of Europe and especially Asia was first made by A. E. Nordenskjöld (1878–79), the North-West passage along the North American coast by R. McClure (1850–53) from the Bering Strait in the direction of the Atlantic Ocean, and in the opposite direction by Roald Amundsen (1903–06). The scientific exploration of the Arctic region began at the end of last century: F. Nansen and O. Sverdrup crossed the South of Greenland in 1888.

Robert E. Peary explored northern Greenland in 1892–1900 and he and M. Henson were the first people to stand on the North Pole (6 April 1909). Richard E. Byrd reached the Pole by air on 6 May 1926, two days later R. Amundsen, L. Ellsworth and U. Nobile did so in an airship; in 1937 the Russian polar explorers I. Papanin and O. Schmidt again used a plane; the Americans reached the Pole under the sea in their nuclear submarine Nautilus on 3 August 1958; Guido Monzino followed Peary's route with a dog team and reached the Pole on 19 May 1971. The Soviet atomic ice-breaker Arktika reached the Pole on 17 August 1977.

ANTARCTICA

Antarctica – the southern Antarctic polar region – derives its name from the Greek word for "opposite the Arctic", "opposite the North". The boundary of Antarctica is given by the Antarctic Circle (66°32' S.Lat.) as well as by the climatic 10°C January isotherm (the warmest), roughly concurrent with the southern timber line; within this boundary **the Antarctic measures 67.84 mn. sq.km** (incl. parts of South America). It comprises the Antarctic continent 14,108,000 sq.km in area, incl. the ice shelf, 13,175,000 sq.km without the ice shelf (i.e. 8.8% of land surface), with 75,570 sq.km of islands and the surrounding sea with the more distant subantarctic islands extending over an area of 13,198 sq.km. Antarctica lies at a distance of 4,000 km from Africa, 3,200 km from Australia and only 1,450 km from South America. The Ross Sea (off the Pacific Ocean) and the Weddell Sea (off the Atlantic Ocean) penetrate deep into the continent and divide it into the larger Eastern Antarctica on the side of the Atlantic and Indian Oceans and the smaller Western Antarctica of the Pacific side, where the large Antarctic Peninsula stretches in the direction of South America. The permanent ice-cap, of mean thickness 2,500 m, leaves only insignificant parts of the coast and the highest rocks free of ice. The average altitude of Antarctica is 2,280 m. The South Pole lies on the South Polar Plateau at a height of 2,800 m above sea level and the thickness of ice there reaches 2,810 m. The highest peak, the Vinson Massif in the Ellsworth Mts. in Western Antarctica is 4,987 m high, Mt. Kirkpatrick in the Transantarctic Mts. in Eastern Antarctica is 4,528 m and the highest active volcano is Mt. Ere-bus, 3,795 m, on Ross I.

The region of the South Pole has a severe, harsh polar **climate**, for the mean summer temperature (January) is −28°C, the July temperature (winter) is about −50°C, with precipitation not exceeding 80 mm in the prevailing calm; by contrast, the Antarctic coast (e.g. Wilkes Land) has the following mean temperatures: January −0.2°C, July −25°C, mean annual temperature −13.9°C, and 340 stormy days (highest number in the world). Absolute minimum temperature was recorded at the Vostok station (3,488 m high): −89.2°C. The lowest annual mean temperature is found at the Pole of Cold: −57.8°C. **Flora:** there exist only 3 species of flowering plants in Antarctica, about 60 varieties of moss and lichen, and microbes, algae, bacteria and fungi live below the surface of the weatherworn rocks. As regards **fauna** there are two species of penguins as well as the skua, a predatory gull-like

page 182

INDEX

The index contains in alphabetical order all geographical names used in the maps. Apart from towns and cities all names are marked with appropriate abbreviations (for example, R. = river, I. = island, L. = lake, etc.). Following each name there is a number signifying the map number, and a letter and a number indicating the section of the map in which the place is located. The letters (marked in red on the maps) refer to sections of latitude, and the numbers (also marked in red) to sections of longitude. For example, "Mamoré, R., 37 D 3" means that the river Mamoré appears on map 37 in square D 3.

Rivers are indexed under the names given them by the country of their source. Thus the Danube comes under Donau and the Rijn under Rhein. For major geographical names, the squares given are those in which the name actually appears. For example, England, 9 B-D 3-5.

In some maps the names of administrative units, states and their subdivisions have been replaced by numbers, which are explained in the legend for the map. In the index this number is given in brackets after the name of the administrative unit.

When there is more than one place with the same name, the country where each is situated is given in brackets. For example, Victoria (Canada) 33 D 7; Victoria (Hong Kong), 19a B 3; Victoria (U.S.A.), 34 F 7. In the case of rivers, the sea, lake or river into which they flow is given, e.g. Negro (Amazonas), R., 37 C 3; Negro (Atlantic Ocean), R., 37 F 3.

ABBREVIATIONS USED IN THE INDEX

Admin. U. = Administrative Unit
Arch. = Archipelago
B. = Bay
C. = Cape
Can. = Canal
Chann. = Channel
Depr. = Depression
Des. = Desert
Fs. = Falls
G. = Gulf
Glac. = Glacier
H., Hs. = Hill, Hills
I., Is. = Island, Islands
L. = Lake

Mt., Mts. = Mountain, Mountains
Pen. = Peninsula
Pk. = Peak
Pl. = Plain
Plat. = Plateau
R. = River
Reg. = Region
Res. = Reserve, Reservoir
S. = Sea
St. = State
Str. = Strait
Sw. = Swamp
Val. = Valley
Vol. = Volcano

ABBREVIATIONS USED IN THE TEXT

m = metre
km = kilometre
sq.m = square metre
sq.km = square kilometre
ha = hectare
kg = kilogramme
ton = metric ton (tonne) = 1,000 kg

cub.m = cubic metre
l = litre
hl = hectolitre
mn. = million
agglom. = agglomeration
R.S.F.S.R. = Russian Soviet Federal Socialist Republic

A

Aachen, 12C2
Aakba, 5aB2
Aare, R., 11C4
Aba, 29D7
Abādān, 21C5
Abadan, 21D6
Abadla, 28A2
Abaetetuba, 38C5
Abagnar Qi, 24B5
Abakaliki, 29D7
Abakan, 16D10,11
Abancay, 38D2
Abashiri, 25B7
Abay, R., 28C6
Abbeville, 11B3
Abéché, 28C5
Abengourou, 29D5
Abenra, 12B3
Aberdeen (U.K.), 10B3
Aberdeen (U.S.A., South Dakota), 34B7
Aberdeen (U.S.A., Washington), 34B7
Aberystwyth, 9C2
Abhā, 28C7
Abhar, 21B5
Abidjan, 29D4,5
Abilene, 34E7
Abilibi, R., 33C,D11
Abisko, 15A6
Abkhaz Autonomous Soviet Socialist Republic, (1) Admin. U., 18D5
Abomey, 29D6
Abong-Mbang, 29E9
Abqaiq, 21D5
Abrantes, 11G1,2
'Abrī, 28B6
Abruzzi (1), Admin. U., 13B3
Abū Ḥamad, 28C6
Abuja, 29C7
Abū Kabīr, 26aB3
Abū Kamāl, 20bB3
Abunā, R., 38D3
Abū Zabad, 28C5
Abū-Zaby, 21E6
Abū Zanīmah, 28B6
Acajutla, 36C3,4
Acapulco, 36C2,3
Acarigua-Araure, 38B3
Accra, 29D5
Achalciche, 18aA1
Achil Island, I., 7E2
Achtubinsk, 18C6
Achtyrka, 18B3
Ačinsk, 16D10,11
Acireale, 13C3
Acklins Island, I., 36B5
Aconcagua, Mt., 37F2,3
Acqui Terme, 13aB2
Acre, Admin. U., 38C2,3
Acton, 9a
Adamaoua, Mts., 26D6
Adam's Bridge, Is., 20aB2
Adamstown, 41F13
Adan, 28C7
Adana, 21aB3
Adapazarı, 21aA2
Ādda, R., 13aA3
Ad Damazin, 28C6
Ad-Dāmir, 28C6
Ad-Dammām, 28B7,8
Ad-Dawḥah, 21D6
Addis Abeba, 28D6
Ad-Dīwānīyah, 21C4,5

Ad-Duwaym, 28C6
Addy, 33aB4
Adelaide, 40D3
Adélie Coast, Reg., 42F22,23
Aden see Adan
Adige, R., 13A2
Adigrat, 28C6,7
Adıyaman, 21aB3
Admiralty Island, Is., 41D4
Ado-Ekiti, 29D7
Adour, R., 11D2
Adra, 11G3
Adrar, 28B2
Adré, 28C5
Adrī, 28B4
Adria, 13aA5,6
Adrian, 33aC4
Adriatic Sea, 5C6
Adwa, 28C6
Adygei Autonomous Region, (7) Admin. U., 18C5
Adzhar Autonomous Soviet Socialist Republic, (2) Admin. U., 18aA1
Adz'vavom, 17A9
Aegean Sea, 14D3
Afyon, 21aB2
Agadez, 29A7
Agadir, 28A1,2
Agalega Islands, Is., 27F10
Agana, 41B4
Agartala, 22B5
Agawa, 34B4
Agboville, 29D4,5
Agde, 11C3
Agen, 11C3
Aginskoje, 24A5
Āgra, 22B3
Agri, R., 13B4
Agrigento, 13C3
Agrinion, 14D3
Agua Prieta, 36A2
Aguascalientes, 36B2
Aguascalientes (1), Admin. U., 36B2
Aguelhok, 29A6
Aguilas, 11G3
Agulhas Negras, Mt., 37E5
Agusan, R., 23C4
Agutaya, 23bB2
Ahar, 18aB2
Ahmadābād, 22B3
Ahmadnagar, 22C3
Ahvāz, 21C5
Ahvenanmaa, Is., 15C6,7
Aibihu, L., 24B2
Aigaioi Nísoi (1), Admin. U., 14D3
Ainaži, 17C2
Aïn Beïda, 27aA2
Aïn Sefra, 28A2,3
Aïr, Mts., 26C5
Aire, R., 7E7
Aisne (02), Admin. U., 11B3
Aisne, R., 11B4
Aix-en-Provence, 11D4
Aizawl, 22B5
Aizu-wakamatsu, 25C6,7

Ajaccio, 11D5
Ajaguz, 24B2
Ajan, 16D15
Ajat, R., 17aC3
Ajdābīyah, 28A5
Ajkino, 17B7
Ajmer, 22B3
Ajo, 34E4
Ak-Dovurak, 24A3
Akesu, 24B2
Aketi, 28D5
Akhelóös, R., 14D2
Akimiski Island, I., 33C11
Akita, 25C6,7
Akjoujt, 28C1
'Akko, 20bB1
Akköy, 21aB1
Aklavik, 33B6
Akola, 22B3
Akordat, 28C6
Akpatok Island, I., 33B13
Ákra Maléa, C., 14D2
Akranes, 15aB2
Ákra Sídheros, C., 14E3
Ákra Spátha, C., 14E2,3
Ákra Taínaron, C., 14D2
Akron, 35C4
Akrotíri, 19cB2
Akrotírion Akámas, C., 19cA1
Akrotírion Apostólou, C., 19cA3
Akrotírion Gátas, C., 19cB1,2
Akrotírion Kormakíti, C., 19cA1
Akrotírion Pidálion, C., 19cB3
Aksaray, 21aB2
Akşehir, 21aB2
Aktogaj, 24B1,2
Akt'ubinsk, 16D,E7
Akulurak, 33B3
Akure, 29D7
Akureyri, 15aB3
Akwanga, 29C8
Ala, 13aA4,5
Alabama, Admin. U., 35E3
Alabama, R., 35E3
Alagir, 18D5
Alagoas (2), Admin. U., 38C6
Alagoinhas, 38D6
Alagón, 11F3
Alajuela, 36B4
Al-'Alamayn, 28A5
Al-'Amārah, 21C5
Al-'Āmirīyah, 26aB1,2
Alamogordo, 34E5
Alamos, 36B2
Alanya, 21aB2
Alapajevsk, 17aB3
Al-'Aqabah, 20bC1
Al-'Arīsh, 21C2
Alaska, Admin. U., 33B3-5
Alaska Peninsula, 33C3,4
Alaska Range, Mts., 31C5,6
Alatyr', 18B6
Al-'Ayn, 21E7
Alaverdi, 18aA1
Alba, 13aB2
Al-Bāb, 20bA2
Albacete, 11G3

Alba-Iulia, 14B2
Al-Bahr al-Abyad, R., 28C6
Al-Bahr al-Azraq see Abay
Al-Bahr al-Jabal, R., 28D6
Albania, St., 13B,C4,5
Albany (Australia), 40D1
Albany (U.S.A., Georgia), 35E4
Albany (U.S.A., New York), 35C6
Albany, R., 33C11
Al-Basrah, 21C5
Al-Bawīṭī, 28B5
Al-Bayḍā', 28A5
Alberga, 13aB2
Alberta, Admin. U., 33C8
Albi, 11D3
Ålborg, 12A3
Alborz, Mts., 19F7
Albuquerque, 34D5
Al-Burayml, 21E7
Albury, 40D4
Alcalá de Henares, 11F3
Alcamo, 13C3
Alcañiz, 11F3
Alcántara, 11G2
Alcira, 11G3
Alcoy, 11G3
Alcudia, 11G4
Aldabra Islands, Is. 30B5
Aldan, 16D14
Aldan, R., 16C15
Alderney, I., 6aA2
Aldershot, 9D4
Aleg, 29A2
Alegrete, 39aC2
Aleksandrija, 18C3
Aleksandrov, 17C5
Aleksandrov Gaj, 18B6
Aleksandrovsk, 17aB2
Aleksandrovsk-Sachalinskij, 16D16
Aleksejevka, 18B4
Aleksin, 18B4
Alençon, 11B3
Alenuihaha Channel, Str., 32A13,14
Alert, 32A13,14
Alès, 11C4
Alessandria, 13A2
Ålesund, 15C3
Aletai, 24B2
Aleutian Islands, Is., 32D2-4
Alexander Archipelago, Is., 33C6
Alexander Bay, 30D2
Alexander I. Island, I., 42F8
Alexandria (Romania), 14C3
Alexandria (U.S.A.), 35E2
Alexandria see Al-Iskandarīyah
Alexandroúpolis, 14C3
Al-Fāshir, 28C5
Al-Fayyūm, 28B5,6
Alfonsine, 13aB2
Al-Fujayrah, 21D7
Algeciras, 11G2
Al-Furāt see Firat
Alger, 28A3
Algeria, St., 28B2,3
Alghero, 13B2
Al-Ghurdaqah, 28B6

page 184

Al-Hadīthah, 21 C 4
Al-Hammadah Al-Hamrá, Des., 26 B 5,6
Al-Hasakah, 20 b A 3
Al-Hillah, 21 C 4
Al-Hoceima, 11 H 2,3
Al-Hudaydah, 28 C 7
Al-Hufrah, 28 B 4
Al-Hufūf, 28 B 7
Aliakmón, R., 14 C 2
Ali-Bajramly, 18 a B 2
Alicante, 11 G 3
Alice, 34 F 7
Alice Springs, 40 C 3
Alida, 34 B 6
Alīgarh, 22 a B 1
Al-Iskandarīyah, 28 A 5,6
Al-Ismāʿīliyah, 28 A 6
Al-Jaghbūb, 28 B 5
Al-Jawf (Libya), 28 B 5
Al-Jawf (Saudi Arabia), 28 B 6
Al-Jīzah, 28 A,B 6
Al-Jubayl, 28 B 7
Al-Junaynah, 28 C 5
Al-Karak, 20 b C 1,2
Al-Kāzimīyah, 21 C 4
Al-Khalīl, 20 b C 1
Al-Khandaq, 28 C 5,6
Al-Khārijah, 28 B 6
Al-Khasab, 21 D 7
Al-Khums, 28 A 4
Al-Khurṭūm, 28 C 6
Al-Khurṭūm Baḥrī, 28 C 6
Alkmaar, 12 B 2
Al-Kufrah Oasis, Reg., 28 B 5
Al-Kuwayt, 21 D 5
Al-Lādhiqīyah, 20 b B 1,2
Allāhābād, 22 B 4
Allentown, 35 C 5
Alleppey, 20 a B 1,2
Aller, R., 12 B 3
Alliance, 34 C 6
Allier (03), Admin. U., 11 C 3
Allier, R., 11 C 3
Allison Harbour, 33 a A 1
Alloa, 10 B 3
Alma, 35 B 6
Alma-Ata, 16 E 9
Almada, 11 F 3
Almadén, 11 G 2
Al-Madīnah, 28 B 6,7
Al-Mahallah al-Kubrā, 26 a A,B 2,1
Al-Manāmah, 21 D 6
Al-Mansūrah, 26 a A,B 3
Al-Manzilah, 26 a A 3
Al-Marj, 28 A 4,5
Al-Maṣīrah, I., 21 E 7
Al-Matarīyah, 26 a A 3
Al- Mawṣil, 21 B 4
Almazán, 11 F 3
Almeirim, 38 C 4
Almería, 11 G 2
Al'metjevsk, 18 B 7
Al-Minyā, 28 B 6,7
Al-Mubarraz, 21 D 5,6
Al-Mudawwarah, 20 b C 1,2
Al-Muglad, 28 C 5
Al-Mukallā, 28 C 7
Al-Mukhā, 28 C 7
Alnwick, 9 B 4
Alofi, 41 E 8,9
Alor Setar, 23 C 1,2
Alotau, 40 B 5
Alpena, 35 B 4
Alpes de Haute-Provence (04), Admin. U., 11 D 4
Alpes (Hautes-) (05), Admin. U., 11 C 4
Alpes-Maritimes (06), Admin. U., 11 C 4
Alpine, 34 E 6
Alps, Mts., 19 E 2-4
Al-Qaḍārif, 28 C 6
Al-Qāhirah, 28 A 5,6
Al-Qāʾim, 20 b B 3
Al-Qāmishlī, 20 b A 3
Al-Qantarah, 26 a B 4
Al-Qasr, 28 B 5
Al-Qaṭīf, 21 D 5
Al-Qayṣūmah, 21 D 5
Al-Qusayr, 28 B 6
Alta, 15 A 7
Altai, Mts., 19 E 10-12
Altaj, 24 B 3
Altamaha, R., 35 E 4
Altamira, 38 C 4
Altanbulag, 24 A 4
Alteelva, R., 15 A 7
Altena, 12 a B 4
Altoona, 35 C 5
Alto Paraguai, 38 D 4
Alturas, 34 C 2
Altus, 34 F 7
Al-ʿUbayyiḍ, 28 C 5,6
Al-Uqṣur, 28 B 6
Alušta, 16 a B 2
Alvdal, 15 C 4
Al-Wajh, 28 B 6,7
Alwar, 22 B 3
Alyangula, 40 B 3
Alyialoúsa, 19 c A 3
Alytus, 18 B 1
Amada Gaza, 29 D 9
Amadjuak Lake, L., 33 B 12
Amadora, 11 G 1
Amakusa-shotō, Is., 25 D 4
Amapá, 38 B 4
Amapá, Admin. U., 38 B 4
Amarillo, 34 D 6
Amasya, 21 a A 3
Amazonas, Admin. U., 38 C 3,4
Amazonas, R., 37 C 2
Ambāla, 22 A 3
Ambanja, 30 C 5
Ambarčik, 16 C 17,18
Ambarnyj, 17 A 4
Ambato, 38 C 2
Ambatondrazaka, 30 C 5
Ambatosoratra, 30 C 5
Amberg, 12 C 3,4
Ambérieu, 11 C 4
Ambidédi, 29 B 3
Ambon, 23 D 4
Ambositra, 30 D 5
Ambovombe, 30 D 5
Ambriz, 30 B 2
Ambrose Channel, Chann., 32 a
Amderma, 16 B,C 8
Amdo, 24 C 3
American Highlands, Reg., 42 G 28,29
American Samoa, Admin. U., 41 c A,B 3,4
Amery, 33 C 10
Amery Ice Shelf, 42 F 29
Ameson, 35 B 4
Amfípolis, 14 C 2,3
Amga, R., 16 C 15
Amguid, 28 B 3
Amiens, 11 B 3
Amirante Islands, Is., 27 E 10
Amlekhganj, 22 a B 3
Ammān, 20 b C 1,2
Ammassalik, 33 B 16
Ammókhostos, 19 c A 2,3
Amnok-kang, R., 25 B 4
Amorgós, I., 14 D 3
Ampanihy, 30 D 5
Amrāvati, 22 B 3
Amritsar, 22 A 3
Amsterdam, 12 B 2
Amudarja, R., 16 E,F 8
Am Timan, 28 C 4,5
Amundsen Gulf, G., 33 A 7
Amundsen-Scott, Station, 42 H
Amundsen Sea, 42 G 11,12
Amuntai, 23 D 3
Amur, R., 16 D 14
Anabar, R., 16 B 13
Anaconda, 34 B 4
Anacortes, 33 a B 2,3
Anadyr', 16 C 19
Anadyr', R., 16 C 19
Anadyrskij Zaliv, B., 16 C 20
'Ānah, 20 b B 3
Anaheim, 34 E 3
Anahim Lake, 33 a A 2
Anambra (1), Admin. U., 29 D 7
Anamur, 21 a B 2
Anapa, 18 D 4
Anápolis, 38 D 4,5
Anār, 21 C 6,7
Anarjokka, R., 15 A 8
Anchorage, 33 B 4,5
Ancona, 13 B 3
Ancud, 39 C 1
Anda, 24 B 6
Åndalsnes, 15 C 3
Andalucía (1), Admin. U., 11 G 2
Andaman Islands, 22 C 5
Andaman Sea, 22 C 5
Andeg, 17 A 8
Anderson, R., 33 B 7
Andes, Mts., 37 C-G 2,3
Andfjorden, Str., 15 A 6
Andhra Pradesh, Admin. U., 22 C 3,4
Andong, 25 C 4
Andorra, 11 F 4
Andorra, St., 11 F 4
Andover, 9 D 4
Andøya, I., 15 A 5,6
Andria, 13 B 4
Andropov see Rybinsk
Andros, I., 14 D 3
Andros Island, I., 35 G 5
Andros Town, 35 G 5
Andújar, 11 G 2
Anécho, 29 D 6
Angara, R., 16 D 11
Ångarsk, 16 b B 1
Ånge, 15 C 5,6
Angeles, 23 b A 2
Angermanälven, R., 15 B,C 6
Angers, 11 C 2
Angicos, 38 C 6
Anglesey, I., 7 E 5
Angmagssalik see Ammassalik
Angoche, 30 C 4,5
Angola, St., 30 C 2,3
Angoulême, 11 C 3
Angra do Heroísmo, 11 a A 3
Anguilla, Admin. U., I., 36 b A 2
Anhui (6), Admin. U., 24 C 5

Aniak, 33 B 4
Anjouan, I., 30 C 5
Anju, 25 C 4
Ankang, 24 C 4,5
Ankara, 21 a A 2
Anna, 18 B 5
Annaba, 28 A 3
An-Nabk, 20 b B 2
An-Nafūd, Des., 19 G 6
An-Najaf, 21 C 4
Annan, 10 C 3
Annan, R., 10 C 3
Annapolis, 35 B 5
Ann Arbor, 35 B 4
An-Nāṣirīyah, 21 C 5
Annecy, 11 C 4
Anniston, 35 E 3
An-Nuḥūd, 28 C 5
Anqing, 24 C 5
Anshan, 24 B 6
Anshun, 24 D 4
Ansongo, 29 B 6
Antalya, 21 a B 3
Antalaha, 30 C 6
Antalya, 21 a B 2
Antalya Körfezi, B., 21 a B 2
Antananarivo, 30 C 5
Antarctica, 42
Antarctic Peninsula, Pen., 42 F,G 6,7
Antequera, 11 G 2
Antigua, I., 36 b A 2
Antigua and Barbuda, St., 36 b A 2
Antofagasta, 39 A 1,2
Antonina, 39 A 5
Antrim, 10 D 6
Antrim (1), Admin. U., 10 D 6
Antrim Mountains, Mts., 7 D 4,5
Antserana, 30 C 5,6
Antsirabe, 30 C,D 5
Antsohihy, 30 C 5
Antwerpen, 11 B 4
Anuradhapura, 20 a B 3
Anvers see Antwerpen
Anxi, 24 B 3
Anyang, 24 C 5
Aomori, 25 B 7
Aosta, 13 A 1
Aotou, 19 a A 4
Aoulef, 28 B 3
Apa, R., 39 A 3
Aparri, 23 b A 2
Apatity, 17 A 4
Ape, 17 C 3
Apeldoorn, 12 B 2
Apia, 41 c A 2
Apoteri, 38 B 3
Appalachian Mountains, Mts., 31 E,F 12,13
Appenines, Mts., 5 C,D 5,6
Appleby, 10 C 3
Appleton, 35 B 3
Apšeronsk, 18 D 4
Apucarana, 39 a B 3
Apure, R., 37 B 3
Apurímac, R., 37 D 2
Arabatskaja Strelka, Pen., 16 a A,B 2
Arabian Peninsula, Pen., 19 G,H 6,7
Arabian Sea, 3
Aracaju, 38 D 6
Aracatuba, 39 a B 3,4
Araçuai, 38 D 5
Arad, 14 B 2
Arafura Sea, 23 D 5

page 185

Aragón (2), Admin. U., 11F3
Aragón, R., 11F3
Araguaia, R., 37D4,5
Araguaina, 38C5
Araguari, 38D5
Arāk, 21C5
Aral'sk, 16E8
Aral'skoje More, L., 16E7,8
Aranda de Duero, 11F3
Aran Islands, Is., 7E2,3
Aran Island, I., 7D3
Aranjuez, 11F3
Araouane, 29A5
Arapiraca, 38C,D6
Arapkir, 21aB3
Araranguá, 39aC4
Araraquara, 39aB4
Aras, R., 21A,B4
Arauca, 38B2
Arauca, R., 38B2
Araxá, 38D5
Arba Minch, 28D6
Arbroath, 10B3
Arcachon, 11C2
Archangel'sk, 16C6
Archipiélago de Colón, Is., Admin. U., 4
Archipiélago de los Chonos, Is., 37G2
Arctic Bay, 33A11
Arctic Ocean, 3
Arctic Red River, 33B6
Ardabīl, 21B5
Ardahan, 18aA1
Ardakān, 21C6
Ardèche (07), Admin. U., 11C4
Ardennes (08), Admin. U., 11B4
Ardennes, Mts., 5B,C5
Ardestān, 21C6
Ards (2), Admin. U., 10D7
Åre, 15C5
Arena, 34B5
Arendal, 15D4
Arenosa, 34a
Arequipa, 38D2
Arezzo, 11F3
Argao, 23bC2
Argentan, 11B2,3
Argenteuil, 11B3
Argentina, St., 39A-D1-2
Argeșul, R., 14B3
Argolikós Kólpos, B., 14D2
Árgos, 14D2
Argostólion, 14D2
Argun', R., 16D13
Argungu, 29B7
Århus, 12A3
Aribinda, 29B5
Arica (Brazil), 38B2
Arica (Chile), 38D2
Ariège (09), Admin. U., 11D3
Aripuanã, R., 38C3,4
Arizona, Admin. U., 34D,E4,5
Arjeplog, 15B6
Arkadak, 18B5
Arkalyk, 16D8
Arkansas, Admin. U., 35E2
Arkansas, R., 34D5
Arklow, 10E6
Arles, 11D4
Arlington (U.S.A., Texas), 34E7

Arlington (U.S.A., Virginia), 35D5
Arlington (U.S.A., Washington), 33aB3
Arlit, 29A7
Armagh, 10D6
Armagh (3), Admin. U., 10D6
Arm'ansk, 16aA3
Armavir, 18C,D5
Armenia, 38B2
Armenian Soviet Socialist Republic, Admin. U., 18aA,B1,2
Armidale, 40D5
Armstrong Station, 35A,B3
Arnaud, R., 33C12
Arnhem, 12B,C2
Arnhem Land, Reg., 40B3
Arnøy, I., 15A7
Arorae, I., 41D7
Arquipélago dos Bijagós, Arch., 29C1,2
Ar-Rab' al-Khāli, Des., 19G,H6,7
Arrah, 22aB3
Ar-Rahad, 28C6
Arraiján, 34a
Ar-Ramādī, 21C4
Arran, I., 7D5
Ar-Raqqah, 20bA,B2
Ar-Riyāḍ, 28B7
Ar-Rutbah, 21C4
Arsenjev, 24B7
Ársos, 19cB1
Árta, 14D2
Artem, 16aB2
Artemisa, 36aA2
Artigas, 39aD2
Artik, 18aA1
Art'om, 25B5
Art'omovsk, 18C4
Art'omovskij, 17aB3
Artvin, 21aA4
Arua, 28D6
Aruba, Admin. U., I., 36C5
Arucas, 26bB2,3
Arunachal Pradesh, Admin. U., 22B5
Arusha, 30B4
Aruvi, R., 22B4
Arvajcheer, 24B4
Arvidsjaur, 15B6,7
Arvika, 15D5
Arzamas, 17C6
Arzgir, 18C5
Aša, 17aB,C2
Asab, 30D2
Asahikawa, 25B7
Asamankese, 29D5
Asansol, 22B4
Asbest, 17aB3
Ascension, I., 27E3
Aschabad, 16F7,8
Ascoli Piceno, 13B3
Aseb, 28D6
Asela, 28D6
Ashburton, R., 40C1
Ashcroft, 33aB3
Asheville, 35D4
Ashford (U.K.), 9D5
Ashford (U.S.A.), 33aC3
Ash Fork, 34D4
Ashington, 9B4
Ashland, 35B2
Ash-Shaqrā', 28B7
Ash-Shāriqah, 21D6,7

Ash-Sharmah, 28B6
Ash-Shihr, 28C7
Ashtabula, 35C4,5
Ashton under Lyne, 9C3,4
Asia, 3
Asiago, 13aA5
Asia Minor, Pen., 19F4,5
Asilah, 11H2
Asino, 16D10
Askino, 17aB2
Askja, Vol., 5A3
Asmera, 28C6
Asola, 13aA4
Asosa, 28C,D6
Aspres, 11C4
As-Sallūm, 28A5
As-Samāwah, 21C4,5
As-Sālihiyah, 26aB3,4
Assen, 12B2
As-Sinbillāwayn, 26aB3
Assis, 39aB3
Assiniboine, R., 34A7
As-Sulaymānīyah (Iraq), 21B5
As-Sulaymānīyah (Saudi Arabia), 28B7
As-Sulayyil, 28B7
Assumption Island, I., 30B5
As-Suwaydā', 20bB2
As-Suways, 28A,B6
Astara, 16F6
Asti, 13A2
Astipálaia, I., 14D3
Astorga, 11F2
Astoria, 34B2
Astove Island, I., 30C5
Astrachan', 16E6,7
Asturias (7), Admin. U., 11F2
Asunción, 39A3
Aswān, 28B6
Asyūṭ, 28B6
Atakpamé, 29D6
Atar, 28B1
Atasu, 24B1
Atbarah, 28C6
Atbarah', R., 28C6
Atebubu, 29D5
Athabasca, 33C8
Athabasca, R., 33C8
Athenry, 10E5
Athens, 10E5
Athens (U.S.A.), 35E4
Athens see Athínai
Athi, R., 30B4
Athínai, 14D2,3
Athlone, 10E6
Athy, 10E6
Ati, 28C4
Atimaono, 41dB2
Atkarsk, 18B6
Atlanta, 35E4
Atlantic City, 35D6
Atlantic Lowlands, Pl., 31F12,13
Atlantic Ocean, 3
Atlas Mountains, Mts., 26A4,5
Atlas Tellien, Mts., 5D5
Atrak, R., 21B7
Ātran, R., 15D5
At-Tā'if, 28B7
Attawapiskat, R., 33C11
At-Tayrīyah, 26aB2
Attu, 32D2
At-Tūr, 28B6
At-Turayf, 20bC2

Aube (10), Admin. U., 11B3
Auburn, 33aC3
Auch, 11D3
Auckland, 40aA2
Auckland Islands, Is., 3
Aude (11), Admin. U., 11D3
Augsburg, 12C3
Augusta (Australia), 40D1
Augusta (U.S.A., Georgia), 35E4
Augusta (U.S.A., Maine), 35C6,7
Augusta (U.S.A., Montana), 34B4
Augustów, 12B6
Auki, 40A6
Aurangābād, 22C3
Aurillac, 11C3
Aurora (U.S.A., Colorado), 34D6
Aurora (U.S.A., Illinois), 35C3
Aurukun, 40B4
Ausiait, 33B14
Austin (U.S.A., Minnesota), 35C2
Austin (U.S.A., Nevada), 34D3
Austin (U.S.A., Texas), 34E7
Australia, St., 40C1-5
Australian Alps, Mts., 40D4
Austria, St. 12C,D3-5
Austvågøy, I., 15A5
Autun, 11C4
Auxerre, 11C3
Avarua, 41F10
Aveiro, 11F1
Aveiro (1), Admin. U., 11F1
Avellino, 13B3
Aves, I., 36bB2
Aveyron (12), Admin. U., 11D3
Avezzano, 13B3
Aviemore, 10B3
Avignon, 11D4
Ávila, 11F2
Avilés, 11F2
Avon (8), Admin. U., 9D3
Avon (English Channel), R., 7E7
Avon (North Sea), R., 7F7
Awasa, 28D6
Awaso, 29D5
Awash, 28D7
Awash, R., 28C7
Awbārī, 28B4
Awjlan, 28B5
Axel Heiberg Island, I., 33A10,11
Axim, 29D5
Axiós, R., 14C2
Ayacucho (Argentina), 39aE2
Ayacucho (Peru), 38D2
Ayamonte, 11G2
Ayancık, 21aA2
Aydın, 21aB1
Áyion Óros, Pen., 14C2,3
Aylesbury, 9D4
Ayorou, 29B6
'Ayoûn el 'Atroûs, 28C2
Ayr, 10C2
Ayvalık, 14D3
Azare, 29C8

Azerbaijan Soviet Socialist Republic, Admin. U., 18a A2
Azores, Is., 11a
Azov, 18 C4
Azovskoje More, S., 16 E5
Azu, 39 B2,3
Az-Zagāziq, 26a B3
Az-Zarqā', 20b B2
Az-Zāwiyah, 28 A4

B

Baba Burnu, C., 19 F4,5
Babajevo, 17 C5
Bāb-el-Mandeb, Chann., 26 C9
Bābol, 21 B6
Babuškin, 17b
Babuyan Islands, Is., 23 B4
Bacabal, 38 C5
Bacău, 14 B1
Bachčisaraj, 16a B1,2
Bachmač, 18 B3
Back, R., 33 B9
Bacolod, 23 B4
Bács-Kiskun (1), Admin. U., 14 B1
Badajoz, 11 G2
Badalona, 11 F4
Badanah, 21 C3,4
Baden-Baden, 12 C3
Baden-Württemberg (1), Admin. U., 12 C3
Bad Ischl, 12 D4
Badulla, 20a C3,4
Bærum, 15 D4
Bafatá, 29 B2
Baffin Island, I., 33 A,B11-15
Baffin Sea, 33 A12,13
Bafing, R., 29 B3
Bafoulabé, 29 B3
Bafoussam, 29 D8
Bāfq, 21 C7
Bafra, 21 A2
Baga, 29 B9
Bagamoyo, 30 B4
Bagansiapi-api, 19b C2
Bagdarin, 16b B3
Bāgē, 39a D3
Baghdād, 21 C4,5
Baghlān, 22 A2
Baguio, 23 B4
Bahamas, St., Is., 35 F5
Baharampur, 22a B3,4
Bahāwalpur, 22 B3
Bahia, Admin. U., 38 D5,6
Bahía Blanca, 39 B2
Bahía Blanca, B., 39 B2,3
Bahia Grande, B., 39 D2
Bahir Dar, 28 C6
Bahrain, St., 21 D6
Bahr al-'Arab, R., 28 D5
Bahr al-Milh, L., 20b B3
Bahr Aouk, R., 28 D4,5
Bahr Azoum, R., 28 C5
Bahr el Ghazal, R., 28 C4
Bahret al-Assad, Res., 21 B3
Baía de Setúbal, B., 11 G1
Baia-Mare, 14 B2
Baichéng, 24 B2
Baidoa, 28 D7
Baie-Comeau, 35 B7
Baie de la Seine, B., 11 B2

Baile Átha Cliath see Dublin
Bailuondo, 30 C2
Bairin Youqi, 25 B2
Baise, 24 D4
Baiyunebo, 24 B4
Baja, 14 B1
Baja California, Pen., 31 F,G9
Baja California Norte (2), Admin. U., 36 B1
Baja California Sur (3), Admin. U., 36 B1
Bajanchongor, 24 B4
Bajangol, 16b B1
Bajan-Uul, 24 B5
Bajkal, 16b B1,2
Bajkal'sk, 16b B1
Bajkonur, 16 E8
Bajo Nuevo, Is., 36 C5
Bajram-Ali, 21 B8
Bakal, 17a C2
Bakel, 29 B2
Baker, 34 C3
Baker Island, I., 41 D8
Baker Lake, 33 B10
Baker Lake, L., 33 B10
Bakersfield, 34 D3
Bakhtarān, 21 C5
Baku, 16 E6,7
Bala (Canada), 33b
Bala (U.K.), 9 C3
Balabac Island, I., 23 C3
Balabac Strait, 23 C3
Ba labakk, 20b B2
Balaklava, 18 C4
Balakleja, 18 B4
Balakovo, 18 B6
Balašov, 18 B5
Balaton, L., 14 B1
Balboa Heights, 34a
Balbriggan, 10 E6,7
Balcarce, 39a E2
Balchaš, 16 E9
Balčík, 14 C4
Baleares (4), Admin. U., 11 G4
Baleares Islas, Is., 11 F,G4
Balearic Islands see Baleares Islas
Bali, I., 23 D3
Balıkesir, 21a B1
Balikpapan, 23 D3
Balintang Channel, 23 B3,4
Balinzuoqi, 25 B2
Balkan Peninsula, Pen., 5 C6,7
Ballarat, 40 D4
Ballater, 10 B3
Ballé, 29 B3
Balleny Islands, Is., 42 F20,1
Ballina, 10 D5
Ballinasloe, 10 E5
Ballycastle, 10 D6
Ballymena, 10 D6
Ballymena (4), Admin. U., 10 D6
Ballymoney, 10 D6
Ballymoney (5), Admin. U., 10 D6
Ballyshannon, 10 D5,6
Balonne, R., 40 C4,5
Balsas, 38 C5
Balsas, R. 36 C2
Balta, 18 C2
Baltic Sea, 15 D,E6,7
Baltijsk, 17 D1,2
Baltim, 26a A3
Baltimore, 35 D5

Bam, 21 D7
Bama, 29 C9
Bamako, 29 B4
Bamba, 29 A5
Bambari, 28 D5
Bamberg, 12 C3
Bambuí, 39a B4
Bamenda, 29 D8
Bāmiān, 22 A2
Bampūr, 21 D8
Banaba, I., 41 D6,7
Banamba, 29 B4
Banana, 30 B2
Banās, R., 22 B3
Banbridge, 10 D6
Banbridge (6), Admin. U., 10 D6
Banbury, 9 C4
Bancroft, 33b
Bānda, 22a B2
Banda Aceh, 23 C1
Banda Sea, 23 D4,5
Bandama, R., 29 C4
Bandar 'Abbās, 21 D7
Bandar-e Anzali, 21 B5
Bandar-e Khomeyni, 21 C5,6
Bandar-e Lengeh, 21 D6
Bandar-e Torkeman, 21 B6
Bandar Seri Begawan, 23 C3
Bandiagara, 29 B5
Bandirma, 21a A1
Bandon, 10 F5
Bandundu, 30 B2
Bandung, 23 D2
Banes, 36a B6
Banff (Canada), 33 C8
Banff (U.K.), 10 B3
Banfora, 29 C4
Bangalore, 22 C3
Bangassou, 28 D5
Bangbu, 24 C5
Banghāzī, 28 A4,5
Bangka,, I., 23 D2
Bangkalan, 23a A3
Bangkok see Krung Thep
Bangladesh, St., 22a B,C4
Bangor (U.K., Northern Ireland), 10 D7
Bangor (U.K., Wales), 9 C,3
Bangor (U.S.A.), 35 C7
Bangui, 28 D4
Banhā, 26a B3
Bani, R., 29 B4
Bani Suwayf, 28 B6
Bāniyās, 20b B1
Banja Luka, 13 A4
Banjarmasin, 23 D3
Banjul, 29 B1
Bank, 18a B2
Bankas, 29 B5
Banks Island, I., 33 A7,8
Banks Strait, Str., 40 E4
Bann, R., 7 D4
Banská Bystrica, 12 C5
Bantry, 10 F5
Bantry Bay, B., 7 F2,3
Banyo, 29 D8,9
Banyuwangi, 23 D3
Baoding, 24 C5
Baoji, 24 C4
Baotou, 24 B4,5
Baoulé, R., 29 C4
Bar, 13 B4
Baracoa, 36a B6
Barakah, R., 28 C6
Bārān, 22a B1
Baranoviči, 18 B2

Baranya (2), Admin. U., 14 B1
Barbacena, 38 E5
Barbados, St., I., 36b B2
Barbar, 28 C6
Barbuda, I., 36a A2
Barcellona, 13 C3
Barcelona, 11 F4
Barcelona-Puerto la Cruz, 38 A3
Barcelos, 38 C3
Barcoo, R., 40 C4
Barddhamān, 22a C3,4
Bardera, 28 D7
Bardi, 13a B3
Bardīyah, 28 A5
Bardsey Island, I., 9 C2
Bardsnehorn, C., 15a B4
Bareilly, 22 B3,4
Barents Sea, 16 B4-7
Barfleur, 6a A3
Bari, 13 B4
Barinas, 38 B2,3
Bāris, 28 B6
Barisāl, 22a C4
Barito, R., 23 D3
Barkley Sound, B., 33 B C1,5
Bar-le-Duc, 11 B4
Barletta, 13 B4
Barmer, 22 B3
Barnaul, 16 D9,10
Barnes, 9a
Barneville-Carteret, 6a A3
Barnouic, Is., 6a A2
Barnsley, 9 C4
Barnstaple, 9 D2
Baro, 29 C7
Baro, R., 28 C6
Barqah, Reg., 28 A5
Barquisimeto, 38 A3
Barra, 38 D5
Barra, I., 7 C4
Barrado Garças, 38 D4
Barragen de Alqueva, Res., 11 G2
Barra Head, C., 7 C4
Barrancabermeja, 38 B2
Barranquilla, 38 A2
Barraute, 35 B5
Barreiras, 38 D5
Barreiro, 11 G1
Barretos, 39a B4
Barrie, 33b
Barrington Tops, Mt., 40 D7
Barrow, 33 A4
Barrow, R., 7 E4
Barrow-in-Furness, 9 B3
Barrow Strait, 33 A10
Barry, 9 D3
Barstow, 31a C,D2
Bartica, 38 B4
Bartın, 21a A2
Bartle Frere, Mt., 40 B4
Barumun, R., 19b D1,2
Barwon, R., 40 C4
Baryš, 18 B6
Basel, 11 C4
Bashi Channel, 24 D6
Basilan Island, I., 23 C4
Basildon, 9 D5
Basilicata (2), Admin. U., 13 B4
Basingstoke, 9 D4
Baskir Autonomous Soviet Socialist Republic, Admin. U., 17a B,C1,2

page 187

Bassano, 34 A4
Bassano del Grappa, 13aA5
Bassari, 29C6
Bassas da India, I., 30D4
Bassein, 22C5
Basse Santa Su, 29B2
Basseterre, 36bA2
Basse Terre, 36bA2
Bassila, 29C6
Bass Strait, Str., 40D4
Bastia, 11D5
Bastogne, 11B4
Bata, 29E8
Batajsk, 18C4,5
Batang, 24C,D3
Batangas, 23B4
Batan Islands, Is., 23A4
Batdâmbâng, 22C6
Bath, 9D3
Bathurst (Australia), 40D4
Bathurst (Canada), 35B7
Bathurst Inlet, 33B9
Bathurst Island, I., (Australia), 40B2
Bathurst Island, I., (Canada), 33A9,10
Batié, 29C5
Batman, 21A3
Batna, 28A3
Baton Rouge, 35E5
Batouri, 29D9
Battersea, 9a
Batticaloa, 20A3
Battle Harbour, 33C14
Batu, Mt., 26D8
Batumi, 16E5,6
Batu Pahat, 19bD3
Baturaja, 23D2
Baubau, 23D4
Bauchi, 29C8
Bauchi (2), Admin. U., 29C8
Baukau, 23D4
Bauru, 38E5
Bawku, 29C5
Bayamo, 36aB5
Bayamón, 36bA1
Baybay, 23bB3,4
Bayburt, 21aA4
Bay City, 35F1
Bayern (2), Admin. U., 12C4
Bayeux, 11B2
Bay of Bengal, B., 22C4
Bay of Biscay, B., 11E,F2,3
Bay of Fundy, B., 33D13
Bayonne, 11D2
Bayreuth, 12C3
Bayrūt, 21aA4
Baza, 11G3
Bazdār, 21D8,9
Beachy Head, C., 7F8
Bear Island see Bjørnøya
Beås, R., 22A3
Beatrice, 35C1
Beau-Bassin, 30aB3
Beauceville-Est, 35B6
Beaufort Sea, 33A5,6
Beaufort West, 30E3
Beauharnois Lock, 33b
Beauly, R., 7C5
Beaumont, 35E2
Beaune, 11C4
Beauvais, 11B3
Beaver, R., 33C9
Beaver, R., 34B2
Beáwar, 22B3
Bebedouro, 39aB4

Béchar, 28A2
Beckley, 35D4
Bedford, 9C4
Bedfordshire (9), Admin. U., 9C4
Bedlington, 9B4
Beechey Point, 33A5
Be'er Sheva', 20bC1
Begna, R., 15C4
Behbehān, 21C6
Behai, 24D4
Beian, 24B6
Beijing, 24C5
Beijing (28), Admin. U., 24B5
Beipiao, 25B3
Beira, 30C4
Beirut see Bayrūt
Beitbridge, 30D3,4
Beja (2), Admin. U., 11G2
Beja, 11G2
Béja, 28A3
Bajaia, 28A3
Béjar, 11F2
Békés (3), Admin. U., 14B2
Békéscsaba, 14B2
Bela, 22B2
Belaja, R., 17aC2
Belaja Cerkov', 18C3
Belcher Islands, Is., 33C11,12
Bel'cy, 18C2
Beled Weyne, 28D7
Belém, 38C5
Belfast, 10D6,7
Belfast (7), Admin. U., 10D7
Belfast Lough, B., 7D5
Belfort, 11C4
Belgaum, 22C3
Belgium, St., 11B3,4
Belgorod, 18B4
Belgorod-Dnestrovskij, 18C2,3
Belgrade see Beograd
Belitung, 23D2
Belize, 36C4
Belize, St., 36C4
Bella Coola, 33aA1,2
Bellary, 22C3
Bella Vista, 39aC4
Belle Fourche, 34C6
Belle-Île, I., 11C2
Belleville, 35C5
Bellevue, 12E4
Bellingham, 34B2
Bellingshausen Sea, 42F,G,8-10
Bello, 38B2
Belluno, 13A2,3
Belmopan, 36C4
Belmullet, 10D5
Belo, 30C5
Belo Horizonte, 38D,E5
Beloje More, S., 16C5,6
Belomorsko-Baltijskij Kanal, Can., 17A2,3
Belopolje, 18B3
Belorečensk, 18D4,5
Beloreck, 17aC2
Belo'ov, 18B4
Beloz'orsk, 17B,C5
Belyj Jar, 16D10
Bembe, 30B2
Bemidji, 35B2
Benavente, 11F2

Benbecula, I., 7C4
Bend, 34C2
Bendaja, 29D3
Bendel (3), Admin. U., 29D7
Bender Beila, 28D7,8
Bendery, 18C2
Bendigo, 40D4
Benevento, 13B3
Bengkalis, 19bD2,3
Bengkulu, 23D2
Beni, R., 38D3
Béni Abbès, 28A2
Beni-Mellal, 28A2
Benin, St., 29C6
Benin City, 29D7
Benjamin Constant, 38C2,3
Ben Lawers, Mt., 7C5
Ben Lomond, Mt., 7C5
Ben Macdhui, Mt., 7C5,6
Ben More (U.K., Mull), Mt., 7C4,5
Ben More (U.K., North West Highlands), Mt., 7B5
Ben Nevis, Mt., 7C5
Benoni, 30D3
Bénoué, R., 29C9
Benue see Bénoué
Benue (4), Admin. U., 29D8
Ben Wyvis, Mt., 7C5
Benxi, 24B6
Benzu, 5aB3
Beograd, 13A5
Berat, 13B4,5
Berbera, 28C7
Berbérati, 28D4
Berck-sur-Mer, 9D5
Berd'ansk, 18C4
Berdičev, 18C2
Beregovo, 18C1
Berens, R., 33A12
Berens River, 33C10
Berežany, 18C1
Bereznik, 17B6
Berezniki, 16D7,8
Berezovka, 18C2
Berezovo, 16C8
Berga, 11F4
Bergama, 21aB1
Bergen, 15C3
Bergerac, 11C3
Berhampur, 22C4
Beringovskij, 16C19
Bering Sea, 33B,C2,3
Bering Strait, Str. 33B3
Berkatit, 16D14
Berkeley, 34D2
Berkner Island, I., 42G,H5,6
Berkshire (10), Admin. U., 9D4
Berlevåg, 15A9
Berlin, 12B4
Berlin (1), Admin. U., 12B4
Bermejo, R., 37E3,4
Bermondsee, 9a
Bermuda, Admin. U., Is., 32F14
Bern, 11C4
Bernburg, 12C3
Beroun, 12C4
Ber'ozka, 18B1,2
Ber'ozovka, 18C3
Ber'ozovsk, 16C8

Berwick-upon-Tweed, 10C3
Besançon, 11C4
Beslan, 18D5
Besni, 21aB3
Bessarabka, 18C2
Bétaré Oya, 29D9
Bethal Green, 9a
Bethel, 33B3
Bethlehem, 30D3
Bethune, 11B3
Béthune, R., 9E5
Betroka, 30D5
Betsiamites, 35B7
Betsiboka, R., 30C5
Bettles Field, 33B4
Bettola, 13aB3
Betwa, R., 22aB1
Beverley, 9C4
Bexhill, 9D5
Beykoz, 14C4
Beyla, 29C3
Beypazarı, 21aA2
Beyşehir, 21aB2
Beyşehir Gölü, L., 21aB2
Bežeck, 17C5
Béziers, 11D3
Bhāgalpur, 22B4
Bhaktapur, 22a B3
Bhatinda, 22A3
Bhātpāra, 22aC4
Bhāvnagar, 22B3
Bhilai, 22B3
Bhopāl, 22B3
Bhubaneswar, 22B,C4
Bhuj, 22B2
Bhutan, St., 22aB4
Biak, 23D5
Biak, I., 23D5
Biała Podlaska, 12B,C6
Białogard, 12B5
Białystok, 12B6
Biarritz, 11D2
Bida, 29C7
Biddeford, 35C6,7
Bideford, 9D2
Biel, 11C4
Bielefeld, 12B3
Bielsko-Biała, 12C5
Bié Plateau, Plat., 26F6
Big Delta, 33B5
Biggar, 34A5
Bighorn, R., 34B5
Bight of Benin, 29D6,7
Bight of Bonny, 29D,E7,8
Big Quill Lake, L., 34A6
Bihać, 13A4
Bihār, 22aB3
Bihār, Admin. U., 22B4
Bijāpur, 22C3
Bījār, 21B5
Bijeljina, 13A4
Bijie, 24D4
Bijsk, 16D10
Bīkāner, 22B3
Bikin, 16E15
Bikini, I., 41B6
Bilāspur, 22B4
Bilbao, 11F3
Bilbays, 26aB3
Bilbino, 16C18,19
Billings, 34B5
Bilma, 28C4
Biloxi, 35F3
Bilqās Qism Awwal, 26aA3
Biltine, 28C5
Bīna-Etāwa, 22aB1
Bindura, 30C4

page 188

Binghamton, 35C5
Bingöl, 21aB4
Binjai, 19bC1
Bintulu, 23C3
Bioko, I., 26D5
Birao, 28C,D5
Biraṭnagar, 22aB3
Birdsville, 40C3
Birdum, 40B3
Birecik, 21aB3
Birendranagar, 22aA2
Bir Hooker, 26aB2
Birjand, 21C7
Birkat Qārūn, L., 26aC2
Birkenhead, 9C3
Birlad, 14B3
Birmingham (U.K.), 9C4
Birmingham (U.S.A.), 35E3
Bir Mogrein, 28B1
Birnin Kebbi, 29B7
Birni Nkonni, 29B7
Birobidžan, 16E15
Birr, 10E6
Birsk, 17aB2
Birtle, 34A6
Biržai; 17C2
Bishoftohen, 12D4
Bisha, 28C6
Bishop, 34D3
Biskra, 28A3
Bislig, 23bC3
Bismarck, 34B6
Bismarck Archipelago, Arch., 41D4,5
Bissau, 29B,C2
Bistriţa, 14B3
Bistriţa, R., 14B3
Bitlis, 21aB4
Bitola, 13B5
Bitterfontein, 30E2
Biu, 29C9
Biwa-ko, L., 25C6
Bizerte, 28,A3,4
Björna, 15C6
Björneya, I., 42C21
Blackburn, 9C3
Blackpool, 9C3
Black Sea, C7,8
Black Volta see Volta Noire
Blackwater, R., (Ireland), 7E3
Blackwater, R., (U.K.), 10D6
Blagodarnyj, 18C5
Blagoevgrad, 14C2
Blagoevgrad (1), Admin. U., 14C2
Blagoveščensk (U.S.S.R., Chabarovsk), 16D14
Blagoveščensk (U.S.S.R., Ufa), 17aB2
Blair Athol, 40C4
Blanca Peak, Mt., 31F10
Blanes, 11C7
Blanquillo, 39aD2
Blantyre, 30C4
Blasket Islands, Is., 7E2
Blida, 28A3
Blind River, 35B4
Blitta, 29C7
Bloemfontein, 30D3
Blois, 11C3
Bloomington, 35C2
Bluefields, 36C4
Blue Mountains, Mts., 40D4,5
Blue Nile see Abay
Bluff Knoll, Mt., 40D1

Blumenau, 39A3,4
Blyth, 9B4
Blythe, 34E3,4
Bo 29C,D3
Boac, 23bB2
Boa Vista, 38B3
Boa Vista, I., 28aB2
Bobo Dioulasso, 29C4,5
Bobrov, 18B5
Bobrujsk, 18B2
Bôca do Acre, 38C3
Bocaranga, 29D9
Bochum, 12aB3
Bodajbo, 16D13
Bodélé, Reg., 26C6
Boden, 15B7
Bodensee, L., 12D3
Bodmin, 9D2
Bodmin Moor, Reg., 7F5
Bodö, 15B5
Bodrum, 21aB1
Boende, 30B3
Boffa, 29C2
Bogdanovič, 17aB3
Bognor Regis, 9D4
Bogor, 23D2
Bogorodskoje, 17b
Bogotá, 38B2
Boguĉar, 18C5
Bogué, 29A2
Bo Hai, R., 24C5,6
Bohemian Forest, Mts., 5C6
Bohol, I., 23C4
Boise, 34C3
Boise City, 34D6
Bojnūrd, 21B7
Bojuru, 39D3
Boké, 29C2
Boknafjorden, B., 15D3
Bokovskaja, 18C5
Bol, 28C4
Bolama, 29C2
Bole, 29C5
Bolgatanga, 29C5
Bolgrad, 18C2
Boli, 25A5
Bolívar, 39aE1
Bolivia, St., 38D3,4
Bollnäs, 15C6
Bologna, 13A2
Bologoje, 17C4
Bol'šaja Gluŝica, 18B7
Bol'šoj Irgiz, R., 18B6
Bol'šoj Kavkaz, Mts., 19E5,6
Bol'šoj Uzen', R., 18B6
Bolton, 9C3
Bolu, 21aA2
Bolzano, 13A2
Boma, 30B2
Bombala, 40D4,5
Bombay, 22C3
Bomi Hills, 29D3
Bom Jesus da Lapa, 38D5
Bornu, R., 28D5
Bonas Hill, H., 7A7
Bonda, 30B2
Bondo, 28D5
Bondoukou, 29C4
Bondowoso, 23aA3
Bong, 29D3
Bongor, 28C4
Bonny, 29D7
Bonthain, 23D3
Bonthe, 29D2
Bontoc, 23bA2

Booué, 30B2
Boquerón, 36aC6
Bor (U.S.S.R.), 17C6
Bor (Yugoslavia), 13A5
Borama, 28C,D7
Borås, 15D5
Borba, 38C4
Bordeaux, 11C2
Borders (55), Admin. U., 9B3
Borđeyri, 15aB2
Bordj Omar Driss, 28B3
Bordo (5), Admin. U., 29B9
Borgarnes, 15aB2
Borgholm, 15D6
Borgo Val di Taro, 13aB3
Borisoglebsk, 18B5
Borisov, 18B2
Borispol', 18B3
Borja, 38C2
Borlänge, 15C5
Bormida, R., 13A2
Borneo, I., 23C,D3
Bornholm, I., 15E5,6
Borongan, 23bB3
Borovići, 17C4
Borovskoj, 17aC3
Borroloola, 40B3
Borsod-Abaúj-Zemplén (4), Admin U., 14A2
Borujerd, 21C5
Borz̄a, 16D13
Bosaso, 28C7
Bosna, R., 13A4
Bosna i Hercegovina, (1), Admin.U., 13A4
Bossangoa, 28D4
Boston (U.K.), 9C4,5
Boston (U.S.A.), 35C6
Boteti, R., 30D3
Botev, Mt., 5C7
Botoşani, 14B3
Botswana, St., 30D3
Bottrop, 12aA2
Botucatu, 39aA4
Bouaké, 29D4
Bouar, 28D4
Bou Arfa, 28A2
Bouches-du-Rhône (13), Admin. U., 11D4
Bou Djébéha, 29A5
Boufarik, 27aA1
Bougainville, I., 40A5
Bougouni, 29C4
Boulder City, 34D3
Boulia, 40C3
Boulogne-sur-Rhône, 11B3
Bouna, 29C5
Boundiali, 29C4
Bounty Islands, Is., 3
Bourail, 41A1
Bouraké, 41A1,2
Bourem, 29A5
Bourg-en-Bresse, 11C4
Bourges, 11C3
Bourg-Saint-Maurice, 11C4
Bourke, 40D4
Bournemouth, 9D4
Bou Saâda, 27aA1
Boutilimit, 29A2
Bouvetöya, I., 3
Bow, R., 34A4
Bowen, 40B4
Bowie, 34E5
Bowling Green, 35D3
Boyle, 10E5
Boyne, R., 7E4
Boyuibe, 38E3
Bozeman, 34B4

Bozoum, 28D4
Bra, 13aB1
Brach, 28B4
Bräcke, 15C5
Brad, 14B2
Bradenton, 35F4
Bradford (U.K.), 9C4
Bradford (U.S.A.), 35C5
Braga, 11F1
Braga (3), Admin. U., 11F1
Bragança (Brazil), 38C5
Bragança (Portugal), 11F2
Brahmaputra see Yaluzangbujiang
Bräila, 14B3
Brainerd, 35B2
Bralorne, 33aB1,2
Branco, I., 28aA1
Branco, R., 38B3
Brandberg, Mt., 26G6
Brandenburg, 12B3,4
Brandon, 33D9
Brandon Mount, Mt., 7E2,3
Br'ansk, 18B3
Brantford, 35C4
Brasília, 38D5
Braşov, 14B3
Brass, 29D7
Bratislava, 12C5
Bratsk, 16D12
Bratskoje Vodochranilišče, Res., 16bA1
Braunschweig, 12B3
Brava, I., 28aB1
Bravo del Norte, R., 36B2
Bray, 10E6,7
Brazeau, 33C8
Brazil, St., 39C2-5
Brazilian Highlands, Hs., 37D4,5
Brazo Casiquiare, R., 36B3
Brazos, R., 34E6,7
Brazzaville, 30B2
Brda, R., 15E6
Breckland, Reg., 7E8
Břeclav, 12C5
Brecon, 9D3
Brecon Beacons, Mt., 7F6
Breda, 12C2
Bregenz, 12D3
Breiðafjörður, B., 15aB1,2
Bremen, 12B3
Bremen (3), Admin. U., 12B3
Bremerhaven, 12B3
Bremerton, 33aC2,3
Brent, Res., 9a
Brent, R., 9a
Brenta, R., 13aA5
Brentwood, 9D5
Brescia, 13A2
Bressay, I., 10a
Brest (France), 11B1
Brest (U.S.S.R.), 16D4
Bretagne, Pen., Reg., 5C4
Brežnev see Naber. Ĉelny
Bria, 28D5
Briançon, 11C4
Bricquebec, 11C2
Bridgeport, 35C6
Bridgetown (Australia), 40D1
Bridgetown (Barbados), 36bB2

page 189

Bridgwater, 9D3
Bridlington, 9B4,5
Bridlington Bay, B., 9B,C4,5
Brig, 11C4,5
Brighton, 9D4,5
Brikama, 29B1
Brindisi, 13B4
Brisbane, 40C5
Bristol, 9D3
Bristol Bay, 33C3,4
Bristol Channel, B., 7F5,6
British Columbia, Admin. U., 33C7
British Islands, Is., 19D1
Brive-la-Gaillarde, 11C3
Brno, 12C5
Broad Law, Mt., 7D6
Brochet, 33C9
Brockville, 33b
Brockway, 34B4
Brodick, 10C2
Brodokalmak, 17aB3
Brody, 18B2
Broken Hill, 40D4
Bronx, 32a
Brooklyn, 32a
Brooks Range, Mts., 31C5,6
Broome, 40B2
Bromsgrove, 9c3
Brownsville, 34F7
Brownsweg see Brokopondo
Brownwood, 34E7
Bruck an der Mur, 12D4
Brue, R., 9C3
Brugge, 11B3
Brunei, St., 23C3
Brunswick, 35E4
Brush, 34C3
Brussel see Bruxelles
Bruxelles, 11B4
Bryan, 35E1
Brzeg, 12C5
Bučač, 18C2
Bucak, 21aB2
Bucaramanga, 38B2
Buccles, 9C5
Buchan Ness, C., 7C7
Buchanan, 29D3
Buchara, 16F8
Buckie, 10B3
Buckinghamshire (11), Admin. U., 9D4
Buckleboo, 40D3
Bucklin, 34D7
Bu Craa, 28B1
Bucureşti, 14B3
Budapest, 14B1
Búdardalur, 15aB2
Budd Coast, Reg., 42F25
Budennovsk, 18D5
Búdir, 15aB2
Budrio, 13aB5
Buea, 29D8
Buenaventura, 38B2
Buenos Aires, 39B2,3
Buenos Aires, Admin. U., 39B2,3
Buerjin, 24B2
Buffalo, 35C5
Bug, R., 18B1
Bugrino, 17A7
Bugul'ma, 18B7
Buguruslan, 18B7
Buhayrat al-Burullus, L., 26aA2,3

Buhayrat al-Manzilah, L., 26aA4
Builth Wells, 9C3
Buinsk, 18B6
Buj, 17C6
Bujnaksk, 18D6
Bujumbura, 30B3,4
Bukama, 30B3
Bukavu, 30B3
Bukittinggi, 23D1,2
Bukoba, 30B4
Bulawayo, 30D3
Bulgan, 24B4
Bulgaria, St. 14C2,3
Bulo Burti, 28D7
Bulu Rantekombola, Mt., 19J13,14
Bumba, 28D5
Bunbury, 40D1
Buncrana, 10D6
Bundaberg, 40C5
Bünyan, 21aB3
Burao, 28D7
Buras, 35F3
Buraydah, 28B7
Burdur, 21aB1,2
Bure, R., 9C5
Bureja, R., 24A7
Bür Fu'ād, 26aA4
Burgas, 14C3
Burgas (2), Admin. U., 14C3
Burgenland (1), Admin. U., 12D5
Burgos, 11F3
Burgsvik, 15D6
Burhānur, 22B3
Burketown, 40B3
Burkina Faso, St., 29B,C4-6
Burlington (U.S.A., Vermont), 35C6
Burlington (U.S.A., Washington), 33aB3
Burma, St., 22B5
Burnaby, 33aB2
Burnie, 40E4
Burnley, 9C3
Burns, 34C3
Bursa, 21aA1
Bür Safājah, 28B6
Bür Sa'īd, 28A6
Bür Sūdān, 28C6
Bür Tawfīq, 26aB,C4
Burton upon-Trent, 9C4
Buru, I., 23D4
Burundi, St., 30B3,4
Bury, 9C3
Bury Saint Edmunds, 9C5
Büshehr, 21D6
Busira, R., 30A,B3
Busselton, 40D1
Busto Arsizio, 13A1,2
Buta, 28D5
Butehaqi, 24B6
Butterworth, 23C1,2
Butt of Lewis, C., 7B4,5
Butuan, 23C4
Buturlinovka, 18B5
Büyük Ağri Daği, Mt., 19F6
Büyükmenderes, R., 21aB1
Bużău, 14B3
Buzaúl, 14B3
Buzuluk, 18B7
Bydgoszcz, 12B5

Byelorussian Soviet Socialist Republic, Admin. U., 16D4,5
Bykovo, 18C6
Bylot Island, I., 33A11,12
Bytom, 12C5

C

Caazapá, 39A3
Cabanatuan, 23B4
Cabimas, 38A2
Cabinda, 30B2
Cabo Bojador, C., 28B1
Cabo Branco, C., 37C6
Cabo Catoche, 31G,H12
Cabo Corrientes, C., 31G9,10
Cabo da Roca, C., 5D3,4
Cabo de Creus, C., 11F4
Cabo de Finisterre, C., 11F1
Cabo de Gata, C., 11G3
Cabo de la Nao, C., 11G4
Cabo Delgado, C., 30C5
Cabo de São. Vicente, C., 11G1
Cabo Horn, C., 37H2,3
Cabo Maisi, C., 36aB6,7
Cabo Orange, C., 37B4,5
Cabo San Antonio, C., 36aA,B1
Cabo San Lucas, C., 36B1,2
Cabo Tres Puntas, C., 37G3,4
Cabot Strait, Str., 31E15
Čačak, 13B5
Cacequi, 39aD3
Cáceres (Brazil), 38D4
Cáceres (Spain), 11G2
Cachoeira de Paulo Afonso, Fs., 37C5,6
Cachoeira do Sul, 39aD3
Cachoeira de Itapemirim, 38E5
Cader Idris, Mt., 7E5,6
Cadiz, 34E3
Cádiz, 11G2
Caen, 11C3
Caernarvon, 9C2
Caernarvon Bay, B., 7E5
Caerphilly, 9C3
Cagan-Aman, 18C6
Cagayan, R., 23B4
Cagayan de Oro, 23C4
Čagda, 16D15
Cagliari, 13C2
Cahirciveen, 10F4
Cahors, 11C3
Caibarien, 36aA5
Caicara, 38B3
Cains, 40B4
Cairo see Al-Qāhirah
Cairo Montenotte, 13aB2
Cajamarca, 38C2
Čajkovskij, 17aB1,2
Calabar, 29D8
Calabozo, 38B3
Calabria (3), Admin. U., 13C4
Calafat, 14C2
Calais, 11B3
Calama, 39A2
Calamar (Colombia, Cartagena), 38A2
Calamar (Colombia, Neiva), 38B2

Calamian Group, Is., 23B3
Calapan, 23bB2
Călăraşi, 14B3
Calbayog, 23B4
Calcutta, 22B4
Caleta Larga, 36aB1
Calgary, 33C8
Calicut, 22C3
Caliente, 34D4
California, Admin. U., 34C,D2,3
Callao, 38D2
Caltanissetta, 13C3
Calvados (14), Admin. U., 11B2
Calvi, 11D5
Calvinia, 30E2,3
Calzada Larga, 34a
Cam, R., 9C4
Camagüey, 36aB4,5
Camaquã, 39aD3
Camaquã, R., 39aD3
Camarones, 39C2
Cambay, 22B3
Camberwell, 9a
Camborne, 9D2
Cambrai, 11B3
Cambrian Mountains, Mts., 7E6
Cambridge (U.K.), 9C5
Cambridge (U.S.A.), 35C6,7
Cambridge Bay, 33B9
Cambridgeshire (12), Admin. U., 9C4
Camden (U.S.A., Arkansas), 35E2
Camden (U.S.A., New York), 35D6
Cameroon, St., 29C-E8,9
Cametá, 38C4
Camiri, 38D3
Camocim, 38C5,6
Camooweal, 40B3
Camopi, 38B4
Campania (4), Admin. U., 13B3
Campbell Island, I., 3
Campbell River, 33aB2
Campbellton, 33D13
Campbeltown, 10C2
Campeche, 36C3
Campeche (4), Admin. U., 36C4
Campina Grande, 38C6
Campinas, 39A4
Campina Verde, 39aA3,4
Campobasso, 13B3
Campo Grande, 38E4
Campo Mourão, 39aB3
Campos, 38E5
Campos Belos, 38D5
Cam-Ranh, 22C6,7
Canada, St., 33C6-13
Canadian, R., 34D6
Canadian Shield see Laurentin Plateau
Çanakkale, 21A1
Çanakkale Boğazı, Str., 21aB1
Canala, 41aA1,2
Canal de la Mona, 36C5,6
Canal du Midi, Can., 11D3
Canal Zone, Admin. U., 36C,D4,5
Cananéia, 39aB4
Canarias (5), see Islas Canarias

Canary Islands see
  Islas Canarias
Canberra, 40D4,5
Canchungo, 29B1
Cancún, 36B4
Canelones, 39aD2
Cangas de Narcea, 11F2
Cangzhou, 24C5
Caniapiscau, R., 33C13
Cankırı, 21aA2
Cannes, 11D4
Canoas, 39aC3
Canoas, R., 39aC3,4
Caño Quebrado, C., 34a
Caño Quebrado, R., 34a
Canso, 33D13
Cantabria (6), Admin. U., 11F2
Cantal (15), Admin. U., 11C3
Canterbury, 9D5
Can-Tho, 22C,D6
Canton, 35C4
Canton see Guangzhou
Canudos, 38C4
Čapajev, 18B7
Čapajevsk, 18B6
Capanema, 38C5
Cap Blanc, C., 28B1
Cap Corse, C., 11D5
Cap d'Ambre, C., 30C5,6
Cap de la Hague, C., 6aA2,3
Cape Adare, C., 42G19,14
Cape Agulhas, C., 30E2,3
Cape Ann, C., 42F31
Cape Blanco, C., 31aB1
Cape Breton Island, C., 31E14,15
Cape Byron, C., 40C5
Cape Canaveral, C., 35F5
Cape Charles, C., 31D15,16
Cape Chidley, C., 33B13
Cape Coast, 29D5
Cape Colbeck, C., 42G15,16
Cape Columbia, C., 42D11-14
Cape Comorin, C., 22D3
Cape Darnley, C., 42F29,30
Cape Dart, C., 42G13,14
Cape Dyer, C., 31C14,15
Cape Farewell, C., 40aB2
Cape Fear, C., 35F5
Cape Flattery, C., 34B1,2
Cape Flying Fish, C., 42F,G16
Cape Froward, C., 37H2
Cape Goodenough, C., 42F24
Cape Hatteras, C., 35D5,6
Cape Horn, C., 39D2
Cape Londonderry, C., 40B2
Capelongo, 30C2
Cape Mendocino, C., 31aB1
Cape Mountains, Mts., 26H6,7
Cape Norvegia, C., 42F,G2,3
Cape of Good Hope, C., 30E2
Cape Palmas, C., 29D4
Cape Poinsett, C., 42F25,26

Cape Prince of Wales, C., 31C4
Cape Province, Admin. U., 30E2,3
Cape Race, C., 33D14
Cape Sable (Canada), C., 33D13
Cape Sable (U.S.A.), C., 35F4
Cape Three Points, C., 29D5
Cape Town, 30E2
Cape Verde, St., Is., 28a
Cape Wrangell, C., 31D1,2
Cape Wrath, C., 7B5
Cape York, C., 40B4
Cape York Peninsula, Pen., 40B4
Cap Lopez, C., 30B1
Cap Murchison, C., 31B11,12
Capo Passero, C., 13C3
Capo Spartivento, C., 13C4
Capo Teulada, C., 13C2
Caprino Veronese, 13aA4
Cap Sainte Marie, C., 30D5
Cap Vert, C., 29B1
Caquetá, R., 37C2
Caracal, 14B3
Caracaraí, 38B3
Caracas, 38,A,B3
Caratinga, 38D5
Carauari, 38C3
Caravaca, 11G3
Caravelas, 38D6
Carbonia, 13C2
Carcassonne, 11D3
Cárdenas, 36aA3
Cardiff, 9D3
Cardigan, 7E5
Cardigan Bay, B., 7E5
Cardžou, 16F8
Carei, 14B2
Carentan, 6aA3
Cariacica, 38D5,6
Caribbean Sea, 36C4,5
Carlisle, 10C3
Carlow, 10E6
Carlow, Admin. U., 10E6
Carlsbad, 34E6
Carlton, 9C4
Carmagnola, 13aB1
Carman, 34A7
Carmarthen, 9D2
Carmarthen Bay, B., 7F5
Carmel Head, C., 7E5
Carmen de Patagones, 39C2
Carnarvon (Austr.), 40C1
Carnarvon (S.Afr.), 30E3
Carn Eige, Mt., 7C5
Carnot, 28D4
Carnsore Point, C., 7E4,5
Carolina, 38C5
Caroline Atoll, I., 41E10,11
Caroline Islands, Arch., 41C3-5
Caroní, R., 38B3
Carozero, 17B5
Carpathian Mountains, Mts. 19E4
Carpatii Meridionali, Mts., 5C7
Carpi, 13aB4,5
Carrara, 13A2
Carrauntoohill, Mt., 7E3

Carrickfergus, 10D7
Carrickfergus (8), Admin. U., 10D7
Carrick on Shannon, 10E5,6
Çarşamba, 21aA3
Carson City, 34D3
Carstairs, 10C3
Cartagena (Colombia), 38A2
Cartagena (Spain), 11G3
Cartwright, 33C14
Caruaru, 38C6
Carúngol, 24B4
Carúpano, 38A3
Carvoeiros, 38aA1
Casablanca, 28A2
Casale Monferrato, 13aA2
Cascade Range, Mts., 31E8
Cascavel, 39A3
Caserta, 13B3
Casey, Station, 42F25,26
Cashel, 10E6
Casiguran, 23bA2
Casilda, 39aD1
Casina, 13aB4
Casper, 34C5
Caspian Sea, 16E,F6,7
Casquets, Is., 6aA2
Cassai, R., 30C2,3
Cassinga, 30C2
Castelfranco Véneto, 13aA5
Castellammare di Stabia, 13B3
Castellón de la Plana, 11F4
Castelo Branco, 11G2
Castelo Branco (5), Admin. U., 11G2
Castilla – La Mancha (7), Admin. U., 11G3
Castilla – León (2), Admin. U., 11F3
Castlebar, 10E5
Castlebay, 10B1
Castlerea, 10E5
Castlereagh (9), Admin. U., 10D7
Castres, 11D3
Castries, 36bB2
Castro, 39C1
Castrop – Rauxel, 12aA3
Castrovillari, 13C4
Catalão, 39aA4
Cataluña (9), Admin. U., 11F4
Catalunya see Cataluña
Catamarca, 39A2
Catamarca (2), Admin. U., 39A2
Catanduaes Island, I., 23B4
Catania, 13C3
Catanzaro, 13C4
Catarman, 23bB2
Catbalogan, 23bB2
Cat Island, I., 35G5
Catrimani, 38B3
Cauayan, 23bB2
Cauca, R., 37B2
Caura, R., 38B3
Cauvery, R., 22C3
Cavalla, R., 29D4
Cavan, 10E6
Cavan, Admin. U., 10D,E6

Cavarzere, 13aA6
Caviana Ilha, I., 37B5
Caxias do Sul, 39aC3
Cayenne, 38B4
Cayman Islands, Is., Admin. U., 36C4
Ceará, Admin. U., 38C5,6
Cebarkul', 17aB,C3
Čeboksarskoje Vodochraniliŝče, Res., 17C6,7
Čeboksary, 17C7
Cebu, 23B4
Cebu, I., 23B4
Cecerleg, 24B4
Cedar City, 34D4
Cedar Rapids, 35C2
Ceduna, 40D3
Cefalù, 13C3
Cegléd, 14B1
Čel'abinsk, 16D7,8
Celaya, 36E,F4
Celebes see Sulawesi
Celebes Sea, 23C3,4
Celinograd, 16D9
Celje, 13A3
Čelkar, 16E7
Celle, 12B3
Celtic Sea, 5B,C4
Ceno, R., 13aB3
Cento, 13aB5
Central (56), Admin. U., 10B2
Central African Republic, St., 28D4,5
Central European Plain, Pl., 4B5-7
Central Plain, Pl., 7E3,4
Ceram Sea, 23D4,5
Čerdyń, 17aA2
Ceremchovo, 16D11,12
Čerepovec, 17C5
Ceres, 38D5
Cerignola, 13B3
Cerkasky, 18C3
Çerkesök, 18D5
Čern'achovsk, 18B1
Černigov, 18B3
Černobyľ, 18B2,3
Černovcy, 16E4
Černovskoje, 17C7
Cerro Bonete, Mt., 37E3
Cerro de Pasco, 38D2
Cerro de Tocorpuri, Mt., 37E3
Cerro Yerupaja, Mt., 37D2
Cero Yogan, Mt., 37H2
Cerskij, 16C19
Červenograd, 18B1
Cervia, 13aB6
Cesena, 13A3
Česká Třebová, 12C4,5
České Budějovice, 12C4
Českaja Guba, B., 16C6,7
Cestas, R., 29D3
Cetinje, 13B4
Ceuta, 28A2
Ceyhan, 21aB3
Ceylânpınar, 21aB3
Chabarovsk, 16E15
Chachapoyas, 38C2
Chaco, Admin. U., 39A2,3
Chad, St., 28C4,5
Chāgai, 21D8
Chaghcharān, 22A2
Chagos Islands, Is., 19J9
Chagres, 34a

page 191

Chagres, R., 34a
Chāh Bahār, 21D8
Chake Chake, 30B4,5
Chala, 38D2
Chalindrey, 11C4
Chal'mer-Ju, 16C7,8
Chalon-sur-Saône, 11C4
Châlons-sur-Marne, 11B4
Cham, 12B5
Chaman, 22A2
Chambal, R., 22B3
Chambéry, 11C4
Chambeshi, R., 30B,C4
Chamgordan, 36C3
Chamonix-Mont-Blanc, 11C4
Champaign, 35C3
Champerico, 36C3
Chañaral, 39A1
Chandīgarh, 22A3
Chandigarh (8), Admin. U., 22A3
Chāndpur, 22aC4
Chandrapur, 22B,C3,4
Chandyga, 16C15
Changajn Nuruu, Mts., 19E9,11,12
Changchun, 24B6
Changde, 24D5
Changdu, 24C3
Changhang, 25C4
Changhua, 25aB1,2
Changjiang see Tongtianhe
Changsha, 24D5
Changzhi, 24C5
Changzhou, 25D2,3
Channel Islands, Admin. U., Is., 6aA2
Channel-Port-aux-Basques, 33D13,14
Chanthaburi, 22C5
Chanty-Mansijsk, 16C8,9
Chaoan, 24D5
Chaohu, L., 25D2
Chaoyang, 25B3
Chāpra, 22B4
Charabali, 18C6
Charaña, 38D3
Charcot Island, I., 42F8
Charente (16), Admin. U., 11C3
Charente, R., 11C3
Charente-Maritime (17), Admin. U., 11C2,3
Chari, R., 28C4
Chārīkār, 22A2,3
Chariton, 35C2
Char'kov, 16D,E5
Charleroi, 11B4
Charleston (U.S.A., South Carolina), 35E5
Charleston (U.S.A., West Virginia), 35D4
Charleville, 40C4
Charleville Mézières, 11B4
Charlotte, 35D4,5
Charlotte Amalie, 36bA1
Charlottetown, 33D13
Charlovka, 17A5
Charovsk, 17C6
Charters Towers, 40B4
Chartres, 11B3
Char Us Nuur, L., 24B3
Chasavjurt, 18D6
Chatanga, 16B12
Chatanga, R., 16B12
Châteaudun, 11B3
Châteauroux, 11C3
Châtellerault, 11C3

Chatgal, 24A4
Chatham (Canada), 33b
Chatham (U.K.), 9D5
Chatham Islands, Is., 41H8
Châtillon, 13aA1
Chattahoochee, R., 35E3,4
Chattanooga, 35D3
Chauk, 22B5
Chaumont, 11B4
Chaves, 11F2
Cheb, 12C4
Chechaouene, 11H2
Checheno – Ingush Autonomous Soviet Socialist Republic (3), Admin. U., 18D6
Cheerchenghe, R., 24C2
Cheju, 25D4
Cheju-do, I., 25D4
Chelan, 33aC3
Chełm, 12C6
Chelmsford, 9D5
Chelsea, 9a
Cheltenham, 9D3,4
Chemult, 34C2
Chenāb, R., 22A3
Cheney, 33aC4
Chengde, 24B5
Chengdu, 24C3
Chengzituan, 25C3
Chépénéhé, 41aA2
Cher, R., 11C3
Cher (18), Admin. U., 11C3
Cherbourg, 11B2
Cherrapunji, 19G11
Cherson, 18C3
Chesapeake Bay, B., 35D5
Cheshire (13), Admin. U., 9C3
Cheshire Plain, Pl., 7E6
Chester, 9C3
Chesterfield, 9C4
Chesterfield Inlet, 33B10,11
Cheta, R., 16B11
Cheviot Hills, Mts., 7D6
Chevrolet, 10E4,5
Chezhou, 24D5
Chiai, 25C4,5
Chiang Mai, 22C5
Chiang Rai, 22C5
Chianje, 30C2
Chiapas (5), Admin. U., 36C3
Ch'iari, 13aA3,4
Chiavari, 13aB3
Chiba, 25C7
Chibougamau, 33D12
Chicago, 35C3
Chichester, 9D4
Chiclayo, 38C1,2
Chico, 34C2
Chicoutimi-Jonquière, 33D12
Chicualacuala, 30D4
Chieti, 13B3
Chifeng, 24B5
Chignik, 33C4
Chihuahua, 36B2
Chihuahua (6), Admin. U., 36B2
Chile, St., 39A-D1,2
Chillán, 39B1
Chilok, 16bB3
Chilpancingo, 36C2,3
Chiltern Hills, Hs., 7F7

Chilung, 25aA,B2
Chimborazo, Mt., 37C2
Chimbote, 38C2
Chimki, 17b
Chimki-Chovrino, 17b
Chimoio, 30C4
China, St., 24C1-5
Chincha Alta, 38D2
Chinchilla, 40C5
Chinde, 30C4
Chin-do, I., 25D4
Chindwin, R., 22B5
Chingola-Chililabombwe, 30C3
Chinhoyi, 30C4
Chinju, 25C4
Chioggia, 13aA6
Chipata, 30C4
Chippenham, 9D3
Chirgis Nuur, L., 24B3
Chirripó, Mt., 31H12
Chiswick, 9a
Chitradurga, 20aA2
Chittagong, 22B5
Chiumbe, R., 30B3
Chivasso, 13aA1,2
Choiseul, I., 40A5
Chojnice, 12B5
Cholet, 11C2
Cholm, 17C4
Choma, 30C3
Ch'ŏnan, 25C4
Ch'ŏngjin, 25B4,5
Ch'ŏngju, 25C4
Chongming, 25D3
Chongqing, 24D4
Chŏnju, 25C4
Chop'or, R., 18B5
Chorej-Ver, 17A9
Chorinsk, 16bB2
Chorog, 24C1
Chorosovo-Mnevniki, 17b
Chorzów, 12C5
Chōshi, 25C7
Chotin, 18C2
Chott Djerid, Sw., 27aB2
Chott Melrhir, L., 27aB2
Chovd, 24B3
Chövsgöl Nuur, L., 24A3
Chrebet Čerskogo, Mts., 19C15,16
Christchurch, 40aB2,7
Christianshåb see Qasigiánguit
Christiansted, 36bA1,2
Christmas Island (Austr.), I., 23E2
Christmas Island (Kiribati), see Kiritimati
Chubut, Admin. U., 39C1,2
Chubut, R., 37G3
Chudat, 18D6
Chumphon, 22C5
Ch'unch'on, 25C4
Ch'ungju, 25C4
Chungli, 25aA,B2
Chuquicamata, 39A2
Chur, 11C5
Churchill, 33C10
Churchill (Canada), R., 33C9
Churchill (Newfoundland), R., 33C13
Churchill Falls, 33C13
Churchill Lake, L., 33C9
Chust, 18C1
Chutte des Passes, 35B6

Chuvash Autonomous Soviet Socialist Republic, Admin. U., 17C7
Chuxiong, 24D4
Chvalynsk, 18B6
Cianjur, 23A1
Ciatura, 18D5
Ciechanów, 12B6
Ciego de Avila, 36aB4,5
Ciénaga, 38A2
Cienfuegos, 36aA3
Cieza, 11G3
Cihanbeyli, 21aB2
Cijulang, 23aA1,2
Cilacap, 23aA,B2
Cil'ma, R., 17A8
Cimarron, R., 34D7
Čimkent, 24B1
Ciml'ansk, 18C5
Ciml'anskoje Vodochranilišče, Res., 18C5
Cimpulung, 14B3
Cincinnati, 35D4
Circle, 33B5
Cirebon, 23D2
Cirencester, 9D3,4
Cirie, 13aA1
Čistopol', 17C8
Čita, 18D13
Citeli – Ckaro, 18aA2
City Island, I., 32a
Ciudad Acuña, 34F6
Ciudad Bolívar, 38B3
Ciudad Camargo, 36C3,4
Ciudad Chetumal, 36C5
Ciudadela, 11G4
Ciudad Guayana, 38B3
Ciudad Jimenez, 36B2
Ciudad Juárez, 35A2
Ciudad Madero, 36B3
Ciudad Mante, 36B3
Ciudad Obregón, 36B2
Ciudad Ojeda, 38A,B2
Ciudad Piar, 38B3
Ciudad Real, 11G2,3
Ciudad Rodrigo, 11F2
Ciudad Victoria, 36B3
Civitavecchia, 13B2
Civril, 21aB1
Cizre, 21aB4
Clacton-on-Sea, 9D5
Clare, Admin. U., 10E5
Clare Island, I., 7E2
Claremorris, 10E5
Clarence Town, 35G5,6
Clark Fork, R., 34B3,4
Clarksdale, 35E2,3
Clarksville, 35D3
Clarsburg, 35D4
Claveria, 23bA2
Clear Island, I., 10F5'
Cleethorpes, 9C4
Clermont-Ferrand, 11C3,4
Cleveland, 35C4
Cleveland (14), Admin. U., 9B4
Clew Bay, B., 7E3
Clifden, 10E4,5
Clinton (Canada), 33aA3
Clinton (U.S.A.), 35D4
Clinton-Colden Lake, L., 33B9
Clipperton, I., 36C2
Clonakilty, 10F5
Cloncurry, 40C4
Clonmel, 10E6
Clovis, 34E6
Cluj-Napoca, 14B2

Clusone, 13aA3
Clwyd (47), Admin. U., 9C3
Clyde, 33A13
Clyde, R., 7D5,6
Clydebank, 10C2
Coahuila (7), Admin. U., 36B2
Coari, 38C3
Coast Land, Reg., 42G2,3
Coast Mountains, Mts., 31D7,8
Coast Ranges, Mts., 31E,F8,9
Coatbridge, 10C2,3
Coats Island, I., 33B11
Coatzacoalcos, 36C3
Cobalt, 33D11,12
Cobar, 40D4
Cobh, 10F5
Cobija, 38D3
Cocalinho, 38D4
Cochabamba, 38D3
Cochin, 22D3
Cochrane, 33D11
Coco, R., 31H12
Cocos Islands, Is., 23E1
Codajás, 38C3
Codigoro, 13aB6
Codó, 38C5
Codogno, 13aA3
Cody, 34C5
Coen, 40B4
Coeur d'Alene, 34B3
Coffs Harbour, 40D5
Cognac, 11C2
Coimbatore, 22C3
Coimbra, 11F1
Cojbalsan, 24B5
Colatina, 38D5
Colby, 34D6
Colchester, 9D5
Coleraine, 10D6
Coleraine (10), Admin. U., 10D6
Colima, 36C2
Colima (8), Admin. U., 36C2
Coll, I., 7C4
Cologna Veneta, 13aA5
Cologne see Köln
Colômbia, 38E5
Colombia, St., 38B2,3
Colombo, 20aC2
Colón (Cuba), 36A5
Colón (Panama), 36D5
Colonia del Sacramento, 39aD2
Colonia Las Heras, 39C2
Colonsay, I., 7C4
Colorado, Admin. U., 34D5,6
Colorado (Atlantic Ocean), R., 39E2
Colorado (G. of Mexico), R., 34F7
Colorado (Pacific Ocean), R., 34E4
Colorado Plateau, Plat., 31F9,10
Colorado Springs, 34D6
Columbia, R., 33C8
Columbus (U.S.A., Georgia), 35E4
Columbus (U.S.A., Mississippi), 35E3
Columbus (U.S.A., Ohio), 35C,D4

Colville, R., 33B4
Colwyn Bay, 9C3
Comacchio, 13aB6
Combra (6), Admin. U., 11F1
Comilla, 22aC4
Como, 13aA2
Comodoro Rivadavia, 39C2
Comoros, St., 30C5
Compiègne, 11B3
Conakry, 29C2
Conceição do Araguaia, 38C4,5
Concepción (Chile), 39B1
Concepción (Paraguay), 39A3
Concepción del Uruguay, 39aD2
Conchos, R., 34F5,6
Concord, 35C6
Concórdia, 39aD2
Côn Dao, Is., 22D6
Conegliano, 13aA6
Congo, R., 30B2
Congo, St., 30A,B2
Congo Basin, Reg., 26D,E6,7
Coniston, 28B4
Connecticut, Admin. U., 35C6
Conselheiro Lafaiete, 39aB5
Consett, 10C4
Constanța, 14B2
Constantine, 28A3
Contwoyto Lake, 33B8,9
Coober Pedy, 40C3
Cookhouse, 30E3
Cook Islands, Is., 41E9,10
Cookstown, 10D6
Cookstown (11), Admin. U., 10D6
Cook Strait, Str., 40aB2
Cooktown, 40B4
Coolgardie, 40D1,2
Coondapoor, 20aA1
Coopers Creek, R., 40C3,4
Coos Bay, 34C2
Čop, 12C6
Copenhagen see København
Copiapó, 39A2
Copparo, 13aB5
Copper, R., 33B5
Copper Harbor, 35B3
Coppermine, 33B8
Coquet, R., 9B4
Coquimbo, 39B2
Coral Harbour, 33B11
Coral Sea, 40B,C4,5
Coral Sea Islands Territory, Reg., 40B4,5
Corantijn, R., 38B4
Corbin, 35D4
Corby, 9C4
Corcaigh see Cork
Cordillera Cantabrica, Mts., 5C4
Cordillera Central, Mts., 37B2
Cordillera de Mérida, Mts., 37A,B2,3
Cordillera Occidental, Mts., 37B2
Cordillera-Oriental, Mts., 37B2
Córdoba (3), Admin. U., 39B2

Córdoba (Argentina), 39B2
Córdoba (Spain), 11G2
Cordova, 33B5
Corinto (Brazil), 39aA5
Corinto (Nicaragua), 36C4
Cork, 10F5
Cork, Admin. U., 10F5
Cork Harbour, B., 7F3,4
Çorlu, 21aA1
Cormoz, 17aB2
Corner Brook, 33D14
Corno Grande, Mt., 5C6
Cornomorskoje, 18C3
Cornth, 35D,E3
Cornwall (Bahamas), 35F5
Cornwall (Canada), 35B6
Cornwall (15), Admin. U., 9D2
Cornwallis Island, 33A10
Coro, 38A3
Coromandel, 39aA4
Coromandel Coast, 20a,A,B3
Coronel Oviedo, 39A3
Coronel Suárez, 39aE1
Corpus Christi, 34F7
Corralillo, 36aA3
Corrèze (19), Admin. U., 11C3
Corrientes, 39A3
Corrientes (4), Admin. U., 39A3
Corse see Corsica
Corse (Haute)- (96), Admin. U., 11D5
Corse-du-Sud (20), Admin. U., 11D5
Corsica, I., 11D5
Corsicana, 35E1
Corte, 11D5
Čortkov, 18C2
Cortland, 35C5
Coruh, R., 21aA4
Çorum, 21aA2
Corumbá, 38D4
Corvallis, 34C2
Corvo, I., 11aA1
Cosenza, 13C4
Cosmoledo Group, Is., 30B5
Costa Rica, St., 36C,D4
Cotabato, 23C4
Coteau-Station, 33b
Côte-d'Or (21), Admin. U., 11C4
Cotentin, Pen., 7G7
Côtes-du-Nord (22), Admin. U., 11B2
Cotonou, 29D6
Cotopaxi, Mt., 37B2
Cotswolds, Hs., 7E,F6,7
Cottbus, 12C4
Cottbus (2), Admin. U., 12C4
Cottondale, 35E3
Council Bluffs, 35C1,2
Courtenay, 33C,D7
Coutances, 6aA3
Coventry, 9C4
Covilhã, 11F2
Covington (U.S.A., Kentucky), 35D4
Covington (U.S.A., Virginia), 35D4,5
Cowes, 9D4
Coxim, 38D4
Cox's Bazar, 22B5
Coyhaique, 39C1

Cradock, 30E3
Craig, 34C5
Craigavon (12), Admin. U., 10D6
Craig Harbour, 33A11
Craiova, 14B2
Cranbrook, 34B3
Crater Lake, 34C2
Cratéus, 38C5,6
Crato, 38C6
Craven Arms, 9C3
Crawford, 34C6
Crawley, 9D4
Cree Lake, L., 33C9
Creil, 11B3
Crema, 13aA3
Cremona, 13A2
Crete see Kriti
Créteil, 11B3
Creuse (23), Admin. U., 11C3
Crewe, 9C3
Crianlarich, 10B2
Ciciúma, 39aC3,4
Crikvenica, 13A3
Cristóbal, 34a
Crkvice, 5C
Crna Gora (2), Admin. U., 13B4
Cross Fell, Mt., 7D6
Cross River (6), Admin. U., 29D8
Crotone, 13C4
Crow Agency, 34B5
Croydon, 40B4
Cruz Alta, 39
Cruz del Eje, 39B2
Cruzeiro do Sul, 38C2
Csongrád (5), Admin. U., 14B2
Ču, 24B1
Ču, R., 24B1
Cuamba, 30C4
Cuando, R., 30C2,3
Cuango, R., 30C2
Cuanza, R., 30C2
Cuba, St., 36B4,5
Cubango, R., 30C2
Ćuchloma, 17C6
Cúcuta, 38B3
Cuddalore, 22C3,4
Cuddapah, 22C3
Čudovo, 17C4
Čudskoje Ozero, L., 17C3
Cue, 40C1
Cuenca (Ecuador), 38C2
Cuenca (Spain), 11F3
Cuernavaca, 36C2,3
Čugujev, 18C4
Cuiabá, 38D4
Cuiabá, R., 38D4
Cuito, R., 30C2,3
Cuito Cuanavale, 30C2,3
Ćukotskij Poluostrov, Pen., 19C20
Ćukotskoje More, S., 16B,C20,21
Culebra, 34a
Culgoa, R., 40C4
Culiacán, 36B2
Culion, 23bB2
Cullera, 11G3
Cullin Hills, Mts., 7C4
Čul'man, 16D14
Ćulym, R., 16D10
Cumaná, 38A3
Cumberland, R., 35D3
Cumberland Peninsula, Pen., 42B12

page 193

Cumbria (16), Admin. U., 9B3
Cumbrian Mountains, Mts., 7D6
Čumikan, 16D15
Cumnock, 10C2
Cuneo, 13A1
Cunnamulla, 40C4
Cuorgnè, 13A1
Čupa, 17A4
Cupar, 10B3
Curaçao, I., 38A3
Curepipe, 30aB3
Curitiba, 39A3,4
Curitibanos, 39aC3,4
Curuzú-Cuatiá, 39aC2
Čusovaja, R., 17aB2
Čusovoj, 17aB2
Cuttack, 22B4
Cuvo, R., 30C2
Cuxhaven, 12B3
Cuyo Islands, Is., 23bB2
Cuzco, 38D2
Cyprus, St., I., 19c
Cyrenaica see Barqah
Czechoslovakia, St., 12C4-6
Częstochowa, 12C5

D

Dabakala, 29C4,5
Dabola, 29C3
Dacca see Dhaka
Dachla, 28B1
Dādra and Nagar Haveli (9), Admin. U., 22B,C3
Daet, 23bB2
Dagana, 29A2
Daghestan Autonomous Soviet Socialist Republic, Admin. U., 18D6
Dagupan, 23B4
Dahengqindao, I., 19D,E13,14
Dahlak Archipelago, Is., 28C6,7
Dahūk, 21aB4
Dajarra, 40C3
Dakar, 29B1
Dakshin Gangotri, Station, 42F34-36
Dalaba, 29C2,3
Dalai, 25A3
Dalai Nur, L., 25B2
Dalälven, R., 15C6
Dalandzadgad, 24B4
Da-Lat, 22D4
Dâlbandin, 21D8
Dalen, 15D4
Dalhart, 34D4
Dalian, 24C4
Dallas, 34E7
Dal'negorsk, 24B7
Dal'nerečensk, 24B7
Daloa, 29D4
Dalol, 26C6
Dalton, 35F4
Daltonganj, 22A B3
Daly, R., 40B3
Daly Waters, 40B3
Damān, 22B3
Damanhūr, 26aA2

Damascus see Dimashq
Dāmodar, R., 22aC3
Damongo, 29C5
Dampier, 40C1
Da-Nang, 22C6
Danau Poso, L., 23D4
Danau Toba, L., 23C1
Danau Towuti, L., 23D4
Dandong, 24B6
Danganliedao, I., 19aB3
Danger Islands see Pukapuka
Dangori, 22B5
Danilov, 17C5,6
Danshui, 19aA3
Danube see Donau
Danville (U.S.A., Illinois), 35C3
Danville (U.S.A., Virginia), 35D4,5
Dapango, 29C6
Dar'ā, 20bB2
Darazo, 29C8
Darbhanga, 22B4
Darby, 34B4
Darchan, 24B4
Dar-el-Beida see Casablanca
Dargan-Ata, 21A8
Darien, 34a
Därjiling, 22B4
Darling, R., 40D4
Darlington, 9B4
Darmouth, 9D3
Darmstadt, 12C3
Darnah, 28A5
Dartmoor, Reg., 7F5,6
Dartmouth, 33D13
Daru, 40A4
Darwen, 9C3
Darwin, 40B3
Daryācheh-ye-Bakhtegān, L., 21D6,7
Daryācheh-ye Namak, L., 21C6
Daryācheh-ye Orūmīyeh, L., 21B4,5
Daryācheh-ye Sīstān, L., 21C7,8
Dasht-e Kavīr, Des., 19F7
Datong, 24B,C5
Daugavpils, 17C3,4
Dauphin, 34A6
Daura, 29B8
Dävangere, 20aA1,2
Davao, 23C4
Davenport (U.S.A., Iowa), 35C2
Davenport (U.S.A., Washington), 33aC4
David, 36D4
David-Gorodok, 18B2
Davis, Station, 42F29
Davis Sea, 42F27
Davis Strait, Str., 33B13,14
Davlekanovo, 17aC1,2
Dawson, 33B6
Dawson Creek, 33C7,8
Dax, 11D2
Daxian, 24C4
Daym Zubayr, 28D5
Dayr az-Zawr, 20bB2,3
Dayton, 35D3,4
Daytona Beach, 35F4,5
De Aar, 30E3
Dead Sea, 20b C1,2
Dearborn, 33b

Dease Lake, 33C6,7
Dease Strait, Str., 33B9
Death Valley, 34D3
Death Valley, Depr., 31aC2
Deblin, 12C6
Debrecen, 14B2
Debre Markos, 28C6
Debre Tabor, 28C6
Decatur (U.S.A., Alabama), 35E3
Decatur (U.S.A., Illinois), 35D3
Decazeville, 11C3
Deccan, Plat., 19G,H9
Dédougou, 29B5
Dedovići, 17C3,4
Dee (Irish Sea), R., 7E6
Dee (North Sea), R., 7C6
Deepdale, 40C1
Degunino, 17b
Deh Bid, 21C6
Dehiwala, 20aC2,3
Dej, 14B2
Delaware, Admin. U., 35D5
Delaware Bay, 35D5,6
Delhi, 22B3
Delicias, 34F5
Dellys, 27aA1
Deloraine, 34B6,7
Del Rio, 34F6
Demidov, 17C4
Demjansk, 17C4
Democratic People's Republic of Korea, St., 25B,C4
Denali see Mount McKinley
Denau, 21B9
Den Helder, 12B2
Denia, 11G4
Denizli, 21aB1
Denmark, St., 12A,B3,4
Denmark Strait, Str., 15aA,B1,2
Denpasar, 23D3
D'Entrecasteaux Islands, Is., 40A5
Denver, 34C,D5
Deoghar, 22aB3
Deptford, 9a
Dera Ismāīl Khān, 22A2,3
Derbent, 18D6
Derby (Australia), 40B2
Derby (U.K.), 9C4
Derbyshire (17), Admin. U., 9C4
De Ridder, 35E2
Derryveagh Mountains, Mts., 7D3,4
Derwent, R., 7D,E7
Dese, 28C6,7
Desenzano del Garda, 13A4
Desierto de Atacama, Des., 37E3
Des Moines, 35C2
Des Moines, R., 35C2
Desna, R., 18B3
Dessau, 12C4
Detroit, 35C4
Deutsche Bay, B., 12B2,3
Deva, 14B2
Deveron, R., 7C6

Devils Lake, 34B7
Devon (18), Admin. U., 9D3
Devon Island, I., 33A10,11
Devonport, 40E4
Dewsbury, 9C4
Dezfūl, 21C5
Dezhou, 25C2
Dhaka, 22B4,5
Dhānbād, 22aC3
Dhankuta, 22B3
Dhaulāgiri, Mt., 19G10
Dherínia, 19cA2,3
Dhodhekánisos, Is., 14D,E3
Dhuburi, 22aB4
Diafarabé, 29B4
Diamantina, R., 40D5
Diamantina, R., 40D3
Diamantino, 38D4
Dibi, 28D7
Dibrugarh, 22B5
Dickinson, 34B6
Didiéni, 29B3
Diébougou, 29C5
Diélette, 6aA3
Diéma, 29B3
Dieppe, 11B3
Difta, 29B9
Digne, 11C4
Digul, R., 23D5,6
Dijon, 11C4
Dikson, 16B9,10
Dikwa, 29B9
Dila, 28D6
Dilī, 23D4
Dilling, 28C5,6
Dilolo, 30C3
Dimashq, 20bB2
Dimbokre, 29D4
Dimitrovgrad (Bulgaria), 14C3
Dimitrovgrad (U.S.S.R.), 18B6
Dinagat Island, I., 23B4
Dinan, 11B2
Dinar, 21aB2
Dinara, Mts., 5C6,7
Dindigul, 20aB2
Dingle, 10E3
Dingle Bay, B., 7E,F2
Dingri, 24D2
Dinguiraye, 29C3
Dingwall, 10B2
Dinslaken, 12aA2
Diplog, 23bC2
Diré, 29A5
Dire Dawa, 28D7
Dirranbandi, 40C4
Disko, I., 33B14
Dispur, 22B5
Disūq, 26aA2
Diu, 22B3
Divnoje, 18C5
Divrigi, 21aB3
Diyālā, R., 21B,C5
Diyarbakır, 21aB4
Dja, R., 29E9
Djado, 28B4
Djambala, 30B2
Djanet, 28B3
Djebel Chélia, Mt., 26A5
Djelfa, 28A3
Djenné, 29B4
Djerba, 27aB3
Djibo, 29B5
Djibouti, 28C7
Djibouti, St., 28C7

Djidjelli, 27 A2
Djilah see Dicle
Djougou, 29 C6
Djúpivogur, 15a B4
Dnepr, R., 16 E5
Dneprodzeržinsk, 18 C3,4
Dnepropetrovsk, 16 E5
Dnestr, R., 18 C1
Dno, 17 C3
Doba, 28 D4
Dobo, 23 D5
Doboj, 13 A4
Dobruš, 18 B3
Dodge City, 34 D7
Dodoma, 30 B4
Dog Creek, 33a A3
Dogondoutchi, 29 B6,7
Doğubayazit, 21a B4
Dolbeau, 35 B6
Dole, 11 C4
Dolgellau, 9 C3
Dolinskaja, 18 C5
Dolores, 39 B3
Dolphin and Union Strait, Str., 33 A,B7,8
D'oma, R., 17a C2
Dombaj, 18 D5
Dombås, 15 C4
Dominica, St. I., 36b B2
Dominican Republic, St., 36 C5,6
Don (Azovskoje more), R., 16 D5
Don (Humber), R., 7 E7
Don (North Sea), R., 7 C6
Donau, R., 12 C3
Doncaster, 9 C4
Dondo, 30 B2
Doneck, 16 E5
Donegal, Reg., 10 D5,6
Donegal Bay, B., 7 D7
Dongao, I., 19a C2
Dongara, 40 C1
Donggala, 23 D3
Donghai, 25 C7
Dongshaqundao, Is., 24 D5
Dongsheng, 24 C4,5
Dongtai, 25 D3
Dongtinghu, L., 24 D5
Dónna, I., 15 B4,5
Dora Baltea, R., 13a A1
Dorchester, 9 D3
Dordogne (24), Admin. U., 11 C3
Dordrecht, 12 C2
Dori, 29 B5
Dornoch, 10 B2
Dornot Fort, B., 7 B,C6
Dorset (19), Admin. U., 9 D3
Dortmund, 12a A3
Dosso, 29 B6
Dothan, 35 E3
Douai, 11 B3
Douala, 29 E8
Doubs (25), Admin. U., 11 C4
Doubs, R., 11 C4
Douentza, 29 B5
Douglas, 9 B2
Doura, R., 7 E7
Dourados, 38 E4
Douro see Duero
Douz, 27 A B2
Dove, R., 7 E7
Dover (U.K.), 9 D5
Dover (U.S.A.), 35 D5

Down (13), Admin. U., 10 D7
Downpatrick, 10 D7
Draguignan, 11 D4
Drakensberg, Mts., 26 G,H7,8
Drake Passage, Str., 39 D2
Dráma, 14 C3
Drammen, 15 D4
Drau, R., 12 D4
Drava see Drau
Dresden, 12 C4
Dresden (3), Admin. U., 12 C4
Drin, R., 13 B5
Drina, R., 13 A4
Drobeta-Turnu-Severin, 14 B2
Drogheda, 10 E6
Drogobyč, 18 C1
Droichead Nua, 10 E6
Drôme (26), Admin. U., 11 C4
Druja, 17 C3
Drummondville, 33b
Druskininkai, 18 B1
Družba (Alma-Ata), 24 B2
Družba (Kursk), 18 B3
Družina, 16 C16
Dry Tortugas, I., 35 G4
Dubā, 21 D3
Dubawnt, R., 33 B9
Dubawnt Lake, L., 33 B9
Dubayy, 21 D6,7
Dubbo, 40 D4
Dublin (Ireland), 10 E6
Dublin (U.S.A.), 35 E4
Dublin, Admin. U., 10 E6
Dubna, 17 C5
Dubno, 18 B2
Dubovka, 18 C5
Dubréka, 29 C2
Dubrovnik, 13 B4
Dubuque, 35 C2
Duchess, 40 C4
Dudinka, 16 C10
Dudley, 9 C3
Duero, R., 11 F3
Duisburg, 12a A3
Dukou, 24 D4
Duku, 29 C8
Dulan, 24 C3
Duluth, 35 B2
Dūmā, 20b B2
Dumaguete, 23 C4
Dumbarton, 10 B,C2
Dumboa, 29 C9
Dumfries, 10 C3
Dumfries and Galloway (57), Admin. U., 9 B3
Dumont d'Urville, Station, 42 F
Dumyāt, 26a A3,4
Duna see Donau
Dunaj see Donau
Dunărea see Donau
Dunaújváros, 14 B1
Dunav see Donau
Duncan, 33a B2
Duncansby Head, C., 7 B6
Dundalk, 10 D6
Dundalk Bay, B., 7 E4,5
Dundee (S. Africa), 30 D4
Dundee (U.K.), 10 B3
Dundrum Bay, B., 7 D5
Dunedin, 40a B7
Dunfermline, 10 B3

Dungannon, 10 D6
Dungannon (14), Admin. U., 10 D6
Dungarvan, 10 E6
Dungas, 29 C8
Dungeness, C., 7 F8
Dunhua, 25 B8
Dunker Beacon, Mt., 7 F6
Dunkirk, 35 C5
Dunkerque, 11 B3
Dunmore Town, 35 F5
Dunnet Head, C., 7 B6
Dún Laoghaire, 10 E6,7
Dunqulah, 28 C5,6
Duns, 10 C3
Duolun, 24 B5
Duque de Caxias, 39a B5
Durance, R., 11 C4
Durango (Mexico), 36 B2
Durango (U.S.A.), 34 D5
Durango (9), Admin. U., 36 B2
Durant, 35 E1
Durazno, 39a D2
Durban, 30 D,E4
Durgāpur, 22 C7
Durham (U.K.), 9 B4
Durham (U.S.A.), 35 D5
Durham (20), Admin. U., 9 B4
Durmitor, Mt., 5 C6
Durrës, 13 B4
Duns, 10 C3
Dushan, 24 D4
Dušanbe, 16 F8,9
Düsseldorf, 12 C2
Dutch Harbor, 32 D4
Duvan, 17a B2
Duyun, 24 D4
Düzce, 21a A2
Dvinskaja Guba, B., 17 A,B5
Dwight David Eisenhower Lock, 33b
Dyersburg, 35 D3
Dyfed (48), Admin. U., 9 D2
Działdowo, 12 B5
Działinka, 24 A6
Dżambul, 24 B1
Dżankoj, 18 C3
Dżanybek, 18 C6
Dzaoudzi, 30 C5
Dżargalant, 24 B5
Dzeržinsk, 17 C6
Dżezkazgan, 16 E8,9
Dżul'fa, 18a B2
Dzuunmod, 24 B4

E

Eagle, 33 B5
Eagle Pass, 34 F6,7
Earn, R., 10 B3
Easky, 10 D5
Eastbourne, 9 D5
East Cape, C., 40a A2,3
East China Sea, 24 C,D6
East Dereham, 9 C5
Eastern Desert, Des., 26 B8
Eastern Ghāts, Mts., 19 H9,10
East European Plain, Pl., 5 A,B7-9
East Falkland, I., 39 D3

East Kilbride, 10 C2
Eastleigh, 9 D4
East London, 30 E3
Eastmain, 33 C12
Eastmain, R., 33 C12
East Retford, 9 C4
East River, Chann., 32a
East Saint Louis, 35 D2,3
East Sussex (21), Admin. U., 9 D5
Eatonville, 33a C3
Eau Claire, 35 C2
Ebbw Vale, 9 D3
Ebebiyin, 29 E8
Eberswalde-Finow, 12 B4
Ebolowa, 29 E8
Ebro, R., 11 F3
Ech Chéliff, 28 A3
Echo Bay, 33 B8
Echuca, 40 D4
Écija, 11 G2
Ecuador, St., 38 C2
Eday, I., 10 A3
Ede, 29 D7
Edéa, 29 E8
Eden, R., 7 D6
Édhessa, 14 C2
Edinburgh, 10 C3
Edirne, 21a A1
Edmundston, 35 B7
Edremit, 21a B1
Edremit Körfezi, B., 14 D3
Eduardo Castex, 39 B2
Edward VII Peninsula, Pen., 42 G15,16
Efate, I., 41 E6
Effingham, 35 D3
Egedesminde see Ausiait
Eger, 14 B2
Egersund, 15 D3
Eğridir, 21a B2
Egypt, St., 28 B5,6
Eha-Amufu, 29 D7
Eigg, I., 7 C4
Eil, 28 D7
Eindhoven, 12 C2
Eirunepé, 38 C3
Eisenach, 12 C4
Eisenerz, 12 D4
Eisenstadt, 12 D5
Ejinaqi, 24 B4
Ekibastuz, 24 A1
Ekonda, 16 C12
El Aaiún, 28 B1
Elat, 20b C2
Elazığ, 21a B3
Elbasan, 13 B4,5
Elbe see Labe
Elbistan, 21a B3
Elblag, 12 B5
El-Borj, 5a B2
El Callao, 38 B4
Elche, 11 G3
El'dikan, 16 C15
Eldorado, 39a C3
Eldoret, 30 A4
Eleskirt, 21a B4
Eleuthera, I., 35 F5
El Fendek, 5a B2
El Ferrol del Caudillo, 11 F1,2
Elgin, 10 B3
El Goléa, 28 A3
Elhovo, 14 C3
Elinghu, L., 24 C3
Elista, 18 C5
Elizabeth, 35 C6
Elizabeth City, 35 D5
El-Jadida, 28 A2
Ełk, 12 B6

page 195

El Kairouan, 28 A3,4
El Kala, 27a A2
El Kasserine, 27a A2
El Kef, 27a A2
Elkhart, 34 D6
Elko, 34 C3
Ellef Ringnes Island, I., 33 A8,9
Ellensburg, 33a C3,4
Ellesmere Island, I., 33 A11
Ellice Islands see Tuvalu
Ellsworth Land, Reg., 42 G9,10
Ellsworth Mountains, Mts., 42 G,H8-10
El Mahdia, 27a A3
El Meghaier, 27a B2
Elmira, 35 C5
El Nido, 23 B3
El Oued, 28 A3
El Paso, 34 E5
El Pico, 38 D3
El Salto, 36 B2
El Salvador, 36 C3,4
El Tigre, 38 B3
El Turbio, 39 D1
Elúru, 22 C4
Elvas, 11 G2
Elverum, 15 C4,5
El Wak, 28 D7
Ely, 9 C5
Emāmrūd, 21 B6,7
Emba, R., 16 E7
Embalse de Alcántara, L., 11 G2
Embalse de Almendra, L., 11 F2
Embalse de Cíjara, L., 11 G2
Embarcación, 39 A2
Embu, 30 B4
Emden, 12 B2
Emerald, 40 C4
Emerson, 34 B2
Emi Koussi, Mt., 26 B6
Emilia-Romagna (7), Admin. U., 13 A2
Emirdağ, 21a B2
Emmen, 12 B2
Empangeni, 30 D4
Empedrado, 39a C2
Emporia, 35 D1
Eskimo Point, 33 B10
Es'Sider, 28 A4
Escobal, 34a
Escuintl, 36 C3
Eséka, 29 E8
Esfahān, 21 C6
Eskifjörður, 15a B4
Eskişehir, 21 a B2
Esla, R., 11 F2
Esmeralda, 38 B3
Esmeraldas, 38 B2
Espanola (Canada), 33a B1
Esperance, 40 D2
Esperanza, Station, 42 F6
Espírito Santo (6), Admin. U., 38 D5
Espíritu Santo, I., 41 B6
Espoo, 15 C8
Esquel, 39 C1
Esquimalt, 33a B2
Essaouira, 28 A1,2
Essen, 12a B3
Essequibo, R., 38 B4
Essex (22), Admin. U., 9 D5
Esslingen, 12 C3
Essonne (91), Admin. U., 11 B3
Estaca de Bares, C., 11 E,F2
Estância, 38 D6
Estonian Soviet Socialist Republic, Admin. U., 16 D4
Etah, 32 B13,14
Empangeni, 30 D4
Enderbury Island, I., 41 D8,9
Enderby Land, Reg., 42 F31,32
Enewetak, I., 41 B6
Engel's, 18 B6
England, Admin. U., 9 B-D3-5
Englewood (Canada), 33a B1
Englewood (U.S.A.), 32a
English Channel, Chann., 7 F,G6,7
Enid, 34 D7
Enna, 13 C3
Ennadai, 33 B9,10
Ennedi, Mts., 26 C7
Enneri Yoo, R., 28 C4
Ennis, 10 E5
Enniscorthy, 10 E6
Enniskillen, 10 D6
Ennistymon, 10 E5
Enontekiö, 15 A7,8
Enschede, 12 B2
Ensenada, 36 A1
Entebbe, 30 A,B4
Entre Ríos (7), Admin. U., 39 B3
Entre Ríos, Reg., 37 E,F4
Enugu, 29 D7
Enumclaw, 33a C3
Épernay, 11 B3,4
Épinal, 11 B4
Episkopi, 19c B1
Epson, 9 D4
Equatorial Guinea, St., 29 E8
Ercis, 21a B4
Erdemli, 21a B2
Erdenet, 24 B4
Erechim, 39a C3
Ereğli (Turkey, İçel), 21a B2
Ereğli (Turkey, Sakarya), 21a A2
Erfurt, 12 C3
Erfurt (4), Admin. U., 12 C3
Ergani, 21a B3,4
Erg Chech, Des., 26 B4
Erg Iguidi, Des., 26 B4
Ergun Zuoqi, 24 A6
Erie, 35 C5
Erigavo, 28 C7
Erimo-misaki, C., 25 B7
Erlian, 24 B5
Ermoúpolis, 14 D3
Ernākulam, 22 C3
Erode, 20a B2
Erigal, Mt., 7 D3
Erris Head, C., 7 D2
Ertil', 18 B5
Erzincan, 21a B3
Erzurum, 21a B4
Esashi, 25 B6,7
Esbjerg, 12 B3
Esch sur Alzette, 11 B4
Ethiopia, St., 28 C,D6,7
Ethiopian Highlands, Plat., 26 C,D8,9
Etna, Vol., 5 D6
Etosha Pan, Sw., 26 F6
Étretat, 9 E5
Eucla, 40 D2
Euclid, 33b
Eugene, 34 C2
Euphrates see Fırat
Eure (27), Admin. U., 11 B3
Eure-et-Loir (28), Admin. U., 11 B3
Eureka (Ellesmere I.), 32 B12
Eureka (U.S.A., California), 34 C2
Eureka (U.S.A., Utah), 34 D4
Europe, 3
Euskadi see País Vasco
Evansville, 35 D3
Evensk, 16 C17
Everett, 34 B2
Everglades, 35 F4
Évian, 11 C4
Évora, 11 G2
Évora (7), Admin. U., 11 G2
Évreux, 11 B3
Évry, 11 B3
Évvoia, I., 14 D2,3
Ewa, 35a B2
Exe, R., 7 F6
Exeter, 9 D3
Exmoor, Reg., 7 F6
Exmouth, 9 D3
Extrtemadura (10), Admin. U., 11 G2
Ezine, 21a B1

F

Faaa, 41d B1
Faaone, 41d B2
Fachi, 29 A8
Facinac, 5a A2
Fada, 28 C5
Fada N'Gourma, 29 B6
Faenza, 13 A5
Fagamalo, 41c A1
Făgăraș 14 B3
Fagernes, 15 C4
Fagurhólsmýri, 15a C3,4
Fahūd, 21 E7
Fa'id, 26a B4
Fairbanks, 33 B5
Fair Head, C., 7 D4
Fair Isle, I., 7 B7
Faisalābād, 22 A3
Faith, 34 B6
Faizābād, 22a B2
Fakenham, 9 C5
Fakfak, 23 D3
Faku, 25 B3
Falcon Reservoir, 34 F7
Fale, 41 D8
Falkirk, 10 B3
Falkland Islands, Admin. U., 39 D2,3
Fall River, 35 C6
Falmouth, 9 D2
Falmouth Bay, B., 7 F5
Falster, I., 12 B4
Falun, 15 C5
Fanano, 13a B4
Fangliao, 25a B2
Fano, 13 B3
Fan-si-pan, Mt., 19 G12
Faraday, Station, 42 F7
Farafangana, 30 D5
Farāh, 22 A2
Farāh, R., 21 C8
Faranah, 29 C3
Fareham, 9 D4
Fargo, 34 B7
Farim, 29 B2
Farmington, 34 D5
Faro (Canada), 33 B6
Faro (Portugal), 11 G2
Faro (8), Admin. U., 11 G1
Farquhar Group, Is., 30 C5,6
Farrukhābād, 22a B1,2
Farwell, 34 E6
Fasā, 21 D6
Faure Range, Mt., 42 H12-15
Fauske, 15 B5
Faxaflói, B., 15a B2
Faxälven, R., 15 B5
Fayetteville (U.S.A., Arkansas), 35 D2
Fayetteville (U.S.A., North Carolina), 35 E5
Fazzān, Reg., 28 B4
Fderik, 28 B1
Fécamp, 11 B3
Federal Capital Territory (20), Admin. U., 29 C7
Federal Republic of Germany, St., 12 B-D2-4
Federated States of Micronesia, Admin. U., 41 C3-6
Fehmarn, I., 12 B3
Feira de Santana, 38 D6
Fejér (6), Admin. U., 14 B1
Felixstowe, 9 D5
Fénérive, 30 C5
Fengcheng, 25 A3
Fengjie, 24 C4,5
Fengning, 25 B2
Feodosija, 18 C,D4
Ferdows, 21 C7
Fergana, 16 E9
Fergus Falls, 35 B1
Fermanagh (15), Admin. U., 10 D6
Fériana, 27a B2
Ferkéssédougou, 29 C4
Fermoy, 10 E5
Ferrara, 13 A2
Fès, 28 A2
Fethiye, 21a B1
Fetlar, I., 7 A7
Feyzābād, 22 A3
Fial., I., 11a A2
Fianarantsoa, 30 D5
Fidenza, 13a B4
Fier, 13 B4
Fife (58), Admin. U., 10 B3
Figueira da Foz, 11 F1
Figueras, 11 F4
Figuig, 28 A2
Fiji, St., Is., 41b
Filchner Ice Shelf, 42 G4,5

page 196

Filingué, 29 B 6
Findhorn, R., 10 B 3
Finike, 21 a B 2
Finistère (29), Admin. U., 11 B 2
Finke, 40 C 3
Finland, St., 15 A-C 7,8
Finlay, R., 33 C 7
Finn, R., 10 D 6
Firenze, 13 B 2
Firenzuola, 13 a B 5
Firmat, 39 a D 1
Firozābād, 22 a B 1
Firth of Clyde, B., 7 D 5
Firth of Forth, B., 7 C 6
Firth of Lorn, B., 7 C 4,5
Firth of Tay, B., 7 C 6
Fish, R., 30 D 2
Fishguard, 9 D 2
Fitzhugh Sound, B., 33 a A 1
Fitzroy, R., 40 B 2
Fitzroy Crossing, 40 B 2
Fizuli, 18 a B 2
Flacq, 11 C 4
Flagstaff, 34 D 4
Flamborough Head, C., 7 D 7,8
Flatey, 15 a B 2
Flathead Lake, L., 34 B 4
Flat Island, I., 30 a A 3
Flaxton, 34 B 6
Fleetwood, 9 C 3
Flekkefjord, 15 D 3
Flensburg, 12 B 3
Flinders, R., 40 C 4
Flin Flon, 33 C 9
Flint (U.K.), 9 C 3
Flint, I., 41 E 10
Flint, R., 35 E 4
Flora, 15 C 3
Florence (Italy) see Firenze
Florence (U.S.A.), 35 E 5
Florencia, 38 B 2
Flores, 38 C 6
Flores (Atlantic Ocean), I., 11 a A 1
Flores (Indian Ocean), I., 23 D 4
Flores Sea, 23 D 3,4
Floriano, 38 C 5
Florianópolis, 39 A 4
Florida, 39 a D 2
Florida, Admin. U., 35 E,F 4
Florida Keys, Is., 35 F,G 4
Flórina, 14 C 2
Fly, R., 41 D 4
Fokku, 29 C 7
Foligno, 13 B 3
Folkestone, 9 D 5
Fond du Lac, 35 C 3
Fontainebleau, 11 B 3
Fonte Boa, 38 C 3
Forcados, 29 D 7
Forfar, 10 B 3
Forli, 13 A 2,3
Formby Point, C., 7 E 6
Formentera, I., 11 G 4
Formiga, 39 a B 4,5

Formosa see Taiwan
Formosa (Argentina), 39 A 3
Formosa (Brazil), 38 D 5
Formosa, Admin. U., 39 A 2,3
Fornovo di Taro, 13 a B 4
Forres, 10 B 3
Forrest, 40 D 2
Forsayth, 40 B 4
Fort Albany, 33 C 11
Fortaleza, 38 C 6
Fort Amador, 34 a
Fort Augustus, 10 B 2
Fort Bragg, 34 D 2
Fort Chipewyan, 33 C 8
Fort Collins, 34 C 5
Fort-de-France, 36 b B 2
Fort Dodge, 35 C 2
Fortescue, R., 40 C 1
Fort George, 33 C 12
Fortín Ayacucho, 38 D 4
Fort Lauderdale, 35 F 4,5
Fort Liard, 33 B 7
Fort Mac Murray, 33 C 8
Fort Myers, 35 F 4
Fort Nelson, 33 C 7
Fort Norman, 33 B 7
Fort Peck, 34 B 5
Fort Peck Lake, Res., 34 B 5,6
Fort Pierce, 35 F 4
Fort Providence, 33 B 8
Fort Randolph, 34 a
Fort Resolution, 33 B 8
Fort Rupert, 33 C 12
Fort Saint John, 33 C 7
Fort Sandeman, 22 A 2
Fort Selkirk, 33 B 6
Fort-Ševčenko, 16 E 7
Fort Severn, 33 C 11
Fort Sherman, 34 a
Fort Simpson, 33 B 7
Fort Smith (Canada), 33 B 8
Fort Smith (U.S.A.), 35 D 2
Fort Stockton, 34 E 6
Fort Vermilion, 33 C 8
Fort Wayne, 35 C 3
Fort Wiliam, 10 B 2
Fort Worth, 34 E 7
Fort Yukon, 33 B 5
Fossil, 31 a B 1,2
Fougères, 11 B 2
Foula, I., 10 a
Foumban, 29 D 8
Foxe Basin, 33 B 11,12
Foxe Channel, 33 B 11,12
Foyle, R., 10 D 6
Foz do Iguaçu, 39 a C 3
Franca, 39 a B 4
France, St., 11 B-D 1-5
Franceville, 30 B 2
Francistown, 30 D 3
Frankfort, 35 D 4
Frankfurt, 12 B 4
Frankfurt (7), Admin. U., 12 B 4
Frankfurt am Main, 12 C 3
Franz, 35 B 4
Fraser, R., 33 C 7,8
Fraserburgh, 10 B 3
Fraser Island, I., 40 C 5
Fray Bentos, 39 a B 2,7
Fredericksburg, 35 D 5
Fredericton, 33 D 13
Frederikshåb see Pâmiut
Frederikshavn, 12 A 3

Fredrikstad, 15 D 4
Freeport, 35 F 5
Freetown, 29 C 2
Fregenal de la Sierra, 11 G 2
Freiburg, 12 C 2,3
Fremont (U.S.A., California), 31 a C 1
Fremont (U.S.A., Nebraska), 35 C 1
French Guiana, Admin. U., 38 B 4
French Polynesia, Admin. U., 41 F 10-12
Fresno, 34 D 3
Fria, 29 C 2
Fribourg, 11 C 4
Frijoles, 34 a
Friuli-Venezia Giulia (6), Admin. U., 13 A 3
Frobisher Bay, 33 B 13
Frolovo, 18 C 5
Frosinone, 13 B 3
Fróya, I., 15 C 4
Frunze, 17 C 4,5
Frutal, 39 a A 4
Fuerte Olimpo, 39 A 3
Fuerteventura, I., 26 b B 2
Fuji, 25 C 6
Fujian (7), Admin. U., 24 D 5
Fuji-San, Vol., 19 F 15
Fukui, 25 C 6
Fukuoka, 25 D 4,5
Fukushima (Japan, Sapporo), 25 B 6,7
Fukushima (Japan, Tokyō), 25 D 5
Fukuyama, 25 D 5
Fulda, 12 C 3
Fulham, 9 a
Fulton, 33 b
Funaco, 38 C 5
Funafuti, I., 41 D 7,8
Funchal, 28 A 1
Funing, 25 D 2,3
Funtua, 29 C 7
Furmanovo, 18 C 6,7
Furneaux Group, Is., 40 D,E 4
Fürth, 12 C 3
Fushun, 24 B 6
Fusong, 25 B 4
Futuna, 41 E 8
Fuxian, 25 C 3
Fuxin, 25 B 3
Fuyu, 25 A 3,4
Fuzhou (China, Fujian), 24 D 5,6
Fuzhou (China, Jiangxi), 24 D 5

G

Gabela, 30 C 2
Gabès, 28 A 4
Gabon, St., 30 A,B 2
Gaborone, 30 D 3
Gabrovo, 14 C 3
Gabrovo (3), Admin. U., 14 C 3
Gachsārān, 21 C 6
Gad'ač, 18 B 3
Gadag, 20 a A 1,7
Gäddede, 15 B 5
Gadsden, 35 E 3

Gaeta, 13 B 3
Gafsa, 28 A 3
Gagarin, 17 C 4,5
Gagnoa, 29 D 4
Gagnon, 33 C 13
Gagra, 18 D 5
Gainesville, 35 F 4
Gainsborough, 9 C 4
Gaiping, 25 B 3
Gairloch, 10 B 2
Gajny, 17 B 8
Gajsin, 18 C 2
Galana, R., 30 B 4
Galapagos Islands see Archipiélago de Colón
Galashiels, 10 C 3
Galaţi, 14 B 3,4
Galela, 23 C 4
Galesburg, 35 C 2
Galič, 17 C 6
Galicia (11), Admin. U., 11 F 1,2
Galka'yo, 28 D 7
Galle, 20 a C 3
Gallipoli, 13 B 4
Gällivare, 15 B 7
Gallup, 34 D 5
Galty Mountains, Mts., 7 E 3,4
Galveston, 35 F 2
Galveston Bay, B., 35 F 2
Gálvez, 39 a D 1
Galway, 10 E 5
Galway Bay, B., 7 E 3
Gamarra, 38 B 2
Gambaga, 29 C 5
Gambela, 28 D 6
Gambell, 33 B 2
Gambia, St., 29 B 1,2
Gambie, R., 29 B 2
Gamboa, 34 a
Gambona, 30 B 2
Gand see Gent
Gandajika, 30 B 3
Gandak, R., 22 B 3
Gander, 33 D 14
Gandhinagar, 22 B 3
Gandia, 11 G 3,4
Ganga, R., 22 B 3
Ganges see Ganga
Gangtok, 22 B 4
Gannett Peak, Mt., 31 E 9,10
Gansu (8), Admin. U., 24 B 3
Ganta, 29 D 3
Ganzhou, 24 D 5
Ganzi, 24 C 4
Gao, 29 A 5
Gaoua, 29 C 5
Gaoual, 29 C 2
Gaoyou, 25 D 2
Gaoyouhu, L., 25 D 2
Gap, 11 C 4
Garafia, 26 b B 2
Garanhuns, 38 C 6
Garapan, 41 B 4
Gard (30), Admin. U., 11 C 4
Garden City, 34 D 6
Gardiner, 34 B 4,5
Gardo, 28 D 7
Gari, 17 a B 3
Garissa, 30 B 4,5
Garmsar, 21 B 6
Garonne (Haute-) (31), Admin. U., 11 D 3
Garonne, R., 11 D 3
Garoua, 29 C 9
Garry Lake, L., 33 B 10
Gartok, 24 C 2

Garut, 23aA1
Gary, 35C3
Gasan-Kuli, 21B6
Gascoyne, R., 40C1
Gashua, 29B8
Gashunu, L., 24B3,4
Gaspé, 33D13
Gatčina, 17C3,4
Gateshead, 9B4
Gatineau, 33b
Gatineau, R., 33b
Gatun, 34a
Gatun, R., 34a
Gatuncillo, 34a
Gatuncillo, R., 34a
Gatun Lake, L., 34a
Gauja, R., 17C2,3
Gaussberg, H., 42F28
Gávdhos, I., 14E3
Gävle, 15C6
Gawso, 29D5
Gaya (India), 22B4
Gaya (Niger), 29B,C6
Gaziantep, 21aB3
Gbarnga, 29D3
Gdańsk, 12B5
Gdov, 17C3
Gdynia, 12B5
Géba, R., 29B2
Gediz, R., 21aB1
Gedser, 11D3
Geelong, 40D4
Geidam, 29B8
Geiju, 24D4
Gela, 13C3
Gelendžik, 18D4
Gelibolu, 21aA1
Gelsenkirchen, 12aA3
Gemlik, 21aA1
General Belgrano I, Station, 42G,H1-4
General Belgrano II, Station, 42G,H2-5
General Juan Madariaga, 39aE2
General Lavalle, 39aE2
General Santos, 23C4
Genesee, R., 33b
Geneva see Genève
Geneva, 33b
Genève, 11C4
Geničensk, 16aA2
Genil, R., 11G2
Genoa see Genova
Genova, 13A2
Gent, 11B3,4
Geokčaj, 18aA2
George, R., 33C13
George V Coast, Reg., 42F21,22
Georgetown (Guyana), 38B4
Georgetown (U.S.A.), 35E5
Georgia, Admin. U., 35E4
Georgian Bay, 34B,C4
Georgian Soviet Socialist Republic, Admin. U., 16E6
Georgijevsk, 18D5
Georgina, R., 40C3
Georgiu Dež, 18B4
Georg von Neumayer, Station, 42F,G1-3
Gera, 12C4
Gera (6), Admin. U., 12C3
Geraldton, 40C1
Gereshk, 21C8
Gerlachovský štít, Mt., 5C6,7

German Democratic Republic, St.,12B,C3,4
Germiston, 30D3
Gerona, 11F4
Gers (32), Admin. U., 11D3
Gevelsberg, 12aB3
Ghāghra, R., 22B4
Ghana, St., 29C,D5
Ghanzi, 30D3
Ghardaïa, 28A3
Gharyān, 28A4
Ghāt, 28B4
Ghazni, 22A2
Ghazzah, 28A6
Gheorghe Gheorghiu-Dej, 14B3
Ghudāmis, 28A3,4
Ghūriān, 21C8
Gibeon, 30D2
Gibraltar, 5aA3
Gibson Desert, Des., 40C2
Giessen, 12C3
Gifu, 25C6
Gigha Island, I., 7D4,5
Gijón, 11F2
Gila, R., 34E5
Gila Bend, 34E4
Gilbert Islands, 41C,D7
Gilgit, 22A3
Gillette, 34C5
Gillingham, 9D5
Giresun, 21aA3
Gironde (33), Admin. U., 11C2
Gironde, Reg., 11C2
Girvan, 10C2
Gisborne, 40aA2
Gisenyi, 30B3
Gitega, 30B3,4
Giurgiu, 14C3
Gjirokastër, 13B4,5
Gjoa Haven, 33B10
Gjøvik, 15C4
Glacier Peak, Mt., 31aA1
Gladstone (Australia), 40C5
Gladstone (Canada), 34A7
Gläma, R., 15C4
Glasgow, 10C2
Glazov, 17C8
Glen Canyon, 34D4
Glendale (U.S.A., Arizona), 34E4
Glendale (U.S.A., Calif.), 34E3
Glendive, 34B5
Glen Innes, 40C5
Glen More, Val., 7C5
Glenrothes, 10B3
Glens Falls, 35C6
Glittertinden, Mt., 5A5
Gliwice, 12C5
Głogów, 12B5
Gloucester, 9D3
Gloucestershire (23), Admin. U., 9D3
Glubokoje, 17C3
Gluchov, 18B3
Gmünd, 12C4
Gniezno, 12B5
Goa, Admin. U., 22C3
Goba, 28D6,7
Gobabis, 30D2
Gobernador Gregores, 39C1,2
Gobi, Des., 19E11-13
Goce Delčev, 14C2

Godāvari, R., 22C3,4
Godhavn see Qeqertarssuaq
Godoy Cruz, 39B2
Godthåb see Núk
Godwin Austen, Mt., 19F9,10
Goiânia, 38D5
Goiás, 38D4
Goiás, Admin. U., 38C,D,4,5
Gökçeada, I., 21aA1
Göksu, R., 21aB2
Gold Coast, 40C5
Gold Coast, Reg., 26D4
Golden Gate, Str., 31aC1
Goldsworthy, 40C2
Golfe de Gabès, G., 28A4
Golfe de Saint-Malo, B., 11B2
Golfe de Tunis, B., 13C2
Golfe du Lion, G., 11D3,4
Golfo de Ana María, B., 36aB4
Golfo de Batabanó, B., 36aA2
Golfo de Cádiz, G., 11G2
Golfo de California, G., 36A,B1,2
Golfo de Campeche, B., 31G11
Golfo de Guacanayabo, B., 36aB4,5
Golfo del Darién, B., 38B2
Golfo de los Mosquitos, B., 36C,D4
Golfo de Panamá, B., 36D5
Golfo de San Jorge, B., 37G3
Golfo de Valencia, B., 11G4
Golfo de Venezuela, B., 38A2
Golfo di Cagliari, B., 13C2
Golfo di Genova, B., 13A,B2
Golfo di Salerno, B., 13B3
Golfo di Taranto, B., 13B,C4
Golfo San Jorge, B., 39C2
Golfo San Matías, B., 37G3
Golmud, 24C3
Golpāyegān, 21C6
Goma, 30B3
Gomati, R., 22aB2
Gombe, 29C8
Gomel', 18B3
Gomera, I., 26bB1,2
Gómez Palacio, 36B2
Gonaïves, 36C5
Gonder, 28C6
Gonggashan, Mt., 19F11,12
Gongola (7), Admin. U., 29C8
Gongola, R., 29C8
Goodwindi, 40C5
Goose Bay, 33C13
Goose Lake, L., 31aB1,2
Göppingen, 12C3

Gora Belucha, Mt., 19D10,11
Gora El'brus, Mt., 19E6
Gora Jamantau, Mt., 5B10
Gora Kazbek, Mt., 5C9
Gorakhpur, 22B4
Gora Munku-Sardyk, Mt., 19D11,12
Gora Mus-Chaja, Mt., 42B32,33
Gora Pobeda, Mt., 42B33,34
Gore, 28D6
Goré, 28D4
Gorey, 10E6
Gorgān, 21B6
Gori, 18D5
Gorizia, 13A3
Gorki, 18D4
Gor'kij, 16D6
Gor'kovskoje Vodochranilišče, Res., 17C6
Görlitz, 12C4
Gorlovka, 18C4
Gorno-Altajsk, 16D10
Gorodnica, 18B2
Gorodovikovsk, 18C5
Gorontalo, 23C4
Gort, 10E5
Goryn', R., 18B2
Gorzów Wielkopolski, 12B4
Gospić, 13A3
Gosport, 9D4
Gostivar, 13B5
Göta Kanal, Can., 15D5,6
Göteborg, 15D4,5
Gotha, 12C3
Gotland, I., 15D6
Gotō-rettō, Is., 25D4
Göttingen, 12C3
Gottwaldov see Zlín
Goulburn, 40D4,5
Goundam, 29A5
Gouré, 29B8
Governador Valadares, 38D5,6
Goya, 39aC2
Göynük, 21aA2
Graciosa, I., 11aA2
Gradaús, 38C4
Grafton, 40C5
Graham Land, Reg., 42F7
Grain Coast, Reg., 26D3,4
Grajaú, R., 38C5
Grampian (59), Admin. U., 10B3
Grampian Mountains, Mts., 7C5,6
Granada (Nicaragua), 36C4
Granada (Spain), 11G3
Granby, 33b
Gran Canaria, I., 26bC3
Gran Chaco, Pl., 37D,E3
Grand Bahama, I., 35F5
Grand Bassam, 29D5
Grand Canal see Yunhe
Grand Canyon, 34D4
Grand Cess, 29D3
Grand Coulee, 34B3
Grande (Madeira), R., 38D3
Grande (Paraná), R., 38E4,5

Grande Baleine, R., 33 C 12
Grande Comore, I., 30 C 5
Grande Prairie, 33 C 8
Grand Erg Occidental, Des., 26 A,B 4,5
Grand Erg Oriental, Des., 26 A,B 5
Grand Forks (Canada), 33 a B 4
Grand Forks (U.S.A.), 34 B 7
Grand Island, 34 C 7
Grand Junction, 34 D 5
Grand-Lahou, 29 D 4
Grand Marais, 35 B 2
Grand' Mère, 35 B 6
Grand Rapids, 35 C 3
Grand Turk, 32 G 13
Grand Union Canal, Can., 9 a
Grangemouth, 10 B,C 3
Granger, 34 C 4,5
Granite City, 35 D 2,3
Grantham, 9 C 4
Grant Land, Reg., 42 D 10,11
Grants Pass, 34 C 2
Granville, 11 B 2
Grass River, R., 33 b
Gravesend, 9 D 5
Grays Thurrock, 9 D 5
Graz, 12 D 4
Gr'azi, 18 B 4,5
Great Abaco, I., 35 F 5
Great Australian Bight, G., 40 D 2,3
Great Barrier Reef, Reg., 40 B,C 4,5
Great Basin, Reg., 31 E,F 9
Great Bear Lake, L., 33 B 7,8
Great Bend, 34 C 7
Great Britain, I., 7 C F 5-7
Great Dividing Range, Mts., 40 B-D 4
Greater Antilles, Is., 36 B,C 4,5
Greater London (1), Admin. U., 9 D 4
Greater Manchester (2), Admin. U., 9 C 3
Great Falls, 34 B 4,5
Great Inagua, I., 36 B 5
Great Karroo, Plat., 26 H 7
Great Ormes Head, C., 7 E 5,6
Great Ouse, R., 7 E 8
Great Plain of China, Pl., 19 F 13,14
Great Plains, Pl., 31 D-F 9-11
Great Ruaha, R., 30 B 4
Great Salt Lake, L., 34 C 4
Great Sandy Desert, Des., 40 C 2
Great Slave Lake, L., 33 B 8
Great Victoria Desert, Des., 40 C 2,3
Great Yarmouth, 9 C 5
Greece, St., 14 C,D 2,3
Greeley, 34 C 6
Green, R., 34 D 4
Green Bay, 35 C 3
Green Bay, B., 35 B 3
Greenland, Admin. U., 33 A,B 15
Greenland Sea, 15 a A 2-4
Greenock, 10 C 2

Greensboro, 35 D 4,5
Greenvale, 40 B 4
Greenville (Liberia), 29 D 3
Greenville (U.S.A., Maine), 35 B 7
Greenville (U.S.A., Mississippi), 35 E 2
Greenville (U.S.A., New York), 33 b
Greenville (U.S.A., South Carolina), 35 E 4
Greenwich, 9 a
Greenwood (U.S.A., Mississippi), 35 E 2,3
Greenwood (U.S.A., South Carolina), 35 E 4
Greifswald, 12 B 4
Gremicha, 17 A 5
Grenada, St., I., 36 b B 2
Grenadine Islands, Is., 36 b B 2
Grenen, C., 12 A 3
Grenoble, 11 C 4
Gretna Green, 10 C 3
Grevenbroich, 12 a B 2
Greymouth, 40 a B 1,2
Griffith, 40 D 4
Grimsby, 9 C 4
Grimsey, I., 15 a A 3
Grímsstaðir, 15 a B 3,4
Grindavík, 15 a C 2
Grodno, 18 B 1
Grong, 15 B 5
Groningen, 12 B 2
Groote Eylandt, I., 40 B 3
Grootfontein, 30 C 2
Grosseto, 13 B 2
Grossglockner, Mt., 5 C 6
Groznyj, 18 D 6
Grudziądz, 12 B 5
Grytviken, Station, 42 E 4
Guadalajara (Mexico), 36 B 2
Guadalajara (Spain), 11 F 3
Guadalamar, R., 11 G 3
Guadalcanal, I., 40 B 5,6
Guadalquivir, R., 11 G 2
Guadeloupe, I., 36 b A 2
Guadiana, R., 11 G 2
Guadix, 11 G 3
Guaíra, 39 A 3
Guajará Mirim, 38 D 3
Gualeguaychú, 39 a D 2
Guam, I., 41 B 4
Guamini, 39 a E 1
Guanajuato (10), Admin. U., 36 B 2
Guane, 36 a A 1
Guangdong (9), Admin. U., 24 D 5
Guanghua, 24 C 5
Guangxi Zhuangzu Zizhiqu (1), Admin. U., 24 D 4
Guangyuan, 24 C 4
Guangzhou, 24 D 5
Guanhe, R., 25 D 2
Guantánamo, 36 a B 6
Guaporé, R., 37 D 3
Guaqui, 38 D 3
Guarapuava, 39 a C 3
Guaratuba, 39 a C 4
Guarda, 11 F 2
Guarda (9), Admin. U., 11 F 2
Guarulhos, 39 a B 4
Guastalla, 13 a B 4
Guatemala, 36 C 3,4
Guatemala, St., 36 C 3,4
Guaviare, R., 37 B 2

Guaxupe, 39 a B 4
Guayaquil, 38 C 1,2
Guaymallén, 39 B 2
Guaymas, 36 B 1
Gubacha, 17 a B 2
Gubkin, 18 B 4
Gudermes, 18 D 6
Güdür, 20 a A 2
Guelma, 27 a A 2
Guelph, 33 b
Guelta Zemmur, 28 B 1
Guemar, 27 a B 2
Guerara, 27 a B 1
Guéret, 11 C 3
Guernsey, I., 6 a A 2
Guerrero (11), Admin. U., 36 C 2
Guiana Highlands, Hs., 37 B 3,4
Guichi, 25 D 2
Guiglo, 29 D 4
Guiiá, 30 D 4
Guildford, 9 D 4
Guilin, 24 D 4,5
Guinea, Reg., 26 D,E 4-6
Guinea, St., 29 C 2,3
Guinea-Bissau, St., 29 B,C 2
Guinguinéo, 29 B 2
Guiyang, 24 D 4
Guizhou (10), Admin. U., 24 D 4
Gujarat, Admin. U., 22 B 2,3
Gujrānwāla, 22 A 3
Gulbarga, 22 C 3
Gulbene, 17 C 3
Gulf of Aden, G., 28 C 7,8
Gulf of Alaska, G., 33 C 5,6
Gulf of Boothia, G., 33 A,B 10,11
Gulf of Bothnia, G., 15 B,C 6,7
Gulf of Cambay, G., 22 B,C 3
Gulf of Carpentaria, G., 40 B 2,3
Gulf of Finland, G., 15 C,D 7,8
Gulf of Guinea, G., 26 D,E 4,5
Gulf of Kutch, G., 22 B 2
Gulf of Mannar, G., 20 a B,C 2
Gulf of Mexico, G., 36 B 3,4
Gulf of Mexico Plain, Pl., 31 F,G 11,12
Gulf of Oman, G., 21 D,E 7
Gulf of Panama, G., 36 D 4
Gulf of Papua, G., 40 A 4
Gulf of Saint Lawrence, G., 33 D 13
Gulf of Sidra, G., 28 A 4
Gulf of Suez, G., 26 a C 4
Gulf of Thailand, G., 22 C,D 6
Gulf of Tonkin, G., 22 B,C 6
Gulf of Trieste, G., 13 A 3
Gulf of Venice, G., 13 B 3
Gulfport, 35 E,F 3
Gulian, 24 A 6
Gulu, 28 D 6
Gümüşhane, 21 a A 3
Guna, 22 B 3
Gunnbjörns Fjeld, Mt., 42 B 15,16
Gunong Tahan, Mt., 19 b B 3

Guntakal, 20 a A 2
Guntūr, 22 C 3,4
Gunung Kerintji, Mt., 19 J 11,12
Gunung Talakmau, Volc., 19 b D 1,2
Gurguéia, R., 38 C 5
Gurjev, 16 E 6,7
Gurupá, 38 C 4
Gurupi, 38 D 5
Gurupi, R., 38 C 5
Gusau, 29 B 7
Gus'-Chrustal'nyj, 17 C 6
Gushan, 25 C 3
Gusinoozersk, 16 b B 2
Gütaşlir, R., 15 D 5
Gutiérrez, 36 C 3
Guwāhāti, 22 B 5
Guyana, St., 38 B 3,4
Guyuan, 25 B 2
Guzmán, 34 E 5
Gvardejskoje, 18 C 3
Gwâdar, 22 B 2
Gwalior, 22 B 3
Gweedore, 10 D 5
Gwent (49), Admin. U., 9 D 3
Gweru, 30 C 3,4
Gwynedd (50), Admin. U., 9 C 2
Gydanskij Poluostrov, Pen., 16 B 9,10
Gympie, 40 C 5
Győr, 14 B 1
Győr-Sopron (7), Admin. U., 14 B 1
Gypsumville, 33 C 10

H

Ha'apai Group, Is., 41 F 8
Haapajärvi, 15 C 8
Haapamäki, 15 C 7,8
Haapsalu, 17 C 2
Haarlem, 12 B 2
Haboro, 25 B 7
Habshān, 21 E 6
Hachinohe, 25 B 7
Hackney, 9 a
Haddington, 10 C 3
Hadejia, 29 B 8
Hadūr Shu'ayb, Mt., 19 H 6
Haeju, 25 C 4
Hafnarfjörður, 15 a B 2
Hafûn, 28 C 8
Hagen, 12 a B 3
Hagerstown, 35 D 5
Haikou, 24 D,E 5
Hā'il, 21 D 4
Hailar, 24 B 5
Hailarhe, R., 24 B 6
Hailey, 34 C 4
Hailong, 24 B 6
Hailun, 24 B 6
Hailuoto, I., 15 B 7,8
Hainandao, I., 24 E 5
Hai-Phong, 22 B 6
Haiti, St., 36 C 5
Haiyang, 25 C 3
Hajdú-Bihar (8), Admin. U., 14 B 2
Hajnówka, 12 B 6
Hakkâri, 21 a B 4
Hakodate, 25 B 7
Halab, 20 b A 2
Halā'ib, 28 C 7
Halawa, 35 a B 3
Halden, 15 D 4

...ax (Canada), 33 D 13	Hartland Point, C., 7 F 5	Hérault (34), Admin. U., 11 D 3	Holsteinsborg see Sisimiut
...fax (U.K.), 9 C 4	Hartlepool, 9 B 4	Hereford, 9 C 3	Holy Cross, 33 B 3
...il, R., 21 D 7	Härüt, R., 21 C 8	Hereford and Worcester (25), Admin. U., 9 C 3	Holyhead, 9 C 2
Halle, 12 C 3	Harwich, 9 D 5		Holy Island, I., 9 C 2
Halle (7), Admin. U., 12 C 3	Haryana (1), Admin. U., 22 B 3	Herma Ness, C., 10a	Hombori, 29 B 5
Halley, Station, 42 G 3,4	Haskovo, 14 C 3	Hermosillo, 36 B 1,2	Homestead, 35 F 4
Halls Creek, 40 B 2	Haskovo (4), Admin. U., 14 C 3	Herne, 12a A 3	Honduras, St., 36 C 4
Halmahera, I., 23 C 4,5	Hassi Messaoud, 28 A 3	Herning, 12 A 3	Hon-Gai, 22 B 6
Halmstad, 15 D 5	Hassi R'Mel, 28 A 3	Hertford, 9 D 4	Hong Kong, 19a B 3
Hamada, 25 C,D 5	Hässleholm, 12 A 4	Hertfordshire (26), Admin. U., 9 D 4	Hong Kong, Admin. U., 19a B 2,3
Hamadān, 21 C 5	Hastings (N.Z.), 40a A 2	Hessen (5), Admin. U., 12 C 3	Hong Kong, I., 19a B 3
Hamāh, 20b B 2	Hastings (U.K.), 9 D 5	Hetian, 24 C 1	Hongshuihe, R., 24 D 4
Hamamatsu, 25 D 6	Hastings (U.S.A.), 34 C 7	Heves (9), Admin. U., 14 B 2	Hongzehu, L., 25 D 2
Hamar, 15 C 4	Ha-Tinh, 22 C 6		Honiara, 40 A 5
Hamburg, 12 B 3	Hattiesburg, 35 E 3	Hexham, 10 C 3	Honiton, 9 D 3
Hamburg (4), Admin. U., 12 B 3	Hattingen, 12a B 3	Hexigten Qi, 24 B 2	Honningsvåg, 15 A 8
Hämeenlinna, 15 C 7,8	Hat Yai, 22 D 5,6	Heysham, 9 B 3	Honokaa, 35a B 4
Hamhŭng, 25 B 4	Haugesund, 15 D 3	Hialeah, 35 F 4	Honolulu, 35a B 2,3
Hami, 24 B 3	Hau Hoi Wan, B., 19a A,B 2	Hiawatha, 34 D 4	Honshū, 1., 25 B,C 5,6
Hamilton (Australia), 40 D 4	Hauts-de-Seine (92), Admin. U., 11 B 3	Hickory, 35 D 4	Hoogly, River Channel, 22 B 4
Hamilton (Bermuda), 32 F 14	Havant, 9 D 4	Hidalgo (12), Admin. U., 36 B 3	Hook Head, C., 10 E 6
Hamilton (Canada), 33 D 11,12	Haverfordwest, 9 D 2	Hidalgo del Parral, 36 B 2	Hooper, 33a C 4
Hamilton (New Zealand), 40a A 2	Havířov, 12 C 5	Hienghène, 41a K 1	Hopa, 21a A 4
Hamilton (U.K.), 10 C 2	Havre, 34 B 5	Hierro, I., 26b C 1,2	Hope, 33 D 7
Hamm, 12a A 4	Hawaii, Admin. U., 35a B,C 2,3	Highland (60), Admin. U., 10 B 2	Hopedale, 33 C 13,14
Hammerfest, 15 A 7,8	Hawaii, I., 35a B 4	High Level, 33 C 8	Hoquiam, 33a C 2
Hammersmith, 9a	Hawaiian Islands, Is., 3	High Willhays, Mt., 7 F 5,6	Horn, C., 15a A 2
Hammond (U.S.A., Indiana), 35 C 3	Hawalli, 21 D 5	High Wycombe, 9 D 4	Hornád, R., 12 C 6
Hammond (U.S.A., Louisiana), 35 E 2,3	Hawi, 35a B 4	Hildesheim, 12 B 3	Hornavan, I., 15 B 6
Hampshire (4), Admin. U., 9 D 4	Hawick, 10 C 3	Hillsborough, 10 D 6,7	Horncastle, 9 C 4,5
Hampstead, 9a	Hawr al-Tharthār, L., 20b B 3	Hilo, 35a C 4	Horsens, 12 B 3
Hāmūn-e-Jaz Mūriān, L., 21 D 7	Hay, R., 33 C 8	Himachal Pradesh, Admin. U., 22 A 3	Horsham (Australia), 40 D 4
Hāmūn-e Şāberī, L., 21 C 8	Hayes, R., 33 C 10	Himalayas, Mts., 19 F, G 9-11	Horsham (U.K.), 8 D 4
Hāmūn-i-Māshkel, L., 22 B 2	Hay River, 33 B 8	Himeji, 25 C,D 5	Horta, 11a A 2
Hana, 35a B 3,4	Hays, 34 D 7	Hims, 20b B 2	Hospitalet, 11 F 4
Hanamaki, 25 C 7	Hazelton, 33 C 7	Hindu Kush, Mts., 19 F 8,9	Hotazel, 30 D 3
Hanau, 12 C 3	Hazen, 34 D 3	Hines Creek, 33 C 8	Hoting, 15 B 6
Hanceville, 33a A 2	Héa, 14 D 2	Hınıs, 21a B 4	Hot Springs, 35 E 2
Hancheng, 24 C 4	Heard Island, I., 3	Hinnøya, I., 15 A 5,6	Hottah Lake, L., 33 B 8
Handan, 24 C 5	Hearst, 33 D 11	Hirosaki, 25 B 6,7	Houailou, 41a A 1
Hangö, 15 D 7	Heavener, 35 E 2	Hiroshima, 25 C,D 5	Houlton, 35 B 7
Hangzhou, 24 C 5,6	Hebei (11), Admin. U., 24 C 5	Hirson, 11 B 3,4	Houma, 35 F 2
Hanna, 34 A 4	Hebron, 33 C 13	Hispaniola, I., 31 H 13,14	Houston, 35 F 1,2
Hannibal, 35 D 2	Hechuan, 24 D 4	Hitachi, 25 C 7	Hove, 9 D 4
Hannover, 12 B 3	Hede, 20b B 1	Hitchin, 9 D 4	Howland Island, I., 41 C 8
Ha-Noi, 22 B 6	Hefa, 20b B 1	Hitiaa, 41 e B 2	Hoxie, 35 D 2
Hanzhong, 24 C 4	Hefei, 24 C 5	Hitra, I., 15 C 3,4	Hoy, I., 7 B 6
Hao, 41 e E 11,12	Hegang, 24 B 7	Hiumaa, I., 17 C 2	Høyanger, 15 C 3
Hāora, 22 B 4	Heidelberg, 12 C 3	Hjørring, 12 A 3	Hradec Králové, 12 C 4,5
Haparanda, 15 B 7,8	Heihe, 24 A 6	Ho, 29 D 6	Hron, R., 12 C 5
Harare, 30 C 2	Heilbronn, 12 C 3	Hoa-Binh, 22 B 6	Hrubieszów, 12 C 6
Harbel, 29 D 3	Heilongjiang (12), Admin. U., 24 B 6	Hobart, 40 E 4	Hrvatska (3), Admin. U., 13 A 4
Harbin, 24 B 6	Heilongjiang, R., 16 D 14	Hobbs, 34 E 6	Hsinchu, 24 D 6
Hardangerfjorden, B., 15 C 3	Heinola, 15 C 8	Hoboken, 32a	Huacho, 38 D 2
Harer, 28 D 7	Heishan, 25 B 3	Hodgson, 34 A 7	Huade, 25 B 3
Hargeysa, 28 D 7	Hejian, 25 C 2	Hódmezővásárhely, 14 B 2	Huaihe, R., 24 C 5
Harirüd, R., 22 A 2	Helena, 34 B 4	Hof, 12 C 3	Huailai, 25 B 2
Harlan, 35 C 1,2	Hellín, 11 G 3	Höfðakaupstaður, 15a A 2,3	Huainan, 24 C 5
Harlow, 9 D 5	Helmand, R., 22 A 2	Höfn, 15a B 4	Huaiyin, 24 C 5
Härnösand, 15 C 6	Helmsdale, 10 A 3	Hofsjökull, Glac., 15a B 3	Hualien, 25a B 2
Haroldswick, 10a	Helong, 25 B 4	Hohhot, 24 B 5	Huallaga, R., 38 C 2
Harper, 29 D 3,4	Helsingborg, 15 D 5	Hokitika, 40a B 1,2	Huambo, 30 C 2
Harris, Reg., 10 B 1	Helsingør, 12 A 3,4	Hokkaidō, I., 25 B 6,7	Huancavelica, 38 D 2
Harrisburg, 35 C 5	Helsinki, 15 C 8	Holbrook, 34 D 4,5	Huancayo, 38 D 2
Harrogate, 9 B,C 4	Hemel Hempstead, 9 D 4	Holdrege, 34 C 6,7	Huanghe, R., 24 C,D 5
Harstad, 15 A 6	Henan (13), Admin. U., 24 C 5	Holguín, 36a B 5,6	Huangshi, 24 C,D 5
Hartbees, R., 30 D, E 3	Henderson Island, I., 41 F 13	Holly Springs, 35 E 2,3	Huánuco, 38 C 2
Hartford, 35 C 6	Hengshui, 25 C 2	Hollywood, 35 F 4,5	Huaraz, 38 C 2
	Hengyang, 24 D 5	Holman Island, 33 A 8	Hubei (14), Admin. U., 24 C 5
	Henzada, 22 C 5	Hólmavík, 15a B 2	Hubli, 22 C 3
	Herāt, 22 A 2	Holstebro, 12 A 3	Huddersfield, 9 C 4
			Hudiksvall, 15 C 6
			Hudson, R., 35 C 6
			Hudson Bay, B., 33 B,C 10,11

page 200

Hudson Strait, Str., 33 B12,13
Hue, 22 C6
Huelva, 11 G2
Huesca, 11 F3
Hughenden, 40 C4
Hugo, 35 E1
Huich'ŏn, 25 B4
Huimin, 25 C2
Huize, 24 D4
Hull, 35 B5
Hulunchi, L., 24 B5
Hulwân, 26a C3
Huma, 24 A6
Humahuaca, 39 A2
Humaitá, 38 C3
Humber, B., 7 E7,8
Humberside (27), Admin. U., 9 C4
Humboldt, R., 34 C3
Húnaflói, B., 15a A,B2
Hunan (15), Admin. U., 24 D5
Hunedoara, 14 B2
Hungary, St., 14 B1,2
Hüngnam, 25 C4
Huntingdon (U.K.), 9 C4
Huntington (U.S.A.), 35 D4
Huntly, 10 B3
Huntsville, 35 E3
Hurao, 24 B7
Huron, 34 C7
Húsavík, 15a A,B3
Hutchinson, 34 D7
Huzhou, 25 D2,3
Hvannadalshnúkur, Mt., 5 A3
Hwange, 30 C3
Hyderābād (India), 22 C3
Hyderābād (Pakistan), 22 B2
Hyesan, 25 B4
Hyrynsalmi, 15 B9
Hyvinkää, 15 C8

I

Ialomiţa, R., 14 B3
Ias Casas, 36 C3
Iaşi, 14 B3
Ibadan, 29 D6,7
Ibagué, 38 B2
Ibar, R., 13 B5
Ibarra, 38 B2
Ibb, 28 C7
Iberian Peninsula, Pen., 5 C,D4
Ibi, 29 C6
Ibiá, 39a A4
Ibicuí, R., 39a C2
Ibicuy, 39 B3
Ibiza, 11 G4
Ibiza, I., 11 G4
'Ibrī, 21 E7
Ica, 38 D2
Içana, 38 B3
Içana, R., 38 B3
Iceland, St., I., 15a
Idaho, Admin. U., 34 B,C3,4
Idaho Falls, 34 C4
Idfū, 26 B6
Ídhra, I., 14 D2
Idlib, 20b B2
Ife, 29 D7
Igarka, 16 C10
Iglesias, 13 C2
Igloolik, 33 B11
Ignoumenítsa, 14 D2

Iguaçu, R., 39 A3
Iguape, 39a B4
Ihiala, 29 D7
Ihosy, 30 D5
Iijoki, R., 15 B8
Iisalmi, 15 C8,9
Ijebu-Ode, 29 D6,7
IJsselmeer, L., 12 B2
Ijuí, R., 39a C2
Ikaría, I., 14 D3
Ikeja, 29 D6
Ikela, 30 B3
Ikerre, 29 D7
Ikom, 29 D8
Ila, 29 C7
Ilagan, 23 B4
Iława, 12 B5
Île Amsterdam, I., 3
Ilebo, 30 B3
Île de Djerba, I., 27a B3
Île de Montréal, I., 33b
Île de Ré, I., 11 C2
Île des Pins, I., 41a B2
Île d'Oléron, I., 11 C2
Île d-Ouessant, I., 11 B1
Île Europa, I., 30 D4,5
Île Jesus, I., 33b
Île Juan de Nova, I., 30 C5
Île Lifou, I., 41a A2
Île Maré, I., 41a A2
Île Perrot, I., 33b
Île Saint-Paul, I., 3
Îles Australes see Îles Toubouai
Îles Chesterfield, Is., 40 B5
Îles Crozet, Is., 3
Îles de la Société, Arch., 41 E10,11
Îles du Vent, Is., 41 E10,11
Îles Gambier, Is., 41 F12
Îles Glorieuses, Is., 30 C5
Ilesha, 29 D7
Îles Kerguélen, Is., 3
Îles Loyauté, Is., 41a A2
Îles Marquises, Is., 3
Îles Toubouai, Is., 41 F10,11
Îles Tuamotu, Arch., 41 E,F11,12
Îles Wallis, Is., 41 E8
Île Uvéa, I., 41a A2
Ilfracombe, 9 D2
Ilgın, 21a B2
Ilha Caviana, I., 38 B5
Ilha de Maracá, I., 38 B5
Ilha de Marajó, I., 37 B,C5
Ilha de Santa Catarina, I., 39a C4
Ilha de São Sebastião, I., 39a B4,5
Ilhas Selvagens, Is., 26b A2,3
Ilhéus, 38 D6
Ili, R., 16 E9
Iliamna Lake, L., 31 D5
Iliamna Volcano, Vol., 31 C4,5
Iliç, 21a B3
Iligan, 23 C4
Ilijcevsk, 18a B1,2
Iljičovsk, 18 C3
Ilapel, 39 B1
Ille-et-Vilaine (35), Admin. U., 11 C2
Illinois, Admin. U., 35 C,D3

Illinois, R., 35 C2
Illizi, 28 B3
Iloilo, 23 B4
Ilorin, 29 C7
Ilulissat, 33 B14,15
Iman, R., 25 A5
Imatra, 15 C9
Imbâbah, 26a B3
Imbituba, 39a C4
Imi, 28 D7
Imo (8), Admin. U., 29 D7
Imola, 13a B5
Imperatriz, 38 C5
Imperia, 13 B2
Impfondo, 28 D4
Imphāl, 22 B5
In Aménas, 28 B3
Inari, 15 A8
Ince Burnu, C., 5 C8
Inch'ŏn, 25 C4
Indalsälven, R., 15 C6
Independence, 35 D2
India, St., 22 B3,4
Indiana, Admin. U., 35 C,D3
Indianapolis, 35 D3
Indian Ocean, 3
Indiga, 17 A7
Indigirka, R., 16 C16
Indo-Gangetic Plain, Pl., 19 F,G9,10
Indonesia, St., 23 C,D1-5
Indore, 22 B3
Indramayu, 23a A2
Indre (36), Admin. U., 11 C3
Indre-et-Loire (37), Admin. U., 11 C3
Indus, R., 22 A4
I-n-Gall, 29 A7
Ingoda, R., 16b B3
Ingolstadt, 12 C3
In Guezzam, 29 A7
Inguri, R., 18 D5
Inhambane, 30 D4
Inharrime, 30 D4
Inhassoro, 30 D4
Inírida, 38 B3
Inishbofin, I., 7 E2
Inn, R., 11 C5
Inner Hebrides, Is., 7 C4
Inner Mongolia, Reg., 24 B4,5
Innisfail, 40 B4
Innsbruck, 12 D3
Inny, R., 10 E6
Inongo, 30 B2
Inowrocław, 12 B5
In Salah, 28 B3
Inukjuaq, 33 C12
Inuvik, 33 B6
Inveraray, 10 B2,3
Invercargill, 40a B1
Inverness, 10 B2,3
Inverurie, 10 B3
Inza, 18 B6
Inžavino, 18 B5
Ioánnina, 14 D2
Iolotan', 21 B8
Iongo, 30 B2
Ionian Sea, 5 D6
Iónioi Nisoi (2), Admin. U., 14 D2
Iónioi Nisoi, Is., 14 D1,2
Íos, I., 14 D3
Iowa, Admin. U., 35 C2
Iowa City, 35 C2
Ípiros (3), Admin. U., 14 D2

Ipoh, 23 C2
Iporanga, 39a B4
Ipswich (Australia), 40 C5
Ipswich (U.K.), 9 C5
Iqe, 24 C3
Iquique, 38 E2
Iquitos, 38 C2
Irajol', 17 B9
Iráklion, 14 E3
Iran, St., 21 B-D5-7
Īrānshahr, 21 D8
Iraq, St., 21 C3-5
Irati, 39a C3
Irbid, 20b B1,2
Irbil, 21 B4
Irbit, 17a B3
Ireland, St., I., 10 E,F5,6
Iri, 25 C4
Irian see New Guinea,
Irian, I., 23 D5
Iringa, 30 B4
Iriri, R., 37 C4
Irish Sea, 7 E5,6
Irkutsk, 16 D12
Irondequoit, 33b
Iron Gate Reservoir, Res., 13 A5
Iron Knob, 40 D3
Iron Mountain, 35 B3
Iron Mountains, Mts., 7 D3,4
Ironwood, 35 B2,3
Iroquois, 33b
Iroquois Dam and Lock, 33b
Iroquois Falls, 35 B4
Irrawaddy, R., 22 C5
Irtyš, R., 16 D9
Irún, 11 F3
Irvine, 10 C2
Isabela, 23 C4
Isachsen, 42 C,D15
Isafjörður, 15a A2
Isar, R., 12 C3,4
Ise, 25 D6
Isel', R., 17a B3
Isère (38), Admin. U., 11 C4
Isère, R., 11 C4
Iserlohn, 12a B4
Ise-wan, B., 25 D6
Seyin, 29 D,C6
Ishikari-wan, B., 25 B7
Ishinomaki, 25 C7
Ishuaia, 36 D2
Isim, R., 16 D8
Isimbaj, 17a C2
Isiolo, 30 A4
Isiro, 28 D5
Iskår, R., 14 C2
İskenderun, 21a B3
İskenderun Körfezi, B., 21a B2,3
İskilip, 21a A2
Isla Alejandro Selkirk, I., 37 F1
Isla Cedros, I., 36 B1
Isla Dawson, I., 39 D1,2
Isla de Alborán, I., 11 H3
Isla de Chiloé, I., 37 G2
Isla de Coiba, I., 36 D4
Isla de Cozumel, I., 36 B4
Isla de Guadalupe, I., 31 G8,9
Isla de la Juventud, I., 36a B2,3
Isla del Rey, I., 36 D5
Isla de Margarita, I., 38 A3
Isla de Pascua, I., 3
Isla de Providencia, I., 36 C4,5

page 201

de San Andrés, I., 6C4,5
Hoste, I., 39D1
..amābād, 22A3
Isla Magdalena, I., 39C1
Isla Navarino, I., 39D2
Island Anticosti, I., 33D13
Island of Newfoundland, I., 33D14
Isla Róbinson Crusoe, I., 37F2
Isla Sala y Gómez, I., 3
Isla San Ambrosio, I., 39A1
Isla San Félix, I., 37E1,2
Islas Canarias, Is., Admin. U., 28A,B1
Islas del Cisne, Is., 36C4
Islas Diego Ramírez, Is., 37H3
Islas Hanover, Is., 39D1
Islas Juan Fernández, Is., 37F1,23
Islas Los Testigos, Is., 36bB2
Islas Revillagigedo, Is., 36C1,2
Isla Tiburón, I., 36B1
Isla Wellington, I., 37G1,2
Islay, I., 7D4
Isle of Man, Admin. U., I., 7D5
Isle of Portland, I., 7F6
Isle of Wight (28), Admin. U., 9D4
Isle of Wight, I., 7F7
Isles of Scilly, Is., 7G4,5
Islington, 9a
Isnā, 28B6
Isoka, 30C4
Isola d' Elba, I., 13B2
Isola di Capri, I., 13B3
Isola di Pantelleria, I., 13C2,3
Isola di Ustica, I., 13C3
Isola Lipari, I., 13C3
Isola Stromboli, I., 13C3
Isole Egadi, Is., 13C2,3
Isole Eolie, Is., 13C3
Isparta, 21aB2
İspir, 21aA4
Israel, St., 20bC1
Issoudun, 11C3
İstanbul, 21aA1
Isthmus of Panama, 37B1,2
Isthmus of Tehuantepec, 31H11
Istrije, Reg., 13A3
Itabuna, 38B6
Itacoatiara, 38C4
Itagüí, 38B2
Itaituba, 38C4
Itají, 39A4
Italy, St., 13A-C1-4
Itanagar, 22B5
Itapeva, 39aB4
Itapicuru, R., 38C5
Itapipoca, 38C6
Itaqui, 39aC2
Itararé, R., 39aB4
Itonamas, R., 38D3
Ittoqqortoormiit, 42C16,17
Ituiutaba, 39aA4
Ituri, 38C3
Ivaí, 39aB3
Ivalo, 15A8,9
Ivalojoki, R., 15A8

Ivangrad, 13B4,5
Ivano-Frankovsk, 18C1
Ivanovo, 17C6
Ivigtut, 33B15
Ivory Coast, Reg., 26D4
Ivory Coast, St., 29C,D4,5
Ivrea, 13aA1
Ivujivik, 33B12
Iwaki, 25C7
Iwo, 29D7
Iwón, 25B4
İzad Khvāst, 21C6
İzberbaš, 18D6
Izma, 17A8
Izma, R., 17B8
Izmail, 18C2
Izmajlovo, 17b
İzmir, 21aB1
İzmir Körfezi, B., 14D3
İzmit, 21aA1
İznik Gölü, L., 14C4
Izuhara, 25D4
Iz'um, 18C4
Izu-shotō, Is., 25D6

J

Jabal al-'Uwaynāt, Mt., 26B7
Jabal ash-Shām, Mt., 19G7
Jabalpur, 22B3,4
Jablanica, 13B4
Jablonovo, 16bB3
Jablonovyj Chrebet, Mts., 19D12,13
Jaboatão, 38C6
Jaca, 11F3
Jacarèzinho, 39aB3
Jáchal, 39B2
Jackson (U.S.A., Michigan), 35C4
Jackson (U.S.A., Mississippi), 35E2
Jacksonville, 35E4
Jacobábád, 22B2
Jacuí, R., 39aD3
Jacuouara, 38C4
Jaén, 11G3
Jaffna, 20aB3
Jagdalpur, 22C4
Jaguarão, 39aD3
Jaguariaíva, 39aB4
Jagüey Grande, 36aA3
Jahrom, 21D6
Jailolo, 23C4
Jaipur, 22B3
Jaisalmer, 22B3
Jajce, 13A4
Jakarta, 23D2
Jakobshavn see Ilulissat
Jakobstad, 15C7
Jakutsk, 16C14,15
Jalālābād, 22A2,3
Jalapa, 36B,C3
Jalingo, 29C8
Jalisco (13), Admin. U., 36C2
Jalón, R., 11F3
Jalta, 18D3
Jaluit, 41C7
Jamaica, 32a
Jamaica, St., 36C5
Jamaica Bay, B., 32a
Jamame, 30A5
Jamanxim, R., 38C4
Jambi, 23D2
Jambol, 14C3
Jambol (5), Admin. U., 14C3

James, R., 34C7
James Bay, B., 33C11,12
Jamestown (Saint Helena) 27F4
Jamestown (U.S.A., New York), 33b
Jamestown (U.S.A., North Dakota), 34B7
Jammu, 22A3
Jammu and Kashmir, Admin. U., 22A3
Jāmnagar, 22B2,3
Jamshedpur, 22B4
Jana, R., 16C15
Janaul, 17aB1,2
Jandaq, 21C6
Jan Mayen, I., 42C18
Januária, 38D5
Japan, St., 25B-D5-7
Japanese Archipelago, Arch., 3
Japurá, R., 37C3
Jaransk, 17C7
Jarcevo, 18A3
Jarega, 17B8
Jarensk, 17B7
Jari, R., 38B4
Jaroslavl' 16D5,6
Jarosław, 12C6
Jarud Qi, 25B3
Jarvis Island, I., 41D9
Jäsk, 21D7
Jaškul', 18C6
Jasper, 33C8
Jataí, 38D4
Jaunpur, 22aB2
Java Sea, 23D2,3
Jawa, I., 23D2,3
Jayapura, 23D6
Jazīreh-ye Khārk, I., 21D5,6
Jazykovo, 18B6
Jbel Tubqāl, Mt., 26A4
Jebba, 29C7
Jędrzejów, 12C6
Jefferson City, 35D2
Jefremov, 18B4
Jega, 29B7
Jegorjevsk, 17C5
Jegorlyk, R., 18C5
Jejsk, 18C4
Jēkabpils, 17C3
Jelan', 18B5
Jelec, 18B4
Jelenia Góra, 12C4
Jelgava, 17C2
Jember, 23D3
Jemca, 17B6
Jemeck, 17B6
Jena, 12C3
Jenakijevo, 18C4
Jenisej, 16C11,12
Jenotajevka, 18C6
Jequié, 38D5
Jerbogačon, 16C12
Jerevan, 16E,F6
Jerez de la Frontera, 11G2
Jersey, I., 6aA2
Jersey City, 35C5,6
Jeršov, 18B6
Jerusalem see Yerushalayim
Jesenice, 13A3
Jessej, 16C11,12
Jessore, 22aC4
Jevpatorija, 18C3
Jezioro Mamry, L., 12B6
Jezioro Śniardwy, L., 12B6
Jhānsi, 22B3

Jhelum, R., 22A3
Jiamusi, 24B7
Ji'an (China, Jiangxi), 24D5
Ji'an (China, Jilin), 25B4
Jiangsu (16), Admin. U., 24C6
Jiangxi (17), Admin. U., 24D5
Jiangzi, 24D2
Jianou, 24C5
Jianping, 25B2,3
Jiaoxian, 24C5,6
Jiaxing, 25D3
Jiayin, 24B6,7
Jiddah, 28B6
Jihlava, 12C4
Jihočeský kraj (2), Admin. U., 12C4
Jihomoravský kraj (6), Admin. U., 12C5
Jilin, 24B6
Jilin (18), Admin. U., 24B6
Jima, 28D6
Jinan, 24C5
Jingdezhen, 24D5
Jinghong, 24D3,4
Jingyuan, 24C4
Jinhua, 24D5,6
Jining (China, Neimenggu Zizhiqu), 24B5
Jining (China, Shandong), 24C5
Jinja, 30A4
Jinshajiang see Tongtianhe
Jinxi, 25B3
Jinxian, 25C3
Jinzhou, 24B6
Jitai, 24B2
Jiujiang, 24D5
Jiuli, R., 14B2
Jiuquan, 24C3
Jixi, 24B7
Joaçaba, 39aC3
João Pessoa, 38C6
João Pinheiro, 39aA4
Jodhpur, 22B3
Joensuu, 15C9
Joetsu, 25C6
Johannesburg, 30D3
Johnson-City, 35D4
Johnston Island, I., 41B9
Johnstons, 35C5
Johor (1), Admin. U., 19bC3
Johor Baharu, 23C2
Joinville, 39A3,4
Jokkmokk, 15B6
Joliet, 35C3
Jolitte, 33b
Jolo, 23C4
Jolo Island, I., 23C4
Jones Sound, Str., 33A11,12
Jönköping, 15D5
Joplin, 35D2
Jordan, R., 20bB1
Jordan, St., 20bB,C2
Jörn, 15B7
Jos, 29C8
Joseph Bonaparte Gulf, G., 40B2
Joškar-Ola, 16D6
Jos Plateau, Plat., 26C,D5
Juárez, 39aE2
Juàzeiro, 38C5
Juàzeiro do Norte, 38C5

page 202

Jubá, 28 D 6
Juba, R., 28 D 7
Júcar, R., 11 G 3
Júcaro, 36a B 4
Juchitán, 36 C 3
Juchnov, 18 B 4
Juen Mina, 34a
Juiz de Fora, 38 E 5
Jujuy, Admin. U., 39 A 2
Julianehåb see Qaqortoq
Jundiaí, 39a B 4
Juneau, 33 C 6
Junín, 39 B 2
Juquia, 39a B 4
Jura (39), Admin. U., 11 C 4
Jura, I., 7 C, D 4,5
Jura, Mts., 5 C 5
Juradó, 38 B 2
Jurgamyš, 17a B 3
Jurla, 17a B 1
Jūrmala, 17 C 2
Juruá, R., 37 C 3
Juruena, 38 D 4
Juruena, R., 37 D 4
Juškozero, 17 B 4
Jutai, R., 38 C 3
Juxian, 25 C 2
Južna Morava, R., 13 B 5
Južno-Sachalinsk, 16 E 16
Južno-Ural'sk, 17a C 3
Južnyj Bug, R., 18 C 2
Jylland, Pen., 12 A,B 3
Jyväskylä, 15 C 8

K

Kaala-Gomen, 41a A 1
Kabala, 29 C 3
Kabalo, 30 B 3
Kabardino-Balkar Autonomous Soviet Socialist Republic (4), Admin. U., 18 D 5
Kabba, 29 D 7
Kabelega Falls, Fs., 26 D 8
Kabinda, 30 C 3
Kabompo, R., 30 C 3
Kābul, 22 A 2
Kabwe, 30 C 3
Kača, 16a B 1
Kachovskoje Vodochranilišče, Res., 18 C 3
Kačug, 16b B 2
Kade, 29 D 5
Kadoma, 30 C 3,4
Kaduna, 29 C 7
Kaduna (9), Admin. U., 29 C 7
Kaduna, R., 29 C 7
Kadūr, 20a A 1,2
Kadžerom, 17 B 9
Kaédi, 28 C 1
Kaesŏng, 25 C 4
Kāf, 20b C 2
Kafan, 18a B 2
Kafanchan, 29 C 8
Kafr ash-Shaykh, 26a A 2,3
Kafue, 30 C 3
Kafue, R., 30 C 3
Kaga Bandoro, 28 D 4,5
Kagan, 21 B 8,9
Kagoshima, 25 D 4,5
Kagul, 18 C 2
Kahemba, 30 B 2

Kahnūj, 21 D 7
Kahoolawe, I., 35a B 3
Kaiama, 29 C 6,7
Kaifeng, 24 C 5
Kailu, 25 B 3
Kaimana, 23 D 5
Kainji Lake,Res., 29 C 7
Kaiserslautern, 12 C 2
Kaiwi Channel, 35a B 3
Kaiyuan, 25 B 3
Kajaani, 15 B 8
Kajabbi, 40 C 3,4
Kākā, 28 C 6
Kākināda, 22 C 4
Kalabāka, 14 B 2
Kalač, 18 B 5
Kalač-na-Donu, 18 C 5
Kaladar, 35 C 5
Kalahari Desert, Des., 26 G 6,7
Kalámai, 14 B 2
Kalimantan see Borneo
Kalamazoo, 35 C 3
Kalan, 21a B 3
Kalančak, 16a A 1
Kalapana, 35a C 4
Kalāt, 22 B 2
Kal'azin, 17 C 5
Kalecik, 21a A 2
Kalemi, 30 B 3
Kalevala, 17 A 4
Kálfafell, 15a B,C 3
Kalgoorlie-Boulder, 40 D 2
Kalianda, 23a A 1
Kalibo, 23b B 2
Kalima, 30 B 3
Kalinin, 16 D 5
Kaliningrad, 16 D 4
Kalininsk, 18 B 5
Kalispell, 34 B 4
Kalisz, 12 C 5
Kalixälven, R., 15 B 7
Kallavesi, L., 15 C 8
Kalmar, 15 D 5,6
Kalmyk Autonomous Socialist Republic, Admin. U., 18 D 5,6
Kaluga, 18 B 4
Kalundborg, 12 B 3
Kaluš, 18 C 1
Kama, R., 16 D 7
Kamaishi, 25 C 7
Kamaši, 21 B 9
Kambalda, 40 D 2
Kamčija, R., 14 C 3
Kamen, 12a A 4
Kamen', Mt., 19 C 11
Kamenec-Podol'skij, 18 C 2
Kamenka, 18 B 5
Kamen'-Kaširskij, 18 B 1,2
Kamennomostskij, 18 D 4,5
Kamenskoje, 16 C 18
Kamensk-Šachtinskij, 18 C 5
Kamensk-Ural'skij, 17a B 3
Kamina, 30 B 3
Kamloops, 33 C 7
Kampala, 30 A 4
Kampar, R., 23 C,D 2
Kâmpóng Saôm, 22 C 6
Kâmpôt, 22 C 6
Kampuchea, St., 22 C 6
Kamsar, 29 C 2
Kamskoje Vodochranilišče, Res., 17a B 2
Kamyšin, 18 B 5,6
Kamyšlov, 17a B 3

Kamyzak, 18 C 6
Kanal Imeni Moskvy, Can., 17 C 5
Kananga, 30 B 3
Kanaš, 17 C 7
Kanawha, R., 35 D 4
Kanazawa, 25 C 6
Kānchipuram, 20a A 2
Kandalakša, 16 C 5
Kandalakskij Zaliv, B., 17 A 4,5
Kandangan, 23 D 3
Kandavu, I., 41b B 2
Kandavu Passage, Str., 41b B 1,2
Kandi, 29 C 6
Kandy, 20a C 3
Kaneohe, 35a B 3
Kanevskoje Vodochranilišče, Res., 18 B,C 3
Kangān, 21 D 6
Kangar, 19b A 2
Kangaré, 29 C 3,4
Kangaroo Island, I., 40 D 3
Kanggye, 25 B 4
Kangiqsualujjuaq, 33 C 13
Kangnŭng, 25 C 4
Kanin Nos, 17 A 6
Kankan, 29 C 3
Kano, 29 B 8
Kano (10), Admin. U., 29 C 8
Kanoya, 25 D 5
Kānpur, 22 B 4
Kansas, Admin. U., 34 D 6,7
Kansas, R., 35 D 1
Kansas City (U.S.A., Kansas), 35 D 1,2
Kansas City (U.S.A., Missouri), 35 D 2
Kansk, 16 D 11
Kansŏng, 25 C 4
Kantchari, 29 B 6
Kantemirovka, 18 C 4
Kanton Island, I., 41 D 8
Kanye, 30 D 3
Kaohsiung, 24 D 5,6
Kaolack, 29 B 1,2
Kap Arkona, C., 12 B 4
Kap Brewster, C., 42 B,C 16,17
Kap Farvel see Uummannarsuaq
Kapiri m'Poshi, 30 C 3
Kap Morris Jesup, C., 42 D 15-18
Kapoeta, 28 D 6
Kaposvár, 14 B 1
Kapsukas, 18 B 1
Kapuas, R., 23 D 2,3
Kapuskasing, 35 B 4
Kapustin Jar, 18 C 6
Karabaš, 17a B 2,3
Karabük, 21 A 2
Karačev, 18 B 3,4
Karachayevo-Cherkessk Autonomous Region (8), Admin. U., 18 D 5
Karāchi, 22 B 2
Karadeniz Boğazi, Str., 21a A 1
Karaganda, 16 E 8,9
Karaidel'skij, 17a B 2
Karaj, 21 B 6

Karakoram Range, Mts., 19 F 9,10
Karaköse, 21a B 4
Karakumy, Des., 19 F 7,8
Karaman, 21a B 2
Karamay, 24 B 2
Karasburg, 30 D 2
Karasjok, 15 A 8
Karasu, 14 C 4
Karawang, 23a A 1
Karbalā', 21 C 4
Kardeljevo, 13 B 4
Kardhítsa, 14 B 2
Kärdla, 17 C 2
Kārdžali, 14 C 3
Kārdžali (6), Admin. U., 14 C 3
Karelian Autonomous Soviet Socialist Rep., Admin. U., 17 A,B 4
Karema, 30 B 3
Karesuando, 15 A 7
Kargopol', 17 B 5
Kariai, 14 C 3
Kariba, 30 C 3
Kārikāl, 20a B 2,3
Karis, 15 C 7
Karjepolje, 17 A 6
Karkheh, R., 21 C 5
Karkinitskij Zaliv, B., 18 C 3
Karl-Marx-Stadt, Karl-Marx-Stadt (8), Admin. U., see Chemnitz
Karlovac, 13 A 4
Karlovy Vary, 12 C 4
Karlshamn, 15 D 5
Karlskrona, 15 D 5,6
Karlsruhe, 12 C 3
Karlstad, 15 D 5
Karmah, 28 C 6
Karmøy, I., 15 D 3
Karnataka, Admin. U., 22 C 3
Karnobat, 14 C 3
Kärnten (2), Admin. U., 12 D 4
Karonga, 30 B 4
Kárpathos, I., 14 E 3
Kárpathos, I., 14 E 3
Karpinsk, 17a B 2,3
Karpogory, 17 B 6,7
Kars, 21a A 4
Karši, 21 B 9
Karskije Vorota, Chann., 16 B,C 7
Karskoje More, S., 16 B 8-10
Karstula, 15 C 7,8
Kartaly, 17a C 3
Kärwär, 20a A 1
Karymskoje, 16b B 3
Kaş, 21a B 1
Kasai see Cassai
Kasama, 30 C 4
Kasempa, 30 C 3
Kasenga, 30 C 3
Kasese, 30 A 4
Kāshān, 21 C 6
Kashi, 24 C 1
Kāshmar, 21 C 6
Kāshmīr, 21 C 6
Kasimov, 18 B 5
Kašin, 17 C 5
Kašira, 18 B 4
Kaskö, 15 C 7
Kasongo, 30 B 3
Kaspijsk, 18 D 6
Kaspijskij, 18 C 6
Kassalā, 28 C 6
Kassel, 12 C 3
Kastamonu, 21a A 2

page 203

...noje, 18B4	Kenema, 29D3	Kętrzyn, 12B6	Kingscourt, 10E6
...a, 30C3	Kenitra, 28A2	Kettering, 9C4	King's Lynn, 9C5
...-Ivanovsk, 17aC2	Kenmare, 10F5	Kettle Falls, 33aB4	Kingsport, 35D4
...ini, 14C2	Kenmare Bay, B., 7F2,3	Key West, 35G4	Kingston (Australia), 40D3
...therine, 40B3	Kennet, R., 7F7	Khalkidhiki, Pen., 14C2	
Kati, 29B4	Kenogami, R., 35A3,4	Khalkis, 14D2	Kingston (Canada), 33D12
Katihār, 22aB3	Kenora, 33D10	Khānaqīn, 21C4,5	
Katiola, 29C4	Kenosha, 35C5	Khaniá, 14E2,3	Kingston (Jamaica), 36C5
Kātmāndu, 22aB3	Kensington, 9a	Kharagpur, 22B4	
Katowice, 12C5	Kent (29), Admin. U., 9D5	Khārān, 22B2	Kingston (New Zealand), 40aB1
Katsina, 29B7		Khāsh, R., 21C8	
Katsina Ala, 29D8	Kentucky, Admin. U., 35D3,4	Khāsh, 21D8	Kingston (Norfolk I.), 41F6
Kattakurgan, 21B9		Khemmarat, 22C6	
Kattegat, Str., 15D4	Kenya, St., 30B4	Khenchela, 27aA2	Kingston upon Hull, 9C4
Katun', R., 24A2	Kepuhi, 35aB3	Khios, 14D3	
Kauai, I., 35aA2	Kepulauan Alor, Is., 23D4	Khon Kaen, 22C6	Kingstown, 36bB2
Kauai Channel, 35aA,B2		Khorramābād, 21C5	Kingswood, 9D3
Kaula Island, I., 35aB1	Kepulauan Anambas, Is., 23C2	Khorramashahr, 21C5	King William I., 33A10
Kaunas, 17C,D2		Khouribga, 28A2	King William's Town, 30E3
Kaura Namoda, 29B7	Kepulauan Aru, Is., 23D5	Khulna, 22aC4	
Kavála, 14C3	Kepulauan Banggai, Is., 23D4	Khurīyā Murīyā, Is., 21F7	Kinkala, 30B2
Kavieng, 41D5			Kinnairds Head, C., 7C7
Kavkaz, 16aB3	Kepulauan Banyak, Is., 23C1	Khvoy, 21B4	
Kawasaki, 25C6		Kibombo, 30B3	Kinnula, 15C8
Kaya, 29B5	Kepulauan Batu, Is., 23D1	Kičmengskij Gorodok, 17B7	Kinross, 10B3
Kayan, R., 23C3	Kepulauan Bunguran Besar, Is., 23C2,3		Kinshasa, 30B2
Kayeli, 23D4		Kidal, 29A6	Kinston, 35D5
Kayes, 29B3	Kepulauan Bunguran Selatan, Is., 23C2,3	Kidatu, 30B4	Kintampo, 29C5
Kayseri, 21aB3		Kidderminster, 9C3	Kintyre, Pen., 7D5
Kazakh Soviet Socialist Republic, Admin. U., 16E7-10	Kepulauan Kai, Is., 23D5	Kidira, 29B2	Kirensk, 16D12,13
	Kepulauan Kangean, Is., 23D3	Kiel, 12B3	Kirgiz Soviet Socialist Republic, Admin. U., 16E3
	Kepulauan Karimata, Is., 23D2	Kelce, 12C6	
Kazan', 16D6,7		Kieler Bay, B., 12B3	Kiri, 30B2
Kazan, R., 33B9	Kepulauan Karimunjawa, Is., 23aA2	Kiffa, 28C1	Kiribati, St., Is., 41C,D7-10
Kazanlāk, 14C3		Kigali, 30B4	
Kazatin, 18C2	Kepulauan Lingga, Is., 23D2	Kigoma-Ujiji, 30B3,4	Kırıkkale, 21aB2
Kāzerūn, 21D6		Kiiv, 16D4,5	Kirillov, 17C5
Kazi-Magomed, 18aA2	Kepulauan Mapia, Is., 23C5	Kijevskoje Vodochranilišče, Res., 18B2,3	Kirinia, 19cA2
Kažym, 17B8			Kiritimati, I., 41C10
Kéa, I., 14D3	Kepulauan Mentawai, Is., 23D1	Kikinda, 13A5	Kirkcaldy, 10B3
Keban Gölü, Res., 21aB3		Kikládhes, 14D3	Kirkcudbright, 10C2
Kébémer, 29B1,2	Kepulauan Riau, Is., 23C2	Kikwit, 30B2	Kirkenes, 15A9
Kebnekaise, Mt., 5A6,7	Kepulauan Sangihe, Is., 23C4	Kilchu, 25B4	Kirkland Lake, 35B4
Kebri Dehar, 28D7		Kildare, 10E6	Kırklareli, 21aA1
Kecskemét, 14B1	Kepulauan Sula, Is., 23D4	Kildare, Admin. U., 10E6	Kirksville, 35C2
Kedah (2), Admin. U., 19bA2	Kepulauan Talaud, Is., 23C4	Kilkee, 10E5	Kirkūk, 21B4
Kediri, 23D3	Kepulauan Tambelan, Is., 23C2	Kilkenny, 10E6	Kirkwall, 10A3
Kédougou, 29B2		Kilkenny, Admin. U., 10E6	Kirov (U.S.S.R., Br'ansk), 18B3
Kedvavom, 17B8	Kepulauan Tanimbar, Is., 23D5		
Keetmanshoop, 30D2		Kilkis, 14C2	Kirov (U.S.S.R., Perm'), 16D6,7
Kefallinia, I., 14D1,2	Kerala, Admin. U., 22C,D3	Kilija, 18C2	
Keffi, 29C7	Kerč', 18C4	Kilimanjaro-Uhuru, Mt., 26E8,9	Kirovabad see Gändžä
Keflavík, 15aB2	Kerčel', 17aB3,4		Kirovakan, 18aA1,2
Keighley, 9C3,4	Kerčenskij Proliv, Str., 18C,D4	Kilis, 21aB3	Kirovgrad, 17aB2
Keitele, L., 15C8		Killarney, 10E5	Kirovo-Čepeck, 17C7,8
Keith, 10B3	Kerema, 40A4	Killybegs, 10D5	Kirovograd, 18C3
Kelafo, 28D7	Kerki, 21B8,9	Kilmarnock, 10C2	Kirovsk, 16C5
Kelang, 23C2	Kérkira, I., 14D1	Kil'mez, 17C8	Kirovskij (U.S.S.R., Astrachan'), 18C6
Kelantan (3), Admin. U., 19bB3	Kérkira, 14D1	Kilombero, R., 30B4	
	Kermadec Islands, Is., 41G8	Kilosa, 30B4	Kirovskij (U.S.S.R., Kamčatka), 16D17
Kelibia, 27aA3		Kilrush, 10E5	
Kelkit, R., 21aA3	Kermān, 21C7	Kilwa Kivinje, 30B4,5	Kirovskoje, 16aB2
Kelloselkä, 15B8,9	Kerme Körfezi, B., 14D3	Kimberley, 30D3	Kirs, 17C8
Kelowna, 33D8	Kérouané, 29C3	Kimberley Plateau, Plat., 40B2	Kirsanov, 18B5
Kelsey Bay, 33aB1,2	Kerrville, 34E7		Kırşehir, 21aB2
Kem', 17A,B4,5	Kerry, Admin. U., 10E,F4	Kimch'aek, 25B4	Kiruna, 15B7
Kem', R., 17B4	Kerulen, R., 24B5	Kimito, 15C7	Kisangani, 30A3
Ké Macina, 29B4	Kesagami Lake, L., 35A5	Kimry, 17C5	Kishi, 29C6
Kemer, 21aB2		Kindersley, 34A5	Kišin'ov, 16E4
Kemerovo, 16D10	Kesten'ga, 17A4	Kindia, 29C2	Kiskunhalas, 14B1
Kemi, 15B8	Keswick, 10C3	Kindu Port-Empain, 30B3	Kislovodsk, 18D5
Kemijärvi, 15B8	Keta, 29D6		Kismaayo, 30B5
Kemijoki, R., 15B9	Ketapang, 23D3	Kinel', 18B7	Kissidougou, 29C3
Kempen, 1B1,2	Ketchikan, 33C6	Kinešma, 17C6	Kisumu, 30A,B4
Kemps's Bay, 35G5	Kete Krachi, 29D5	King City, 34D2	Kita, 29B3
Kempten, 12D3		Kingcome Inlet, 33aA1	Kitakami, R., 25C7
Ken, R., 22aB2		King Island, I., 40E4	Kitakyūshū, 25D5
Kenai, 33B4		Kingissepa, 17C2	Kitami, 24B7
Kendal, 9B3			
Kendari, 23D4			

page 204

Kitchener, 35 C 4
Kithira, I., 14 D 2
Kitimat, 33 C 3
Kitinen, R., 15 B 8
Kittilä, 15 B 8
Kitwe-Kalulushi, 30 C 3
Kizel, 17 a B 2
Kızıl, R., 21 a B 3
Kizl'ar, 18 D 6
Kiz'oma, 17 B 6
Kizyl-Arvat, 21 B 7
Kizyl-Kaja, 21 A 7
Kjustendil (7), Admin. U., 14 C 2
Kjustendil, 14 C 2
Kladno, 12 C 4
Klagenfurt, 12 D 4
Klaipėda, 12 B 6
Klamath, R., 34 C 2
Klamath Falls, 34 C 2
Klarälven, R., 15 C 5
Klatovy, 12 C 4
Kletskij, 18 C 5
Klin, 17 C 5
Klincy, 18 B 3
Kłodzko, 12 C 5
Knight Klinakini, R., 33 a A, B 1, 2
Knin, 13 A 4
Knoxville, 35 D 4
Knud Rasmussen Land, Reg., 42 C, D 12-14
Knysna, 30 E 3
Kobenhavn, 12 B 3, 4
Koblenz, 12 C 2
Kobrin, 18 B 1
Kobuk, R., 33 B 4
Kocaeli see Izmit
Kočevo, 13 A 4
Koch Bihār, 22 a B 4
Kōchi, 25 D 5
Kočubej, 18 D 6
Kodiak, 33 C 4
Kodiak Island, I., 33 C 4
Kodino, 17 B 5, 6
Kodok, 29 D 5
Koforidua, 29 D 5
Kōfu, 25 C 4
Kohima, 22 B 5
Kohtla Järve, 17 C 3
Kojda, 17 A 6
Kojgorodok, 17 B 8
Kokčetav, 16 D 8
Kokemäenjoki, R., 15 C 7
Kokkola, 15 C 7
Koko Kyunzu, Is., 22 C 5
Kokonau, 23 D 5
Kokstad, 30 E 3
Kolār, 20 a A 2
Kolari, 15 B 7, 8
Kolda, 29 B 2
Kolding, 12 B 3
Kolhāpur, 22 C 3
Kolín, 12 C 4
Kolobrzeg, 12 B 4
Kologriv, 17 C 6
Kolomna, 18 A 4
Kolomyja, 18 C 2
Kolonia, 41 C 5
Kolpaševo, 16 D 9, 10
Kolpino, 17 C 4
Kolpny, 18 B 4
Kólpos Ammókhostou, B., 19 c A 2, 3

Kólpos Lárnakos, B., 19 c B 2, 3
Kólpos Mórfou, B., 19 c A 1
Kólpos Orfanoú, B., 14 C 2, 3
Kólpos Patraïkós, B., 14 D 2
Kólpos Thermaïkós, B., 14 C, D 2
Kol'skij Poluostrov, Pen., 17 A 5
Kolva, R., 17 A 9
Kolwezi, 30 C 3
Kolyma, R., 16 C 17
Kolymskij Chrebet, Mts., 19 C 17, 18
Komadugu Yobe, R., 29 B 9
Komandorskije Ostrova, Is., 16 D 18
Komárno, 12 D 5
Komárom (10), Admin. U., 14 B 1
Komatipoort, 30 D 4
Komatsu, 25 C 6
Komi Autonomous Soviet Socialist Republic, Admin. U., 17 B 7-9
Kommunarsk, 18 C 4
Komoé, R., 29 C 4
Komofini, 14 C 3
Komrat, 14 B 4
Komsomolec, 17 a C 3
Komsomol'skij, 18 C 6
Komsomol'sk-na-Amure, 16 D, E 15
Kona, 29 B 9
Konda, R., 17 a A, B 4
Kondoa Irangi, 30 B 4
Kondopoga, 17 B 4
Koné, 41 A 1
Kong, 29 C 4
Kong Christian IX.s Land, Reg., 42 B, C 15, 16
Kong Christian X.s Land, Reg., 42 C 15, 16
Kong Frederik VIII.s Land, Reg., 42 C, D 16
Kong Frederik IX.s Land, Reg., 42 B 14
Kongolo, 30 B 3
Kongsberg, 15 D 4
Kongsvinger, 15 C 5
Konin, 12 B 5
Könkämäälven, R., 15 A 7
Konoša, 17 B 6
Konotop, 18 B 3
Kon'ovo, 17 B 5
Konstantinovsk, 18 C 5
Kontagora, 29 C 7
Kontiomäki, 15 B 9
Konya, 21 a B 2
Ko Phuket, I., 22 D 5
Korab, Mt., 5 C 7
Kor'akskoje Nagorje, Mts., 42 B 35, 36
Kor'ažma, 17 B 7
Korçë, 13 B 5
Korea Bay, 25 C 3
Korea Strait, Str., 25 D 4
Korenovsk, 18 C 4
Korf, 16 C 18
Korhogo, 29 C 4
Korinthiakós Kólpos, B., 14 D 2

Kórinthos, 14 D 2
Köriyama, 25 C 7
Korkino, 17 a C 3
Koro, I., 41 b A 2
Korodougou, 29 B 4
Korogwe, 30 B 4
Koror, 41 C 3
Koror, I., 41 C 3
Körös, R., 14 B 2
Koro Sea, 41 b A, B 2
Korosten', 18 B 2
Korsakov, 16 E 16
Korsør, 12 B 3
Kortamyš, 17 a C 3
Kortrijk, 11 B 3
Kos, I., 14 D 3
Kościan, 12 B 5
Košice, 12 C 6
Koslan, 17 B 7
Kosŏng, 25 C 4
Kosovo (6a), Admin. U., 13 B 5
Kosrae, I., 41 C 6
Kostomukša, 17 B 4
Kostroma, 17 C 6
Kostrzyn, 12 B 4
Kost'ukoviči, 18 B 3
Koszalin, 12 B 5
Kota, 22 B 3
Kota Baharu, 23 C 2
Kota Kinabalu, 23 C 3
Kotel'nič, 17 C 7
Kotel'nikovo, 18 C 5
Kotka, 15 C 8
Kotlas, 16 C 6
Kotor, 13 B 4
Kotovo, 18 B 5
Kotovsk (U.S.S.R., Kišin'ov), 18 C 2
Kotovsk (U.S.S.R., Tambov), 18 B 5
Kotto, R., 28 D 5
Kotuj, R., 16 C 12
Kotzebue, 33 B 3
Koudougou, 29 B 5
Koulikoro, 29 B 4
Koumac, 41 a A 1
Koundara, 29 B 2
Koungheul, 29 B 2
Kouroussa, 29 C 3
Kousseri, 29 B, C 9
Koutiala, 29 B 4
Kouvola, 15 C 8
Kovdor, 17 A 4
Kovel', 18 B 1
Kovrov, 17 C 6
Kovylkino, 18 B 5
Kowloon, 19 a B 3
Kowŏn, 25 C 4
Koyukuk, R., 33 B 4
Köyçeri, 21 a B 3
Kozan, 21 a B 3
Kozáni, 14 C 2
Kozhikode see Calicut
Koz'modemjansk, 17 C 7
Kpalimé, 29 D 6
Kpandu, 29 D 6
Kra Buri, 22 C 5
Krâchéh, 22 C 6
Kragero, 15 D 4
Kragujevac, 13 A 5
Krakatau see Rakata
Kraków, 12 C 5, 6
Kraljevo, 13 B 5
Kramatorsk, 18 C 4
Kramfors, 15 C 6
Kranj, 13 A 3
Krasino, 16 B 8
Krasnoarmejsk, 18 B 5, 6
Krasnoborsk, 17 B 7
Krasnodar, 16 E 5, 6

Krasnograd, 18 C 4
Krasnogvardejskoje, 18 C 5
Krasnojarsk, 16 D 11
Krasnokamsk, 17 a B 2
Krasnoperekopsk, 18 C 3
Krasnosel'je, 17 A 5
Krasnoturjinsk, 17 a B 3
Krasnoufimsk, 17 a B 2
Krasnoural'sk, 17 a B 3
Krasnoviŝersk, 17 a A 2
Krasnovodsk, 16 E 7
Krasnyj Kut, 18 B 6
Krasnyj Luč, 18 C 4
Krefeld, 12 a B 2
Kremenčug, 18 C 3
Kremenčugskoje Vodochraniliŝče, Res., 18 C 3
Krems an der Donau, 12 C 4
Kribi, 29 E 8
Kričov, 18 B 3
Krishna, R., 22 C 3
Kristiansand, 15 D 3, 4
Kristianstad, 15 D, E 5
Kristiansund, 15 C 3
Kristinestad, 15 C 7
Kríti (4), Admin. U., 14 E 3
Kríti, I., 14 E 2, 3
Krivoj Rog, 18 C 3
Kronštadt, 17 C 3
Kropotkin, 18 C 5
Krosno, 12 C 6
Krugersdorp, 30 D 3
Krung Thep, 22 C 6
Kruševac, 13 B 5
Krymsk, 18 C 4
Krymskij, Poluostrov, Pen., 18 C 3, 4
Krzyż, 12 B 5
Ksar-el-Kebir, 28 A 2
Ksar-es-Seghir, 5 a B 2
Ksar-es-Souk, 28 A 2
Kstovo, 17 C 6
Kuala Lipis, 19 b B 3
Kuala Lumpur, 23 C 2
Kuala Terengganu, 23 C 2
Kuancheng, 25 B 2
Kuandian, 25 B 3, 4
Kuantan, 23 C 2
Kuba, 18 D 6
Kuban', R., 18 D 5
Kuche, 24 B 2
Kuching, 23 C 3
Kudat, 23 C 3
Kudus, 23 a A 2
Kudymkar, 17 a B 1
Kuerle, 24 B 2
Kufstein, 12 D 4
Kuhmo, 15 B 9
Kuito, 30 C 2
Kujbyšev, 16 D 6, 7
Kujbyševskoje Vodochraniliŝče, Res., 18 B 6
Kujeda, 17 a B 2
Kukawa, 29 B 9
Kuldīga, 17 C 2
Kulgera, 40 C 3
Kuloj, R., 17 A 6
Kulu, 21 a B 2
Kulunda, 25 B 3
Kuma, R., 18 D 5
Kumamoto, 25 D 5
Kumanovo, 13 B 5
Kumasi, 29 C 5
Kumba, 29 D 8
Kumbakonam, 20 a B 2
Kunc'ovo, 17 b

page 205

, 17aB2
shanmai, Mts., 9-11
ng, 24D4
n, 25C4
Kununurra, 40B2,3
Kuopio, 15C8
Kupa, R., 13A3,4
Kupang, 23D,E4
Kup'ansk, 18C4
Kura, R., 18aA1
Kuraymah, 28C6
K'urdami, 18aA2
Kure, 25D5
Kurejka, R., 16C10,11
Kurgan, 16D8
Kurgan-T'ube, 21B9
Kuril'skije Ostrova, Is., 16E16,17
Kurnool, 22C3
Kursk, 16D5
Kurskij Zaliv, B., 12B6
Kurtalan, 21aB4
Kurume, 25D5
Kurumkan, 16bB3
Kurunegala, 20aC3
Kuşadası Körfezi, B., 14D3
Kusary, 18D6
Kuščinskij, 18aA2
Kuščovskaja, 18C4,5
Kuş Gölü, L., 14C3
Kushiro, 25B7
Kuška, 16F8
Kuskokwim, R., 33B4
Kustanaj, 16D8
Küsti, 28C6
Kušva, 17aB2
Kütahya, 21aB1
Kutaisi, 18D5
Kūt al-Imāra, 21C5
Kutno, 12B5
Kutu, 30B2
Kutum, 28C5
Kuujjuaq, 33C13
Kuusamo, 15B8
Kuwait, St., 21D5
Kuzneck, 18B6
Kuzomen', 17A5,6
Kvalöya, 15A7,8
Kvalöya, I., 15A6
Kvarner, B., 13A3
Kvikkjokk, 15B6
Kwa, R., 30B2
Kwajalein, I., 41C6
Kwangju, 25C4
Kwango see Cuango
Kwara (11), Admin. U., 29C7
Kwekwe, 30C3
Kwilu, R., 30B2
Kyle of Lochalsh, 10B2
Kyŏngju, 25C4
Kyōto, 25C5
Kyuquot, 33aB1
Kyūshū, I., 25D5
Kyzyl, 16D11
Kyzylkum, Des., 19E8
Kzyl-Orda, 16E8

L

Laba, R., 18D5
Labé, 29C2,3
Labe, R., 12C4
Labinsk, 18D5
Labrador, Reg., 33C12,13

Labrador City, 33C13
Labrador Peninsula, Pen., 31D13,14
Labrador Sea, 33C14
Lábrea, 38C3
Labuhan, 23aA1
Labytnangi, 16C8
Laç, 13B4
La Caldera, Mt., 26bB1
Lac à l'Eau-Claire, 33C12
Lac aux-Sables, 35B6
Lac de Kossou, Res., 29D4
La Ceiba, 36C4
Lac Evans, L., 35A5
Lachlan, R., 40D4
L'achovskije Ostrova, Is., 16B14-16
Lac Kivu, L., 30B3
Lac La Martre, L., 33B7,8
Lac Mai-Ndombe, L., 30B2
Lac Minuto, L., 33C12
Lac Mistassini, L., 33C12
La Coruña, 11F1
Lacq, 11D2
La Crosse, 35C2
Lac Saint-Jean, L., 33D12,13
Lac Saint Louis, L., 33b
Lac Seul, L., 35A2
Lacul Razelm, L., 14B4
Lacul Sinoe, L., 14B4
La Dorada, 38B2
Ladožskoje Ozero, L., 16C5
Ladysmith, 30D3
Lae, 41D4
La Esperanza, 38D3
Lafa, 25B4
Lafayette, 35E2
Lafayette, 35C3
Lafia, 29C8
La Foa, 41aA1,4
Lagan, 15D5
Lagarto, R., 34a
Lågen, R., 15C,D4
Lågen (Mjøsa), R., 15C4
Laghouat, 28A3
Lagoa dos Patos, L., 37F4
Lagoa Mirim, L., 37F4,5
Lago Argentino, L., 39D1
Lago Buenos Aires, L., 39C1
Lago de Maracaibo, L., 37A2,3
Lago de Nicaragua, L., 36C4
Lago de Poopó, L., 37D3
Lago di Como, L., 13A2
Lago di Garda, L., 13A2
Lago d'Iseo, L., 13aA3
Lago Maggiore, L., 13A1,2
Lagos (Nigeria), 29D6
Lagos (Portugal), 11G1
Lagos (12), Admin. U., 29D6
Lago Titicaca, L., 37D3
Lago Viedma, L., 39C1
La Grande, R., 33C12
La Grange, 35E3,4
La Guaira, 38A4
Laguna (Brazil), 39aC4
Laguna (Panama), 34a
Laguna Iberá, L., 39aC2
La Habana, 36aA2
Lahaina, 35aB3

La Have du Puits, 6aA3
Lahore, 22A3
Lahti, 15C8
Laï, 28D4
Lainioälven, R., 15A,B7
Lairg, 10A2
Laiyang, 25C3
Laizhouwan, B., 25C2,3
Laja, R., 17A9
Lajes, 39aC3
Lajes do Pico, 11aA2
La Junta (Mexico), 36B2
La Junta (U.S.A.), 34D6
Lake Abaya, L., 28D6
Lake Abitibi, L., 35B4,5
Lake Albert, L., 28D5,6
Lake Amadeus, L., 40C2,3
Lake Athabasca, L., 33C9
Lake Bangweulu, L., 30C4
Lake Barlee, L., 40C1
Lake Cabora Bassa, Res., 30C4
Lake Carnegie, L., 40C2
Lake Chad, L., 29B9
Lake Champlain, L., 35C6
Lake Charles, 35E2
Lake Cowan, L., 40D2
Lake Edward, L., 30B3
Lake Erie, L., 35C4,5
Lake Eyasi, L., 30B4
Lake Eyre, L., 40C3
Lake Frome, L., 40D4
Lake Gairdner, L., 40C3
Lake Geneva, L., 11C4
Lake Harbour, 33B12,13
Lake Huron, L., 35B,C4
Lake Kariba, Res., 30C3
Lake Kyoga, L., 27D8
Lake Natron, L., 30B4
Lake Nipigon, L., 33D11
Lake Nipissing, L., 35B4,5
Lake Nyasa, L., 30C4
Lake of the Woods, L., 33D10
Lake Ohrid, L., 41bB3
Lake Okeechobee, L., 35F4,5
Lake Ontario, L., 35C5
Lake Placid, 35B6
Lake Portchartrain, L., 35E2,3
Lake Powell, Res., 34D4,5
Lake Prespa, L., 13B5
Lake Rudolf see Lake Turkana
Lake Rukwa, L., 30B4
Lake Saint Clair, L., 33b
Lake Saint Francis, L., 33b
Lake Saint Lawrence, L., 33b
Lake Sakakawea, L., 34B6
Lake Scutari, L., 13B4
Lakeside, 34C4
Lake Simcoe, L., 33b

Lake Superior, L., 35B2,3
Lake Tahoe, L., 34D3
Lake Tana, L., 28C6
Lake Tanganyika, L., 30B3,4
Lake Taupo, L., 40aA2
Lake Te Anau, L., 40aB1
Lake Torrens, L., 40D3
Lake Turkana, L., 28D6
Lake Victoria, L., 30B4
Lakeview, 34C2,3
Lake Volta, Res., 29D5
Lake Winnipeg, L., 33C10
Lake Winnipegosis, L., 33C9
Lakewood, 34D5
Lakonikós Kólpos, B., 14D2
Laksefjorden, B., 15A8
Lakselv, 15A8
Lakshadweep, Admin. U., 22C3
La Laguna, 26bB2
La Linea, 11G2
Lalitpur (India), 22aB1
Lalitpur (Nepal), 22aB3
La Maddalena, 13B2
Le Malbaie, 35B6
La Matanza, 39aB2,3
Lambaréné, 30B1,2
Lambasa, 41bA2
Lambert Glacier, Glac., 42F,G29,30
Lamego, 11F2
Lamezia Terme, 13C3,4
Lamia, 14D2
Lammermuir Hills, Mts., 7D6
Lampang, 22C5
Lampeter, 9C2
Lamu, 30B5
Lanai, I., 35aB3
Lanark, 10C3
Lancangjiang, R., 24C,D3
Lancashire (30), Admin. U., 9C3
Lancaster (Canada), 35B7
Lancaster (U.K.), 9B3
Lancaster Sound, Str., 33A11,12
Landeck, 12D3
Lander, 34C5
Lane (40), Admin. U., 11C2
Land's End, C., 7F4,5
Landshut, 12C4
Langon, 11C2
Langøya, 15A5
Langsa, 23C1
Lang-Son, 22B6
Lansing, 35C4
Lanzarote, I., 26bB3,4
Lanzhou, 24C4
Laoag, 23B4
Lao-Cai, 22B6
Laohahe, R., 25B2
Laois, Admin. U., 10E6
Laon, 11B3
La Oroya, 38D2
Lapa, 39aC4
La Palma, 36D5
La Palma, I., 26bB2
La Paloma, 39aD3
La Pampa, Admin. U., 39B2
La Paz (Argentina), 39aB2
La Paz (Bolivia), 38D3
La Paz (Mexico), 36B1,2

La Perla, 34 F 6
La Perouse Strait, 25 A 7
Lápithos, 19c A 2
La Plata, 39 B 3
Lappeenranta, 15 C 8
Lappland, Reg., 5 A 7
L'Aquila, 13 B 3
Lår, 21 D 6
Larache, 28 A 2
Laramie, 34 C 5
Laredo, 34 F 7
Largeau, 28 C 4
Largs, 10 C 2
La Rioja, 39 A 2
La Rioja (11), Admin. U.,
  (Argentina), 39 A 2
La Rioja (12), Admin. U.,
  (Spain), 11 F 3
Lárisa, 14 D 2
Lárkäna, 22 B 2
Lárnax, 19c B 2
Larne, 10 D 7
Larne (16), Admin. U.,
  10 D 7
La Rochelle, 11 C 2
La Roche-sur-Yon, 11 C 2
Larsen Ice Shelf, 42 F, G 6
Las Anod, 28 D 7
Las Cascadas, 34a
Las Cruces, 34 E 5
La Serena, 39 A 1
La Serre, 35 B 5
Las Flores, 39 B 2,3
Lashio, 22 B 5
Lashkar Gäh, 22 A 2
Las Palmas, 28 B 1
La Spezia, 13 A 2
Las Piedras, 39a D 2,3
Las Plumas, 39 C 2
Lassen Peak, Vol., 31a B 1
Las Truchas, 36 C 2
Las Vegas, 34 D 3
Latina, 13 B 3
La Tuque, 35 B 6
Latvian Soviet Socialist
  Republic, Admin. U.,
  16 D 4
Lau Group, Is., 41b A,B 3
Launceston (Tasmania),
  40 E 4
Launceston (U.K.), 9 D 2
La Unión, 36 C 4
Laura, 40 B 4
Laure, 35 E 3
Laurentin Plateau, Plat.,
  31 C,D 10,11
Lauria, 13 B,C 3,4
Lausanne, 11 C 4
Lautoka, 41b A 1
Laval (Canada), 33 D 12
Laval (France), 11 B 2
Laverton, 40 C 2
Lavras, 39a B 5
Lavumisa, 30 D 4
Lawra, 29 C 5
Lawton, 34 E 7
Lazio (7), Admin. U., 13 B 3
Lea, R., 7 F 7
Leader, 34 A 5
Learmonth, 40 C 1
Lebanon, St., 20b B 1,2
Lebesby, 15 A 8
Lębork, 12 B 5
Lebu, 39 B 1
Lecco, 13 A 2
Lech, R., 12 C 3
Lecce, 13 B 4
Le Creusot, 11 C 3,4
Le Croisic, 11 C 2
Led'anaja, Mt., 42 B 36

Leduc, 33 C 8
Lee, R., 7 F 3
Leeds, 9 C 4
Leeuwarden, 12 B 2
Leeward Islands, Is.,
  36b A,B 2
Legazpi, 23 B 4
Legnago, 13a A 5
Legnano, 13a A 5
Legnica, 12 C 5
Leh, 22 A 3
Le Havre, 11 B 3
Leicester, 9 C 4
Leicestershire (31),
  Admin. U., 9 C 4
Leichlingen, 12a B 3
Leiden, 12 B 2
Leigh Creek, 40 D 3
Leikanger, 15 C 3
Leipzig, 12 C 4
Leipzig (9), Admin. U.,
  12 C 4
Leiria, 11 G 1
Leiria (10), Admin. U.,
  11 G 1
Leith Hill, H., 7 F 7,8
Le Mans, 11 B 3
Le Mars, 35 C 1
Lemesós, 19c B 2
Lena, R., 16 D 12
Lendery, 17 B 4
Leninabad, 21 A 9
Leninakan, 18a A 1
Leningrad, 16 C,D 5
Leningradskaja, Station,
  42 F 20,21
Lenino, 16a B 2
Leninogorsk, 24 A 2
Leninsk, 16 E 8
Leninskoje, 17 C 7
Lenkoran ̀, 18a B 2
Lenne, R., 12a B 4
Lens, 11 B 3
Lensk, 16 C 13
Lenvik, 15 A 6
Léo, 29 C 5
Leoben, 12 D 4
Leominster, 9 C 3
León (Mexico), 36 B 2
León (Nicaragua), 36 C 4
León (Spain), 11 F 2
Leonárison, 19c A 3
Leonora, 40 C 2
Lepel', 18 B 2
Le Port, 30a B 1
Le Puy, 11 C 3
Léré, 29 C 9
Le Relais, 33b
Lérida, 11 F 4
Lerma, 11 F 3
Lervick, 10a
Les Ecris, Mt., 5 C 5
Leskovac, 13 B 5
Lesnoj, 17 C 8
Lesosibirsk, 16 D 11
Lesotho, St., 30 D,E 3
Lesozavodsk, 25 A 5
Les Sables-d'Olonne,
  11 C 2
Lessay, 6a A 3
Lesser Antilles, Is., 38 A 3
Leśukonskoje, 17 B 7
Lésvos, I., 14 D 3
Leszno, 12 C 5
Lethbridge, 33 D 8
Lethem, 38 B 4
Letiahau, R., 30 D 3
Leticia, 38 C 2,3
Letka, 17 C 7
Le Tréport, 11 B 3
Letterkenny, 10 D 6

Leulumoega, 41c A 1
Leuven, 11 B 4
Levádhia, 14 D 2
Levanger, 15 C 4
Levaši, 18 D 6
Levice, 12 C 5
Lévka, 19c A 1
Levkás, I., 14 D 2
Levkónoikon, 19c A 2
Levkosía, 19c A 2
Lev Tolstoj, 18 B 4,5
Levuka, 41b A 2
Lewes, 9 D 5
Lewis, I., 7 B,C 4
Lewisham, 9a
Lewiston (U.S.A., Idaho),
  34 B 3
Lewiston (U.S.A., Maine),
  35 C 6,7
Lexington-Fayette, 35 D 4
Leyte, I., 23 B 4
Leyton, 9a
L'gov, 18 B 4
Lhasa, 22 B 5
Lhokseumawe, 23 C 1
Lianyungang, 24 C 5,6
Liaocheng, 25 C 2
Liaodongwan, B., 25 B 3
Liaohe, R., 25 B 3
Liaoning (19), Admin. U.,
  24 B 6
Liaoyang, 25 B 3
Liaoyuan, 25 B 4
Liard, R., 33 B 6,7
Libenge, 28 D 4
Liberal, 34 D 6
Liberec, 12 C 4
Liberia, St., 29 D 3
Libourne, 11 C 2
Libreville, 30 A 1,2
Libya, St., 28 B 4,5
Libyan Desert, Des.,
  26 B 6,7
Licata, 13 C 3
Lichinga, 30 C 4
Lichoslavl', 17 C 5
Lida, 18 B 2
Liechtenstein, St., 12 D 3
Liège, 11 B 4
Lieksa, 15 C 9
Lienz, 12 D 4
Liepāja, 16 D 3,4
Liffey, R., 7 E 4
Lifford, 10 D 6
Liguria (8), Admin. U.,
  13 A 2
Ligurian Sea, 13 B 2
Lihue, 35a B 2
Lijiang, 24 D 3,4
Likasi, 30 C 3
Lille, 11 B 3
Lillehammer, 15 C 4
Lillooet, 33a B 3
Lilongwe, 30 C 4
Lim, R., 14 B 1
Lima, 38 D 2
Limavady, 10 D 6
Limavady (17), Admin. U.,
  10 D 6
Limay, R., 39 B 2
Limbe, 29 D 8
Limburg, 12 C 3
Limeira, 39a B 4
Limerick, 10 E 5
Limerick, Admin. U., 10 E 5
Limfjorden, Str., 12 A 3
Límnos, I., 14 D 3
Limoges, 11 C 3
Limón, 36 D 4
Limon, 34 D 6
Limpopo, R., 30 D 3

Linares (Chile), 39 B 1
Linares (Mexico), 34 G 7
Linares (Spain), 11 G 3
Lincoln (U.K.), 9 C 4
Lincoln (U.S.A.), 35 C 1
Lincoln Sea, 42 D 13,14
Lincolnshire (32),
  Admin. U., 9 C 5
Lind, 34 B 3
Lindesnes, C., 15 D 3
Lindhos, 14 D 3,4
Lindi, 34 B 4
Lindi, R., 30 A 3
Lindsay, 33b
Line Islands, Is.,
  41 C,D 9,10
Linfen, 24 C 5
Lingayen, 23 B 3,4
Lingling, 24 D 5
Linguère, 29 B 2
Lingyuan, 25 B 2
Linhai, 24 D 6
Linhares, 38 D 6
Linhe, 24 B 4
Linjiang, 25 B 4
Linköping, 15 D 5,6
Linkou, 25 A 4,5
Linqing, 25 C 2
Lins, 39a B 4
Linxi, 24 B 5
Linxia, 24 C 4
Linyi, 24 C 5
Linz, 12 C 4
Lipa, 23b B 2
Lipeck, 18 B 4
Lippe, R., 12a A 2
Lisala, 28 D 5
Lisboa, 11 G 1
Lisboa (11), Admin. U.,
  11 G 1
Lisbon see Lisboa
Lisburn, 10 D 6,7
Lisburn (18), Admin. U.,
  10 D 6
Lishui, 25 E 2,3
Lismore, 40 C 5
Listowel, 10 E 5
Lithuanian Soviet Socialist
  Rep., Admin. U., 16 D 4
Little Abaco Island, I.,
  35 F 5
Little Colorado, R., 34 D 4
Little Minch, Str., 7 C 4
Little Missouri, R., 34 B 6
Little Rock, 35 E 2
Liuan, 25 D 2
Liuzhou, 24 D 4,5
Live Oak, 35 E 4
Liverpool, 9 C 3
Liverpool Bay, B., 9 C 3
Livingstone see Maramba
Livny, 18 B 4
Livorno, 13 B 2
Lizard Point, C., 7 G 5
Ljubljana, 13 A 3
Ljungan, R., 15 C 6
Ljusnan, R., 15 C 6
Llandrindod Wells, 9 C 3
Llanelli, 9 D 2
Llanes, 11 F 2
Llano Estacado, Plat.,
  31 F 10
Llanos, Pl., 37 B 2,3
Lleyn Peninsula, P., 7 E 5
Lloydminster, 33 C 8,9
Loberia, 39 B 3
Lobito, 30 C 2
Lobva, 17a B 3
Locarno, 11 C 5
Loch Awe, L., 7 C 5
Lochboisdale, 10 B 1

page 207

...richt, L., 10 B 2	Loop Head, C., 7 E 2,3	Lubilash, R., 30 B 3	Lynn Lake, 33 C 9,10
...yne, B., 10 B,C 2	Lop Nur, L., 24 B 3	Lublin, 12 C 6	Lyon, 11 C 4
...innhe, B., 7 C 5	Lopydino, 17 B 8	L'ublino, 17b	Lyster Station, 33b
...ochy, L., 10 B 2	Lorain, 35 C 4	Lubny, 18 B,C 3	Lys'va, 17a B 2
Loch Lomond, L., 7 C 5	Lorca, 11 G 3	L'ubotin, 18 B,C 4	Lytton, 33 C 7
Loch Maree, L., 7 C 5	Lord Howe Island, I., 41 G 6	Lubudi, 30 B 3	
Lochnagar, Mt., 7 C 6	Loreto, 36 B 1	Lubuklinggau, 23 D 2	
Loch Ness, L., 7 C 5	Lorient, 11 C 2	Lubumbashi, 30 C 3	**M**
Loch Rannoch, L., 7 C 5,6	Los Alamos, 34 D 5	Lucca, 13 B 2	
Loch Shin, L., 7 B 5	Los Angeles (Chile), 39 B 1	Luce Bay, B., 7 D 5	Ma'ān, 20 b C 1,2
Loch Tay, L., 7 C 5,6	Los Ángeles (U.S.A.), 34 E 2,3	Lucélia, 39 a B 3	Maanshan, 25 D 2
Lockport, 33b	Los Barrios, 5 a A 2,3	Lucena (Philippines), 23 b B 2	Ma'arrat an-Nu'mān, 20 b B 2
Loc-Ninh, 22 C 6	Los Mochis, 36 B 2	Lucena (Spain), 11 G 2	Maas see Meuse
Locri, 13 C 4	Lot (46), Admin. U., 11 C 3	Lučenec, 12 C 5	Maas, R., 12 C 2
Lodejnoje Pole, 17 B 4	Lot, R., 11 C 3	Luck, 18 B 2	Maasin, 23 b B 2,3
Lodi, 13 a A 3	Lota, 39 B 1	Lucknow, 22 B 4	Maastricht, 12 C 2
Lodja, 30 B 3	Lot-et-Garonne (47), Admin. U., 11 C 3	Lüderitz, 30 D 2	Mac Alester, 35 D 1,2
Lodwar, 28 D 6	Lothian (61), Admin. U., 9 B 3	Ludgate, 35 B 4	Mac Allen, 34 F 7
Łódź, 12 C 5	Louangphrabang, 22 C 6	Ludhiāna, 22 A 3	Macapá, 38 B 4
Lofoten, Is., 15 A 5	Loubomo, 30 B 2	Ludvika, 15 C 5	Macau, 38 C 6
Logan, 34 C 4	Louchi, 17 A 4	Ludwigshafen, 12 C 2,3	Macau, Admin. U., 19 a B 2
Logone, R., 28 D 4	Louga, 29 B 1	Luena, 30 C 2,3	Macaúba, 38 D 4,5
Logroño, 11 F 3	Lough Allen, L., 7 D 3	Lufki, 35 E 2	Mac Cammon, 34 C 4
Loir, R., 11 C 3	Loughborough, 9 C 4	Luga, 17 C 3	Macclesfield, 9 C 3
Loire (42), Admin. U., 11 C 4	Lough Conn, L., 7 D 3	Luga, R., 17 C 3	Mac Clintock Channel, 33 A 9,10
Loire, R., 11 C 4	Lough Corrib, L., 7 E 3	Lugano, 11 C 5	Mac Clure Strait, 33 A 7,8
Loire-Atlantique (44), Admin. U., 11 C 2	Lough Derg, L., 7 E 3,4	Lugenda, R., 30 C 4	Macdonnel Ranges, Mts., 40 C 3
Loire (Haute-) (43), Admin. U., 11 C 3	Lough Erne, L., 7 D 4	Lugnaquillia Mount, Mt., 7 E 4,5	Maceió, 38 C 6
Loiret (45), Admin. U., 11 C 3	Lough Foyle, B., 7 D 4	Lugo (Italy), 13 a B 5	Macenta, 29 C 3
Loir-et-Cher (41), Admin. U., 11 C 3	Lough Mask, L., 7 E 3	Lugo (Spain), 11 F 2	Macerata, 13 B 3
Loja, 38 C 2	Lough Neagh, L., 7 D 4	Lugoj, 14 B 2	Mac Grath, 33 B 4
Lojo, 15 C 7	Loughrea, 10 E 5	Luimneach see Limerick	Machačkala, 16 E 6,7
Lokka, 15 A 8,9	Lough Ree, L., 7 E 4	Lukojanov, 17 C 6,7	Machala, 38 C 1,2
Lokoja, 29 D 7	Lough Swily, L., 7 D 4	Łuków, 12 C 6	Macharadze, 18 D 5
Lol, R., 28 D 5	Louisiana, Admin. U., 35 E 2	Lukuga, R., 30 B 3	Machias, 35 C 7
Lolland, I., 12 B 3	Louisville, 35 D 3	Lulea, 15 B 7	Machilipatnam, 22 C 4
Lom, 14 C 2	Lourdes, 11 D 2,3	Luleälven, R., 15 B 7	Machupicchu, 38 D 2
Loma Mansa, Mt., 26 D 3	Lousiade Archipelago, Arch. 40 B 5	Lüleburgaz, 13 B 6	Machynlleth, 9 C 3
Lomami, R., 30 B 3	Louth, 9 C 4,5	Lulua, R., 30 B 3	Mackay (Australia), 40 C 4
Lomas de Zamora, 39 B 3	Louth, Admin. U., 10 E 6	Lumajang, 23 a B 3	Mackay (U.S.A.), 34 C 4
Lombardia (9), Admin. U., 13 A 2	Lovat, R., 17 C 4	Lumbala, 30 C 3	Mackay see Linden
Lombok, I., 23 D 3	Loveč, 14 C 3	Lund, 12 B 4	Mackenzie, R., 33 B 7,8
Lomé, 29 D 6	Loveč (8), Admin. U., 14 C 3	Lundazi, 30 C 3	Mackenzie, Bay, 33 A,B 5,6
Lomela, 30 B 3	Lovelock, 34 C 3	Lundy, I., 9 D 2	Mackenzie King Island, I., 33 A 8,9
Lomello, 13 a A 2	Lovozero, 17 A 4,5	Lüneburg, 12 B 3	Mackenzie Mountains, Mts., 31 C 7,8
Lompoc, 34 E 2	Lowell, 35 C 6	Lüneville, 11 B 4	Mackinaw City, 35 B 4
Łomża, 12 B 6	Lower Hutt, 40 a B 7	Lunga, R., 30 C 3	Mac Kinney, 34 E 7
London (Canada), 33 D 11	Lower Lough Erne, L., 7 D 4	Lüni, R., 22 B 3	Maclear, 30 E 3
London (U.K.), 9 D 4	Lowestoft, 9 C 5	Luninec, 18 B 2	Macomb, 35 C 2
Londonderry, 10 D 6	Łowicz, 12 B 5	Luning, 34 D 3	Macomba, 34a
Londonderry (19), Admin. U., 10 D 6	Lozère (48), Admin. U., 11 C 3	Lunino, 18 B 3	Macon, 35 E 4
Londrina, 39 a B 3	Lozovaja, 18 C 4	Lunsar, 29 C 2	Mâcon, 11 C 4
Long Beach, 34 E 3	Loz'va, R., 17 a A 3	Luohe, 24 C 5	Mac Pherson, 34 D 7
Long Eaton, 9 C 4	Luachimo, 30 B 3	Luoyang, 24 C 5	Macquarie, R., 40 D 4
Longford, 10 E 6	Lualaba, R., 30 B 3	Lúrio, R., 30 C 4	Macquarie Islands, Is., 42 E 20,21
Longford, Admin. U., 10 E 6	Luanda, 30 B 2	Lusaka, 30 C 3	Mac Robertson Land, Reg., 42 F,G 29-31
Longgang, 19 a A 3	Luanda-Katanga Plateau, Plat., 26 E,F 6,7	Lusambo, 30 B 3	Macroom, 10 F 5
Longhua, 25 B 5,6	Luangue, R., 30 B 2,3	Lussanvira, 39 a B 3	Madagascar, St., I., 30 C,D 5
Long Island (Atlantic Ocean), I., 35 C 6	Luangwa, R., 30 C 3	Luton, 9 D 4	Madang, 41 D 4
Long Island (Caribbean Sea), I., 35 G 5	Luanhe, R., 25 B 2	Luuq, 28 D 7	Madawaska, R., 33b
Long Island Sound, Str., 32a	Luanping, 25 B 2	Luvua, R., 30 B 3	Madden Dam, 34a
Longlac, 35 B 3	Luanshya, 30 C 3	Luwuk, 23 D 4	Madeira, Admin. U., I., 28 A 1
Longreach, 40 C 4	Luapula, R., 30 C 3	Luxembourg, 11 B 4	Madeira, R., 38 C 3
Long Sault, 33b	Luarca, 11 F 2	Luxembourg, St., 11 B 4	Madhya Pradesh, Admin. U., 22 B,C 3,4
Long Sault Dam, 33b	Luau, 30 C 3	Luxor see Al-Uqsur	Madina do Boé, 29 C 2
Longueuil, 33b	Luba, 29 E 8	Luza, 17 B 7	Madīnat ash-Sha'b, 28 C 7
Longuyon, 11 B 4	Lubang Islands, Is., 23 b B 1,2	Luza, R., 17 B 7	Madison, 35 C 2,3
Longview, 35 E 2	Lubango, 30 C 2	Luzern, 11 C 4,5	
Longyearbyen, 42 C 20,21	Lubbock, 34 E 6	Lyckele, 15 B 6	
Lønsdal, 15 B 5	Lübeck, 12 B 3	Lyme Bay, 7 F 6	
Lons-le-Saunier, 11 C 4		Lynchburg, 35 D 5	

page 208

Madisonville, 35 D3
Madiun, 23 D3
Madras, 22 C4
Madre de Dios, R., 38 D2,3
Madrid, 11 F3
Madrid (1), Admin. U., 11 F3
Maduo, 24 C3
Madura, I., 23 D3
Madurai, 22 C,D3
Maebashi, 25 C6
Maevatanana, 30 C5
Mafia Island, I., 30 B5
Magadan, 16 C,D16,17
Magadi, 30 B4
Magdagači, 16 D14
Magdalena, R., 37 B2
Magdeburg, 12 B3
Magdeburg (10), Admin. U., 12 B3
Magelang, 23 D2,3
Magenta, 13 A2,3
Maghera, 10 D6
Magherafelt, 10 D6
Magherafelt (20), Admin. U., 10 D6
Magnet, 40 C1
Magnitogorsk, 16 D7
Magog, 35 B6
Magwe, 22 B5
Mahajanga, 30 C5
Mahakam, R., 23 C,D3
Mahānadi, R., 22 B4
Mahārāshtra, Admin. U., 22 B3
Mahattat Harad, 28 B7
Mahe, 20 aB1
Mahébourg, 30 aB3,4
Mahé Island, I., 27 E10
Mahnomen, 34 B7
Maho, 20 aC3
Mahón, 11 G4
Maidstone, 9 D5
Maiduguri, 29 C9
Main, R., 12 C3
Maine, Admin. U., 35 B7
Maine-et-Loire (49), Admin. U., 11 C2
Mainland (Orkney Is.), I., 7 B6
Mainland (Shetland Is.), I., 7 A7
Maintirano, 30 C5
Mainz, 12 C3
Maio, I., 28 aB3
Maipú, 39 aE2
Maiquetía, 38 A,B3
Maitland, 40 D5
Maizuru, 25 C6
Maja, R., 16 D15
Majene, 23 D4
Majkop, 18 D5
Majskij, I., 41 C7
Maka, 29 B2
Makarjev, 17 C6
Makarska, 13 B4
Makassar see Ujung Pandang
Makat, 6 C10
Makedhonía (5), Admin. U., 14 C2
Makedonija (4), Admin. U., 13 B5
Makejevka, 18 C4
Makeni, 29 C2,3
Makgadikgadi Pans, Pl., 30 D3
Makkah, 28 B6,7
Makokou, 30 A2

Makoua, 30 A2
Maksatícha, 17 C5
Mäkü, 21 aB4
Makumbako, 30 B4
Makurdi, 29 D8
Malabar Coast, 20 aA,B1,2
Malabo, 29 E8
Malacca, 23 C2
Málaga, 11 G2
Malaita, I., 40 A6
Malakāl, 28 D6
Malang, 23 D3
Malange, 30 B2
Malanville, 29 C6
Mälaren, L., 15 D6
Malargüe, 39 B2
Malatya, 21 aB3
Malawi, St., 30 C4
Malawi see Lake Nyasa
Malaya, Admin. U., 23 C2
Malay Peninsula, 19b
Malaysia, St., 23 C2,3
Malazgirt, 21 aB4
Malbork, 12 B5
Malden Island, I., 41 D10
Maldives, St., Is., 22 D3
Maldonado, 39 aE3
Malé, 22 D3
Malen'ga, 17 B5
Mali, St., 29 A,B3-6
Malili, 23 D4
Malindi, 30 B5
Malin Head, C., 7 D4
Mallaig, 10 B2
Mallawi, 28 B5,6
Mallorca, I., 11 G4
Mallow, 10 E5
Malmö, 15 E5
Malmyž, 17 C7
Målselv, 15 A6
Malta, St., I., 13 D3
Maluku, Arch., 23 C,D4,5
Malung, 15 C5
Matyj Uzon', R., 18 B,C6
Mamaja, 14 B4
Mamberamo, R., 23 D5
Mamburao, 23 bB2
Mamfe, 29 D8
Mamoré, R., 37 D3
Mamou, 29 C2,3
Mampong, 29 D5
Man, 29 D4
Mana (French Guyana), 38 B4
Mana (Hawaiian Is.), 35 A A1,2
Manacor, 11 G4
Manado, 23 C4
Managhan, 10 D6
Managua, 36 C4
Manakara, 30 D5
Mananjary, 30 D5
Ma'nasi, 24 B2
Manaus, 38 C3,4
Manavgat, 21 aB2
Manche (50), Admin. U., 11 B2
Manchester (U.K.), 9 C3
Manchester (U.S.A.), 35 C6
Mand, R., 21 D6
Manda, 30 C4
Mandal, 15 D3
Mandalay, 22 B5
Mandalgov', 24 B4
Mandritsara, 30 C5
Manfredonia, 13 B3,4
Mangaia, I., 41 F10

Mangalia, 14 C4
Mangalore, 22 C3
Mango, I., 41 bA3
Mangochi, 30 C4
Mangoky, R., 30 D5
Mangui, 24 A6
Mangya, 24 C3
Manhattan (U.S.A., Kansas), 35 D1
Manhattan (U.S.A., New York), 32a
Maniamba, 30 C4
Manica, 30 C4
Manicoré, 38 C3
Manihi, I., 41 E11
Manihiki, I., 41 E9,10
Manila, 23 B4
Manila Bay, 23 bB2
Manipur (2), Admin. U., 22 B5
Manisa, 21 aB1
Manitoba, Admin. U., 33 C10
Manitoulin Island, I., 35 B4
Maniitsoq (Sukkertoppen), 33 B14
Maniwaki, 35 B5
Manizales, 38 B2
Mankato, 35 C2
Mankono, 29 C4
Mankota, 34 B5
Manna, 23 D2
Mannar, 20 aB2,3
Mannheim, 12 C3
Manokwari, 23 D5
Monono, 30 B3
Manresa, 11 F4
Mansa, 30 C3
Mansel Island, I., 33 B11,12
Mansfield (U.K.), 9 C4
Mansfield (U.S.A.), 33b
Manta, 38 C1,2
Mantova, 13 A2
Manturovo, 17 C6
Mäntyluoto, 15 C7
Manua Islands, Is., 41 cB4
Manuelzinho, 38 C4
Manukau, 40 aA2
Manyč, R., 18 C5
Manyoni, 30 B4
Manzanares, 11 G3
Manzanillo (Cuba), 36 aB5
Manzanillo (Mexico), 36 C2
Manzhouli, 24 B5
Mao, 28 C4
Maoming, 24 D5
Mapuera, R., 38 C4
Maputo, 30 D4
Maraā, 38 C3
Marabá, 38 C5
Maracaibo, 38 A2
Maracay, 38 A3
Maradi, 29 B7
Marae, 41 dB1
Marâgheh, 21 B5
Maramba, 30 C3
Marand, 21 B5
Maranhão, Admin. U., 38 C5
Marañón, R., 37 C2
Maraş, 21 aB3
Marathon, 35 B3
Marawī, 28 C6
Marbella, 11 G2
Marble Bar, 40 C2
Marble Canyon, 34 D4

Marburg an der Lahn, 12 C3
March, 9 C5
Marcha, R., 16 C13
Marche (10), Admin. U., 13 B3
Mar del Plata, 39 B3
Mardin, 21 aB4
Merengo, 33 aC4
Marganec, 18 C3,4
Margate, 9 D5
Margerøya, I., 15 A8
Mariana Islands, Is., 3
Mariánské Lázně, 12 C4
Marias, R., 34 B4
Maribor, 13 A3
Marica, R., 14 C3
Marîdī, 28 D5
Marie Byrd Land, Reg., 42 G12-14
Mariehamn, 15 C6,7
Mariental, 30 D2
Mariestad, 15 D5
Marília, 38 E4,5
Marinduque Island, I., 23 bB2
Maringá, 39 A3
Marka, 28 D7
Markovo, 16 C18,19
Marks, 18 B6
Marl, 12 aA3
Marmagao, 20 aA1
Marmande, 11 C3
Marne (51), Admin. U., 11 B4
Marne, R., 11 B3
Marne (Haute-) (52), Admin. U., 11 B,C4
Maroantsetra, 30 C5,6
Maromokotro, Mt., 26 F9,10
Maroua, 29 C9
Marovoay, 30 C5
Marquette, 35 B3
Marrakech, 28 A2
Marree, 40 C3
Marsabit, 30 B6
Marsala, 13 C3
Mars'aty, 17 aA3
Marseille, 11 D4
Marshall (Liberia), 29 D3
Marshall (U.S.A.), 35 F2
Marshall Islands, Admin. U., 41 B,C7
Marsh Island, I., 35 F2
Martaban, 22 C5
Martapura, 23 D3
Martí, 36 aB5
Martil, 5 aB3
Martin, 12 C5
Martinique, Admin. U., I., 36 bB2
Mary, 21 B8
Maryborough, 40 C5
Maryland, Admin. U., 35 D5
Maryport, 10 C3
Maryville, 35 C2
Marzūq, 28 B4
Masai Steppe, Pl., 26 E8
Masan, 25 C4
Masbate, 23 bB2
Masbate Island, I., 23 bB4
Mascarene Islands, Is., 26 F,G10,11
Maseru, 30 D3
Masjed Soleymān, 21 C5,6

page 209

, 21 B 7,8
ur-Raqq, 28 D 5
28 D 6
ity, 35 C 2
21 E 7
Massa, 13a B 4
Massachusetts, Admin. U., 35 C 6
Massakori, 29 B 9
Massangena, 30 D 4
Massena, 33b
Masset, 33 C 6
Massif Central, Mts., 5 C 5
Masuda, 25 D 5
Masvingo, 30 D 4
Matadi, 30 B 2
Matagalpa, 36 C 4
Matam, 29 B 2
Matamoros, 36 B 3
Matane, 35 B 7
Matanzas, 36a A 3
Matara, 20a C 3
Mataram, 23 D 3
Mata Utu, 41 E 8
Matautu, 41 c A 2
Matehuala, 36 B 2
Matera, 13 B 4
Matészalka, 14 B 2
Mateur, 27a A 2,3
Mathura, 22 B 3
Matlock, 9 C 4
Mato Grosso, 38 D 4
Mato Grosso, Admin. U., 38 D 4
Mato Grosso do Sul, Admin. U., 38 D,E 4
Matrah, 21 E 7
Matrūh, 28 A 5
Matsue, 25 C 5
Matsumae, 25 B 6,7
Matsumoto, 25 C 6
Matsuyama, 25 D 5
Mattawa, 35 B 7
Mattawamkeag, 35 B 7
Matuku, I., 41 b B 2
Maturín, 38 B 3
Maubeuge, 11 B 3
Maués, 38 C 4
Maui, I., 41 B 10
Maun, 30 C 3
Mauna Kea, Vol., 3
Mauritania, St., 28 B,C 1,2
Mauritius, St., 30a B 2,3
Mava, 23 D 6
Mawson Station, 42 F 30
Mawson Coast, Reg., 42 F 30,31
Mayenne (53), Admin. U., 11 C 2
Mayo, 33 B 6
Mayo, Admin. U., 10 D,E 5
Mayotte, I., 30 C 5
Maysville, 35 D 4
Mayumba, 30 B 2
Mazabuka, 30 C 3
Mazār-e-Sharīf, 22 A 2
Mazatlán, 36 C 2
Mažeikiai, 17 C 2
Mazilovo, 17 b
Mazirbe, 17 C 2
Mba, 41 b A 1
Mbabane, 30 D 4
Mbala, 30 C 3
Mbalmayo, 29 E 8
Mbandaka, 30 A,B 2
M'Banza Congo, 30 B 2
Mbanza-Ngungu, 30 B 2
Mbarara, 30 B 4
Mbengga, I., 41 b B 2
Mbeya, 30 B 3
Mbinda, 30 B 2

Mbout, 29 A 2
Mbua, 41 b A 2
Mbuji-Mayi, 30 B 3
Mbutha, 41 b A 2,3
Mcensk, 18 B 4
Mchinji, 30 C 4
Mc Murdo, Station, 42 G 18-20
Mdiq, 5a B 3
Meadville, 33b
Meath, Admin. U., 10 E 6
Mecca see Makkah
Mechelen, 11 B 4
Mecklenburgen Bay, B., 12 B 3,4
Medan, 23 C 1
Médéa, 27a A 1
Medellín, 38 B 2
Médenine, 28 A 4
Mederdra, 29 A 2
Medford, 34 C 2
Medgidia, 14 B 4
Mediaş, 14 B 3
Medicine Hat, 33 C,D 8
Medina del Campo, 11 F 2
Mediterranean Sea, 3
Medvedica, R., 18 B 4
Medvedkovo, 17 b
Medvežjegorsk, 17 B 4
Meekatharra, 40 C 1
Meerut, 22 B 3
Mega, 28 D 6
Mégara, 14 D 2
Meghalaya (3), Admin. U., 22 B 5
Mehdia, 27a A 1
Meiganga, 29 D 9
Meiktila, 22 B 5
Meixian, 24 D 5
Mejillones, 39 A 1
Mekele, 28 C 6,7
Meknès, 28 A 2
Mekong see Lancangjiang
Mekoryuk, 33 B 3
Melaka, 19 b C 3
Melaka (4), Admin. U., 19 b C 3
Melanesia, Arch., 41 C-E 4-6
Melbourne, 40 D 4
Melenki, 17 C 6
Melilla, 28 A 2
Melitopol', 18 C 4
Mělník, 12 C 2
Melo, 39 a D 3
Melun, 11 B 3
Melville, 34 A 6
Melville Island (Australia), I., 40 B 3
Melville Island (Canada), I., 33 A 8,9
Melville Peninsula, Pen., 33 B 11
Memmingen, 12 C,D 3
Memphis, 35 D 2
Menai Strait, Str., 7 E 5
Ménaka, 29 A,B 6
Mende, 11 C 3
Mendoza, 39 B 2
Mendoza (12), Admin. U., 39 B 2
Mengzi, 24 D 2
Menominee, 35 B 3
Menongue, 30 C 2
Menorca, I., 11 F,G 4
Mentok, 23 D 2
Menzies, 40 C 2
Meppel, 12 B 2
Merak, 23 a A 1
Merano, 13 A 2
Merauke, 23 D 5,6

Merced, 34 D 2
Mercedes (Argentina), 39 A 3
Mercedes (Uruguay), 39 a D 2
Merefa, 18 C 4
Meriç, R., 14 C 3
Mérida (Mexico), 36 B 4
Mérida (Spain), 11 G 2
Mérida (Venezuela), 38 B 2
Meridian, 35 E 3
Merirumã, 38 B 4
Merredin, 40 D 1
Merrick, Mt., 7 D 5
Merritt, 33 a B 3
Mersa Fatma, 28 C 7
Merseburg, 12 C 3
Mersey, R., 7 E 6
Merseyside (3), Admin. U., 9 C 3
Mersin, 21 a B 2
Merthyr Tydfil, 9 D 3
Merzifon, 21 a A 3
Mesa, 34 E 4
Meščura, 17 B 8
Mesewa, 28 C 6
Mesolóngion, 14 D 2
Mesopotamia, Reg., 19 F 6
Messalo, R., 30 C 4,5
Messaría, Pl., 19 c A 2
Messina (Sicilia), 13 C 3
Messina (South Africa), 30 D 3,4
Messiniakós Kólpos, B., 14 D 2
Mestre, 13 a A 6
Meta, R., 37 B 2
Metairie, 35 E,F 2
Metaline Falls, 33 a B 4,5
Metán, 39 A 2
Metz, 11 B 4
Meurthe-et-Moselle (54), Admin. U., 11 B 4
Meuse (55), Admin. U., 11 B 4
Meuse, R., 11 B 4
Meymaneh, 22 A 2
Mexicali, 36 A 1
Mexican Plateau, Plat., 31 G 10
Mexico, 35 D 2
México, 36 C 3
México (14), Admin. U., 36 C 3
Mexico, St., 36 A-C 2,3
Mexico Beach, 35 F 3
Međurečenskij, 17 a B 3,4
Meyer', 16 C 6
Mezen', 17 B 7
Mezenskaja Guba, B., 17 A 6
Mežozernyj, 17 a C 2,3
Miami, 35 F 4,5
Miāneh, 21 B 5
Miānwāli, 22 A 3
Mianyang, 24 C 3
Miass, 17 a B,C 3
Miass, R., 17 a B,C 3
Micha-Cchakaja, 18 D 5
Michajlovka (U.S.S.R., Kamyšin), 18 B 5
Michajlovka (U.S.S.R., Zaporožje), 18 C 3,4
Michalovce, 12 C 6
Michel, 34 B 4
Michigan, Admin. U., 35 B,C 3,4
Michikamau Lake, L., 33 C 13

Michoacán (15), Admin. U., 36 B 2
Micronesia, Arch., 41 B,C 3-6
Mičurin, 14 C 3,4
Mičurinsk, 18 B 5
Middelburg, 30 E 3
Middlesboro, 35 D 4
Middlesbrough, 9 B 4
Midelt, 28 A 2
Mid Glamorgan (51), Admin. U., 9 D 3
Midland, 34 E 6
Midway Islands, Is., 3
Midwest City, 34 D 7
Mielec, 12 C 6
Miercurea-Ciuc, 14 B 3
Mieres, 11 F 2
Mihajlovgrad, 14 C 2
Mihajlovgrad (9), Admin. U., 14 C 2
Mikkeli, 15 C 8
Mikun', 17 B 8
Milan see Milano
Milano, 13 A 2
Milás, 21 a B 1
Mildura, 40 D 4
Miles, 33 a C 4
Miles City, 34 B 6
Milford Haven, 9 D 2
Milk, R., 34 B 4
Millau, 11 C 3
Mille Lacs Lake, 35 B 2
Millerovo, 18 C 5
Milo, R., 29 C 3
Milos, I., 14 D 3
Milwaukee, 35 C 3
Mimmaya, 25 B 7
Minas, 39 a D 2,3
Minas de Riotinto, 11 G 2
Minas Gerais, Admin. U., 38 D 5
Minatitlán, 36 C 3
Mincio, R., 13 a A 4
Mindanao, I., 23 C 4
Mindanao Sea, 23 b C 2
Mindelo, 28 a A 1
Mindoro, I., 23 B 3,4
Mindoro Strait, 23 B 3,4
Mineiros, 38 D 4
Mineral'nyje Vody, 18 D 5
Mingečaur, 18 a A 2
Mingečaurskoje Vodochranilišče, Res., 18 a A 2
Minho see Miño
Minitonas, 34 A 6
Minna, 29 C 7
Minneapolis, 35 C 1,2
Minnesota, Admin. U., 35 B,C 1,2
Miño, R., 11 F 2
Minot, 34 B 6
Minsk, 18 B 2
Minusinsk, 16 D 11
Mira, 13 a A 6
Miraflores, 34 a
Miramar, 39 a E 2
Miranda de Ebro, 11 F 3
Mirandola, 13 a B 5
Mirbāt, 21 F 6,7
Mirgorod, 18 B,C 3
Miri, 23 C 3
Mirjāveh, 21 D 8
Mirnyj, 16 C 13
Mirnyj, Station, 42 F 27
Mironovka, 18 C 3
Mirpur Khās, 22 B 2
Mirzāpur, 22 a B 2
Mishan, 25 A 5

page 210

Misiones (13), Admin. U., 39A3
Miskolc, 14A2
Mismār, 28C6
Misrātah, 28A4
Missinaibi, R., 35A4
Mississauga, 33b
Mississippi, Admin. U., 35E2,3
Mississippi, R., 35B2
Mississippi Lowlands, Pl., 31F11,12
Missoula, 34B4
Missouri, Admin. U., 35D2
Missouri, R., 34B5
Mitchell, 34C7
Mitchell, R., 40B4
Mīt Ghamr, 26aB3
Mitilíni, 14D3
Mito, 25C7
Mittellandkanal, Can., 12B2,3
Mitú, 38B2
Mitwaba, 30B3
Miyake-jima, I., 25D6,7
Miyako, 25C7
Miyakonojō, 25D5
Miyazaki, 25D5
Mizdah, 28A4
Mizen Head, C., 7F2,3
Mizoram (7), Admin. U., 22B5
Mizque, 38D3
Mizuho, Station, 42G32
Mjøsa, L., 15C4
Mława, 12B6
Mmabatho, 30D3
Moab, 34D5
Moala, I., 41bB2
Moanda, 30B2
Moba, 30B3
Moberly, 35D2
Mobile, 35E3
Mobile Bay, B., 35E,F3
Moçambique, 30C5
Mochudi, 30D3
Mocímboa da Praia, 30C5
Moclips, 34B2
Mocoa, 38B2
Mocuba, 30C4
Modaomen, B., 19aB1
Modena, 13A2
Moers, 12aB2
Moffat, 10C3
Mogil'ov, 18B3
Mogil'ov-Podol'skij, 18C2
Mogoča, 16D13
Mogzon, 16bB3
Mohács, 14B2
Mohammedia, 11H2
Mohéli, I., 30C5
Moirans, 11C4
Moisie, R., 33C13
Mojave, 34D3
Mojave Desert, Des., 31aC,D2
Mokolo, 29C9
Mokp'o, 25D4
Moldavian Soviet Socialist Republic, Admin. U., 18C2
Molde, 15C3
Moldoveanu, Mt., 5C7
Molepolole, 30D3
Molfetta, 13B4
Molise (11), Admin. U., 13B3
Mollendo, 38D2
Molodečno, 18B2

Molodežnaja, Station, 42G34,35
Molokai, I., 35aB3
Molopo, R., 30D3
Molucca Sea, 23C,D4
Mombasa, 30B4,5
Mombetsu, 25B7
Mén, I., 12B4
Monaco, 11D4
Monaco, St., 11D4
Monaghan, 10D6
Monaghan, Admin. U., 10D,E6
Moncalieri, 13aA,B1
Mončegorsk, 17A4
Mönchengladbach, 12aB1,2
Monclova, 36B2
Moncton, 33D13
Mondovi, 13aB1
Monet, 35B5
Monforte de Lemos, 11F2
Mongo, 28C4
Mongolia, St., 24B3-5
Mongu, 30C3
Monmouth, 9D3
Mono, R., 29D6
Monroe (U.S.A., Louisiana), 35E2
Monroe (U.S.A., Washington) 33aC3
Monrovia, 29D2
Mons, 11B3
Monselice, 13aA5
Montana, Admin. U., 34B5
Montauban, 11C3
Montbard, 11C4
Montbéliard, 11C4
Mont Blanc, Mt., 5C5
Mont Cameroun, Mt., 26D5,6
Mont-de-Marsan, 11D2
Montebelluna, 13aA5,6
Montebourg, 6aA3
Monte Caseros, 39aD2
Monte Cinto, Mt., 5C5
Montélimar, 11C4
Monte Lirio, 34a
Montemorelos, 34F7
Montenegro, 39aC3
Montego Bay, 36C5
Montería, 38B2
Montes Claros, 38D5
Montevideo, 39aD,E2
Mont Forel, Mt., 42B14,15
Montgomery, 35E3
Monticello, 34D5
Mont-Joli, 33D13
Mont Laurier, 35B5
Montlucon, 11C3
Montmartin-sur-Mer, 6aA3
Montpelier (U.S.A.), 35C5
Montpellier (France), 11D3
Montréal, 33D12
Montreux, 11C4
Montrose, 10B3
Montserrat, Admin. U., 36bA2
Monza, 13A2
Monzón, 11F4
Moorea, I., 41dB1
Moorhead, 34B7
Moosehead Lake, L., 33b
Moose Jaw, 33C9
Moosonee, 33C11
Mopti, 29B4,5

Mora, 15C5
Morādābād, 22B3,4
Moramanga, 30C5
Moratuwa, 20aC2,3
Morava, R., 12C5
Morawhanna, 38B3,4
Moray Firth, B., 7B,C6
Morbihan (56), Admin. U., 11C2
Mordovian Autonomous Soviet Socialist Rep., Admin. U., 18B5,6
Morecambe, 9B3
Morecambe Bay, B., 7D,E6
Morehead City, 35E5
More Laptevych, S., 16B13-15
Morelia, 36C2
Morella, 11F3,4
Morelos (16), Admin. U., 36C3
Mórfou, 19cA1
Morghāb, R., 21B8,9
Morioka, 25C7
Morlaix, 11B2
Morocco, St., 28A,B2
Morogoro, 30B4
Morombe, 30D5
Morón, 36aA4
Mörön, 24B3,4
Morondava, 30D5
Moroni see Njazidja
Morotai, I., 23C4
Morozovsk, 18C5
Morpeth, 9B4
Morrinhos, 38D5
Morristown, 35D4
Moršansk, 18B5
Mortara, 13aA2
Moscow, 34B3
Moscow see Moskva
Mosel see Moselle
Moselle (57), Admin. U., 11B4
Moselle, R., 11B4
Moses Lake, 34B3
Moshi, 30B4
Mosjøen, 15B5
Moskva, 16D5,6
Moskva, R., 17C5
Moss, 15D4
Mossel Bay, 30E3
Mossoró, 38D6
Most, 12C4
Mostar, 13B4
Mostardas, 39aB3
Motala, 15D5
Motherwell, 10C3
Motril, 11G3
Moudjéria, 29A2
Mouila, 30B2
Moulins, 11C3
Moulmein, 22C6
Moundou, 28D4
Mount Adams, Mt., 31aA1
Mountain Nile see Al-Bahr al-Jabal
Mountains Nimba, Mts., 26D4
Mount Amundsen, Mt., 42F,G26
Mount Aspiring, Mt., 40aB1
Mount Augustus, Mt., 40C1
Mount Columbia, Mt., 31D9,10
Mount Cook, Mt., 40aB1

Mount Cooke, Mt., 40D1
Mount Elbert, Mt., 31F9,10
Mount Elgon, Mt., 26D8
Mount Elkins, Mt., 42F31
Mount Erebus, Mt., 42G19,20
Mount Everest, Mt., 19G10,11
Mount Forest, 33b
Mount Gambier, 40D3,4
Mount Hawkes, Mt., 42H5-8
Mount Hood, Mt., 31aA1
Mount Isa, 40C3
Mount Jefferson, Mt., 31aC2
Mount Kenya/Kirinyaga, Vol., 26D8
Mount Kinabalu, Mt., 19 I 13
Mount Kirkpatrick, Mt., 42H20-24
Mount Kosciusko, Mt., 40D4,5
Mount Leinster, Mt., 7E4
Mount Liebig, Mt., 40C3
Mount Linn, Mt., 31aB1
Mount Lister, Mt., 42G21,22
Mount Logan, Mt., 31C6,7
Mount Markham, Mt., 42H21-23
Mount Mc Kinley, Mt., 31C5,6
Mount Meharry, Mt., 40C1
Mount Menzies, Mt., 42G30,31
Mount Meru, Vol., 26E8
Mount Minto, Mt., 42G19
Mount Mitchell, Mt., 31F12,13
Mount Olympus, Mt., 31aA1
Mount Ord, Mt., 40B2
Mount Pinos, Mt., 31aD2
Mount Pleasant, 35E2
Mount Rainier, Mt., 31aA1
Mount Ratz, Mt., 42A5,6
Mount Robson, Mt., 31D8,9
Mount Roraima, Mt., 37B3,4
Mount Saint Elias, Mt., 31C7
Mount Saint Helens, Vol., 31aA1
Mount's Bay, B., 9D,E2
Mount Shasta, Mt., 31aB1
Mount Sidley, Mt., 42G12,13
Mount Victoria, Mt., 40A4
Mount Waddington, Mt., 31D8,9
Mount Wells, Mt., 40B2
Mount Whitney, Mt., 31aC2
Mount Woodroffe, Mt., 40C2,3
Moura (Brazil), 38C3
Moura (Portugal), 11G2
Mourdiah, 29B4
Mourne, R., 7D4
Mourne Mountains, Mts., 7D4,5
Moyale, 28D6
Moyamba, 29C2
Moyle (21), Admin. U., 10D6
Moyobamba, 38C2

page 211

17C5	Musoma, 30B4	Nähded, 22C3	Naryn (Abakan), 24A3
...que, St., 30C,D4	Musselburgh, 10C3	Nahr al-Āsī, R., 20bA,B2	Naryn (Alma-Ata), 24B1
...ique Channel,	Mustafakemalpaşa,	Nahr al-Khābūr, R.,	Naryn, R., 24B1
...)4,5	14C,D3,4	20bA,B3	Nashville-Davidson, 35D3
...,18D5	Mustvee, 17C3	Na'in, 21C6	Näsik, 22B,C3
Mozyr', 18B2	Mūt, 28B5	Nairn, 10B3	Nassau, 35F5
Mpanda, 30B4	Mutare, 30C4	Nairobi, 30B4	Nassau, I., 41E9
Mpika, 30C4	Mutnyj Materik, 17A8	Najin, 25B5	Nässjö, 15D5
M'Sila, 27aA1	Mutton Bay, 33C14	Nakhchevan Autonomous	Natal (Brazil), 38C6
Mtwara, 30C5	Mutuali, 30C4	Soviet Socialist	Natal (Sumatera), 19bD1
Muang Khammouan,	Muzaffarpur, 22aB3	Republic (5), Admin. U.,	Natal, Admin. U., 30D3,4
22C6	Mwanza (Tanzania), 30B4	18aB2	Natchez, 35E2
Muar, 19bC,D3	Mwanza (Zambia), 30B3	Nakhon Ratchasima,	Nateva Bay, B., 41bA2,3
Muarabungo, 23D2	Mwaya, 30B4	22C6	Natitingou, 29C6
Mubi, 29C9	Mweelrea, Mt., 7E2,3	Nakhon Sawan, 22C5,6	Nauru, St., I., 41C6
Mucusso, 30C3	Mweka, 30B3	Nakhon Si Thammarat,	Nauški, 16D12
Mudanjiang, 24B6	Mwene-Ditu, 30B3	22D5,6	Nausori, 41bA2
Mudanjiang, R., 25B4	Myanaung, 22C5	Nakina, 33C11	Nauta, 38B2
Mudanya, 21aA1	Myeik, 22C5	Naknek, 33C4	Navan, 10E6
Mufulira, 30C3	Myeik Kyunzu, 22C,D5	Nakskov, 12B3	Navarra (15), Admin. U.,
Muğla, 21aB1	Myingyan, 22B5	Nakuru, 30B4	11F3
Muhammad Qawl, 28B6	Myitkyinā, 22B5	Nal'čik, 18D5	Naviti, I., 41bA1
Mui Bai-Bung, C., 22D6	Myla, 17A8	Nālūt, 28A4	Navfa, 18B3
Mujezerskij, 17B4	Mymensingh, 22aB4	Namacunde, 30C2	Navoi, 21A9
Mukačevo, 18C1	Mys Arktičeskij, C.,	Namangan, 16E9	Năvplion, 14D2
Mukden see Shenyang	16A10-12	Namapa, 30C4,5	Navrongo, 29C5
Mulan, 15A4	Mys Čeľuskin, 16B12,13	Namche Bazar, 22aB3	Navua, 41bB2
Mulengzhen, 25B5	Mys Čeľuskin, C.,	Nam-Dinh, 22B6	Nawābshāh, 22B1
Mülheim, 11C4	19B12-14	Namhu, I., 24C3	Náxos, I., 14D3
Mulhouse, 11C4	Mys Deževa, C.,	Namibe, 30C2	Nayarit (17), Admin. U.,
Mulhacén, Mt., 5D4	19B,C20	Namibia, St.,	36B2
Mulinghe, R., 25A5	Mys Fligeli, C., 42D25,26	30C,D2	Nāy Band, 21D6
Mull, I., 7C4,5	Mys Kriljon, C., 25A7	Namlea, 23D4	Nayoro, 25B7
Mullet Peninsula, Pen.,	Mys Lopatka, C.,	Nampa, 34C0	Nazaré, 38D6
7D2	19D17,18	Namp'o, 25C3,4	N'azepetrovsk, 17B8
Mullewa, 40C1	Mys Navarin, C., 42B1	Nampula, 30C4	Nazerat, 20bB1
Mullingar, 10E6	Mysore, 22C3	Namsos, 15B4	Nazilli, 21aB1
Mull of Galloway, C., 7D5	Mys Saryč, C., 18D3	Nam Tok, 22C5	Nazret, 28D6
Mull of Kintyre, C., 7D5	Mys Šmidta, 16B20	Namuhu, L., 24C3	Nazwā, 21E7
Mulobezi, 30C3	Mys Želanija, 16B8	Namur, 11B4	N'Dalatando, 30B2
Multān, 22A3	My-Tho, 22C6	Nanaimo, 33aB2	Ndendé, 30B2
Mumra, 18C6	Mytišči, 17C5	Nanchang, 24D5	Ndjamena, 28C4
München, 12C3,4	Mzuzu, 30C4	Nanchong, 24C4	Ndola, 30C3
Muncie, 35C3,4		Nancy, 11B4	Neah Bay, 33aB2
Mungbere, 28D5		Nanded, 22C3	Néa Páfos, 19bC1
Munger, 22aB3	**N**	Nänded, 22C3	Neápolis, 14D2
Munich see München		Nanduri, 41bA2	Neath, 9D3
Münster, 12C2	Naas, 10E6	Nanga-Eboko, 29D8,9	Nebit-Dag, 21B6
Muonio, 15A7,8	Nabeul, 27aA3	Nänga Parbat, Mt., 19F9	Nebolči, 17C4
Muqdisho, 28D7	Nabire, 23D5	Nânga Parbat, Mt., 19F9	Nebraska, Admin. U.,
Mur, R., 12D4	Nabq, 21D2	Nanjing, 24C5	34C6,7
Muradiye, 21aB4	Nābulus, 20bB1	Nanning, 24D4	Neches, R., 35E1
Muraši, 17C7	Nacala, 30C5	Nanortalik, 33B15	Necochea, 39B2,3
Murat, R., 21aB4	Nachičevan, 16F6	Nanping, 24D5	Nefta, 27aB2
Muratkovo, 17aB3	Nachingwea, 30C4	Nansei-shotō, Is., 24D6	Neftegorsk, 18B7
Murchison, R., 40C1	Nachodka, 16E15	Nantes, 11C2	Neftekamsk, 17aB1,2
Murcia, 11G3	Nadon, 11H3	Nantong, 24C6	Neftekumsk, 18D5,6
Murcia (14), Admin. U.,	Nadvoicy, 17B4	Nantou, 19aA2	Negeri Sembilan (5),
11G3	Nadvornaja, 18C1	Nanumea, I., 41D7	Admin. U., 19bC3
Mureşul, R., 14B3	Nadym, 16C9	Nanyang, 24C5	Negombo, 20aC2
Murgab, 24C1	Næstved, 12B3	Nanyang'u, L., 25C2	Negro (Amazonas), R.,
Murgab see Morghāb	Naft-e Safid, 21C5,6	Nanyuki, 30A,B4	37C3
Murkong Selek, 22B5	Naga, 23D4	Nanyunhe, R., 25C2	Negro (Atlantic Ocean),
Murmansk, 16C5	Nāgāland (4), Admin. U.,	Napanee, 33b	R., 37F3
Murom, 17C6	22B5	Napier, 40A2	Negro (Uruguay), R.,
Muroran, 25B7	Nagano, 25C6	Naples see Napoli	39aD2,3
Murray, R., 40D4	Nagaoka, 25C6	Napo, R., 38C2	Negros, I., 23C4
Murray Bridge, 40D3,4	Nägappattinam, 20aB2,3	Napoli, 13B3	Neijiang, 24D4
Murrumbidgee, R., 40D4	Nagar Pārkar, 22B3	Nara (Japan), 25D6	Nei Mongol Zizhiqu (2),
Mururoa, I., 41F12	Nagasaki, 25D4	Nara (Mali), 29B4	Admin. U., 24B4-6
Murwāra, 22aC2	Nagatino, 17b	Narbonne, 11D3	Neisse see Nysa Lužicka
Muş, 21aB4	Nāgercoil, 20aB2	Narew, R., 12B6	Neiva, 38B2
Musa, Mt., 5aB3	Nagorno-Karabakh	Narmada, R., 22B3	Nejva, R., 17aB3
Musala, Mt., 5C7	Autonomous Region (9),	Narodnaja, Mt., 19C7,8	Nelidovo, 17C4
Musan, 25B4	Admin. U., 18aB2	Narrogin, 40D1	Nellore, 22C3,4
Mūs'a Qal'eh, 21C8	Nagorsk, 17C8	Narssaq, 33B15	Nelson, 40aB2
Musgrave Ranges, Mts.,	Nagoya, 25C6	Narva, 17C3	Nelson, R., 33C10
40C3	Nágpur, 22B3	Narva, R., 17C3	Néma, 28C2
Musi, R., 23D2	Naggu, 24C3	Narvik, 15A6	Neman, R., 18B2
Muskegon, 35C3	Nagykanizsa, 14B1		Nemuro, 25B8
Muskogee, 35D1	Naha, 24D6		

page 212

Nenagh, 10 E 5
Nenana, 33 B 5
Nene, R., 7 E 7
Nenjiang, 24 B 6
Nenjiang, R., 25 A 3
Nepal, St., 22a A,B2,3
Népālganj, 22a A 2
Nephin, Mt., 7 D 3
Nerechta, 17 C 6
Neretva, R., 13 B 4
Nerja, 11 G 3
Ner'ungri, 16 D 14
Nes', 17 A 6
Neskaupstadur, 15a B 4
Nesna, 15 B 5
Nestor Falls, 35 B 2
Néstos, R., 14 C 3
Netherlands, St., 12 B,C 1,2
Netherlands Antilles, Admin. U., 38 A 3
Nettilling Lake, L., 33 B 13
Neubrandenburg, 12 B 4
Neubrandenburg (11), Admin. U., 12 B 4
Neuchâtel, 11 C 4
Neufchâtel-en-Bray, 9 E 5
Neumünster, 12 B 3
Neuquén, 39 B 2
Neuquén, Admin. U., 39 B,C 1,2
Neuquén, R., 39 B 1,2
Neuruppin, 12 B 4
Neusiedler See, L., 12 D 5
Neuss, 12 B 2
Neustrelitz, 12 B 4
Neuwied, 12 C 2
Neva, R., 17 C 4
Nevada, 35 D 2
Nevada, Admin. U., 34 D 3
Nevado Ancohuma, Mt., 37 D 3
Nevado Auzangate, Mt., 37 D 2,3
Nevado de Huascarán, Mt., 37 C 2
Nevado del Huila, Mt., 37 B 2
Nevel', 17 C 3,4
Nevers, 11 C 2
Nevinnomyssk, 18 D 5
Nevis, I., 36b A 2
Nevjansk, 17a B 3
Nevşehir, 21a B 2
New Amsterdam, 38 B 4
Newark, 35 C 6
Newark Bay, B., 32a
Newark-upon-Trent, 9 C 4
New Bedford, 35 C 6
New Bern, 35 D 5
New Britain see Birara
New Brunswick, Admin. U., 33 D 13
Newbury, 9 D 4
New Caledonia, I., 41a
Newcastle, 40 D 5
Newcastle under Lyme, 9 C 3
Newcastle upon Tyne, 9 B 4
Newcastle Waters, 40 B 3
Newcastle, West, 10 E 5
New Delhi, 22 B 3
Newfoundland, Admin. U., 33 C,D 13,14
New Georgia, I., 40 A 5
New Guinea, I., 41 D 3,4
Newhalem, 33a B 1
New Hampshire, Admin. U., 33 D 12
Newhaven, 9 D 5

New Haven, 35 C 6
New Hebrides see Vanuatu
New Ireland see Tombara
New Jersey, Admin. U., 35 D 5,6
New Jilm, 35 C 1,2
New Kowloon, 19a B 3
Newman, 40 C 1,2
Newmarket, 9 C 5
New Meadows, 34 C 3,4
New Mexico, Admin. U., 34 D,E 5,6
New Orleans, 35 F 2,3
New Plymouth, 40a A 2
Newport (U.K., Cardiff), 9 D 3
Newport (U.K., Portsmouth), 9 D 4
Newport (U.S.A.), 35 C 6
Newport News, 35 D 5
New Providence, I., 35 F 5
Newquay, 9 D 2
New Rochelle, 32a
Newry, 10 D 6
Newry and Mourne (22), Admin. U., 10 D 6
New South Wales, Admin. U., 40 D 4,5
Newton Abbot, 9 D 3
Newton Falls, 33b
Newtonmore, 10 B 2,3
Newton Saint Boswells, 10 C 3
Newton Stewart, 10 C 2
Newtown, 9 C 3
Newtownabbey, 10 D 6,7
Newtownabbey (23), Admin. U., 10 D 7
Newtownards, 10 D 7
New Westminster, 33a B 2,3
New York, 35 C 6
New York, Admin. U., 35 C 5,6
New Zealand, St., Is., 40a
Neyrīz, 21 D 6
Neyshābūr, 21 B 7
Nežin, 18 B 3
Ngaliema, Mts., 26 D 7,8
Ngaoundéré, 29 D 9
Ngau, I., 41b A,B 2
Nguigmi, 29 B 9
Nguru, 29 B 8
Nha-Trang, 22 C 6,7
Nhulunbuy, 40 B 3
Niafounké, 29 B 4
Niagara Falls, 35 C 5
Niagara Falls, Fs., 33b
Niagassola, 29 B 3
Niamey, 29 B 6
Nica, R., 17a B 3
Nicaragua, St., 36 C 4
Nice, 11 D 4
Nicobar Islands, Is., 22 D 5
Nicolls Town, 35 F 5
Nicosia see Levkosia
Niederösterreich (3), Admin. U., 12 C 4
Niedersachsen (6), Admin. U., 12 B 3
Nièvre (58), Admin. U., 11 C 3
Niğde, 21a B 2
Niger (fjord), B., 15 C 3
Niger, R., 29 C 7
Niger, St., 29 A,B 6-9
Nigeria, St., 29 C 7,8

Niigata, 25 C 6
Niihama, 25 D 5
Niihau, I., 35a B 1,2
Nijmegen, 12 C 2
Nikel', 17 A 4
Nikolajev, 18 C 3
Nikolajevsk, 18 B 6
Nikolajevsk-na-Amure, 16 D 15,16
Nikol'sk, 17 C 7
Nikopol', 18 C 3
Nikšić, 13 B 4
Nile, R., 28 C 6
Nile Delta – Suez Canal, 26a
Nîmes, 11 D 3
Nimule, 28 D 6
Ningan, 25 B 4
Ningbo, 24 D 6
Ningwu, 24 C 5
Ningxia Huizu Zizhiqu (3), Admin. U., 24 C 4
Niobrara, R., 34 C 6
Niono, 29 B 4
Nioro du Sahel, 29 B 3
Niort, 11 C 2
Nipigon, 33 D 11
Nipton, 34 D 3
Niquero, 36a B,C 5
Niš, 13 B 5
Nissan, R., 12 A 4
Niteroi, 39 A 4
Nith, R., 7 D 6
Nitra, 12 C 5
Niue Island, I., 41 E 9
Nizāmābād, 22 C 3
Nižn'aja Peša, 17 A 7
Nižn'aja Tunguska, R., 16 C 10,11
Nižn'aja Tura, 17a B 2
Nižnegansk, 16 D 12,13
Nižnegorskij, 18 C 3,4
Nižnejansk, 16 B 15,16
Nižnekamsk, 17 C 8
Nižnekamskoje Vodochraniłišče, Res., 17a B 1,2
Nižneleninskoje, 24 B 7
Nižneudinsk, 16 D 11,12
Nižnevartovsk, 16 C 9,10
Nižnije Sergi, 17a B 2
Nižnij Lomov, 18 B 5
Nižnij Tagil, 17a B 2
Njazidja, 30 C 5
Nkawkaw, 29 D 5
Nkayi, 30 B 2
Nkongsamba, 29 D 8
Noatak, 33 B 3
Noatak, R., 33 B 4
Nobeoka, 25 D 5
Nogales (Mexico), 36 A 1
Nogales (U.S.A.), 34 E 4
Nográd (11), Admin. U., 14 B 1
Nok Kundi, 21 D 8
Nolinsk, 17 C 7,8
Nome, 33 B 3
Nong'an, 25 B 4
Nong Khai, 22 C 5
Nootka, 33a B 1
Nootka Sound, B., 33a B 1
Noranda, 35 B 5
Nord, 42 D 17
Nord (59), Admin. U., 11 B 3
Nordaustlandet, I., 42 C 21-23
Nordfjord, B., 15 C 3
Nordfold, 15 B 5,6
Nordhausen, 12 C 3
Nordkapp, C., 15 A 8
Nordkinn, C., 15 A 8,9

Nordostrundingen, C., 42 D 17-19
Nordreisa, 15 A 7
Nordrhein – Westfalen (7), Admin. U., 12 C 2
Nore, R., 7 E 4
Norfolk (U.S.A., Nebraska), 34 C 7
Norfolk (U.S.A., Virginia), 35 D 5
Norfolk (33), Admin. U., 9 C 5
Norfolk Island, I., 41 F 6,7
Noril'sk, 16 C 10,11
Normada, R., 19 D 9
Norman, 34 D 7
Normandie, Pen. and Reg., 5 C 4,5
Normanton, 40 B 4
Norman Wells, 33 B 7
Norrköping, 15 D 6
Norrtälje, 15 D 6
Norseman, 40 D 2
Northallerton, 9 B 4
Northam, 40 D 1
North America, 3
Northampton, 9 C 4
Northamptonshire (34), Admin. U., 9 C 4
North Battleford, 33 C 8,9
North Bay, 33 D 12
North Canadian, R., 34 D 6,7
North Cape, C., 40a A 2
North Carolina, Admin. U., 35 D 4,5
North Channel, Str., 7 D 5
North Dakota, Admin. U., 34 B 6,7
North Down (24), Admin. U., 10 D 7
North Downs, Hs., 7 F 7,8
Northern Ireland, Admin. U., 10 D 6,7
Northern Mariana Islands, Admin. U., 41 B 4
Northern Territorry, Admin. U., 40 C,B 2,3
North Esk, R., 10 B 3
North European Plain, Pl., 5 B 5-7
North Foreland, C., 7 F 8
North Frisian Islands, Is., 12 B 3
North Island, I., 40a A 2
North Little Rock, 35 D,E 2
North Magnetic Pole, 31 B 8-10
North Ossetian Autonomous Soviet Socialist Republic (6), Admin. U., 18 D 5
North Platte, 34 C 6,7
North Platte, R., 34 C 6
North Pole, 42 D
North Rona, I. 7 B 5
North Saskatchewan, R., 33 C 8,9
North Sea, 5 B 5
North Tyne, R., 10 C 3
North Uist, I., 7 C 3,4
Northumberland (35), Admin. U., 9 B 3
North Vancouver, 33a B,2,3
North West Cape, C., 40 C 1
North West Highlands, Hs., 7 B,C 5
Northwest Territories, Admin. U., 33 C 7-13

...k, 30D11,12
...k Moors, Mt.,
...
...rkshire, (36),
... U., 9B4
Norton, 9B4
Norton Sound, Str., 42B2
Norway, St., 15A-D3-8
Norway House, 33C10
Norwegian Sea, 15A,B3-6
Norwich, 9C5
Noshiro, 25B6,7
Nosovaja, 17A8,9
Nossop, R., 30D3
Nosy-Be, 30C5
Noteč, R., 12B5
Nottaway, R., 33C10
Nottingham, 9C4
Nottinghamshire, (37), Admin. U., 9C4
Nouadhibou, 28B1
Nouakchott, 28C1
Nouamrhar, 29A1
Nouméa, 41aB2
Nova, 11F1
Nova Iguaçu, 39A4
Novaja Kachovka, 18C5
Novaja Kazanka, 18C6
Novaja Laľa, 17aB2,3
Novaja Zemľa, Is., 16B7,8
Nova Olinda-do Norte, 38C4
Novara, 13A2
Nova Scotia, Admin. U., 33D13
Novgorod, 16D5
Novgorod-Severskij, 18B3
Novi Ligure, 13aB2
Novi Pazar, 13B5
Novi Sad, 13A4
Novoaleksandrovsk, 18C5
Novoaleksejevka, 16aA2
Novoanninskij, 18B5
Novoburejskij, 24B6,7
Novočeboksarsk, 17C7
Novočerkassk, 18C5
Novochopjorsk, 18B5
Novodvinsk, 17B6
Novograd-Volynskij, 18B2
Nôvo Hamburgo, 39aC3,4
Novokačalinsk, 25A5
Novokujbyševsk, 18B6,7
Novokuzneck, 16D10
Novolazarevskaja, Stantion, 42F,G20,21
Novomichajlovka, 25B5
Novomoskovsk (U.S.S.R., Dneprpetrovsk), 18C3,4
Novomoskovsk (U.S.S.R., Tula), 18B4
Novopolock, 17C3
Novorossijsk, 16E5,6
Novorzev, 17C3,4
Novošachtinsk, 18C4,5
Novosibirsk, 16D9,10
Novosibirskije Ostrova, Is., 16B15-18
Novosokoľniki, 17C3,4
Novoukrajinka, 18C3
Novouzensk, 18B6
Novozybkov, 18B3
Novyj Bor, 17A8
Novyj Bug, 18C3
Novyje Kuzminki, 17b
Novyj Port, 16C9
Nowy Sącz, 12C6
Nsawam, 29D5
Nsukka, 29D7

Nubian Desert, Des., 26B8
N'uchča, 17B7
Nudo Coropuna, Mt., 37D2
Nueces, R., 34F7
Nueltin Lake, L., 33B10
Nueva Gerona, 36aB2
Nueve de Julio, 39aE1
Nuevitas, 36aB5
Nuevo Chagres, 34a
Nuevo Laredo, 36B2,3
Nuevo León (18), Admin. U., 36B2,3
Nujiang, R., 24C3
Nūk, 33B14
N'uksenica, 17B6
Nuku'alofa, 41F8
Nukus, 16E7,8
Nulato, 33B4
Nullarbor Plain, Pl., 40D2,3
Numan, 29C8,9
Numazu, 25C,D6
Nuneaton, 9C4
Nunivak Island, I., 33C3
Nuoro, 13B2
N'urba, 16C13
Nurlat, 18B7
Nurmes, 15C9
Nürnberg, 12B3
Nusaybin, 21aB4
Nushki, 22B2
Nyala, 28C5
Nyborg, 12B3
Nyeri, 30B4
Nyíregyháza, 14A,B2
Nykøbing Falster, 12B3,4
Nyköping, 15A3
Nyong, R., 29E8
Nysa, 12C5
Nysa Łużicka, R., 12C4
Nytva, 17aB1,2
Nzérékoré, 29D3
Nzi, R., 29D4

O

Oahu, 42B2
Oahu, I., 41B10
Oakland, 34D2
Oak Ridge, 35D4
Oamaru, 40aB2
Oates Coast, Reg., 42F,G20,21
Oaxaca, 36C3
Oaxaca (19), Admin. U., 36C3
Ob', R., 16D10
Oba, 35B4
Oban, 10B2
Obbia, 28D7
Oberhausen, 12aB2
Oberösterreich (4), Admin. U., 12C4
Óbidos, 38C4
Obihiro, 25B7
Objačevo, 17B7,8
Obluče, 24B7
Obninsk, 18A4
Obojan', 18B4
Obskaja Guba, B., 16B,C9
Obuasi, 29D5
Očakovo, 17b
Ocala, 35F4
Očamčira, 18D5
Ocean Falls, 33C7
Oceanside, 34E3
Ocha, 16D16
Ochansk, 17aB1,2

Ochil Hills, Mts., 7C6
Ochotsk, 16D16
Odda, 15C3
Oddur, 28D7
Ödemiş, 21aB1
Odense, 12B3
Oder see Odra
Odessa (U.S.A.), 34E6
Odessa (U.S.S.R.), 16E5
Odienné, 29C4
Odra, R., 12C5
Ofanto, R., 13B3,4
Offa, 29C7
Offaly, Admin. U., 10E6
Offenbach, 12C3
Ogasawara Guntō, Is., 4
Ogbomosho, 29C7
Ogden, 34C4
Ogdensburg, 35C5
Oglio, R., 13aA4
Ogoja, 29D8
Ogoki, 35A3
Ogoki, R., 35A3
Ogooué, R., 30B2
Ogun (14), Admin. U., 29D6
Ohata, 25B7
Ohio, Admin. U., 35C4
Ohio, R., 35D4
Ohře, R., 12C4
Ohrid, 13B5
Oiapoque, 38B4
Oich, R., L., 7C5
Oil City, 35C5
Oise (60), Admin. U., 11B3
Oise, R., 11B3
Ōita, 25D5
Ojinaga, 36B2
Ojm'akon, 16C15,16
Ojos del Salado, Mt., 37E3
Oka (Angara), R., 16B1
Oka (Volga), R., 16D5
Okahandja, 30D2
Okavango, R., 30C3
Okayama, 25D5
Okehampton, 9D2,3
Okene, 29D7
Okha, 22B2
Oki-guntō, Is., 25C5
Okinawa-jima, I., 24D6
Okitipupa, 29D7
Oklahoma, Admin. U., 34D7
Oklahoma City, 34D7
Oksino, 17A8
Oksovskij, 17B5
Okťabr'skij (U.S.S.R., Kujbyšev), 18B7
Okťabr'skij (U.S.S.R., Minsk), 18B2
Okťabr'skij (U.S.S.R., Vologda), 17B6
Okťabr'skoje, 16aB1,2
Oktember'an, 18aA1
Okulovka, 17C4
Okun'ov Nos, 17A8
Okushiri-tō, I., 25B6
Ólafsvík, 15aB1,2
Öland, I., 15D6
Olavarria, 39B2
Olbia, 13B2
Oldenburg, 12B2,3
Oldham, 9C3,4
Olean, 35C5
Olenegorsk, 17A4
Olen'ok, 16C12,13
Olen'ok, R., 16B,C13,14
Oleśnica, 12C5
Ol'ga, 25B6

Ölgij, 24B2,3
Olifants (Atlantic Ocean), R., 30D2
Olifants (Indian Ocean), R., 30D4
Ólimbos (Cyprus), Mt., 19cB1
Ólimbos (Greece), Mt., 5D7
Olinda, 38C6
Oliveira, 39aB4,5
Ollagüe, 39A2
Ol'okma, R., 16D13,14
Ol'okminsk, 16C14
Olomouc, 12C5
Olonec, 17B4
Olongapo, 23B3,4
Olov'annaja, 16bB4
Olsztyn, 12B6
Oltu, 21aA4
Oltul, R., 14B3
Olympia, 34B2
Omagh, 10D6
Omagh (25), Admin. U., 10D6
Omaha, 35C1
Omak, 33aB4
Oman, St., 21D-F6,7
Omaruru, 30D2
Omatako see Omuramba
Omo, R., 28D6
Omolon, 16C18
Omolon, R., 16C17,18
Omsk, 16D9
Omuramba, R., 30C,D2
Ōmuta, 25D5
Omutninsk, 17C8
Ondangua, 30C2
Ondjiva, 30C2
Ondo, 29D7
Ondo (15), Admin. U., 29D7
Ondörchaan, 24B4,5
Onega, 17B5
Onega, R., 17B5
Oneida Lake, L., 33b
Onežskaja Guba, B., 17B5
Onežskoje Ozero, L., 16C5,6
Ongjin, 25C3,4
Onitsha, 29D7
Onon, R., 16D13
Onslow, 40C1
Onsong, 25B4,5
Ontario, Admin. U., 33C10,11
Oodnadatta, 40C3
Oostende, 11B3
Opanake, 20aC3
Oparino, 17C7
Opatija, 13A3
Opava, 12C5
Opelika, 35E3
Opheim, 34B5
Opobo, 29D7
Opočka, 17C3
Opole, 12C5
Opua, 40aA2
Oradea, 14B2
Oran, 28A2
Orange (Australia), 40D4
Orange (France), 11C3
Orange, R., 30E3
Orange Free State, Admin. U., 30D3
Orbetello, 13B2
Orbost, 40D4
Orcadas, Is., 42F5
Orchon, R., 24B4
Ord, R., 40B2
Ordu, 21aA3

page 214

Ordžonikidze, 16E6
Örebro, 15D5
Orechovo-Zujevo, 17C5
Oregon, Admin. U., 34C2,3
Orellana, 38C2
Orenburg, 16D7
Orense (Argentina), 39aE2
Orense (Spain), 11F2
Orihuela, 11G3
Orillia, 35C5
Orinoco, R., 37B3
Orion, 34B4
Orissa, Admin. U., 22B,C4
Oristano, 13C2
Orivesi, L., 15C9
Orizaba, 36C3
Orkanger, 15C4
Orkney (64), Admin. U., 10A3
Orkney Islands, Is., 7B6
Orlando, 35F4
Orléans, 11C3
Ormara, 21D8
Ormea, 13aB1
Ormoc, 23B4
Orne (61), Admin. U., 11B2
Örnsköldsvik, 15C6
Or'ol, 16D5
Oron, 20bC1
Oroquieta, 23bC2
Orosháza, 14B2
Orša, 18B3
Orsk, 16D7,8
Ørsta, 15C3
Ortigueira, 11F1,2
Orümïyeh, 21B4,5
Oruro, 38D3
Orzinuovi, 13aA3,4
Oš, 24B1
Osa, 17aB2
Ōsaka, 25D6
Osasco, 39aB4
Oshawa, 35C5
Oshogbo, 29D7
Oshwe, 30B2,3
Osijek, 13A4
Osipoviči, 18B2
Oskarshamn, 15D6
Oskol, R., 18B4
Oslo, 15C,D4
Oslofjorden, B., 15D4
Osmaniye, 21aB3
Osnabrück, 12B2,3
Osorno, 39C1
Osoyoos, 33aB4
Ostankino, 17b
Ostaškov, 17C4
Oster, 18B3
Österdaälven, R., 15C5
Östersund, 15C5
Ostfriesische Inseln, Is., 12B2
Ostiglia, 13aA5
Ostrava, 12C4
Ostrołęka, 12B6
Ostrov, 17C3
Ostrov Ajon, I., 16B18
Ostrov Belyj, I., 16B8,9
Ostrov Bir'učij, I., 16aA2
Ostrov Boľševik, I., 16B10,11
Ostrov De-Longa, I., 16B17,18
Ostrov Iturup, I., 25A,B4
Ostrov Karaginskij, I., 16D17
Ostrov Kolgujev, I., 16C6,7

Ostrov Komsomolec, I., 16A9-11
Ostrov Koteľnyj, I., 16B14,15
Ostrov Kunašir, I., 25B8
Ostrov Novaja Sibiŕ, I., 16B17
Ostrov Oktabŕskoj Revoľucii, I., 16B8-11
Ostrov Oľchon, I., 16bB2
Ostrov Sachalin, I., 16D,E16
Ostrov Vajgač, I., 16B7,8
Ostrov Vrangeľa, I., 16B19,20
Ostrowiec Świętokrzyski, 12C6
Ostrów Mazowiecka, 12B6
Ostrów Wielkopolski, 12C5
Ōsumi-kaikyō, Str., 25D5
Ōsumi-shotō, Is., 25D5
Oswego, 35C5
Otaru, 25B7
Otavi, 30C2
Oti, R., 29C6
Otjiwarongo, 30D2
Otok Brač, I., 13B4
Otok Cres, I., 13A3
Otok Dugi, I., 13A3
Otok Hvar, I., 13B4
Otok Korčula, I., 13B4
Otok Krk, I., 13A3
Otok Mljet, I., 13B4
Otok Pag, I., 13A3
Otok Palagruža, I., 13B4
Otok Vis, I., 13B3,4
Otoskwin, R., 35A2
Otra, R., 15D3
Otradnyj, 18B7
Otranto, 18B4
Ōtsu, 25C6
Otta, 15C4
Ottawa (Canada), 33D12
Ottawa (U.S.A.), 35D1,2
Ottawa, R., 33D12
Ottawa Islands, Is., 33B,C11,12
Ottone, 13aB3
Oturkpo, 29D7,8
Ouagadougou, 29B5
Ouahigouya, 29B5
Ouahran see Oran
Ouargla, 28A3
Ouarzazate, 28A2
Oubangui, R., 26D6
Oubangui see Ubangi
Oubatche, 41aA1
Oudtschoorn, 30E3
Oued Azaouak, R., 29A6
Oued Chéliff, R., 28A3
Oued Daoura, R., 28A2
Oued Draâ, R., 28A2
Oued Haouach, R., 28C4
Oued Irhazrhar, R., 28B3
Oued Moulouya, R., 28A2
Oued Mya, R., 28B3
Oued Sala, R., 28C5
Oued Saoura, R., 28B2
Oued Sebou, R., 11H2
Oued Tamanrasset, R., 28B3
Oued Zem, 28A2
Ouémé, R., 29D6
Ouessa, 29C5
Ouesso, 29D4
Ouezzane, 11H2
Ouham, R., 28D4
Ouidah, 29D6

Oujda, 28A2
Oulainen, 15B8
Ouled Djellal, 27aB1,2
Oulu, 15B8
Oulujärvi, L., 15B8
Oulujoki, R., 15B8
Oum Chalouba, 28C5
Ounasjoki, R., 15B8
Ouniaga Kébir, 28C5
Ourinhos, 39aB4
Ouro Prêto, 39aB5
Ouse, R., 7E7
Outer Hebrides, Is., 7B,C4
Outjo, 30D2
Ovada, 13aB2
Ovalle, 39B1
Ovar, 11F1
Övertomea, 15B7
Oviedo, 11F2
Ovruč, 18B2
Owando, 30B2
Owensboro, 35D3
Owen Sound, 35C4
Owerri, 29D7
Owo, 29D7
Owyhee, R., 31aB2
Oxford, 9D4
Oxfordshire (38), Admin. U., 9D4
Oxnard, 34E3
Oyem, 28D4
Oyo, 29D6,7
Oyo (16), Admin. U., 29C6
Ozamiz, 23bC2
Ozero Alakoľ, L., 24B1,2
Ozero Bajkal, L., 16D2
Ozero Balchaš, L., 16E9
Ozero Baskunčak, L., 18C6
Ozero Beloje, L., 17B5
Ozero Čany, L., 16D9
Ozero Chanka, L., 24B7
Ozero Donuzlav, L., 16aB1
Ozero Eľton, L., 18C6
Ozero Iľmen', L., 17C4
Ozero Imandra, L., 17A4
Ozero Issyk-Kuľ, L., 19E9,10
Ozero Kubenskoje, L., 17C5
Ozero Kujto, L., 17A4
Ozero Laca, L., 17B5
Ozero Manyč Gudilo, L., 18C5
Ozero N'uk, L., 17B4
Ozero P'aozero, L., 17A3,4
Ozero Sasyk, L., 16aB1
Ozero Segozero, L., 17B4
Ozero Sevan, L., 18aA2
Ozero Tajmyr, L., 16B12,13
Ozero Tengiz, L., 16D8
Ozero Topozero, L., 17A4
Ozero Umbozero, L., 17A4,5
Ozero Vože, L., 17B5
Ozero Vogozero, L., 17B5
Ozero Zajsan, L., 16E10
Ozinki, 18B6

P

Paarl, 30E2
Pabianice, 12C5
Pabna, 22aB,C4
Pacasmayo, 38C1,2
Pachuca, 36B3
Pacific Coast of U.S.A., 31a
Pacific Ocean, 3
Padang, 23D1,2
Padangsidempuan, 19bD1
Paddington, 9a
Padma, R., 22aC4
Padova, 13A2
Paducah, 35D2
Paea, 41dB1
Paektusan, Mt., 19E14,15
Pagadian, 23C4
Pagalu, I., 30B1
Pago Pago, 41cB3
Pahala, 35aC4
Pahang (5), Admin. U., 19bB,C3
Pahang, R., 19bC3
Paignton, 9D3
Päijänne, L., 15C8
Paisley, 10C2
País Valenciano (16), Admin. U., 11G3
País Vasco (17), Admin. U., 11F3
Paita, 41aB2
Paja, 34a
Pakistan, St., 22A,B2,3
Pakokku, 22B5
Pakxé, 22B6
Pala, 29C9
Palaikhóri, 19cB1
Palana, 16D17
Palanan, 23bA2
Palanga, 17C2
Palangkaraya, 23D3
Palau, Admin. U., Is., 41C3
Palawan, I., 23B3
Paleleh, 23C4
Palembang, 23D2
Palencia, 11F2
Palermo, 13C3
Palestine, 35F1,2
Palk Strait, 20aB2,3
Pallasovka, 18B6
Paľma, 17B5
Palma (Baleares Is.), 11G4
Palma (Mozambique), 30C4,5
Palmas, 39aC3
Palmeira, 39aC3,4
Palmer, 33B5
Palmer Station, 42F7
Palmer Land, Reg., 42F,G7
Palmerston, 41E9
Palmerston North, 40aB2
Palmi, 13C3,4
Palmira, 38B2
Palm Springs, 34E3
Palmyra Archipelago, Is., 41C9
Paloma, 34a
Palopo, 23D3,4
Palu (Sulawesi), 23D3
Palu (Turkey), 21aB3,4
Pam, 41aA1
Pama, 29C6
Pamir, Mts., 19F9
Pamiut, 33B15

Sound, B., 35D5
   4D6
   Reg., 37F3,4
   a, 11F3
   2C3
Panamá, 36D5
Panamá, St., 36D4,5
Panama Canal, Can., 37A1,2
Panama City, 35E3
Panaro, R., 13A2
Panay, I., 23B4
Pančevo, 13A5
Panch'iao, 25aB2
P'andž, R., 24C1
Panevėžys, 17C2,3
Pangkalpinang, 23D2
Pangnirtung, 33B13
Pankshin, 29C5
Páno Levkara, 19cB2
Pante Makassar, 23D4
Pánuco, R., 36B3
Paola, 13C3,4
Papeete, 41dB1
Papenoo, 41dA,B2
Papetoai, 41dA1
Papua-New Guinea, St., 41D4,5
Pará, Admin. U., 38C4
Pará, R., 38C5
Parabuduro, 40C1
Paracel Is., 22C6,7
Paraguai, R., 38D4
Paraguay, St., 39A2,3
Paraguay see Paraguai
Paraíba do Sul, R., 38E5
Parakou, 29C6
Paramaribo, 38B4
Paramonga, 38D2
Paraná, 39B2,3
Paraná, Admin. U., 39A3
Paraná, R., 37E4
Paranaguá, 39A4
Paranaíba, R., 37D5
Paranapanema, R., 39B3
Parc des Laurentides, Park, 33b
Parc du Mont Tremblant, Park, 33b
Pardubice, 12C4
Parepare, 23D3
Parintins, 38C4
Paris, 11B3
Parkano, 15C7
Parkersburg, 35D4
Parksville, 33aB2
Parma (Italy), 13A2
Parma (U.S.A.), 35C4
Parnaíba, 38C5
Parnaíba, R., 37C5
Pärnu, 17C2
Parrett, R., 7F6
Parry Sound, 33D11,12
Parsons Miami, 35D1
Partizansk, 25B5
Paru, R., 38C4
Pasadena (U.S.A., California), 34E3
Pasadena (U.S.A., Texas), 35F1,2
Pașcani, 14B3
Pasco, 34C3
Pas-de-Calais (62), Admin. U, 11B3
Pas de Calais, Chann., 11B3
P'asina, R., 16B10,11
Pasni, 21D8

Paso de los Vientos, Str., 36B,C5
Passage de la Déroute, Str., 6aA2,3
Passage of Tiree, Str., 7C4
Passaic, 32a
Passau, 12C4
Passo Fundo, 39A3
Passos, 38E5
Pasto, 38B2
Pasuruan, 23aA3
Patagonia, Reg., 37G,H2,3
Pataz, 38C2
Pate Island, I., 30B5
Paterson, 32a
Patiāla, 22A,B3
P'atichatki, 18C3
P'atigorsk, 18D5
Patna, 22B4
Patos de Minas, 39aA4
Pátrai, 14D2
Patrakijevka, 17B6
Patrocínio, 39aA4
Pattani, 22D6
Pau, 11D2
Paulatuk, 33B7
Paulistana, 38C5
Paulo Afonso, 38C6
Pavia, 13A2
Pavlodar, 16D9
Pavlograd, 18C4
Pavlovo, 17C6
Pavlovsk, 18B5
Pavlovskaja, 18C4
Pavullo nel Frignano, 13aB4
Payakumbuh, 23D2
Paysandú, 39aA3
Pazar, 21aA4
Pazardžik, 14C3
Pazardžik (10), Admin. U., 14C3
Peace, R., 33C7
Peach Springs, 34D4
Pearl, R., 35E3
Peary Land, Reg., 42D14-16
Peć, 13B5
Pečenga, 16B,C5
Pečora, 16C7,8
Pečora, R., 16C7
Pecos, 34E6
Pecos, R., 34D6
Pécs, 14B1
Pedias, R., 19cA2
Pedro Afonso, 38C5
Pedro Cays, Is., 36C5
Pedro Juan Caballero, 39A3
Pedro Miguel, 34a
Peebles, 10C3
Peel, 9B2
Peel, R., 33B6
Pegli, 13aB2
Pegu, 22C5
Pehuajó, 39aE1
Peixian, 25D2
Pekalongan, 23D2,3
Pekan, 19bC3
Pekanbaru, 23C2
Peking see Beijing
Peledui, 16D13
Pelee Island, I., 33b
Pello, 15B7,8
Pelly, R., 33B6
Pelly Bay, 33B10,11
Pelopónnisos (6), Admin. U., 14D2

Pelopónnisos, Pen., 14D2
Pelotas, 39B3
Pelotas, R., 39aC3
Pelym, 17aB3
Pelym, R., 17aA3
Pematangsiantar, 23C1
Pemba, 30C5
Pemba Island, I., 30B5
Pemberton, 33aB3
Pembroke (Canada), 35B5
Pembroke (U.K.), 9D2
Peñarroya Pueblonuevo, 11G2
Pendembu, 29C3
Pendleton, 34B3
P'enghu Liehtao, Is., 25aB1
Penglai, 25C3
Península Valdés, Pen., 37G3
Penner, R., 20aA2
Pennines, Mts., 7D,E6,7
Pennsylvania, Admin. U., 35C4,5
Peno, 17C4
Ponong, 40D3
Penonomé, 36D4
Penrhyn, I., 41D9,10
Penrith, 10C3
Pensacola, 35E3
Pensacola Mountains, Mts., 42H
Penticton, 34B3
Pentland Firth, Str., 7B6
Penza, 16D6
Penzance, 9D2
Peoria, 35C3
Pepel, 29C3
Perabumuliti, 23D2
Perak (7), Admin. U., 19bB2
Perak, R., 19bB2
Pereira, 38B2
Pereľub, 18B7
Pereslavľ-Zalesskij, 17C5
Pergamino, 39B2
Péribonca, R., 33C12
Périers, 6aA3
Périgueux, 11C3
Perito Moreno, 39C1,2
Perlis (8), Admin. U., 19bA2
Perm', 16D7
Pernambuco, Admin. U., 38C5,6
Pernik, 14C2
Pernik (11), Admin. U., 14C2
Perovo, 17b
Perpignan, 11D3
Perry Island, 33B9
Persian Gulf, G., 21D5,6
Perth (Australia), 40D1
Perth (U.K.), 10B3
Peru, St., 38C,D2
Perugia, 13B3
Pervomajsk, 18C3
Pervomajskij, 18B5
Pervouralsk, 17aB2
Pesaro, 13B3
Pescara, 13B3
Pescara, R., 13B3
Peshāwar, 22A3
Peshkopi, 13B5
Pest (12), Admin. U., 14B1
Pestovo, 17C5
Petaling Jaya, 19bC2

Peterborough (Australia), 40D3,4
Peterborough (Canada), 35C5
Peterborough (U.K.), 9C4
Peterhead, 10B3,4
Peter I. Island, I., 42F9
Petermann Berg, Mt., 42C16,17
Petersburg (Canada), 33C6
Petersburg (U.S.A.), 35D5
Petrič, 14C2
Petrolina, 38C5
Petropavlovsk, 16D8,9
Petropavlovsk-Kamčatskij, 16D17,18
Petrópolis, 39A4
Petrosani, 14B2
Petrovsk, 18B6
Petrovsko Razumovskoje, 17b
Petrovsk-Zabajkaľskij, 16bB2
Petrozavodsk, 16C5
Pevek, 16C19
Peza, R., 17A7
Pforzheim, 12C3
Phan-Rang, 22C6
Phatthalung, 19bA1
Philadelphia, 35C5
Philippines, St., Is., 23B,C4
Philippine Sea, 3
Phitsanulok, 22C6
Phnum Pénh, 22C6
Phoenix, 34E4
Phoenix Islands, Is., 41D8
Phong Saly, 22B6
Phuket, 22D5
Piacenza, 13A2
Piadena, 13aA4
Piangil, 40D4
Piatra-Neamt, 14B3
Piave, R., 13A3
Piauí, Admin. U., 38C5
Pibor, R., 28D6
Picacho, 34E4
Pico, I., 11aA2,3
Pico Bolívar, Mt., 37B2,3
Pico Cristóbal Colón, Mt., 37A2
Pico da Bandeira, Mt., 37D,E5
Pico da Neblina, Mt., 37B3
Pico de Aneto, Mt., 5C4,5
Pico de Teide, Mt., 26bB2,3
Pico Duarte, Mt., 31H13,14
Picton, 40aB2
Pidurutalagala, Mt., 19I10
Piedras Negras, 36B2
Pieksämäki, 15C8
Pielinen, L., 15C9
Piemonte (12), Admin. U., 13A1
Pierre, 34C6
Piešťany, 12C5
Pietermaritzburg, 30D4
Pietersburg, 30D3
Pik Kommunizma, Mt., 19E,F8,9
Pik Pobedy, Mt., 19E10
Piła, 12B5
Pilcomayo, R., 37E3,4
Pilica, R., 12C6
Pinang, 23C1,2

page 216

Pinang (9), Admin. U., 19B2
Pınarbaşı, 21aB3
Pinar del Río, 36aA1,2
Píndhos, Óros, Mts., 5C,D7
Pine Bluff, 35E2
Pine Creek, 40B3
Pinega, 17B6
Pinega, R., 17B7
Pine Point, 33B8
Pinghu, 19aA3
Pingliang, 24C4
P'ingtung, 25aB2
Pingxiang, 24D4
Piniós, R., 14D2
Pinsk, 18B2
Pin'ug, 17B7
Pioche, 34D4
Piotrków Trybunalski, 12C5
Pipestone, 34C7
Pipestone, R., 35A2
Pipinas, 39aE2
Piquiri, R., 39aB4
Piracicaba, 39aB4
Pirapora, 38D5
Pir'atin, 18B3
Pírgos, 14D2
Piripiri, 38C5
Pirot, 13B5
Pisa, 13B2
Pisagua, 38D2
Pisco, 38D2
Písek, 12C4
Pisogne, 13aA4
Pisuerga, R., 11F2,3
Pita, 29C2
Pitcairn Island, I., 41F12
Piteå, 15B7
Piteälven, R., 15B6,7
Piteşti, 14B3
Pitlochry, 10B3
Pittsburgh, 35C4,5
Pittsfield, 35C6
Piura, 38C1,2
Plain of France, Pl., 5C6,7
Plain of Po, Pl., 13a
Plainview, 34E6
Planalto do Mato Grosso, Plat., 37D7
Plasencia, 11F2
Plast, 17aC3
Plateau (17), Admin. U., 29C8
Plateau of Iran, Plat., 19F7
Plateau of Shotts, Plat., 5D5
Plato Usť Urt, Plat., 19E7
Platte, R., 34C7
Platte Island, I., 27E10
Plattsburgh, 35C6
Plauen, 12C4
Plavsk, 18B4
Pleseck, 17B6
Pleven, 14B3
Pleven (12), Admin. U., 14C3
Ploče see Kardeljevo
Płock, 12B5
Ploieşti, 14B3
Plovdiv, 14C3
Plovdiv (13), Admin. U., 14C3
Plymouth (Lesser Antilles), 36bA2

Plymouth (U.K.), 9D2,3
Plynlimon, Mt., 7E5,6
Plzeň, 12C4
Pô, 29C5
Po, R., 13A1
Pobé, 29D6
Pocatello, 34C4
Poços de Caldas, 39aB4
Podkamennaja Tunguska, R., 16C,D11,12
Podoľsk, 17C5
Podor, 29A2
Podporožje, 17B4
Pogradec, 13B5
Pogranicnyj, 25B5
P'ohang, 25C4
Pohnpei, I., 41C5,6
Point Barrow, C., 31B4,5
Pointe-à-Pitre, 36bA2
Pointe des Almadies, C., 26C2,3
Pointe du Raz, C., 11C1
Pointe-Noire, 30B2
Point Hope, 33B3
Poitiers, 11C3
Pokhara, 22aA2,3
Pok Liu Chao, I., 19aB3
Pokrovsk-Uraľskij, 17aA2
Poland, St., 12B4-6
Poľarnyj, 17A5
Polati, 21aB2
Pole of Inaccessibility, 42G,H30-93
Polesje, Reg., 5B7
Polevskoj, 17aB3
Pólis, 19cA1
Polock, 17C3
Pologi, 18aB2
Poltava, 18C3
Polunočnoje, 6A10,11
Poluostrov Jamal, Pen., 16B8,9
Poluostrov Kamčatka, Pen. 16C,D17,18
Poluostrov Kanin, Pen., 17A6,7
Poluostrov Tajmyr, Pen., 16B10-12
Polynésia, Arch., 41A-F8-11
Pomeranian Bay see Zatoka Pomorska
Pomorie, 14C3
Pomozdino, 17B8
Pompano Beach, 35F4,5
Ponca City, 34D7
Ponce, 36C6
Pondicherry, 22C3,4
Pondicherry (11), Admin. U., 22C3
Pond Inlet, 33A12
Ponferrada, 11F2
Ponérihouen, 41aA1
Ponoj, R., 17A5
Ponorogo, 23aA,B2
Ponta Delgada, 11aB3,4
Ponta Grossa, 39A3
Ponta Porã, 38E4
Pontevedra, 11F1
Pontiac, 33b
Pontianak, 23D2
Pontivy, 11B2
Pontoise, 11B3
Pontremoli, 13aB3,4
Pontypool, 9D3
Pontypridd, 9D3
Poole, 9D3,4
Popayan, 38B2
Poplar, 9a
Poplar Bluff, 35D2

Popondetta, 41D4
Poprad, 12C6
Porangatu, 28D4,5
Porbandar, 22B2
Porcupine, R., 33B5
Pordenone, 13A3
Pori, 15C7
Porpoise Bay, B., 42F24
Porsangen, B., 15A8
Portadown, 10D6
Portage-la-Prairie, 34A7
Port Alberni, 33aB2
Portalegre, 11G2
Portalegre (12), Admin. U., 11G2
Port Alfred, 30E3
Port-Alice, 33aA1
Port Angeles, 33aB,C2
Port Arthur, 35F2
Port Augusta, 40D3
Port-au-Prince, 36C5
Port Austin, 33C4
Port Canaveral, 35F4,5
Port-Cartier, 33C13
Port Elizabeth, 30E3
Port Ellen, 10C1,2
Port-Gentil, 30B1
Port Harcourt, 29D7
Port Hardy, 33C7
Porthcawl, 9D3
Port Hedland, 40C1
Port Henry, 33b
Porthmadog, 9C2,3
Port Huron, 35C4
Port-Iľič, 18aB2
Portimão, 11G1
Portland (Australia), 40D3,4
Portland (U.S.A., Maine), 35C6,7
Portland (U.S.A., Oregon), 34B2
Port Laoise, 10E6
Port Lincoln, 40D3
Port Loko, 29C2
Port Louis, 30aB3
Port Macquarie, 40D5
Port Moresby, 41D4
Port Nelson, 33C10
Port Nolloth, 30D2
Porto, 11F1
Porto (13), Admin. U., 11F1
Pôrto Alegre, 39A3,4
Porto Amboim, 30C2
Porto Armuelles, 36D4
Pôrto Artur, 38D4
Porto Barrios, 36C4
Porto Cortés, 36D4
Porto de San José, 36C3
Porto Esperança, 38D,E4
Portoferraio, 13B2
Port of Spain, 38A3,4
Portogruaro, 13aA6
Pôrto Inglês, 28aB2
Portolaguera, 13aA6
Pôrto Nacional, 38D5
Porto-Novo, 29D6
Porto Tolle, 13aB3,4
Porto Torres, 13B2
Pôrto União, 39aC3
Porto Valter, 38C2
Porto-Vecchio, 11D5
Pôrto Velho, 38C3
Portoviejo, 38C1,2

Port Pirie, 40D3
Port Radium see Echo Bay
Portree, 10B1
Port Renfrew, 33aB2
Port Rowan, 35C4
Port Said see Bür Sa'īd
Port Shepstone, 30E4
Portsmouth (U.K.), 9D4
Portsmouth (U.S.A., Ohio), 35D4
Portsmouth (U.S.A., Virginia), 35D5
Port Sudan see Bür Südän
Port Talbot, 9D3
Port Townsend, 33aB3
Portugal, St., 11F,G1,2
Posadas, 39A3
Pošechonje-Volodarsk, 17C5
Posjet, 25B5
Poso, 23D3
Poste de la Baleine, 33C12
Postojna, 13A3
Potenza, 13B3
Potgietersrus, 30D3
Poti, 18D5
Potiskum, 29C8
Po Toi Group, Is., 19aB3
Potomac, R., 35D5
Potosí, 38D3
Potrerillos, 39A2
Potsdam, 12B4
Potsdam (12), Admin. U., 12B4
Pouso Alegre (Cáceres), 38D4
Pouso Alegre (Rio de Janeiro), 39aB4
Povoação, 11aB4
Povorino, 18B5
Povungnituk, 33B12
Powder, R., 34B5
Powell River, 33aB2
Power Houses Bearnarois, 33b
Power Houses Moses-Saunders, 33b
Powys (52), Admin. U., 9C3
Poyanghu, L., 24D5
Poza Rica de Hidalgo, 36B3
Poznań, 12B5
Pozoblanco, 11G2
Prague see Praha
Praha, 12C4
Prahovo, 13A5
Praia, 28aB2
Praia da Vitória, 11aA3,4
Prato, 13B2
Praya, 23aB4
Přerov, 12C5
Prescott, 34E4
Presidente Epitácio, 38E4
Presidente Prudente, 39aB3
Prešov, 12C6
Presque Isle, 35B7
Presqu'île de Taiarapu, C., 41dB2
Preston, 9C3
Pretoria, 30D3
Pribeľskij, 17aC2
Prieska, 30D3
Prijedor, 13A4

page 217

...ja
...ost', Pl.,
   5
Primorsk, 17B3
Primorskij, 16aB2
Primorsko-Achtarsk, 18C4
Prince Albert, 33C9
Prince Charles Island, I., 33B12
Prince Edward Island, I., Admin. U., 33D13
Prince Edward Islands, Is., 3
Prince George, 33C7
Prince of Wales Island, I., 33A9,10
Prince Patrick Island, I., 33A7,8
Prince Rupert, 33C6,7
Princess Astrid Coast, Reg., 42G35,36
Princeton, 33aB3
Principe, I., 28F2
Principe da Beira, 38D3
Prioz'orsk, 17B4
Prip'at', R., 18B1,2
Priština, 13B5
Privas, 11C4
Privolžskaja Vozvyšennost', Plat., 5B,C9
Prizren, 13B5
Probolinggo, 23aA3
Prochladnyj, 18D5
Procter, 34B3
Progreso, 36B3,4
Proletarsk, 18C5
Proletarskij, 18B4
Proliv Longa, Chann., 16B,C19,20
Proliv Matočkin Šar, Chann., 16B6,7
Proliv Vil'kickogo, Chann., 16B11-13
Prome, 22C5
Propriá, 38D6
Prostějov, 12C5
Provadija, 14C3
Providence, 35C6
Providence Island, I., 30B6
Providenija, 16C20
Provo, 34C4
Prudhoe Bay, 33A5
Prut see Prutul
Prutul, R., 14A3
Prydz Bay, B., 42F29
Przemyśl, 12C6
Prževal'sk, 16E9,10
Przylądek Rozewie, C., 12B5
Pskov, 16D4,5
Pskovskoje Ozero, L., 17C3
Ps'ol, R., 18B4
Puako, 35aB3,4
Puán, 39aE1
Puapua, 41cA1
Pucallpa, 38C2
Pudož, 17B5
Puebla, 36C3
Puebla (20), Admin. U., 36C3
Pueblo, 34C5,6
Puente Genil, 11G2
Puerto Aisén, 39C1
Puerto Angel, 36C3
Puerto Ayacucho, 38B3

Puerto Berío, 38B2
Puerto Cabello, 38A3
Puerto Cabezas, 36C4
Puerto Carreño, 38B3
Puerto de la Cruz, 26bB2
Puerto del Rosario, 26bB4
Puerto Deseado, 39C2
Puerto Inírida see Obando
Puerto la Cruz, 38A3
Puertollano, 11G2,3
Puerto Lobos, 39C2
Puerto Madryn, 39C2
Puerto Maldonado, 38D3
Puerto Montt, 39C1
Puerto Natales, 39D1
Puerto Peñasco, 36A1
Puerto Pilón, 34a
Puerto Princesa, 23C3
Puerto Rico, Admin. U., 36C6
Puerto Sastre, 39A3
Puerto Suárez, 38D4
Puerto Williams, 39D2
Pugačov, 18B6
Puglia (13), Admin. U., 13B4
Pukapuka, Is., 41E9
Pukch'ŏng, 25B4
Puksoozero, 17B6
Pula, 13A3
Pulau Ambon, I., 23D4
Pulau Babar, I., 23D4
Pulau Bacan, I., 23D4
Pulau Banggi, I., 23C3
Pulau Bawean, I., 23aA3
Pulau Butung, I., 23D4
Pulau Enggano, I., 23D2
Pulau Kabaena, I., 23D4
Pulau Kobroor, I., 23D5
Pulau Larat, I., 23D5
Pulau Laut, I., 23D3
Pulau Lomblen, I., 23D4
Pulau Mangole, I., 23D4
Pulau Misool, I., 23D5
Pulau Moa, I., 23D4
Pulau Nias, I., 23C1
Pulau Obi, I., 23D4
Pulau Pagai Selatan, I., 23D1,2
Pulau Pagai Utara, I., 23D1,2
Pulau Panaitan, I., 23D2
Pulau Peleng, I., 23D4
Pulau Pini, I., 19bD1
Pulau Rakata, I., 23aA1
Pulau Roti, I., 23E4
Pulau Sanana, I., 23D4
Pulau Satengar, I., 23aA4
Pulau Sawu, I., 23E4
Pulau Selayar, I., 23D4
Pulau Selaru, I., 23D5
Pulau Siberut, I., 23D1
Pulau Simeulue, I., 23C1
Pulau Sipora, I., 23D1,2
Pulau Taliabu, I., 23D4
Pulau Ternate, I., 23C4
Pulau Waigeo, I., 23C5
Pulau Wetar, I., 23D4
Pulau Wokam, I., 23D5
Pulau Yamdena, I., 23D5
Pulau Yapen, I., 23D5
Pulau Yos Sudarsa, I., 23D5
Puławy, 12C6
Punaauia, 41dB1
Punakha, 22aB4
Puncak Jaya, Mt., 3
Pune, 22C3

Punia, 30B3
Punjab, Admin. U., 23A3
Puno, 38D2
Punta Alto, 39aE1
Punta Arenas, 39D1
Punta Gallinas, C., 37A2
Punta Mariato, C., 31 I 12,13
Punta Marroquí, C., 11G2
Punta Pariñas, C., 37C1,2
Puntarenas, 36C4
Punto Fijo, 38A2,3
Pur, R., 16C9
Purus, R., 38C3
Purwokerto, 23aA2
Purworejo, 23aA,B2
Pusan, 25C4
Puškin, 17C4
Puškino (U.S.S.R., Moskva), 17C5
Puškino (U.S.S.R., Saratov), 18B6
Pušlachta, 17B5
Putao, 22B5
Putian, 25aA1
Putozersk, 5A10
Puttalam, 20aB2,3
Putumayo, 38C2
Putumayo, R., 37C2
Putussibau, 23C3
Puulavesi, L., 15C8
Puy-de-Dôme (63), Admin. U., 11C3
Puy de Sancy, Mt., 5C4,5
Pwllheli, 9C2
Pyinmana, 22C5
P'yŏnggang, 25C4
P'yŏngyang, 25C3,4
Pyramid Lake, L., 34D3
Pyrenees, Mts., 5C4,5
Pyrénées-Atlantiques (64), Admin. U., 11D2
Pyrénées (Hautes-) (65), Admin. U., 11D3
Pyrénées-Orientales (66), Admin. U., 11D3
Pyšma, R., 17aB3,4

Q

Qalāt, 22A2
Qal'eh-ye Now, 22A2
Qānāq, 33A12,13
Qandahār, 22A2
Qaqortoq, 33B15
Qareh Sū, R., 21B5,6
Qasigiánguit, 33B14,15
Qasr Abā as-Sa'ūd, 28C7
Qasr al-Burayqah, 28A,B4,5
Qasr al-Farâfirah, 28B5
Qatar, St., 21D,E6
Qattara Depression, Depr., 26A,B7
Qazvīn, 21B5
Qeqertarssuaq, 33B14
Qeshm, Yam., 21D7
Qianjin, 24B7
Qiemo, 24C2
Qilianshanmai, Mts., 19F11,12
Qilinhu, L., 24C2
Qimen, 25E2
Qinā, 28B7
Qingdao, 24C6

Qinghai (20), Admin. U., 24C3
Qinghai, L., 24C4
Qingyang, 24C4
Qinhuangdao, 25C2,3
Qiongzhouhaixia, Str., 22B6,7
Qiqihar, 24B6
Qizān, 28C7
Qolleh-ye Damāvand, Mt., 19F7
Qom, 21C6
Qom, R., 21C5,6
Qomisheh, 21C6
Qondūz, 22A2
Qualāta, 28C2
Quan-Long, 22D6
Quanzhou, 24D5
Qu'Appelle, R., 34A6
Quarai, R., 39aD2
Quatre Bornes, 30aB3,4
Qučhān, 21B7
Québec, 33D12
Québec, Admin. U., 33C12,13
Queen Charlotte Islands, Is., 33C6
Queen Elizabeth Islands, Is., 33A8-10
Queen Mary Land, Reg., 42F,G27
Queen Maud Land, Reg., 42G34-36
Queens, 32a
Queensland, Admin. U., 40B,C4
Queenstown (South Africa), 30E3
Queenstown (Tasmania), 40E4
Quelimane, 30C4
Querétaro, 36B2,3
Querétaro (21), Admin. U., 36B3
Quesnel, 33C7
Quetta, 22A2
Quezaltenango, 36C3
Quezon City, 23B4
Quibdó, 38B2
Quilmes, 39aD2
Quilon, 20aB2
Quilpie, 40C4
Quimper, 11C1,2
Quinhagak, 33C3
Qui-Nhon, 22C6,7
Quintana Roo (22), Admin. U., 36C4
Quito, 38C2
Quixadá, 38C6
Qujing, 24D4
Qytet Stalin, 13B4

R

Raahe, 15B7,8
Ra'akoski, 17A3
Raasay, I., 7C5
Raba, 23D3
Rába, R., 12D5
Rabat, 28A2
Rabaul, 41D5
Rachal, 34F7
Rach-Gia, 22C,D6
Rachov, 18C1
Racibórz, 12C5
Racine, 35C3
Radom, 12C6
Radomsko, 12C5
Radomyśl', 18B2
Rafaela, 39aD1

Rafsanjān, 21 C6,7
Raga, 28 D5
Ragusa, 13 C3
Rahīmyār Khān, 22 B3
Raiatea, I., 41 E10
Rainy Lake, L., 35 B2
Raipur, 22 B4
Raisin, R., 33b
Rājahmundry, 22 C4
Rajapalaiyam, 20 aB2
Rājasthān, Admin. U., 22 B3
Rājkot, 22 B3
Rājshāhi, 22 B4
Rakahanga, I., 41 D,E9
Rakvere, 17 C3
Raleigh, 35 D5
Rambi, I., 41 bA3
Rāmhormoz, 21 C5,6
Ramon', 18 B4
Rāmpur, 22 aA1
Ramsey, 9 B2
Ramsgate, 9 D5
Rana, 15 B5
Rancagua, 39 B1
Rānchī, 22 B4
Randers, 12 A3
Ranger, 34 E7
Rangoon, 22 C5
Rangpur, 22 B4
Rantauprapat, 23 C1,2
Ranua, 15 B8
Rapa, I., 41 F11
Rapallo, 13 aB3
Rapid City, 34 C6
Räpti, R., 22 aB2
Rarotonga, I., 41 F9
Ra's ad Daqm, 21 F7
Ras Addar, C., 27 aB3
Ra's al-Hadd, C., 21 E8
Ra's al-Khaymah, 21 D6,7
Ra's an-Naqb, 20 bC1,2
Ras Ben Sekka, C., 28 A3,4
Ras Gharib, 28 B6
Rās Hafūn, C., 26 C10
Rashīd, 26 aA2
Rasht, 21 B5
Raso, I., 28 aA1
Rás Sabartil, C., 5 aB1,2
Rathlin Island, I., 7 D4
Ratingen, 12 aB2
Ratlām, 22 B3
Raurkela, 22 B4
Rauma, 15 C7
Ravenna, 13 A3
Ravensthorpe, 40 D2
Rāvi, R., 22 A3
Rawalpindi, 22 A3
Rawāndūz, 21 aB4
Rawlinna, 40 D2
Rawson, 39 C2
R'azan', 16 D5,6
Razdol'noje, 16 aB1
Razgrad, 14 C3
Razgrad (14), Admin. U., 14 C3
R'ažsk, 18 B5
Reading (U.K.), 9 D4
Reading (U.S.), 35 C5
Reboly, 17 B4
Recife, 38 C6
Recklinghausen, 12 aA3
Reconquista, 39 aC2
Redcar, 9 B4

Red Deer, 33 C8
Red Deer, R., 33 C8
Redding, 34 C2
Redditch, 9 C4
Redeyef, 27 aB2
Red Lake, L., 35 B2
Redon, 11 C2
Red (Mississippi), R., 34 E6
Red (Winnipeg, L.), R., 34 A7
Red Sea, 28 B,C6,7
Redstone, 33 aA2
Reed City, 35 C3
Regaia, 5 aB2
Regensburg, 12 C4
Reggane, 28 B3
Reggio di Calabria, 13 C3,4
Reggio-nell'Emilia, 13 A2
Regina, 33 C9
Rehoboth, 30 D2
Reigate, 9 D4,5
Reims, 11 B3,4
Reindeer Lake, L., 33 C9
Reinosa, 11 F2
Reliance, 33 B9
Rembang, 23 aA2
Remscheid, 12 aB3
Renfrew, 33b
Reni, 14 B4
Renmore, 33b
Rennell Island, I., 40 B5,6
Rennes, 11 B2
Reno, 34 D3
Reno, R., 13 aB5
Reo, 23 D4
Reprêsa Itaipu, Res., 38 E5
Reprêsa de Furnas, Res., 39 aB,C3
Reprêsa Tucuruí, Res., 38 C4,5
Republic, 34 B3
Republican, R., 34 C6,7
Republic of Korea, St., 25 C4
Requena, 11 G3
Réservoir Cabonga, Res., 35 B5
Réservoir Gouin, Res., 33 D12
Réservoir Lagdo, Res., 29 C9
Réservoir Mbakaou, Res., 29 D9
Reshui, 24 C3,4
Resistencia, 39 A2,3
Reşiţa, 14 B2
Resolute, 33 A10
Resolution Island, I., 33 B13
Restinga, 5 aB3
Réthimnon, 14 E3
Réunion, Admin. U., I., 30 aB1,2
Reus, 11 F4
Reut, 18 C2
Revda, 17 aB2,3
Revelstoke, 33 C8
Rewa, 22 aB2
Rexford, 34 B3,4
Rey, 21 B6
Rey Bouba, 29 C9
Reyes, 38 D3
Reykjavík, 15 aB2
Reynosa, 36 B3
Rež, R., 17 aB3
Rēzekne, 17 C3
Rhein, R., 12 D3

Rheinland-Pfalz (8), Admin. U., 12 C2
Rhin (Bas-) (67), Admin. U., 11 B4
Rhin (Haut-) (68), Admin. U., 11 C4
Rhode Island, (R.I.), Admin. U., 35 C6
Rhodope Mountains, Mts., 5 C7
Rhondda, 9 D3
Rhône (69), Admin. U., 11 C4
Rhône, R., 11 C4
Rhourd-el-Baguel, 28 A3
Rhum, I., 7 C4
Rhyl, 9 C3
Ribadeo, 11 F2
Ribble, R., 7 E6
Ribe, 12 B3
Ribeira Grande, 28 aA1
Ribeirão Prêto, 38 E5
Riberalta, 38 D3
Richmond, 35 D5
Ridgeway, 34 D5
Riesa, 12 C4
Rieti, 13 B3
Rifstangi, C., 15 aA3,4
Rīga, 16 D4
Riihimäki, 15 C7,8
Rijeka, 13 A3
Rijn see Rhein
Rikaze, 24 D2
Rikers Island, I., 32a
Rimini, 13 A3
Rîmnicu-Vîlcea, 14 B3
Rincon, 34 E5
Ringerike, 15 C4
Ringvassøya, I., 15 A6
Rio Balsas, 36 C3
Riobamba, 38 C2
Rio Branco, 38 C3
Río Cuarto, 39 B2
Río de la Plata, G., 37 F4
Rio de Janeiro, 39 A4
Rio de Janeiro (17), Admin. U., 39 A4
Rio do Sul, 39 aC4
Río Gallegos, 39 D2
Rio Grande, 39 B3
Río Grande, 39 D2
Rio Grande, R., 34 E5
Rio Grande de Santiago, R., 36 B2
Rio Grande do Norte (18), Admin. U., 38 C6
Rio Grande do Sul, Admin. U., 39 A3
Ríohacha, 38 A2
Rio Negro, 39 aC3,4
Río Negro, Admin. U., 39 B,C1,2
Rioni, R., 18 D5
Ripon, 9 B4
Rishiri-tō, I., 25 A7
Riva, 13 aA4
Rivadavia, 39 C2
Rivera, 39 aD2
Rivers (18), Admin. U., 29 D7
Riverside, 34 E3
Rivière à Pierre, 33b
Rivière des Prairies, R., 33b
Rivière-du-Loup, 35 B7
Rize, 21 A4
Rizokárpason, 19 cA3
Rížskij Zaliv, B., 17 C2
Road Town, 36b A1

Roanne, 11 C4
Roanoke, 35 D4,5
Roanoke, R., 35 D5
Robertsport, 29 D3
Roboré, 38 D4
Rocas Formigas, I., 11 aB4
Rocha, 39 aD3
Rochdale, 9 C3,4
Rochefort, 11 C2
Roches Douvres, Is., 6 aA2
Rochester (U.S.A., Minnesota), 35 C2
Rochester (U.S.A., New York), 35 C5
Rock Bay, 33 aB1,2
Rockford, 35 C2,3
Rockhampton, 40 C5
Rock Hill, 35 E4
Rock Island, 35 C2,3
Rock Springs, 34 C5
Rocky Mountains, Mts., 31 D-F 8-10
Rødby, 12 B3
Rodez, 11 C3
Ródhos, 14 D3,4
Ródhos, I., 14 D3,4
Rodrigues, I., 26 F11
Roebourne, 40 C1
Rohtak, 22 B3
Roja, 17 C2
Rojas, 39 aD1
Rokan, R., 19 bD2
Rokel, R., 29 C2
Roma (Australia), 40 C4
Roma (Italy), 13 B3
Romagnano Sesia, 13 aA2
Roman, 14 B3
Romania, St., 14 B2,3
Romanovka, 16 bB3
Romans, 11 C4
Romblon, 23 bB2
Rome (U.S.A., Georgia), 35 E3,4
Rome (U.S.A., New York), 33b
Rome see Roma
Romny, 18 B3
Ronda, 11 G2
Rondônia, 38 D3
Rondônia, Admin. U., 38 D3
Rondonópolis, 38 D4
Rønne, 15 E5
Ronne Ice Shelf, 42 G6
Roosevelt, R., 38 C3
Roosevelt Island, I., 42 G17-19
Roper, R., 40 B3
Roque, 34a
Roraima, Admin. U., 38 B3
Røros, 15 C4
Rosalia, 33 aC4
Rosario (Argentina), 39 B2
Rosario (Azores), 11 aA1
Rosario (Mexico), 34 F5
Roscommon, 10 E5
Roscommon, Admin. U., 10 E5
Roscrea, 10 E6
Roseau, 36b B2
Roseburg, 34 C2
Rosenheim, 12 D3,4
Rosignol, 38 B4
Roşiori-de-Vede, 14 B3
Roskilde, 12 B4
Rosl'atino, 17 C6

page 219

18B3
10E6
Shelf, 42H17-19
nd, I.,
19
Rosso, 28C1
Rossoš', 18B3
Ross River, 33B6
Ross Sea, 42G17-19
Rostock, 12B4
Rostock (13), Admin. U., 12B4
Rostov, 17C5
Rostov-na-Donu, 16E5,6
Roswell, 34E6
Rothera, Station, 42F7,8
Rotherham, 9C4
Roto, 40D4
Rotorua, 40aA2
Rotterdam, 12C1,2
Rotuma, I., 41E7
Roubaix, 11B3
Rouen, 11B3
Round Island, I., 30aA3,4
Rousay, I., 7B6
Rouses Point, 33b
Rovaniemi, 15B8
Rovato, 13aA3,4
Rovereto, 13aA5
Rovigo, 13aA5
Rovno, 18B2
Rovnoje, 18B6
Roxas (Philippines, Palawan), 23bB1
Roxas (Philippines, Panay), 23B4
Royal Leamington Spa, 9C4
Royan, 11C2
Rozel, 6aA2,3
Rtiščevo, 18B5
Ruapehu, Mt., 40aA2
Rubcovsk, 24A2
Rubežnoje, 18C4
Rudnaja Pristan', 25B6
Rudničnyj, 17C3
Rudnyj, 17aC3
Rufiji, R., 30B4
Rufisque, 29B1
Rugao, 25D3
Rugby, 9C4
Ruhr, R., 12B4
Rügen, I., 12B4
Rui Barbosa, 38D5
Ruki, R., 30B2
Rum Jungle, 40B3
Rumoi, 25B7
Ruoqiang, 24C2
Rurutu, I., 41F10
Ruse, 14C3
Ruse (15), Admin. U., 14C3
Russian Soviet Federal Socialist Republic, Admin. U., 16C,D5-18
Russkaja, Station, 42G14,15
Ruston, 35E2
Ruth, 34D4
Rutland, 33C6
Ruvuma, R., 30C4
Ruzajevka, 18B5
Rwanda, St., 30B3,4
Rybačje, 24B1
Rybinskoje Vodochranilišče, Res., 17C5
Rybnica, 18C2
Rybnik, 12C5
Ryl'sk, 18B3
Ryōtsu, 25C6

Ryukyu Is. see Nansei-shotō
Rzeszów, 12C6
Ržev, 17C4

S

Saarbrücken, 12C2
Saaremaa, I., 17C2
Saarland (9), Admin. U., 12C2
Saavedra, 39aE1
Sabadell, 11F4
Sabah, Admin. U., 23C3
Sabhah, 28B4
Sabinas, 36B2
Sabine, R., 35E2
Sable Island, I., 33D13
Sabzevār, 21B7
Sacanana, 39C2
Saččhere, 18D5
Sachrisabz, 21B9
Sachs Harbour, 33A7
Šachty, 18C5
Šachunja, 17C7
Sacramento, 34D2
Sacramento, R., 34C,D2
Sa'dah, 28C7
Sadiola, 29B3
Sado, I., 25C6
Sado, R., 11G1
Šadrinsk, 17aB3
Saffāniyah, 21D5
Safi, 28A2
Safid, R., 21B5
Safonovo, 17A7
Saga (China), 24D2
Saga (Japan), 25D5
Sagami-nada, B., 25C,D6
Sagar (India, Karnataka), 20aA1
Sāgar (India, Madhya Pradesh), 22B3
Saginaw, 35C4
Saginaw Bay, B., 35C4
Saguenay, R., 35B6
Sagunto, 11G3,4
Sahara, Des., 26B3-8
Sahāranpur, 22B3
Sahel, Reg., 26C3,4
Saïda, 28A3
Sa'idābād, 21D7
Saidpur, 22aB4
Saigon see Thanh-pho Ho Chi Minh
Saihan Toroi, 24B3,4
Sai Kung, 19aB3
Saim, 17aA3
Saimaa, L., 15C9
Saimaa Canal, Can., 15C8,9
Saimbeyli, 21aB3
Saint Albans, 9D4
Saint Andrews, 10B3
Saint Annes, 6aA2
Saint Anthony, 33C14
Saint Aubin, 6aA2
Saint Augustine, 35F4
Saint Austell, 9D2
Saint Bees Head, C., 7D5,6
Saint-Benoît, 30aC1
Saint Brides Bay, B., 7F5
Saint-Brieuc, 11B2
Saint Catharines, 33b
Saint Catherine Lock, 33b

Saint Christopher, I., 36bA2
Saint Christopher and Nevis, St., 36bA1,2
Saint Cloud, 35B2
Saint Croix, 36bA1
Saint David's Head, C., 7F4,5
Saint-Denis, 30aB1
Saint-Dié, 11B4
Saint-Dizier, 11B4
Saint-Donat, 33b
Sainte-Anne-des-Monts, 35B7
Saintes, 11C2
Sainte-Foy, 35B6
Saint-Étienne, 11C3,4
Saint-Gaudens, 11D3
Saint George Island, I., 35F3
Saint George's, 36bB2
Saint George's Channel, Chann., 7E,F4,5
Saint Helena, I., 27F4
Saint Helens, 9C3
Saint Helier, 6aA2,3
Saint-Hyacinthe, 33b
Saint Ives, 9D2
Saint-Jean, 33b
Saint-Jérôme, 33b
Saint John, 33D13
Saint John, R., 35B7
Saint John's (Canada), 33D14
Saint John's (Lesser Antilles), 36bA2
Saint Joseph, 35D1
Saint Kilda, I., 7C3
Saint Lambert Lock, 33b
Saint-Laurent see Saint Lawrence
Saint Lawrence, R., 33D12
Saint Lawrence Island, I., 33B2,3
Saint-Lô, 11B2
Saint-Louis (Réunion), 30aC1
Saint-Louis (Senegal), 29A,B1
Saint Louis (U.S.A.), 35D2
Saint Lucia, St., I., 36bB2
Saint Magnus Bay, B., 7A6,7
Saint-Malo, 11B2
Saint Martin, 36bA2
Saint Mary, 6aA2
Saint Matthew Island, I., 32E2
Saint Maurice, R., 35B6
Saint-Nazaire, 11C2
Saint Pancras, 9a
Saint-Paul (Réunion), 30aC1
Saint Paul (U.S.A.), 35B2
Saint Paul, R., 29D3
Saint Peter Port, 6aA2
Saint Petersburg, 35F4
Saint-Pierre (Réunion), 30aC1
Saint-Pierre (St. Pierre et Miquelon), 33D14
Saint-Pierre-Église, 6aA3
Saint Pierre et Miquelon, Admin. U., 33D14
Saint Quentin, 11B3
Saint Regis River, R., 33b
Saint Sampson, 6aA2

Saint Thomas, 33b
Saint-Tropez, 11D4
Saint-Valéry-sur-Somme, 9D5
Saint Vincent, I., 36bB2
Saint Vincent and Grenadines, St., 36bB2
Sajak, 24B1
Sajnšand, 24B4,5
Sak, R., 30E3
Sakai, 25D6
Sakākah, 28B7
Sakarya, R., 21aA2
Sakata, 25C6
Sakchu, 25B3,4
Saki, 16aB1
Sakishima-shotō, Is., 24D6
Sakrivier, 30E3
Sal, I., 28aA2
Salado (Colorado), R., 37F3
Salado (Paraná), R., 37E3
Salaga, 29C5
Salailua, 41cA1
Salālah, 28B6
Šalālah, 21F6
Salamanca, 11F2
Salani, 41cB2
Salar de Uyuni, Sw., 37E3
Salavat, 17aC2
Salawati, 1,23D4,5
Saldanha, 30E2
Saldo, R., 37E3
Salechard, 16C8
Salem (India), 22C3
Salem (U.S.A.), 34C2
Salerno, 13B3
Salford, 9C3
Salgótarján, 14A1
Salihli, 21aB1
Salima, 30C4
Salina, 34D7
Salina Cruz, 36C3
Salinas (Ecuador), 38C1
Salinas (U.S.A.), 34D2
Salisbury (U.K.), 9D4
Salisbury (U.S.A.), 35D5
Salisbury (Zimbabwe) see Harare
Salisbury Plain, Pl., 7F6,7
Saljany, 18aB2
Salkirk, 10C3
Salmon, R., 34B3
Salo, 15C7
Saló, 13aA4
Salonika see Thessaloniki
Salop (39), Admin. U., 9C3
Sal Rei, 28aA2
Sal'sk, 18C5
Salso, R., 13C3
Salsomaggiore, 13aB3,4
Salta, 39D2
Salta, Admin. U., 39A2
Saltcoats, 10C2
Saltillo, 36B2
Salt Lake City, 34C4
Salto, 39aD2
Salto Ángel, Fs., 37B3
Salton Sea, L., 34E3
Saltos do Iguaçu, Fs., 37E4
Salvador, 38D6
Salween see Nujiang

page 220

Salzburg, 12 D 4
Salzburg (5), Admin. U., 12 D 4
Salzgitter, 12 B,C 3
Sama de Langreo, 11 F 2
Samar, I., 23 B 4
Samarinda, 23 D 3
Samarkand, 16 E,F 8
Sāmarrā', 21 C 4
Samary, 17 a B 2
Sambalpur, 22 B 4
Sambava, 30 C 5,6
Sambor, 12 C 3
Samch'ŏk, 25 C 4
Samoa, St. Is., 41 c A 1,2
Sámos, 14 D 3
Sámos, I., 14 D 3
Samothráki, I., 14 C 3
Sampit, 23 D 3
Samsun, 21 a A 3
Samur, R., 18 a A 2
San, 29 B 4
San, R., 12 C 6
San'ā', 28 C 7
Sanae, Station, 42 F,G 1,2
Sanaga, R., 29 D 8
San Ángelo, 34 E 6,7
Sanandaj, 21 B 5
San Antonio, 34 F 7
San Antonio Oeste, 39 C 2
San Bernardino, 34 E 3
San Bernardo, 39 B 1,2
San Bonifacio, 13 a A 5
San Carlos (Philippines), 23 b B 4
San Carlos (Uruguay), 39 a B 3
San Carlos (U.S.A), 34 E 4,5
San Carlos de Bariloche, 39 C 2
Sánchez (Dominican Rep.), 36 C 6
Sánchez (Mexico), 36 B 2
San Clemente Island, I., 34 E 3
San Cristobal, 39 a D 1
San Cristóbal (Mexico), 36 C 3
San Cristóbal (Venezuela), 38 B 2
San Cristóbal, I., 40 B 5,6
Sancti-Spíritus, 36 a B 3,4
Sandakan, 23 C 3
Sandaré, 29 B 3
Sanday, I., 7 B 6
Sandefjord, 15 D 4
San Diego, 34 E 3
Sandnes, 15 D 3
Sandoa, 30 B 3
Sandomierz, 12 C 6
San Donà di Piave, 13 a A 6
Sandpoint, 34 B 4
Sandstone, 40 C 1,2
Sandusky, 33 b
Sandviken, 15 C 6
Sandykači, 21 B 8
Sandy Lake, 33 C 9
San Felipe (Mexico), 36 A 1
San Felipe (Venezuela), 38 B 3
San Fernando (Mexico), 34 G 7
San Fernando (Philippines), 23 B 3,4
San Fernando (Trinidad), 38 B 3,4

San Fernando de Apure, 38 B 2
Sanford, 35 D 5
San Francisco (Argentina), 39 B 2
San Francisco (U.S.A.), 34 D 2
Sangar, 16 C 14,15
Sangaredi, 29 C 2
Sangay, Vol., 37 C 2
Sangha, R., 28 D 4
Sāngli, 22 C 3
Sango, 30 D 4
Sangüesa, 11 F 3
San Ignacio, 38 D 3
San Javier, 39 a D 2
San Joaquin, R., 34 D 2,3
San José (Costa Rica), 36 D 4
San Jose (Philippines-Luzon), 23 b A 2
San Jose (Philippines-Panay), 23 b B 2
San José (U.S.A), 34 D 2
San José de Chiquitos, 38 D 3,4
San José del Cabo, 36 B 2
San Juan (Argentina), 39 B 2
San Juan (Puerto Rico), 36 C 6
San Juan (17), Admin. U., 39 B 2
San Juan, R., 34 D 4,5
San Juan Bautista, 39 a C 2
San Julián, 39 C 2
Sankt Gallen, 11 C 5
Sankt Moritz, 11 C 5
Sankt Pölten, 12 C 4
Sankuru, R., 30 B 3
San Lorenzo (Argentina), 39 a D 1
San Lorenzo (Ecuador), 38 B 1,2
San Lorenzo de El Escorial, 11 F 2
San Luis (Argentina), 39 B 2
San Luis (Mexico), 34 F 5
San Luis (18), Admin. U., 39 B 2
San Luis Obispo, 34 D 2
San Luis Potosí, 36 B 2
San Luis Potosí (23), Admin. U., 36 B 2
San Marino, 13 B 3
San Marino, St., 13 B 3
San Martin, R., 38 D 3
Sanmaur, 35 B 6
San Miguel, 36 C 4
San Miguel, R., 38 D 3
San Miguel de Tucumán, 39 A 2
San Miguelito, 34 a
Sanming, 24 D 5
Sännär, 28 C 6
San Nicolás (Argentina), 39 a D 1,2
San Nicolás (Peru), 38 D 2
Sanniquellie, 29 D 3
Sanok, 12 C 6
San Pablo, 23 B 4
San Pedro, 39 A 3
San-Pédro, 29 D 4
San Pedro Sula, 36 C 4
San Rafael, 39 B 2
San Remo, 13 A,B 1

San Roque, 5 a A 3
San Salvador, 36 C 3,4
San Salvador (Watling Island), 35 G 5,6
San Salvador de Jujuy, 39 A 2
Sansanné-Mango, 29 C 6
San Sebastián, 11 F 3
San Sebastián de la Gomera, 26 b B,C 2
San Severo, 13 B 3
Santa Ana (Bolivia), 38 D 3
Santa Ana (Mexico), 36 A 1
Santa Ana (Salvador), 36 C 4
Santa Barbara, 34 E 2,3
Santa Catarina, Admin. U., 39 A 3,4
Santa Clara, 36 a A 3,4
Santa Clara de Olimar, 39 a D 3
Santa Cruz (Argentina), 39 D 2
Santa Cruz (Philippines), 23 b B 2
Santa Cruz, Admin. U., 39 C 1,2
Santa Cruz da Graciosa, 11 a A 2,3
Santa Cruz das Flores, 11 a A 1
Santa Cruz de la Palma, 26 b B,C 1
Santa Cruz de la Sierra, 38 D 3
Santa Cruz del Sur, 36 a B 4,5
Santa Cruz de Tenerife, 28 B 1
Santa Cruz Isla, I., 41 E 6
Santa Cruz Islands, Is., 3
Santa Elena, 38 C 1
Santa Elena de Uairen, 38 B 3
Santa Fe (Argentina), 39 B 2,3
Santa Fe (U.S.A.), 34 D 5
Santa Fe, Admin. U., 39 A,B 2,3
Santa Fé, 36 a B 2
Santa Isabel, I., 40 A 5,6
Santa Lucía, 36 a B 5,6
Santa Luzia, I., 28 a A 1,2
Santa Maria (Brazil), 39 A 3
Santa Maria (Cape Verde), 28 a A 2
Santa Maria, I., 11 a B 4
Santa Marta, 38 A 2
Santa Monica, 34 E 3
Santander, 11 F 2,3
Santarém (Brazil), 38 C 4
Santarém (Portugal), 11 G 1
Santarém (14), Admin. U., 11 G 1
Santa Rita, 34 E 5
Santa Rosa (Argentina), 39 B 2
Santa Rosa (Brazil), 39 A 3
Santa Rosa (U.S.A.), 34 D 2
Santa Rosalía, 36 B 1
Šantarskije Ostrova, Is., 16 D 15,16
Santa Vitória do Palmar, 39 a B 3
Santee, R., 35 E 5

Santiago (Brazil), 39 a C 2,3
Santiago (Chile), 39 B 1
Santiago (Dominican Rep.), 36 C 5,6
Santiago (Panama), 36 D 4
Santiago de Compostela, 11 F 1,2
Santiago de Cuba, 36 a B,C 5,6
Santiago del Estero, 39 A 2
Santiago del Estero (21), Admin. U., 39 A 2
Santo André, 39 A 4
Santo Ângelo, 39 a C 3
Santo Antão, I., 28 a A 1
Santo Antônio-do Içá, 38 C 3
Santo Domingo, 36 C 5,6
Santos, 39 A 4
San Valentin, Mt., 37 G 2
Sanxiang, 19 a B 1
Sanzao, 19 a B 1
Sanzaodao, I., 19 a B 1,2
São Borja, 39 a C 2
São Filipe, 28 a B 1
São Francisco, R., 37 D 5
São Francisco do Sul, 39 A 4
São Gabriel, 39 B 3
São Joaquim, 39 a C 3,4
São Jorge, I., 11 a A 2,3
São José do Rio Prêto, 39 a B 3,4
São Leopoldo, 39 a C 3,4
São Lourenço do Sul, 39 a B 3
São Luís, 38 C 5
São Miguel, I., 11 a A 3
Saône (Haute-) (70), Admin. U., 11 C 4
Saône, R., 11 C 4
Saône-et-Loire (71), Admin. U., 11 C 4
São Nicolau, 28 a A 1,2
São Paulo, 39 A 4
São Paulo, Admin. U., 38 E 4,5
São Tiago, I., 28 a B 1,2
São Tomé, 30 A 1
São Tomé and Principe, St., 30 A 1
São Vicente, 39 a B 4
São Vicente, I., 28 a A 1
São Vicente de Baracaldo see Baracaldo
Sapele, 29 D 7
Sapitwa, Mt., 26 F 8
Šapkina, R., 17 A 8
Sapporo, 25 B 7
Sapri, 13 B 3
Sapt Kosi, R., 22 a B 3
Saqqez, 21 B 5
Sarajevo, 13 B 4
Saransk, 18 B 6
Sarapul, 17 a B 1
Sarasota, 35 F 4
Saratov, 16 D 6
Saratovskoje Vodochranilišče, Res., 18 B 6
Sarawak, Admin. U., 23 C 3
Sardegna, I., 13 B,C 2
Sardegna (14), Admin. U., 13 B 2

page 221

1B9

!1aA4
C4
Sarja, 17C7
Sark, I., 6aA2
Şarkışla, 21aB3
Sarmi, 23D5
Sarmiento, 39C2
Särna, 15C5
Sarnia, 33b
Sarny, 18B2
Saronikós Kólpos, B., 14D2
Saros Körfezi, B., 14C3
Sarpa, 18C6
Sartène, 11D5
Sarthe (72), Admin. U., 11C3
Sarysu, R., 16E8
Sāsarām, 22aB2,3
Sasebo, 25D4
Saskatchewan, Admin. U., 33C,D9
Saskatchewan, R., 33C9
Saskatoon, 33C9
Sasovo, 18B5
Sassandra, 29D4
Sassandra, R., 29D4
Sassari, 13B2
Sassnitz, 12B4
Sasso Narconi, 13aB5
Sassuolo, 13aB4
Satadougou, 29B3
Sata-misaki, C., 25D5
Sataua, 41cA1
Satna, 22aB2
Satsunan-shotō, Is., 24D6
Satu Mare, 14B2
Sauda, 15D3
Sauðárkrókur, 15aB4
Saudi Arabia, St., 28B6-8
Sault Sainte Marie (Canada), 33D11
Sault Sainte Marie (U.S.A.), 33D11
Saumlaki, 23D5
Saumur, 11C2,3
Saurimo, 30B2,3
Sava, R., 13A3
Savai'i, I., 41cA1,1
Savalou, 29C,D6
Savannah, 35E4
Savannah, R., 35E4
Savannakhet, 22C6
Savé, 29C6
Save, R., 30D4
Savigliano, 13aB1
Šavnik, 13B4
Savoie (73), Admin.U., 11C4
Savoie (Haute-) (74), Admin. U., 11C4
Savona, 13A2
Savonlinna, 15C9
Savusavu, 41bA2
Savu Sea, 23D,E4
Sawākin, 28C6
Sawel, Mt., 7D4
Sawdirī, 28C5
Sawhāj, 28B6
Sawknah, 28B4
Say, 29B6
Sayan Mountains, Mts., 19D10,11
Saydā, 20bB1
Sayhūt, 28C8

Sba, 28B2,3
Scafell Pikes, Mt., 7D6
Scandinavia, Pen., 19C2-4
Scapa Flow, Str., 10A3
Scarborough (Tobago), 36bC2
Scarborough (U.K.), 9B4
Šćeljajur, 17A8
Schefferville, 33C13
Schelde, R., 12C1,2
Schenectady, 35C6
Schio, 13aA5
Schleswig, 12B3
Schleswig-Holstein (10), Admin. U., 12B3
Schwedt, 12B4
Schweinfurt, 12C3
Schwerin, 12B3
Schwerin (14), Admin. U., 12B3
Schwerte, 12aB4
Schwyz, 11C5
Sciacca, 13C3
Šçigry, 18B4
Scilly, I., 41E10
Škokino, 18B4
Scoresbysund see Ittoqqortoormiit
Ščors, 18B3
Scotland, Admin. U., 10A-C2,3
Scott Base, Station, 42G18,19
Scott City, 34C6
Scott Island, I., 42F18
Scottsbluff, 34C6
Scranfon, 35B5,6
Šćučje Ozero, 17aB2
Scunthorpe, 9C4
Sea of Crete, 14D,E2,3
Sea of Japan, 25B,C5,6
Sea of Marmara, 21aA1
Sea of Okhotsk, 3
Seattle, 34B2
Sebež, 17C3
Şebinkarahisar, 21aA3
Secchia, 13aB4
Sechelt, 33aB2
Sedalia, 35D2
Sedan, 11B4
Sedok, 18D5
Seeheim, 30D2
Sefadu, 29C3
Sefrou, 11H2
Segeža, 17B4
Ségou, 29B4
Segovia, 11F2
Segre, R., 11F4
Séguéla, 29D4
Segura, R., 11G3
Seinäjoki, 15C7
Seine, R., 11C4
Seine-et-Marne (77), Admin. U., 11B3
Seine-Maritime (76), Admin. U., 11B3
Seine-Saint-Denis (93), Admin. U., 11B3
Sejmčan, 16C17
Šejm, R., 18B4
Šeki, 18D6
Sekondi-Takoradi, 29D5
Selangor (10), Admin. U., 19bC2
Selat Karimata, Str., 23D2,3
Selat Makasar, Str., 23D3

Selat Mentawai, Str., 19bD1
Selat Sunda, Str., 23D2
Selby, 9C4
Selebi-Pikwe, 30D3
Selenga see Selenge Mörön
Selenga, R., 16bB2
Selenge Mörön, R., 24B3,4
Selenginsk, 16bB2
Selfoss, 15aC2
Sélibaby, 29B2
Selma, 35E3
Selvas, Reg., 37C2-4
Semara, 28B1
Semarang, 23D3
Sembé, 29E9
Semipalatinsk, 16D10
Semnān, 21B6
Sem'onov, 17C6,7
Sena, 30C4
Sendai (Japan, Honshū), 25C7
Sendai (Japan, Kyūshū), 25D5
Seneca, 34C3
Sénégal, R., 29B2
Senegal, St., 29A,B1-3
Senhor do Bonfim, 38D5
Senja, I., 15A6
Senkursk, 17B6
Sens, 11B3
Seo de Urgel, 11F4
Šepetovka, 18B2
Sept-Îles, 33C13
Sequoia National Park, Park, 31aC1,2
Serafimovič, 18C5
Seram, I., 23D4,5
Serang, 23D2
Serdobsk, 18B5
Sereflikoçhisar, 21aB2
Seremban, 23C2
Sergač, 17C7
Serginskij, 16C8
Sergipe (22), Admin. U., 38C6
Serov, 16C,D7
Serowe, 30D3
Serpuchov, 18B4
Serra do Mar, Mts., 37E4,5
Serra dos Carajás, 38C4
Serra Geral de Goiás, Mts., 37D5
Sérrai, 14C2
Serra Môco, Mt., 26F6
Sertã, 11F2
Sesto San Giovanni, 13aA2,3
Sestri Levante, 13aB3
Setafe, 11F3
Sete Lagoas, 39a4,5
Sétif, 28A3
Setúbal, 11G1
Setúbal (15), Admin. U., 11G1
Sevard Peninsula, Pen., 31C4,5
Sevastopol', 16E5
Ševčenko, 16E7
Severnaja Dvina, R., 16C6
Severnaja Zeml'a, Is., 16A,B12,13
Severn (Canada), R., 33C10
Severn (U.K.), R., 7E6
Severodoneck, 18C4

Severodvinsk, 17B5
Severo-Jenisejsk, 16C11
Severomoravský kraj (7), Admin. U., 12C5
Severomorsk, 17A4
Severskij Donec, R., 18C4
Sevier, R., 34D4
Sevilla (Colombia), 38B2
Sevilla (Spain), 11G2
Sèvres (Deux-) (79), Admin. U., 11C2
Sewa, R., 29C3
Seward, 33B4,5
Seychelles, St., Is., 30B5,6
Seydisfjördur, 15aB4
Seyhan, R., 21aB3
Seymour, 35D3
Sfax, 28A4
Sfîntu-Gheorghe (Braşov), 14B3
Sfîntu-Gheorghe (Constanţa), 14B4
's-Gravenhage, 12B1,2
Shaanxi (21), Admin. U., 24C4
Shackleton Ice Shelf, 42F27
Shāhjahānpur, 22aB1,2
Shaki, 29C9
Shandī, 28C6
Shandong (22), Admin. U., 24C5
Shanghai, 24C6
Shanghai (29), Admin. U., 24C6
Shangrao, 24D5
Shangzi, 25A4
Shanhaiguan, 25B,C2,3
Shannon, I., 42C17
Shannon, R., 7D,E3
Shantou, 24D5
Shanxi (23), Admin. U., 24C5
Shaoguan, 24D5
Shaoxing, 24C,D6
Shaoyang, 24D5
Shapinsay, I., 10A3
Shari, 25B7
Shashi, 24C5
Sha Tin, 19aB3
Shawinigan, 33b
Shaykh 'Uthmān, 28C7
Shebele, R., 28D7
Sheberghān, 21B9
Sheboygan, 35C3
Sheffield (U.K.), 9C4
Sheffield (U.S.A.), 35E3
Shelby, 34B4
Shendam, 29C8
Shenyang, 24B6
Shenzhen, 19aA3
Sherbrooke, 35B6
Sheridan, 34C5
Sheringham, 9C5
Sherridon, 33C9
Shetland (65), Admin. U., 10aA1
Shetland Islands, Is., 7A,B7
Shexian, 25E2
Sheyenne, R., 34B7
Shibīn al- Kawm, 26aB2,3
Shibīn al-Qanātir, 26aB3
Shijiazhuang, 24C5
Shijiusuo, 24C5,6
Shika, 25aB2

page 222

hikoku, I., 25D5
hillong, 22B5
himoga, 22C3
himonoseki, 25D5
hinyanga, 30B4
hiono-zaki, C., 25D6
hiráz, 21D6
hiretoko-misaki, C., 25B8
hirvân, 21B7
hishaldin Volcano, Vol., 31D3,4
hivpuri, 22aB1
hizuishan, 24C4
hizuoka, 25D6
hkodër, 13B4
horeditch, 9a
howa, Station, 42F33
hreveport, 35E2
hrewsbury, 25A4
huangcheng, 25A4
huangliao, 24B6
huangyashan, 24B7
hubrá al-Khaymah, 26aB3
hucheng, 25D2
hulan, 25B4
hunyi, 25B2
huqrâ', 28C7
hūr, R., 21B5
hūrāb, R., 21C7
hūsf, 21C7
hushtar, 21C5
huyang, 25D2
hwebo, 22B5
iyenne, R., 34B7
ak, R., 19bD2
älkot, 22A3
argao Island, I., 23C4
auliai, 6B7
oaj, 6B10
oenik, 13B3
oi, 22B2
oir, Reg., 19D8-11
oiu, 14B3
oolga, 23C1
ou, 23C3
out, 28D4
chote-Alin, Mts., 19D,E15
chuan (24), Admin. U., 24C4
cilia (15), Admin. U., 13C3
cilia, I., 13C3
cuani, 38D2
di bel Abbès, 28A2,3
di Ifni, 28B1
di Kacem, 11H2
di Sâlim, 26aA2,3
dney, 34C6
dlce, 12B6
agen, 12C3
em Réap, 22C6
na, 13B2
radz, 12C5
rra Colorada, 39C2
rra de Córdoba, Mts., 37E,F3
rra Leone, St., 29C2,3
rra Madre Occidental, Mts., 31C10
rra Madre Oriental, Mts., 31G10,11
rra Mojada, 36B2
rra Morena, Mts., D4

Sierra Nevada (Spain), Mts., 5D4
Sierra Nevada (U.S.A.), Mts., 31F8,9
Sig, 17A4
Sighetul Marmației, 14B3
Siglufjörður, 15aA3
Signy, I., 42F5
Sigüenza, 11F3
Siguiri, 29C3
Siirt, 21aB4
Sikasso, 29C4
Sikeston, 35D2
Sikia, 14C2,3
Sikkim, Admin. U., 22B4
Sil, R., 11F2
Šilega, 15bB3
Silifke, 21aB2
Sílíguri, 22aB4
Silistra (16), Admin. U., 14C3
Siljan, L., 15C5
Šilka, 16bB4
Šilka, R., 16D13
Šilovo, 18B5
Silvassa, 22B3
Šimanovsk, 24A6
Simferopol', 18D3
Simikot, 22B4
Simla, 22A3
Simpson Desert, Des., 40C3
Sinaia, 14B3
Sinaia Peninsula, Pen., 26A,B8
Sinaloa (24), Admin. U., 36B2
Sincelejo, 38B2
Sind, R., 22aB1
Sindangbarang, 23aA1
Sines, 11G1
Singapore, 23C2
Singapore, St., 23C2
Singaraja, 23D3
Singatoka, 41bB1
Singida, 30B4
Singkawang, 23C2,3
Sinjah, 28C6
Sinkiang, Admin. U., see Xinjiang Weiwuer Zizhiqu
Sinkiang, Reg., 24B,C1-3
Sinnûris, 26aC2,3
Sinop, 21aA3
Sintang, 23C3
Sinŭiju, 25B3,4
Siófok, 14B1
Sion, 11C4
Sioux City, 35C1
Sioux Falls, 35C1
Sioux Lookout, 33C10
Siping, 24B6
Siple Island, I., 42G13
Siracusa, 13C3
Sirăjganj, 22aB4
Siretul, R., 14B3
Síros, I., 14D3
Sisak, 13A4
Sishen, 30D3
Sisimiut, 33B14
Sistema Central, Mts., 5C4
Sistema Ibérico, Mts., 5C4
Sitía, 14E3
Sitka, 33C6
Sittwe, 22B5

Situbondo, 23aA3
Sivas, 21aB3
Siverek, 21aB3
Sivrihisar, 21aB2
Sīwah, 28B5
Sjælland, I., 12B4
Skadovsk, 18C3
Skagerrak, Str., 15D3,4
Skagway, 33C6
Skárdu, 22A3
Skarżysko-Kamienna, 12C6
Skeena, R., 33C7
Skegness, 9C5
Skellefteå, 15B7
Skellefteälven, R., 15B6
Skibbereen, 10F5
Skibotn, 15A7
Skien, 15D4
Skierniewice, 12C6
Skikda, 28A3
Skipton, 9C4
Skíros, I., 14D3
Skopin, 18B5
Skopje, 13B5
Skövde, 15D5
Skovorodino, 16D14
Skye, I., 7C4,5
Slaney, R., 7E4
Slatina, 14B3
Slav'ansk, 18C4
Slav'ansk-na-Kubani, 18C4
Slave, R., 33C8
Slave Coast, Reg., 26D5
Slave Lake, L., 33C8
Slavonski Brod, 13A4
Sleaford, 9C4
Slea Head, C., 8E2
Slieve Bloom Mountains, Mts., 7E4
Slieve Donard, Mt., 7D5
Sligo, 10D5
Sligo, Admin. U., 10D5
Sligo Bay, B., 7D3
Slite, 15D6
Sliven, 14C3
Sliven (17), Admin. U., 14C3
Slobodskoj, 17C8
Slobozia, 14B3
Slonim, 18B2
Slough, 9D4
Slovenija (5), Admin. U., 13A3
Sluck, 18B2
Sl'ud'anka, 16bB1
Słupsk, 12B5
Smela, 18C3
Smethwick, 9C3
Smithers, 33C7
Smiths Falls, 33b
Smith Sound, Str., 42C11
Smoky-Falls, 35B4
Smȩła, I., 15C3
Smolensk, 16D5
Smol'an, 14C3
Smoljan (18), Admin. U., 14C3
Smorgon', 18B2
Snaefell, Mt., 7D5
Snag, 33B6
Snake, R., 34C3
Snasa, 15B5
Snězka, Mt., 5B6
Snigir'ovka, 18C3
Snoqualmie, 33aC3
Snowdon, Mt., 7E5,6
Sobat, R., 28D6

Sobrado, 38C4
Sobral, 38C5,6
Soči, 18D4
Socorro, 34E5
Sodankylä, 15B8
Södertälje, 15D6
Sofia see Sofija
Sofija (town) (19), Admin. U., 14C2
Sofija, 14C2
Sofija (20), Admin. U., 14C2
Sogamoso, 38B2
Sognefjorden, B., 15C3
Sohano, 41D5
Sohag, 28C6
Soho, 9a
Soitué, 39B2
Šojna, 17A6
Söke, 21aB1
Sokodé, 29C6
Sokol, 17C6
Sokol'niki, 17b
Sokolo, 29B4
Soko Islands, Is., 19aB2,3
Sokoto, 29B7
Sokoto (19), Admin. U., 29B7
Sokoto, R., 29B7
Solápur, 22C3
Soligalič, 17C6
Soligorsk, 18B2
Solihull, 9C4
Solikamsk, 17aB2
Solingen, 12aB2,3
Sollefteå, 15C6
Soller, 11G4
Solna, 15D6
Solo, R., 23aA3
Solomon Islands, St., Is., 40A5,6
Sovoveckije Ostrova, Is., 17A5
Solway Firth, B., 7D6
Solwezi, 30C3
Soma, 21aB1
Somalia, St., 28C,D7
Somali Peninsula, Pen., 26D9
Sombor, 13A4
Somerset (40), Admin. U., 9D3
Somerset Island, I., 33A10
Someşul, R., 14B2
Somme (80), Admin. U., 11B3
Somme, R., 11B3
Somogy (13), Admin. U., 14B1
Somosomo, 41bA3
Son, R., 22B4
Sondrio, 13A2
Song Da, R., 22B6
Songea, 30C4
Songhla, 22D6
Song Hong, R., 22B6
Songhu, R., 25B4
Songhuajiang, Res., 24B6
Songhuajiang, R., 24B6
Songnim, 25C4
Songo, 30C4
Sonkovo, 17C5
Sonora, 34E6
Sonora (25), Admin. U., 36B1
Sonsorol Islands, Is., 41C2,3
Sopot, 12B6
Sopron, 14B1
Sorel, 33b

, 13aA3
 F3
, 33aB4
, 18B7
 8C2
 23D5
Soroti, 28D6
Séréya, I., 15A7
Sorsele, 15B6
Sortavala, 17B4
Sosna, R., 18B4
Sosnogorsk, 17B8
Sosnovka, 18B5
Sosnowiec, 12C5
Šostka, 18B3
Sos'va, 17aB3
Sos'va, R., 17aB3
Soubré, 29D4
Souillac, 30aB3
Souk Ahras, 27aA2
Sŏul, 25C4
Sound of Harris, Str., 7C4
Sound of Jura, Str., 7C,D5
Souris, R., 34B6
Souro, 38C5
Sousse, 28A4
South Africa, St., 30D,E2-4
South America, St.
Southampton, 9D4
Southampton Island, I., 33B11
South Australia, Admin. U., 40C,D3
South Bend, 33C3
South Carolina, Admin. U., 35E4,5
South China Sea, S., 23C6,7
South Dakota, Admin. U., 34C6,7
South Downs, Hs., 7F7,8
South East Cape, C., 40E4
South East Point, C., 40D4
Southend-on-Sea, 9D5
South Esk, R., 10B3
Southern Alps, Mts., 40aB1,2
Southern Cross, 40D1,2
Southern Uplands, Mts., 7D5,6
South Georgia, I., 37H6
South Glamorgan (53), Admin. U., 9D3
South Island, I., 40aB2
South Magnetic Pole 42F23
South Orkney Islands, Is., 42E,F5
South Ossetian Autonomous Region (10), Admin. U., 18D5
South Platte, R., 34C6
South Pole, 42H
Southport, 9C3
South Ronaldsay, I., 7B6
South Sandwich Islands, Is., 42E,F2,3
South Saskatchewan, R., 33C8,9
South Shetland Islands, Is., 42F6,7
South Shields, 9B4
South Tyne, R., 10C3
South Uist, I., 7C4
Southwest Cape, C., 40aB1,2

South Yemen see Yemen
South Yorkshire, (4), Admin. U., 9C4
Sovetsk (U.S.S.R., Kaliningrad), 15E7
Sovetsk (U.S.S.R., Kirov), 17C7
Sovetskaja Gavan', 16E15,16
Sovetskij, 16aB7
Sovetskoje, 18C5
Sŏya, 25A7
Soyo, 30B2
Soż, R., 18B3
Sozopol, 14C3
Spain, St., 11F,G2,3
Spalding, 9C4
Spanish Head, C., 9B2
Sparta, 35D3
Spartanburg, 35D,E4
Spárti, 14D2
Spassk-Dal'nij, 25B5
Spence Bay, 33B10
Spencer Gulf, G., 40D3
Spences Bridge, 33aB3
Spey, R., 7C4
Spithead, B., 7F7
Split, 13B4
Spokane, 34B3
Spoleto, 12C3
Spratly Island, I., 23C3
Springbok, 30D2
Springdale, 33C3
Springfield (U.S.A., Illinois), 35D2,3
Springfield (U.S.A., Massachusetts), 35C6
Springfield (U.S.A., Missouri), 35D2
Springfield (U.S.A., Ohio), 35C4
Springfontein, 30E3
Springs, 30D3
Spurn Head, C., 7E8
Squamish, 33D7
Squaw Valley, 34D2
Srbija (6), Admin. U., 13A5
Srednekolymsk, 16C16,17
Srednerusskaja Vozvyšennost', Plat., 19D,E5
Sredne-Sibirskoje Ploskogorje, Plat., 19C11-13
Sretensk, 24A5
Sri Lanka, St., I., 20aB3
Srīnagar, 22A3
Stachanov, 18C4
Stafford, 9C3
Staffordshire (41), Admin. U., 9C3
Staines, 9D4
Stamford, 9C4
Standish, 35C4
Stanhope, 10C3
Stanley, 39D3
Stanley Falls, Fs., 26D7
Stanovoj Chrebet, Mts., 19D14,15
Stanovoje Nagorje, Mts., 19D13,14
Staraja Russa, 17C4
Stara Planina, Mts., 5C7
Stara Zagora, 14C3

Stara Zagora (21), Admin. U., 14C3
Starbuck Island, I., 41D10
Stargard Szczeciński, 12B4
Starobel'sk, 18C4
Starokonstantinov, 18C2
Starominskaja, 18C4
Start Point, C., 7F6
Staryj Krym, 16aB2
Staryj Oskol, 18B4
Staten Island, 32a
Stavanger, 15D3
Stavropol', 16E6
Steenkool, 23D5
Steep Point, C., 40C1
Stehekin, 33aB3
Steiermark (6), Admin. U., 12D4
Steinkjer, 15B,C4,5
Stendal, 12B3
Stepanakert, 18a,AB2
Stepney, 9a
Stephenville, 33D14
Stereá Ellas (7), Admin. U., 14D2
Sterlitamak, 17aC2
Steubenville, 35C4
Stevenage, 9D4,5
Stewart, 33C6,7
Stewart, R., 33B6
Stewart Island, I., 40aB1,2
Steyr, 12C4
Stikine, R., 33C6
Štip, 13B5
Stirling, 10B2,3
Stockholm, 15D6
Stockport, 9C3,4
Stockton (U.K.), 9B4
Stockton (U.S.A.), 34D2
Stoeng Tréng, 22C6
Stoke Newington, 9a
Stoke on Trent, 9C3
Stonehaven, 10B3
Storavan, L., 15B6
Stord, I., 15D3
Stóren, 15C4
Stornoway, 10A1
Storožëvsk, 17B8
Storsjön, L., 15C5
Storuman, 15B6
Stour (Atlantic Ocean), R., 7F6,7
Stour (North Sea), R., 7F8
Stowmarket, 9C5
Strabane, 10D6
Strabane (26), Admin. U., 10D6
Stradella, 13aA3
Strait of Bonifacio, Str., 13B2
Strait of Dover, Str., 7F8
Strait of Gibraltar, Str., 5A,B2,3
Strait of Hormuz, Str., 21D7
Strait of Juan de Fuca, Str., 33aB1,2
Strait of Magellan, Str., 39D2
Strait of Malacca, Str., 23C1,2
Strait of Otranto, Str., 13B,C4
Strait of Sicily, Str., 13C2,3
Straits of Florida, Str., 35F,G4,5

Stralsund, 12B4
Strand, 30E2
Strangford Lough, B., 7D4,5
Stranraer, 10C2
Strasbourg, 11B4,5
Stratford, 33b
Stratford upon-Avon, 9C4
Strathclyde (62), Admin. U., 9B2
Strathmore, Reg., 7C6
Straubing, 12C4
Středočeský kraj (1), Admin. U., 12C4
Stredoslovenský kraj (9), Admin. U., 12C5
Strel'na, 17A5
Stretford, 9C3
Stretto di Messina, Str., 13C3
Strimón, R., 14C2
Stromness, 10A3
Strömstad, 15D4
Stronsay, I., 7B6
Struga, 13B5
Strugi-Krasnyje, 17C3
Stryj, 18C1
Sturgis, 34A6
Stuttgart, 12C3
Stykkishólmur, 15A2
Suao, 25aB2
Subotica, 13A4
Suceava, 14B3
Suchaja, 16bB2
Suchbaatar, 24A4
Sučhiničí, 18B4
Suchona, R., 17C6
Suchumi, 16E5,6
Suck, R., 7E3
Sucre, 38D3
Sucuaro, 38B3
Suda, R., 17C5
Sudak, 16aB2
Sudan, Reg., 26C4-7
Sudan, St., 28B,C5,6
Sudbury (Canada), 33B11
Sudbury (U.K.), 9C5
Sue, R., 28D5
Suez see As-Suways
Suez Canal, Can., 26A8
Suffolk (42), Admin. U., 9C5
Suhār, 21E7
Suhl, 12C3
Suhl (15), Admin. U., 12C3
Suide, 24C4,5
Suihua, 25A4
Suir, R., 7E4
Šuja, 17C6
Sukabumi, 23aA1
Sukkertoppen see Maniitsoq
Sukkozero, 17B4
Sukkur, 22B2
Suksun, 17aB2
Sulawesi, I., 23C,D3,4
Sulina, 14B4
Sullana, 38C1,2
Sulu Archipelago, Is., 23C3,4
Sulu Sea, 23C3,4
Sultan, 34B4
Sumatra, I., 23C,D1,2
Sumba, I., 23D,E3,4
Sumbawa, I., 23D3
Sumbawa Besar, 23D3

page 224

Sumbe, 30C2
Sumber, 24B4
Sumburgh Head, C., 7B7
Sumen, 14C3
Šumen (22), Admin. U., 14C3
Sumenep, 23aA3
Šumerlja, 17C7
Sumgait, 18aA2
Šumicha, 17aB3
Šumperk, 12C5
Sumy, 18B3
Sunch'ŏn, 25D4
Sunderland, 9B4
Sundsvall, 15C6
Šungaj, 18B2
Sungurlu, 21aA2
Sunnyvale, 34D2
Sunyani, 29D5
Suoche, 24C7
Suomussalmi, 15B8,9
Superior, 35B2
Suqian, 25D2
Suquṭrā, I., 26C10
Sūr (Lebanon), 20B7
Sūr (Oman), 21E7
Sura, R., 18B6
Surabaya, 23D3
Surakarta, 23D3
Sūrān, 21D8
Surat, 22B3
Surat Thani, 22D5
Surgut (U.S.S.R., Kujbyšev), 18B7
Surgut (U.S.S.R., Nižnevartovsk), 16C9
Surigao, 23C4
Surinam, St., 38B4
Surovo, 16bA2
Surrey, 34B6
Surrey (43), Admin. U., 9D4
Surt, 28A4
Susitna, R., 33B4
Susuman, 16C16
Sutlej, R., 22A3
Suva, 41bB2
Suwalki, 12B6
Suwarrow, I., 41E9
Suwŏn, 25C4
Suxian, 25D2
Suzhou, 24C5,6
Suzu-misaki, C., 25C6
Svalbard, Admin. U., Is., 4
Svatovo, 18C4
Sveg, 15C5
Svendborg, 12B3
Sverdlovsk (U.S.S.R., Čel'abinsk), 16D7,8
Sverdlovsk (U.S.S.R., Doneck), 18C4,5
Sverdrup Islands, Is., 42C,D8,9
Svetlogorsk (U.S.S.R., Gomel'), 18B2,3
Svetlogorsk (U.S.S.R., Kaliningrad), 15E6,7
Svetlograd, 18C5
Svir', R., 17B4
Svirsk, 16bB1
Svištov, 14C3
Svobodnyj, 24A6
Svolvær, 15A5
Swains Island, I., 41E8,9
Swakopmund, 30D2
Swale, R., 9B4
Swan Hill, 40D4
Swansea, 9D2,3
Swaziland, St., 30D4

Sweden, St., 15B-D5-7
Sweetwater, 34E6
Swift, 33C9
Swift Current, 33C,D9
Swindon, 9D4
Świnoujście, 12B4
Switzerland, St., 11C4,5
Syčovka, 17C4
Sydney (Austr.), 40D5
Sydney (Canada), 33D13,14
Syktyvkar, 16C7
Sylt, I., 12B3
Sylva, R., 17aB2
Syracuse, 35C5
Syrdarja, R., 16E8
Syria, St., 20B,A,B2,3
Syrian Desert, Des., 26A8
Sysola, R., 17B8
Syzran', 18B6
Szabolcs-Szatmár (14), Admin. U., 14A2
Szczecin, 12B4
Szczecinek, 12B5
Szczytno, 12B6
Szeged, 14B2
Székesfehérvár, 14B1
Szekszárd, 14B1
Szentes, 14B2
Szombathely, 14B1
Szolnok, 14B2
Szolnok (15), Admin. U., 14B2

T

Tabaco, 23bB2
Tabankort, 29A6
Tabarka, 27aA2
Tabas, 21C7
Tabasco (26), Admin. U., 36C3
Tabelbala, 28B2
Tabla, 29B6
Tablas Island, I., 23B4
Tábor, 12C4
Tabora, 30B4
Tabory, 17aB3
Tabou, 29D4
Tabrīz, 21B5
Tabuaeran, I., 41C10
Tabūk, 28B6
Tacheng, 24B2
Tachta-Bazar, 21B8
Tacloban, 23bB2,3
Tacna, 38D2
Tacoma, 34B2
Tacuarembó, 39D2
Tadinou, 41aA2
Tadoussac, 33D12,13
Tadzhik Soviet Socialist Republic, Admin. U., 16F8,9
Taegu, 25C4
Taejŏn, 25C4
Taft, 34D3
Taganrog, 18C4
Tagbilaran, 23bC2
Tagdempt, 28A3
Tagil, R., 17aB3
Tagula Island, I., 40B5
Tagus see Tajo
Tahat, Mt., 26B5
Tahiti, I., 41d
Tahoua, 29B7
Tahsis, 33aB1
Tahuna, 23C4
Taï, 29D4

Tai'an, 25C2
T'aichung, 24D6
Taihu, L., 25D2,3
Tailai, 24B6
T'ainan, 24D5,6
Tai O, 19aB2
T'aipei, 24D6
Taiping, 23C2
Tai Po, 19aB3
Taitung, 25aB2
Taivalkoski, 15B8,9
Taiwan (25), Admin. U., 24D6
Taiwan, I., 25a
Taiwan Strait, Str., 24D5,6
Taiyuan, 24C5
Taizhou, 25D2,3
Tai'zz, 28C7
Tajo, R., 11F3
Takamatsu, 25D5
Takaoka, 25C6
Takapuna, 40aA2
Takasaki, 25C6
Takikawa, 25B7
Talara, 38C1
Talavera de la Reina, 11G2
Talawdī, 28C5,6
Talca, 39B1
Talcahuano, 39B1
Taldy-Kurgan, 16E9
Talica, 17aB3
Tall 'Afar, 20bA3
Tallahassee, 35E4
Tallinn, 16D4
Tal'noje, 18C3
Talorza, 29A2
Talsi, 17C2
Taltal, 39A1
Tamale, 29C5
Taman', 16aB3
Tamanrasset, 28B3
Tamar, R., 7F5
Tamaulipas (27), Admin. U., 36B3
Tambacounda, 29B2
Tambao, 29B5,6
Tambo, 40C4
Tambov, 16D6
Tamchaket, 29A3
Tamil Nadu, Admin. U., 22C3
Tampa, 35F4
Tampa Bay, B., 35F4
Tampere, 15C7,8
Tampico, 36B3
Tamrida, 27C10
Tamsagbulag, 24B5
Tamworth, 40D5
Tana, 15A9
Tana (Kenya), R., 30B5
Tana (Nor.-Fin.), R., 15A8
Tanabe, 25D6
Tanacross, 33B5
Tanafjorden, B., 15A9
Tanahmerah, 23D5,6
Tanami, 40B2,3
Tanana, 33B4
Tanana, R., 33B5
Tanaro, R., 13aB2
Tandag, 23bC3
Tandil, 39B3
Tanega-shima, I., 25D5
Tanga, 30B4
Tanger, 28A2
Tangjia, 19aB2
Tangshan, 24C5
Tangtouxia, 19aA3

Tanjungbalai, 19bC1,2
Tanjung Buru, C., 19I12
Tanjung Datu, C., 23C2
Tanjung Mangkalihat, C., 23C3,4
Tanjungpandan, 23D2
Tanjung Perkam, C., 23D5
Tanjungpinang, 23C2
Tanjung Selatan, C., 23D3
Tanjungselor, 23C3
Tanjung Torawitan, C., 23C4
Tanjung Vals, C., 23D5
Tânout, 29B8
Tantā, 28A6
Tanzania, St., 30B,C4
Taoan, 24B6
Taolanaro, 30D5
Taoudenni, 28B2
Taourirt, 11H3
Tapa, 17C3
Tapachula, 36C3
Tapajós, R., 37C4
Tapanliieh, 25aB2
Tapanuauara, 38C3
Tapauá, 38C3
Tāpi, R., 22B3
Taqâtu' Hayyâ, 28C6
Taquari, R., 38D4
Tarābulus (Lebanon), 20B7
Tarābulus (Libya), 28A4
Tarābulus, Reg., 28A,B4
Tarakan, 23C3
Taranto, 13B4
Taravo, R., 13B2
Tarawa, 41C7
Tarawa Island, I., 41C7
Tarbert (U.K., Outer Hebrides), 10B1
Tarbert (U.K., Scotland), 10C2
Tarbes, 11D3
Tarcoola, 40D3
Tarfaya, 28B1
Târgovişte, 14C3
Târgovişte (23), Admin. U., 14C3
Tarif, 21E6
Tarifa, 5aA2
Tarija, 38E3
Tarīm, 28C7
Tarimhe, R., 24B2
Tarim Pendi, Des., 19F9,10
Tarin-Kowt, 22A2
Tarkwa, 29D5
Tarlac, 23B3,4
Tarn (81), Admin. U., 11D3
Tarn, R., 11C3
Tarn-et-Garonne (82), Admin. U., 11D3
Tarnobrzeg, 12C6
Tarnów, 12C6
Taro, R., 13aB4
Taroudant, 28A2
Tarrafal, 29B1
Tarragona, 11F4
Tarrasa, 11F4
Tarsus, 21aB2
Tartu, 17C3
Tartūs, 20B1
Tarum, R., 23aA1
Tarutung, 12bC1
Tašauz, 16E7
Tasikmalaya, 23D2
Taškent, 16E8
Tasmania, I., 40E4

41 H5,6	Temr'uk, 18C4	The Sound, Str., 12A,B4	Timaru, 40aB2
10	Temuco, 39B1	Thetford, 9C5	Timaševsk, 18C4
I E12	Tenasserim, 22C5	Thetford Mines, 35B6	Timbédra, 29A3
ous Soviet	Ténéré, Reg., 26B,C5,6	The Wash, B., 7E8	Timbuktu see Tombouctou
oublic,	Tenerife, I., 28B1	The Weald, Hs., 7F7,8	Timimoun, 28B3
Admin. U., 17C7,8	Ténès, 27aA1	The Wrekin, Mt., 7E6,7	Timișoara, 14B2
Tatarbunary, 18C2	Tengchong, 24D3	Thicket Portage, 33C10	Timmins, 33D11
Tatarskij Proliv, Chann.,	Tenkodogo, 29C5	Thiers, 12D1,2	Timón, 38C5
16D,E16	Tennessee, Admin. U.,	Thiès, 29B1	Timor, I., 23D4
Tateyama, 25D6,7	35D3,4	Thimbu, 22aB4	Timor Sea, 23E4
Tatlayoko Lake, L.,	Tennessee, R., 35E3	Thingeyri, 15aB2	Tinaca Point, C.,
33aA2	Tenom, 23C3	Thingvellir, 15aB2	23C4
Tatvan, 21aB4	Teófilo Otoni, 38D5	Thio, 41aA2	Tindouf, 28B2
Taubaté, 39A4	Tepic, 36B2	Thionville, 11B4	Tîngrêla, 29C4
Taunggyi, 22B5	Teplice, 12C4	Thíra, 14D3	Tinogasta, 39A2
Taunoa, 41dB2	Téra, 29B6	Thirsk, 9B4	Tínos, I., 14D3
Taunton, 9D3	Teraina, I., 41C10	Thisted, 12A3	Tin Zaouaten, 29A6
Tauragé, 18A1	Teramo, 13B3	Thistilfjördur, B.,	Tipperary, 10E5,6
Tautira, 41dB2	Tercan, 21aB4	15aA4	Tipperary, Admin. U.,
Tauz, 18A2	Terceira, I., 11aA3	Thithia, I., 41bA3	10E5,6
Tavda, 17aB4	Terek, R., 18D5	Thívai, 14D2	Tiradentes, 39aB5
Tavda, R., 17aB3	Terengganu (11), Admin.	Thjórsá, R., 15aB3	Tirana see Tiranë
Taveuni, I., 41bA3	U., 19bB3	Thomasville, 35E4	Tiranë, 13B4
Tavoy, 22C5	Teresina, 38C5	Thompson, 33C10	Tiraspol', 18C2,3
Tavşanlı, 21aB1	Teresinha, 38B4	Thomson, R.,	Tire, 21aB1
Taw, R., 9D3	Termez, 16F8	40C4	Tirebolu, 21aA3
Tawau, 23C3	Ternate, 23C4	Thorshavn, 6A4	Tiree, I., 7C4
Tawkar, 28C6	Ternej, 25A6	Thórshöfn, 15aA3,4	Tîrgovişte, 14B3
Tay, R., 7C6	Terni, 13B3	Thouars, 11C2,3	Tîrgu-Jiu, 14B2
Taymá', 21D3	Ternopol', 18C2	Thráki (9), Admin. U.,	Tîrgu Mureş, 14B3
Tayside (63), Admin. U.,	Terre Haute, 35D3	14C3	Tirl'anskij, 17aC2
10B3	Territoire de Belfort (90),	Three Forks, 34B4	Tirol (7), Admin. U.,
Tayua, 41bA1	Admin. U., 11C4	Thule see Qânâq,	12D3
Taz, R., 16C10	Terry, 34B5	33A12,13	Tirso, R., 13B2
Tazovskij, 16C9,10	Teruel, 11F3	Thun, 11C4	Tiruchchirāppalli, 22C3
Tbilisi, 16E6	Teseney, 28C6	Thunder Bay, 33D10,11	Tirunelveli, 22D3
Tchien, 29D3	Teslin, 33B6	Thurles, 10E6	Tirupati, 20aA2
Tczew, 12B5	Tessalit, 28B3	Thursday Island, I.,	Tiruppur, 20aB2
Tearaght Island, I.,	Tessaoua, 29B7,8	40B4	Tisa, R., 12C6
7E2	Tete, 30C5	Thurso, 10A3	Tista, R., 22aB4
Tébessa, 28A3	Tétouan, 28A2	Thurston Island, I.,	Tisza see Tisa
Tebingtinggi, 19bC1,2	Tetovo, 13B5	42F,G10	Tit' Ary, 16B14
Tecuci, 14B3	Tevere, R., 13B3	Tianjin, 24C5	Titograd, 13B4
Tedžen, 21B8	Teviot, R., 10C3	Tianjin (30), Admin. U.,	Titovo Užice, 13B4
Tedžen, R., 21B8	Texada Island, I.,	24C5	Titov Veles, 13B5
Tees, R., 7D7	33aB2	Tianjun, 24C3	Tivoli, 13B3
Tefé, 38C3	Texarkana, 35E2	Tianshui, 24C4	Tizimín, 36B4
Tegal, 23D2	Texas, Admin. U.,	Tiarei, 41dB2	Tizi Ouzou, 28A3
Tegucigalpa, 36C4	34E6,7	Tiassalé, 29D4	Tiznit, 28B2
Tehrān, 21B6	Tezpur, 22A5	Tiavea, 41cA2	Tkvarčeli, 18D5
Teifi, R., 7E5	Thabana Ntlenyana, Mt.,	Tibagí, R., 39aB3	Tlaxcala (28), Admin. U.,
Tejkovo, 17C6	26G7	Tibati, 29D9	36C3
Tejo see Tajo	Thailand, St., 22C5,6	Tibesti, Mts., 26B6	Tlemcen, 28A3
Tekeli, 24B1	Thames (Canada), R.,	Tibet, Admin. U., see	Toamasina, 30C5,6
Tekirdağ, 13B6	33b	Xizang Zizhiqu	Toanoano, 41dB2
Telavi, 18D6	Thames (U.K.), R., 7F7	Tibet, Region,	Tobago, I., 38A3,4
Tel Aviv-Yafo, 20bB1	Thāna, 22C3	19F10,11	Tobermory, 10B1
Telemba, 16bB3	Thanh-Hoa, 22C6	Tichît, 28C2	Tobi, I., 23C5
Teles Pires, R., 37C,D4	Thanh-phô Hô Chi Minh,	Tichoreck, 18C5	Tobol, 17aC3
Télimélé, 29C2	22C6	Tichvin, 17C4	Tobol, R., 16D8
Telok Anson, 19bB,C2	Thanjāvūr, 22C3,4	Ticino, R., 13aA2,3	Tobol'sk, 16D8,9
Telukbetung, 23D2	Thar Desert, Des.,	Tidjikdja, 28C1	Tobseda, 17A8
Teluk Bone, B., 23D4	19G8,9	Tieling, 25B3	Tocantins, R., 37D5
Teluk Cenderawasih, B.,	Thásos, I., 14C3	Tien Shan, Mts., 19E9-11	Tocopilla, 39A1
23D5	The Cheviot, Mt., 7D6,7	Tientsin see Tiajin	Todenyang, 28D6
Teluk Mandar, B.,	The Dalles, 34B2	Tierra del Fuego, Admin.	Tofino, 33aB2
23D3	Thedford, 34C6	U., 39D2	Togo, St., 29C,D6
Teluk Sarera, B.,	The Fens, Reg., 7E7,8	Tierra del Fuego, I.,	Tokat, 21aA3
23D5	Thelon, R., 33B9	37H3,4	Tokelau Islands, Is.,
Teluk Tolo, B.,	The Minch, Str.,	Tietê, R., 37E5	41D8
23D4	7B,C4,5	Tifton, 35E4	Tokmak, 18C4
Teluk Tomini, B.,	The Naze, C., 7F8	Tigre, R., 38C2	Tokushima, 25D5
23C,D4	The Needles, C., 7F6,7	Tigris see Dicle	Tōkyō, 25C6,7
Tema, 29D5,6	Theodore, 40C4,5	Tijuana, 36A1	Tolbuhin, 14C3
Temae, 41dA1	The Pas, 33C9	Tikrît, 21C4	Tolbuhin (24), Admin. U.,
Teme, R., 7E6	The Peaks, Mt., 7E6,7	Tiksi, 16B14,15	14C4
Temirtau, 16D9	The Ruhr Basin, Reg., 12a	Tilburg, 12C2	Toledo (Brazil),
Temnikov, 18B5	Thessalia (8), Admin. U.,	Tillabéry, 29B6	39aB3
Temple, 34E7	14D2	Tillamook, 34B2	Toledo (Spain), 11G2,3
	Thessaloníki, 14C2	Timanskij Kr'až, Hs.,	Toledo (U.S.A., Ohio),
		5A9,10	35C4

page 226

oledo (U.S.A., Oregon), 34C2
olga, 27aB2
oliara, 30D5
oljatti, 18B6
olna (16), Admin. U., 14B1
olob, 10a
oluca, 36C2,3
omakomai, 25B7
omaszów Mazowiecki, 12C6
ombara, I., 41D5
ombouctou, 29A5
ombua, 30C2
omini, 23C4
omo, R., 38B3
om Price, 40C1
omsk, 16D10
one, R., 25C7
onekåbon, 21B6
onga, St. Is., 41E,F8
ongareva see Penrhyn
ongatapu Group, Is., 41F8
ongch'ŏn, 25C4
ongchuan, 24C4
onghua, 25B4
ongjosŏn-man, B., 25C4
ongliao, 24B6
ongling, 25D2
ongtianhe, R., 24C3
ongue, 10A2
ongyu, 25B6
ongxian, 25C2
onié Sab, L., 22C6
nsberg, 15D4
ora-Chem, 24A3
oowoomba, 40C5
opeka, 35D1
opolobampo, 36B2
rbat-e Heydarieh, 21B7,8
rino, 13A1
rlino, 17aB3
rmes, R., 11F2
rnealviken, 15B7
rnetråsk, L., 15A6,7
ronto, 33D11,12
ropec, 17C4
ros Dağlari, Mts., 19F5
rquay, 9D3
rre del Greco, 13B3
rrelavega, 11F2
rreón, 36B2
rres, 39aC4
rres Novas, 11G1
rres Strait, Str., 10A,B4
rsby, 15C5
rtoli, 13C2
rtona, 13aB2
rtosa, 11F4
ruń, 12B5
ry Island, I., 10D5
żok, 17C4
scana (16), Admin. U., 13B2
sno, 17C4
stado, 39A2
sya, 21aA2
t'ma, 17aB3
toya, I., 41bB3
tori, 25C5
uba (Ivory Coast), 29C4
uba (Senegal), 29B2
ugan, 29B5
uggourt, 28A3
ukoto, 29B3

Toul, 11B4
Touléplou, 29D3
Toulon, 11D4
Toulouse, 11D3
Toungoo, 22C5
Tourcoing, 11B3
Tours, 11C3
Townbridge, 9D3
Townsville, 40B4
Toyama, 25C6
Toyohashi, 25D6
Toyota, 25C6
Tozeur, 28A3
Trabzon, 21aA3
Tracade, 35B7
Tracadie, 35B7
Trail, 33D8
Tralee, 10E5
Tramore, 15E6
Trang, 22D5
Transantarctic Mountains, Mts., 42G,H1
Trans-Carpathian Region (11), Admin. U., 18C1
Transkei, Admin. U., 30E3,4
Transvaal, Admin. U., 30D3,4
Trapani, 13C3
Traverse City, 35C3,4
Trby, 15D4
Trebbia, R., 13aB3
Treinta y Tres, 39aD3
Trelew, 39C2
Trelleborg, 15E5
Tremadoc Bay, B., 7E5
Tremp, 11F4
Trenčín, 12C5
Trent, R., 7E7
Trentino-Alto Adige (17), Admin. U., 13A2
Trento, 13A2
Trenton (Canada), 33b
Trenton (U.S.A.), 35C,D6
Tres Arroyos, 39aE1
Três Lagoas, 38E4
Treviso, 13A3
Trichūr, 20aB2
Trier, 12C2
Trieste, 13A3
Tríkala, 14D2
Tríkomon, 19cA2
Trim, 10E6
Trincomalee, 20aB3
Trinidad (Bolivia), 38D3
Trinidad (Cuba), 36B3,4
Trinidad (Uruguay), 39aD2
Trinidad (U.S.A.), 34D5,6
Trinidad, I., 37A3,4
Trinidad and Tobago, St., 38A3,4
Trinity, R., 34E7
Tripoli see Tarābulus
Tripura (5), Admin. U., 22B5
Tristan da Cunha Group, Is., 3
Trivandrum, 22D3
Trnava, 12C5
Trogir, 13B4
Troick, 17aC3
Troicko-Pečorsk, 17B9
Trois-Rivières, 33D12
Trollhättan, 15D5
Tromsø, 15A6

Trondheim, 15C4
Trondheimsfjorden, B., 15C4
Troon, 10C2
Troy, 35E3
Troyes, 11B4
Trujillo, 38C2
Trujillo, 11G2
Truk Islands, Is., 41C5
Truro (Canada), 39D13
Truro (U.K.), 9D2
Tsao, 30D3
Tsavo, 30B4
Tshane, 30D3
Tshela, 30B2
Tshikapa, 30B3
Tsu, 25D6
Tsuen Wan, 19aB3
Tsugaru-kaikyō, Str., 25B6,7
Tsumeb, 30C2
Tsuruga, 25C6
Tsuruoka, 25C6
Tsushima, Is., 25D4
Tsushima-kaikyō, Str., 25D4,5
Tual, 10E5
Tuam, 10E5
Tuapse, 18D4
Tuasivi, 41cA1
Tuban, 23aA3
Tubarão, 39aC4
Tubaruri, 38C4,5
Tudela, 11F3
Tudmur, 20bB2
Tuen Mun, 19aB2
Tugela Falls, Fs., 26G7,8
Tuguegarao, 23B4
Tuktoyaktuk, 33B6
Tula, 16D5
Tulare, 34D3
Tulcea, 14B4
Tul'čin, 17aC5
Tullahoma, 35D3
Tullamore, 10E6
Tulle, 11C3
Tuloma, R., 17A4
Tulsa, 35D1
Tulufan, 24C3
Tulun, 16bB1
Tulungagung, 23aB2
Tumaco, 38B2
Tumbes, 38C1
T'umen', 16D8
Tumenjiang, R., 25B4,5
Tummo, 28B4
Tunas de Zara, 36aB3,4
Tunbridge, 9D5
Tunbridge Wells, 9D5
Tundža, R., 14C3
Tunis, 28A3,4
Tunisia, St., 28A3,4
Tunja, 38A3
Tunxi, 25E2
Tuotuo Heyan, 24C3
Tupelo, 35E3
Tupiza, 38E3
Tura, 16C12
Tura, R., 17aB3

Turanskaja Nizmennosť, Pl., 19E,F7,8
Turbat, 22B2
Turbo, 38B2
Turda, 14B2
Turgutlu, 14D3
Turia, R., 11G3
Terib'orka, 15A10
Turin see Torino
Turinsk, 17aB3
Turka (RSFSR), 16bB2
Turka (U.S.S.R.), 18C1
Turkey, St., 21aA,B1-4
Turkmen Soviet Socialist Republic, Admin. U., 16F7,8
Turks and Caicos Islands, Admin. U., 37B3,4
Turku, 15C7
Turnu-Măgurele, 14C3
Turtle Lake, 35B2
Turuchansk, 16C10,11
Tuscaloosa, 35E3
Tušino, 17b
Tuticorin, 20aB2
Tutrakan, 14B,C3
Tuttlingen, 12D3
Tutuila, I., 41cB3
Tuvalu, St., Is., 41D,E7
Tuxtla, 36C3
Túy, 11F1
Tuz Gölü, L., 21aB2
Tuzla, 13A4
Tyler, 35E1
Tymovskoje, 16D16
Tynda, 16D14
Tyne, R., 7D6,7
Tyne and Wear (5), Admin. U., 9B4
Tynemouth, 9B4
Tyrrhyauz, 18D5
Tyrrhenian Sea, 13B,C2,3
Tywi, R., 7F5
Tywyn, 9C2
Tweed, R., 7D6
Twin Falls, 34C3,4

U

Uad Atui, R., 28B1
Uaupés, R., 38B3
Ubagan, R., 17aC3
Ubangi, R., 28D5
Úbeda, 11G3
Uberaba, 38D5
Uberlândia, 38D5
Ubinas, Mt., 37D2
Udon Ratchathani, 22C6
Ubundi, 30B3
Ucayali, R., 37C2
Uchta, 16C7
Udaipur, 22B3
Uda, R., 16bB3
Uddevalla, 15D4
Uddjaur, L., 15B6
Udine, 13A3
Udmurt Autonomous Soviet Socialist Republic, Admin. U., 17C8
Udon Thani, 22C6
Uele, R., 28D5
Ušlen, 16c20,21
U'zen, 12B3
Ūfa, 16D7
Uganda, St., 30B4
Uglič, 17C5

page 227

Ujung Pandang, 23D3
Ulaanbaatar, 24B4
Ulaangom, 24B3
Ulan-Ude, 16D12
Uliastaj, 24B3
Uliga, 41C7
Uljanovsk, 16D6
Ullapool, 10B2
Ullŭng-do, I., 25C5
Ulm, 12C3
Ulsan, 25C4
Ulugh Muztagh, Mt., 19F10,11
Ulukışla, 21aB2
Ukmerge, 17C2
Ukrainian Soviet Socialist Republic, Admin. U., 16E4,5
Uman', 18C3
Ūmanak, 33A14
Umba, 17A4
Umbria (18), Admin. U., 13B3
Umeå, 15C7
Umeälven, R., 15B6
Umfors, 15B5
Umiat, 33B4
Umm Durmān, 28C5,6
Umm-Qasr, 21C5
Umtata, 30D2
Umuarama, 39A3
Una, R., 13A4
Unalakleet, 33B3
Unalaska, I., 31D4
'Unayzah, 28B7
Undu Cape, C., 41bA3
Uneča, 18B3
Ungava Bay, B., 33C13
Ungava Peninsula, Pen., 31C,D13
Ungeny, 18C2
Uni, 17C6
Unimak Island, I., 31D4,5
Union City, 32a
Union of Soviet Socialist Republics, St., 16C6-17
United Arab Emirates, St., 21D,E6,7
United Kingdom, St., 8B-E7,8
United States, St., 32F9-12
Unna, 12aB3
Unst, I., 7A7
Unža, R., 17C6
Upata, 38B3
Upernavik, 33A14
Upington, 30D3
Upolu, I., 41cB2
Upper Lough Erne, L., 7D4
Upper Volta see Burkina Faso
Uppsala, 15D6
Uraj, 17A3
Urakawa, 25C6
Ural, R., 16E7
Ural'sk, 16D7
Ural'skije Gory, Mts., 19C,D7,8
Uranium City, 33C9
Urawa, 25C6

Urda, 18C6
Ure, R., 7D7
Urengoj, 16C9,10
Urfa, 21aB3
Urgal see Čekunda
Urgenč, 21A8
Uria, 14D3
Uruapan, 36C2
Urubamba, R., 38D2
Uruguai, R., 39A3
Uruguaiana, 39A3
Uruguay, R., see Uruguai
Uruguay, St., 39aD2,3
Ürümqi, 24B2
Ur'upinsk, 18B5
Uržum, 17C7
Usa, R., 17A9
Uşak, 21aB1
Usakos, 30D2
Usedom, I., 12B4
Usinsk, 17A9
Usman', 18B4,5
Usolje, 17aB2
Usolje-Sibirskoje, 16bB1
Ussuri, R., 16E15
Ussurijsk, 16E15
Usť-Barguzin, 16bB2,3
Usť-Cil'ma, 17A8
Ústí nad Labem, 12C4
Ustinov see Iževsk
Ustka, 12B5
Usť-Kamčatsk, 16D18
Usť-Kamenogorsk, 16D,E9,10
Usť-Katav, 17aB,C2
Usť-Kulom, 17B8
Usť-Kut, 16C12
Usť-Luga, 17C3
Usť-Nera, 16C16
Usť-Ordynskij, 16bB1,2
Usť-Pinega, 17B6
Usť-Usa, 17A9
Utah, Admin. U., 34D4
Utah Lake, L., 34C4
Utajärvi, 15B8
Utena, 17C3
Utete, 30B4
Utica, 35C5,6
Utrecht, 12B2
Utrera, 11G2
Utsjoki, 15A8
Utsunomiya, 25C6,7
Uttar Pradesh, Admin. U., 22B3,4
Uummannarsuaq, C., 33C15
Uusikaupunki, 15C7
Uvalde, 34F7
Uvarovo, 18B5
Uvea, 41aA2
Uvira, 30B3
Uvs Nuur, L., 24A,B3
Uwajima, 25D5
Uyuni, 38E3
Uzbek Soviet Socialist Republic, Admin. U., 16E,F7,8
Užgorod, 18C1
Uzlovaja, 18B4

V

Vaal, R., 30D3
Vaasa, 15C7
Vác, 14B1
Vacaria, 39aC3
Vadodara, 22B3
Vadsö, 15A9

Vaduz, 11C5
Vaga, R., 17B6
Váh, R., 12C5
Vaiaku, 41D7
Vaileka, 41bA2
Vairao, 41dB2
Vaitoto, 41dB2
Valdagno, 13aA5
Valdajskaja Vozvyšennosť, Admin. U., 5B8
Val-de-Marne (94), Admin. U., 11B3
Valdepeñas, 11G3
Valdez, 33B5
Valdivia, 39B1
Val-d'Oise (95), Admin. U., 11B3
Val-d'Or, 35B5
Valence, 11C4
Valencia (Spain), 11G3
Valencia (Venezuela), 38A,B3
Valencia Island, I., 7F2
Valencia, 38B2
Valenciennes, 12C1
Vale of York, Reg., 7D7
Valera, 38B2
Valga, 17C3
Valjevo, 13A4
Valladolid (Mexico), 36B4
Valladolid (Spain), 11F2
Valle d'Aosta (19), Admin. U. 13A1
Valledupar, 38A2
Vallée de l'Azaquak, Val., 26C5
Vallejo, 34D2
Vallenar, 39A1
Valletta, 13D3
Valley City, 34B7
Valleyfield, 33b
Valli di Comacchio, B., 13A3
Valmiera, 17C2,3
Valognes, 6aA3
Valok, 16aB2
Valparaíso, 39B1
Valujki, 18B4
Valverde, 26bC2
Van, 21aB4
Van Gölü, L., 21aB4
Vanna, I., 15A6
Vännäs, 15B,C6,7
Vannes, 11C2
Vansbro, 15C5
Vantaa, 15C8
Vanua Levu, I., 41bA2
Vanua Mbalavu, I., 41bA3
Vanuatu, St., Is., 41E6,7
Var (83), Admin. U., 11D4
Varallo, 13aA2
Vārānasi, 22B4
Varangerfjorden, B., 15A9
Varanger Halvöya, Pen., 15A9
Varaždin, 13A3,4
Varberg, 15D5

Vardar, R., 13B5
Vardö, 15A9
Varese, 13aA2
Varginha, 39aB4
Varkaus, 15C8,9
Varna, 14C3,4
Varna (20), Admin. U., 14C3
Värnamo, 15D5
Vartsilja, 17B4
Varzi, 13aB3
Vas (17), Admin. U., 14B1
Vaška, R., 17B7
Vaslui, 14B3
Västerås, 15D6
Västervik, 15D6
Vasto, 13B3
Vatican City, St., 13B2,3
V'atka, R., 17C8
Vatnajökull, Glacier, 15aB3
Vatneyri, 15aB1,2
Vatra Dornei, 14B3
Vättern, L., 15D5
Vatulele, I., 41bB1
Vaucluse (84), Admin. U., 11C4
Vaughn, 34E5
Vaupés, R., 37B2,3
Vava'u Group, Is., 41E8
Växjö, 15D5
Važgort, 17B7
V'az'ma, 17C4
Vega, I., 15B4
Veintcinco de Mayo, 39aE1,2
Vejle, 12B3
Velas, 11aA2
Velbert, 12aB2,3
Velikaja, R., 17C3
Velika Morava, R., 13A,B5
Velikije Luki, 17C4
Velikij Ustug, 17B7
Veliko Tărnovo, 14C3
Veliko Tărnovo (26), Admin. U., 14C3
Velikovisočnoje, 17A8
Vélingara, 29B2
Veliž, 17C4
Vellore, 22C3
Veľsk, 17B6
Vendée (85), Admin. U., 11C2
Vendenga, 17B7
Vendôme, 11C3
Veneto (20), Admin. U., 13A2,3
Venezia, 13A3
Venezuela, St., 38A,B2,3
Venice see Venezia
Venta, R., 17C2
Ventnor, 9D4
Ventspils, 17C2
Veracruz, 36C3
Veracruz (29), Admin. U., 36B3
Verāval, 22B2,3
Vercelli, 13aA2
Verchn'aja Salda, 17aB3
Verchn'aja Tojma, 17B7
Verchn'aja Tura, 17aB2
Verchn'aja Zolotica, 17A6
Verchnetulomskij, 17A4
Verchneural'sk, 17aC2,3

page 228

Verchnij Baskunčak, 18C6
Verchnij Ufalej, 17aB3
Verchojansk, 16C15
Verchojanskij Chrebet, Mts., 19B,C14,15
Verchoturje, 17aB3
Verchovažje, 17B6
Verden, 12B3
Verdun (Canada), 33b
Verdun (France), 11B4
Vereeniging, 30D3
Vereščagino, 16C10,11
Verin, 11F2
Vermont, Admin. U., 35C6
Vernon, 34E7
Véroia, 14C2
Verona, 13A2
Versailles, 11B3
Veselovskoje Vodochranilišče, Res., 18C5
Vesjegonsk, 17C5
Vesoul, 11C4
Vesterålen, Is., 15A5,6
Vestfjorden, B., 15A5,6
Vestmannaeyjar, 15aC4
Vestspitsbergen, I., 42C21,22
Vesuvio, Vol., 5C6
Veszprém, 14B1
Veszprém (18), Admin. U., 14B1
Vetluga, 17B7
Vetluga, R., 17C7
Vetlužkij, 17B7
Viana do Castelo, 11F1
Viana do Castelo (16), Admin. U., 11F1
Viangchan, 22C6
Viareggio, 13B2
Viborg, 12A3
Vicenza, 13A2
Vich, 11F4
Vichigasta, 39A2
Vichy, 11C3
Vicklow Mountains, Mts., 7E4
Vicksburg, 35E2
Victor Harbour, 40D3
Victoria (Austr.), Admin. U., 40D4
Victoria (Canada), 33D7
Victoria (Hong Kong), 19aB3
Victoria (Seychelles), 27E10
Victoria (U.S.A.), 34F7
Victoria, R., 40B3
Victoria Beach, 34A7
Victoria de Las Tunas, 36aB4,5
Victoria Falls, 30C3
Victoria Land, I., 33A,B8,9
Victoria Land, Reg., 42G20,21
Victoria Nile, R., 29D6
Victoria River Downs, 40B3
Victoria Strait, Str., 33A,B9,10
Victoriaville, 33b
Vičuga, 17C6
Vidin, 14C2
Vidin (27), Admin. U., 14C2
Viedma, 39C2
Vienna see Wien
Vienne, 11C4

Vienne (86), Admin. U., 11C3
Vienne (Hautes-) (87), Admin. U., 11C3
Vienne, R., 11C3
Vientiane see Viangchan
Viersen, 12aB1
Vierzon, 11C3
Vietnam, St., 22B,C6
Vigan, 23bA2
Vigevano, 13aA2,3
Vigo, 11F1
Vijayawāda, 22C3,4
Vijosë, R., 13B4,5
Vík, 15aC3
Vikna, I., 15B4
Vila, 41E6
Vila da Ribeira Brava, 28aA1,2
Vila do Porto, 11aB4
Vila Nova de Gaia, 11F1
Vila Real, 11F2
Vila Real (17), Admin. U., 11F2
Vila Real de Santo António, 11G2
Vila Velha, 38E5
Vilejka, 18B2
Vilhelmina, 15B6
Vilhena, 38D3
Vilija, R., 18B2
Viljandi, 17C3
Villa Bittencourt, 38C3
Villach, 12D4
Villa Dolores, 39B2
Villaguay, 39aD2
Villahermosa, 36C3
Villa María, 39B2
Villa Montes, 38B3
Villarrobledo, 11G3
Villavicencio, 38B2
Villena, 11G3
Villeurbanne, 11C4
Vilnius, 16D4
Vil'uj, R., 16C13
Vil'ujsk, 16C14
Vimmerby, 15D5,6
Viña del Mar, 39B1,2
Vinaroz, 11F4
Vincennes, 35D3
Vindelälven, R., 16B6
Vinh, 22C6
Vinh-Long, 22C,D6
Vinkovci, 13A4
Vinnica, 16E4
Vinson Massif, Mt., 42G,H8,9
Virac, 23bB2
Viranşehir, 21aB3
Virginia, 35B2
Virginia, Admin. U., 35D4,5
Virginia Beach, 35D5,6
Virgin Islands, Admin. U., Is., 36bA1
Virovitica, 13A4
Visby, 15D6
Viscount Melville Sound, Str., 33A8-10
Višera, R., 17aA,B2
Viseu, 11F2
Viseu (18), Admin. U., 11F1
Viseu de Sus, 14B3
Vishākhapatnam, 22C4
Vitebsk, 17C4
Viterbo, 13B3
Viti Levu, I., 41bA2

Vitim, R., 16D13
Vitoria, 11F3
Vitória, 38E5,6
Vitória da Conquista, 38D5
Vivero, 11F2
Vizianagaram, 22C4
Vizinga, 17B7
Vladimir, 17C6
Vladimirskij Tupik, 17C4
Vladimir-Volynskij, 18B1
Vladivostok, 16E15
Vlissingen, 12C1
Vlorë, 13B4
Vltava, R., 12C4
Vochma, 17C7
Vodla, R., 17B5
Voe, 10a
Voghera, 13aB3
Voh, 41aA1
Voi, 30B4
Voinjama, 29C3
Vojkovo, 16aB1
Vojvodina (6b), Admin. U., 13B5
Voj-Vož, 17B8
Volcán Citlaltépetl, Vol., 31H11
Volcán de Colima, Vol., 31H10
Volcán Guallatiri, Vol., 37D2,3
Volcan Karisimbi, Vol., 26E7,8
Volcán Lanin, Vol., 37F2
Volcán Lascar, Vol., 37E3
Volcán Llullaillaco, Vol., 37E3
Volcano Maipó, Vol., 37F2
Volcano Osorno, Vol., 37G2
Volcán Popocatépetl, Vol., 31H10,11
Volčansk, 18B4
Volcán Tajumulco, Vol., 31H11,12
Volchov, 17C4
Volchov, R., 17C4
Volga, R., 16D5
Volgo-Baltijskij Kanal, Can., 17B5
Volgodonsk, 18C5
Volgograd, 16E6
Volgogradskoje Vodochranilišče, Res., 18C6
Volkovysk, 18B1
Volnovacha, 18C4
Vologda, 16D5,6
Volonga, 17A7
Vólos, 14D2
Volovo, 18B4
Vol'sk, 18B6
Volta, R., 29D6
Volta Blanche, R., 29B5
Volta Noire, R., 29C4
Volta Redonda, 39aB4,5
Volta Rouge, R., 29C5
Volžskij, 18C5,6
Vopnafjörður, 15aB4
Vorarlberg (8), Admin. U., 12D3
Vorīai Sporádhes, Is., 14D2,3
Vorkuta, 17C8
Voronež, 16D5,6

Vorošilovgrad see Lugan.
Vørterkaka Nunatak, Mt., 42G33,34
Vosges (88), Admin. U., 11B,C4
Voss, 15C3
Vostočno-Sibirskoje More, S., 16B16-19
Vostok, Station, 42G26
Vostok Island, I., 41E10
Votkinsk, 17aB1
Votkinskoje Vodochranilišče, Res., 17aB2
Vožajol', 17B8
Vožega, 17B6
Vožgora, 17B7
Voznesensk, 18C3
Vraca, 14C2
Vraca (28), Admin. U., 14C2
Vranje, 13B5
Vrbas, R., 13A4
Vršac, 13A5
Vryburg, 30D3
Vulkan Ključevskaja Sopka, Vol., 19D18
Vung-Tau, 22C6
Vunindawa, 41bA2
Vuoksa, R., 17B3
Vuotso, 15A8
Vya, 34C3
Vyborg, 16C4,5
Vyčegda, R., 17B8
Vychino, 17b
Východočeský kraj (5), Admin. U., 12C5
Východoslovenský kraj (10), Admin. U., 12C6
Vyksa, 17C6
Vym, R., 17B8
Vyšnij Voločok, 17C4
Vytegra, 17B5

W

Wa, 29C5
Wabash, R., 35D3
Waco, 34E7
Waddān, 28B4
Waddeneilanden, Is., 12B2
Waddenzee, S., 12B2
Wadebridge, 9D2
Wādī an-Naṭrūn, Depr., 26aB2
Wādī Ḥalfā, 28B6
Wad Madani, 28C6
Wager Bay, 33B10
Wagga Wagga, 40D4
Waha, 28B4
Wahai, 23D4,5
Wahpeton, 34B7
Waialua, 35aB2
Waikato, R., 40aA2
Wailuku, 35aB3,4
Waingapu, 27C4
Wainwright, 33A4
Wajima, 25C5
Wajir, 28D7
Wakayama, 25D6
Wakefield, 9C4
Wake Island, Admin. U., I., 41B6
Wakkanai, 25A7
Wakre, 23D5
Wałbrzych, 12C5
Walcott, 34C5
Wales, 33B3

Wallasey, 9C3
Walla Walla, 34B3
Wallis and Futuna, Admin. U., 41E8
Walney Isle, I., 9B3
Walsall, 9C4
Walvisbaai, 30D2
Wanganui, 40aA2
Wanshanqundao, Is., 19aB2,3
Wanxian, 24C4
Warangal, 22C3
Warburton Creek, R., 40C3
Ware, 33C7
Warren (U.S.A., Michigan), 33b
Warren (U.S.A., North Dakota), 34B7
Warren (U.S.A., Ohio), 35C4
Warrenton, 30D3
Warri, 29D7
Warrington, 9C3
Warrnambool, 40D4
Warsaw see Warszawa
Warszawa, 12B6
Warta, R., 12C5
Warwick (Austr.), 40C5
Warwick (U.K.), 9C4
Warwickshire (44), Admin. U., 9C4
Wasatch Mountains, Mts., 31E,F9
Washington, 35D5
Washington, Admin. U., 34B2,3
Watampone, 23D4
Waterbury, 35C6
Waterford, 10E6
Waterford, Admin. U., 10E6
Waterloo, 35C2
Waterville, 33aC3
Watertown (U.S.A., New York), 35C5,6
Watertown (U.S.A., South Dakota), 34C7
Watford, 9D4
Watling Island see San Salvador, 35G5,6
Watrous, 34A5
Watson, 34A6
Watson Lake, 33B7
Waugh, 33D11
Waukegan, 33C5
Wausau, 35B,C2,3
Wauwatosa, 35C3
Waveney, R., 9C5
Wāw, 28D5
Wawa, 33D11
Waycross, 35E4
Waynesboro, 35D5
Wear, R., 9B4
Weddell Sea, 42F,G3-5
Weed, 34C2
Weichang, 25B2
Weifang, 24C5,6
Weihai, 24C6
Weihe, R., 24C4,5

Weipa, 40B4
Weishanhu, L., 25D2
Weldya, 28C6,7
Welkom, 30D3
Welland, R., 7E7
Welland Canal, Can., 33b
Wellesley Island, I., 40B3,4
Wellington, 40aB2
Wells (U.K.), 9D3
Wells (U.S.A.), 34C3,4
Wellton, 34E4
Wels, 12C4
Welshpool, 9C3
Wembley, 9a
Wenatchee, 33aC3
Wendeng, 25C3
Wendover, 34C4
Wentworth, 40D4
Wenzhou, 24D6
Wesel, 12aA2
Weser, R., 12C3
Wessel Islands, Is., 40B3
West Bengal (6), Admin. U., 22B4
Westberlin, 12B4
West Brigford, 9C4
West Bromwich, 9C4
Western Australia, Admin. U., 40C1,2
Western Desert, Des., 26B7
Western Ghâts, Mts., 19G,H9
Western Isles (66), Admin. U., 10B1
Western Sahara, Admin. U., 28B1
West Falkland, I., 37H3
West Glamorgan (54), Admin. U., 9D3
West Ham, 9a
West Ice Shelf, 42F28
Westmeath, Admin. U., 10E6
West Midlands (6), Admin. U., 9C3
West Nicholson, 30D3
Weston-super-Mare, 9D3
West Palm Beach, 35F4,5
West Point (U.S.A., Kentucky), 35D3
West Point (U.S.A., Virginia), 35D5
Westport (New Zealand), 40aB2
Westport (U.K.), 10E5
Westray, I., 7B6
West Sussex (45), Admin. U., 9D4
West Virginia, Admin. U., 35D4,5
West Wyalong, 40D4
West Yellowstone, 34B,C4,5
West Yorkshire (7), Admin. U., 9C4
Wewak, 41D4
Wexford, 10E6
Wexford, Admin. U., 10E6
Wexford Harbour, B., 7E4,5
Weybury, 34B6
Weymouth, 9D3
Whakatane, 40aA2
Whalsay, I., 10aA1
Whangarei, 40aA2
Wharfe, R., 7E7

Wheeling, 35C,D4,5
Whernside, Mt., 7D6
Whitby, 9B4
White (U.S.A., Arkansas), R., 35D2
White (U.S.A., South Dakota), R., 34C6
Whitehaven, 10C3
Whitehorse, 33B6
White Mountain Peak, Mt., 31aC2
White Nile see Al-Bahr al-Abyad
White Sea see Beloje More
White Volta see Volta Blanche
Whitney, 35B5
Whitstable, 9D5
Whyalla, 40D3
Wichita, 34D7
Wichita Falls, 34E7
Wick, 10A3
Wickenburg, 34E4
Wicklow, 10E6,7
Wicklow, Admin. U., 10E6
Widnes, 9C3
Wieliczka, 12C6
Wiemar, 12C3
Wien, 12C5
Wien (9), Admin. U., 12C5
Wiener Neustadt, 12D4,5
Wiesbaden, 12C2,3
Wigan, 9C3
Wigtown, 10C2
Wilhelmshaven, 12B2
Wilkes-Barre, 35C5
Wilkes Land, Reg., 42F,G23-25
Willamette, R., 31aA,B1
Willemstad, 38A3
Willesden, 9a
Williams Lake, 33C7
Williamsport, 35C5
Willmar, 35B1
Willow, 33B4
Wilmington (U.S.A., North Carolina), 35E5
Wilmington (U.S.A., Pennsylvania), 35D5
Wilson, 35D5
Wilton, 9D4
Wiltshire (46), Admin. U., 9D4
Wiluna, 40C2
Winchester (U.K.), 9D4
Winchester (U.S.A.), 35D5
Windermere, L., 9B3
Windhoek, 30D2
Windsor (Canada), 33D11
Windsor (U.K.), 9D4
Windward Islands, Is., 36bB2
Winfield, 34D7
Winisk, 33C11
Winisk, R., 33C11
Winneba, 29D5
Winnemucca, 34C3
Winnipeg, 33C,D10
Winnipeg, L., 35A1,2
Winnipegosis, 34A6
Winona, 35C2
Winslow, 34E4
Winstom-Salem, 35D4
Winterthur, 11C5
Winton, 40C4
Wisbech, 9C5
Wisconsin, Admin. U., 35B,C2,3

Wisconsin, R., 35C2,3
Wiseman, 33B4
Wisła, R., 12C6
Wismar, 12B3
Witchurch, 9C3
Witham, R., 7E7
Witten, 12aB3
Wittenberg, 12C4
Wittenberge, 12B3,4
Włocławek, 12B5
Woking, 9D4
Wolfsburg, 12B3
Wollaston Lake, L., 33C9
Wollongong, 40D5
Wolverhampton, 9C3
Wŏnju, 25C4
Wonosobo, 23aA2
Wŏnsan, 25C4
Wood, 34C6
Wood Buffalo National Park, Park, 31D8,9
Woodward, 34D7
Woomera, 40D3
Worcester (South Africa), 30E2,3
Worcester (U.K.), 9C3
Worcester (U.S.A.), 35C6
Workington, 10C3
Worms, 12C3
Worthing, 9D4
Wrangell, 33C6
Wrexham, 9C3
Wrigley, 33B7
Wrocław, 12C5
Wudu, 24C4
Wuhai, 24C4
Wuhan, 24C5
Wuhu, 24C5
Wukari, 29D8
Wulanhaote, 24B6
Wuppertal, 12aB3
Wurno, 29B7
Würzburg, 12C3
Wusu, 24B2
Wuwei, 24C4
Wuxi, 24C6
Wuyuan, 24B4
Wuzhou, 24D5
Wye, R., 7E6
Wyndham, 40B2
Wyoming, Admin. U., 34C4,5

X

Xai-Xai, 30D4
Xangongo, 30C2
Xánthi, 14C3
Xiamen, 24D5
Xi'an, 24C4
Xiangfan, 24C5
Xiangkhoang, 22C6
Xiangshan, 25E3
Xiangtan, 24D5
Xichang, 24D5
Xiguitui, 24B6
Xihe, R., 25B3
Xijiang, R., 37C4
Xilotimbou, 19cA,B2
Xingú, R., 37D4
Xining, 24C4
Xinjiang Uygur Zizhiqu (4), Admin. U., 24B2
Xinjin, 25C3
Xinmin, 25B3
Xinxiang, 24C5

page 230

Kinyang, 24C5
Kizang Zizhiqu (5), Admin. U., 24C2
Kuanhua, 25B2
Kuzhou, 24C5

'aan, 24C,D4
'akima, 34B2
'aku-shima, I., 25D4,5
akutat, 33C5,6
ala, 19bA2
algoo, 40C1
alinga, 28D5
alongjiang, R., 24C3
alujiang see Amnok-kang
aluzangbujiang, R., 22B4,5
amagata, 25C6,7
amaguchi, 25D5
amoussoukro, 29F4
ampi Sound, 40B2
amuna, R., 22B3,4
an'an, 24C4
anbu'al-Bahr, 28B6
ancheng, 24C6
angzhou, 25D2
anji, 24B6
ankton, 34C7
ntai, 24C6
nzhou, 25C2
oundé, 29E8
p, I., 41C3
qui, R., 36A,B2
araka, 40C4
are, R., 7E1
ren, 41D6
rí, R., 38B2
sawa, I., 41bA1
sawa Group, Is., 41bA1
té, 41aB2
tsushiro, 25D5
vari, R., 38C2
xian, 24E4
zd, 21C6
zoo, R., 35E2
22C5
I, I., 7A7
lowknife, 33B8
low Sea, 24C6
lowstone, R., 34B4,5
lowstone Lake, L., 34C4,5
wa, 29C7
nassoe, 35E4
nen, St., 28C7
di, 29C5
vil, 9D3
üshalayim, 20bC1
il, R., 21aA3
u, 22B5
, 39aC2
n, 24D4
ang, 24B6
un, 24B6
, 25C2
h, 25A4
huan, 24C4
ng, 24B2
an, 24D4
ui, 25C2
ng, 24D5
g, 25D2
rnio, 15B7,8

Ylivieska, 15B8
Yogyakarta, 23D2,3
Yokadouma, 29E9
Yoko, 29D9
Yokohama, 25C6,7
Yokosuka, 25C6,7
Yola, 29C9
Yonago, 25C5
Yongdinghe, R., 25C2
Yonkers, 35C6
Yonne, R., 11C3
York, 9C4
Yorkton, 33C9
Yosemite National Park, Park, 34C2
Yōsu, 25D4
Youghal, 10F6
Youngstown, 35C4,5
Yozgat, 21aB2,3
Ystad, 15E5
Yuanjiang, R., 24D4,5
Yuba City, 34D2
Yubari, 25B7
Yucatan (30), Admin. U., 36B,C4
Yucatán, Reg., 31G,H11,12
Yucatán Strait, 36B4
Yuci, 24C5
Yuen Long, 19aB2,3
Yueyang, 24D5
Yugoslavia, St., 13A,B3-5
Yujiang, R., 24D4
Yukon, Admin. U., 33B6
Yukon, R., 33B6
Yulin (China, Guangxi Zhuang Z.), 24D5
Yulin (China, Shǎnxī), 24C4,5
Yuma, 34E4
Yumen, 24C3
Yuncheng, 24C5
Yunhe, Can., 24C5
Yunnan (26), Admin. U., 24D4
Yupanyang, B., 25D3
Yu Shan, Mt., 19G14
Yushu (China, Jilin), 25B4
Yushu (China, Qinghai), 24C3
Yutian, 24C2
Yuty, 39aC2
Yvelines (78), Admin. U., 11B3

Z

Zābol, 21C8
Zabrze, 12C5
Zacatecas, 36B2
Zacatecas (31), Admin. U., 36B2
Zacharvan', 17A9
Zadar, 13A3
Zafra, 11G2
Zagnanado, 29D6
Zagorsk, 17C5
Zagreb, 13A3,4
Zágros, Mts., 19F,G6,7
Zāhedān, 21D8
Zahlah, 20bB1,2
Zaire, R., 30A3
Zaïre, St., 30B2,3
Zaječar, 13B5
Zakataly, 18D6

Zākhū, 21aB4
Zákinthos, 14D2
Zákinthos, I., 14D2
Zakopane, 12C5,6
Zala (19), Admin. U., 14B1
Zalaegerszeg, 12D5
Zalari, 16bB1
Zalău, 14B2
Zaliv Kara-Bogaz-Gol, B., 21A6
Zaliv Šelichova, B.,16C17
Zaliv Petra Velikogo, B., 25B5
Zambeze see Zambèze
Zambèze, R., 30C3
Zambezi, 30C3
Zambezi see Zambèze
Zambia, St., 30C3,4
Zamboanga, 23C4
Zamora, 11F3
Zamość, 12C6
Zanjān, 21B5
Zanzibar, 30B4,5
Zanzibar Island, I., 30B4,5
Zaozhuang, 25D2
Zapadnaja Dvina, 17C4
Zapadnaja Dvina, R., 18A2
Zapadna Morava, R., 13B5
Zapadno-Sibirskaja Ravnina, Pl., 19C,D8-10
Západočeský kraj (3), Admin. U., 12C4
Západoslovenský kraj (8), Admin. U., 12C5
Zapala, 39B1
Zaporožje, 18C4
Zara, 21aB3
Zaragoza, 11F3
Zarajsk, 18B4
Zarand, 21C7
Zaranj, 22A2
Zárate, 39aD2
Zaria, 29C7
Žarkovskij, 17C4
Žarma, 24B2
Žary, 12C4
Zarzis, 27aB3
Zatoka Gdańska, B., 12B5
Zatoka Pomorska, B., 12B4
Zavolžje, 17C6
Zawiłah, 28B4
Ždanov see Mariupol'
Zeebrugge, 11B3
Zeehan, 40E4
Zeja, R., 24A6
Zelenčukskaja,18D5
Zelenoborskij, 17A4
Zelenograd, 17C5
Železnodorožnyj, 17B8
Železnogorsk, 17C7
Zel'onodol'sk, 17C7
Zemetčino, 18B5
Zemio, 28D5
Zeml'a Franca Iosifa, Is., 16A6-9
Zeml'a Georga, I., 16A,B6
Zenica, 13A4
Zeravšan, R., 21B9
Zešart, 17B7
Zestafoni, 18D5
Zgorzelec, 12C4
Zhalinghu, L., 24C3
Zhangjiakou, 24B5

Zhangmutou, 19aA3
Zhangye, 24C4
Zhangzhou, 25AB1
Zhanjiang, 24D5
Zhaxigang, 24C1,2
Zhejiang (27), Admin. U., 24D6
Zhengzhou, 24C5
Zhenjiang, 25D2,3
Zhijiang, 24D4
Zhongshan, 19aA1
Zhongwei, 24C4
Zhoushanqundao, Is., 25D,E3
Zhuangaerpendi, Reg., 19E10
Zhucheng, 25C2
Zhuhai, 19aB2
Zhujiangkou, B., 19aA,B2
Zhuzhou, 24D5
Zibo, 24C5
Zielona Góra, 12C4
Ziftá, 26aB3
Žigalovo, 16bB2
Žiganск, 16C14
Zigong, 24D4
Ziguinchor, 29B1
Zile, 21aA3
Žilina, 12C5
Zima, 16bB1
Zimbabwe, St., 30C3,4
Zimi, 29D3
Zimovniki, 18C5
Zinder, 29B8
Zingst, 12B4
Žitomir, 18B2,3
Zlatoust, 17aB2
Žlobin, 18B2,3
Žmerinka, 18C2
Znojmo, 12C5
Zolotonoša, 18C3
Zomba, 30C4
Zonguldak, 21aA2
Zouar, 28B4
Zouîrât, 28B1
Zrenjanin, 13A5
Zuénoula, 29D4
Zug, 11C5
Zuja, 16aB2
Zujevka, 17C8
Żukovka, 18B3
Zumbo, 30C4
Zungeru, 29C7
Zunhua, 25B2
Zunyi, 24D4
Zürich, 11C5
Zuru, 29C7
Zuwārah, 28A4
Zvishavane, 30D3,4
Zvolen, 12C5
Zvornik, 13A4
Zwickau, 12C4
Zwolle, 12B3
Zyr'anka, 16C17
Zyr'anovsk, 16E10
Żyrardów, 12B6

CHANGES IN THE INDEX SEE PAGE 232

page 231

... IN THE INDEX:

... 11F3
...g (4),
..., 12 B 4
Brokopondo, 38B4
Čekunda, 16D15
Chemnitz, 12C4
Damān and Diu (10),
  Admin. U., 22B3
Gjandža, 18aA2
Iževsk, 16D7
Linden, 38B4
Lugansk, 18C4
Mariupol', 16E5
Mecklenburg-Vorpommern
  (8), Admin. U., 12 B 4
Naber. Čelny, 17C8
Obando, 38B3
Rybinsk, 17C5
Sachsen (13), Admin. U.,
  12 C 4
Sachsen-Anhalt (14),
  Admin. U., 12 B 3
Thüringen (16),
  Admin. U., 12 C 3
Zlín, 12C5